LAW AND PSYCHOLOGY

CURRENT LEGAL ISSUES 2006
VOLUME 9

Law and Psychology

Current Legal Issues 2006

VOLUME 9

Edited by

BELINDA BROOKS–GORDON

Lecturer in Psychology
Birkbeck College, London

and

MICHAEL FREEMAN

Professor of English Law
University College London

OXFORD
UNIVERSITY PRESS

OXFORD
UNIVERSITY PRESS

Great Clarendon Street, Oxford OX2 6DP

Oxford University Press is a department of the University of Oxford.
It furthers the University's objective of excellence in research, scholarship,
and education by publishing worldwide in

Oxford New York

Auckland Cape Town Dar es Salaam Hong Kong Karachi
Kuala Lumpur Madrid Melbourne Mexico City Nairobi
New Delhi Shanghai Taipei Toronto

With offices in

Argentina Austria Brazil Chile Czech Republic France Greece
Guatemala Hungary Italy Japan Poland Portugal Singapore
South Korea Switzerland Thailand Turkey Ukraine Vietnam

Oxford is a registered trade mark of Oxford University Press
in the UK and in certain other countries

Published in the United States
by Oxford University Press Inc., New York

British Library Cataloguing in Publication Data

Data available

Library of Congress Cataloging in Publication Data

Law and psychology / edited by Belinda Brooks–Gordon and Michael
Freeman.
    p. cm. — (Current legal issues; v. 9)
Includes bibliographical references and index.
ISBN-13: 978–0–19–921139–5
ISBN-10: 0–19–921139–6
1. Law—Psychological aspects.   I. Brooks–Gordon, Belinda.
II. Freeman, Michael D. A.
K346.L377 2006
340'.19—dc22

                                                        2006027129

Typeset by Newgen Imaging Systems (P) Ltd., Chennai, India
Printed in Great Britain
on acid-free paper by
Biddles Ltd., King's Lynn

ISBN 0–19–921139–6 (Hbk.)   978–0–19–921139–5

1 3 5 7 9 10 8 6 4 2

General Editor's Preface

UCL Law School held its ninth international interdisciplinary colloquium in July 2005, in the immediate aftermath of 7/7. This book is the product of the colloquium. My thanks are to Dr Belinda Brooks-Gordon who helped me convene the colloquium, to Lisa Penfold who ably administered it—a task rendered the more difficult by the events of the previous week—and to Priscilla Saporu and Linda Thomas without whose administrative and secretarial support the book would not have seen the light of day. My co-convenor and I are also very grateful to those who chaired sessions, in particular to Baroness Hale of Richmond who took the chair at the Public Lecture by Stephen Frosh.

The next volume in this series, to be published in 2007, is on 'Law and Philosophy'. The 2007 colloquium—on 2 and 3 July 2007—is on 'Law and Bioethics'. Enquiries about this may be addressed to Lisa Penfold at <lisa.penfold@ucl.ac.uk>.

Professor Michael Freeman

March 2006

Contents

List of Tables

List of Figures

Notes on Contributors

Michael Freeman is Professor of English Law at UCL and the Editor of the interdisciplinary series of which this is the ninth volume. He was formerly the editor of *Current Legal Problems* and is the editor of the *International Journal of Children's Rights* and co-editor of the *International Journal of Law in Context*. He is the author of a number of books including *Introduction to Jurisprudence* (7th edn, Sweet & Maxwell, 2001), a new edition of which is in preparation. He also writes on family law, medical law, and medical ethics.

Belinda Brooks-Gordon is University Lecturer and Programme Director of the MSc Family and Systemic Psychotherapy at Birkbeck, University of London. Her research on the sex industry addresses the psychological, political, methodological, and human rights issues surrounding sex work, sex workers, and their clients. A chartered psychologist with a PhD from the University of Cambridge Law Faculty, she has written on sexual offending for the Home Office Offending Behaviour Programmes Unit and conducted systematic reviews for the Department of Health on psychological interventions for sexual offenders. Recent publications include *Sexuality Repositioned* (Hart Publishing, 2004) and *The Price of Sex* (Willan Publishing, 2006).

Jenny McEwan was appointed Professor of Criminal Law at Exeter University in 1999. She has published widely on various aspects of the law of evidence. Her interest in the function and efficacy of the criminal trial has led to involvement in some campaigning television programmes. In 1995 she played a major role in *The Big Picture* 'Criminal Injustice' BBC 2, and in 1996 *Verdict*: 'The Persuaders' BBC 2. Her books include *Evidence and the Adversarial Process: The Modern Law* (Hart Publishing, 1998) and *The Verdict of the Court: Passing Judgment in Law and Psychology* (Hart Publishing, 2003).

Bruce J Winick is Professor of Law and Professor of Psychiatry and Behavioural Sciences at the University of Miami in Coral Gables, Florida, where he has taught since 1974. He is co-founder of the school of social enquiry known as therapeutic jurisprudence.

Mandeep K Dhami is a lecturer in Criminology at the Institute of Criminology, University of Cambridge. She is on the editorial board of the *Journal of Analyses of Social Issues and Public Policy*. Her research interests include legal decision making, imprisonment, and restorative justice, and she has published widely in these areas. She is currently principal investigator on a Home Office project entitled 'Sentencing and its Outcomes' that aims to examine the factors that influence sentencing decisions in the English criminal justice system and explore the effectiveness of different types of sentences in reducing reconvictions.

Oliver R Goodenough has written on a wide variety of subjects relating to law and cognitive science. With Semir Zeki, he edited the 2004 special issue of the Philosophical Transactions of the Royal Society devoted to Law and the Brain, recently reprinted in book form by Oxford University Press. Currently a Professor at the Vermont Law School, Goodenough has also been a visiting Research Fellow at the Zoology Department at the University of Cambridge, a Lecturer at the University of Pennsylvania Law School, an

Adjunct Professor at Dartmouth's Thayer School of Engineering, and a visiting Professor at Humboldt University in Berlin.

Paul H Robinson is one of the world's leading experts on criminal law. He served as a federal prosecutor, as counsel for the US Senate Subcommittee on Criminal Law, and as one of the original commissioners of the US Sentencing Commission. He is the author of a dozen books, as well as scholarly articles in nearly every top US law review. Robinson, who has given scholarly lectures and assisted in criminal code reform throughout the world, led the only two recent criminal code reform projects in the United States and, under United Nations sponsorship, is currently drafting for the Maldives the first Islamic criminal code to use a modern code format.

Paul Dougan is Deputy Director of the LLM International Law Programmes at Brunel University, West London. After studying for science degrees at Oxford and Glasgow Universities, he qualified in law and his current research focuses upon issues in intellectual property law, transnational law, and international trade law, with forthcoming books in all three of these areas. He is a visiting lecturer on the MSc information Security programme at University College London and sits on the education committee of the Chartered Institute of Patent Agents.

Michael King is Professor in the School of Social Sciences and Law, Brunel University, UK. He has degrees in both law and psychology and has written on the relationship between the two disciplines. His books include *Psychology in and out of Court* (Pergamon, 1986), *How the Law Thinks about Children* (with C Piper, Arena, 1995) and *A Better World for Children* (Routledge, 1997). More recently, he has concentrated on the contribution of Niklas Luhmann's theory of autopoietic systems to understanding the relationship between law and psychology and, in particular, its application to decisions concerning children.

Fernand Gobet is Professor of Cognitive Psychology and Director of the Centre for the Study of Expertise at Brunel University. His research is oriented towards the psychology of expertise, the acquisition of language, computational modelling of cognitive process, computational scientific discovery, and evolutionary computation. His latest book, *Moves in Mind* (Psychology Press, 2004) provides a systematic study of the psychology of board games.

Jeffrey J Rachlinski received his BA and MA in Psychology from the Johns Hopkins University in 1988, his JD from Stanford Law School in 1993, and his PhD in Psychology in 1994. In 1994 he joined the faculty at the Cornell Law School and has taught as a visiting professor at the University of Chicago Law School, the University of Virginia Law School, the University of Pennsylvania Law School, Yale Law School, and Harvard Law School. His interests primarily involve the application of cognitive and social psychology to law.

Michael E Lamb is currently Professor of Psychology in the Social Sciences at the University of Cambridge. He received his PhD in Developmental Psychology from Yale University in 1976, an honorary doctorate in the Social Sciences from the University of Göteborg, Sweden in 1995, an Honorary Doctorate of Civil Law from the University of East Anglia in July 2006, and the 2003/4 James McKeen Cattell Award for Lifetime Contributions to Applied Psychological Research from the American Psychological Society. He has written many articles on children's testimony as well as *Investigative Interviews of*

Children (American Psychological Association, 1998). *Child Sexual Abuse: Disclosure, Delay, and Denial* will appear in 2007.

Anneli S Larsson PhD, is Research Associate at the Faculty of Social and Political Sciences, University of Cambridge. She received her PhD from Göteborg University, Sweden. Dr Larsson conducts research on interviewing techniques that help children to recount past experiences. She has a strong interest in promoting and protecting the rights of vulnerable groups such as abused and neglected children. Her research involves the assessment of factors that influence the accuracy and completeness of child abuse victims' reports. Her long-term intention is to work for a thorough and systematic implementation of relevant research findings within concerned authorities, establishments, and organizations.

Sarah Henderson is a Lecturer in Psychology at The Robert Gordon University, Aberdeen. Her main focus of interest is in the field of psychology and law, specifically in memory and memory disorders, and she is currently conducting research into the area of interviewing techniques in forensic settings.

Linda Taylor is a qualified solicitor and notary public in local government with a specialist research interest in forensic psychology. She has been an Honorary Lecturer to the Division of Forensic Psychology at Glasgow Caledonian University since 2004, is a former lecturer in law at The Robert Gordon University, Aberdeen and has authored a number of papers in the field of psychology and law.

Aldert Vrij is Professor of Applied Psychology at the University of Portsmouth. His main research interest is deception, particularly non-verbal aspects of deception (eg how liars behave), verbal aspects of deception (eg what they say), people's ability to detect deceit, and ways to improve this ability. He has published almost 300 articles and book chapters and six books to date, the majority of which are related to deception. His book, *Detecting Lies and Deceit,* published by Wiley in 2000, provides a comprehensive overview of non-verbal, verbal, and physiological correlates of deception. He is at present editor of *Legal and Criminological Psychology*.

Andrew Roberts is a Lecturer in the School of Law at the University of Warwick. His research interests lie in the field of criminal procedure. He has published a number of articles on eyewitness identification procedures.

Helen L Westcott is a Senior Lecturer at The Open University in Milton Keynes, and a member of the International Centre for Comparative Criminological Research. She has a long-standing interest in issues concerning child sexual abuse and interviewing children, along with cross-examination practice, and the abuse of children who are disabled. She is a Chartered Forensic Psychologist, and she publishes and presents widely on topics related to children's evidence (eg *Children's Testimony*, Wiley, 2002, with Professors Graham Davies and Ray Bull). She was a member of the writing team that produced the 2002 Home Office Guidance *Achieving Best Evidence in Criminal Proceedings*, and she works closely with practitioners and policy-makers.

Nicholas Bala has been a Professor at the Faculty of Law at Queen's University in Kingston Ontario, Canada since 1980. His main area of teaching and research interest is family and children's law. He has done a considerable amount of work with psychologists, and presently heads an interdisciplinary research team doing work on child witness issues.

Katherine Duvall Antonacopoulos worked as a research assistant for Professor Nicholas Bala when this chapter was written in the summer of 2005. She graduated with an LLB from Queen's University in the spring of 2006, and she is now an articling student at the Ontario Office of the Children's Lawyer.

Elizabeth Gilchrist is a Chartered Forensic Psychologist and is currently Reader in Forensic Psychology at the University of Kent. Her expertise is in the area of domestic violence, fear of crime, criminal justice decision-making and impact of victimization. She has both clinical and research experience with perpetrators and victim/survivors of domestic violence. She led the national study, funded by the Home Office, to explore criminogenic need in domestic violent offenders, which involved research with perpetrators and victim/survivors. She is also a part-time psychologist member of the Parole Board.

Cynthia Willis Esqueda has held a joint appointment in the University of Nebraska-Lincoln Department of Psychology and the Institute for Ethnic Studies since joining the faculty in 1991. She received her PhD in Social Psychology from the University of Kansas. Her research focuses on the impact of ethnic/racial stereotypes on cognitive processing of social information and interpretations of social behaviour in the legal system. She teaches courses in social psychology, as well as ethnic studies and has taught in the US Federal Bureau of Prisons. She is of Old Settler Cherokee descent.

Melissa Tehee is a graduate student in Social Psychology at Western Washington University in Bellingham, Washington. She has worked with the Independence Center (residential and outpatient drug and alcohol treatment center) through BrayanLGH Medical Center and for the Rape/Spouse Abuse Crisis Center on the crisis line, both in Lincoln, Nebraska. She is Cherokee from Tahlequah, Oklahoma.

Lizzie Barmes is a Reader in the Faculty of Laws, University College London. She is a specialist in employment and equality law, with a background in practice and in law reform work for the Law Commission. Her current research interests include workplace bullying, discriminatory harassment, and the common law of the contract of employment.

Peter Bartlett is Nottinghamshire Healthcare NHS Trust Professor of Mental Health Law at the University of Nottingham. He is author of *Blackstone's Guide to the Mental Capacity Act 2005* (OUP, 2006), *The Poor Law of Lunacy: The Administration of Pauper Lunatics in Nineteenth-Century England* (Cassell, 1999), and, with Ralph Sandland, *Mental Health Law: Policy and Practice* (2nd edn, OUP, 2003), as well as a wide variety of articles on law and mental health.

Neil Vidmar is Russell M Robinson II Professor of Law at Duke Law School and holds a secondary appointment in the Psychology Department at Duke University. Vidmar has testified or consulted as an expert on jury behaviour for trials in the United States, Canada, England, Australia, and New Zealand.

Judith Fordham is a Senior Lecturer in Law and Forensic Science at the University of Western Australia. She teaches law students criminal law and evidence, teaches scientists about the legal system and how to give expert evidence, and teaches expert evidence to outside agencies including doctors, fingerprint, blood spatter, and other analysts. She continues to practise as a senior barrister, taking forensically interesting cases. She teaches advocacy and is Immediate Past President of the Australian & New Zealand Association for Psychiatry, Psychology & Law (WA), Vice President of the Criminal Lawyers Association, and a Member of the Law Society Council.

Julia Fionda is a Senior Lecturer in Law and Director of the Institute of Criminal Justice at Southampton University. Her teaching and research interests lie in criminal justice, youth justice, and criminal law and her publications include *Public Prosecutors and Discretion: A Comparative Study* (OUP, 1995), *Devils and Angels: Youth, Policy and Crime* (Hart Publishing, 2005) and *Legal Concepts of Childhood* (Hart Publishing, 2001).

Robert Jago is a Lecturer in Law at the University of Surrey. His teaching and research interests lie in criminal justice, family law, and public law. He has extensive research experience in the field, having worked on projects evaluating young offender regimes (at Cambridge University) and parenting support projects (at Kent University).

Rachel Manning is a Lecturer in Social Psychology at the University of the West of England. Her teaching and research interests include pro- and anti-social behaviour, the history and development of research on bystander intervention, the links between social and environmental psychology, and the use of multi-research programmes.

Diane King is a researcher and PhD student at the Institute of Education, London University. She has a BA in English and Psychology from Queen's University Belfast and an MA in Psychology of Education from the Institute of Education. She is a qualified teacher and has taught in secondary schools, and in further and higher education. Her research interests are autism, special needs, and language. She has contributed to several publications in the areas.

Ya'ir Ronen LLD (Child Law), MA (Educational Counselling) is a lecturer at the Department of Social Work at Ben Gurion University of the Negev, Israel. His research interests include children's rights, social justice, human rights advocacy, and multiculturalism. He is involved in efforts to reform child law and policy in Israel.

Robert Mason, PhD is an Emeritus Professor at the Survey Research Center, Department of Statistics, Oregon State University. He received his doctorate from Stanford University in 1962 and has devoted his professional life to studying communication processes, survey methodology, and compliance with tax laws. The study on which this chapter is based was supported by a grant from the American Bar Foundation.

Safaa Amer works as a survey statistician with the National Opinion Research Center (NORC) at the University of Chicago. She received her Bachelor of Science degree in Statistics from the Faculty of Economics and Political Sciences at Cairo University, Egypt in 1996, her Master of Science in Statistics from Oregon State University in 2000, and her PhD in Statistics from Oregon State University in 2005.

Susan Block-Lieb teaches bankruptcy and commercial law courses at Fordham Law School, including advanced courses on Bankruptcy, Corporate Reorganization in Bankruptcy, International Insolvency Law, Consumer Protection Law and Secured Transactions. She is a delegate from the American Bar Association to UNCITRAL's Insolvency Working Group, Chair of the Subcommittee on International Bankruptcy to the ABA's Business Bankruptcy section, and treasurer and a member of the Board of

Directors for the Coalition for Consumer Bankruptcy Debtor Education. Together with Professor Karen Cross, she was the recipient of a 2002 New York State Bar Association President's Pro Bono Service Attorney Award. She is a prolific writer of law review and other articles.

Edward J Janger is a Professor of Law at Brooklyn Law School. He has also taught at the University of Pennsylvania, Washington University in Saint Louris, and Ohio State University. In 2004 Professor Janger served as the Robert M Zinman Scholar-in-Residence at the American Bankruptcy Institute, and he is currently the consultant to the United States Federal Bankruptcy Rules Advisory Committee. He has written extensively on the subjects of bankruptcy law and data privacy, and his most recent work has been published in the *Michigan Law Review*, *Texas Law Review*, *Willian and Mary Law Review* and *Minnesota Law Review*.

Helen J Self has campaigned for many years for legal justice for sex workers through her lecturing, writing, and reports on government papers and police initiatives. She has a BA in Social Science (history, sociology, social policy and law) and a PhD in Law from the University of Kent. Her thesis, entitled 'Prostitution, Women and Misuse of the Law. The Fallen Daughters of Eve' was published by Frank Cass in 2003. She has been a board member of the International Alliance of Women for six years and a member of the Josephine Butler Society Executive Committee for ten.

Stephen Frosh is Pro-Vice-Master, Professor of Psychology, and Director of the Centre for Psychosocial Studies at Birkbeck College, University of London. He was previously a Consultant Clinical Psychologist and Vice Dean at the Tavistock Clinic, London. His many books include *Hate and the 'Jewish Science': Anti-Semitism, Nazism and Psychoanalysis* (Palgrave, 2005), *For and Against Psychoanalysis* (Routledge, 2006), *Young Masculinities* (with Ann Phoenix and Rob Pattman, Palgrave, 2002), and *The Politics of Psychoanalysis* (Palgrave, 1999).

1

Law and Psychology: Issues for Today

Belinda Brooks-Gordon and Michael Freeman

Lawyers' interests in psychology and psychologists' interests in law can be traced back a long way. Indeed, questions of a psychological nature were being asked about law long before psychology emerged as a discrete discipline. Thus, for example, the 1833 Commissioners in England were 'proud' to acknowledge their debt to Cesare Beccaria.[1] But they were much less confident than Beccaria that 'all relevant circumstances and aggravations could be expressed adequately in legal precepts'.[2] Also, in contrast to Beccaria, the factors they were willing to take cognizance of in distinguishing among 'gradations of crime, shades of guilt, and choices of punishment included a number of the offender's subjective character-istics', which, of course, Beccaria would have rejected 'as likely to lead to bias and inequality'.[3] Even at this early stage, then, law was grappling with nascent psychology and not finding its conclusions completely palatable.

Today, the disciplines of law and psychology have a more comfortable co-existence. Indeed, they may be said to be inextricably intertwined. Several journals have emerged to promote this interaction, notably *Law and Human Behavior*[4] and *Behavioral Sciences and the Law*.[5] It is not uncommon for law reviews, particularly in the United States, to devote whole issues to questions of law and psychology.[6] This is not surprising, for psychology underpins many legal decisions and is at the root of many legal principles. To take some obvious examples, legal evidence may rest upon mental state or degree of harm, on issues of duress or trauma, or questions may arise as to the limits of provocation as in the many notorious cases where battered women have killed violent husbands.[7] Legal decisions may also depend upon predictions about future behaviour, for

---

[1] L Radzinowicz and R Hood, *A History of English Criminal Law*, vol 5 (London, 1986) 726.
[2] ibid 727.   [3] ibid.   [4] Now in its 30th year of publication.
[5] 2006 is the 24th year of the publication of this work.
[6] eg see (2004) 69(4) *Missouri Law Review*.
[7] See *R v Thornton* [1992] 1 All ER 306; *R v Ahluwalia* [1992] 4 All ER 889. And see P Brett, 'The Physiology of Provocation' [1970] *Criminal Law Review* 634 (which shows that legal assumptions are not borne out by psychological/physiological evidence). See also A Browne, *When Battered Women Kill* (New York, 1987).

example determining which placement is in a child's best interests[8] or whether an offender should be released from an institution, a prison, or a mental hospital.[9] There are legal principles which are rooted in doctrines of free will. The relationship between thought and behaviour is inherently psychological.

The disciplines are most obviously related in the criminal law. All serious crimes and most minor offences require proof that the defendant had the relevant blameworthy state of mind.[10] The traditional term for the state of mind that must be proved—*mens rea*—is sometimes used to include all degrees of fault, including negligence. But whilst it may be obvious that intention and recklessness are mental states, it is more difficult to conceptualize negligence as a state of mind. Recently, in *R v G* Lord Bingham stated that it was 'a salutary principle' that conviction of serious crime should depend on proof 'not simply that the defendant caused an injurious result to another but that his state of mind when so acting was culpable'.[11] But despite his strong endorsement of the subjectivist position, Parliament in the United Kingdom shows a fondness for creating serious offences in which the fault element is explicitly objective: examples include many sexual offences in the Sexual Offences Act 2003 and some of the money laundering offences in the Proceeds of Crime Act 2002.

But, as the contributions to this volume make very clear, the impact of psychology upon law goes way beyond the criminal process. There have never been more opportunities than in today's evidence-based culture for psychologists to contribute to the legal process, both at the stage of policy-making—witness the debates on law and sexuality during the passage of the Sexual Offences Act of 2003[12]—and during trial processes. Examples can be found in the area of family law. For example, the clinical psychologist, using theoretical and empirical models as guides, can provide information to help a court to determine whether a child is suffering or is likely to suffer significant harm as a result of a deficit in care by a parent. And child psychiatrists also have contributions to make.[13] Nor is this the only area of family law litigation where clinical psychology can make its mark—there are many issues adjacent to divorce where children's welfare is at

---

[8] See R Mnookin, 'Child Custody Adjudication: Judicial Functions In The Face of Indeterminacy' (1975) 39 *Law and Contemporary Problems* 226.

[9] See DP Farrington and R Tarling (eds), *Prediction in Criminology* (Albany, NY, 1985). See also Special Issue of *Law and Human Behavior* (2005) 29(1).

[10] JC Smith, 'The Guilty Mind In The Criminal Law' (1960) 76 LQR 78.

[11] [2004] 1 AC 1034, 1055.

[12] See A Bainham and B Brooks-Gordon, 'Reforming The Law on Sexual Offences' in B Brooks-Gordon, L Gelsthorpe, M Johnson, and A Bainham (eds), *Sexuality Repositioned: Diversity and the Law* (Oxford, 2004) 260–96.

[13] Required for a care or supervision order under s 31(2) of the Children Act 1989; and see D Jones, A Bentovim, H Cameron, E Vizard, and S Wolkind, 'Significant Harm in Context: the Child Psychiatrist's Contribution' in M Adcock, R White, and A Hollows (eds), *Significant Harm* (Croydon, 1991) 125–36. 'Significant harm' is defined by clinical psychologists, much as it is by lawyers, as extreme delays in the child's cognitive, emotional, social, or behavioural development that is attributable to inadequate parenting.

stake—but whether the courts use psychological research when they can rely on their common sense, as they see it, and their own personal experiences may be doubted.[14]

There are some important landmarks in law and psychology, and a number of significant texts have helped to define the subdisciplines which have emerged. One of the earliest books was Haward's *Forensic Psychology*.[15] Three years before this a conference in Oxford led to Sally Lloyd-Bostock's *Psychology in Legal Contexts*.[16] This concentrated on the reliability of witness evidence, on interrogation and confession, the psychologist as expert (including a piece by Lionel Haward), legal language and communication (this examined whether legal jargon was a restrictive practice),[17] and the applications of psychology in areas of substantive law, including family violence.[18]

There have been important studies into eyewitness testimony; Elizabeth Loftus's appeared in 1979.[19] Her main reason for writing this was a long-standing concern with cases in which an innocent person has, as a result of false identification, been gaoled. She has since co-edited (with Gary Wells) *Eyewitness Testimony: Psychological Perspectives*[20]—this included a legal response to the 'inherent dangers' of eyewitness identification testimony.[21] And there is now a handbook written by Wells[22] and in addition several other studies,[23] and a considerable body of psychological research which examines in detail the criteria which affect the quality of identification evidence.[24]

There are also important overviews, for example by Hollin[25] and by Blackburn.[26] Blackburn addresses, albeit briefly, the problem of role ambiguity and the ethical dilemmas this may cause. Who is the client? Of course, it is not just in the context of law that this arises—it clearly occurs in health and education as well—but here there are issues of liberty at stake. A significant development is Bull and Carson's edited volume offering a comprehensive handbook.[27] It provides a framework for the three subdisciplines that, McGuire argues, have emerged in forensic psychology.[28] These are *criminological* psychology, which provides

---

[14] See P Harnett, 'The Contribution of Clinical Psychologists to Family Law Proceedings in England' (1995) 6 *The Journal of Forensic Psychiatry* 173. [15] (London, 1981).

[16] (London, 1981).

[17] It would be nice to think that this has influenced the Woolf reforms, but we think this unlikely.

[18] By Michael Freeman (who has no recollection of writing this!).

[19] (Cambridge, Mass, 1979). [20] (New York, 1984).

[21] By Joseph Grano (see 315–35).

[22] *Eyewitness Identification: A System Handbook* (Toronto, 1988). For some of the latest developments, see O Machin, L Zimmerman, and R S Malpass (2005) 29 *Law and Human Behavior* 303–21.

[23] Including B Clifford and R Bull, *The Psychology of Person Identification* (London, 1978).

[24] See B Cutler and S Penrod, *Mistaken Identification: The Eyewitness, Psychology and the Law* (New York, 1995) and G Wells and E Olson, 'Eyewitness Identification' (2003) 54 *Annual Review* of *Psychology* 277. [25] *The Psychology of Crime* (London, 1989).

[26] *The Psychology of Criminal Conduct* (Chichester, 1993).

[27] *Handbook of Psychology in Legal Contexts* (Chichester, 1995).

[28] *Understanding Psychology and Crime* (Maidenhead, 2004).

explanations for and an understanding of offending behaviour—using direct research with offender populations in prison, probation, juvenile justice, and allied settings; *legal* psychology involving such things as the study of juries, decision-making process, eyewitness testimony, employment and discrimination issues, family law including child protection, and the scientific and ethical aspects of expert witness testimony; and *forensic* psychology, which includes research into memory for faces and events, witness reliability, interviewing vulnerable witnesses, false confessions, mental health tribunals, and hostage-taking. There is also *investigative* psychology, which includes offender-profiling[29] and explores crime scene analysis.

The history of the relationship of psychology with legal practice has been charted by Kapardis. He describes some recent influences on the inter-disciplinary enterprise such as the foundation in 1981 of the APA Psychology and Law Section, the setting up of the British Psychological Society Forensic Section, and the establishment of the European Association of Psychology and Law. There is now greater opportunity than there ever was for lawyers and psychologists to meet and to collaborate in a productive way.

This volume seeks to explore all the main areas of psychology:

   (1) attribution (social knowledge and explanation);

   (2) social identity (self-motives, self-esteem, impression management);

   (3) values, beliefs and attitudes and their relationship to behaviour;

   (4) persuasion and attitude change (arguments and behaviour);

   (5) compliance and social influence (including obedience and conformity);

   (6) groups (group cohesion, socialization, group structure);

   (7) leadership and decision-making;

   (8) prejudice (stigma and discrimination);

   (9) inter-group behaviour (relative deprivation, realistic conflict);

  (10) aggression (personal and situational factors);

  (11) cognition and language communication; and

  (12) culture (norms, contact between cultures).

And in doing so to relate them to law and its processes. The relationship of law and psychology is considered first in the three chapters by Jenny McEwan, Bruce Winick and Mandeep Dhami (Chapters 2 to 4). McEwan describes the points of contact between psychologists and lawyers since the Devlin Report of 1976[30] to analyse the classical psychological concept of attribution and how it has been used. Winick shows how therapeutic jurisprudence[31] can enhance the relationship

---

[29] See B Turvey, *Criminal Profiling* (London, 2002).

[30] *Evidence of Identification in Criminal Cases* (London, 1976).

[31] A term he coined together with David Wexler. See also Special Issue of *Contemporary Issues in Law* (2004) 7(1).

between psychology and law. Both McEwan and Winick discuss the contribution psychologists have made to the legal system. McEwan discusses confession evidence, identification evidence, and vulnerable witnesses—Winick, by contrast, offers a psychological approach to law that provides a new focus for law and psychology scholarship. He identifies new roles and contexts for clinical psychologists working in the legal system for transformative work, especially in the mental health system and offender rehabilitation. He offers a new lens though which to examine the legal system which both raises new questions and sets a new research agenda for immigration, juvenile justice, and human rights law.[32]

Dhami also bridges the divide between 'psychological reality' and 'legal idealism' in her study of magistrates' bail decisions in pre-trial cases. The performance of legal decision-makers is often divergent from, or in conflict with, legal ideals. Dhami presents original findings before scrutinizing the explanations for this practice, such as cognitive capabilities and task conditions, and offering potential interventions for change. Psychological research explains the inconsistencies in magistrates' decision-making, and why they do not work in accordance with due process considerations.

The law's relationship to the study of cognition is evaluated in the three chapters by Oliver Goodenough (Chapter 5); Paul Dougan, Fernand Gobet, and Michael King (Chapter 7); and Jeffrey Rachlinski (Chapter 8). Goodenough takes a provocative look at what psychology has offered the law. He argues that the limitations of some psychological models have prevented them from being foundational in law. His somewhat controversial chapter sets the scene for the chapters by Dougan and his colleagues and by Rachlinski. Dougan, Gobet and King use computational modelling to contrast legal and scientific communications. Rachlinski explores individual differences in the making of cognitive errors to consider the possibility of reducing the incidence of such errors in an identifiable group of people in the context of marketing techniques. This analysis shows that individual differences in cognitive errors cannot be overlooked.

Chapter 6—by Paul Robinson—shows how psychology is changing the debate about the theory of punishment. Psychology has been more successful, it may be thought, in helping the law to get its best evidence in forensic settings. Indeed, achieving the best evidence in such settings may be considered to be a major contribution of psychological scholarship to the legal process. It is certainly one of the ways in which psychology has altered the process of information gathering and analysis. In Chapter 9, Michael Lamb and Anneli Larsson explore developmentally appropriate interview techniques. In a state-of-the-art chapter, they encapsulate current understanding of the factors which affect children's ability to provide accurate information about experienced events. They discuss how to retrieve information, and how it can be communicated more effectively. They review

---

[32] For another application see C Shaffer, 'Therapeutic Domestic Violence Courts: An Efficient Approach to Adjudication?' (2004) 27 *Seattle University Law Review* 981–97.

current protocols to show how the interviewer can improve performance by changing his or her own behaviour so as to help children to retrieve as much remembered detail as possible, uncontaminated by the interviewer's own beliefs and expectations.

Sarah Henderson and Linda Taylor (Chapter 10) show how external stimuli, such as inappropriate questioning, can affect individual recall, especially in the preliminary legal interview and subsequent court process. They consider the impact of various questioning styles on recall, including complex syntax and vocabulary.

In Chapter 11, Aldert Vrij and Samantha Mann examine the extent to which the two lie detection methods of physiological response and speech content meet the criteria required for the admission of expert scientific evidence in criminal cases, according to the standard set by the *Daubert* decision of the US Supreme Court.[33] (Though it should be stressed this was not a criminal case.)

The major advances in our understanding of eyewitness identification— already referred to in this introduction—are explored further by Andrew Roberts (Chapter 12). He puts forward a theoretical framework into which this decision-making process can be placed. He demonstrates how the various aspects of procedure relate to, and might be affected by, what precedes and what follows in the legal process.

Helen Westcott's essay (Chapter 13) concludes this part of the collection. She examines where the gaps remain in current understandings of evidence, and she looks to the future by forging a new research agenda.

A number of chapters in this volume explore issues of family law: questions about the best interests of the child and about domestic violence featuring prominently. Nicholas Bala and Katherine Duvall Antonacopoulos (Chapter 14) focus on the clinical assessment by experts and mental health professionals as court-appointed assessors. Their chapter explores the influence of assessors. It investigates some of the controversies in the system as it exists and asks questions about the value of assessments as a source of information for judges and as assistance in reaching settlements. The extent to which it promotes the best interests of the child is also examined.

There are two contributions on domestic violence. Elizabeth Gilchrist (Chapter 15) reviews the research on domestic violence with a view to constructing typologies of perpetrators. With a focus on the best interests of children she reports on an ongoing study to explore issues related to risk and to child protection. Our understanding of domestic violence is further explored in relation to ethnicity and prejudice by Cynthia Willis Esqueda and Melissa Tehee

---

[33] 113 S Ct 2786 (1993). There is an extensive literature on this case including B Black, F Ayala, and C Saffron-Brinks (1994) 72 *Texas Law Review* 715, and J Sanders (1994) 78 *Minnesota Law Review* 1387.

(Chapter 16). They describe new legal and psychological approaches to violence against women in their research with Native American women.[34]

The theme of aggression permeates the chapters by Lizzie Barmes and Peter Bartlett (Chapters 17 and 18). Barmes examines psychological research on workplace bullying. She raises challenging questions about the application of learning derived from outside her own discipline of law to appraise legal responses to a growing social problem. The analysis of power issues and aggressive behaviour is taken a stage further by Bartlett, who considers the psychological issues raised by gay homicides. Drawing on data from a large study, he argues that these homicides are sufficiently similar to form a coherent subject for investigative study.

The development of human rights laws has given a new emphasis to the right of defendants to a fair trial. The problems of ensuring that this happens are aggravated when the trial is for terrorism. Neil Vidmar (Chapter 19) explores one aspect in particular of this problem: can we find jurors with sufficient impartiality to try such cases? Jurors will come to court against a background of intense media coverage, much, if not most, of it highly prejudicial to the defendant. Psychological research shows how prejudicial attitudes and beliefs can affect trial processes. Vidmar breaks down the dimensions of prejudice and advocates trial judges taking extraordinary steps to ensure a jury which can provide a fair trial.

Judith Fordham (Chapter 20) is also concerned to explore how juries process evidence, in particular how they assimilate, evaluate, and use expert testimony.

Justice for juveniles is a theme that runs though the next group of chapters. In the first of these (Chapter 21) Julia Fionda, Robert Jago, and Rachel Manning provide a critique of anti-social behaviour orders (ASBOs), which were introduced in England in 1998 as part of New Labour's 'respect' agenda. There is a concern now that these are over-used and are stigmatizing and, ultimately, criminalizing young people in particular. Far too many ASBOs have been imposed on learning disabled young people: estimates put the proportion as high as a third of such orders. Because ASBOs restrict space, they can be seen as an example of conflict over territory. Fionda and her colleagues challenge some manifestly outdated assumptions about the nature of group behaviour, and they look widely at some of the implications of these orders, for example at the criminogenic effects of 'grounding' young people.

Michael and Diane King (Chapter 22) are concerned about another group of young people, those with autism. They examine the ways in which legal decisions relating to the education of such children are taken. By applying a theoretical approach that concentrates on the interface between different social systems, they raise key questions about the claims of justice and how the educational needs of children with autism are met.

---

[34] For work on sexual abuse across American cultures—though this does not discuss Native Americans—see L Aronson Fontes, *Sexual Abuse in Nine American Cultures* (Thousand Oaks, California, 1995).

Ya'ir Ronen (Chapter 23) explores society's conflict over collective memory and the question of responsibility to minority groups. His chapter describes how professionals who fail to perceive this conflict can also fail to respond to individual suffering. By focusing on child protection and the public response to the victimization of young offenders, he shows how psychotherapists, judges, legislators, and also legal scholars can project meanings of their choice on to our collective and personal pasts. Such projections can then become part of the 'history' or 'the facts'.

In Chapters 24 and 25, issues relating to finance are addressed. Robert Mason and Safaa Amer discuss the dynamics of tax payment. How are we to persuade people to pay their taxes? What they found was that the persuasive force of a sanction threat is undermined because people interpret the message as being there to influence others rather than themselves. They look also at media messages: how these impact or are discounted and how this affects tax compliance.

Susan Block-Lieb and Edward Janger examine the mediated risk in consumer credit and bankruptcy (Chapter 25). In the light of the US Bankruptcy Act of 2005, they question the empirical accuracy of the picture painted of paradigmatic debtors by proponents of the legislation. They offer instead a more plausible and more problematic scenario of honest borrowing and inadvertent but crushing debt. Financial literacy, with large sanctions for the financially illiterate, is inevitable in the current climate. These two chapters illustrate important new terrain in which fruitful collaboration between law and psychology can take place.

In the final two chapters Helen Self (Chapter 26) explores the regulation of prostitution and Stephen Frosh (Chapter 27) the attitudes of the Nazis towards the 'Jewish science' of psychoanalysis. Although not immediately obvious, there is a link in these expositions. Both provide historical accounts of prejudice and intolerance. Self first explores the coercive intent running through prostitution legislation before we reach the 'New Labour' rhetoric of 'protecting the vulnerable', with its accompanying claims to be 'victim-centred'. She shows how the prostitute was constructed as 'the other' by the disciplines of psychology, psychiatry, and the law. She then explores the contemporary legal context, including the police strategy documents which have demonized clients but at the same time and paradoxically created a climate of greater vulnerability for sex workers.[35]

In Chapter 27, Stephen Frosh's paper reproduces the public lecture given at the end of the colloquium. It is about a clash of cultures, about prejudice and racism and the power of the state and of professional organizations. It describes and analyses what happens when the state tries to control science.[36] It offers, we believe, salutary lessons way beyond its immediate subject.

---

[35] An interesting comparison is with Victorian England: see the classic account by JR Walkowitz, *Prostitution and Victorian Society—women, class and the state* (Cambridge, 1980).

[36] An example of a text he does not discuss but which is highly pertinent, is O Weininger's *Sex and Character* (London, 1906) (previously published in Germany in 1903). And see further MC Nussbaum, *Hiding from Humanity—Disgust, Shame and the Law* (Princeton, NJ, 2004) 108.

As was said in the Preface, this colloquium was held against the backdrop of the London bombings. We would like to think that the productive discussions that took place at the colloquium and which are reflected in this volume contribute a little to our understanding of these events. The interface between law and psychology is not a bad place to begin exploring the issues of fear and control which surrounded the events of that day. The events gave the colloquium and this book a new relevance. It is clear to us that volumes such as this can promote understanding. We would hope that policy-makers will find important insights in this book and that researchers will investigate further some of the newer terrain explored herein.

2

Breaking Down the Barriers

Jenny McEwan

An Interdisciplinary Subject?

My question in this chapter is whether law and psychology is really an inter-disciplinary field, or whether it is simply the case that scholars are carrying out work in law and in psychology which infrequently, and perhaps by accident, overlaps. My argument is that although there are many areas of common interest, it is only rarely that practitioners in either discipline become aware of this, and it is almost unheard of for them to work together. The fields where common interest has been identified are well known; for example, there is a huge literature available in the fields of criminology and victimology. Psychologists and other behavioural specialists have in fact led the debate on patterns of crime and the disposal of offenders.

In other areas of law, also largely on the criminal side of the legal system, it might be thought that the two areas of expertise are increasingly coming together, even in the United Kingdom, which is far less adventurous than the United States in this respect. Back in the mid-1970s, the Devlin Report[1] could be regarded as a breakthrough in its reliance on psychological research. It was immediately followed by the Court of Appeal's decision in *Turnbull*,[2] where the Court reacted to the empirical evidence cited by Devlin. In all identification cases, finders of fact must be warned of the risk of error. From then on, it seemed to be established practice for major inquiries into the criminal justice system to commission their own empirical studies. Two successive Royal Commissions on the criminal justice system sponsored empirical research.[3] More recently, Sir Robin Auld commissioned a literature review of jury research to inform his inquiry into the workings

---

[1] *Report of the Departmental Committee on Evidence of Identification* (Cmnd 338, 1976).
[2] [1977] 2 QB 871.
[3] *Report of the Royal Commission on Criminal Procedure* (Phillips Report) (Cmnd 8092, 1981); *Report of the Royal Commission on Criminal Justice* (Runciman Report) (Cm 2263, 1993); More recently, the Law Commission did the same, commissioning the Oxford studies by Sally Lloyd-Bostock into jury and magistrates' reactions to bad character evidence. Her findings were published

of the criminal courts.[4] In discussion of certain areas of substantive law he demonstrates a high degree of awareness of and respect for experimental and observational empirical work. This endorsement has helped to make that research more familiar to a large circle of criminal practitioners. The Criminal Bar Association of England and Wales, generally perceived to be a conservative institution, recently commissioned Neil Kibble's research into the operation of the 'rape shield' legislation of 1999.[5] Criminal lawyers had already been showing increasing awareness of Professor Gudjonsson's work on confessions. Its significance has been such that convictions from the relatively distant past are even now being reassessed; only recently, a conviction from 1978 was overturned on the ground that a confession obtained in circumstances that may have rendered it coerced-compliant should have been excluded from evidence.[6]

But why were lawyers willing to take account in these areas of their activities of the results of psychological research? Would the disturbing literature on false confessions ever have seen the legal light of day if Gudjonsson had not become involved in the notorious miscarriages of justice involving the Guildford Four and the Birmingham Six?[7] The modification of the law on identification, which might appear on the surface to have been influenced primarily by the work of psychologists, and to have been motivated by the desire to ensure the fairness of trials, also followed a dramatic campaign of vocal public disquiet.[8] The Devlin Report on identification evidence was commissioned in response to two other well-publicized miscarriages of justice, one of which was uncovered by the pressure group, Justice.[9] However, by the time the Report was published, the country was reeling from the sabotage by the 'Free George Davis' campaigners of a cricket pitch at Headingley in 1975. The match was abandoned, costing the England team a likely victory over Australia. This event was followed by the prosecution of Peter Hain (now Secretary of State for Northern Ireland, then President of the Young Liberals) in 1976 for bank robbery. He was identified by three schoolboys and a cashier. He had a high public profile because of his campaign to stop tours

---

as Appendices to each of the following: Law Commission, *Evidence in Criminal Proceedings: Previous Misconduct of a Defendant* (Law Com No 141, Cm 1996); Law Commission, *Evidence of Bad Character in Criminal Proceedings* (Law Com No 273, Cm 5257, 2001).

[4] Sir Robin Auld, *Criminal Courts Review*, (London, 2001;<http://www.criminal-courts-review.org.uk>).

[5] N Kibble, *Judicial Perspectives on Section 41 of the Youth Justice and Criminal Evidence Act 1999* (Aberystwyth, 2004). [6] *Blackburn The Times*, 10 June 2005.

[7] GH Gudjonsson, *The Psychology of Interrogations, Confessions, and Testimony* (Chichester, 1992).

[8] Parl Debs HC, vol 761, col 553; see R Brandon and C Davies, *Wrongful Imprisonment* (London, 1973).

[9] The case of Luke Dougherty; his conviction in 1972 for shoplifting was quashed by the Court of Appeal in 1974. The other case, that of Laszlo Viraj, involved convictions for various theft and firearm offences in 1969. The convictions appeared unsafe in the light of articles found in the possession of another man, arrested for other offences in 1971. Viraj was granted a Free Pardon in 1974: *Report of the Departmental Committee on Evidence of Identification*, n 1 above.

of South Africa by rugby and cricket teams. He produced an alibi, and was acquitted. The issue of mistaken identification had become a matter of general concern. Similarly, public pressure might account for the scale of the changes to the criminal justice process that have taken place over the last twenty years to accommodate children and other vulnerable witnesses. Would so much notice have been taken of their plight had it not been for the campaigning of such notable figures as Esther Rantzen, the television personality and founder of ChildLine?[10] Would Parliament and judges have become so aware of the invidious effects of cross-examination in trials of sexual offences and of the rape myths attached to complainants without the furore following Lynn Ferguson's award-winning documentary for Channel 4?[11]

The Auld Review breaks new ground insofar as we find a respected judge citing psychological research on the question of demeanour evidence. He expressed doubts as to the evidential value of demeanour as a means of assessing a witness's reliability, and, in consequence, suggested that the rule against hearsay should be given much less prominence in criminal trials.[12] While Auld should be congratulated for the breadth of his Review, at the same time it has to be conceded that the hearsay rule has caused the legal system itself a great deal of inconvenience. This became dramatically apparent when the House of Lords decided the case of *Kearley*.[13] This case involved a prosecution for dealing in drugs. While the police searched the defendant's flat, they intercepted ten telephone calls and received seven visitors at the door who, thinking they were talking to 'Chippie' (as Kearley was known), asked him to supply them with drugs. The officers' evidence was held to be inadmissible hearsay. The conviction had to be quashed,[14] despite the power of the common-sense inference that he must be a dealer. In this context, Auld's suggestion that there should be less emphasis on demeanour and therefore less insistence that the maker of the statement must appear in court to be cross-examined could be seen as a manifestation of disillusion with the exclusionary power of a rule that has become so technical it is almost impossible to comprehend. Parliament has not, however, gone as far as Auld recommended. Although the ambit of the rule against hearsay was considerably reduced by the provisions of the Criminal Justice Act 2003, neither Parliament nor a powerful lobby within the legal profession showed any inclination to abolish it altogether.[15] And outside the thorny context of hearsay, judicial reliance on demeanour as a clue to credibility seems as unshakeable as ever. For

---

[10] See eg *Minutes of Evidence*, HC Joint Committee on Human Rights, (17 June 2002) 331.
[11] 'Dispatches: Getting Away with Rape', Channel 4, 16 February 1994. See also S Lees, *Carnal Knowledge: Rape on Trial* (London, 2002).   [12] Auld, n 4 above, 11.79–11.80.
[13] [1992] 2 All ER 345.
[14] A Pyrrhic victory, since Kearley had died by the time his conviction was overturned.
[15] See Briefings on the Criminal Justice Bill 2003 by the General Council of the Bar, <http://www.Barcouncil.org.uk/documents/BriefingOntheCriminalJusticeBillMar03.doc>; and Liberty, <http://www.liberty-human-rights.org.uk>.

example, in the recent case, *Armstrong v First York*,[16] the claimants were the driver of and passenger in a car which was hit by the defendant's bus. The parties jointly instructed a forensic motor vehicle engineer whose evidence suggested that the claimants were lying. The judge said that he could find no error in the expert's evidence, but thought that there must be one, since the claimants struck him as 'blameless and honest'. His decision was upheld by the Court of Appeal.

Similarly, it could be said that psychology became part of the debate about evidence of the bad character of the defendant at the point when the law was seen to be becoming unmanageable. The Anglo-American law of evidence attempts to differentiate highly probative bad character evidence from that which is merely prejudicial; this has led to much confusion. Exceptions to the rule were incoherent, and, as with all flawed rules of criminal evidence, led to unmeritorious but sometimes-successful appeals. The Law Commission noted in 1997 that 'The House of Lords has considered similar fact evidence twice in the past five years',[17] and that the Court of Appeal had been required to consider section 1 of the Criminal Evidence Act 1898 nineteen times in the previous six years.[18] This was largely due to the law in the area being 'difficult to comprehend, embodied . . . in a series of judgments that are not always reconcilable'.[19] In response to this disarray, many lawyers (myself included) have resorted to empirical evidence to undermine the premise on which the exclusionary rule is founded, namely the assumption that fact-finders who learn of the defendant's previous misconduct will be disproportionately biased against the accused. Auld does the same, quoting empirical studies which try to assess the reactions of juries and magistrates where such evidence is admitted.[20] Meanwhile, lawyers who object to relaxation of the bad character rules have adopted a similar strategy. Thus we find the same empirical data being used to support arguments on both sides of the previous misconduct debate.[21] Cynical sociologists accused lawyers some time ago of a 'cherry-picking' attitude to social science.[22] Whether or not that is fair, it cannot be denied that the controversy surrounding hearsay and bad character evidence is to some extent coloured by an ideology that may encourage a selective attitude to the empirical evidence that is marshalled for or against reform.

[16] *The Times*, 19 January 2005.
[17] Law Commission, *Evidence in Criminal Proceedings: Previous Misconduct of a Defendant*, n 3 above, 1.2.   [18] ibid, 1.4.
[19] *Report of the Royal Commission on Criminal Justice* (Runciman Report), n 3 above, 8.30.
[20] Auld, n 4 above, 11.118.
[21] Arguing for relaxation of the rules, Auld, n 4 above, 11.119: J McEwan, 'Previous Misconduct at the Crossroads: Which Way Ahead'? [2002] *Criminal Law Review* 180. *Contra*, Law Commission, *Evidence of Bad Character in Criminal Proceedings*, n 3 above, 6.57–6.61; C Tapper, 'Criminal Justice Act 2003' [2004] *Criminal Law Review* 533; R Munday, 'What Constitutes "Other Reprehensible Behaviour" under the Bad Character Provisions of the Criminal Justice Act 2003?' [2005] *Criminal Law Review* 24.
[22] R Cotterrell, 'Why Must Legal Rules Be Interpreted Sociologically?' (1998) 25 *British Journal of Law and Society* 171.

Not Going Far Enough

Confession Evidence

What concessions have been made in England and Wales to the results of research into the psychology behind an innocent person confessing to the police? Although it is clear that the experience of being held on arrest and questioned by police is inevitably intimidating and stressful,[23] courts seem to have little sympathy for defendants who cannot cope.[24] The confession will not necessarily be excluded from evidence. Under section 76(2)(b) of the Police and Criminal Evidence Act 1984 (PACE), in a case where it is represented to the court that a confession was or may have been obtained 'in consequence of anything said or done which was likely to render unreliable any confession which might be made by him in consequence thereof', the confession is inadmissible unless the prosecution proves beyond reasonable doubt that the confession was not so obtained. However, this provision applies only when something was 'said or done' to the suspect that could have such an effect; therefore a confession obtained in consequence of anxiety alone or even illness falls outside its scope, unless the police have behaved improperly.[25] A defence argument that such a confession should be excluded must be made under section 78 of PACE, which gives the court a discretion to exclude if it considers that the admission of the evidence would have an adverse effect on the fairness of the proceedings. Here the burden rests on the defence to convince the court that potential unreliability should prevent the confession being admitted into evidence.

The discretionary nature of section 78 inevitably renders trials somewhat unpredictable. For example, in the *Kilner* case,[26] the defendant had a low IQ, epilepsy, and became hysterical when he found himself in difficulties. There had been no misconduct by the police, but the confession was not admitted in evidence. In contrast, the trial judge in the *McKenzie* case[27] did not exclude the defendant's confession. McKenzie had been arrested on suspicion of arson, which he duly admitted in interview. Unprompted, he then went on to confess to twelve murders, ten of which the police did not believe he had committed. He was nevertheless tried for the remaining two murders although there was no other evidence to implicate him. He was convicted. On appeal, Professor Gudjonsson gave expert evidence of McKenzie's suggestible and compliant personality,[28] and McKenzie's conviction was quashed. In terms of precedent, the importance of the *McKenzie* case is the judgment that in cases where a

---

[23] eg B Irving and L Hilgendorf, *Police Interrogation: The Psychological Approach*: B Irving, *Police Interrogation: A Case Study of Current Practice* Royal Commission on Criminal Procedure Research Studies Nos 1 and 2 (HMSO: London, 1980).   [24] *Fulling* [1987] 2 All ER 65.
[25] *Goldenberg* [1987] 2 All ER 65.   [26] [1976] Crim LR 740.
[27] (1992) 96 Cr App R 98.   [28] Gudjonsson, n 7 above, 243–7.

prosecution case depends wholly upon a confession made by a defendant who suffers from a significant degree of mental handicap and the confession is unconvincing to the point where a jury, properly directed, could not properly convict upon it, the judge should stop the case altogether.

The problem with *McKenzie* is that it applies only where there is no other evidence to suggest that the confession is true. Numerous cases where a false confession appeared to be confirmed by circumstantial or other evidence linking the suspect to the crime, some of which are described in Gudjonsson's book, suggest that it is relatively easy to find some evidence in support. It is worrying that courts do not appear to feel obliged to stop the case, for example, if this supporting evidence consists of the level of detail in the confession. In the *Bailey* case[29] the suspect suffered from serious learning disability. She confessed to a friend, and then to police, that she was responsible for a fire in which an elderly woman died. There was no appropriate adult present at her interview with the police, who were not aware of Bailey's disability. She later retracted the confession she had made to the police, but then confessed again in the presence of a solicitor and a social worker. The prosecution was allowed to go forward, despite the evidence of learning disability, on the ground that she displayed such remorse, and the later confession contained so much detail, that the jury should consider it. The idea that the suspect's guilt is confirmed by his knowing things that only the perpetrator of the crime would know is highly dangerous. Kassin and Wrightsman give the example of Clifton Lawson, who was eighteen, but had an IQ of 70, the emotional maturity of a five-year-old, and 'disturbed mental conditioning'.[30] His confession to the rape and murder of an elderly woman contained details that only the police and the killer would know. He was saved from disaster by the discovery that fingerprints at the scene were not his. It transpired that Lawson had overheard the police and the Forensic Medical Examiner discussing details of the case. He confessed because he wanted to leave the police station and go to choir practice.

Should the court decide that a particular confession is admissible, the defence are entitled to argue that nevertheless the circumstances in which it was made render it so unreliable that it should not be taken by the finder of fact to indicate guilt.[31] To this end they may call on expert evidence as long as the accused does not occupy the category of the 'normal' individual whose likely reaction to being interrogated the magistrates or jurors are apparently entirely capable of assessing for themselves. Expert evidence on the reliability of the confession is allowed for defendants with a personality disorder or learning difficulties, but the judgment in the *Ward* case refers to personality disorders so severe as properly to be characterized as mental disorders,[32] and even if expert evidence is heard in such a case,

---

[29] 26 January 1995.
[30] SM Kassin and LS Wrightsman *The American Jury on Trial* (New York, 1988) 87.
[31] *Wong Kam-Ming v R* [1980] AC 247. [32] *Ward* [1993] 3 All ER 577.

the jury should be directed that they do not have to accept it.[33] If a confession is allowed to go to the jury, there is a substantial risk that they will disregard the expert evidence and convict. The intuitive notion that confessions are strong evidence of guilt is difficult to dispel. Acquittals following confession evidence are rare.[34] Although mock jurors are likely to disregard confessions obtained after threats of violence from the police, they tend to act on those obtained in response to an offer of leniency, even if given an explanation of the relationship between hopes of advantage and involuntariness in law.[35] Police officers also find it hard to believe that a confession may not be true.[36] In some jurisdictions, such as France, the psychology of false confessions is simply not recognized.[37]

Identification Evidence

I shall not here go into the question of the wisdom of generalizing from the methodology of laboratory experiments on eyewitness evidence to the concrete criminal case, on which there is much literature.[38] The Devlin Report indicated numerous instances of genuine miscarriages of justice that resulted from mistaken identification. There are some notable near misses too, as in the case of Patrick Murphy. A cab driver was abducted by a man intending to plant a bomb. Murphy was selected at an identification by three people including the cab driver. Eleven members of his local Alcoholics Anonymous meeting had to sacrifice their anonymity in order to confirm his alibi.[39] The gravity of the danger is insufficiently addressed in the *Turnbull* decision, particularly regarding cases where the identification evidence is weak. Although it was held that a trial should be stopped if the prosecution case rests entirely upon poor quality identification evidence, this is less reassuring than it seems. In the *Weeder* case[40] it was held that one poor quality identification can be supported by another, which means that the case can proceed and potentially lead to a conviction. This disregards the massive literature showing that there is no safety in numbers. Indeed, the Court of Appeal recently

---

[33] *O'Brien, Hall and Sherwood The Times*, 16 February 2005.

[34] J Baldwin and M McConville, *Confessions in Crown Court Trials* (Royal Commission on Criminal Procedure Research Study No 5 (HMSO: London, 1980); R Underwager and H Wakefield, 'False Confessions and Police Deception' (1992) 10 *American Journal of Psychology* 49.

[35] EE Jones, 'The Rocky Road from Acts to Dispositions' (1979) 34 *American Psychologist* 107.

[36] T Williamson, *Strategic Charges in Police Interrogation*' unpublished PhD thesis, University of Kent.

[37] J Hodgson, 'Comparing Legal Cultures: the Comparativist as a Participant Observer' in D Nelken (ed), *Contrasting Criminal Justice* (Aldershot, 2000).

[38] M King, *Psychology in or out of Court* (London, 1986); S Lloyd-Bostock, 'Juries and Jury Research in Context' in G Davies, S Lloyd-Bostock, K MacMurran, and C Wilson, (eds) *Psychology Law and Criminal Justice* (Berlin, 1996); R Hastie, S Penrod, and N Pennington, *Inside the Jury* (Cambridge, Mass, 1983); JC Yuille and JL Cutshall 'A Field Study of Eyewitness Memory of a Crime' (1986) 71 *Journal of Applied Psychology* 291.

[39] PB Ainsworth, *Psychology, Law and Eyewitness Testimony* (Chichester, 1998) 80.

[40] (1980) 71 Cr App R 228.

appeared to accept that a number of 'fleeting glimpse' identifications could support each other, even though it is not clear that they all related to the same person. In the case of Barry George, whose conviction for murdering Jill Dando was upheld in 2002,[41] some of the sightings were four hours apart.

According to a large body of psychological research,[42] the warning given to finders of fact in those identification cases that do proceed is unlikely to be effective. There is, however, reason to believe that an explanation from an expert witness would have more power,[43] but it is unlikely that courts in the United Kingdom would allow this, since:

The fact that an expert witness has impressive scientific qualifications does not by that fact alone make his opinion on matters of human nature and behaviour within the limits of normality any more helpful than that of the jurors themselves; but there is a danger that they may think that it does.[44]

Vulnerable Witnesses

An avalanche of real-life research into the effect of cross-examination on vulnerable witnesses has led to a series of measures to avoid unnecessary stress.[45] The most notable of these are the live link[46] and the videotaped interview.[47] First children, and then other vulnerable witnesses, have been assisted by these special measures. A powerful lobby had argued for videotaped interviews to allow the testimony of child witnesses to be recorded at a time when events are reasonably fresh in their memory. Included in this lobby were John Spencer and Rhona Flin, whose book in fact represents a rare collaboration between lawyer and psychologist, and has been highly influential.[48] The success of the child-centred measures encouraged the Government to think about overcoming some of the practical problems confronting some categories of adult witness.

---

[41] *George (Barry Michael) The Times*, 30 August 2002.

[42] eg WA Wagenaar, PJ van Koppen, and HM Crombag, *Anchored Narratives: the Psychology of Criminal Evidence* (Hemel Hempstead, 1993); KD Williams, EF Loftus, and KA Deffenbacher, 'Eyewitness testimony' in DK Kagehiro and WS Laufer (eds), *Handbook of Psychology and Law* (New York, 1992); BL Cutler and SD Penrod, *Mistaken Identification: The Eyewitness, Psychology and Law* (Cambridge, 1995) 255–64.

[43] ibid, 225–51; GL Wells, RCL Lindsay, and JP Tousignant, 'Effects of Expert Psychiatric Advice on Human Performance in Judging the Validity of Eyewitness Testimony' (1980) 4 *Law and Human Behavior* 275.　　　　　　　　　　[44] *Turner* [1975] 1 All ER 70 *per* Lawton LJ, 74.

[45] For a summary, see L Ellison, *The Adversarial Process and the Vulnerable Witness* (Oxford, 2001).

[46] The use of CCTV began with child witnesses in the Criminal Justice Act 1988, s 32. Eligibility for the live link has been extended from the vulnerable witnesses identified in the Youth Justice and Criminal Evidence Act 1999 to all witnesses: Criminal Justice Act 2003, s 51.

[47] Originally introduced in Criminal Justice Act 1991, s 54, for children only; extended to vulnerable witnesses generally, Youth Justice and Criminal Evidence Act 1999, s 27; extended to all eyewitnesses, Criminal Justice Act 2003, s 137.

[48] J Spencer and R Flin, *The Evidence of Children: the Law and the Psychology* (2nd edn, London, 1993) 105.

Hence, some of the studies that have led to the introduction and improvement of the operation of these measures have in fact been conducted on behalf of Government Departments.[49] The most recent survey, amongst adult vulnerable witnesses, found satisfaction rates levels to be high; 98 per cent of witnesses who used the live link or videotaped interview felt they had been able to say all they wanted to say.[50] Special measures are now to be provided to other kinds of witness, under the Criminal Justice Act 2003.

A cynical view of the motivation here is that it is merely pragmatic. Although, in theory, neither to encourage witnesses to come forward nor to facilitate testimony is a prosecution-centred activity, in practice, special measures are most commonly used by witnesses for the prosecution. It is clearly advantageous to the prosecution if the testimony of alleged victims can be delivered as clearly and confidently as possible. In contrast, there seems to be little concern about enabling the accused person to give the most fluent testimony possible. In England and Wales even child defendants are denied special measures, although legislation has recently been introduced that remedies this for Scotland.[51] In England and Wales, therefore, we have seen cases in the youth court where the defendant has been younger than the child prosecution witnesses, but the accusers have had the protection of special measures. The legislation specifically excludes an accused person from the special measures provisions. The House of Lords, in an appeal heard in 2005,[52] considered that this situation did not amount to a breach of the right to a fair trial under Article 6 of the European Convention on Human Rights. Baroness Hale conceded that many child defendants may have serious communication difficulties:

The child defendants appearing [in the youth court] are often amongst the most disadvantaged and the least able to give a good account of themselves. They lack the support and guidance of responsible parents. They lack the support of the local social services authority. They lack basic educational and literacy skills. They lack emotional and social maturity. They often have the experience of violence or other abuse within the home. Increasing numbers are being committed for trial in the Crown Court where these disadvantages will be even more disabling.[53]

The answer to that problem, she concluded, could not be to deprive other child witnesses of special measures; that would be to have the worst of all possible

---

[49] eg G Davies and E Noon, *An Evaluation of the Live Link for Child Witnesses* (London, 1991); K Murray, *Live Television Link: an Evaluation of its use by Child Witnesses in Scottish Criminal Trials* (Edinburgh, 1995); G Davies, C Wilson, R Mitchell, and J Milson, *Videotaping Children's Evidence: an Evaluation* (Home Office: London, 1995); Social Services Inspectorate, *The Child, the Court and the Video* (London, 1994).

[50] Home Office Research Study 283, *Are Special Measures Working? Evidence from Surveys of Vulnerable and Intimidated Witnesses* (London, 2004).

[51] Vulnerable Witnesses (Scotland) Act 2004, s 1, amending Criminal Procedure (Scotland) Act 1995, s 1.   [52] *R (on the application of D) v Camberwell Green Youth Court* [2005] 1 All ER 999.

[53] ibid, 1017.

worlds. In any case, there are obvious practical difficulties regarding the production of a video-recorded interview to replace the evidence in chief of a juvenile defendant. Also, some of the measures are inappropriate, being designed specifically to shield the witness from the defendant.[54] Significantly, however, Baroness Hale[55] was unconvinced by the suggestion[56] that the courts have no inherent power to allow the live link to a defendant in a criminal case. It remains to be seen whether youth courts will feel encouraged to allow CCTV links for juvenile defendants who lack communication skills.

Like child witnesses for the prosecution, alleged victims of sexual offences are eligible for special measures[57] and also protection from cross-examination by the accused in person.[58] However, many criminal justice systems across the world are still struggling to adjust in the light of descriptions, drawn from observation studies and interviews, of the trauma suffered by those complainants who give evidence. In addition, it is not clear that finders of fact have sufficient information to give appropriate weight to the evidence they hear of complainants' behaviour and general character. Most ordinary people harbour a stereotypical picture of rape, in which a stranger assailant, who is probably an unattractive social and mental misfit, employs some violence in an outdoor attack. On the victim's part there should be resistance.[59] Violence and premeditation are seen as integral to stranger rape but not acquaintance or date rape,[60] although in Lees' study[61] the most violence was found in cases where the parties had had consensual sex in the past (20 per cent of the total). Nevertheless, in her study, only 33 per cent of the alleged acquaintance rapes led to a conviction, whereas all the stranger rapes did so. Even a brief acquaintance with the defendant seems likely to prompt an acquittal.[62] Indeed, one of the rape allegations made against Ian Huntley, who subsequently went on to murder two young girls, was not proceeded with because nightclub CCTV footage showed the complainant dancing with him in an intimate

---

[54] ibid.   [55] ibid, 1018.

[56] In *R (on the application of S) v Waltham Forest Youth Court* [2004] All ER 590.

[57] Youth Justice and Criminal Evidence Act 1999, s 17(4) in fact creates a presumption in favour of special measures for complainants in sexual cases.

[58] Youth Justice and Criminal Evidence Act 1999, ss 34 and 35.

[59] KM Ryan, 'Rape and Seduction Scripts' (1988) 12 *Psychology of Women Quarterly* 237; S Estrich, *Real Rape: How the Legal System Victimises Women Who Say No* (Boston, 1987); A Clarke, J Moran-Ellis, and J Sleney, *Attitudes to Date Rape and Relationship Rape: a Qualitative Study*, Sentencing Advisory Panel Research Report No 2 (London, 2002), <http://www.sentencing-advisory-panel.gov.uk/research; JE Workman and EW Freeburg, 'An Examination of Date Rape, Victim Dress and Perceiver Variables Within the Context of Attribution Theory' (1999) *Sex Roles: A Journal of Research* 413–14.

[60] JVP Check and NM Malamuth, 'Sex Role Stereotyping and Reactions to Depictions of Stranger versus Acquaintance Rape' (1983) 45 *Journal of Personality and Social Psychology* 344.

[61] Lees, n 11 above.

[62] G LaFree, *Rape and Criminal Justice: the Social Construction of Sexual Assault* (Belmont, Calif, 1989); J Harris and S Grace, *A Question of Evidence: Investigating and Prosecuting Rape in the 1990s*, HORS 196 (London, 1999); Check and Malamuth, n 60 above.

way.[63] Apparently eager or encouraging behaviour from the woman is at odds with the 'rape script'. [64] In acquaintance rape cases the features commonly associated with rape are absent, so it is difficult to obtain convictions in acquaintance rape cases. [65]

Although the 'rape script' represents only a tiny minority of genuine rape cases, there is no mechanism to alert the jury to this. In any event, it may be difficult to dispel the stereotype if a strong psychological imperative lies behind it. Doubts as to whether a situation amounts to rape without clear indicators such as serious violence from the offender and spirited resistance from the victim may be explained according to the theory of Just World. According to Lerner,[66] people are more comfortable believing the world to be a fair and predictable place in which there is a reasonable fit between merit and reward. An event in which a person suffers serious injury without somehow being responsible threatens the belief that the world is just. In well-known experiments, it was found that where people are asked to observe someone apparently being punished severely but are powerless to help, they react by rejecting the victim and finding her unsympathetic.[67] There are obvious parallels with a rape trial here. The jury are confronted both with a description of a serious attack on the complainant, and they also have to watch her being subjected to a hostile and often degrading cross-examination. If we wish to dispel the false expectations that operate in sexual cases, the *Turnbull* solution of a judicial warning is unlikely to have much effect. Perhaps an expert account of what rape cases look like in reality should be allowed. There are many 'rape myths' that are candidates for expert evidence, such as the expectation that a genuine victim would report the

---

[63] J Smith, 'It Has Never Been Easier to Get Away With Rape' *The Times*, 2 July 2004. The school at which Huntley was employed as a caretaker would not have employed him had the Head been aware of a string of sexual offences, in relation to a number of different women and young girls, of which Huntley had been accused. Huntley was convicted of murdering two ten-year-old girls, Holly Wells and Jessica Chapman, in 2002.

[64] Harris and Grace, n 62 above, 57; HL Littleton and D Axsom, 'Rape and Seduction Scripts of University Students: Implications for Rape Attributions and Unacknowledged Rape' (2003) 49 *Sex Roles: a Journal of Research* 465; B Krahe, 'Police Officers' Definition of Rape: a Prototype Study', (1991) 1 *Journal of Community and Applied Social Psychology* 223; Ryan, n 59 above; RS Shotland and L Goodstein, 'Just Because She Doesn't Want To Doesn't Mean It's Rape' (1983) 46 *Social Psychology Quarterly* 220; Clarke, Moran-Ellis, and Sleney, n 59 above. On script theory generally, RP Abelson, 'The Structure of Belief Systems' in K Colby and R Schank (eds), *Computer Simulations of Thought and Language* (San Francisco, Calif, 1973).

[65] Ryan, n 59 above; Estrich, n 59 above; Clarke, Moran-Ellis and Sleney, n 59 above.

[66] MJ Lerner, 'Evaluation of Performance as a Function of Performer's Reward and Attractiveness' (1965) 1 *Journal of Personality and Social Psychology* 355. Doubted, AL Chaikin and JM Darley, 'Victim or Perpetrator: Defensive Attribution of Responsibility and the Need for Order' (1973) 25 *Journal of Personality and Social Psychology* 268.

[67] MJ Lerner and CH Simmons, 'Observer's Reaction to the Innocent Victim' (1966) 4 *Journal of Personality and Social Psychology* 203.

offences as soon as possible. Reform in this direction is currently being contemplated by the Government.[68]

It is claimed that such a shift has occurred in relation to evidence of the previous sexual experience of complainants in rape cases. This has been one of the most hotly debated issues in criminal law over the last few years. Legislatures in countries all over the world have tried, with varying degrees of success, to devise a workable 'rape shield' to limit the use of sexual history in rape trials. Rather less attention has been paid to the issue of the relevance of the complainant's behaviour, arguably short of coming within the sexual behaviour category, that might be vaguely suggestive that he or she is of a flirtatious disposition.[69] A number of studies suggest that both kinds of evidence are highly damaging to a prosecution case in a sexual offence trial. For example, LaFree, whose methodology included trial observation and interviews with jurors, criminal practitioners, and judges, found that a complainant was less likely to be believed if she had had sex outside marriage.[70] A jury that hears such evidence in a case where the defence is consent is more likely to acquit than one that does not.[71] But Neil Kibble has expressed a note of caution against studies that take as a starting point that there is no proper, non-prejudicial use of such evidence apart from the question of the defendant's belief in consent. He accuses some researchers of assuming that any use by a mock jury of the evidence for any other purpose demonstrates 'the prejudicial impact of the evidence'.[72] Neil Kibble himself presents a reassuring picture of judicial enlightenment. His interviews with judges show them to approach the question of relevance and admissibility thoughtfully and with awareness of the dangers. If the evidence had to be admitted, they wanted to keep to a minimum the sexual content of any descriptions of previous incidents in the complainant's life. Historically, however, there has been a yawning chasm between lawyers' descriptions of their own practices in court and the reality as exposed by observational studies. One of the points of disagreement is, inevitably, the actual relevance of the evidence to the issue at trial. But there are encouraging signs in the case law[73] and in the recent Home Office study[74] into

[68] Office for Criminal Justice Reform, *Convicting Rapists and Protecting Victims* (Consultation Paper, London, 2006).

[69] J McEwan, 'Proving Consent in Sexual Cases: Legislative Change and Cultural Evolution' [2005] *International Journal of Evidence and Proof* 1.   [70] LaFree, n 62 above.

[71] K Cotton, 'Evidence Regarding the Prior Sexual History of an Alleged Rape Victim: its Effect on the Perceived Guilt of the Accused' (1975) 33 *University of Toronto Law Review* 165; E Borgida and N Brekke, 'Psycholegal Research on Rape Trials' in AW Burgess (ed), *Rape and Sexual Assault* (New York, 1985).

[72] N Kibble, *Judicial Perspectives on Section 41 of the Youth Justice and Criminal Evidence Act 1999* (Aberystwyth, 2004) 177.   [73] eg *Mokrecovas* [2002] 1 Cr App R 226.

[74] Home Office Research Study 283, *Are Special Measures Working? Evidence from Surveys of Vulnerable and Intimidated Witnesses* (London, 2004).

vulnerable witnesses. Few of those interviewed (of whom 15 per cent were victims of sexual offences) considered that they had been asked irrelevant questions about events in the past.

Largely Uncharted Waters

The points of contact between law and psychology mentioned so far are known as such by practitioners in both fields. But there are many areas of psychological research that have bearing on legal practice, or the content of the law itself, which are less well known. In some areas, it is not clear that the experimenters themselves are aware of the potential relevance of their work to the law. Attribution theory is not often quoted in publications that lawyers are likely to read. Back in 1979 Sally Lloyd-Bostock, in the *Modern Law Review*,[75] demonstrated the way attribution theory might assist lawyers with concepts like causation, 'the reasonable man', 'commonsense' and responsibility. She explained:

Judgements of causes and responsibility are reached by an active, constructive, process which goes beyond the information given and is therefore subject to various forms of error and bias; are structured by as well as expressed in language; and are influenced by the motives, values, experiences, and other characteristics of the judger, the specific context, and the anticipated consequence.[76]

Celia Wells took up the challenge in her book *Corporations and Criminal Responsibility*,[77] in which she drew upon attribution theory. Nevertheless, since then there has been a surprising lack of interest displayed in most of the legal literature. Some years ago, of course, the issue would not have arisen, as psychologists were more concerned with investigating how people react to the behaviour of others, for example whether they would intervene in a particular situation, whether they would be hostile or attracted to another person. It was Heider[78] who realized that these reactions inevitably flow from judgements that had been made about the motivations of that other person, so attributions of responsibility were at the root of reactions to the behaviour of others.[79] Despite this, the fact that now both practising lawyers and psychologists spend a great deal of their time trying to predict how people answer the question 'Why?'[80] seems to be lost on many of them.

---

[75] S Lloyd-Bostock, 'The Ordinary Man, and the Psychology of Attributing Causes and Responsibility' (1979) 42 *Modern Law Review* 143.   [76] ibid, 167.
  [77] (Oxford, 2001).
  [78] F Heider, *The Psychology of Interpersonal Relations* (New York, 1958).
  [79] HH Kelley, 'Attribution Theory in Social Psychology' in D Levine (ed), *Nebraska Symposium on Motivation* (Nebraska, 1967).
  [80] HH Kelley, *Attribution in Social Interaction* (Morristown, NJ, 1971) 1.

Judgements about causation, for example, are made by most of us on a daily basis. According to Kelley, observers base causal judgements upon the covariation model, if they have sufficient information for that. Otherwise, they will rely on an interpretational framework based upon experience, their observations of people in various situations.[81] If behaviour is inconsistent with prior expectation, it will be attributed to external causes.[82] Causation is also of central importance in most areas of the law. However, attribution theory may not be the most appealing one on the causation issue in the legal context. For example, Ward[83] argues that attribution theory does not reflect the way judges, in arriving at causation judgments, search for narrative coherence, relying heavily on biographical narratives, assessments of individual credibility, and analogical reasoning. Fincham and Jaspars have also expressed doubt[84] that individuals construct their causal attributions in a systematic manner as part of their cognition, and not as part of their cultural system. They suggest also that legal inquiry is less concerned with the perceived relationship between behaviour and an unspecified internal or external cause than with the narrower issue of the connection between behaviour and its outcome.

Most of the legal tests for causation rest on the concept of foreseeability, which, as Lloyd-Bostock indicated, is also a focus of attribution theory. But it is clear that causation judgments arrived at by courts are not simple applications of a foreseeability test. Courts can be seen to manipulate the test in order to achieve the result they think morally right. I have suggested[85] that nevertheless the verdict in the *Pagett* case[86] is explicable in terms of attribution theory, since Pagett had the opportunity to behave otherwise. He used his pregnant girlfriend, Gail, as a shield during his attempt to escape from the police. He fired over her head at the police, they returned fire and a police bullet killed her. To convict Pagett of her manslaughter required the jury to regard the police action, although it was a breach of official guidelines, as a foreseeable consequence of his. However, the fact that responsibility was allotted to him is unsurprising, given that Pagett could have chosen from a number of alternative actions other than firing at the police over Gail's head. Another factor according to attribution theory is that his motives would not have attracted social approval. The correspondent inference theory[87]

---

[81] HH Kelley, 'Causal Schemata and the Attribution Process' in EE James, DE Kanouse, HH Kelley, RE Nisbett, S Valins, and B Weiner (eds), *Attribution: Perceiving the Causes of Behaviour* (Morristown, NJ, 1971).

[82] JA Kulik, 'Confirmatory Attribution and the Perpetuation of Social Beliefs' (1983) 44 *Journal of Personality and Social Psychology* 1171.

[83] T Ward, 'Psychiatric Evidence and Judicial Fact-Finding' (1999) 3 *International Journal of Evidence and Proof* 180.

[84] FD Fincham and JM Jaspars, 'Attribution of Responsibility: from Man the Scientist to Man as Lawyer' in L Berkowitz (ed) (1980) 13 *Advances in Experimental Psychology* 82.

[85] J McEwan, *The Verdict of the Court: Passing Judgment in Law and Psychology* (Oxford, 2003) 43.

[86] (1983) 76 Cr App R 279.

[87] EE Jones and KE Davis, 'From Acts to Dispositions: the Attribution Process in Person Perception' in L Berkowitz (ed), *Advances in Experimental Social Psychology*, vol 2 (New York, 1965).

holds that attributions of responsibility take account of factors such as motive and the observer's own role, plus environmental factors, that limit the actor's freedom of choice. Internal attributions are made if there are few uncommon effects, that is, those produced by the action that could not be produced by alternative courses of action.[88] On the other hand, the case of *Videan v British Transport Commissioner*[89] is probably more readily explicable by reference to the Just World theory of attribution. A railwayman saw that his own toddler son was crawling on the railway line, just as a trolley was coming rapidly towards him. The father threw himself at the young child and saved him, but was himself fatally struck by the trolley. The Court of Appeal decided that it was not reasonably foreseeable that the little boy would be on the railway line at a small station, but nevertheless also decided that the father's heroic leap to save him from the approaching trolley, was reasonably foreseeable. Fleming ascribes the decision to the court's high regard for the rescuer.[90]

Clearly psychology has much to offer the law in terms of understanding judgments about causation. Cultural expectations colour the operation of the foreseeability analysis and the interpretation of that famous legal personality, the 'reasonable man'. There is no doubt that psychology could tell us much about this individual. He is frequently described by judges as 'ordinary'—'the man on the Clapham omnibus', more recently, the 'traveller on the London Underground'.[91] In terms of his personality, he is apparently 'free both from over-apprehension and from over-confidence',[92] He has 'customary phlegm'[93] and is of 'a normal standard of susceptibility'.[94] Exposed to unpleasantness at the scenes of road traffic accidents, apparently the 'ordinary frequenter of the streets has sufficient fortitude to endure such incidents as occur from time to time in them'.[95] The reasonable man is likely to offer assistance after such accidents, but 'the law must take us to be sufficiently robust to help at accidents that are a daily occurrence without suffering a psychological breakdown'.[96] Even when an accident amounts to a 'disaster', psychological trauma would not be a foreseeable outcome in every case.[97] On the other hand, 'suppose, for example, that a scholar's life's work of research or composition were destroyed before his eyes as a result of a defendant's careless conduct'; he might well sustain psychiatric illness as a result.[98] After the Hillsborough football stadium disaster, some police officers were found to have suffered psychiatric illness as a result of their involvement with the many dead and injured. The judge at first instance, Waller J, thought that even though the

---

[88] Heider, n 78 above.   [89] [1963] 2 QB 650.
[90] JG Fleming, *An Introduction to the Law of Torts* (Oxford, 1985).
[91] *MacFarlane v Tayside Health Board* [1994] 4 All ER 961, 977.
[92] *Glasgow Corp v Muir* [1943] AC 448, 457.
[93] *Bourhill v Young* [1943] AC 92, *per* Lord Porter at 117.
[94] ibid, *per* Lord Wright at 110.   [95] ibid, *per* Lord Porter at 117.
[96] *White v Chief Constable of South Yorkshire* [1999] 1 All ER 1, 6.
[97] *McFarlane v EE Caledonia Ltd* [1994] 2 All ER 1.
[98] *Attia v British Gas plc* [1988] QB 304, *per* Bingham LJ at 320.

circumstances were exceptional, their illnesses were not foreseeable, because we would expect a professional rescuer to possess 'extraordinary phlegm'.[99] However, the House of Lords thought the 'nature and scale of the catastrophe' together with the officers' direct involvement in it, rendered their training and experience insufficient protection against psychological injury.[100]

We can see in this and many other pronouncements about foreseeability the operation of heuristics in jury and judicial reasoning. One of the most dangerous is the representativeness heuristic,[101] which makes the layman insensitive to base-rate information.[102] There is evidence of the difficulty of dispelling the power of the Base Rate Fallacy, possibly because base rate information is comparatively pallid and imageless; it might be better utilized if vivid examples are provided.[103] Frequently, the data supplied in competition with base rate information is more immediately striking. Vividness of image may account in part for the conviction of Sally Clark for murdering her two sons. At her trial the expert witness, Professor Sir Roy Meadow, testified that the chance of two cot deaths occurring without human intervention in one family in the same social group as the Clark family was 1 in 73 million. He then expressed the likelihood in these terms:

It's the chance of backing that long odds outsider at the Grand National, you know: let's say it's an 80 to 1 chance, you back the winner last year, then the next year there's another horse at 80 to 1 . . . you back it again and it wins . . . So it's the same with cot deaths. You have to say two unlikely events have happened and together it's very, very, very, unlikely.

One of the editors of the report on which Professor Meadow had relied for his figures gave evidence for the defence, to explain that squaring the figure for the incidence of one cot death in a family was an illegitimate oversimplification, and that the figures had in any event been produced to identify families at high risk of sudden infant death in order to target resources. At the second appeal, Lord Justice Judge considered that it would have been the headline figure of 1 in 73 million that would be uppermost in the jury's minds 'with the graphic reference by Professor Meadow to the chances of backing long odds winners of the Grand National year after year'.[104]

---

[99] *Frost v Chief Constable of Sourth Yorkshire Police* [1997] 1 All ER 540, 547.

[100] *White v Chief Constable South Yorkshire Police*, n 96 above, 29.

[101] D Kahneman and A Tversky, 'Subjective Probability: a Judgment of Representativeness' (1972) 3 *Cognitive Psychology* 430; A Tversky and D Kahneman, 'Availability: a Heuristic for Judging Frequency and Probability' (1973) 5 *Cognitive Psychology* 207.

[102] A Tversky and D Kahneman, 'Evidential Impact of Base Rates' in D Kahneman, P Slovic, and A Tversky (eds), *Judgment under Uncertainty: Heuristics and Biases* (Cambridge, 1982).

[103] R Nisbett, E Borgida, R Crandell, and H Reed, 'Popular Induction: Information is not necessarily informative' in JS Carroll and JW Payne (eds), *Cognition and Social Behaviour* (New York, 1976).

[104] *Clark* [2003] EWCA 11020; [2003] 2 FCR 44, para 178. The Court of Appeal at the first appeal had accepted that the statistic was wrong according to the Royal Statistical Society. However, it was held that the error was of minimal significance, and had not affected the jury verdict. *Clark* 2 October 2000, <http://www.lexis-nexis.com/professional>. Court of Appeal (CD); see B Mahendra, 'Science and Uncertainty in the Miscarriage of Justice' [2001] *New Law Journal* 1686.

Our apparent inability to express these likelihoods accurately, and the regularity with which lawyers and expert witnesses fall into the 'Prosecutor's Fallacy' trap[105] has led to convictions which have had to be set aside as unsafe, not only in the Sudden Infant Death Syndrome (SIDS) cases such as *Clark*, but in DNA-based cases such as *Deen*.[106] Here, also, an expert was guilty of this common error. So great has been the impact of this particular mistake in DNA evidence cases that the Court of Appeal has ruled that any scientist who introduces into evidence in a criminal trial the results of a DNA comparison should explain not only his methodology, but also the operation of the 'random occurrence ratio'. It may be appropriate to indicate how many people with matching characteristics are likely to be found in the United Kingdom or in a more limited relevant sub-group.[107] Whether or not the expert witness has sufficient grasp of statistics to do so is another matter: 'the mistake has been to assume that an expert in blood is also an expert on probability, and unfortunately, many are not'.[108] Professor Meadow is a paediatrician, not a statistician, for instance. And even when the science is presented entirely accurately, courts are reluctant to tie the jury down. 'Jurors evaluate evidence and reach a conclusion not by means of a formula, mathematical or otherwise, but by the joint application of their common sense and knowledge of the world to the evidence before them.'[109]

Human cognitive heuristics and weakness, such as the tendency people have to exaggerate the probability of likely events and the improbability of unlikely events,[110] affect their receptiveness to arguments made in a legal setting. Psychologists are also addressing the issue of the persuasive effect of arguments. It has been suggested that individuals test arguments by weighing them against a hypothesis they are testing.[111] But making decisions in complex cases can be seen as necessarily having to resolve a variety of factors including information, values, and goals (constraint satisfaction). This means that the content of a judgment may be affected by personal goals related to the decision, but also by whether a decision has to be made, and then whether there is a desire to reach an accurate decision.[112] Holyoak and Simon found individuals' ratings of agreement with

---

[105] cf DJ Baldwin and P Donnelly, 'The Prosecutor's Fallacy and DNA evidence' [1984] *Criminal Law Review* 711. This and other common statistical errors have been set out in MJ Saks and RF Kidd, 'Human Information Processing and Adjudication: Trial by Heuristics' (1980–1981) 15 *Law and Society Review* 123.   [106] *The Times*, 10 January, 1994.

[107] *Doheny and Adams* [1997] 1 Cr App R 369.

[108] B Robertson and GA Vignaux, 'Expert Evidence: Law, Practice and Probability' (1992) 12 *Oxford Journal of Legal Studies* 392.

[109] *Adams* [1996] 2 Cr App R 467.

[110] S Lichtenstein, B Fischoff, and LD Phillips, 'Calibrations of Probabilities: the State of the Art to 1980' in D Kahneman, P Slovic, and A Tversky (eds), *Judgment under Uncertainty: Heuristics and Biases* (Cambridge, 1982).

[111] RM Hogarth and HJ Einhorn, 'Order Effects in Belief Updating: the Belief-Adustment Model' (1992) 24 *Cognitive Psychology* 1.

[112] S Simon, LB Pham, QA Le, and KJ Holyoak, 'The Emergence of Coherence Over the Course of Decision-Making' (2001) 27 *Journal of Experimental Psychology/Learning, Memory and Cognition* 1250.

presented arguments gradually cohered as the case material was understood. It seems that people may give inferences different weight when they know that they have to reach a decision, so that the decision has stronger support. Afterwards they may have trouble recalling the assessments they made prior to reaching the decision.[113] The process perhaps therefore could be modelled as a process of constraint satisfaction in which an ambiguous situation has to be interpreted to impose coherence on it.

Green and McCloy[114] also investigate the causal relationship of argument to decision. Holyoak and Simon had assessed as a preliminary whether or not the individual subject agreed in principle with an argument that would subsequently be raised in a specific scenario, but Green and McCloy are working on whether or not an argument will be as persuasive in context as it is in the abstract. They also attempt to measure the effect of counter-argument. It seems clear from their work so far that the strength of an argument or counter-argument may be undermined by background evidence. They found that verdicts are determined by the strength of the counter-argument, but these in turn may be undermined by background evidence provided. They used, as one example, a scenario employed by Holyoak and Simon: P Company is declared by D, over the internet, to be failing financially. After this, P's share price drops dramatically. Mock juror ratings for the strength of D's initial defence argument, that P's share price was falling before publication and therefore was unaffected by D's action, were revised once background information, that all share prices in the sector were falling for several weeks beforehand, was supplied. D's argument thus gained a much higher rating in the light of this information. The authors conclude that individuals consider one and often two causal possibilities, using arguments and relevant background information (whether previously known or supplied) to construct a mental model of the original state of affairs. The mental model consists of a set of causally connected conceptual entities (actual share price, market information, and so on) against which the party's claim is tested. In effect, individuals attempt to explain an event by process of a mental simulation, an explanation Green and McCloy regard as entirely compatible with Pennington and Hastie's story model of interpretation.

Also of potential interest to lawyers is the work being done on the effect of language, for example in quantity information. This concerns representations of risk, probability, or frequency, and is common in everyday life. Labels describing the content of food, for instance, are not neutral in their effect. Whether the information is given in linguistic or numerical form, its presentation automatically entails a particular perspective, for example the difference between, 'a few of the passengers were injured' and 'few of the passengers were injured'. Using the phrase, 'few of' focuses attention of the passengers that were *not* injured. Yet

[113] KJ Holyoak and D Simon, 'Bidirectional Reasoning in Decision-Making by Constraint Satisfaction' (1999) 128 *Journal of Experimental Psychology/General* 3.
[114] DW Green and R McCloy (2003) 9 *Thinking and Reasoning* 307.

research has shown that these expressions, along with 'not many', denote the same proportions. Reactions to a label containing the phrase such as '95% fat free' are different from those inspired by 'contains 5% fat'. Advertisers intuitively exploit the more positive inferences drawn from the former. Those positive inferences also lead to a stronger perception of the product as a healthy thing, and affect subjects' receptiveness to further information on the healthiness or unhealthiness of the product.[115] An advocate armed with knowledge derived from psychological work on persuasion would find it even easier to manipulate the finders of fact.

Why so Little?

To a non-psychologist, reading work on argumentation and persuasion represents a considerable challenge. It is likely that the researchers themselves are far more interested in the significance of their findings to the processes of cognition than their implications for the legal system. Thus the context in which the research takes place is unfamiliar to a reader from a legal background, who consequently may struggle to assess the potential usefulness of the research in the legal sphere. The same is true of some other kinds of experimental work, and it is possible that there is a large body of psychological research, of which lawyers are entirely unaware, that could inform and improve legal scholarship. The problem is exacerbated if the results are published in periodicals that only psychologists tend to read.

I have argued above that lawyers take very little notice of the work done by psychologists unless it serves their immediate purpose. One of their stock defences against work that has inconvenient content is to stress the difficulty of generalizing from experimental work to the courtroom—a problem acknowledged by everyone in the field. Against this background, the recent publication by the Department of Constitutional Affairs of a consultation paper to consider the merits of repealing section 8 of the Contempt of Court Act 1981 in order to permit meaningful research into how the jury system operates[116] is very welcome. But lawyers are less aware than they should be of the relevance of some laboratory work. Few attend the International Conference on Psychology and Law. This is not entirely due to the insularity of a conservative profession. Many of the papers presented at the International Conferences,[117] where presumably

---

[115] LM Moxey and AJ Sanford, 'Prior Expectation and the Interpretation of Natural Language Quantifiers' (1993) 5 *European Journal of Cognitive Psychology* 73.

[116] Department of Constitutional Affairs, *Jury Research and Impropriety*, Consultation Paper (London, 2005). Confusingly, the consultation is inspired partly by the decision in *O'Connor and Mirza* [2004] 1 All ER 925, which confirmed the confidentiality of deliberations in the jury room. However, here the issue might be thought to be rather more of protection of the jury from illegitimate pressure in relation to the trial than concern with the prospect of research into decision-making.

[117] eg *Programme, Abstracts*, Psychology and Law: International Interdisciplinary Conference, Edinburgh, 7–12 July 2003 (Southampton, 2003).

researchers want to communicate across the boundary between the two disciplines, deliver fairly stark descriptions of method and result. It is not always clear what, if any, implications for the law the exercise would have. This may explain the relative absence of lawyers from the Conference, which in turn affects the dissemination of the information and ideas presented there. In addition, it affects the level of collaborative work between the two disciplines, of which there is very little.

The field of psychology and law is dominated by psychologists, who sometimes appear mainly to write for each other's benefit. There are, of course, some notable publications that pull psychological experimental findings together, either in relation to a particular issue, such as eyewitness evidence, or across a wide range of psycholegal concerns, such as Professor Kapardis' book *Psychology and Law*.[118] But there are relatively few people working in the area who have qualifications in each discipline, for example Professor Thompson in Australia and Professor Lloyd-Bostock in the United Kingdom. Experience in police work has proved an invaluable bridge between the law and psychology (Gudjonsson, Williamson, Ainsworth), but there is no equivalent on the non-criminal side of the law. The heart of the law consists of the legal rules themselves and the way in which judgments are made; this is largely unexplored. To do that may require collaborative work. Attribution research may measure responses in terms of 'cause', 'blame', 'responsibility', and sometimes 'sanction', but much of it was not in fact designed to analyse the way in which legal judgments are made,[119] and consequently the terms are used in a manner that is too loose to reflect the separate elements of responsibility in a legal sense. A mutually informed common evolution in psychology and law can develop only when experimenters take account of the legal context in which the rules or phenomena concerned actually operate.

---

[118] A Kapardis, *Psychology and Law: a Critical Introduction* (Cambridge, 1997).
[119] eg GR Semin and ASR Manstead, *The Accountability of Conduct* (London, 1983).

3

Therapeutic Jurisprudence: Enhancing the Relationship Between Law and Psychology

*Bruce J Winick**

Introduction

Psychology and psychologists have made an enormous contribution to the legal system. Psychological principles inform many legal rules. For example, the deterrence of the criminal sanction and the incentive structures reflected in many tax law provisions are grounded in psychological explanations of how people behave. Many legal rules are based on assumptions concerning human behaviour, and a traditional role of law and psychology scholarship has been the empirical testing of the validity of these assumptions. Not only can psychological research increase our understanding of the myriad kinds of human behaviour that law seeks to regulate and the best ways of doing so, but it can enlighten us concerning how legal rules and institutions actually function and can be improved.

Moreover, psychologists provide a significant service to the courts and other legal institutions. Many psychologists perform evaluations for the courts and needed expert testimony on a variety of legal issues. Some provide consultation to lawyers on issues including, for example, jury selection and trial strategy. Some have provided treatment to individuals involved in various legal processes, including criminal offenders, children and adolescents in family or juvenile court, families in distress, and people suffering from mental illness who sometimes are required by the courts to participate in treatment.

These are the traditional ways in which psychology and psychologists have contributed to the legal system. If they are to function more effectively, legal professionals and the law itself need to understand and apply the insights, principles, and approaches of psychology much more than they do at present. The professional disciplines of law and psychology, and the conceptual categories they embody, are limited and limiting. They are artificial and inevitably

* Correspondence should be addressed to the author at <bwinick@law.miami.edu>.

imprisoning. We mistakenly view our professional disciplines as self-contained and isolated bodies of knowledge and skills. In fact, these two disciplines overlap much more than we seem to realize. Law is a system that seeks to channel human behaviour, and psychology is the science of how people learn and behave. To be effective, law therefore must master the lessons of psychology, and because many of the significant rules and constraints that shape human behaviour are legal in nature, psychology must understand the techniques and concepts of law. Law, properly understood, is a system of applied psychology, and in our increasingly law-dominated societies, law is an important determinant of human behaviour. The borders between law and psychology therefore must be open, allowing the free passage of ideas. To function effectively as members of each discipline, we must increasingly understand the language and culture of the other. Both professions must be expanded to allow a greater degree of interdisciplinary exchange.

An important way of promoting such interdisciplinary cross-fertilization is the branch of legal scholarship known as therapeutic jurisprudence. As will be seen, therapeutic jurisprudence embodies a psychological approach to law—one that applies the insights and principles of psychology to the examination of legal rules and practices and to their improvement. It provides a new focus for law and psychology scholarship, identifying a variety of issues in need of theoretical and empirical examination. Many of these are issues that have not previously been thought of, but which are essential to law reform. The law is not a static system; rather, it is always changing as legislatures, courts, and administrative agencies respond to developing knowledge about how legal rules and practices actually function and seek to reshape them to better achieve their objectives. Law reform is an important theme of therapeutic jurisprudence, and scholars applying the approach have succeeded in offering an enormous range of proposals for legal change in a wide variety of legal contexts.

In addition, therapeutic jurisprudence identifies a number of new roles and contexts for clinical psychologists working in the legal system. This is especially so for clinicians working in the mental health system and in offender rehabilitation, fields that have been significantly expanded and transformed as a result of therapeutic jurisprudence analysis. Moreover, therapeutic jurisprudence has created and will continue to create increased demand for psychologists working in the courts and in consultation with practising attorneys.

The approach of therapeutic jurisprudence is transformative, changing the way we look at the legal system and at the roles of legal actors. This transformation will provide new incentives for judges, legislatures, administrative officials, and practising lawyers to understand the insights and approaches of psychology. Moreover, as a result of the increased interest that therapeutic jurisprudence has generated in research on legal rules and processes and the increasing role it has produced for psychologists working within the legal system, therapeutic jurisprudence has also been transformative for psychology. As a result, both disciplines have undergone a significant expansion and the area of their overlapping interest has grown considerably.

In the following section, this paper will explain the approach of therapeutic jurisprudence. It will then illustrate its growing impact on the field of law and psychology by reviewing how therapeutic jurisprudence has transformed various areas of law, legal practice, and legal education. Finally, the paper will illustrate how therapeutic jurisprudence can be used to map a new research agenda for law and psychology scholarship that would be highly useful for the legal system. Empirical work examining the therapeutic consequences of legal arrangements and therapeutic jurisprudence reform proposals has begun to emerge, but the extent of such work still remains disappointingly small. It is hoped that this paper will prompt research psychologists and other social scientists to understand better the potential of therapeutic jurisprudence for identifying important questions for empirical investigation.

The Approach of Therapeutic Jurisprudence

Therapeutic jurisprudence is an interdisciplinary approach to legal scholarship and law reform that sees law itself as a therapeutic agent.[1] The basic insight of therapeutic jurisprudence is that legal rules, legal practices, and the way legal actors (such as judges, lawyers, governmental officials, police officers, and expert witnesses testifying in court) play their roles impose consequences on the mental health and emotional wellbeing of those affected. Therapeutic jurisprudence calls for the study of these consequences with the tools of the behavioural sciences. The aim is to better understand law and how it applies, and reshape it to minimize its anti-therapeutic effects and maximize its therapeutic potential. Therapeutic jurisprudence is interdisciplinary in that it brings insights from psychology and the social sciences to bear on legal questions, and it is empirical in that it calls for the testing of hypotheses concerning how the law functions and can be improved. Much of the existing therapeutic jurisprudence literature is conceptual in nature, although some of it contains an empirical component.[2] One hope of this paper

---

[1] DB Wexler and BJ Winick, *Essays in Therapeutic Jurisprudence* (Durham, NC, 1991); DB Wexler and BJ Winick (eds), *Law in a Therapeutic Key: Developments in Therapeutic Jurisprudence* (Durham, NC, 1996); BJ Winick, 'The Jurisprudence of Therapeutic Jurisprudence' (1997) 3 *Psychology, Public Policy and Law* (hereinafter PPPL) 184. Readers interested in more information should visit the International Network on Therapeutic Jurisprudence website at <http://www.therapeuticjurisprudence.org/>—a resource containing a comprehensive bibliography and notices of upcoming activities.

[2] See eg E Anderson, M Levine, A Sharma, L Feretti, K Steinberg, and L Wallace, 'Coercive Uses of Mandatory Reporting in Therapeutic Relationships' in Wexler and Winick, *Law in a Therapeutic Key*, n 1 above, 895; DJ Chase and PF Hora, 'The Implications of Therapeutic Jurisprudence for Judicial Satisfaction' (2000) 37 *Court Review* 12; B Feldthusen, 'The Civil Action for Sexual Battery: Therapeutic Jurisprudence?' in Wexler and Winick (eds), *Law in a*

is to encourage psychologists and other social scientists to perform more theoretical work on legal issues and more empirical research testing therapeutic jurisprudence hypotheses and applications.

Therapeutic jurisprudence suggests that law should value psychological health, should strive to avoid imposing anti-therapeutic consequences whenever possible, and when consistent with other values served by law, should attempt to bring about healing and wellness. It does not privilege therapeutic values over others. Rather, it seeks to ascertain whether law's anti-therapeutic effects can be reduced and its therapeutic consequences enhanced, without subordinating due process and other justice values.

Although at first blush, therapeutic jurisprudence might appear to be paternalistic, its principal proponents have disavowed governmental paternalism,[3] and much therapeutic jurisprudence work has stressed the psychological value of individual autonomy.[4] Governmental paternalism is often perceived by its recipients as offensive, disempowering, and dehumanizing. Moreover, it often provokes feelings of resentment and psychological reactance.[5] People subject to coercion frequently do not function as effectively as those permitted self-determination.[6] Rather than extolling paternalism, therapeutic jurisprudence work has frequently relied upon the psychological benefits of allowing people

---

Therapeutic Key, n 1 above, 845; A Greer, M O'Regan, and A Traverso, 'Therapeutic Jurisprudence and Patients' Perceptions of Procedural Due Process of Civil Commitment Hearings' in Wexler and Winick (eds), *Law in a Therapeutic Key*, n 1 above, 923; U Holmberg, and SA Christianshon, 'Murderers' and Sexual Offenders' Experiences of Police Interviews and Their Inclination to Admit or Deny Crimes' (2002) 20 *Behavioral Sciences and the Law* (hereinafter BSL) 31; PF Hora and DJ Chase, 'Judicial Satisfaction When Judging in a Therapeutic Key' (2003/2004) 7 *Contemporary Issues in Law* 8; KA Kamin and JJ Rachlinski, 'Ex Post≠Ex Ante: Determining Liability in Hindsight' in Wexler and Winick (eds), *Law in a Therapeutic Key*, n 1 above, 979; CL Kennedy, 'Judicial Behavior and the Civil Commitment Petitioner' in BJ Winick and DB Wexler (eds), *Judging in a Therapeutic Key: Therapeutic Jurisprudence and the Courts* (Durham, NC, 2003) 158; CJ Petrucci, 'The Judge-Defendant Interaction: Toward a Shared Respect Process' in Winick and Wexler, *Judging in a Therapeutic Key*, above, 148; NG Poythress and SL Brodsky, 'In the Wake of a Negligent Release Law Suit: An Investigation of Professional Consequences and Institutional Impact on a State Psychiatric Hospital' in Wexler and Winick (eds), *Law in a Therapeutic Key*, n 1 above, 875; DW Shuman, JA Hamilton, and CE Daley, 'The Health Effects of Jury Service' in Wexler and Winick (eds), *Law in a Therapeutic Key*, n 1 above, 949; J Susman, 'Resolving Hospital Conflicts: A Study on Therapeutic Jurisprudence' in Wexler and Winick (eds), *Law in a Therapeutic Key*, n 1 above, 907; JM Zito, J Vitrai, and TJ Craig, 'Toward a Therapeutic Jurisprudence Analysis of Mediation Refusal in the Court Review Model' in Wexler and Winick (eds), *Law in a Therapeutic Key*, n 1 above, 935.

  [3] DB Wexler and BJ Winick, 'Patients, Professionals, and the Path of Therapeutic Jurisprudence: A Response to Petrila' in Wexler and Winick (eds), *Law in a Therapeutic Key*, n 1 above, 707.

  [4] See eg BJ Winick, *The Right to Refuse Mental Health Treatment* (Washington, DC, 1997) ch 17; BJ Winick, 'On Autonomy: Legal and Psychological Perspectives' (1992) 37 *Villanova Law Review* 1705.

  [5] SS Brehm and JW Brehm, *Psychological Reactance: A Theory of Freedom and Control* (New York, 1981).

  [6] eg BJ Winick, *Civil Commitment: A Therapeutic Jurisprudence Model* (Durham, NC, 2005) ch 2; Winick, *Right to Refuse*, n 4 above, ch 17; Winick, n 4 above; BJ Winick, 'Coercion and Mental Health Treatment' (1997) 74 *Denver Law Review* 1145.

voluntary choice in a wide variety of matters.[7] Legal arrangements that permit individuals to make decisions for themselves, rather than those based on governmental paternalism, are generally more conducive to psychological well-being, and therefore are favoured by therapeutic jurisprudence.

Therapeutic jurisprudence does not suggest that therapeutic considerations should trump other considerations. Law often serves other ends that are equally or more important than the therapeutic. Therapeutic jurisprudence seeks convergence between therapeutic and other values, and suggests that such convergence is the path to true law reform. When therapeutic and other values served by law conflict, therapeutic jurisprudence cannot resolve the conflict. Rather, therapeutic jurisprudence helps to make this conflict more visible and sharpens the issues for further debate. Sometimes therapeutic considerations may strongly outweigh other values, and thus point the way to law reform. Although the weighing of therapeutic against other values may be a task that some might describe as weighing apples and oranges, it is possible to weigh differing values, even those thought of as incommensurable.[8] When therapeutic and other normative values do not converge, creative solutions can often be found that permit maximized balancing among such values with a minimization of conflict.[9]

Therapeutic jurisprudence therefore is a scholarly approach for bringing mental health insights into the development and reshaping of law. It originated in scholarly work in mental health law,[10] and has since spread across the legal landscape, emerging as a mental health approach to law generally.[11] Therapeutic jurisprudence has examined issues not only in mental health law, but also in such diverse fields as criminal law, juvenile and family law, health law, disability law, immigration law, bankruptcy law, tort law, contract and commercial law, trusts and estates, evidence law, and constitutional law.[12] Moreover, therapeutic jurisprudence has become increasingly international in character, and has been used in examining legal rules and practices in a variety of countries in addition to the United States.[13] Therapeutic jurisprudence thus looks at legal rules, practices, and the roles of legal actors to assess their therapeutic impact and to see how they

---

[7] eg Winick and Wexler (eds), *Judging in a Therapeutic Key*, n 2 above, 156, 182, 185; BJ Winick, 'Therapeutic Jurisprudence and Problem Solving Courts' (2003) *Fordham Urban Law Journal* 1055, 1071–8; Winick, n 4 above.

[8] K Kress 'Therapeutic Jurisprudence and the Resolution of Value Conflicts: What We Can Realistically Expect In Practice, From Theory' (1999) 17 BSL 556–88; National Judicial Institute, *Judging in the 21st Century: A Problem-solving Approach* (2005) <http://www.nji.ca/Public/publication.htm> (last accessed 21 September 2005).

[9] BJ Winick, 'Applying the Law Therapeutically in Domestic Violence Cases' (2000) 69 *University of Missouri Kansas City Law Review* 33, 79.

[10] Wexler and Winick, *Essays*, n 1 above.

[11] Wexler and Winick (eds), *Law in a Therapeutic Key*, n 1 above.

[12] *Law in a Therapeutic Key*, n 1 above.

[13] *Symposium, International Perspectives on Therapeutic Jurisprudence, Part One* AJ Tomkins and D Carson (eds), (1999) 17 BSL 553; *Symposium, International Perspectives on Therapeutic*

can be revamped to increase therapeutic outcomes. It is a form of law and society scholarship in that it involves interdisciplinary examination of the legal system that seeks to reform the way in which law and social institutions function.

An important development in therapeutic jurisprudence has been its emphasis on how law is applied by various legal actors, such as lawyers, judges, administrators, police officers, and expert witnesses. Even if the legal rule in question remains unchanged, the way it is applied by these legal actors can make an enormous difference for the psychological well-being of those affected. Therapeutic jurisprudence calls upon these professionals to reframe their professional roles. In addition to their other functions, these professionals should see themselves as therapeutic agents. They can have positive or negative effects on those whose lives they touch. It is hoped that this awareness will cause them to act in ways that minimize the likelihood that their actions will impose negative psychological effects and maximize their potential to advance psychological well-being.

In regard to lawyering, therapeutic jurisprudence has been integrated with preventive law to develop a new model of legal practice that values the psychological well-being of the client, that seeks to avoid legal problems through creative problem-solving approaches, legal drafting, and the use of alternative dispute resolution mechanisms, and that contemplates lawyers who practice their profession with an ethic of care, emotional intelligence, and increased interpersonal skills.[14] Therapeutic jurisprudence has also had an important impact on legal education, particularly in the area of clinical legal education and skills training.[15] It suggests that law students, practising lawyers, and even judges be taught the principles and approaches of psychology in order to enhance their professional functioning. Therapeutic jurisprudence courses and insights have begun to permeate the law school curriculum, and clinical (or experiential) legal education in particular.

Not only is the lawyer, in how she functions in the law office and courtroom, a therapeutic agent, but so is the judge, in how she performs her judicial duties. The past fifteen years have witnessed the emergence of exciting new developments in the courts that include a variety of specialized, treatment-oriented tribunals, applying principles of therapeutic jurisprudence to help people appearing before them to solve a variety of psychosocial problems that precipitate court involvement, many of which are of a recurring nature.[16] These include drug treatment

---

Jurisprudence, Part Two AJ Tomkins and D Carson (eds), (2000) 18 BSL 411; K Diesfeld and I Freckleton (eds), *Involuntary Detention and Therapeutic Jurisprudence: International Perspectives on Civil Commitment* (Aldershot, Hampshire, 2003).

[14] DP Stolle, DB Wexler, and BJ Winick (eds), *Practicing Therapeutic Jurisprudence: Law as a Helping Profession* (Durham, NC, 2000); *Symposium: Therapeutic Jurisprudence and Preventive Law: Transforming Legal Practice and Education* (1999) 5 PPPL 793 (BJ Winick, DB Wexler, and EA Dauer, guest eds).

[15] *Symposium, Therapeutic Jurisprudence and Clinical Legal Education and Skills Training* (2005) 17 *St Thomas Law Review* 403 (BJ Winick and DB Wexler, guest eds).

[16] Winick and Wexler (eds), *Judging in a Therapeutic Key*, n 2 above; Winick, n 7 above.

court, domestic violence court, mental health court, unified family court, teen court or youth court, community court, and reentry court.[17] Judges in these specialized courts, as well as judges generally, are increasingly using the approaches of therapeutic jurisprudence in a new effort to assist litigants to achieve rehabilitation and otherwise solve a variety of social and emotional problems that contribute to their court involvement.[18]

How Therapeutic Jurisprudence has Transformed Law and Psychology: Several Illustrations

Therapeutic jurisprudence thus can be seen as providing a new lens through which to examine the legal system. What are the therapeutic and antitherapeutic consequences of legal rules, legal practices, and the ways in which various legal actors perform their roles? Looking at legal issues in this way generates a host of theoretical and empirical questions. Therapeutic jurisprudence work frequently involves speculation about how principles of psychology, developed in other contexts, might apply to various legal arrangements. Such scholarly speculation about therapeutic consequences of various legal rules and practices or law reform proposals can generate useful hypotheses. Whether these hypotheses are true, however, requires empirical investigation, and provides an invitation for psychological research.[19] Like much of traditional law and psychology and social science in law, therapeutic jurisprudence examines law with the tools of the behavioural sciences.[20] But therapeutic jurisprudence has a more narrow focus. Unlike these other interdisciplinary approaches, it does not seek generally to examine law's untested assumptions or measure its impact or effectiveness. Much law and psychology and social science in law scholarship has traditionally been dominated by research into law's consequences.[21] Therapeutic jurisprudence is concerned

[17] Winick and Wexler (eds), *Judging in a Therapeutic Key*, n 2 above; National Judicial Institute, *Judging for the 21st Century*, n 8 above; BJ Winick and DB Wexler, 'Drug Treatment Court: Therapeutic Jurisprudence Applied' (2002) 18 *Touro Law Review* 479; Winick, n 4 above; *Symposium, Mental Health Courts* (2005) 11 (4) PPPL 505–632 (BJ Winick and S Stefan, guest eds); JQ La Fond and BJ Winick, 'Sex Offender Reentry Courts: A Proposal for Managing the Risk of Returning Sex Offenders to the Community' (2004) 34 *Seton Hall Law Review* 1173; AR Shiff and DB Wexler, 'Teen Court: A Therapeutic Jurisprudence Perspective', in Wexler and Winick (eds), *Law in a Therapeutic Key*, n 1 above, 287.
[18] *Symposium: Special Issue on Therapeutic Jurisprudence* (2000) 37 *Court Review* 1; W Schma, 'Judging for the New Millennium' (Spring, 2000) 37 *Court Review* 4.
[19] CJ Petrucci, DB Wexler, and BJ Winick, 'Therapeutic Jurisprudence: An Invitation to Social Scientists', in D Carson and R Bull (eds), *The Handbook of Psychology in Legal Contexts* (2nd edn, Hoboken, NJ, 2002) 579.   [20] Winick, n 1 above, 184.
[21] eg J O'Reilly and BD Sales, 'Privacy for the Institutionalized Mentally Ill: Are Court-Ordered Standards Effective?' (1987) 11 *Law and Human Behavior* 41; BD Sales, 'The Legal Regulation of Psychology: Professional and Scientific Interactions' in CJ Scheirer and BI Hammonds (eds), *Psychology and the Law* (Washington, DC 1983) 9; A Sarat, 'Legal Effectiveness and Social Studies of Law: On The Unfortunate Persistence of Research Tradition' (1985) 9 *Legal Studies Forum* 23.

with the more narrow set of consequences. It seeks to apply social science to examine law's impact on the mental health of the people it affects.[22] Therapeutic jurisprudence calls for the use of psychological and behavioural science research to explore these consequences theoretically and empirically.

This need for theoretical and empirical research is a niche that psychological and other forms of social science research can fill. Moreover, unlike general empirical research on the consequences of law, which may not be of interest to courts, legislatures, and others involved in law reform, empirical work on law's consequences for the psychological wellbeing of those affected will often be highly relevant to law reform efforts.

Therapeutic jurisprudence scholarship has transformed many areas of law and legal practice. It has had an especially significant impact on mental health law, the area in which it started.[23] Therapeutic jurisprudence work has examined a range of mental health law issues, including the criteria for civil commitment; the procedures that should be applied in the civil commitment hearing; the standards that should govern competence to consent to voluntary hospitalization; how rights within mental hospitals should be defined and applied; the wisdom of new legal approaches requiring preventive outpatient commitment and its alternatives; how preventive outpatient commitment should be applied, if adopted; how competence to manage property should be ascertained and how guardianship should function; the use of advance directive instruments for mental hospitalization and treatment; the use of mental health courts to divert individuals with mental illness from the criminal justice process; how the legal insanity defence functions and can be improved; and incompetency to stand trial and how the doctrines of incompetency to stand trial and to be executed function and can be reshaped.[24]

Prior to the advent of therapeutic jurisprudence, mental health law reform efforts had been dominated by a rights-based approach aimed at protecting the civil liberties of people with mental illness. While therapeutic jurisprudence scholars have applauded the emergence of a legal model for civil commitment and other mental health law doctrines, they have also noted the excesses of this model. Although providing much needed protection for the civil liberties of patients, the legal model often neglected their therapeutic needs. Therapeutic jurisprudence has now emerged as a new and dominant paradigm for law reform efforts and scholarly research in the field of mental health law.

Therapeutic jurisprudence has also had a dramatic impact on the criminal process. Although the rehabilitative ideal had fallen into decline starting in the

---

[22] C Slobogin, 'Therapeutic Jurisprudence: Five Dilemmas to Ponder' (1995) 1 PPPL 1, 193.

[23] Winick, *Civil Commitment*, n 6 above, 7; Wexler and Winick, *Essays*, n 1 above; BJ Winick, *Therapeutic Jurisprudence Applied: Essays on Mental Health Law* (Durham, NC, 1997).

[24] See, Diesfeld and Freckleton, *Involuntary Detention and Therapeutic Jurisprudence*, n 13 above; MJ Perlin, *The Hidden Prejudice* (Washington, DC, 2000); MJ Perlin, *The Jurisprudence of the Insanity Defense* (Durham, NC, 1994); Wexler and Winick, n 1 above; Winick, *Civil Commitment*, n 6 above; Winick, n 23 above.

1970s, recent research has sparked a revived interest in offender rehabilitation and in how the legal system can make use of it.[25] Therapeutic jurisprudence scholarship has suggested that criminal courts, prosecutors, and criminal defence attorneys make use of these new rehabilitative models in an effort to facilitate the rehabilitation of criminal offenders.[26]

The emergence of a variety of problem-solving courts designed to achieve offender rehabilitation can be seen as a therapeutic jurisprudence development inasmuch as the judges, prosecutors, and defence attorneys in these courts explicitly use the legal process in an effort to achieve therapeutic outcomes.[27] In drug treatment court, for example, defendants with substance abuse problems are given the option of engaging in substance abuse treatment under the supervision of the court as an alternative to having their cases processed in criminal court. Offenders enter into a behavioural contract with the court in which they agree to remain drug free, to submit to periodic urinalysis drug testing, and to report to court periodically for monitoring by the judge concerning their progress in treatment. The judge, functioning as a member of the treatment team, applies principles of psychology to facilitate treatment compliance. When the individual's drug test reveals that he has been taking drugs, the judge sanctions the defendant, applying agreed-upon penalties ranging from a judicial scolding to short-term imprisonment. When drug testing reveals that the defendant has remained drug-free, the judge praises the individual and invites those present in the courtroom to applaud his success, thereby reinforcing pro-social behaviour. After a period of approximately one and one-half to two years, offenders who succeed in drug treatment court 'graduate' and their charges are dismissed. This occurs at a 'graduation' ceremony held in court and attended by the individual's family and friends, at which the arresting officer sometimes awards him his diploma. Many offenders thereby succeed in ending their substance abuse problems and experience a significant reduction in recidivism compared to those processed in a more typical criminal court.[28]

The approach of drug treatment court has been adapted to deal with various other areas of offender rehabilitation. These include domestic violence court,

---

[25] See eg J McGuire (ed), *What Works?: Reducing Reoffending* (Hoboken, NJ, 1995).

[26] See eg A Birgden, 'Dealing with the Resistant Criminal Client: A Psychologically-Minded Strategy for More Effective Legal Counseling' (2002) 38(2) *Criminal Law Bulletin* 255; C Clarke and J Neuhard, 'Making the Case: Therapeutic Jurisprudence and Problem Solving Practices Positively Impact Clients, the Justice Systems and Communities They Serve' (2005) 17 *St Thomas Law Review* 781; DB Wexler, 'Robes and Rehabilitation: How Judges Can Help Offenders "Make Good"' (2001) 38 *Court Review* 18; DB Wexler, 'Therapeutic Jurisprudence and the Rehabilitative Role of the Criminal Defense Lawyer' (2005) 17(3) *St Thomas Law Review* 743.

[27] See Winick and Wexler (eds), *Judging in a Therapeutic Key*, n 2 above; Winick, n 7 above.

[28] See eg S Belenko, 'Research on Drug Treatment Courts' in Winick and Wexler (eds), *Judging in a Therapeutic Key*, n 2 above, 27–8; P Hora, 'A Dozen Years of Drug Treatment Courts: Uncovering our Theoretical Foundation and the Construction of a Mainstream Paradigm' in L Harrison, F Scarpitti, M Amir, and S Einstein (eds), *Drug Courts: Current Issues and Future Perspectives* (Washington, DC, 2002).

designed to encourage perpetrators of domestic violence to enter into treatment, as well as to address the needs of the victim.[29] They also include mental health court, in which individuals with untreated mental illness who commit minor crimes are diverted from jail by a judicial process designed to encourage them to accept treatment in the community.[30] Although originating in misdemeanour cases, this model has recently been extended to the processing of felony cases in which mental illness is a significant component of the offence.[31] Teen court or youth court is another application of therapeutic jurisprudence principles, designed to facilitate the rehabilitation of youthful offenders.[32] In this model, juvenile offenders who have been through the teen court process play the role of prosecutors and jurors in future cases, role-playing which allows them better to understand the consequences of criminal wrongdoing and that functions as an inoculation of empathy training. A proposed model—sex offender re-entry court—would apply the problem-solving court approach to sex offenders, facilitating their rehabilitation and monitoring and supervising the graduated release into the community of those who successfully undergo treatment.[33]

These developments have led to a new and revolutionary role for judges, prosecutors, and defence attorneys, one that requires the understanding of basic principles and approaches of psychology.[34] These new courts provide significant research opportunities for psychologists as well as opportunities to assist the courts in achieving their rehabilitative goals. Increasing numbers of psychologists and allied professionals will be employed in these new court models and in the community programmes they will spawn.

Therapeutic jurisprudence has also had a transformative effect on the practice of law. The lawyer functioning in the courtroom or the law office is a therapeutic agent, directly affecting the psychological well-being of the client. Just as physicians need to be taught 'bedside manner', lawyers need to be taught 'desk side manner'. To be effective interviewers and counsellors, lawyers need to improve their emotional intelligence, their listening skills, and their ability to interpret non-verbal forms of communication, to be empathic to clients in distress, to identify and deal effectively with denial and other forms of client resistance that may arise in the counselling of the client, and to understand transference and

---

[29] See eg Winick, n 4 above.
[30] See eg *Symposium on Mental Health Courts*, (2005) 11(4) PPPL 505–632; RA Boothroyd, CC Mercado, NG Poythress, A Christy, and J Petrila, 'Clinical Outcomes of Defendants in Mental Health Court' (July 2005) 56 *Psychiatric Services* 829.
[31] See, eg C Fisler, 'Building Trust and Managing Risk: A Look at a Felony Mental Health Court' (2005) 11(4) PPPL 587–604.   [32] Shiff and Wexler, n 17 above.
[33] La Fond and Winick, n 17 above; JQ La Fond and BJ Winick, 'Sex Offender Reentry Courts: A Cost Effective Proposal for Managing Sex Offender Risk in the Community' in R Prentky, E Janus, and M Seto (eds), *Sexually Coercive Behavior: Understanding and Management* (New York, 2003) 300.
[34] See Winick and Wexler (eds), *Judging in a Therapeutic Key*, n 2 above (discussing principles of psychology and social work that judges functioning in problem-solving courts should apply).

counter-transference occurring in the attorney/client relationship.[35] They need to be client-centred counsellors, empowering their clients to make decisions for themselves rather than merely telling them what to do in a paternalistic fashion. They need to improve their interpersonal skills and their ability to communicate more effectively in the professional relationship. These are psychological skills, and psychologists have much to teach lawyers about how to understand and apply them effectively in legal practice.

Moreover, psychologists have much to teach lawyers concerning how best to deal with the 'psycho-legal soft spots' that arise in the attorney/client relationship.[36] This concept, which grows out of the integration of therapeutic jurisprudence with preventive law,[37] refers to the predictable emotional reactions that clients will encounter in the legal process. Court involvement or dealing with serious legal problems like divorce, criminal accusation, bankruptcy, or betrayal by a business partner can produce intense stress, fear, anger, sadness, depression, hard and hurt feelings, and other emotional difficulties. The stress of engaging in litigation, either as plaintiff or defendant, itself produces intense psychological distress.[38] Therapeutic jurisprudence has sensitized lawyers to the need to understand these 'psycholegal soft spots' and how to deal with them.[39] Lawyers can

---

[35] Birgden, n 26 above; S Keeva, 'Beyond the Words: Understanding What Your Client is Really Saying Makes for Successful Lawyering' (January 1999) 85 *American Bar Association Journal* 60; LG Mills, 'Affective Lawyering: The Emotional Dimensions of the Lawyer-Client Relation' in Stolle *et al*, *Practicing Therapeutic Jurisprudence*, n 14 above, 419; see eg MA Silver, 'Love, Hate and Other Emotional Interference in the Lawyer/Client Relationship' (1999) 6 *Clinical Law Review* 259; BJ Winick, 'Client Denial and Resistance in the Advance Directive Context: Reflections on How Attorneys Can Identify and Deal with a Psycholegal Soft Spot' (1998) 4 PPPL 901.

[36] MW Patry, DB Wexler, DP Stolle, and AJ Tomkins, 'Better Legal Counseling Through Empirical Research: Identifying Psycholegal Soft Spots and Strategies' in Stolle *et al*, *Practicing Therapeutic Jurisprudence*, n 14 above, 69; DB Wexler, 'Practicing Therapeutic Jurisprudence: Psycholegal Soft Spots and Strategies' in Stolle *et al*, *Practicing Therapeutic Jurisprudence*, n 14 above, 45; Winick, n 35 above.

[37] DP Stolle, DB Wexler, BJ Winick, and EA Dauer, 'Integrating Preventive Law and Therapeutic Jurisprudence: A Law and Psychology Based Approach to Lawyering' (1997) 34 *California Western Law Review* 15.

[38] 'Being a party in litigation is an extremely stressful event. It ranks near the death of a loved one, the loss of a job, and the experience of a grave illness. Indeed, Judge Learned Hand complained that "as a litigant I should dread a lawsuit beyond almost anything else short of sickness and death." There is little worse than being sued. Litigation requires the expenditure of huge sums of money and takes the litigant away from employment and personal endeavors. It is particularly difficult for the defendant, who is involuntarily made to play this role. However, it may be almost as stressful to be the plaintiff in a lawsuit. Plaintiffs have been harmed in some fashion, and rather than putting the pain and loss behind them and beginning the healing process, a lawsuit makes them relive the painful episode in ways that may prevent healing.' BJ Winick, 'Therapeutic Jurisprudence and the Role of Counsel in Litigation' (2000) 37 *California Western Law Review* 108; see also BS Dohrenwend *et al*, 'Exemplification of a Method for Scaling Life Events: The PERI Life Events Scale' (1978) 19 *Journal of Health and Social Behavior* 205; 'Learned Hand, The Deficiencies of Trials to Reach the Heart of the Matter, Address Before the Association of the Bar of the City of New York' (17 November 1921), quoted in DW Louisell *et al* (eds), *Pleading and Procedure: State and Federal* (6th edn, Westbury, NY, 1989) 36, 37.   [39] See eg Stolle *et al*, *Practicing Therapeutic Jurisprudence*, n 14 above.

benefit from consultation with psychologists concerning how to identify and deal with these issues, and from psychological research on these problems. In this way, the law office itself can be considered a laboratory for psychological research and a new context for psychological consultation.

Therapeutic jurisprudence has thus begun to transform the way in which legal professionals deal with their clients.[40] This transformation has increased the need for lawyers to understand the basic principles and approaches of psychology; these skills now are being taught in law schools,[41] and in continuing legal education programs for practising lawyers. Psychologists have much to contribute to the education of lawyers in this regard.

These examples merely illustrate the many ways in which therapeutic jurisprudence has had a transformative effect on legal rules and practices, on judging, on the practice of law, and on legal education. Some therapeutic jurisprudence proposals have been implemented, but many others are, at this stage, merely suggestions for how legal rules and practices can be improved. How have the reforms that have already been implemented been working? How can those not yet implemented be refined and adapted for practical application? In what additional ways can law and legal practices be improved so as to increase psychological well-being? These are questions that psychology and psychologists can help the legal system to answer, in the process contributing immensely to significant improvements in the functioning of the legal system. Therapeutic jurisprudence calls upon psychologists to contribute their skills to the improvement of law and our society generally by examining and helping the legal system to answer these questions. Therapeutic jurisprudence thus provides a range of new opportunities for psychology, reinvigorating and expanding the field of law and psychology.

An Agenda for Future Psychological Research

A perusal of the therapeutic jurisprudence literature,[42] reveals a long list of questions that are ripe for empirical research, the results of which will be of considerable importance to the legal system. Psychology can make an enormous contribution to law by helping it to answer these questions. Many of these are questions that otherwise might well go unasked. Examples can be drawn from many areas of law.

---

[40] See eg DB Wexler and BJ Winick, 'Putting Therapeutic Jurisprudence to Work in the Law Office' (May 2003) 89 *American Bar Association Journal* 54.

[41] BJ Winick, 'Using Therapeutic Jurisprudence in Teaching Lawyering Skills: Meeting the Challenge of the New ABA Standards' (2005) 17 *St Thomas Law Review* 429.

[42] For an up-to-date bibliography of therapeutic jurisprudence work, see the website of the International Network on Therapeutic Jurisprudence, <http://www.therapeuticjurisprudence. org>.

In mental health law, for example, existing therapeutic jurisprudence scholarship raises questions such as:

- What are the therapeutic consequences of considering antisocial personality disorder[43] or paedophilia[44] to be mental disorders sufficient as predicates for civil commitment?

- Is recognition of a legal right to refuse mental health treatment likely to be therapeutic or antitherapeutic for those with mental illness, and how should such a right be implemented so as to increase therapeutic outcomes?[45]

- Is recognition of the legal insanity defence likely to produce self-attributional effects that will be antitherapeutic for those who successfully raise it, and if so, how can they be mitigated?[46]

- As presently administered, does the incompetency to stand trial doctrine in the criminal process impose needless antitherapeutic consequences for those found incompetent, and how can it be restructured to avoid these negative consequences and expedite the restoration of competence for trial?[47]

- Do existing civil commitment hearings impose antitherapeutic consequences for those affected, and how can psychological theory be used to restructure such hearings to increase the potential of a positive response to civil commitment?[48]

- Is court-ordered preventive outpatient commitment more or less likely than consensual approaches to improve the mental health of those affected, and if adopted, how can it be applied so as to increase its therapeutic potential?[49]

- How can police officers executing civil commitment orders act with regard to the people they are transporting to the hospital so as to increase the therapeutic potential of commitment?[50]

- Is voluntary hospitalization more therapeutic than involuntary commitment, and how can voluntary admission be facilitated?[51]

---

[43] See BJ Winick, 'Ambiguities in the Legal Meaning and Significance of Mental Illness' (1995) 1 PPPL 534.
[44] BJ Winick, 'Sex Offender Law in the 1990s: A Therapeutic Jurisprudence Analysis' (1998) 4 PPPL 505.   [45] See Winick, *The Right to Refuse*, n 4 above.
[46] See Perlin, *The Jurisprudence of the Insanity Defense*, n 24 above.
[47] See BJ Winick, 'Restructuring Competency to Stand Trial' (1985) 32 *University of California Los Angeles Law Review* 921; BJ Winick, 'Reforming Incompetency to Stand Trial and Plead Guilty: A Restated Proposal and a Response to Professor Bonnie' (1995) 85 *Journal of Criminal Law and Criminology* 571; BJ Winick, 'Incompetency to Stand Trial: An Assessment of Costs and Benefits, and a Proposal for Reform' (1987) 39 *Rutgers Law Review* 243.
[48] See Winick, *Civil Commitment*, n 6 above; BJ Winick, 'Therapeutic Jurisprudence and the Civil Commitment Hearing' (1999) 10 *Journal of Contemporary Legal Issues* 37.
[49] See Winick, *Right to Refuse*, n 4 above, ch 9; BJ Winick, 'Outpatient Commitment: A Therapeutic Jurisprudence Analysis' (2003) 9 PPPL 107.   [50] See Winick, n 1 above, 202.
[51] See eg Winick, *Civil Commitment*, n 6 above, ch 7; American Psychiatric Association, *Consent to Voluntary Hospitalization, Task Force Report No. 34* (Washington, DC, 1993); BJ Winick,

- What are the antitherapeutic consequences of labelling people with mental illness as incompetent—to make treatment decisions, to manage their property, to consent to voluntary hospitalization, to vote, to marry, and to stand trial in the criminal process—and can revised legal standards for measuring incompetency or procedures for ascertaining it or alternative legal labels mitigate these negative consequences?[52]

- What are the therapeutic consequences of allowing people with mental illness to make future decisions about their hospitalization and treatment by executing advance directive instruments or health care proxies?[53]

- What are the antitherapeutic consequences that might ensue for people suffering from dementia or other serious mental disorders who are precluded from participation in research because they are deemed insufficiently competent to provide informed consent to such research?[54]

- What are the therapeutic implications of recognizing an evidentiary psychotherapist-patient privilege,[55] and of recognizing exceptions to such a privilege that require therapists to divulge threats of violence by their patients[56] or to report incidents of past violence or abuse to governmental protective services agencies?[57]

In the criminal process, examples include:

- Can a judge's colloquy with a criminal defendant at a hearing on acceptance of a guilty plea influence the defendant's acceptance of responsibility, with consequent positive effects for his rehabilitation?[58]

'Competency to Consent to Voluntary Hospitalization: A Therapeutic Jurisprudence Analysis of Zinermon v. Burch' (1991) 14 *International Journal of Law and Psychiatry* 169; BJ Winick, 'Voluntary Hospitalization After Zinermon v. Burch' (September, 1991) 21 *Psychiatric Annals* 1; BJ Winick, 'How to Handle Voluntary Hospitalization After Zinermon v. Burch' (1994) 21 *Administration and Policy in Mental Health* 395.

[52] See eg BJ Winick, 'The Side Effects of Incompetency Labeling and the Implications for Mental Health Law' (1995) 1 PPPL 6.

[53] See eg BJ Winick (ed), *Symposium, Advance Directive Instruments for Health and Mental Health Care: Legal, Ethical, and Clinical Issues* (1998) 4 PPPL 577; BJ Winick, 'Advance Directive Instruments for Those with Mental Illness' (1996) 51 *University of Miami Law Review* 57.

[54] BJ Winick and KW Goodman, 'A Therapeutic Jurisprudence Perspective on Participation in Research by Subjects with Reduced Capacity to Consent: A Comment on Drs. Kim and Appelbaum' (forthcoming, 2006) BSL.

[55] See eg BJ Winick, 'The Psychotherapist-Patient Privilege: A Therapeutic Jurisprudence View' (1996) 50 *University of Miami Law Review* 249.

[56] See eg DB Wexler, 'Patients, Therapists, and Third Parties: The Victimological Virtues of Tarasoff' (1979) 2 *International Journal of Law and Psychiatry* 1.

[57] See eg M Levine, 'A Therapeutic Jurisprudence Analysis of Mandated Reporting of Child Maltreatment by Psychotherapists' in Wexler and Winick (eds), *Law in a Therapeutic Key*, n 1 above, 323.

[58] DB Wexler and BJ Winick, 'Therapeutic Jurisprudence and Criminal Justice Mental Health Issues' (1992) 16 *Mental & Physical Disability Law Reporter* 225.

- Does permitting defendants to plead *nolo contendere* reinforce psychological defence mechanisms like denial, minimization, or rationalization in ways that prevent rehabilitation and perpetuate recidivism?[59]

- How can sentencing judges conduct sentencing hearings in a manner likely to increase a criminal defendant's compliance with conditions of probation?[60]

- Is sentence bargaining or charge bargaining more conducive to offender rehabilitation?[61]

- How should a judge in a domestic violence court deal with victims of abuse so as to facilitate their healing?[62]

- Does teen court or youth court promote rehabilitation by having youths serve as attorneys for victims in teen court proceedings?[63]

- How can judges serving in drug treatment courts minimize the perception of coercion on the part of defendants accepting this kind of diversion from the criminal process, and what is the impact of the perception of coercion in this context on successful substance abuse treatment?[64]

- How should criminal defence attorneys counsel their clients about accepting diversion to drug treatment court so as to facilitate their recovery without sacrificing their legal rights?[65]

- How can police officers interrogate criminal defendants in ways that promote rehabilitation?[66]

- How can restorative justice approaches be imported into the criminal justice process in ways that increase both offender rehabilitation and healing on the part of the victim of the crime?[67]

- How can a sentencing judge use the scheduling of sentencing hearings to increase the potential of offender rehabilitation?[68]

[59] S Bibas, 'Using Plea Procedures to Combat Denial and Minimization' in Winick and Wexler (eds), *Judging In A Therapeutic Key*, n 2 above, 165–76; Wexler and Winick, n 58 above; DB Wexler, 'Therapeutic Jurisprudence and the Criminal Courts' (1993) 35 *William and Mary Law Review* 279–99.　　　　　　　　　　　　　　　　　　　　[60] Wexler, n 59 above.

[61] ibid; Wexler and Winick, n 58 above.　　　[62] Winick, n 4 above.

[63] Shiff and Wexler, n 17 above; DB Wexler, 'Just Some Juvenile Thinking About Delinquent Behavior: A Therapeutic Jurisprudence Approach to Relapse Prevention Planning and Youth Advisory Juries' (2000) 69(1) *University of Missouri Kansas City Law Review* 93.

[64] Winick and Wexler, n 17 above; Winick, n 7 above.

[65] M Reisig, 'The Difficult Role of the Defense Lawyer in a Post-Adjudication Drug Treatment Court: Accommodating Therapeutic Jurisprudence and Due Process' (2002) 38 *Criminal Law Bulletin* 216.　　　　　　　　　　　　　　[66] Holmberg and Christianshon, n 2 above.

[67] See J Braithwaite, 'Restorative Justice and Therapeutic Jurisprudence' (2002) 38 *Criminal Law Bulletin* 244; TJ Scheff, 'Community Conferences: Shame and Anger in Therapeutic Jurisprudence' (1999) 67 *Revista Juridica Universidad de Puerto Rico* 97.

[68] See BJ Winick, 'Redefining the Role of the Criminal Defense Lawyer at Plea Bargaining and Sentencing: A Therapeutic Jurisprudence/Preventive Law Model' (1999) 5 PPPL 1051.

- How can criminal defence attorneys use motivational interviewing to increase the potential that their clients will accept rehabilitation?[69]
- How can they use relapse prevention planning models to achieve a rehabilitative form of probation for their clients rather than incarceration?[70]
- Can convincing criminal offenders to apologize to their victims increase the potential for their rehabilitation?[71]
- Do mandatory arrest and prosecution policies in domestic violence cases pose antitherapeutic effects for the victims of domestic violence, and if so, how can arrest and prosecution practices in this area be structured so as to reduce these consequences without providing a symbolic endorsement of domestic violence?[72]
- How can criminal justice processes be adjusted so as to respond more effectively to the therapeutic needs of crime victims?[73]
- How can prison practices be reshaped so as to increase the potential of offender rehabilitation?[74]
- How can criminal offenders who have served their sentences be more effectively dealt with in ways that will better prepare them for reentry and reintegration into the community?[75]

Similarly, therapeutic jurisprudence has raised a long list of novel questions in need of empirical investigation across a wide variety of other legal areas:

- Do juveniles in foster care facing civil commitment respond more effectively to such commitment if they are given a hearing beforehand, and if so, would therapeutic outcomes be increased if they are represented by counsel rather than a *guardian ad litem*?[76]

---

[69] Birgden, n 26 above.   [70] Wexler, n 63 above.

[71] See C Petrucci, 'Apology in the Criminal Justice Setting: Evidence for Including Apology as an Additional Component in the Legal System' (2002) 20 BSL 1.

[72] See LG Mills, 'Killing Her Softly: Intimate Abuse and the Violence of State Intervention' (1999) 113 *Harvard Law Review* 550; Winick, n 4 above, 70–87.

[73] RP Wiebe, 'The Mental Health Implications of Crime Victims' Rights' in Wexler and Winick (eds), *Law in a Therapeutic Key*, n 1 above, 213.

[74] See eg F Cohen and JA Dvoskin, 'Therapeutic Jurisprudence and Corrections: A Glimpse, in Law in a Therapeutic Key' in Wexler and Winick (eds), *Law in a Therapeutic Key*, n 1 above, 149.

[75] See eg La Fond and Winick, n 17 above; S Maruna and TP LeBel, 'Welcome Home? Examining the "Reentry Court" Concept from a Strengths-based Perspective' (2003) 4 *Western Criminology Review*, <http://wcr.sonoma.edu/v4n2/manuscripts/marunalebel.pdf> (last accessed 16 September 2005); FS Taxman, and MH Thanner, 'Probation From a Therapeutic Perspective: Results From the Field' (2004) 7(1) *Contemporary Issues in Law* 39; J Travis, 'But They All Come Back: Rethinking Prisoner Reentry', *Sentencing & Corrections: Issues for the 21st Century*, No 7 (National Institute of Justice, US Department of Justice, May 2000), available at <http://www.ncjrs.org/pdffiles1/nij/181413.pdf> (last visited 16 September 2005).

[76] BJ Winick and GL Wren, 'Do Juveniles facing Civil Commitment Have a Right to Counsel?: A Therapeutic Jurisprudence Brief' (2002) 17 *University of Cincinnati Law Review* 115; see *In Re* Amendment to the Rules of Juvenile Procedure, 804 So 2d 1206 (Fla 2001) and Amendment to the Rules of Juvenile Procedure, 842 So 2d 763 (Fla 2003).

- Would juveniles facing transfer of their cases to adult criminal court respond more effectively to rehabilitative efforts if they received a hearing on whether they should be so transferred?[77]

- What are the therapeutic implications of various constitutional rights, such as freedom of expression, the right to privacy, and the right to procedural due process when the government seeks to deprive an individual of her liberty or property?[78]

- How can the informed consent doctrine in health law be defined and applied by physicians so as to increase the therapeutic potential of the doctor/patient relationship?[79]

- What are the therapeutic benefits and disadvantages of legal recognition of a right to physician assisted suicide?[80]

- Do people who have been involved in accidents experience more effective psychological healing as a result of fault or no-fault tort liability systems?[81]

- Does the 'don't ask, don't tell' policy of the US military impose antitherapeutic consequences on gay and lesbian members of the armed services?[82]

- What is the therapeutic impact—on former offenders, on members of the community, and on police officers—of mandatory reporting and notification laws for discharged sex offenders?[83]

- What are the psychological consequences when tortfeasors deny their liability rather than acknowledging it and apologizing to the victim?[84]

- What are the negative self-attributional effects that occur when individuals are given certain legal labels—juvenile delinquent, sexually violent predator,

---

[77] See TJ Mescall II, 'Legally Induced Participation and Waiver of Juvenile Courts: A Therapeutic Jurisprudence Analysis' (1999) 68 *Revista Juridica University of Puerto Rico* 707; Winick, n 68 above, 1078–9.

[78] See eg Winick, *Civil Commitment*, n 6 above, chs 6 and 8; Winick, n 4 above; BJ Winick, 'Therapeutic Jurisprudence and the Civil Commitment Hearing' (1999) 10 *Journal of Contemporary Issues in Law* 37.

[79] See eg C Sprung and BJ Winick, 'Informed Consent in Theory and Practice: Legal and Medical Perspectives on the Informed Consent Doctrine and a Proposed Reconceptualization' (1989) 17 *Critical Care Medicine* 346; BJ Winick, 'The MacArthur Treatment Competence Study: Legal and Therapeutic Implications' (1996) 2 PPPL 137–66; Winick, *Right to Refuse*, n 4 above, ch 18.

[80] See KL Cerminara and AM Perez, 'Death: A Look At Oregon's Law' (2000) 6 PPPL 503.

[81] See DW Shuman, 'The Psychology of Compensation in Tort Law' (1994) 43 *University of Kansas Law Review* 39.

[82] K Kavanagh, 'Don't Ask, Don't Tell: Deception Required, Disclosure Denied' in Wexler and Winick (eds), *Law in a Therapeutic Key*, n 1 above, 343.

[83] See BJ Winick, 'A Therapeutic Jurisprudence Analysis of Sex Offender Registration and Community Notification Laws' in BJ Winick and JQ La Fond (eds), *Protecting Society from Sexually Dangerous Offenders: Law, Justice, and Therapy* (Washington, DC, 2003) 213.

[84] JR Cohen, 'The Culture of Legal Denial' (2005) 84 *Nebraska Law Review* 247; JR Cohen, 'The Immorality of Denial' (2005) 79 *Tulane Law Review* 903.

or learning disabled, for example—and how can these be reduced or eliminated?[85]

- What are the emotional reactions of individuals filing for bankruptcy, and how can bankruptcy lawyers counsel them in order to avoid their experiencing negative consequences in this regard?[86]

- What are the likely emotional reactions of people consulting with immigration lawyers who have claims for political asylum, and how can such lawyers effectively interview and counsel them concerning such claims?[87] How can lawyers overcome various psychological barriers to the settlement of the civil dispute, thereby avoiding litigation?[88] What are the therapeutic consequences of litigation and the various methods of alternative dispute resolution for the client?[89]

These are merely illustrative of the many novel issues that therapeutic jurisprudence has identified. They constitute a research agenda for psychologists and other social scientists interested in studying the legal system. While there may be other consequences that the law will and should take into account, the therapeutic dimensions of these legal rules and practices are quite important in thinking about how the law should be restructured. These questions are grist for the mill of generations of psychological researchers and graduate students. Moreover, unlike much of the psychological research on the legal system that has been performed in the past, exploration of the therapeutic and antitherapeutic consequences of various legal arrangements and practices will be of great interest to legal audiences and helpful in improving the law's functioning.

As mentioned earlier, therapeutic jurisprudence is concerned not only with changing legal rules, but also with examining and reforming the ways in which they are applied by various legal actors. Through the use of psychological insights and approaches, therapeutic jurisprudence has done much to change how judges and lawyers function within the legal system. The expanding array of problem-solving courts, in which judges explicitly play a role in facilitating the rehabilitative process, provides an important example of the impact of therapeutic jurisprudence. This represents a new and expanded role for the judiciary, one that

---

[85] Winick, n 52 above; BJ Winick, 'A Therapeutic Jurisprudence Assessment of Sexually Violent Predator Laws' in Winick and La Fond (eds), *Protecting Society*, n 83 above, 317.

[86] ML Stines, 'Must We Bankrupt the Spirit Also?: The Benefits of Incorporating Therapeutic Jurisprudence Into Law School Bankruptcy Assistance Programs' (2005) 17 *St Thomas Law Review* 855.

[87] EH Cruz, 'Validation Through Other Means: How Immigration Clinics Can Give Immigrants a Voice When Bureaucracy Has Left Them Speechless' (2005) 17 *St Thomas Law Review* 811; I Loreen, 'Therapeutic Jurisprudence and the Law School Asylum Clinic' (2005) 17 *St Thomas Law Review* 835.

[88] BJ Winick, 'Settling the Civil Dispute: A Therapeutic Jurisprudence/Preventive Law Model' in MA Silver (ed), *The Affective Assistance of Counsel: Practicing Law as a Healing Profession* (forthcoming, Durham, NC, 2006).   [89] Winick, n 88 above.

has revolutionized our concept of courts and judges. Although courts generally have in the past used the services of psychologists and other clinicians, typically in performing evaluations of a variety of issues that are relevant to the legal process, this development greatly expands the potential for psychology and psychologists to contribute to the judicial process. How effective are these new courts? How can judges act so as to increase their ability to motivate offenders to accept rehabilitation and successfully undergo it? How can judges increase treatment compliance? How can judges make more effective use of the emerging tools of risk assessment? How should judges deal with denial, minimization, and rationalization on the part of offenders in these special courts? These are all questions that would benefit immeasurably from psychological research and consultation.

To achieve these new rehabilitative objectives, the courts will increasingly need the services of clinical psychologists in various evaluation and treatment roles. Problem-solving court judges need training in such psychological tools as motivational interviewing and behavioural contracting, and in how to apply the insights of the research on the psychology of procedural justice. If judges are to be successful in these new therapeutic missions, they will need the assistance of increased psychological research and evaluation and treatment services.

Conclusion

This paper has described the approach of therapeutic jurisprudence, an interdisciplinary field of legal scholarship that has an explicit law reform agenda. Therapeutic jurisprudence is a law and psychology approach to studying and improving the legal system. It has revitalized the field of law and psychology, and greatly expanded the interdisciplinary exchange between these two disciplines and professions. It provides new opportunities for psychology and psychologists to contribute to the legal system, identifying a wide range of issues that should be the subject of psychological research. In addition, it provides new opportunities for clinical psychologists to function in the courts and the law office.

Therapeutic jurisprudence has begun to transform our understanding of the legal system and of the roles of legal professionals. Similarly, therapeutic jurisprudence has greatly enlarged the opportunities for psychology and psychologists to contribute to the legal system. In the process, therapeutic jurisprudence has greatly expanded the field of law and psychology, and promises increasingly to do so. It has greatly invigorated the marriage of law and psychology, providing new opportunities for interdisciplinary cross-fertilization. It invites psychologists to join hands with lawyers in a new and exciting adventure that can do much to transform society and improve the psychological wellbeing of all of its members.

4

Legal Decision Making: Psychological Reality Meets Legal Idealism[1]

Mandeep K Dhami[2]

> The decisions of magistrates are indeed complex, each case is an individual case. (Lay magistrate)
>
> The situation [of bail decision making] depends on an enormous weight of balancing information, together with our experience and training. (Lay magistrate)
>
> We are trained to question, and to assess carefully the evidence we are given. (Member of Council of the Magistrates' Association)

In Konecni and Ebbesen's (1984) terms, these quotations highlight the mythology of legal decision making. Legal decision making encompasses a variety of decisions made by different actors in numerous contexts on a range of cases. Decisions may be made in criminal and civil cases. I will consider decisions made in criminal cases. Decisions on such cases may be made by defendants (offenders), victims, witnesses, and police at the crime and investigation stages; by prosecution, defence, judges, and juries at the court stage; and by probation officers, prison staff, and parole boards at the prison and parole stages. I will consider decisions made by judges in court, with a focus on pre-trial decisions, namely the bail decision. The aim of this chapter is to compare the psychological reality of legal decision making with the models of ideal legal practice. In the first section, I describe the bail decision making task in the English criminal justice system with a specific focus on the characteristics of the decision makers and the decision. In the second section, I describe two models of ideal legal practice, namely due process and crime control. In the third section, I review some of my past

[1] The research reviewed in this chapter was funded by City University, London. The author received the Poster Award from the Society of Judgment and Decision Making in 1998, the De Finetti PhD Student Prize from the European Association for Decision Making in 1999, and the SPSSI Social Issues Dissertation Award, Division 9 of APA in 2001–02 for the research reviewed in this chapter. The author is particularly grateful to Peter Ayton for his helpful comments on this research. [2] Please send correspondence to <mkd25@cam.ac.uk>.

research on the psychological process of bail decision making that demonstrates how the performance of legal decision makers is often divergent or in conflict with legal ideals. I also present some new findings on how people perceive real and ideal practice in the context of bail. In the final section, I discuss how we can bridge the divide between the reality of legal decision making as demonstrated by psychological research and the ideal practice of legal decision making as proposed in law by exploring potential explanations for practice and potential interventions for change.

Bail in the English Criminal Justice System

The Decision Makers

In the English criminal justice system, over 95 per cent of all criminal cases are dealt with from start to finish in the magistrates' courts. The vast majority (around 28,000) of decision makers in these courts are lay magistrates.[3] These lay judges are local people. They do not necessarily have any legal qualifications, although they are given some specific training. They make decisions in court as a bench of two or three, on an unpaid, part-time basis. According to the Department of Constitutional Affairs, which is responsible for appointing magistrates, 'sound judgment: to be able to think logically, weigh arguments and reach a sound decision' is one of the six essential qualities of a magistrate.

The Decision

One of the most frequent decisions made by magistrates is the bail decision, because it arises each time a case is adjourned for trial, sentence, or appeal. In the English system, the bail decision is categorical.[4] Should the defendant be bailed (released) unconditionally until the next court hearing? Should the defendant be bailed with non-financial conditions such as curfew or financial conditions such as a surety or security?[5] Or, should the defendant be denied bail and remanded into custody (imprisonment)? Clearly, the defendant may perceive having conditions imposed on bail or being remanded into custody as punitive measures, whether or not they are intended as such by decision makers.

---

[3] A tiny minority (around 180) are district or deputy district judges (previously known as stipendiary magistrates). They are legally qualified and experienced, and they make decisions alone on a full-time, paid basis. The term magistrate will be applied to this group also unless otherwise stated.

[4] This is similar to the Canadian system. There is no monetary bail similar to that in other jurisdictions, such as the US and Australia. The English bail system nevertheless shares several important features with the bail systems of other jurisdictions, such as Canada, the US, and Australia.

[5] A surety is where a third party agrees to pay the court a sum of money if the defendant absconds. A defendant may be required to deposit a security (money) with the court until next appearance at court.

Consequences

The bail decision is important not only because it has ramifications for all those involved, but also because it may affect later decisions in a case. Compared to their bailed counterparts, remanded defendants are more likely to lose their homes, jobs, and contact with their families (Hammond, 1988). Remand prisoners place a financial burden on the penal system (White, 1999), and pose a practical challenge in terms of finding accommodation and regimes, which in turn may explain their increased likelihood of committing suicide in prison relative to other prison populations (Liebling, 1999). Attaching conditions to bail curtails a defendant's liberty and interferes with his/her daily life (Raine and Willson, 1994). However, if more defendants were bailed, the public might be at increased risk of being victimized by those who offend on bail (Brown, 1998), and the police may be unable to track down all defendants who abscond on bail (Parliament, House of Commons Public Accounts Committee, 2005). Finally, evidence suggests that compared to their bailed counterparts, defendants who are denied bail and remanded in custody are more likely to plead guilty (Davies, 1971; Kellough and Wortley, 2002). If their case goes to trial, they are more likely to be convicted. And, if convicted, they are more likely to receive a custodial sentence.

Law and Court Factors

The magistrates' bail decision making process is governed by the Bail Act 1976 and its subsequent revisions.[6] This legislation is vague and ill-defined, and thus affords magistrates considerable discretion in how they make bail decisions. Section 4 of the Act provides a general right to bail for unconvicted and convicted defendants awaiting a pre-sentence report. There are, however, several statutory exceptions to this right. Part 1 of Schedule 1 to the Act sets out grounds for denying bail to defendants accused or convicted of imprisonable offences. For instance, bail may be denied if the court is 'satisfied that there are substantial grounds for believing' that the defendant would abscond, offend, or obstruct justice, if released on bail. In order to judge these risks, the law states that the court should have 'regard to' specific cues such as the nature and seriousness of the charge, the defendant's community ties, previous convictions, bail record, the prosecution case, and 'any others which appear to be relevant'. Importantly, this discretion is not sufficiently controlled by guidelines or training.

　　Other features of the bail decision making task include the fact that there are no formal rules of procedure for bail hearings, so information may be presented in any order. Often seemingly relevant information, such as the defendant's community

---

[6] Significant revisions have been made by the Criminal Justice Act 1988, ss 153–155; the Bail (Amendment) Act 1993; the Criminal Justice and Public Order Act 1994, ss 25–30 and Sch 3; the Crime and Disorder Act 1998, ss 54–56; the Criminal Justice and Police Act 2001, Pt 6; and the Criminal Justice and Courts Services Act 2000, s 58.

ties, may be unavailable to magistrates because of insufficient time to collect information in the period between when a defendant is arrested and bought before the court the next morning. When information is available, magistrates do not necessarily know how to use it because they do not know which cues actually predict absconding, offending, or obstructing justice on bail (eg are weak community ties predictive of absconding?). And magistrates cannot easily learn how to use cues because they do not receive any systematic outcome feedback (eg they don't know what happened to a defendant whom they bailed). Magistrates also face heavy caseloads and so are working under time pressure. Finally, their working pattern is sporadic because they are only required to sit on the bench a minimum of twenty-six times over the course of a year.

Process, Outcomes, and Goals

Drawing on Egon Brunswik's (1952) description of cognitive tasks, the bail decision making task, like all legal decision making tasks, is probabilistic. It requires the decision maker to select, weight, and integrate proximal interrelated cues (pieces of information) that make up a case to predict a distal criterion which is not perfectly predictable. For instance, in order for a magistrate to decide whether to release a defendant on bail or remand him in custody, she must predict the likelihood of the defendant absconding. The case comprises cues such as the defendant's age, offence, and community ties. In one case, the defendant may be young, charged with a serious assault, and may not have any permanent residence. In another case, the defendant may also be young, but may be charged with a minor burglary, and be residing with his family. The strength of a defendant's community ties may be a better predictor of him absconding than the seriousness of the offence with which he is charged. However, not all defendants without a permanent residence will abscond and some defendants with a permanent residence may abscond. When considering the cues that the magistrate may use to predict absconding on bail, the defendant's gender may be highly related to the type of offence with which he is charged, and she may consider the strength of the defendant's community ties. However, in some cases this information may be unavailable, and so she may consider the defendant's age, if she believes age to be related to community ties. Typically, there may be no single cue or combination of cues that allows the perfect prediction of absconding on bail.

Thus, there are two types of error that could result: type I and type II (eg denying bail to defendants who are unlikely to abscond and granting bail to those who are, resepectively). The former is also known as a false positive and the latter as a false negative. The inverse relationship between the two types of errors means, for example, that minimizing the probability of making a type I error maximizes the probability of making a type II error. Given that legal decision making tasks are inherently probabilistic, it is no surprise that legal decision making is not necessarily related to discovering the truth or making the correct decision. Accuracy is not the main aim of a legal decision. For instance, a trial does not establish whether the defendant is innocent of the offence he/she has been charged with, but whether the evidence is sufficient, 'beyond a reasonable doubt', to establish guilt. Similarly, a successful appeal against conviction does not establish the defendant's innocence; it merely states that the correct procedures were not adhered to. Indeed, it would be difficult, if not impossible, to assess the accuracy of legal decisions. For instance, it can never be known whether a specific defendant who was remanded in custody would have absconded if he were released on bail.

Thus, when making legal decisions, decision makers must balance an individual defendant's rights against society's rights. At the pre-trial bail stage, magistrates must balance a defendant's right to pre-trial liberty and society's right to be protected against those defendants who offend on bail and support society's views on defendants who abscond and obstruct justice. The aim is to make a decision or reach this balance following a particular set of procedures. Indeed, social psychological research has demonstrated that in addition to wanting fair outcomes (distributive fairness), people are often highly concerned with the fairness of the process used to arrive at the outcomes (procedural fairness) (eg Folger and Konovsky, 1989). Fair procedures may be used as a proxy for the fairness of outcomes (eg van den Bos, Lind, and Wilke, 2001). The quality of legal decisions is judged not just in terms of the outcomes, but largely in terms of the procedures used to get to those outcomes. Thus, an examination of how magistrates make bail decisions can help us to evaluate their performance.

Models of Ideal Legal Practice

Various theoretical frameworks have been developed to describe, explain, and evaluate how legal decisions are generally made, and how the criminal justice system operates (see eg Bottoms and McClean, 1976; Davies, Croall, and Tryer, 1995; Griffiths, 1970; King, 1981; Packer, 1968).[7] Packer's (1968) due process and crime control models are by far the most widely known. These two models make a statement regarding the function of the criminal justice system and the goals and roles of the agencies operating within the system. Both models represent ideal types or, in Packer's (1968) terms, 'normative' models that lie at two opposite ends of a continuum.

Crime Control

In the crime control model, the aim is to minimize type II errors (ie the number of guilty defendants who are set free). The model minimizes the adversarial

---

[7] The specific models are: Packer's (1968) due process model and crime control model; King's (1981) medical model, bureaucratic model, status passage model, and power model; Bottoms and McClean's (1976) liberal bureaucratic model; Griffiths' (1970) family model; and the just desserts model described by Davies *et al* (1995). King (1981) states that the system is best described by some features of a number of these models, rather than by any one model.

aspect of the judicial process. The function of the justice system is to repress crime, and a failure in controlling crime would result in public disorder. The law abiding society, who are the victims of crime, need to be protected from deviant individuals. There are only limited resources available for dealing with crime. Thus, there is an emphasis upon efficiency and a high rate of detection, and conviction is ensured through speed and finality. Speed can be achieved by adopting informal and uniform practices. 'Facts can be established more quickly through interrogation in a police station than through the formal process of examination and cross-examination . . . Routine, stereotyped procedures are essential . . . The model . . . must be an administrative, almost managerial model' (Packer, 1968, 159). Thus, the system is like an 'assembly-line conveyor belt' where individuals are screened at each stage (ibid). Those that are probably innocent are filtered out early in the process by the police. The remainder are either expected to plead guilty or are then rushed through to conviction in court by prosecutors. There is thus a presumption of guilt. Finality is achieved through minimizing opportunities for challenge. Errors, which are defined in terms of acquittals or successful appeals, are redefined as due to a technicality, thus maintaining faith in the police and prosecution. Finally, as a deterrent, the whole experience is supposed to be unpleasant for the defendant.

Due Process

By contrast, in the due process model the aim is to minimize type I errors (ie the number of innocent defendants who are convicted). The model places the adversarial aspect at the centre of the justice process. The police may be unreliable and prone to errors in their gathering of the facts, not simply for self-serving reasons, but also because witnesses may not accurately recall events, for example. Therefore, an 'obstacle course' is placed along the process, and there is 'an insistence on formal, adjudicative, adversary fact-finding processes in which the factual case against the accused is publicly heard by an impartial tribunal and is evaluated only after the accused has had a full opportunity to discredit the case against him' (Packer, 1968, 163–4). The due process model 'resembles a factory that has to devote a substantial part of its input to quality control' and so the manner in which cases are dealt with is deemed more important than the quantity of cases dealt with (ibid, 165). Factual guilt is set aside for the notion of legal guilt. For instance, cases must be dealt with by the court that has the power to deal with them, in an appropriate venue, within a limited period of time, the defendant cannot be tried for the same case twice, and he/she may plead insanity. Rules govern police powers and the admissibility of evidence, there is a presumption of innocence, and the burden of proof is placed on the prosecution. Defendants have the right to a defence solicitor, and they must be treated equally. A conviction of guilt can only be upheld if the case has been dealt with according to procedural guidelines. As an acknowledgement of the fallibility of the system, there are opportunities to re-open a case. Thus, the police and prosecution are made aware of the need to adhere to rules, as otherwise factually guilty defendants will go free. The rule-abiding behaviour of the system acts as an exemplar to the public, who should also abide by the law. Finally, the due process model aims to control the power of the state against an individual.

Ideal Model for Bail

Packer (1968) saw the relevance of the due process and crime control models for decisions at the bail stage. Although the Bail Act 1976 contains due process and crime control principles, it also affords magistrates much discretion in which of these principles is enforced, and how they are enforced. The training given to magistrates does not differentiate between crime control and due process and does not structure their discretion (for example Judicial Studies Board, 2005; Waterside Press, 2003). However, the conception of justice in the Anglo-American system is synonymous with the due process model. For instance, in the *Hobson* case, Holroyd J declared that 'it is a maxim of English law that ten guilty men should escape rather than one innocent man should suffer' (1823 1 Lew CC 261). Although pre-trial decisions such as the bail decision lack regulation, due process ideals are often recommended as ways to regulate such decisions and recommended as the ideal practice to which magistrates should aspire when making bail decisions (eg Galligan, 1987).

Psychological Research on Bail Decision Making

Packer's (1968) two models can be translated into two different types of decision making processes. In the crime control model, there is an emphasis on efficiency, speed, and finality. Translating this into decision making processes we could say that magistrates should search and weight only evidence of guilt and not integrate evidence of innocence. Essentially, they should be non-compensatory and fast and frugal. By contrast, in the due process model, there is an emphasis on adherence to an adversarial, adjudicative, fact finding procedure. Translating this into decision making processes, we could say that magistrates should search for all relevant information, and weight and integrate evidence for and against the defendant appropriately. Essentially, they should be compensatory, slow, and careful. In past research, I have examined whether magistrates making bail decisions behave according to the due process or crime control models. In particular, I have measured the extent to which two different types of psychological strategies that map onto either the due process or crime control models, capture and predict magistrates' bail decision making behaviour.

Compensatory Strategies

Compensatory decision strategies, such as the statistical regression model and the non-statistical Franklin's rule and Dawes' rule, embody aspects of the procedure proposed by the due process model.[8] These models search through all of the available cues, and weight and integrate multiple cues in a compensatory way when making a decision. For example, seriousness of offence may be given greater weight than defendant's gender, but both cues will be integrated to form a decision. Franklin's rule differentially weights cues, while Dawes' rule weights them equally.

As Equation 1 illustrates below, in Franklin's rule, for each case the value of a cue is multiplied by the predetermined cue weight and summed across all cues. If the sum is equal or greater to a predetermined threshold then the case will be treated punitively (ie bailed with conditions or remanded into custody), and if the sum is less than the threshold then the case is treated non-punitively (ie bailed unconditionally). Similarly, as Equation 2 illustrates, in Dawes' rule, for each case the cue values are summed across all cues, and if the sum is equal to or greater than the threshold the case is treated punitively, otherwise the case is treated non-punitively (for details of how the cue values, weights, and thresholds are computed see Dhami and Ayton, 2001).

> *Equation 1*
> Example case is made up of gender(0)(0.72) + race(1)(0.67) + age(0)(0.67) + offence(1)(0.78) + prosecution request(1)(0.72) + previous convictions and bail record(0)(0.73) + prosecution case(0)(0.78) + community ties(1)(0.67) + police bail decision(1)(0.67) = 3.51
> Threshold for a magistrate is 3.52. Therefore, this case would be treated non-punitively.

> *Equation 2*
> Example case is made up of gender(0) + race(1) + age(0) + offence(1) + prosecution request(1) + previous convictions and bail record(0) + prosecution case(0) + community ties(1) + police bail decision(1) = 5
> Threshold for a magistrate is 5.89. Therefore, this case would be treated punitively.

Traditionally, decision researchers have used compensatory models to infer the judgment process from the judgments made (see Cooksey, 1996; Dawes and Corrigan, 1974; Hammond *et al*, 1975; Slovic and Lichtenstein, 1971). Studies have typically found that such models are valid descriptors of legal decision making as they provide a good fit to individuals' judgment data (eg Ebbesen and

---

[8] Franklin's rule is named after Benjamin Franklin, who described the procedure for the model, while Dawes' rule is named after Robyn Dawes, who showed that equal-weighted models can approximate the performance of differential weighted models.

Konecni, 1975; Sensibaugh and Allgeier, 1996; York, 1992). More recently, however, some psychologists have suggested that these compensatory models are not psychologically plausible because they require attention, memory, and computational capacities that are beyond the human mind, and would be difficult to achieve under certain task conditions such as time pressure and lack of information (eg Dhami and Harries, 2001; Gigerenzer, Todd, and the ABC Research Group, 1999). Furthermore, these models provide only a static view of decision making, by implying that the same cues are used in the same way in every case.

Non-compensatory Strategies

Researchers have proposed simple heuristics as alternatives to models such as Franklin's rule and Dawes' rule (Dhami and Harries, 2001; Gigerenzer *et al*, 1999). Many of these are non-compensatory, 'fast and frugal' decision strategies. Non-compensatory strategies, such as the Matching Heuristic, embody aspects of the procedure proposed by the crime control model (Dhami and Ayton, 1998). This model only searches through a tiny subset of the available cues in rank order, and bases a decision on one cue alone, disregarding all others no matter how relevant they may seem.

As Figure 4.1 illustrates, in the Matching Heuristic, for each case, the values of a predetermined number of cues (K) are searched in a predetermined order. If a cue has a critical value, then the case is treated punitively, otherwise the value of the next cue is searched. This process continues until the Kth cue is reached, and if by this time none of the cues has a critical value, the case is treated non-punitively. Here, different cues may be used to make decisions on different cases. Once a decision is made on the basis of a cue that attains a critical value, the values of other cues cannot alter it, and so the strategy is non-compensatory (for details of how the critical cue values, cue rank ordering, and K are computed see Dhami and Ayton, 2001).

Bail Decisions on Simulated Cases

In one study, I examined how individual magistrates made bail decisions on simulated cases (see Dhami and Ayton, 2001). Is their decision making better described and predicted by a compensatory or a non-compensatory strategy? Are magistrates using legal or extra-legal cues? To what extent does magistrates' self-reported cue use correspond to their cue use as suggested by strategies that best predict their behaviour? Does the same magistrate make a consistent decision on the same case presented on another occasion? Do different magistrates agree as to the decision to be made on the same case? How confident are magistrates in their bail decisions?

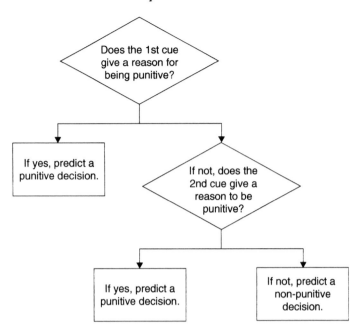

Figure 4.1. The Matching Heuristic ($K = 2$)

A postal survey was conducted of eighty-one magistrates from a random sample of forty-four courts throughout England and Wales. Magistrates had on average thirteen years of experience on the bench. Forty-six magistrates sat in courts located in metropolitan areas and the remainder sat in provincial courts.

Magistrates were asked to make bail decisions on forty-one simulated cases. Twenty-seven cases were used to capture magistrates' bail decision making policies, seven cases were used to cross-validate these captured policies, and seven cases were duplicates from the former set of twenty-seven cases used to measure the consistency of decisions. The cases comprised an orthogonal (fractional-factorial) combination of nine legal and extra-legal cues which were selected on the basis of a task analysis. The 'legal' cues, such as offence and community ties, were those that are explicitly mentioned in the Bail Act 1976, whereas the extra-legal cues, such as gender and police bail decision, were those that past research has indicated that magistrates may be using. After reading each case, magistrates first made a decision (ie unconditional bail, conditional bail, or remand in custody), and then rated their confidence in their decision on an 11-point scale (marked from 'absolutely uncertain' to 'absolutely certain'). Finally, magistrates ranked the nine cues in order of the importance they attached to them when making their decisions.

The data was analysed for each magistrate separately (for details of the analyses see Dhami and Ayton, 2001). There were few differences in the decision making behaviour of lay magistrates and district judges, magistrates with more and less experience on the bench, and magistrates located in metropolitan and provincial courts.

Each magistrate's decisions made on the duplicate cases were compared with the originals to measure intra-individual consistency in bail decisions using Cohen's Kappa statistic. Across magistrates, Kappa ranged from zero to one, with an average of 0.69, indicating some degree of inconsistency in bail decisions.[9] There was also disagreement across magistrates as to the decision to be made on the twenty-seven cases. Magistrates disagreed with the modal decision on from four to twenty-five cases, with an average of fifteen cases. Despite the intra- and inter-individual inconsistency in bail decision making, magistrates were highly confident in their decisions. Across magistrates, the post-decisional confidence ratings over the twenty-seven cases ranged from 6 to 10, with an average of 8. This high level of confidence may reflect magistrates' need to gain public support rather than their actual confidence in their decisions (Allwood and Grahag, 1999), although confidence is likely to be boosted by the knowledge that they were appointed partly because of their 'sound judgement'.

In order to capture magistrates' bail decision making policies, the bail decision was divided into punitive (conditional bail or remand in custody) versus non-punitive (bail unconditionally). The policy of each magistrate was captured using two compensatory strategies (ie Franklin's rule and Dawes' rule) and one non-compensatory strategy (ie Matching Heuristic). Franklin's rule and Dawes' rule both *a priori* assume use of all nine cues that were available to magistrates, whereas cue use is an empirical issue for the Matching Heuristic, which used only one cue for 75 per cent of the magistrates. The three strategies were developed on twenty-seven of the forty-one cases, and each strategy's ability to predict magistrates' decisions was first tested on these cases. Then, the strategies were cross-validated on another seven cases. Figure 4.2 presents a box plot showing the median fit of the strategies across magistrates at both the modelling and cross-validation (holdout) stages. All three models on average performed above chance level in predicting magistrates' decisions (which for a binary decision: punitive versus non-punitive is 50 per cent). At the modelling stage, on average both the Matching Heuristic, and Franklin's rule outperformed Dawes' rule. However, at the cross-validation stage, the Matching Heuristic, which based decisions on only one cue, was a better predictor of magistrates' decisions than Franklin's rule, which used all nine cues. In fact, the Matching Heuristic correctly predicted on average 66 per cent of magistrates' decisions on these simulated cases.

---

[9] All averages refer to means unless otherwise stated.

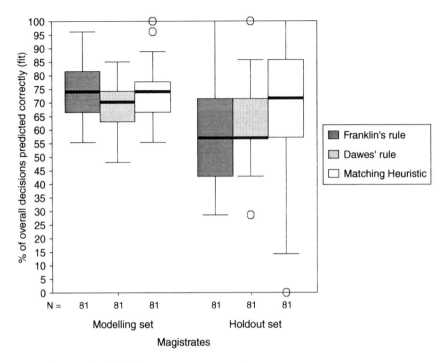

Figure 4.2. Median fit of the strategies across magistrates
Source: Adapted from Dhami and Ayton, 2001.

According to the Matching Heuristic, the majority of magistrates searched and used legal cues, such as previous convictions and bail record, seriousness of offence, prosecution request, community ties, and strength of prosecution case. However, a minority of magistrates did use extra-legal cues, such as the defendant's gender, police bail decision, and defendant's age and race. Interestingly, different magistrates used different cues to make bail decisions on the same set of cases.

For each magistrate, the rank order of the nine cues as described by the Matching Heuristic was compared with the magistrate's self-reported rank order. Across magistrates, Kendall's tau-b correlations between the captured and self-reported ranks ranged from −0.39 to 0.67, with an average of 0.09. As Figure 4.3 shows, on average, magistrates ranked extra-legal cues as not very important to their decisions, but the Matching Heuristic, which was a good predictor of their decisions, indicated that these were important cues. Conversely, magistrates ranked legal cues as very important to their decisions but the Matching Heuristic indicated otherwise. These findings may reflect a lack of insight, as suggested by

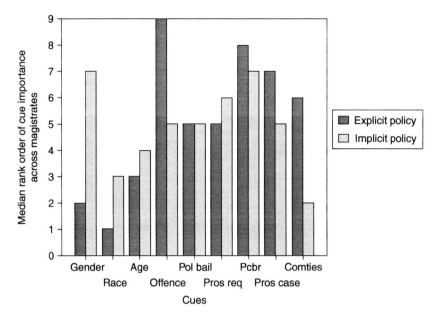

Figure 4.3. Median captured (implicit) and self-reported (explicit) cue importance (9 = most important)

Source: Adapted from Dhami and Ayton, 2001.

some researchers (eg Sensibaugh and Allgeier, 1996; Summers, Taliaferro, and Fletcher, 1970), or an inability to articulate cognitive behaviour (Nisbett and Wilson, 1977). In the legal domain, there may also be an element of social desirability response bias such that magistrates tell researchers what they 'ought' to be doing rather than what they are 'actually' doing, or what they privately think they are doing (Konecni and Ebbesen, 1984). Hence, the importance of studying magistrates' behaviour rather than their self-reports.

Bail Decisions on Real Cases

In another study, I examined benches of magistrates making bail decisions on real cases in the courtroom (see Dhami, 2003). Does the finding that individual magistrates use a non-compensatory strategy when making bail decisions on simulated cases generalize to benches' bail decisions made on real cases? How long does it take magistrates to make bail decisions?

Two observers recorded the bail decisions made in two courts, one outside London (court A) and one inside London (court B), over a four-month period. Magistrates' courts are open to the public, and the court managers granted permission to observe from the defence and media benches as well as access to all written information provided to magistrates during a bail hearing. Importantly, magistrates did not know that they were being observed for research purposes. In total, 159 bail decisions made by 25 benches were observed in court A and 183 decisions made by 32 benches were observed in court B. Details of the cases presented (ie 25 cues that can be divided into those referring to the defendant's personal characteristics, the offence, the defendant's previous record, and the bail hearing) and the decisions made were recorded using a structured coding scheme that was developed on the basis of a task analysis. The duration of the hearing was measured using a stopwatch.

Information was often unavailable to magistrates on the defendant's previous convictions, bail record and community ties, and the police bail decision. There was also little redundancy of information as indicated by low inter-cue correlations.[10] The average duration of bail hearings was only seven to ten minutes in courts A and B, respectively. Indeed the rapidity of the hearings lends convergent validity to the idea that magistrates may be using a non-compensatory, fast and frugal decision strategy.

In this study, I captured each court's bail decision making policy because individual benches do not make a sufficient number of decisions for analysis and benches are not stable groups, as individual magistrates rotate across benches. Franklin's rule and Dawes' rule both assume the use of all available cues (ie 25 cues). By contrast, for both courts, the Matching Heuristic used only 3 cues. The predictive validity of the strategies was tested for each court ten times, after randomly selecting cases used to develop the strategies and sixty cases used to cross-validate them. Figures 4.4 and 4.5 present box plots showing the median fit of each strategy across the ten tests at the modelling and cross-validation stages for court A and B, respectively. All three models performed exceptionally well in predicting both courts' bail decisions at the modelling stage, with an average of over 75 per cent accuracy. However, as in the previous study, at cross-validation, the Matching Heuristic was the best predictor of benches' bail decisions. In fact, it correctly predicted on average 92 per cent of court A's decisions and 85 per cent of court B's decisions.

According to the Matching Heuristic, when a case appears in court A, the bench will make a punitive decision if the prosecution requested a punitive decision. If the prosecution request was non-punitive or no request was made, then the bench will make a punitive decision if the previous court made a punitive decision on the case. However, if the previous court was non-punitive or if this is the first time the case is appearing in court, then the bench will make a punitive decision if the police made a punitive decision on the case after arrest. However, if the police decision was non-punitive or is unknown, then the bench will make a

---

[10] From an analysis perspective, this makes it easier to determine the effect of each cue on the bail decision, independent of the other cues.

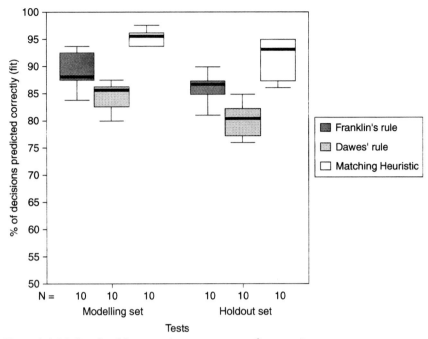

Figure 4.4. Median fit of the strategies across ten tests for court A

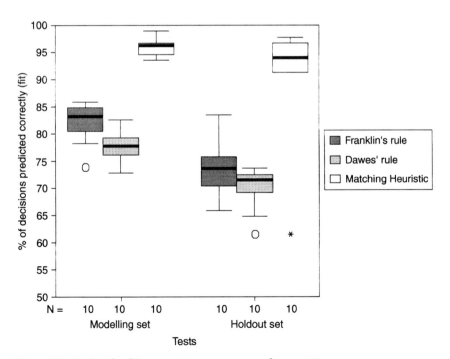

Figure 4.5. Median fit of the strategies across ten tests for court B

non-punitive decision. No other cue is used. A remarkably similar 'passing-the-buck' approach was used by court B, which follows the punitive decisions of the previous court and the police, and also makes a punitive decision if the defendant has a previous conviction for a similar offence. Finally, the Bail Act 1976 states that magistrates should behave punitively when information is unavailable (ie remand in custody while gathering sufficient information to make a decision). However, the Matching Heuristic shows that magistrates are better predicted when they are non-punitive in this situation.

The fact that there were few inter-correlations among the cues suggests that none of the previous legal actors' decisions were associated with any of the other legal or extra-legal cues in the case. Thus, it is unclear what information the prosecution, police, and previous bench used when making their decisions. The decision making strategies of these other legal actors warrants investigation.

Other Studies of Bail Decision Making

Other studies of magistrates' bail decision making have examined magistrates' imposition of conditions to bail (Dhami, 2004), magistrates' interpretation of the legal threshold for denying bail (Dhami and Ayton, 2005), the source of disagreement among magistrates' bail decisions (Dhami, 2005), and the effectiveness of a policy initiative designed to reduce magistrates' decisions to deny bail and remand in custody (Dhami, 2002). The main findings of these studies are described briefly.

Magistrates must balance a defendant's rights to liberty at the pre-trial stage against the public's right to be protected against defendants who may offend on bail and assure society that defendants will be bought to justice. Therefore, when magistrates believe that a defendant may pose a risk of absconding, offending, or obstructing justice if released on bail unconditionally, they often decide to attach conditions to bail rather than release the defendant unconditionally or remand him/her in custody. Dhami (2004) found that when deciding on conditional bail, magistrates imposed on average two conditions to bail, and these were a limited variety of conditions such as residing at a specified address, reporting to the police station, and not contacting witnesses.

The law on bail states that bail should be denied if there are 'substantial grounds' for believing that a defendant would abscond, offend, or obstruct justice while on bail. Thus, the phrase substantial grounds is a threshold for remanding a defendant in custody. Dhami and Ayton (2005) found that, on average, lay magistrates denied bail to defendants when they judged their risk of absconding, offending, and obstructing justice to be 47 per cent, 37 per cent, and 42 per cent, respectively. There were also wide intra- and inter-individual differences in how magistrates interpreted the phrase. Furthermore, less experienced magistrates adopted a lower threshold, implying that they were more stringent.

It is a reasonable requirement that a defendant be treated similarly by two different judges, and it is apparent that if two judges make different decisions on the same case, one must be erroneous. Dhami (2005) reported that the percentage of magistrates disagreeing with the modal decision across cases could be partly predicted by variability in magistrates' earlier risk judgements of absconding on these cases. In turn, the variability in these risk judgements was reliably predicted by three case cues: defendant's community ties, seriousness of offence, and defendant's previous convictions and bail record.

Finally, just and defensible legal decisions can only be made if decision makers have access to relevant information on a case. As a response to the problem of limited information, and in order to reduce unnecessary remands in custody, Bail Information Schemes were introduced in the late 1980s. These schemes assume that defendants with strong community ties, such as a fixed residence and employment, are less likely to abscond and so could be granted bail. Probation officers collect, verify, and provide largely positive information about a defendant's community ties to the prosecution and defence, who then relay it to the court. Dhami (2002) demonstrated that these schemes had no significant effect on magistrates' bail decisions or their consistency and agreement in decisions. Rather, the schemes served to further increase magistrates' confidence in their decisions.

Study on Perceptions of Bail Decision Making Practice

The psychological research findings reviewed above demonstrate that the real practice of magistrates' bail decision making departs from the ideal practice as represented in the law on bail and the due process model to which the English criminal justice system aspires. Magistrates who use non-compensatory strategies or simple, fast and frugal heuristics are behaving akin to the crime control model. They are performing as an 'assembly-line conveyor belt'. By contrast, the due process model sets up an 'obstacle course'. There is an old adage that 'when due process is observed, justice is served'. Importantly, the ideal of due process is a normative model and it is unclear to what extent society in general and participants in the criminal justice system, such as offenders and professionals, support this model.

As Buck and Miller (1994) note, when considering outcomes, people not only think about whether they could have been better or worse, they also reflect on the fairness of the outcomes (distributive justice) and the fairness of the procedures used to allocate the outcomes (procedural justice). Due process emphasizes the notion of procedural fairness, and social psychological research has demonstrated that people are often concerned about this (see Tyler, 1997). If there is insufficient or unavailable information regarding the fairness of outcomes, people may refer to the fairness of procedures that led to the outcomes. Fair procedures may thus be used as an albeit imperfect cue to fair outcomes (Folger, 1984; Folger,

Rosenfield, Grove, and Cokran, 1979). Procedures may also be outcomes in themselves (Leventhal, 1980; Leventhal, Karuza, and Fry, 1980). Essentially, unfair procedures may lead people to feel the same as they would when they experience unfair outcomes (Folger and Kass, 2000). According to Leventhal (1980), procedural fairness requires consistency, bias-suppression, accuracy, correctability, representativeness, and ethicality.

In a recent study, I examined whether the legal ideal was perceived to be better practice relative to the practice demonstrated by research. Are magistrates who use a compensatory strategy such as Franklin's rule when making bail decisions perceived to make fewer errors, and be fairer, more consistent, and less biased, than magistrates who use a non-compensatory strategy such as the Matching Heuristic?

A sample of forty medium security prisoners and forty-one criminal justice professionals (ie prison governors, senior probation officers, and police officers) completed a survey. They each read a brief description of a real bail case taken from Dhami (2003), and a description of a hypothetical benches' decision making process and decision on the case. Then they were asked to rate the: (1) fairness of the magistrates' decision; (2) fairness of the magistrates' decision making process; (3) likelihood that the magistrates would deny bail to defendants who are unlikely to abscond, offend, or obstruct justice (type I error); (4) likelihood that the magistrates would grant bail to defendants who are likely to abscond, offend, or obstruct justice (type II error); (5) likelihood that the magistrates would deny bail to defendants who are likely to abscond, offend or obstruct justice; (6) likelihood that the magistrates would grant bail to defendants who are unlikely to abscond, offend or obstruct justice; (7) chances that the magistrates would make a different decision on the same case if it was presented on another occasion; and (8) likelihood that the magistrates would be biased. Ratings were made on 0 to 100 point scales. In addition, participants were asked (9) how much they thought magistrates should aim to guard society's right to be protected versus a defendant's right to freedom on an 11-point scale marked 'society's right' and 'defendant's right' on the first and last points, respectively. Half of the participants were randomly assigned to read about a bench that used a non-compensatory strategy (ie Matching Heuristic), while the other half read about a bench that used a compensatory strategy (ie Franklin's rule). The decision made (ie punitive or non-punitive) was counterbalanced across the two conditions such that a random half of the 'compensatory' group read that the decision was punitive and the other half read that the decision was non-punitive. Similarly, half of the 'non-compensatory' group read about a punitive decision and half read about a non-punitive decision.

For analysis, the data was combined across decision type (ie punitive or non-punitive) and participant type (ie prisoners and the criminal justice professionals). Independent samples *t*-tests revealed that, on average, both the compensatory and non-compensatory groups believed that magistrates should aim slightly more to guarding society's right to be protected (see Table 4.1). As Table 4.1 shows, on

Table 4.1. Statistical comparison between compensatory and non-compensatory groups' perceptions of magistrates' bail decision making

Measure	Compensatory Group		Non-compensatory Group		Test Statistic
	M	SD	M	SD	
Decision aim	5.08	2.00	5.61	2.10	$t[79] = 1.17, p = 0.244$
Type I error	40.00	25.13	46.34	26.15	$t[78] = 1.10, p = 0.273$
Type II error	30.25	27.50	31.95	26.76	$t[79] = 0.28, p = 0.779$
Correctly deny bail	72.50	24.47	76.34	23.95	$t[79] = 0.71, p = 0.477$
Correctly grant bail	65.75	19.73	64.15	23.56	$t[79] = 0.33, p = 0.741$
Fair decision process	54.00	26.49	40.24	27.88	$t[79] = 2.28, p = 0.026$
Fair decision	56.25	26.09	39.51	25.69	$t[79] = 2.91, p = 0.005$
Inconsistency	43.50	25.58	49.76	26.97	$t[79] = 2.05, p = 0.044$
Bias	44.50	27.54	60.24	25.64	$t[79] = 2.66, p = 0.009$

M = mean
SD = standard deviation

average, both groups believed that magistrates would be equally likely to make a type I and type II error, and to make the correct decision (ie deny bail to defendants who would be likely to abscond, offend, or obstruct justice, and grant bail to defendants who are unlikely to behave in this way; see Table 4.1). However, on average, participants in the compensatory group believed that the magistrates' decision and decision making process were significantly fairer than did participants in the non-compensatory group. On average, compared to participants in the non-compensatory group, participants in the compensatory group also believed that the magistrates were less likely to make a different decision on the same case presented to them on another occasion. Finally, on average, participants in the compensatory group believed that the magistrates were less likely to be biased than did participants in the non-compensatory group. Therefore, on the whole, prisoners and criminal justice professionals tend to have more positive perceptions of magistrates who behave according to the due process model than the crime control model.

Bridging the Divide between Psychology and Law

To summarize, the psychological research on magistrates' bail decision making has shown that, on average, magistrates are internally inconsistent in their decisions; different magistrates disagree as to the decision to be made on the same case, which can be partly explained by their variability in earlier risk judgments; magistrates attach a limited variety of conditions to bail; magistrates have a relatively low and variable interpretation of the legal threshold for denying bail; magistrates make bail decisions fairly rapidly; magistrates' bail decision making strategies are fast and frugal and sometimes rely on extra-legal cues; magistrates' self-reported cue use when making bail decisions differs from their captured cue use; and Bail Information Schemes do not have the intended effect of reducing remands in custody. However, magistrates are highly confident in their decisions. This picture of magistrates' decision making behaviour does not correspond with the ideal practice as proposed in the law on bail and legal theories. Furthermore, magistrates' practice is perceived to be inconsistent, unfair, and biased by prisoners and criminal justice professionals. Thus, there is a divide between the reality and the ideal of bail decision making. In order to bridge this divide it is necessary to understand why magistrates behave the way they do so that efforts can be made to improve their decision making.

Explaining Legal Decision Making

To date, psychological research has aimed to describe how magistrates make bail decisions. The next step is to explain their behaviour. One explanation for magistrates' performance is likely to lie in the fact that they are, after all, only human. The human mind is characterized by limited attention, memory, and information processing capacities (eg Kahneman, 1973; Miller, 1956). Several psychologists have pointed out that unaided human judgement cannot meet the demands of compensatory decision strategies (eg Gigerenzer *et al*, 1999; Simon, 1956, 1987, 1990), and that people may choose strategies that reduce cognitive effort (eg Payne, Bettman, and Johnson, 1993). This is particularly likely under specific task conditions.

Another explanation may, therefore, lie in the nature of the decision making task that magistrates are expected to perform. As is the case for many other legal decision makers, magistrates are often expected to perform under suboptimal conditions. For instance, there are no formal rules of procedure for bail hearings; seemingly relevant information is often unavailable; magistrates do not know the objective predictive validity of different case cues; they are faced with heavy caseloads; and they work on a sporadic basis. Research in cognitive psychology shows that these types of factors can influence the decision making processes used such that decision makers may be less consistent in their decisions; they may use simple decision making strategies; and may ignore relevant information (eg Davis and Davis, 1996; Edland, 1979; Payne *et al*, 1993; Rieskamp and Hoffrage, 1999). As task complexity increases, people switch to simple non-compensatory strategies (eg Timmermans, 1993). There is also evidence showing that when groups make decisions involving shared responsibility, as in the case of benches of magistrates, they tend to use few cues (Weldon and Gargano, 1985).

Importantly, magistrates' ability to perform well is likely to be hampered by the fact that the law on bail does not provide them with sufficient guidance on how decisions ought to be made. Neither is this situation remedied by the training and further guidelines provided to magistrates. Therefore, there is ample opportunity for magistrates to interpret and apply the law differently (even on similar cases), and for magistrates to be influenced by socially undesirable or extra-legal cues.

Future research on magistrates' bail decision making could aim to measure the effects of certain task conditions on bail decisions with the goal of determining a set of courtroom conditions (including legislative wording) that can facilitate acceptable performance. Indeed, a body of research that systematically examines the effect of task conditions and cognitive capabilities on legal decision making, can help us to find ways in which legal decision making can be improved.

Improving Legal Decision Making

Previous attempts to improve bail decision making have frequently focused on changing the characteristics of the decision makers. For example, proposals have been made to increase the demographic representativeness of the magistracy (Brown, 1991; Darbyshire, 1997a, 1997b), and to replace lay magistrates with district judges, or make them work more closely with these judges (Narey, 1997). The research, however, shows that there is little difference in the performance of lay magistrates and district judges (Dhami and Ayton, 2001). Furthermore, there are few differences in the performance of more and less experienced magistrates and district judges (Dhami and Ayton, 2001). Both groups have limited cognitive abilities, and both work under essentially the same suboptimal conditions. Therefore, replacing one judge with another may not be sufficient to improve performance. Other interventions are necessary.

The fact that human performance is often contingent on both cognitive capabilities and task conditions suggests that interventions for change or improving legal decision making should adopt a dual focus on the legal decision makers and the legal decision making task. Magistrates' cognitive processing limitations could be overcome by providing them with a cognitive aid that helps them to implement the law. Cognitive aids have been recommended in other judgment domains, such as psychiatry (eg Erdman, 1988), and are not a new concept in the legal domain (eg Larsen, Yelon, and Irving, 1997). Magistrates' consistency and disagreement could be improved by providing them with cognitive feedback of their own and other magistrates' bail decision making policies, respectively.[11] Cognitive feedback has been shown to be effective in other domains, such as medicine (Kirwan *et al*, 1983). However, in the legal domain, where the objectively correct decision is difficult to determine reliably, feedback of policies may result in the consistent and/or agreed use of a policy that leads to type I errors.

[11] Cognitive feedback involves providing information about the formal properties of the task (eg objective cue validities and inter-cue correlations), the individual's judgment policy, (ie cue utilization validities, and consistency), and the match between properties of the environment and the individual's judgement policy (eg accuracy) (see Doherty and Balzer, 1988).

The magistrates' bail decision making task is characterized by a number of conditions that may impede good decision making, and which could be altered to improve performance. Interventions that remedy or overcome these conditions could be useful. For instance, consistent use of information could be achieved by introducing statutory rules of procedure for bail hearings. Inconsistency and use of simple strategies could be eliminated, by reducing the time pressure under which magistrates work (for example by reducing the number of cases that must be dealt with in one court session).

Other efforts to reduce inconsistency, disagreement and use of extra-legal cues could involve reducing the discretion afforded magistrates by the law on bail. This can be done either by directly revising the legislation or by providing well-defined and structured guidelines. There have been many calls for a reduction in judicial discretion in pre-trial (eg Goldkamp, 1993), conviction (eg Kagehiro, 1990), sentencing (eg Nash, 1992), and parole decisions (eg Carroll *et al*, 1982). Guidelines appear to be effective in reducing sentencing disparities (eg Anderson, Kling, and Stith, 1999; Meeker, Jesilow, and Aranda, 1992), and increasing the accountability and transparency of pre-trial decisions (eg Galligan, 1987; Goldkamp and Gottfredson, 1985; Goldkamp *et al*, 1995; Stanfiel, 1983). Guidelines may also help improve the equity and effectiveness of judges' decisions (see Goldkamp and Gottfredson, 1985; Goldkamp *et al*, 1995, ch 15).

In terms of revising the law on bail, the catch-all category in the Bail Act 1976 (ie allowing consideration of any other factors that appear to be relevant) could be unpacked into its component parts, and a scheme for weighting cues could be incorporated that is informed by at least some objective measures of the relative predictive validities of the cues. In addition, magistrates could be provided with information on which conditions are effective in reducing absconding, offending, and obstructing justice while on bail. Thus, research needs to be directed at measuring cue validities and effectiveness of bail conditions. Although measuring the predictive validity of different cues is inherently problematic in the legal domain, there is much to be gleaned from the successful approaches adopted by researchers identifying predictors of dangerousness (see Monahan, 1982; Monahan and Steadman, 1994).[12] In fact, some headway has been made on the determination

---

[12] A scientific approach to bail risk assessment and decision making would require randomized controlled trials where a sample of defendants matched on important characteristics, such as community ties and criminal history, were either randomly bailed or remanded in custody. Clearly, this is unethical. A statistical approach would at best provide only a partial measure of the objective predictive validity of the information because it would never be known how many defendants who were remanded in custody would have offended if they had not been imprisoned. The two groups (bailed defendants and defendants remanded in custody) differ in many ways and so generalizations cannot be made from one sample to the other. Furthermore, although it is relatively easy to discover if a bailed defendant failed to surrender to custody, it is impossible to measure exactly how many defendants who were released on bail actually offended or interfered with witnesses/obstructed justice. Crimes and obstructions of justice may not be detected, or if detected, may not be reported, and some crimes may not be recorded. In order to overcome these difficulties, defendants

of predictive validities of various cues in the US (eg Goldkamp and Gottfredson, 1985; Nussbaum *et al*, 1994) and Australian bail systems (eg Weatherburn, Quinn, and Rich, 1987). In the United Kingdom, Brown (1998) has reported that the nature of the offence, the length of time on bail, and the defendant's previous convictions were associated with offending on bail. Clearly, more research is needed.

Finally, it is worth considering that if statistical data could be collected and a decision rule could be formulated, it is conceivable that magistrates could be replaced by an automated system. There is considerable literature attesting to the efficacy of actuarial prediction (eg Dawes, 1971; Meehl, 1954), and actuarial models are already being used in other aspects of the criminal justice system (eg Copas, Marshall, and Tarling, 1996; Ditchfield, 1997).

Support for Change

Clearly, different interventions may have more or less support from the public and policy makers. The survey of prisoners and criminal justice professionals reported earlier, also asked them to rate the extent to which they favoured different ways of helping magistrates to improve their bail decision making. It was found that, on average, these groups were most strongly in favour of providing magistrates with more accurate, reliable, and relevant information to enable them to make better decisions. There was also some favour for providing magistrates with follow-up feedback about what happened to a defendant when he/she was released on bail or remanded in custody; ensuring that information about each case is presented in the same way and in the same order; and giving magistrates a computer device that helps them to remember the information presented and helps them to weight and combine it to form a decision. Interestingly, prisoners and criminal justice professionals least favoured reducing judicial discretion by making laws and guidelines more clear and less vague. Finally, both groups were, on average, more in favour of changing the type of people that become judges, than replacing judges with automated systems.

Any attempt to improve performance needs to take into consideration the idea that decision makers may be resistant and reluctant to change. As research demonstrates, magistrates are overconfident in their decision making, and thus may not be amenable to change (Dhami, 2002, 2004, 2005; Dhami and Ayton, 2001). Nevertheless, an awareness of the magnitude and significance of legal decisions, such as magistrates' bail decisions, may highlight the urgency with which practice needs to be improved.

---

could be asked to self-report crimes, however, self-reports may be unreliable due to problems with remembering and they may also be invalid due to respondents providing socially desirable responses or responses that will not incriminate them.

Conclusions

Legal decisions are regularly criticized by organizations supporting victims, groups representing defendants, and professional agencies such as the police. Criticism is directed both at the existing legal rules and procedures and the individuals who are formally trained and entrusted to apply them. The research on magistrates' bail decision making reviewed here involved 385 lay magistrates and district judges from 159 magistrates' courts in England and Wales. It demonstrated that, amongst other things, magistrates do not work in accordance with due process considerations. Although the due process model requires cognitive capacities that are beyond the unaided human mind, the criminal justice system aspires to this model, and those who work in the system or are subject to it support this model. The fact that the bail decision is considered to be a straightforward legal decision raises concerns about performance on other more complex and less frequent tasks, such as sentencing.

Legal decisions have consequences for both the public purse and the lives of the public. Therefore, it is crucial that further research shows why legal decision makers are sometimes inconsistent, in disagreement, or use simple decision strategies and extra-legal cues. The findings of such research can help us to change the way in which judges think and behave by helping us to overcome their cognitive limitations and their suboptimal task conditions. A full understanding of how legal decision makers behave is essential to developing appropriate tools for training, evaluating, and aiding legal decision making.

References

Allwood, CM, and Granhag, PA (1999). 'Feelings of confidence and the realism of confidence judgments in everyday life'. In P Juslin and H Montgomery (eds) *Judgment and decision making: New-Brunswikian and process-tracing approaches* 123–46. Hillsdale, NJ.

Anderson, JM, Kling, JR, and Stith, K (1999). 'Measuring interjudge sentencing disparity: Before and after the federal sentencing guidelines'. *Journal of Law and Economics* 42: 271–307.

Bottoms, AE and McClean, JD (1976). *Defendants in the criminal process.* London.

Brown, D (1998). *Offending on bail and the police use of conditional bail.* Research Findings No 72. London: Home Office.

Brown, S (1991). *Magistrates at work—sentencing and social structure.* Buckingham.

Brunswik, E (1952). *The conceptual framework of psychology.* Chicago.

Buck, ML and Miller, DT (1994). 'Reactions to incongruous negative life events'. *Social Justice Research* 7: 29–46.

Carroll, JS, Wiener, RL, Coates, D, Galegher, J, and Alibrio, JJ (1982). 'Evaluation, diagnosis, and prediction in parole decision making'. *Law and Society Review*, 17: 199–228.

Cooksey, RW (1996). *Judgment analysis: Theory, methods, and applications.* San Diego, Calif.

Copas, JB, Marshall, P, and Tarling, R (1996). *Predicting reoffending for discretionary conditional release*. HORS No 150. London: HMSO.

Darbyshire, P (1997a). 'An essay on the importance and neglect of the magistracy'. *Criminal Law Review* 627–43.

——(1997b). 'For the new Lord Chancellor—some causes for concern about magistrates'. *Criminal Law Review* 861–74.

Davies, C (1971). 'Pre-trial imprisonment: A Liverpool study'. *British Journal of Criminology* 11: 32–48.

Davis, CE, and Davis, EB (1996). 'Information load and consistency of decisions'. *Psychological Reports* 79: 279–88.

Davis, M, Croall, H, and Tryer, J (1995). *Criminal justice. An introduction to the criminal justice system in England and Wales*. Harlow.

Dawes, RM (1971). 'A case study of graduate admissions: Applications of three principles of human decision making'. *American Psychologist* 26: 180–8.

——and Corrigan, B (1974). 'Linear models in decision making'. *Psychological Bulletin* 81: 95–106.

Dhami, MK (2002). 'Do bail information schemes really affect bail decisions?' *The Howard Journal of Criminal Justice* 41: 245–62.

——(2003). 'Psychological models of professional decision-making'. *Psychological Science* 14: 175–80.

——(2004). 'Conditional bail decision making in the magistrates' court'. *The Howard Journal of Criminal Justice* 43: 27–46.

——(2005). 'From discretion to disagreement: Explaining disparities in judges' pre-trial decisions'. *Behavioral Sciences and the Law* 23: 367–86.

——and Ayton, P (1998). Legal decision making the fast and frugal way. Paper presented at the 1998 Meeting of the Society for Judgment and Decision Making, 21–23 November 1998, Dallas.

——and Ayton, P (2001). 'Bailing and jailing the fast and frugal way'. *Journal of Behavioral Decision Making* 14: 141–68.

——and —— (2005). Judicial interpretations of the threshold for denying bail in the English criminal justice system. Manuscript submitted for publication.

——and Harries, C (2001). 'Fast and frugal versus regression models of human judgment'. *Thinking and Reasoning* 7: 5–27.

Ditchfield, J (1997). 'Actuarial prediction and risk assessment'. *Prison Service Journal* 113.

Doherty, ME, and Balzer, WK (1988). 'Cognitive feedback'. In B Brehmer and CRB Joyce (eds) *Human judgment: The SJT view* 163–97. Amsterdam.

Ebbesen, EB, and Konecni, VJ (1975). 'Decision making and information integration in the courts. The setting of bail'. *Journal of Personality and Social Psychology* 32: 805–21.

Edland, A (1979). *On cognitive processes under time stress: A selective review of the literature on time stress and related stress*. Reports from the Department of Psychology, University of Stockholm, Suppl 68, 31.

Erdman, HP (1988). 'Computer consultation in psychiatry'. *Psychiatric Annals* 18: 209–16.

Folger, R (1984). 'Emerging issues in the social psychology of justice'. In R Folger (ed) *The sense of injustice: Social Psychological Perspectives* 3–24. New York.

——Rosenfield, D, Grove, J, and Cokran, L (1979). 'Effects of voice and peer opinions on responses to inequity'. *Journal of Personality and Social Psychology* 37: 2253–61.

Folger, R and Konovsky, MA (1989). 'Effects of procedural and distributive justice on reactions to pay raise decisions'. *Academy of Management Journal* 32: 115–30.

——and Kass, EE (2000) 'Social comparison and fairness. A counterfactual simulation of perspective'. In JM Suls and L Wheeler (eds) *Handbook of social comparison: Theory and research* 423–41. New York.

Galligan, DJ (1987). 'Regulating pre-trial decisions'. In IH Dennis (ed) *Criminal law and justice* 177–202. London.

Gigerenzer, G, Todd, PM, and the ABC Research Group (1999). *Simple heuristics that make us smart.* New York.

Goldkamp, JS (1993). 'Judicial responsibility for pretrial release decisionmaking and the information role of pretrial services'. *Federal Probation* 57: 28–35.

—— and Gottfredson, MR (1985). *Policy guidelines for bail: An experiment in court reform.* Philadelphia, Pa.

—— Gottfredson, MR, Jones, PR, and Weiland, D (1995). *Personal liberty and community safety. Pretrial release in the criminal court.* New York.

——, —— and Gottfredson, DM (1988). *Decisionmaking in criminal justice: Toward the rational exercise of discretion.* New York.

Griffiths, J (1970). 'Ideology in criminal procedure or a third 'model' of the criminal process'. *Yale Law Journal* 79: 358–417.

Hammond, D (1988). 'The effects of remand'. *Prison Service Journal.* January.

Hammond, KR, Stewart, TR, Brehmer, B, and Steinmann, DO (1975). 'Social judgment theory'. In MF Kaplan, and S Schwartz (eds) *Human judgment and decision processes* 271–317. New York.

Judicial Studies Board (2005). *Adult court bench book.* <http://www.jsboard.co.uk/ magistrates/adult_court/complete.pdf>.

Kagehiro, DK (1990). 'Defining the standard of proof in jury instructions'. *Psychological Science* 1: 194–200.

Kahneman, D (1973). *Attention and effort.* Englewood Cliffs, NJ.

Kellough, G and Wortley, S (2002). 'Remand for plea'. *British Journal of Criminology* 42: 182–210.

King, M (1981). *The framework of criminal justice.* London.

Kirwan, JR, Chaput de Saintonge, DM, Joyce, CRB, and Currey, HLF (1983). 'Clinical judgement analysis—practical application in rheumatoid arthritis'. *British Journal of Rheumatology* 22: 18–23.

Konecni, VJ, and Ebbesen, EB (1984). 'The mythology of legal decision making'. *International Journal of Law and Psychiatry* 7: 5–18.

Larsen, CR, Yelon, S, and Irving, PD (1997). 'Legal decision models: Training aids and job aids for professionals'. *Journal of Criminal Justice* 25: 49–60.

Leventhal, GG, Karuza, J, and Fry, WR (1980). 'Beyond fairness. A theory of allocation processes'. In G Mikula (ed) *Justice and social interaction* 167–218. New York.

Leventhal, GS (1980) 'What should be done with equity theory? New approaches to the study of fairness in social relationships'. In KJ Gergen, MS Greenbers, and RH Willis (eds) *Social exchange: Advances in theory and research* 27–53. New York.

Liebling, A (1999). 'Prison suicide and prisoner coping'. In M Tonry and J Petersillia (eds) *Prisons* 283–359. Chicago, Ill.

Meehl, PE (1954). *Clinical versus statistical prediction: A theoretical analysis and a review of the evidence*. Minneapolis.

Meeker, JW, Jesilow, P, and Aranda, J (1992). 'Bias in sentencing—A preliminary analysis of community-service'. *Behavioral Sciences and the Law* 10: 197–206.

Miller, GA (1956). 'The magic number seven, plus or minus two: Some limits on our capacity for processing information'. *Psychological Review* 63: 81–93.

Monahan, J (1982). 'Clinical prediction of violent behavior'. *Psychiatric annals* 12: 509–13.

——and HJ Steadman (1994). 'Toward a rejuvenation of risk assessment research'. In J Monahan and HJ Steadman (eds) *Violence and mental disorder: Developments in risk assessment* 1–17. Chicago, Ill.

Narey, M (1997). *Review of delay in the criminal justice system*. London: Home Office.

Nash, M (1992). 'Dangerousness Revisited'. *International Journal of the Sociology of Law* 20: 337–49.

Nisbett, RE, and Wilson, TD (1977). 'Telling more than we can know: Verbal reports on mental processes'. *Psychological Review* 84: 231–59.

Nussbaum, D, Lang, M, Chan, B, and Riviere, R (1994). 'Characterization of elopers during remand: Can they be predicted? The METFORS experience'. *American Journal of Forensic Psychology* 12: 17–37.

Packer, HL (1968). *The limits of the criminal sanction*. Stanford, Calif.

Parliament, House of Commons Public Accounts Committee (2005). *Facing Justice: Tackling Defendants' Non-Attendance at Court*. London.

Payne, JW, Bettman, JR, and Johnson, EJ (1993). *The adaptive decision maker*. Cambridge.

Raine, JW, and Willson, MJ (1994). *Conditional bail or bail with conditions? The use and effectiveness of bail conditions*. London: Home Office.

Rieskamp, J and Hoffrage, U (1999). 'When do people use simple heuristics, and how can we tell?' In G Gigerenzer, PM Todd, and the ABC Research Group (eds) *Simple heuristics that make us smart* 141–67. New York.

Sensibaugh, CC and Allgeier, ER (1996). 'Factors considered by Ohio juvenile court judges in judicial bypass judgments: A policy-capturing approach'. *Politics and Life Sciences* 15: 35–47.

Simon, HA (1956). 'Rational choice and the structure of the environment'. *Psychological Review* 63: 129–38.

——(1987). 'Rational decision making in business organizations'. In L Green and JH Kagel (eds) *Advances in behavioral economics*, vol 1, 18–47. Norwood, NJ.

——(1990). 'Invariants of human behavior'. *Annual Review of Psychology* 41: 1–19.

Slovic, P and Lichtenstein, S (1971). 'Comparison of Bayesian and regression approaches to the study of information processing in judgement'. *Organisational Behavior and Human Performance* 6: 649–744.

Stanfiel, JD (1983). 'Criminal justice decisionmaking: Discretion vs. equity'. *Federal Probation* 46: 36–41.

Summers, DA, Taliaferro, JD, and Fletcher, DJ (1970). 'Subjective vs objective description of judgment policy'. *Psychonomic Science* 18: 249–50.

Timmermans, D (1993). 'The impact of task complexity on information use in multi-attribute decision making'. *Journal of Behavioral Making* 6: 95–111.

Tyler, TR (1997). 'Citizen discontent with legal procedures'. *American Journal of Comparative Law* 45: 869–902.

Waterside Press (2003). *Magistrates' bench handbook*. Winchester.

Weatherburn, D, Quinn, M, and Rich, G (1987). 'Drug charges, bail decisions and absconding'. *Australian and New Zealand Journal of Criminology* 20: 95–109.

Weldon E, and Gargano, GM (1985). 'Cognitive effort in additive task groups: The effects of shared responsibility on the quality of multiattribute judgments'. *Organizational Behavior and Human Decision Processes* 36: 348–61.

White, P (1999). *The prison population in 1998: A statistical review*. Research Findings No 94. London: Home Office.

Van den Bos, K, Lind, EA, and Wilke, HAM (2001). 'The psychology of procedural and distributive justice viewed from the perspective of *fairness* heuristic theory'. In R Cropanzano (ed) *Justice in the workplace: From theory to practice*, vol 2, 49–66. Mahwah, NJ.

York, KM (1992). 'A policy capturing analysis of federal district and appellate court sexual harassment cases'. *Employee Responsibilities and Rights Journal* 5: 173–84.

5

Can Cognitive Neuroscience Make Psychology a Foundational Discipline for the Study of Law?

Oliver R Goodenough

Why has Psychology Made only Marginal Contributions to the Study of Law?

Psychology and law share a basic preoccupation: understanding the nature of human thought and action (eg Foley, 1993; Horowitz and Willging, 1984; Kapardis, 2003). Law can be seen as an implicit, if somewhat naive, science of mind (Goodenough, 2001; Goodenough and Prehn, 2004); psychology is the explicit science. The two disciplines have had a long and often productive interaction (eg Kapardis, 2003), and the papers in this volume demonstrate the breadth of knowledge which this interaction can helped to produce. Nonetheless, the interaction has been far less compelling than one might expect. The collaboration has been fruitful on many specific issues of legal research, where the focus has often, but not exclusively, been on criminal behaviour, punishment, and other forms of pathology. Notwithstanding, or perhaps even consistent with, these localized successes, psychology has not become a foundational discipline for the study of law. It has failed to provide an overarching framework informing the field as a whole. Rather, in honesty, one must admit that psychology has made important, but essentially marginal contributions.

Treatments of law and psychology contain a recurring lament that less has been done to advance common interests than should be possible. For instance, Kapardis (2003) asks: 'Why, then, has it taken so long for the field of psychology and law to develop when, as some authors would argue, psychologists and lawyers do have a lot of common ground?' Law and psychology authors generally note that progress is being made (eg Foley, 1993; Horowitz and Willging, 1984; Kapardis, 2003), but fulfillment of the productive potential that they feel exists seems always around the corner.

The need for better models of thought and behaviour in legal scholarship is certainly there. Legal scholarship, and the law itself, often reflects implicit, unexamined approaches that hark back to a time when philosophy, introspection, and subjective inquiry provided our psychology. A prevalent traditional theory is the Cartesian model, incorporating both a physical/mental dualism and the notion that the mind operates as a unitary organ of thought (Goodenough, 2001). A classic metaphor of this approach is the 'homunculus', Latin for 'little man'. The image is of a little, rational figure at the centre of our thinking, like a captain on the bridge of a ship, barking out orders to a sometimes emotional, befuddled, and inattentive crew.

While there has been considerable room for improvement on this, through the twentieth century the emerging science of psychology did not fill the void in the law. Freudian insights had some impact (Frank, 1930), but the limitations of the psychoanalytic model prevented it from becoming foundational in law. The behaviorist approach, described further below, dominated academic psychology around the middle of the century. It operated on the conviction that behaviour, and not the internal mental states of an actor, was the proper sphere of study (eg Skinner, 1953; Watson, 1924). Behaviourism eschewed creating a large, unifying understanding of the kind that foundational approaches must supply. Rather, under this influence the interchange between law and psychology continued to look at behavioural particulars.

In the United States, at any rate, the foundational role for legal studies that psychology could have filled has been occupied by economics instead. The simplified mental modelling of neoclassical economics may be woefully incomplete, but it has captured the field. There is a triumphalism in the tone of law and economics writers that contrasts with the more tentative tone of law and psychology. As early as 1988, Cooter and Ulen could write: 'Law and economics is one of the most rapidly growing areas of specialization among both economists and legal scholars.' By 2005, Samuels flatly declares: 'Neoclassical law and economics enjoys a hegemonic position.'

At the risk of being yet another writer declaring prematurely that law will *soon* take proper notice of the insights of psychology, I believe that we are on the verge of a fundamental change. Psychology itself has developed considerably over the past several decades, as the cognitive approaches pioneered in the 1960s have spread and matured (Gazzaniga *et al*, 2002; Goodenough and Prehn, 2004; Miller, 1962). This new knowledge has begun to percolate into the legal academy, both directly through the work of psychologically trained and sophisticated scholars (see, for example, this volume), but also through the correction that psychology has been providing to economics. Imbued with psychological knowledge and methods 'behavioural economics' (eg Camerer, 2004; Korobkin and Ulen, 2002) and 'experimental economics' (eg Smith, 1982) both look beyond simple rationality assumptions and investigate what people actually think and do.

Psychology itself is in the midst of a disciplinary growth spurt. The pace of advance in the cognitive approach has only accelerated in recent years, driven to a large degree by the addition of new tools and approaches from the physical science of the brain. The combined discipline, often called cognitive neuroscience (Gazzaniga *et al*, 2002), has integrated the study of behaviour, mind, and brain, and is now beginning to provide a unified, predictive understanding of the processes of human thought and their connection to action (Gazzaniga *et al*, 2002; Zeki and Goodenough, 2004). True to its hegemonic character, economics is capturing many of these ideas, creating neuroeconomics as a new subdiscipline (Chorvath and McCabe, 2004; Glimcher, 2003; Zak, 2004). While neuroeconomics may be the path to improved psychology for some in the law (Hoffman, 2004), I believe that the straight road will do the job even better. Cognitive neuroscience can make psychology a foundational discipline for the study of law.

Some of the obstacles to this transition lie with psychology. Careful researchers can err on the side of caution when asked to make the kind of observations about the bigger picture that the legal scholars hunger for (Goodenough and Prehn, 2004). The greater obstacles lie with the law. In order for cognitive psychology and neuroscience to provide a fundamental framework for legal scholars, the lawyers will need at least a basic understanding of the new models and methods. This paper, therefore, will first provide an introduction to the developments of cognitive neuroscience for those with little background. Readers with some knowledge on the psychology side will be wise to skip over much of this material. It will also sketch out two applications at the intersection of law and psychology, one dealing with a particular concern, intellectual property, and the other dealing with some of the enduring, fundamental questions of legal studies: the relationship of moral and legal judgments and the role of law. By contrasting the cognitive approach to each of these, at least briefly, with possible economic analysis, I hope to demonstrate how psychology, enriched by neuroscience, can provide more satisfactory answers.

As a final point of introduction, Greely (2005) has usefully divided the intersection of law and psychology into three categories. First of all, there is the law of psychology, covering such diverse topics as informed consent, duties of therapists, and health care funding. Secondly, there is the psychology of thought and behaviour which is of interest to the law. This includes not only criminal, abnormal, and pathological phenomena, but also the mental basis of honesty, reliability, peacemaking, and other law-regarding behaviours. Thirdly, there is the psychology of law itself. What are we up to in our minds and brains when we make law, bring a knowledge of law to our decisions about our own behaviour, and apply rules of law in judging the behaviour of others? This paper will focus only on the second and third—applying psychology to thought and behaviour of interest to law and to the thought and behaviour of law itself.

Importance of the Cognitive Revolution

It was not so long ago that *behaviourism* was an important, perhaps even dominant, approach in psychology. Lacking tools to probe scientifically the workings of thought, and wary of the fuzziness and subjectivity of philosophical introspection, the behaviourists focused on behaviour, and not the internal mental states of an actor, as the proper sphere of study (eg Skinner, 1953; Watson, 1924). The brain and its workings were a 'black box', unsusceptible and inappropriate as a matter for serious study. While this approach yielded results of value, it was unnecessarily constricted, and over the past half century, cognitive approaches to reasoning and judgement have largely replaced behaviourism in psychology (eg Gazzaniga *et al*, 2002; Goodenough and Prehn, 2004; Miller, 1962; Neisser, 1967). This is not to say that behavioural observation and data are not still central in research; it is just that brain processes are now critical elements in the mix as well.

This is a significant development. Consider a science of automobile mechanics based only on the observations of a driver at the wheel, with no opportunity to open the bonnet of the car. Good insights could be achieved through a strictly behavioural approach to the automobile, but it takes little imagination to foresee the revolution in understanding that would occur if we could expose the engine, braking systems, and other components to a functional review. We are in the early stages of just such a revolution in our understanding of the brain. This revolution will profoundly alter some of our approaches to questions of both law and psychology; it will also leave some relatively intact (Greely, 2004; Greene and Cohen, 2004; Morse, 2004). The depth and unity which it brings has the potential to make psychology a necessary touchstone for understanding not only behaviour of interest to law but also the processes of law itself.

The cognitive revolution allows us to investigate how people think, charting the many ways that we humans move from observation to decision to action. Key elements in this approach are: (1) richer cognitive models, (2) an understanding of the strategic dimensions of thought and action, and (3) technical and methodological advances. The investigation has shed light on processes that are conscious and unconscious, rational and emotional, learned and automatic, social and selfish (Goodenough and Prehn, 2004). All of these, in isolation and in interaction, are on the table.

Brain Basics for Legal Scholars

A short review of the physiology of the brain will help those without a background in neurology to understanding the importance of these elements. Further detail is available in Zak (2004), and Gazzaniga *et al* (2002) and from many other print and online sources.

The brain is not physically a homogenous, undifferentiated organ; rather, it consists of a number of different regions and components. A good starting point is the distinction between the upper and outer layers of the brain, principally the cerebrum and its outermost part, the cortex (from the Latin for 'bark'), and the inner and lower portions, made up of a number of organs, many of which are linked under the label of the lymbic system. The outer layers are divided into two distinct hemispheres, right and left, which are connected by a mass of communication channels in the corpus callosum. The two hemispheres are, confusingly, linked functionally to the opposite sides of the body. The left brain controls the right hand, the right brain the left hand, and so forth. Some brain functions related to perception and thought are likewise relatively localized on one side or the other; others are distributed bi-laterally. Humans are distinguished from even our nearest primate relatives by the high degree of cortical development.

Key components in the inner and lower portions of the brain are the cerebellum, the amygdala, the thalamus and hypothalamus, the hippocampus, and the brain stem. Some of these areas are linked to such 'automatic' functions as temperature control, breathing, etc. Others, particularly those in the lymbic system, can provide different, often quicker, pathways to decision, often linked to emotional arousal and inaccessible to consciousness. These elements do not operate in isolation from the cortex, however. For instance, there are connections back and forth between the amygdala—a key component in the generation and perception of emotion—and nearby regions of the frontal lobe (see below). This communication can help the inhibitions and judgments of the frontal area to affect our emotional states and can allow emotional reactions to inform our more deliberative processes.

Once beyond this most basic set of distinctions, the physical descriptions quickly become challenging to the non-specialist. Brain physiology has several labeling systems, some based in Latin, others in the names of discoverers, and others still in numbers and letters. For instance, the cortex is subdivided into four principal regions—the frontal lobes, the parietal lobes, the temporal lobes, and the occipital lobes, each with a matching region in the left and right hemispheres. There are some relatively gross-level functional distinctions between each of these. The occipital lobes, at the back of the head, are where much of our primary visual processing takes place. The parietal lobes, in the middle near the top of the head, are involved in hearing, sensory perception, and spatial relations. The temporal lobes, lower down on the sides, play a role in speech and hearing. The frontal lobes are involved in memory, many reasoning processes, emotional modulation, and behavioural control.

These lobes are further subdivided into more specific regions, with such involved names as the ventromedial prefrontal cortex and the orbitofrontal cortex. Even more specificity is possible using Brodmann area designations (a numbering system for brain regions), various numerical coordinate systems, and conventional names, such as Werneke's Region or the auditory cortext. A mastery of the distinctions at this level and beyond is important to the specialist, but a detailed knowledge of the brain as a whole is not necessary for an appreciation of the overall approach of cognitive neuroscience.

Moving to micro-anatomy, the cellular workhorse of the brain is the neuron—a specialized cell which has a lot of electro/chemical connectors to other neurons in the same region and, sometimes, to those in other regions of the brain. These work by sending messages back and forth over the map of connections. Neurons act by cumulating their inputs, and if the total is weighty enough, by sending out a signal in return. The actual communication across the gaps between the neurons is made by various neurochemical agents, including such popularly recognized chemicals as dopamine, testosterone, and serotonin. The general levels of these in the brain, together with the number and efficacy of receptors in the neurons, all modulate the kinds of communication that takes place, influencing our thought and behaviour.

Richer Cognitive Models

Research in cognitive psychology and neuroscience is revealing a complex picture of thought. It rejects the unitary model of thought that has flourished in some schools of philosophy and psychology since Descartes (Damasio, 1994; Restak, 1994). Rather, human mental processes are multiple and complex, often the product of different physical systems activating different parts and combinations of the anatomy described above. Our brains are constantly working, not always successfully, to balance, integrate, and reconcile this diversity into a relatively coherent set of thoughts and actions. This model of complexity stands in contrast to the rational actor model of classical economics. While the kind of means/ends rationality assumed by economics is a reasonable approximation of some human mental processes, behavioural- and neuroeconomics are bringing an understanding of this complexity to the 'dismal science' as well (eg Korobkin and Ulen, 2002; Zak, 2004).

This complexity model helps us to understand better the difference between conscious and unconscious mental processes. Consciousness itself has still not received an adequate explanation, but it has been put into reasonable perspective. The 'workspace' of consciousness (Baars *et al*, 1998; Dehaene and Naccache, 2001) accommodates some of our modes of thinking, but many of our most competent mental abilities appear to operate outside its scope. This approach, explored by Gladwell (2005) in the best-selling popular book *Blink*, helps us to understand that people use intuitive approaches to reach trivial and important conclusions all the time.

Put simply, intuition is a concept we use to describe mental processes that are not directly accessible to conscious monitoring or participation. Viewed this way, the property of intuition has more to do with the boundaries of self-awareness than it does with the actual competence or incompetence of the mental processes so labeled. There is no reason to suppose that intuitive processes are simple or inaccurate just because they aren't directly involved in conscious thought. (Goodenough and Prehn, 2004)

Nobel Prize winner Daniel Kahneman (2002) argues for a 'dual process model' which has room for both intuitive and deliberative processes:

The essence of such a model is that judgments can be produced in two ways (and in various mixtures of the two): a rapid, associative, automatic, and effortless intuitive process (sometimes called System 1), and a slower, rule-governed, deliberate and effortful process (System 2). System 2 'knows' some of the rules that intuitive reasoning is prone to violate, and sometimes intervenes to correct or replace erroneous intuitive judgments. Thus, errors of intuition occur when two conditions are satisfied: System 1 generates the error and System 2 fails to correct. (References omitted)

Another traditional distinction is between 'rational', or cognitive, decision making on the one hand and 'emotional', or affective, on the other. To begin with, we can usefully separate the idea of emotion as a 'sensation of arousal that we monitor in ourselves and others', from emotion as a functional piece of how we sort out important from unimportant mental processes (Goodenough and Prehn, 2004). Experimenters have been making steady progress in identifying the functional properties of emotion seen in this latter role (eg Dolan, 2002; Morris and Dolan, 2004; Phelps, 2002; Rolls, 1999). Their results suggest that emotion gives salience to perceptions and conclusions as the brain works, indicating importance and urgency. Damasio has called this property a 'somatic marker' (Damasio, 1994). This works for memory: events that are associated with emotional arousal are much more likely to be assimilated into long-term memory (Morris and Dolan, 2004). It also works for attention: we attend to objects in our perception that have emotional content (Anderson and Phelps, 2001). Emotion is also a goad to action, differentiating an irresistible conclusion from idle speculation (Hume, 1739; Rolls, 1999; Schwartz, 2000). This research suggests that affective and cognitive processes are often partners in thought, rather than necessary opposites.

Research on the sensation that emotional arousal brings suggests that this self-monitoring is a somewhat indirect avenue for conscious processes to access the responses of the intuitive systems running in parallel. This is not to say that all intuitive processes are emotional or vice versa. Experienced drivers on a familiar road can find they have traveled several miles 'unconsciously', but without emotion (Goodenough and Prehn, 2004).

This recognition of complexity reflects another important principle: the brain is, at least in part, specialized at the anatomical level as well. Recent technical advances, particularly imaging techniques such as PET and fMRI, discussed below, allow us to measure the brain activity in specific structures and relate the result to particular kinds of mental tasks. This research has created a picture of a mix of specialization and integration (Gazzaniga *et al*, 2002; Goodenough and Prehn, 2004). While some kinds of activity can be linked to very specific regions, many mental tasks are more distributed, sometimes involving a network of functional regions. Some of the elements in the network may be mobilized for use in a number of different kinds of tasks. Other physiological components, even those used as part of a distributed task, may have a relatively dedicated role linked to that task itself.

Complex social judgements, such as moral decision making, implicate this more distributed pattern (Goodenough and Prehn, 2004; Moll *et al*, 2005). A number of different research programmes have implicated a system involving the ventromedial prefrontal cortex, orbitofrontal cortex, posterior cingulate cortex, and posterior superior temporal sulcus (Goodenough and Prehn, 2004). Many of the identified components of this network have been linked to other tasks, for example, control of behaviour, processing of socially relevant cues, memory and processing of emotional stimuli (Greene and Haidt, 2002). In this sense there is not a 'moral centre' of the brain (Casebeer and Churchland, 2003), although pieces of the network may be relatively dedicated to aspects of moral judgement tasks.

Whether relatively regionalized or distributed, mental tasks vary in the degree of specialization in all or part of the anatomy involved in the task. The visual cortex, for instance, has very specialized structures, down to quite specific groups of neurons, which respond to such characteristics as colour, borders of objects, alignment of edges, etc (Zeki, 1999). Such relatively specific structures and capacities are sometimes called primitives or priors (Goodenough and Prehn, 2004). The degree to which such dedicated equipment is present in more complex cognitive tasks is an important question, and the subject of a great deal of ongoing empirical work. Where they do exist, priors can provide excellent cognitive shortcuts, but they can also shape and constrain the way we can approach particular kinds of thinking.

A final piece of the picture of complexity is the multiple sources of information that guide the brain as it works to convert sensation into thought and action. Science has moved well beyond the arid 'nurture/nature' debate: we are a mix of the two, with different proportions in different contexts. For instance, our ability to create and use language has its roots both in our genetic material and in the brain which gets constructed as the genetic programme interacts with the environment during development (Pinker, 1994). Some aspects of the form of the language may be partly rooted in our in genetic heritage—the noun/verb distinction, for instance, may be the result of some kind of prior. Other aspects are both culturally dependent and constrained by the physiology of our vocal tracts and hearing.

The emerging picture of our mental processes is not a simple one; why should that surprise us? Nonetheless, cognitive science is developing an increasingly coherent account both of the general principles of thought and of the activity related to specific kinds of mental tasks. Cognitive science is also developing a better formal understanding of the nature of these tasks.

Strategic Role of Thought in a Social Context

Much of our thinking concerns our relations with other humans. We are a gregarious, social species, pack animals like wolves and chimps. Many of our day-to-day concerns involve our position in the pack, how we work with others to achieve both individual and group ends, and similar problems and opportunities of group living. These problems and opportunities can be summarized as present- ing 'strategic' issues, that is issues that involve assessing and working with the needs and desires of other actors, engaged in similar kinds of assessments (eg Binmore, 1998; Camerer 2003, 2004; Dixit and Skeath, 2004). Chess is a strategic game; computer solitaire is not. On a number of indices, humans have a highly developed set of strategic mental capacities, capacities that are particularly important for thought and behavior of interest to the law.

Cognitive neuroscience looks to game theory and other formal approaches to strategic problems to help make predictions and provide explanations about our social thinking. For instance, the optimal response to a behavioural opportunity may not be the same for the actor, a person acted upon, or a third party observer asked to judge the behaviour (Goodenough and Prehn, 2004). We tend to think of the failure of people to apply the same standards to themselves as they apply to others as hypocritical—and in a sense so it is. But given the functional specializa- tion present in many intellectual processes, this 'failure' may also be a natural result of different strategic options being accessible through different pathways depending on the strategic presentation of the problem. The admirable but challenging idea that we should judge ourselves as we judge others may be a late arrival to our mental landscape, one in which the law may play an important supporting role.

Game theory itself is not a static or fully realized field. We are all tempted to draw bleak conclusions from our first acquaintance with the selfish, cooperation destroying, dominant strategies predicted in some kinds of strategic interac- tions. But humans clearly avoid these pitfalls much of the time. Agents can often recast the games in which they take part into forms with dominant cooperative strategies, 'outwitting Nash' in the process. Recognizing and dealing with strategic situations involves the ability to perceive an active other and to think from their perspective about a joint problem and is frequently called the 'theory of mind' capability (Baron-Cohen *et al*, 1993; Coricelli *et al*, 2000; Goodenough, 2004).

Methodological Advances

Cognitive science now routinely postulates and tests hypotheses about thought, itself. Research has linked behaviour, thought, and physical processes in the brain to a degree unimaginable a generation ago. That does not mean a rejection of all that went before; the traditional taxonomies of psychology and of law were themselves the product of decades, even centuries, of observation and analysis. They provide a good starting point for investigations following the new paradigm. New techniques encourage us to build on prior experiments and approaches, rather than reject them. The behavioural data produced using long-established psychological methods is still very much part of the mix (Goodenough and Prehn, 2004).

What we can now add to the picture are ways to investigate the physiological processes which produce our cognition. Several of the principal tools for getting inside the skull and underneath the bonnet depend on means of measuring blood flow to regions of the brain. It is well established that particularly active regions of the brain can call on an increase in the flow of oxygenated blood to help support the increased metabolic activity involved. This effect, which follows the onset of activity by a short, predictable interval, can be measured by imaging techniques such as fMRI, PET, and near-infrared measurement (Frackowiak *et al*, 2004, *passim*; Goodenough and Prehn, 2004).

While these techniques have produced very exciting results, and have greatly assisted in creating the functional understanding discussed above, a few cautions are in order (Goodenough and Prehn, 2004). First of all, the resolution of these techniques, while ever increasing, must still refer to brain regions rather than to particular neuronal connections. Secondly, imaging techniques identify areas of relatively increased and decreased activity, but that in and of itself does not show a 'centre' for the behaviour or cognitive task implicated in the experiment. As discussed above, some kinds of mental processing are distributed across a relatively disbursed network, or invoke capacities shared in other kinds of brain work. For instance, visual processing begins in the visual cortex in the occipital lobes at the back of the head (eg Zeki, 1999), and activities as diverse as reading, driving, ogling, and gazing at the stars will all show activation there.

Finally, there is the 'lights up' fallacy. The measurements actually produced by the functional imaging machines consist of three-dimensional coordinates linked with some kind of physical measurement that provides a reliable proxy for blood-flow. In order to present this information in a compelling fashion, it is often mapped onto the outline of a brain in a graphic manner that puts bright spots on regions of activity. This has led to people casually talking about brain anatomy 'lighting up'. Of course, nothing could be further from the truth. The pretty, glowing pictures are artefacts of illustration, and are not some kind of actual picture being taken when the machines are at work (Goodenough and Prehn, 2004).

Another cluster of techniques looks to measure the electrical activity of the brain. Like blood-flow, electrical impulses can be linked to cognitive processes. Techniques such as EEG and MEG give excellent resolution from a temporal standpoint, but only quite general spatial association. In animal studies and in some rare human cases it is possible to implant sensors directly into particular neurons, with sometimes spectacular results in linking anatomy to function (Glimcher, 2003).

Neurochemistry is another measurable component of brain activity. So far, there are only limited means to locate chemical activity spatially; using blood measures, we can get a fairly generalized idea of the major chemical currents in our brains. Even such rough measures have led to insights into such behaviours as aggression and sexual interest, linked to testosterone (Mazur and Booth, 1998), and nurturing and trust, linked to oxytocin (Zak *et al*, 2005).

Before there were methods for contemporaneous measurement of brain activity, injuries to particular parts of the brain allowed researchers to make links between anatomy and function. These 'lesion studies' depend on tragedies such as strokes, accidents, and birth defects to create subjects whose mental deficits have an identifiable physical basis. The cooperation of such unlucky subjects is still an important source of data about the brain (Goodenough and Prehn, 2004; Moll *et al*, 2005).

Where Does this Take Us? A Pair of Applications

The advances of cognitive neuroscience, together with the insights of traditional psychology, have created an approach to questions of thought and behaviour that has explanatory and predictive powers that transcend specific instances and extend across an array of legal questions, characteristics of foundational discipline for law. Furthermore, hypotheses about thought itself can now be tested using imaging as well as more traditional techniques. The implications of this new science for the law are best understood through illustration. The remainder of this paper will suggest two applications, one relating to a specific legal field and the other broadly jurisprudential. Both are more at the stage of hypothesis formation than proven fact, although each is in the early stage of an empirical investigation.

Why do Good People Steal Intellectual Property?

Intellectual property law has a deeply seated problem. The difficulty is not doctrinal; on the contrary, the doctrine of intellectual property is well understood. The basic rules of such areas as patent, trademark, and copyright have been worked out and have become widely accepted in law throughout the world. There may be debates over particulars and national variations, but these are largely driven by policy and politics, and not by failures in understanding. The integration of new technologies into the framework presents challenges, but the existing paradigm has so far been up to the task (Goodenough, 2002).

What is not well understood is the psychology of intellectual property. The intractable problem for IP regimes is not in stating coherent doctrinal rules or even in disseminating knowledge about them to the general public. Rather, it is in getting people to take them seriously, not just as a matter of possible punishment, but as a real instance of right and wrong. In a field where technology is making law-breaking easy and offenders relatively hard to catch, it is important to find ways to make law-respecting emotionally compelling (Goodenough, 2002).

Two personal anecdotes, both of which cannot be fully attributed, illustrate the intractability of the problem. I was describing this line of reasoning about intellectual property to the in-house counsel of a major media production company. He admitted that many of his fellow workers at the company frequently made and used bootleg copies, even though their jobs depended on the fact that others would pay. As the in-house counsel succinctly put it: 'What's that about?'

At the other end of the spectrum, the students at America's military academies are governed by honour codes, widely accepted, respected, and observed among the students, that include an undertaking not to steal. Theft of personal items on these campuses is very low. I have been told, however, that internet usage records suggest that a significant number of these normally honor code-respecting students have engaged in unauthorized file-sharing. A unitary, Cartesian brain should make the connection; these highly intelligent and motived students do not.

Cognitive psychology and neuroscience suggest possible answers to this dilemma. First of all, the simple comprehension of a rule is not necessarily enough to create compliance with it. As discussed above, the involvement of emotion both serves as a 'tag' that grabs mental attention to a problem and gives impetus to moving from contemplation to action. It is clear that our brains are able to make an emotional link to judgements about the taking of physical property, whether it is our own or someone else's. Guilt and inhibition follow. The data, and my stories, suggest that the emotional link is much harder to create for intangibles in general and intellectual property in particular.

It is possible that there are certain priors and primitives relating to our capacity to conceptualize, emotionally engage with, and implement rules of property, and that these are linked to a physical perception of the item in question (Goodenough and Prehn, 2004). If this is true, then the problem with intellectual property would not be a failure in the logic and good policy of the rules, but rather with the ability of the typical human brain to make the mental connections that will give them force, allowing broad, self-motivating compliance. Perhaps normally 'good' people do not have the cognitive capacity to easily realize that 'good' includes respecting copyright and patent rights.

So what is the deeply rooted psychology relating to information? After all, it is the spread and use of information that is at the heart of the intellectual property. Humans seem readily to understand the idea of secrecy (even if they do not keep secrets all that well). Perhaps we have 'equipment' that helps us in this perception. Once a secret is out, however, information may seem fair game. Paradoxically for this approach, most intellectual property makes its money by being released out into the world.

A further explanation may lie in the different strategic positions occupied by players in the IP story, differences that may manifest themselves in discontinuities between the psychology and motivation of IP creators, of IP developers and marketers, and of IP consumers and users. Creators often seem more attuned to the rewards of acclaim than to monetary return, although most feel that this acclaim should include the resources to live decently and to continue to pursue creation. The Grateful Dead approach suggests that consumers and users are willing to give very high levels of acclaim, even devotion, to good creators, and to provide adequate resources to the creators, even while they share the products of creation among themselves for free. In each of these cases personal respect, not a sense of property, is a sufficient motivator.

IP developers and marketers, by contrast, make investments which can be readily justified and rewarded through a property convention. Until recent innovations in copying technology made them trivial to circumvent and hard to enforce, property-based legal prohibitions worked pretty well for the record companies, film studios, and computer software manufacturers (Goodenough, 2002). (It is worth noting that some marketers make respect work for them—the National Public Radio fund-raising model for US non-profit radio depends on it.) A traditional economic approach has a hard time accounting for such differences in preferences; cognitive psychology suggests we should look for it.

The final advantage of the cognitive approaches is that they give us tools to test hypotheses such as these. An empirical programme could combine traditional behavioural and attitude assessments with imaging and other brain function techniques in an experimental programme aimed at unravelling the cognitive treatment of property and intellectual property. We already have models and technical tools to chart the differences in emotional involvement and processing on which the hypotheses rest. Psychology has the potential to change an intractable puzzle of normative judgement into a factual question that while challenging, is able to be competently investigated.

How Does Law Differ from Moral Judgement and What Does It Add?

A classic puzzle of jurisprudence, perhaps *the* classic puzzle, is the relation of law to morality. Many writers, from philosophers to judges, using a variety of intellectual approaches, from religion to utilitarianism, have taken a stab at an answer (for a partial survey, see Goodenough, 2001; Goodenough and Prehn, 2004). As discussed above, neuroscience is providing a clearer and clearer picture of the system of intuitive moral judgment. Generally quick in response and linked to emotion, such systems work reasonably well among friends, family, and in a small community. Repeat play, outcome interdependency, and other links help to create a web of reliable expectations in such a context (Gintis *et al*, 2005).

The quick, intuitive system, however, has limitations, particularly around questions of reliability, consistency, and openness to abuse. Furthermore, its very quickness can be a problem. Lynchings are hot, quick events, driven by intuitive judgements (Goodenough and Prehn, 2004). Supported by language generally, and written language in particular, law can externalize some of its information content, and even recruit new, cooler brain functions to normative issues.

Richerson and Boyd (1999) have suggested that culture can provide cognitive 'work-arounds', patches in our thinking that create new options for better outcomes. I believe that the law provides just such an extension. Indeed, the law can recruit many approaches from across the pallet of human mental processing. As we suggested in Goodenough and Prehn (2004):

Law is neither all reason nor all emotion; it is neither all explicit rules nor intuitively accessed principles of justice; it is a composite. In some instances, such as the American standard for determining negligence, law makes an explicit appeal to intuitive processes of risk assessment and avoidance, asking the question what would a 'reasonable person' have done in a like circumstance (Restatement 2nd of Torts, §283). In establishing the requirements for the waiver of a warranty on goods sold in normal commerce, law provides an explicit, word based rule in the Uniform Commercial code that operates through deductive logic application. (UCC §2–316)

Viewed in this light, law and intuitive morality are not so much in opposition as supplementary. Law is potentially a more complete system. Its recruitment possibilities open up additional, sometimes superior, approaches to settling disputes, both within communities and at the national and even international level. Zak and Knack (2001) have demonstrated a firm link between a reliable rule of law and higher rates of growth in economies around the world. This is consistent with the notion advanced by law and economics that law gravitates toward utility enhancing solutions (eg Posner, 1998), but the economics version is essentially a 'black box' theory. Cognitive approaches suggest the mechanism.

Once again, this insight produces a testable hypothesis. A preliminary experiment, using fMRI neuroimaging to compare activation patterns, has given it support (Goodenough and Prehn, 2004; Schultz *et al*, 2001). Subjects were asked to assess whether the manufacturer should be held liable in a series of product injury scenarios. In some instances they were told to use their intuitive sense of justice; in others they were asked to apply a formal legal rule, expressed in the form of a multi-part deductive syllogism, in still others they used both approaches, pitted against each other. The results, while not fully conclusive, suggest anatomical differences in processing between these two approaches. While the intuitive justice patterns were broadly congruent with those appearing in other intuitive moral judgement experiments, the legal rule application had activations in common with those in other deductive logic experiments (Goodenough and Prehn, 2004). More investigation is needed to test the hypothesis fully, but this early result suggests that we may well find confirmation for the approach.

Making Psychology a Foundational Discipline for the Law

I have argued that until recently psychology has not been a foundational discipline for the law, ie a discipline with broad explanatory and predictive possibility. Rather, it has been a useful tool for shedding light on specific behavioural questions in particular areas of doctrine. The addition of cognitive neuroscience to traditional psychology creates a new, testable model of functional complexity and specificity and provides the tools to make empirical investigations. These methods can convert what have previously been intractable normative questions into matters of factual investigation. Furthermore, the approach can be generalized across a wide range of matters of interest to the study of law.

As legal scholars and practitioners become familiar with the new science, this increased power, scope, and applicability will inevitably draw more and more of them to use psychology in their work, not just in connection with limited questions but increasingly as a source of understanding for the broad and basic questions at the heart of the law.

References

Anderson, AK and Phelps, EA (2001). 'Lesions of the human amygdala impair enhanced perception of emotionally salient events'. *Nature* 411: 305–9.

—— —— (2002). 'Is the human amygdala critical for the subjective experience of emotion? Evidence of intact dispositional affect in patients with amygdala lesions'. *Journal of Cognitive Neuroscience* 14: 709–20.

Baars, BJ, Newman, J, and Taylor, JG (1998). 'Neuronal mechanisms of consciousness: A Relational Global Workspace framework'. In S Hameroff, A Kaszniak, and J Laukes (eds) *Toward a Science of Consciousness II: The second Tucson discussions and debates* 269–78. Cambridge, Mass.

Baron-Cohen, S, Tager-Flusberg, H, and Cohen, DJ (1993). *Understanding Other Minds*. Oxford.

Binmore, K (1998). *Just Playing: Game Theory and the Social Contract*. Cambridge, Mass.

Boyd, R and Richerson, PJ (1982). 'Cultural transmission and the evolution of cooperative behavior'. *Human Ecology* 10: 325–51.

Camerer, CF (2003). 'Behavioral studies of strategic thinking in games'. *Trends in Cognitive Sciences* 7: 225–31.

Camerer, CF (2004). 'Behavioral Game Theory: Prediction of Human Behavior in Strategic Situations'. In CF Camerer, G Loewenstein, and M Rabin *Advances in Behavioral Economics* 374–92. Princeton, NJ.

Chorvat, T and McCabe, K (2004). 'The brain and the law'. *Philosphical Transctions of the Royal Society*, London B, 359: 1727–36.

Cooter, R, and Ulen, T (1988). *Law and Economics*. Glenview, Ill.

Coricelli, G, McCabe, K, and Smith, V (2000). 'Theory-of-Mind Mechanism in Personal Exchange'. In G Hatano, N Okada, and H Tanabe (eds) *Affective Minds* 249–59. Amsterdam.

Damasio, AR (1994). *Descartes' Error: Emotion, Reason, and the Human Brain*. New York.

Dixit, A and Skeath, S (2004). *Games of Strategy* (2nd edn). New York.

Dolan, RJ (1999). 'On the neurology of morals'. *Nature Neuroscience* 2: 297–9.

—— (2002). 'Emotion, cognition, and behavior'. *Science* 298: 1191–4.

Foley, LA (1993). *A Psychological View of the Legal System*. Madison, Wisc.

Frackowiak, RS, Friston, KJ, Frith, CD, Dolan, RJ, Price, CJ, Zeki, S, Ashburner, J, and Penny, W (2004). *Human Brain Function* (2nd edn). San Diego.

Frank, J (1930). *Law and the Modern Mind*. New York.

Gazzaniga, MS, Ivry, RB, and Mangum, GR (2002). *Cognitive Neuroscience: The Biology of the Mind*. New York.

Gintis, H, Bowles, S, Boyd, RT, and Fehr, E (eds) (2005). *Moral Sentiments and Material Interests: The Foundations of Cooperation in Economic Life (Economic Learning and Social Evolution)*. Cambridge, Mass.

Gladwell, M (2005). *Blink: The Power of Thinking Without Thinking*. New York.

Glimcher, PW (2003). *Decisions, Uncertainty, and the Brain: The Science of Neuroeconomics*. Cambridge, Mass.

Goodenough, OR (2001). 'Mapping Cortical Areas Associated with Legal Reasoning and with Moral Intuition'. *Jurimetrics* 41: 429–42.

—— (2002). 'The Future of Intellectual Property: Broadening the Sense of "Ought"'. *European Intellectual Property Review* 24: 6–8.

—— and Prehn, K (2005). 'A neuroscientifc approach to normative judgment in law and justice'. *Philosophical Transactions of the Royal Society*, London B, 359: 1709–26.

Greely, HT (2005). 'Frontier Issues: Neuroscience'. Presented at *Where are Law, Ethics and the Life Sciences Headed? Frontier Issues*. University of Minnesota Law School, 20 May 2005.

Greene, J, and Cohen, J (2004). 'For the law, neuroscience changes nothing and everything'. *Philosophical Transactions of the Royal Society*, London B, 359: 1775–85.

Hoffman, MB (2004). 'The neuroeconomic path of the law'. *Philosophical Transactions of the Royal Society*, London B, 359: 1667–76.

Hume, D (1739–40). *A Treatise of Human Nature*. Variously reprinted, available at <http://www.socsci.mcmaster.ca>.

Kahneman, D (2002). *Autobiography*. Stockholm: Nobel Museum, available at <http://www.nobel.se/economics/laureates/2002/kahneman-autobio.html>.

Kapardis, A (2003). *Psychology and Law: A Critical Introduction* (2nd edn). Cambridge.

Korobkin, RB and Ulen, TS (2002). 'Law and Behavioral Science: Removing the Rationality Assumption from Law and Economics'. *California Law Review* 88: 1051–144.

Kosfeld, M, Heinrichs, M, Zak, PJ, Fishcbacher, U, and Fehr, E (2005). 'Oxytocin increases trust in humans'. *Nature* 435: 673–6.

Lloyd-Bostock, SMA (1981). 'Introduction: Does Psychology have a Practical Contribution to make to Law?' In SMA Lloyd-Bostock (ed) *Psychology in Legal Contexts: Applications and Limitations* ix–xix. London.

Mazur, A and Booth, A (1998). 'Testosterone and dominance in men'. *Behavioral and Brain Sciences* 21: 353–97.

Miller, G (1962). *Psychology, the Science of Mental Life*. New York.

Moll, J, Zahn, R, de Oliveira-Souza, R, Krueger, F and Grafman, J (2005). 'The neural basis of human moral cognition'. *Nature Reviews Neuroscience* 6: 799–809.

Morris, J and Dolan, R (2004). 'Functional Neuroanatomy of Human Emotion'. In RSJ Frackowiak *et al* (eds) *Human Brain Function* (2nd edn) 365–96. San Diego.

Phelps, EA (2002). 'The cognitive neuroscience of emotion'. In MS Gazzaniga, RB Ivry, and GR Mangun (eds) *Cognitive Neuroscience: The Biology of the Mind* (2nd edn) 537–556. New York.

Pinker, S (1994). *The Language Instinct: How the Mind Creates Language*. New York.

Posner, RA (1998). *Economic Analysis of Law*. New York.

Restak, RM (1994). *The Modular Brain: How New Discoveries in Neuroscience are Answering Age-Old Questions About Memory, Free Will, Consciousness, and Personal Identity*. New York.

Richerson, PJ and Boyd, R (1999). 'Complex societies: The evolutionary origins of a crude superorganism'. *Human Nature* 10: 253–89.

Rolls, ET (1999). *The Brain and Emotion*. Oxford.

Samuels, WJ (2005). 'Some Thoughts on the Study of Law and Economics and on the Role of Government'. In M Oppenheimer and N Mercuro (eds) *Law and Economics: Alternative Economic Approaches to Legal and Regulatory Issues*. Armonk, NY.

Schultz, J, Goodenough, OR, Frackowiak, R, and Frith, CD (2001). 'Cortical regions associated with the sense of justice and with legal rules'. *Neuroimage* 13: S473.

Schwarz, N (2000). 'Emotion, cognition, and decision making'. *Cognition and Emotion* 14: 433–40.

Smith, VL (1982). 'Microeconomic Systems as an Experimental Science'. *American Economic Review* 72: 923–55.

Zak, PJ (2005). 'Neuroeconomics'. *Philosophical Transactions of the Royal Society*, London B, 359: 1737–48.

—— and Knack, S (2001). 'Trust and Growth'. *The Economic Journal* 111: 295–321.

—— Kurzban, R, and Matzner, WT (2005). 'Oxytocin is associated with human trustworthiness'. *Hormones and Behavior*, 48: 522–7.

Zeki, S (1990). 'The motion pathways of the visual cortex'. In C Blakemore (ed) *Vision: Coding and Efficiency* 321–45. Cambridge.

—— (1999). *Inner Vision: An Exploration of Art and the Brain*. Oxford.

—— and Goodenough, OR (2004). 'Law and the brain: introduction'. *Philosphical Transactions Royal Society*, London B, 359: 1661–5.

6

How Psychology is Changing the Punishment Theory Debate

Paul H Robinson*

These are exciting times in punishment theory. For nearly a half century there have been what seem like irreconcilable disagreements about how punishment should be distributed. The deontologists argue for a distribution that tracks an offender's blameworthiness. The utilitarians urge a distribution of punishment that maximizes deterrents or rehabilitation or incapacitation, whichever will best reduce future crime. For the deontologists, doing justice is a value in itself and needs no further justification. For the utilitarians, some future benefit is required to justify the imposition of punishment. The desert-based distribution of the deontologists looks almost exclusively to the past, focusing on the conduct and state of mind of the offender at the time of the offence. The utilitarian calculations look primarily to the future: how to avoid future crime most effectively.

This irreconcilable dispute is not simply academic. Penal code writers, sentencing guideline drafters, judges interpreting the provisions of either, and judges exercising sentencing discretion all were caught in the middle of this apparently irreconcilable disagreement. According to which of the alternative guiding principles should the code or guideline provision be drafted or interpreted or should sentencing discretion be exercised?

The Model Penal Code, promulgated in 1962 by the American Law Institute, reflected the ambivalence of the situation: when it set out the purposes of the criminal code and the purposes that should guide its interpretation and its grant of discretion in Section 1.02, it listed all of these alternative principles for the distribution of liability and punishment without distinguishing among them. Because it did not define the interrelation among these alternative distributive principles, it presented a significant practical problem. Different distributive principles produce different punishment results and the absence of a defined interrelation among the alternative principles fails to give a decision maker needed guidance as to which principle to follow when they conflict. In sentencing the

* The author thanks Thomas O'Brien and Cat-Uyen Vo for their useful research assistance.

elderly Nazi concentration camp torturer, for example, a dangerousness distributive principle would suggest no punishment while a desert or general deterrence distributive principle would suggest significant punishment. On the other hand, it is not unusual to have an offender commit a minor offence but under circumstances that predict future more serious offences, which similarly would suggest quite different sentences depending upon whether the distributive principle is incapacitation of the dangerousness or deterrence or desert.

What is exciting about our present times is that the stalemate of the last several decades has been, if not broken, significantly altered to avoid the practical problems. A recent report of the American Law Institute illustrates the point. It proposes changing the Code's 'purposes' section, Section 1.02. This is the first proposed change to the Model Penal Code since its promulgation in 1962. I will talk more about the proposed change later.[1]

What has changed in the punishment theory debate and why? The answers to these questions put psychology in a prominent role. Let me briefly describe the contribution that it has made, which has come from the cumulative effect of many very different aspects of psychology.

The changes are of two sorts. First is a general disappointment in the effectiveness of the utilitarian distributive principles of deterrence, rehabilitation, and incapacitation of the dangerous. Let me give a quick walk through the basis for this disappointment, taking up each of these alternative utilitarian mechanisms in turn.

Deterrence

The dominant distributive principle of the past several decades has been deterrence. Any distributive principle for punishment will provide some kind of deterrent effect by virtue of its threat of sanction upon violation. But setting deterrence as the distributive principle for liability and punishment means having liability and punishment rules formulated to maximize deterrent effect. And it is this project—formulating liability and punishment rules to maximize deterrence—about which there is increasing reason for scepticism.[2]

Effective deterrence requires at least three things. First, for a particular code rule formulation or sentencing policy to have deterrent effect, the target of that deterrent effect must know of the rule formulation or policy. Yet the existing studies suggest that this is rarely the case. People often think they know the legal rule but are commonly wrong. Most frequently, people think the rule is as they think it should be—their own intuitions about what a just rule would be—in other

---

[1] See *Preliminary Draft*, n 24 below.
[2] See generally P Robinson and J Darley, 'Does Criminal Law Deter? A Behavioral Science Investigation' [hereinafter 'Deter'], (2004) 24 OJLS 173; P Robinson and J Darley, 'The Role of Deterrence in the Formulation of Criminal Law Rules: At Its Worst When Doing Its Best' [hereinafter 'Role'] (2003) 91 *Georgetown Law Journal* 949.

words, they assume desert-based rules. But a deterrence-based rule can provide greater deterrence than a desert-based rule. It can only do so by *deviating* from desert, in other words, by deviating from the rule that people assume exists. Thus, the very instances in which the deterrence-based rule could provide more deterrence are just those situations in which people will not know the deterrence-based rule.[3]

Secondly, to have an effective deterrent effect, a target must be able to bring knowledge of the rule to bear on his own conduct. Yet the evidence is that drugs, alcohol, anger, fear, group arousal, group identity shift, impulsiveness, and other distortion effects are common in situations in which crimes are committed and are in fact disproportionately greater in the very people that are meant to be the target of the deterrent threat.[4] Thus, even if a person knew of the rule that was designed to deter his conduct, the chances are high that the rule would have no effect on him because one of these common distorting effects would be present to prevent the person from bringing the knowledge of the rule to bear in avoiding the violation.

Finally, even if an actor knows of the rule and has the capacity to bring the rule to bear in governing his conduct, there will be no deterrent effect unless the person perceives that the cost of engaging in the prohibited conduct is greater than the perceived benefits of doing so. Bentham famously suggests that the decision here will depend upon the actor's perceptions of three specific aspects of the threat: the probability of punishment, the intensity (or amount) of punishment, and the delay between violation and punishment.[5]

As to the perceived probability of punishment, there is good reason to think that the present criminal justice system does not present a terribly effective deterrent threat. Consider, for example, animal studies that demonstrate the importance of probability of punishment. In one study, for example, if pigeons are trained to get food by pressing a bar and then are shocked when they press the bar, the shock can deter further pressing. If the frequency with which they are shocked is decreased from 100 per cent to 50 per cent, the result is a 30 per cent decrease in the suppression of the conduct. If the frequency is reduced to being shocked 10 per cent of the time, suppression disappears. This illustrates that the probability of punishment can have a real effect. One, of course, must have some caution in applying lessons from studies of lower animals to the conduct of humans, but it does at least give us some pause when we realize that the probability of punishment in the criminal justice system is for most offences quite low, 100 to 1 or 50 to 1. (It is only for offences like homicide or aggravated assault that the punishment rate increases to 50 per cent for homicide and something less for aggravated assault.)[6]

    [3] Robinson and Darley, 'Role', n 2 above, 983–92.
    [4] Robinson and Darley, 'Deter', n 2 above, 178–82.
    [5] J Bentham, *The Theory of Legislation* (1931 edn) 322–6, 336. See also Robinson and Darley, 'Deter', n 2 above, 175–97.   [6] Robinson and Darley, ibid, 193–5.

Oddly, what helps us in this respect is that other studies confirm that humans tend to exaggerate the probability of rare events. Thus, the targets of deterrence may overestimate the likelihood of punishment.[7] The difficulty here is that those persons who are most prone toward committing criminal offences are the persons who have special incentives to sort out exactly what the real probabilities are. Anderson concludes after his studies of offenders in prison that 76 per cent of active offenders committing serious offences simply do not think seriously about the possibility of punishment in their calculations and are therefore willing to commit the offence.[8]

The second factor—the perceived amount of punishment threatened—presents a somewhat different situation. There is no question that it is within the ability of the criminal justice system to impose some punishment bite. But a successful deterrence programme requires something more; it requires that the amount of punishment be modulated to achieve the deterrent purpose. For example, a deterrence-based system requires, all other things being equal, a threat of greater punishment for more serious offences than for less serious offences. This assures, for example, that some additional deterrent threat is available to deter an offender who has committed an offence from further committing some more serious offence.[9]

But the available studies suggest that the dynamics at work here are very complex and unpredictable given our current amount of information. First, we know that people's perception of the amount of punishment threatened will be discounted by the fact that it does not occur immediately but will occur at some time in the sometimes distant future. A different kind of complexity is seen in animal studies again. If pigeons are trained to get food by pushing a lever, then are shocked to deter them from pressing it, a certain level of shock will deter, in one study 80 volts. But consider the effect when the pigeon is initially shocked only with 60 volts—which will not suppress the pushing—and then shocked with 70, then 80 volts, and so on, increasing the voltage incrementally, an efficient approach in a deterrence system for finding the point of suppression (so as not to punish more than is needed). With the incremental increases, the 80 volt shock will no longer suppress the conduct. It is as if the earlier shockings have taught the pigeon that it can in fact withstand the shock. In fact, in this study, the voltage was increased incrementally to 300 volts before it suppressed the conduct. This could make one somewhat uncomfortable about our standard practice of giving low punishment to a first time offender and then increasing it upon each repetition of the conduct. The incremental increase approach may make good sense from a deterrence point of view—it supposedly avoids the waste of punishment in excess

---

[7] See ibid, 184.

[8] D Anderson, 'The Deterrence Hypothesis and Picking Pockets at the Pickpocket's Hanging' (2002) 4 *American Law and Economic Review* 295.

[9] Robinson and Darley, 'Deter', n 2 above, 185–6.

of that necessary to deter conduct—but its effect may simply be to educate offenders that they can in fact withstand the punishment threatened.[10]

Another sort of complexity is found in the 'subjective well being' studies. Both lottery winners and paraplegics from car accidents have a natural tendency to revert back to their prior affective state with the passage of time; they are no more or less well off emotionally than before the chance event. This reflects what we know to be the normal human capacity to adapt to one's situation. This same adaptive mechanism works in relation to imprisonment as well. The punitive bite of the prison experience is greatest at the start, which is why most prison suicides occur in the first few days of imprisonment. The punitive bite decreases over time as the person adapts to their situation, and adjusts their expectations accordingly. The effect of this is that punishment becomes increasingly less cost efficient. The cost of imprisonment is the same for each unit of time—often US $30,000 per year—but the punitive bite that we get from each year's punishment decreases over time, such that the cost per punishment unit increases as the prison term gets longer.[11]

But in fact this adaptive mechanism has even more seriously complicating effects when combined with what is called the 'duration neglect' effect. Daniel Kahneman reports a study in which he gives a minor medical-like operation with a certain amount of pain for a certain duration and then gives the subject a second operation that has the same amount of pain for the exact same duration as the first but continues for an additional period without a break during which the amount of the pain is gradually reduced. He then tells the subject that one of the two procedures needs to be repeated and asks subjects which they would prefer to repeat. They prefer to repeat the second rather than the first, even though it has all of the pain of the first and more! What the experiment demonstrates is that it is not the duration of the pain that is of significance but rather two other factors: the maximum intensity and the end point intensity. Because the second operation reduced the pain at the end, it reduced the end point intensity and thereby became perceived as less painful.[12]

The effect of duration neglect for imprisonment practices is quite troubling. With the natural adaptation effect that reduces the punitive bite of prison as the period becomes longer, the end point intensity decreases over time with the possibility that a longer prison term may be perceived as having less punitive bite than a shorter prison term! These results have not been confirmed with human subjects but the point here is simply to illustrate the level of complexity of the dynamics at work in a deterrence system and to suggest that that complexity is at the moment well beyond our ability reliably to predict deterrent effects and to modulate punitive bite as a deterrence-based system requires.

[10] Robinson and Darley, 'Deter', n 2 above, 186–7.   [11] ibid, 187–93.
[12] D Redelmeier and D Kahneman, ' "Patients" Memories of Painful Medical Treatments: Real Time and Retrospective Evaluations of Two Minimally Invasive Procedures' (1996) 116 *Pain* 3.

The last factor that affects the perceived extent of a deterrent threat is the delay between the punishment and the violation. Consider the study of hungry dogs who were given two bowls of food, one tasty, one not. Once the dogs had come to understand their preference, an experimenter strikes the dog on the nose with a newspaper—which I am told is quite painful to dogs—as soon as the dog eats from the preferred bowl, or 5 seconds after he eats from the preferred bowl, or 15 seconds after he eats. The dogs are then let back into the room with the experimenter not present and are timed to see how long it takes them to return to eat from the preferred bowl. The dogs for whom the punishment was delayed by 15 seconds return to the preferred bowl in 3 minutes. The dogs for whom the punishment was delayed only 5 seconds take dramatically longer to return to the preferred bowl, 8 days. The dogs who were punished immediately did not return to the preferred bowl for 2 weeks. Again, the point here is to demonstrate that delay in punishment can have a very dramatic effect in the effectiveness of punishment. One cannot directly translate these results to the effect of delay in punishment on humans but it is again somewhat unsettling when one appreciates that in the criminal justice system the punishment is typically delayed 7 months on average for guilty pleas and 13 months on average for trial.[13]

Compare these troubling results for the criminal justice system in projecting a perception of serious costs to a violation as compared to the perceived benefits of the violation. The probability of gaining the benefit is likely to be seen as high, because the perceived chances of being caught are low. The amount of the benefit typically is quite clear, and can be overwhelming if the person is an addict committing the offense to buy drugs, which is common. Finally, the delay in benefits will be minimal, since it will come soon after the violation, in contrast to perceived long delay before the threatened punishment. On balance, it seems difficult to imagine that the perceived costs will exceed the perceived benefits.

The larger point here in relation to deterrence as a distributive principle is to say that tripping any one of these three hurdles—a failure to know the deterrence-base rule, an inability to bring that rule to bear on one's conduct, or a failure to perceive the cost of a violation as exceeding its benefits—is fatal to any deterrent effect. Further, even if all of these three hurdles can be cleared, it will not be uncommon to have some kind of cumulative disabling effect. For example, a person may know the rule but be a bit fuzzy on its contours, may be able to control his conduct to some extent yet have some impairment in full clarity and control, and may perceive some potential cost to a violation but may see the perceived cost and the perceived benefits as quite close in amount. But even if the system's intended deterrent effect is not lost by stumbling over one of the three hurdles, which may be the rule rather than the exception, the remaining deterrent effect in the lucky case described immediately above may be one of trivial

[13] RL Solomon, LH Turner, and MS Lessac, 'Some Effects of Delay of Punishment on Resistance to Temptation in Dogs' (1968) 8 *Journal of Personality and Social Psychology* 233.

deterrent effect. Indeed, if one looks at studies of rule or policy changes designed to increase deterrent effect, the results suggest that success is rare and, where it does exists, is modest or trivial, and unpredictable.[14]

The conclusion that one can draw from all of this is that constructing liability and punishment rules and policies based on a deterrence distributive principle makes little sense unless there is reason to believe that the prerequisites to deterrence exist and that we have the information and the understanding needed to know how to produce the desired deterrent effect. The difficulty is that those situations seem to be very much the exception rather than the rule.

Rehabilitation

There is every reason to try to rehabilitate offenders. Even if its success is quite modest, as seems to be the case, its use commonly can justify the costs. But the issue at stake here is not whether to try to rehabilitate but rather whether to use rehabilitation as the guiding principle in deciding whom and how much to punish.

It seems difficult to conceive of a criminal justice system that took seriously rehabilitation as its primary distributive principle, for such a system would distribute punishment based solely upon whether somebody could be rehabilitated. And the possibility of such might well be the unusual case, in which case most offenders would not be punished. There would seem to be few people who would take this view, in part because it would so seriously conflict with what people conceive of as what a 'criminal justice' system ought to be doing. That is, such a distribution would regularly fail to do justice and fail to protect the community.

What makes somewhat more sense would be using rehabilitation not as a sole distributive principle for punishment liability but rather as part of a dual principle with incapacitation of the dangerous. Persons would be rehabilitated if possible and, if not, would be preventively detained while they remained dangerous.

Incapacitation

Unlike deterrence and rehabilitation, whose effectiveness seems to be quite limited, it seems relatively clear that incapacitation does work. Putting potential offenders in prison or otherwise incapacitating them so they cannot commit offenses (at least offenses against the community outside of prison) can avoid crimes. The complications with using incapacitation as a distributive principle in whole or in part lies in the fact that, while it can provide some protection, it provides much less protection than would be possible, and at a much greater cost than

---

[14] Robinson and Darley, 'Deter', n 2 above, 197–204.

would be necessary, if such preventive detention were provided openly, rather than if it were provided in the guise of criminal justice.[15]

That is, if a society wishes to have a system of preventive detention that restricts people's liberty not for a past wrong done but based upon a prediction of future dangerousness, then that preventive program can more effectively, more fairly, and more cheaply be provided by an open preventive detention system of a civil nature—analogous to the current system for the civil commitment of persons who are dangerously mentally ill, infected with a contagious disease, or, in some jurisdictions, addicted to drugs—rather than attempting to dress such preventive detention up as criminal justice.

To give just one example, when preventive detention is pursued through a criminal justice system, the prediction of future dangerousness typically is not done simply through a clinical examination by those best trained to predict future criminality using all available information. Instead, to keep the appearance of criminal justice, the prediction of future dangerousness is made instead by a correlate of future dangerousness—prior criminal conduct—that seems more relevant to doing justice. Our ability to predict future criminality under the best of circumstances is quite limited; the effectiveness of past criminal conduct to predict future criminal conduct is even worse.[16] By relying upon this significantly less reliable predictor, we either provide less protection to society than we could provide under an open preventive detention system or we produce more unfairness by imprisoning more 'false positives'—persons who would not in fact commit an offense if they had not been imprisoned—or we do both, getting worse protection while causing greater unfairness. In other words, that kind of flawed system—relying upon less accurate predictive factors than necessary in order to disguise the system as being one of criminal justice rather than preventive detention—is both unfair to persons to be detained and to the community to be protected.[17]

But these inefficiencies and unfairness are not the most serious problem with an incapacitative distributive principle for criminal justice. The real problem is that an incapacitation distributive principle (either combined with a rehabilitation principle or not) produces distributions of criminal liability and punishment that seriously conflict with principles of justice that the community shares and that they expect to be embodied in their criminal justice system. And the perception of a criminal justice system that regularly does injustice in some cases and fails to do justice in others is something that will have its own effect in undercutting efficient crime control.[18] This is the second general development in punishment theory to which psychology has contributed: it has led us to understand that the real power

---

[15] See generally P Robinson, 'Punishing Dangerousness: Cloaking Preventative Detention as Criminal Justice' (2001) 114 *Harvard Law Review* 1429, 1450–4.   [16] ibid, 1450.
[17] ibid, 1451–5.   [18] ibid, 1439–41, 1443–4.

of control over people's conduct is not the threat of official sanction but rather the power of social influence and internalized norms.[19]

The Crimogenic Effect of Injustices and Failures of Justice

The effective operation of the criminal justice system depends upon the cooperation, or at least the acquiescence, of those involved in it—offenders, judges, jurors, witnesses, prosecutors, police, and others. To the extent that people see the system as unjust, as in conflict with their own intuitions about justice, that acquiescence and cooperation is likely to fade and be replaced with subversion.

Consider the effect of an incapacitation distributive principle on the system's reputation for doing justice. The elderly Nazi concentration camp commandant may be perceived as deserving significant punishment but, because he is not dangerous, no preventive detention is required and an incapacitation distributive principle would impose no punishment. On the other hand, a minor offence, meriting little if any punishment, may be committed by a person who is predicted to be dangerous in the future, and consequently would receive substantial punishment under an incapacitation principle. Thus, an incapacitative principle will undercut the criminal justice system's reputation for doing justice.

Note that a desert-based system does necessarily provide some degree of preventive detention as it imposes deserved punishment. Thus, an incapacitation-based system can provide greater preventive detention only in those instances where it *deviates* from a desert distribution. In other words, the traditional utilitarian mechanisms are preferred over a desert distribution only to the extent that they deviate from desert. But it is just these deviations from desert—injustices or failures of justice—which will prompt subversion of the system as well as other detrimental effects.

The Power of Social Influence and Internalized Norms, and Criminal Law's Ability to Harness that Power

The other detrimental effects to which I refer here may in practice be the more important. While the real power of social control lies in social influence and internalized norms, law is not irrelevant to these powers. A criminal law that has gained a reputation for reliably stating what is and is not morally condemnable from the point of view of the community, is a criminal law that can have positive influence in guiding conduct in borderline cases where the community may not yet have a clear sense of whether conduct is condemnable or not. Consider, for example,

---

[19] P Robinson and J Darley, 'The Utility of Desert' (1997) 91 *Northwestern University Law Review* 453, 468–71.

insider trading. We live in a complex society in which many harms are more abstract and more subtle than taking others' property or striking another over the head. Insider-trading is conduct that on its face may not seem clearly condemnable but if the criminal law announces it to be so and that criminal law has otherwise earned credibility with the community in making reliable judgements regarding what is condemnable, the community may be more inclined to see the conduct as condemnable and therefore to be avoided.[20]

Law may have an even more powerful impact in another way: in its ability to shape community norms generally. Drunk driving, domestic violence, and date rape are all instances in which we have seen changes in community views and in the common internalization of norms. The law cannot shape these kinds of changes in norms by itself; calling something criminal by itself cannot make it condemnable. This is in part the lesson of Prohibition in the United States. However, the law can be an active participant in the public discussions that do effectively shape norms when it adds its voice to that of the larger discussion.[21]

But these effects—gaining compliance in borderline cases and in shaping norms—are possible only if the criminal law has earned moral credibility with the community. To the extent that the criminal law distributes liability and punishment based upon distributive principles that conflict with the community's shared intuitions of justice—deterrence, rehabilitation, and incapacitation would all do—the criminal law's moral credibility is undercut and its ability to harness these powerful effects in influencing conduct is undermined.[22]

The Utility of Desert

The conclusion that one can come to on these facts is that the utilitarian who wishes to avoid future crime most effectively may well end up preferring a desert distribution of liability and punishment. By tracking a community's shared intuitions of justice, the criminal law can build its moral credibility and then use that influence in select situations, such as drunk driving, domestic violence, and date rape, to help shape community norms.[23]

The most striking thing about this conclusion, of course, is that this argument in support of a desert distributive principle is utilitarian in nature rather than deontological. In other words, while the dispute of the past half century has been resolved, as a practical matter it has come to common ground. The deontologists still believe that doing justice is a value in itself and requires no beneficial future consequences to justify it, while utilitarians still can only justify punishment if it produces future beneficial consequences, such as reducing crime. But both utilitarians and deontologists may come to the same conclusions of preferring a desert distributive principle, albeit for quite different reasons.

[20] ibid.   [21] ibid, 471–6.   [22] ibid, 477–8.   [23] ibid, 485–8.

In light of this background, it should be no surprise to hear that the American Law Institute committee's proposal for revising the Model Penal Code's 'purposes' section is one that would give complete priority to doing justice. Under the proposal, the traditional utilitarian mechanisms of deterrence, rehabilitation, and incapacitation can be given play only if they are not inconsistent with an offender's deserved punishment and if there is some evidence to think that they would be effective in that situation.[24]

---

[24] The text of the proposal provides:

§ 1.02(2). Purposes; Principles of Construction.
(2) The general purposes of the provisions governing sentencing and corrections, to be discharged by the many official actors within the sentencing and corrections system, are:
  (a) in decisions affecting the sentencing and correction of individual offenders:
    (i) to render punishment within a range of severity proportionate to the gravity of offenses, the harms done to crime victims, and the blameworthiness of offenders;
    (ii) when possible with realistic prospect of success, to serve goals of offender rehabilitation, general deterrence, incapacitation of dangerous offenders, and restoration of crime victims and communities, provided that these goals are pursued within the boundaries of sentence severity permitted in subsection (a)(i) and (ii); and
    (iii) to render sentences no more severe than necessary to achieve the applicable purposes from subsections (a)(i) and (ii); . . .

Model Penal Code: Sentencing, Preliminary Draft No 3 (28 May 2004) 4–5.

7

Modelling Systematic Communication Differences between Law and Science

Paul Dougan, Fernand Gobet, and Michael King[1]

Overview of Main System Approaches

In reaction to classical, analytical science, which studies phenomena by reducing them into more manageable parts, the twentieth century has witnessed a number of influential theorists who have argued that 'the whole is more than the sum of its parts', and that science should study the complexity of entire systems. Systems are defined as comprising both parts and the relations between these parts. This stance has since permeated almost all sciences, and is essential to the study of artificial systems such as computers. It has also been central in the study of communication in society.

One of the first and also most ambitious systemic approaches was proposed by the biologist von Bertalanffy,[2] who as early as in the 1920s tried to develop a general theory of systems. His aim was to identify and formalize abstract principles that apply to all systems, be they physical, biological, psychological, or sociological. Von Bertalanffy was first of all interested in mathematical laws that characterized systems in different scientific fields, and showed that a small number of systems of differential equations can explain natural and social phenomena in different fields.

Further mathematical formulation of systems behaviour was carried out by Wiener, in his work on cybernetics,[3] which can be defined as the science of communication and control in animals and machines. While working on anti-aircraft fire control, Wiener had noted the importance of feedback control, input, output, prediction, and stability. In his book, he generalized these concepts to biology and the social sciences. While Wiener's work and related

---

[1] Please send all correspondence to the authors at: School of Social Sciences and Law, Brunel University, Uxbridge, Middlesex, UB8 3PH.

[2] L von Bertalanffy, *General System Theory* (1973).

[3] N Wiener, *Cybernetics* (1948); WR Ashby, *An Introduction to Cybernetics* (1964).

research in control engineering and computer science focused on reactive systems (sometimes called first-order cybernetics), second-order cybernetics stresses that systems are autonomous and display a spontaneous activity. Prominent researchers in this second approach include von Foerster,[4] Maturana, and Varela.[5]

Simon[6] noted that hierarchical systems, which consist of subsystems that in turn have their own further subsystems, are omnipresent in human-made environments and artefacts, but also in nature. He argued that such hierarchical systems are more likely to evolve than non-hierarchical systems, other things being equal. Another important contribution of Simon in this context is the notion of nearly-decomposable systems. Interactions will be large within a subsystem, but smaller between subsystems, to the point that subsystems can often be treated independently, at least as a first approximation. This has important implications for the study of systems: the assumption of near-decomposability enables the researcher to focus on one level of the hierarchy (say psychology) in the search of scientific laws, and ignore lower levels (eg chemistry) and higher levels (eg sociology). A similar idea is present in the recent concept of emergence, where laws at one level of analysis are not derivable from the laws at a lower level, although they do depend on them. One good example of 'emergence' is offered by living beings, whose behaviour can be seen as emergent from the level below—physical mechanisms. While living beings are constrained by the laws of physics, biological laws of physiology or evolution cannot be derived from the laws of physics. Emergence has been referred to as 'vertical causality' by Collier.[7]

Systems and Communication

Shannon's theory of communication[8] revolutionized the concept of communication in engineering and had substantial impact in several fields of scientific investigation. The proposed measure for information contents—in bits (binary units)—enables, among other things, the provision of formal definitions for concepts such as information gain, redundancy, and channel capacity. The theory showed how codes can be error-correcting, as indeed natural languages are, which made it possible to specify how much information a system can send per unit of time through a limited channel. Finally, there is a direct correspondence

---

[4] H von Foerster, *Observing systems: Selected papers of Heinz von Foerster* (1981).

[5] H Maturana, and FJ Varela, *Autopoiesis and cognition: The realization of the living* (1980).

[6] HA Simon, 'The architecture of complexity' (1962) 106 *Proceedings of the American Philosophical Society* 467–82.

[7] A Collier, 'Stratified Explanation and Marx's Conception of History' in M Archer, R Bhaskar, A Collier, T Lawson, and A Norrie (eds), *Critical Realism—Essential Readings* (1998) 258–81.

[8] CE Shannon, 'A mathematical theory of communication' (1948) *Bell System Technical Journal*, July and October; CE Shannon and W Weaver, *The mathematical theory of communication* (1949).

between the concept of information and that of negative entropy in thermodynamics, although the exact consequences of this isomorphism are still not understood. Aspects of von Bertalanffy, Wiener, and Shannon's work were used by Watzlawick[9] and his colleagues at Palo Alto to develop a theory of human communication, with an emphasis on applications in psychotherapy. In particular, they provided a 'double-bind' theory of schizophrenia, where paradoxical messages in the family environment are seen as causal to the development of this illness. The theory was summarized in five axioms of communication. For example, the first axiom stipulates that 'one cannot not communicate'.

In sociology, the functionalist Talcott Parsons[10] forcibly defended the idea that society can be seen as systems embedded within larger systems: individuals within small groups, small groups within the community, and the community within society. All of these systems are subsystems of *action*, and thus the study of social sciences becomes a science of action. Following the biological principle of homeostasis (the maintenance of a stable state), social systems aim to maintain equilibrium and thus to reduce by negative feedback the effect of external perturbations that disturb the balance among the elements of a given subsystem. The evolution of a system can be divided into four processes. After *division*, where subsystems are created from an extant system, these subsystems become more efficient through *adaptation*. By *inclusion*, elements that were originally excluded from subsystems are incorporated into them. Finally, by *generalization of values*, systems increase their legitimacy.

Niklas Luhmann: Social Systems as Systems of Communication

Of particular interest in this context is Niklas Luhmann's sociological and systems theory. While influenced by scholars such as Parsons, Maturana, Varela, and von Foerster, whose work we have just briefly reviewed, Luhmann's originality is to consider that functionally differentiated subsystems organize meaning, and not, for example, action, as proposed by Parsons.

In Niklas Luhmann's theoretical scheme, systems of communication do not relate to one another directly in an input-output fashion, but rather one system reproduces the communications of the other using its own unique code and programmes.[11] Research to date has been unable to explain this phenomenon, and has therefore attracted criticism from some commentators who have rejected Luhmannian systems theory as not producing hypotheses which are susceptible to empirical verification.[12] Luhmann conducted his research in an idiosyncratic

---

[9] P Watzlawick, J Beavin, and D Jackson, *Pragmatics of human communication: A study of interactional patterns, pathologies and paradoxes* (1967).   [10] T Parsons, *The Social System* (1951).
[11] N Luhmann, *Soziale Systeme: Grundriss einer allgemeinen Theorie* (1984), trans by J Bednarz, Jr as *Social Systems* (1995).
[12] D Zolo, 'Function, meaning, complexity: The epistemological premises of Niklas Luhmann's "sociological enlightenment"' (1986) 16 *Philosophy of the Social Sciences* 115–27; G Wagner, 'Am

fashion, denying the appropriateness of such empiricism as a way of testing his social theories. However, the detailed nature of Luhmann's 'Gedankenwelt'[13] supports, to some extent at least, the validity of this approach. Although Luhmann's theories can now be considered to be rather more 'mature' in form, they still operate in their own conceptual world and it is not clear how the concepts relate on a clearly identifiable empirical basis.

Luhmann's theory of 'autopoietic systems'[14] claims that what distinguishes a living system from a non-living one, ie the 'essence' of the living system, is that it has its own internal logic, being able to perpetuate itself by reproducing its elements while maintaining an organization of these elements that is characteristic of it. The means of obtaining a 'true' understanding of such a system, therefore, is by focusing on this very process of self-production and self-organization. Luhmann's writings are full of explanations about how different systems 'maintain' their identity and distinguish their communications from those of other systems, and his conceptualization of social systems provided him with an ability to abstract from the individual and allowed him to make descriptions of modern society that are compelling to a degree unmatched by any other theories. However, this approach departs from the traditional view of how science works, ie through the patient accumulation of knowledge gathered through empirical investigation. The role, therefore, of Luhmannian system theory is to explore conceptual models without concern for their immediate applicability, thus possibly coming across ideas that would not otherwise have been found that may be of explanatory value in the empirical sciences.

Our Research

According to Luhmann's social theory, modern societies are differentiated into functional subsystems, that determine the way they interact with their environment and will 'code' information in different ways. Thus, the legal system is specialized for processing information in terms of the distinction legal/illegal, and psychology, as a science, is specialized for doing so in terms of the distinction true/false. It is easy to see that both types of activity are 'programmed' by being formalized in a highly detailed manner: the function of judges is to make legal decisions on the basis of statutes and precedents as laid out in legal texts and not on the basis of what they personally find to accord with 'common sense'.

Ende der systemtheoretischen Soziologie: Niklas Luhmann und die Dialektik' (1994) *Zeitschrift für Soziologie* 275–91; G Wagner, 'The end of Luhmann's social systems theory' (1997) 27 *Philosophy of the Social Sciences* 387–409.

[13] Literally 'Imaginary World'.
[14] This is an extension and application to the social sciences of a biological theory originally developed by the Chilean neuroscientists Humberto Maturana and Francisco Varela: Maturana and Varela, n 5 above.

The implication that law and psychology, indeed law and virtually any other science-based discipline, might communicate similar (but not exactly the same) information in dissimilar ways, has ramifications beyond mere justification for an intellectual endeavour. There are serious implications for the manner in which expert psychological evidence may be interpreted by judge, jury, and lawyers in a courtroom setting, etc. The mere process of a judge attempting to paraphrase or re-state the evidence of an expert psychologist would, according to Luhmann, result in a necessity for one system of communication to reproduce the communications of the other. From an empirical perspective this ought to result in a definable and measurable difference in the syntactic and semantic structure of the communications. How, then, are we to deconstruct these communications so as to provide evidence of these differences, if they do indeed exist?

Many theories and methods exist for the extraction and representation of the contextual usage of words through the statistical computations applied to large corpora of text, both for syntactic and semantic analysis. Computational models of the construction of syntactic structures include the Pooled Adjacent Context Model (PAC),[15] the Syntagmatic Paradigmatic model (SP),[16] and the Model of Syntax Acquisition in Children (MOSAIC).[17] Computational models of the construction of semantic representations include, mostly famously, Latent Semantic Analysis (LSA)[18] but also Hyperspace Analogue to Language (HAL),[19] Sparse Random Context Representation (SRCR),[20] and Word Association Space (WAS).[21] All of these models attempt to elucidate the difference, or indeed similarity, of word and passage meaning through the statistical analysis of large text corpora. However, whilst each of these methods is capable of extracting lexical, grammatical, or semantic information from the statistics of word use, the

[15] M Redington, N Chater, and S Finch, 'Distributional information: A powerful cue for acquiring syntactic categories' (1998) 22 *Cognitive Science* 425–69.

[16] S Dennis and M Harrington, 'The Syntagmatic Paradigmatic Model: A distributed instance-based model of sentence processing', *The Second Workshop on Natural Language Processing and Neural Networks*, 30 November 2001, Tokyo.

[17] D Freudenthal, JM Pine, and F Gobet, 'Modelling the development of children's use of optional infinitives in English and Dutch using MOSAIC' (in press). *Cognitive Science*; F Gobet, D Freudenthal, and JM Pine, 'Modelling syntactic development in a cross-linguistic context' (2004) *Proceedings of the COLING 2004 Workshop 'Psychocomputational Models of Human Language Acquisition'* 53–60.

[18] TK Landauer and ST Dumais, 'A solution to Plato's problem: The Latent Semantic Analysis theory of acquisition, induction and representation of knowledge' (1997) 105 *Psychological Review* 221–40.

[19] C Burgess, 'From simple associations to the building blocks of language: Modelling meaning in memory with the HAL model' (1998) 30 *Behavior Research Methods, Instruments, & Computers* 188–98.

[20] M Sahlgren, 'Vector-based semantic analysis: representing word meaning based on random labels' (2001) *Semantic Knowledge Acquisition and Categorisation Workshop at ESSLLI '01, Helsinki, Finland*; M Sahlgren, 'Towards a flexible model of word meaning' (2002) *AAAI Spring Symposium 2002*.

[21] M Steyvers, RM Shiffrin, and DL Nelson, 'Word Association Spaces for predicting semantic similarity effects in episodic memory' in A Healy (ed), *Cognitive Psychology and its Applications: Festschrift in Honor of Lyle Bourne, Walter Kintsch, and Thomas Landauer* (2004).

type of information captured by each of the methods appears to differ in character. The underlying principles for each method, however, are broadly similar, insofar as the totality of information about all the contexts in which given words do and do not appear provides a set of mutual constraints that largely determines the similarity of meaning of words and sets of words to each other. Headline uses of this *textual analysis* have included accurately measuring the learnability of passages by individual students[22] and the quality and quantity of knowledge contained in an essay, the latter effectively presaging a future time when student academic work might be assessed by computers.

Comparison of the Available Models of Word Meaning Construction

Latent Semantic Analysis,[23] the best known of all these theories, uses as its input a corpus of free text, with the relevant contextual unit being the paragraph. An analysis of word occurrences within all paragraphs leads to a representation of the meaning and relationship of words as vectors. The mechanism implemented in LSA makes it possible to compare words semantically. It also has the advantage of capturing higher-order co-occurrences,[24] ie, the way words not necessarily adjacent to each other are related, and the meaning of a text, ie its compositionality as a linear combination of the meaning of its words. The semantic representations generated by LSA have been extensively tested in the literature[25] and it is regarded as a very successful theory indeed. Hyperspace Analogue to Language (HAL)[26] is both a model of semantic memory and a method for deriving lexical information from a corpus of text. It is broadly similar to LSA but differs in some significant ways. It ignores higher-order co-occurrences between words, since the vectors generated by the analysis are merely direct co-occurrence vectors. Finally, rather than paragraphs, HAL uses a sliding window of a few words as unit of context. This maintains information about lexical distance.

Sparse Random Context Representation (SRCR)[27] is similarly based upon the operation of a sliding window mode of analysis applied to a large corpus of text. Each word within the corpus is accorded an initial random vector representation

[22] TK Landauer, PW Foltz, and D Laham, 'Introduction to Latent Semantic Analysis' (1998) 25 *Discourse Processes* 259–84.

[23] TK Landauer, 'On the computational basis of learning and cognition: Arguments from LSA' in N Ross (ed), *The Psychology of Learning and Motivation* (2002) 41, 43–84.

[24] A Kontostathis, and WM Pottenger, 'Detecting patterns in the LSI term matrix' (2002) *Workshop on the Foundation of Data Mining and Discovery, IEEE International Conference on Data Mining.*

[25] PW Foltz, 'Latent Semantic Analysis for text-based research' (1996) 282 *Behavior Research Methods, Instruments and Computers* 197–202; MBW Wolfe, ME Schreiner, B Rehder, D Laham, PW Foltz, W Kintsch, and TK Landauer, 'Learning from text: Matching readers and texts by Latent Semantic Analysis' (1998) 25 *Discourse Processes* 309–36.   [26] Burgess, n 19 above.

[27] Sahlgren, n 20 above (2002).

which is then modified by the vectors of the co-occurring words but with a 'multi-plying factor' dependent upon their distance to the current word within the window. This incremental mechanism has, in some circumstances, generated more impressive results than LSA, particularly on the well-known TOEFL test for ascertaining proficiency in English as a second language. Like HAL, SRCR does not take into account higher-order co-occurrences, which could again be viewed as something of a shortcoming. Word Association Space (WAS)[28] is based upon 'association norms' rather than upon a corpus of text. 'Associates' are provided for a large number (5,000) of words and the use of scaling methods enables each word to be uniquely located in a high-dimensional representational space. Great reliance is placed upon 'singular value decomposition' (SVD), the same mathematical alogrithm that LSA uses. With SVD, words occuring in similar contexts end up in similar regions in the representational hyperspace. The idea is that words that appear within similar contexts or similar associative relationships are placed in similar regions in the space.

Choice of ICAN over Competing Methods

After analysis of the benefits and disadvantages of these various theories, one theory in particular emerged as the leading candidate for use in the current research project. Incremental Construction of an Associative Network (ICAN),[29] as with the other theories, is a computational method for examining and comparing the hidden structures of large bodies of text. This technique, we argue, is able to offer a measure of objectivity to comparisons between the way in which different Luhmannian social subsystems (law and science) communicate, thereby illuminating the nature of the relationship(s) between them.

Features of ICAN compared with the other models are usefully summarized in graphical form in Table 7.1.[30]

The selection of this theory was in recognition of the perceived existing limitations of the other methods of extracting lexical information from the statistics of word use. In particular, as input, a corpus of free text is cognitively more plausible than somewhat contrived 'association norms', so therefore ICAN, as well as some of the other methods, delivers improvements over, for instance, WAS. Similarly, all the models, apart from ICAN, are based on a vector representation of word meaning. The resulting multi-dimensional geography of the 'semantic space' can accrue from a statistical analysis which keeps hundreds of unlabelled dimensions (as in LSA or SCRC), the most variant words (as in HAL), words with the greatest

---

[28] Steyvers *et al*, n 21 above.

[29] B Lemaire, and G Denhière, 'Incremental Construction of an Associative Network from a Corpus' (2004) *Proceedings of the 26th Annual Meeting of the Cognitive Science Society* 825–30.

[30] This table has been adapted from Lemaire and Denhière, n 29 above, 827.

Table 7.1. Features of different computational models used for the construction of word meaning

Model	Input	Representation	Memory updating	Unit of context	Higher order co-occurrences
ICAN	**Corpus**	**Network**	**Incremental**	**Sliding window**	Yes
LSA	Corpus	Vectors	Not incremental	Paragraph	Yes
HAL	Corpus	Vectors	Incremental	Sliding window	No
SCRC	Corpus	Vectors	Incremental	Sliding window	No
WAS	Association Norms	Vectors	Not incremental	N/A	No

frequency[31] or a ready-constructed checklist of words, taken either from a thesaurus[32] or selected as being representative across various sub-corpora.[33]

One recognized advantage of the vector representation is that it delivers a simpler measurement of word similarity, with the angle between the corresponding vectors or some measure thereof generally being used. But the use of vectors also has significant disadvantages. For example, in order to find which words are most similar to a specified target, one has to scan all vectors. This procedure lacks computational elegance and is also an implausible memory mechanism from a cognitive point of view. In addition, representing meanings as vectors requires the assumption that similarity is symmetrical. However, substantial empirical research into language and memory has established that this assumption cannot be maintained.[34] In ICAN, there is a network of words with simple numerical oriented links between nodes, an 'oriented graph', and this is a far more elegant and accurate means of illustrating semantic similarity. What is particularly important is the retention of the often asymmetric relationship between particular terms.

A problem that affects both the LSA and WAS models is the fact that they are not incremental in nature, ie there is no way of updating the semantic space with a 'new unit of context' without having to redo the whole process, which is computationally very costly. So, although these models can represent a new

---

[31] JP Levy, JA Bullinaria, 'Learning lexical properties from word usage patterns: which context words should be used?' in R French and JP Sougne (eds), *Connectionist Models of Learning, Development and Evolution: Proceedings of the Sixth Neural Computation and Psychology Workshop* (2001) 273–82.

[32] V Prince, and M Lafourcade, 'Mixing semantic networks and conceptual vectors: the case of hyperonymy', *2nd IEEE International Conference on Cognitive Informatics* (2003) 121–8.

[33] W Lowe and S McDonald, 'The direct route: mediated priming in semantic space' in MA Gernsbacher and SD Derry (eds), *Proceedings of the 22nd Annual Meeting of the Cognitive Science Society* (2000) 675–80.

[34] A Tversky, 'Features of similarity' (1977) 84(4) *Psychological Review* 327–52. An example may be, for instance, the word 'bird', which is a very close neighbour of 'swallow', but it cannot be said that the opposite, ie the word 'swallow', leads one immediately to think of the word 'bird'.

paragraph by a vector—that is, by a linear combination of its constituent words—there in no change in the semantic space following this operation. An incremental model, such as ICAN, is computationally preferable, since we will see improvements in our results instantaneously, but the model is also cognitively more plausible since the processing of new texts will surely modify the semantic memory, even if it only does so by a small amount.

Semantic relationships between terms in a corpus of text are derived from the occurrences of words within particular contexts and the size of these contexts is of significant importance. Computer simulations[35] and empirical studies in psychology both indicate that a context comprising a few words before and after the particular word being analysed should be sufficient. A whole paragraph, however, is likely to be too large a unit, a unit chosen as the default by the likes of LSA, due to computational limitation. Models using paragraphs use the context as a 'bag of words' and do not keep information about the lexical distance. With its sliding window, ICAN can use distance between words if necessary.

A further refinement that the ICAN model delivers over the other models, apart from LSA, is in consideration of the higher-order co-occurrences of words. This is the occurrence relationship between words that are not found together within the particular units considered. The importance of higher-order co-occurences in the latent structure of meaning is well established.[36] Thus, although two words may never be present together within *same* context, it is vital that the alogrithm consider them as associated if they do occur within *similar* contexts.[37]

As has been shown, there are numerous reasons why the ICAN model was selected. What now follows is an explanation of how this model actually constructs the semantic space by analysis of the corpora of text that are used as input.

Methodology

Like the other models that have already been mentioned, the ICAN model uses as its input free text corpora and engages in analysis of these bodies of terms to produce a computational representation of word meanings. The model uses a network representation of semantic space rather than a vector representation,

---

[35] C Burgess, 'From simple associations to the building blocks of language: Modelling meaning in memory with the HAL model' (1998) 30 *Behavior Research Methods, Instruments, and Computers* 188–98.   [36] Kontostathis and Pottenger, n 24 above.

[37] eg, word A is said to be a second-order co-occurrence of B if it co-occurs with C which also happens to co-occur with B. If C were a second-order co-occurrence of B, A would be considered as a third-order co-occurrence of B, etc. See Lemaire and Denhière, n 29 above, 826.

which is preferable since the network is likely to be a more accurate rendering of the relationship between words and terms in actual human memory. Through the use of computational analysis, each word within the corpus of text is associated with a set of neighbours, and each association allocated a 'weight' or degree of importance. When ICAN processes text, associations for each word are updated online. New links can be added to the network using information about co-occurrence, and a link between a pair of words can be removed if the association strength between these two words falls below a certain threshold. Thus, ICAN is incremental in nature.

Table 7.2 indicates the rules that are employed during the computational analysis. Links between words are updated by taking into account the results of previous simulations by the inventors of the ICAN method.[38]

As the model uses a sliding window as unit of analysis, both the preceding and following contexts affect the way each word within the corpus of text is processed. The size of the window is variable and can be modified. Lemaire and Denhière have shown,[39] as illustrated in Table 7.3, that a window size of 11 (ie five preceding and five following terms) produces the best correlation with human data. In the current research, we used a window of five words, therefore with two words in a preceding context and two words in a following context. Although this is clearly below the optimal value obtained by Lemaire and Denhière, it was considered sufficient at this stage of research, as it allowed flexibility in carrying out exploratory studies. (With our implementation of ICAN, running one simulation with a window of 11 took more than one day.) We take up the question of window size in the discussion.

Table 7.2. Types of relationships between two words (W1 and W2), and effect of the rules on the way similarity is encoded in the network

Rules	Relationship	Effect of rule on similarity
Rule 1	Co-occurrence of W1 and W2	Strongly increases the W1-W2 similarity
Rule 2	Occurrence of W1 without W2 or W2 without W1	Decreases the W1-W2 similarity
Rule 3	Second and third-order co-occurrence of W1 and W2	Slightly increases the W1-W2 similarity

[38] B Lemaire and G Denhière, (Submitted). Effects of higher-order Co-occurrences on semantic similarity of words. The simulation here was on 13,637 paragraphs of a corpus of text.

[39] Lemaire and Denhière, n 29 above, 829. Other studies also support this conclusion: window sizes of 10 are used in Burgess, n 19, above, as well as Lowe and McDonald, n 33 above; see also, JP Levy, JA Bullinaria, and M Patel, 'Explorations in the derivation of semantic representations from word co-occurrence statistics' (1998) 10 *South Pacific Journal of Psychology* 99–111. In this paper, researchers found best performance for a window size from 8 to 14.

Table 7.3. Effect of sliding window size on the way ICAN matches association norms between words for nine-year-old children

Window Size	Correlation with human data
3 (1+1+1)	0.34
5 (2+1+2)	0.38
7 (3+1+3)	0.44
9 (4+1+4)	0.48
11 (5+1+5)	**0.50**
13 (6+1+6)	0.49
15 (7+1+7)	0.47

Source: Lemaire and Denhière, 2004.[40]

Table 7.4. Algorithm used for updating the weights of the links between nodes in the network

Let us call each word W, its preceding context C1 . . . Ck and its following context Ck + 1 . . . C2k. The sliding window is therefore [C1 C2 . . . Ck W Ck + 1 Ck + 2 . . . C2k]. Three learning situations can occur:

Effect of 'Direct Co-occurrence'	If the link $WC_i (i = 1\ to\ 2k)$ does not exist, create it with a weight of 0.5, otherwise reinforce it by increasing its weight p by setting it to $p + (1-p)/2$.
Effect of 'Second-order Co-occurrence'	Let p be the weight of the W-C_i link. For each M linked to C_i with weight m, reinforce the link W-M (if such a link does not exist, create it with a weight of $p * m$, otherwise increase the weight q by setting it to $q + A(1-q)(p * m)$. In our simulations, the parameter A was set to 0.02.
Effect of 'Occurrence without Co-occurrence'	Reduce the links between W and its other neighbours (if the weights were p, set them to a fraction of p, eg $0.9p$). If some of them fall under a threshold value (eg 0.1), then remove these links.

This algorithm has been developed by Lemaire and Denhière.

Analysis of the section of text will modify the association network according to the algorithm listed in Table 7.4.[41] (See Figure 7.3 for a graphical illustration of this algorithm.) Functional words (eg 'the', 'for', 'whilst') are not being taken into account in this calculation. For simplicity, the third-order co-occurrence effect was not employed in our analysis.

For our study k = 2, therefore the sliding window was [C1 C2 W C3 C4] with W being the word at the centre of the sliding window, which will naturally change

[40] Taken from Lemaire and Denhière, n 29 above, 829.
[41] This table is created from information contained in ibid, 827.

as computation progresses. Using the algorithm in the table above we will arrive at a measure of similarity between two particular words in the corpus, W1 and W2. The similarity is the combination of the links of the shortest path between W1 and W2.[42]

Our Input Data

In order to attempt to make a valid comparison between law and science (with social sciences as an example) as systems of communication, it was essential that we 'control' our input data in terms of subject matter. In all cases, our chosen topic was related to the convicted 'moors murderer' Myra Hindley. Four academic journal articles were chosen for the science system[43] and three appropriate law cases were chosen from the LexisNexis Professional database[44] for the law system. Before filtering, the law texts comprised a corpus of 45,115 words, and the social science texts 34,135 words. The differential between the size of each corpus was not considered problematic for this pilot study, but in future a smaller disparity would be preferable. The law cases were downloaded as text files and the social sciences files as Adobe Acrobat (PDF) files and then converted to text files. The bodies of text from each system were then subjected to a filtering process, this initially comprising some obvious editing, such as the removal of page numbers and page headers.

Example of text at Stage 1
These crimes, known as the 'Moors Murders' are deeply embedded in the collective consciousness of our society [. . .]

Stage 2 of the process was the automatic removal of 'function words' from the bodies of text. For the selection of function words, lists available on the internet were used.[45] Note that the definition of 'function words' is rather liberal in this context, as the lists contain, in addition to articles, pronouns, prepositions, and

---

[42] If W2 is connected to W1, similarity is defined as the weight of the link; if W1 is connected to Z which is connected to W2, similarity is defined as the combination of the two weights. If W2 does not belong to the neighbours of W1's neighbours, similarity is defined as 0.

[43] JM Schone, 'The hardest case of all: Myra Hindley, life sentences, and the rule of law' (2000) 28(4) *International Journal of the Sociology of Law* 273–89; GT Viki, K Massey, and B Masser, 'When chivalry backfires: Benevolent sexism and attitudes toward Myra Hindley' (2005) 10 *Legal and Criminological Psychology* 109–20; J Winter, 'The truth will out? The role of judicial advocacy and gender in verdict construction' (2002) 11(3) *Social and Legal Studies* 343–67; E Storrs, ' "Our Scapegoat": An Exploration of Media Representations of Myra Hindley and Rosemary West' (2004) 11(1) *Theology and Sexuality* 9–28.

[44] *R v Secretary of State for the Home Department, ex p Hindley* [2000] 1 QB 152, CA; *Hindley v Higgins and anor,* CA (Civil Division) (unreported 1983); *R v Secretary of State for the Home Department, ex p Hindley* [1998] QB 751 (Divisional Court).

[45] The following two lists were used: <http://www.dcs.gla.ac.uk/idom/ir_resources/linguistic_utils/stop_words> and <http://www.lextek.com/manuals/onix/stopwords2.html>.

conjunctions, empty words such as 'certainly' and 'hopefully', which do not add much to the meaning of a text. In addition to this automatic process, further scanning of the filtered files identified some additional function words that had not yet been removed, and these were added to the database. Finally, all typographical characters other than letters were removed, including numerical characters, resulting in quite radically filtered files:

Example of text at Stage 2
[. . .] crimes moors murders deeply embedded collective consciousness society [. . .]

Stage 3 of the process of preparing the bodies of text for lexical analysis was to concatenate the files into single files, one for the law system and one for the social sciences system. Boundaries between the original files were clearly indicated, to avoid the creation of spurious links between nodes, which could have occurred if words belonging to different files were included in the same window.

After this third stage, the filtered social science file contained 15,792 words in total and 4,360 unique terms, whereas the law file contained 18,252 words and 2,839 different terms; 1,459 different terms appeared to be common to both files.

Construction of the Semantic Network

The bodies of text were now prepared and ready to be subjected to lexical analysis and, from the resulting data, subsequent construction of the associative network. Initially the semantic network is empty. As 'learning' develops (ie as the sliding window analysis progresses), the network acquires 'nodes', which encode terms, and 'links', which connect any two given nodes. A link has a particular weight, a numerical value between 0 and 1, which, roughly speaking, encodes the probability that two terms appear in the same context and which can therefore be interpreted as a measure of similarity between words.

In terms of providing input data for the algorithm described in Table 7.4 above, a sliding window of five words was moved through each concatenated file, starting from the beginning. Figure 7.1 below illustrates this process.

Step 1
     [. . .] **crimes moors** | murders | *deeply embedded* [. . .]

Step 2
     [. . .] **moors murders** | deeply | *embedded collective* [. . .]
Preceding context | Centre of the sliding window | *Following context*

Figure 7.1. Illustration of the way the sliding window moves through the input file

Example

[. . .] crimes moors murders deeply embedded [. . .]
$$\rightarrow$$
(murders **crimes**)
(murders **moors**)
(murders *deeply*)
(murders *embedded*)

Figure 7.2. Illustration of the way pairs of words are extacted from the input, using the centre of the window as anchor

For the construction of the network, the algorithm received as input pairs of terms formed between the centre of the window and the other words in the rest of the window. The combinations for the 5 term window is illustrated in Figure 7.2 and there are clearly four pairwise combinations. Note that distance (within the window) was not taken into consideration.

Although details of the mathematical aspects of the update algorithm are given in Table 7.4 above, the effect of the algorithm can be presented in diagrammatic form in Figure 7.3 below. It is important that the system verify that the words in the window are all encoded as nodes and then update the weights between the node representing the centre and other nodes in the network.

While extremely simple, this algorithm is costly computationally, because the same operations have to be repeated again and again, in particular when many nodes are linked to a given node. The summary statistics in Table 7.5 below indicate the large numbers of both links and individual nodes of which the system must take account. However, it is only by creating such a multi-dimensional semantic space that we can properly understand the very complex relationships between terms contained within the corpus.

Results

Luhmann proposed that different social systems encode information using different binary codes and programmes. A plausible consequence is that communications within those systems, for example law cases for the law system and academic journal articles for the (social) science system, should have not only different surface structures, for example style and convention, but also different semantic structures. However, it is critical to control the input to the two systems, insofar as this should relate as nearly as possible to identical topics.

This is what our empirical study has aimed to elucidate, ie to provide some scientific evidence to support Luhmann's theory about social systems. We

Panel 1

The weight between two linked words is increased
(or a link is added)

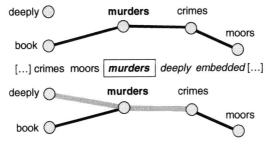

Panel 2

Nodes that are two links away also see their
weight increased, but less than in case 1

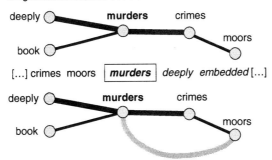

Panel 3

The weight between two nodes that do not occur
in the same window is slightly decreased

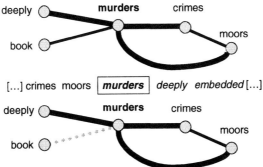

Figure 7.3. Illustration of the way the weights of the links connecting nodes in the network are updated

The diagrams depict the effect of each of the three learning mechanisms, and show a diminutive network before and after the presentation of a list of words.

Panel 1: co-occurrence of two words strongly increase their similarity;

Panel 2: second-order co-occurrence of words leads to a smaller increase of similarity than first-order co-occurrence;

Panel 3: occurrence of a word without another decreases the similarity between words.

(Note that the thickness of the links is proportional to their weights).

attempted to test the hypothesis in two ways, first, by looking at summary statistics derived from the two networks and, secondly, by analysing in detail the properties of sub-networks of both the law and social science networks, encoding selected terms which were categorized as being 'law', 'social sciences', or 'neutral' terms.

Statistics for the Two Networks

Table 7.5 below, sets out the various summary statistics for the two networks (social sciences and law).

What is noteworthy is that, although the science file has fewer words in total, there are more different words, and also more links. However, the branching factor is higher for law. Several explanations may account for these differences. The greater number of different terms within the science file could be related to the specific use of scientific 'jargon', within that system, words that are highly unlikely to appear within the common usage of another system. The higher branching factor for law may relate to the manifold contexts in which law may seek to employ the same terms. One important point to note is that the distribution of the number of links per node is more or less the same between the two networks, ie when viewed in graphical format (see Figure 7.4 below), a clear skewed bell curve shape emerges in both cases.

Comparison of the Two Networks on Target Terms within and without the Domain

A comparison of sub-networks was then undertaken for ten specifically-selected terms within the law terms, social science terms, and neutral terms, ie terms not deemed proprietary to either law or social sciences (see Table 7.6). The law terms appeared at least fifty-seven times in both input files, and the science terms at least twenty-two times. As for the neutral terms, they appeared with similar frequency in both the law and science input. As a consequence, all the target terms were present in both networks.

Table 7.5. Summary statistics for the law network and the social science network

	Law Network	Science Network
Total number of nodes	2,839	4,360
Total number of links	1,687,229	1,962,028
Average branching factor (ie number of links per node)	594	450

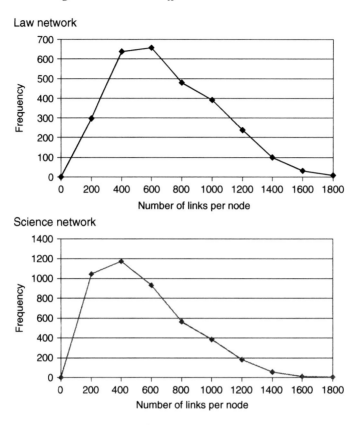

Figure 7.4. Frequency distribution of the number of links per node for the law network and the science network

Table 7.6. The ten target terms for law and social science, as well as the ten neutral terms

System	Terms
Law	tariff sentence case parole justice mandatory statement judicial retribution unlawful
Social Science	sexual construction relationship study structure behaviour violence family narrative truth
Neutral	summary context work death basis criticism public concept article questions

For each network, we looked up the weights between the nodes encoding terms of each kind (law terms, social science terms, and neutral terms). We tested whether the weights were statistically different between the two networks with paired t-tests.[46] Remarkably, given the shortcomings of this pilot study, the results were very clear-cut (see Table 7.7 below). On average, the law network has higher weights for law terms than did the science network (the difference was statistically significant). The pattern is reversed with the science terms (again, the difference was statistically significant). Finally, there were *no* differences between the two networks with respect to the neutral terms.

This is represented visually in Figure 7.5 below. Although there were actually ten terms, the Figure has been simplified to five terms, and is for illustration only. Also, while there are two links between two terms (from A to B, and from B to A), the Figure depicts the average between the two, for clarity's sake.

Table 7.7. Average weights between terms for law, science, and neutral terms, as a function of the type of network

	Average weight between 10 terms		
	Law terms	Science terms	Neutral terms
Law network	0.203	0.120	0.142
Science network	0.176	0.192	0.136
Significance value	p < 0.05	p < 0.001	non-significant

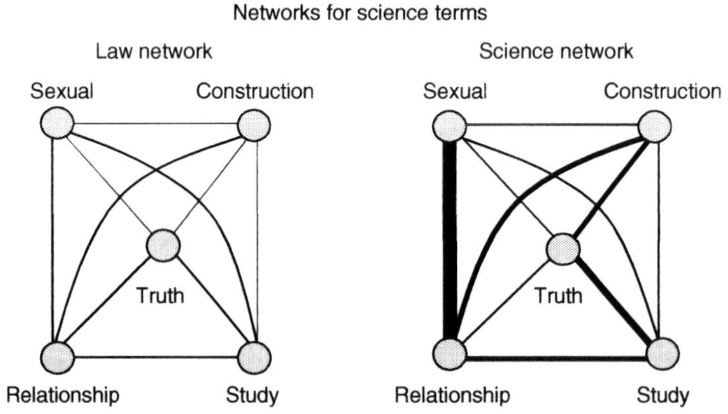

Figure 7.5. Simplified graphical representation of how five nodes representing science terms are connected within each network

The thickness of the line is proportional to the weight of the link.

[46] CH Howell, *Statistical methods for psychology* (1987).

Conclusion

A number of influential systems theories, including those of von Foerster, Maturana, and Luhmann, argue that 'the whole is more than the sum of its parts' and that systems ought to be viewed as comprising both their constituent elements and the resultant relationships between those elements. The latter theory of Niklas Luhmann differentiated social systems such as law and science, claiming that each has its own specialized medium of communication, coding information in different ways. That law and science might code and indeed communicate a similar body of information in dissimilar ways ought to be problematic to anyone concerned with the administration of justice. The recent controversies surrounding the cases of Infant Cot Death syndrome and Shaken Baby syndrome[47] in the United Kingdom, highlight the problems of scientists communicating their findings in a courtroom setting, only to have this information restated and reinterpreted by lawyers, judges, and juries.

The sophisticated approaches of these theorists to a better understanding of the functioning of systems have, to date, not been vindicated in terms of empirical studies conducted under strict scientific conditions. However, our own empirical analysis with the admittedly limited ambit of 'social systems', has demonstrated measurable and statistically reliable differences in the semantic structure between the law and science systems of communication, as inferred by the networks developed using the ICAN algorithm. The terms related to a particular domain had a higher average weight within the network associated with this domain than with the network associated with the other domain. There were no differences for the neutral terms.

In spite of these encouraging results, our study suffers from a number of limitations. First, more sophisticated methods could be developed in the future for filtering the input files. Secondly, larger corpora of text are necessary to test the robustness of our results. Thirdly, a larger sliding window would accord more closely with the reality of the way semantic memory actually functions, as previously estimated in the literature (see the description of ICAN). A window limited to five terms provides a context that is too limited, although it is not obvious why this should affect one network more than the other. Fourthly, the resulting networks could be compared using more sophisticated methods, sensitive not only to the average weights of the links, but also to the structure of the networks. Finally, it would be desirable to extend our approach to other social systems to establish whether the pattern we have uncovered here generalizes to social systems as a whole.

[47] See Paul Dougan's article, 'How are the Courts to make sense of Modern Science?' *The Times*, 28 June 2005, 3.

Although only a preliminary study, this work has shown that it is possible, at least to a first approximation, to formalize the concept of 'communication' within systems theory, and then to use this formalism to compare communications between different social systems. Although we do not claim to be providing scientific proof, as such, for Luhmann's theory of social systems, the results are statistically significant insofar as they do confirm measurable differences between the semantic structures of the law and science systems of communication. As well as highlighting problems that might result from such differences, we believe that our work has practical applications in the long term, in that it may help to develop tools that will alleviate the difficulty that social systems have in exchanging meaningful communications.

8

Cognitive Errors, Individual Differences, and Paternalism

Jeffrey J Rachlinski

Introduction

Restricting individual choice in a free society is as perilous as it is essential. Because the aggregation of individual choices directs the production of goods and services, meddling with these choices risks misdirecting the economy. But if collective foolishness governs individual choice, then allowing an unchecked market to direct the economy can produce an undesirable allocation of resources. Public perception of the role of government reflects this tension. People expect that government will respect their desires and commonly resent restrictions on choice, but people also expect that government will protect them from market forces that would exploit their weaknesses. Evidence that people make poor decisions favours restricting individual choice.[1] But what of evidence that decision making skills vary?

Scholars applying the psychology of judgment and choice (ie Behavioural Law and Economics, or BLE) to the legal system have largely assumed that consumers share identical cognitive processes and vulnerabilities.[2] Rarely do scholars seriously consider the implications of a mixture of wisdom and foolishness for legal policy. In the jargon of psychology, legal scholarship adopts a

---

[1] *See* C Camerer *et al*, *Regulation for Conservatives: Behavioral Economics and the Case for Asymmetric Paternalism*, 151 U. PENN. L. REV. 1211, 1212 (2003) ('To the extent that errors identified by behavioral research lead people not to behave in their own interests, paternalism may prove useful.'); C Jolls, CR Sunstein & RT Thaler, *A Behavioral Approach to Law and Economics*, 50 STAN. L. REV. 1471 (1996) ('bounded rationality pushes toward a sort of anti-antipaternalism'); JJ Rachlinski, *The Uncertain Psychological Case for Paternalism*, 97 NW. U. L. REV. 1165 (2003) ('Recognition of the fallibility of human judgment and the research that identifies this fallibility commonly inspire calls for imposing constraints on individual choice.').

[2] *See* G Mitchell, *Why Law and Economics' Perfect Rationality Should Not Be Traded for Behavioral Law and Economics' Equal Incompetence*, 91 GEO. L.J. 67 (2002) ('behavioral law and economics treats all legal actors in all situations as if they were equally predisposed to commit errors of judgment and choice.')

nomothetic approach—treating all people as having identical cognitive abilities. In contrast, reality almost certainly supports an ideographic approach—treating people as having various cognitive abilities.[3] Given the complexity of human cognition and the incredible variation in attitudes, beliefs, intelligence, and experience among consumers, they almost certainly do not commit identical errors. Legal scholars have nevertheless proceeded under the unexamined assumption that consumers are sufficiently similar that a nomothetic approach is appropriate.

To be sure, no BLE scholar has ever embraced the proposition that all people in all settings commit cognitive error to exactly the same extent.[4] Indeed, much of the BLE literature discussing the differences between lay and expert assessments of risk depends on the faith (sometimes misplaced) that experts will avoid the cognitive errors that plague lay persons. Similarly, calls to replace juries with judges in civil trials commonly arise from a belief that judges avoid cognitive errors that juries commit.[5] Others have argued that organizational settings can balance and correct mistakes that different individuals might make, implicitly recognizing differential abilities.[6] The nomothetic commitment in BLE is limited to the assumption that every member of an identifiable group of people relies on cognitive processes that are sufficiently similar that differences within the group do not undermine policies designed to protect the group from suffering undesirable consequences of faulty decision making. With the notable exception of a paper by Camerer and his co-authors endorsing a soft form of paternalism,[7] BLE embraces that nomothetic assumption.

This paper explores the value of an ideographic approach in behavioural law and economics. The first section assesses the sensibility of the assumption that individual variation in cognitive style does not exist by tracing the origin of the assumption and by assessing evidence that individual variation is widespread. The second section assesses possible markers of individual variation in cognitive styles. The final section discusses how the law can and should respond to individual differences in cognitive ability.

---

[3] For a review of the 'nomothetic' and 'ideographic' approaches within the social sciences, see PT Manicas (1998), Social science, history of philosophy of. In E Craig (ed), *Routledge Encyclopedia of Philosophy*. London: Routledge. Retrieved August 8, 2005, from <http://www.rep.routledge.com/article/R015>.

[4] *See* RA Prentice, *Chicago Man, K-T Man, and the Future of Behavioral Law and Economics*, 56 VANDERBILT L. REV. 1663, 1722 (2003) (calling the concern that BLE embraces uniform cognitive error 'an enormous straw man').

[5] *See* CR Sunstein, D Kahneman & D Schkade, *Assessing Punitive Damages (With Notes on Cognition and Valuation in Law)*, 107 YALE L.J. 2071, 2113 (1998) (relying on cognitive limitations of jurors to conclude that 'judges should decide on the appropriate level of punitive damages').

[6] *See* C Heath, RP Larrick & J Klayman, *Cognitive Repairs: How Organizational Practices Can Compensate for Individual Shortcomings*, 20 RESEARCH IN ORGANIZATIONAL BEHAVIOR 1 (1998); Rachlinski, n 1 above, at 1214–19.   [7] Camerer *et al*, n 1 above.

The Simplifying Nomothetic Assumption

The Nomothetic Roots of Behavioural Law and Economics

Why would proponents of a psychological analysis of law so firmly embrace the assumption that all people share similar cognitive abilities? It is, after all, almost certainly a false assumption. It seems strange that those who embrace psychology and deride rational choice theory for its adherence to false simplifications would themselves pursue a similar course. As Jolls, Sunstein, and Thaler put it, the point of behavioural law and economics is to bring more accurate assumptions concerning human behaviour to law so as to produce, 'law with a greater R-squared'.[8]

The nomothetic foundation of behavioural law and economics represents a methodological commitment that runs to the very roots of the field. The phenomena that BLE scholars frequently discuss: framing, adjustment and anchoring, the representativess heuristic, cognitive availability, the hindsight bias, the endowment effect, norms of reciprocity, hyperbolic discounting, and so forth, are usually discussed as if they affect everyone. But this assumption does not arise from BLE itself. Rather, it arises from the fields that originally documented these phenomena: the cognitive psychology of judgement and choice and behavioural economics. Both of these fields, in turn, embrace a largely nomothetic view of human cognition because they also, in turn, arose from fields that embrace a nomothetic view.

For its part, the psychology of judgement and choice mimics the methodological approach of psychologists studying memory and perception. Memory researchers are certainly aware that people's mnemonic abilities vary, just as those who study perception know that visual and auditory acuity vary. Nevertheless, the basic cognitive mechanisms underlying the mnemonic and perceptual systems are truly nomothetic. Even people with good memory, for example, find recognition easier than recall and remember words at the beginning and end of words lists better than those words in the middle. Similarly, everyone sees the illusion of apparent motion that is the foundation of the motion picture industry. Given the success of researchers studying memory and perception in identifying universal cognitive processes across people of varying abilities, it only made sense for researchers to pursue a similar nomothetic approach to the psychology of judgement and choice.

Behavioural economics embraced a nomothetic approach for slightly different reasons. The earliest proponents of the field of behavioural economics were well aware of the growing work in psychology and borrowed from it (just as psychologists borrowed back from behavioural economics). But the behavioural economic commitment to nomotheticism arises from another source as well. Early work in

---

[8] Jolls *et al*, note 1 above, 1487.

behavioural economics had, as its goal, undermining the assumption of full rationality implicit in rational choice theory. Rational choice theory itself is a nomothetic theory. It assumes everyone engages in the selfish pursuit of their own goals at all times. Rational choice allows for variance in knowledge, preferences, and abilities, but the fundamental assumption of rationality does not vary from person to person.

Given the nomothetic commitments of both cognitive psychology and of behavioural economics, it is not surprising that behavioural law and economics incorporates the assumption that people's cognitive abilities do not vary. The nomothetic assumption is not part of BLE because it is necessarily accurate, or even because it is sufficiently accurate so as to constitute a useful simplification. Rather, the nomothetic assumption is simply carried along into legal analysis as an unexamined stowaway.

Nomothetic Versus Ideograph Methodology

To see how the nomothetic assumption functions, consider a typical experiment from the cognitive psychology of judgement and choice. To demonstrate framing effects, Tversky and Kahneman presented two groups of subjects with a decision about which of two vaccines would be appropriate for combating the onset of an oncoming Asian disease.[9] One vaccine carries some probability of saving all of the potential victims, while the other vaccine will save some fraction of the potential victims for sure. Half of the subjects read a description of the problem that poses the outcomes as saving lives (the 'gain' frame) and the other half of the subjects read a description of the problem that poses the outcomes as losing lives (the 'loss' frame). Life being the mutually exclusive and exhaustive alternative to death, the problem could be described, or framed, either way. And yet the frame affects the result. When the vaccines present potential gains, 72 per cent of the subjects favoured the certain outcome of saving some lives, whereas when the vaccines present potential losses, 78 per cent of the subjects favoured the risky option.

This well-known, often criticized, and widely replicated study illustrates well the nomothetic approach implicit in Tversky and Kahneman's work.[10] They conclude that the results demonstrate the power of framing in choice, in that they show a reversal of preferences between the two decision frames. Tversky and Kahneman therefore describe the choice as a violation of the rational choice assumption that preferences are invariant. They further support this claim by reference to numerous studies that replicate their result in many contexts.

---

[9] *See* D Kahneman & A Tversky, *Choices, Values, and Frames*, 39 AM. PSYCHOLOGIST 341, 343 (1984).

[10] *See generally*, IP Levin *et al*, *A New Look at Framing Effects: Distribution of Effect Sizes, Individual Differences, and Independence of Types of Effects*, 88 ORG. BEHAV. & HUMAN DECISION PROCESSES 411 (2002) (reviewing the literature on framing).

As they state: 'The failure of invariance is both pervasive and robust.' The conclusion is indisputable, in one sense. An overwhelming majority of subjects prefer the safe option when the choices are described as a gain and the risky option when the choices are described as a loss. Were this a democratic decision, society's choice would vary with the frame.

The data suggests, however, that a change in frame would not alter the choice of all of the subjects in the Asian disease problem. Among the subjects in the gain frame, 28 per cent chose the riskier option. Presumably, these subjects would have chosen the risky option in the loss frame as well, and thus the frame did not alter their decision. Similarly, the 22 per cent of the subjects in the loss frame who chose the safe option would have chosen that option in the gain frame as well. In effect, half of the subjects were unaffected by frame. A nomothetic researcher might respond that these subjects were indeed influenced by frame, but their preferences were sufficiently strong that the frame did not alter their choice. Figure 8.1 (below) represents the nomothetic interpretation of the Asian disease problem.

Figure 8.1 assumes that people's preferences for the two options vary along a continuum, represented by the position on the abscissa. Because the choice is binary, the middle of the graph reflects a cut-off point; people with a preference that falls on the right side of the cut-off prefer the risky option while those people with a preference that falls on the left side of the cut-off prefer the certain option.

The bell curves in Figure 8.1 represent the distribution of preferences among all individuals that the two different decision frames produce. The gains frame produces a distribution of preferences that puts most of the subjects on the left side of the midpoint. Following the nomothetic interpretation of the data, altering the problem to the loss frame uniformly shifts the distribution of preferences. The distribution of preferences in the loss frame lies largely on the right side of the midpoint. The 'failure of invariance' to which Tversky and Kahneman refer is thus reflected in a shift in preferences among everyone in the population. Even though

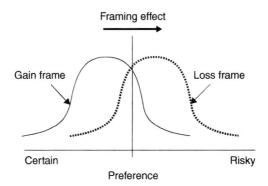

Figure 8.1. Nomothetic interpretation of vaccine problem

the framing effect influences all of the subjects' preferences, it only affects the ultimate choice of a few of the subjects.

Figure 8.2 (below) represents the ideographic interpretation of the Asian disease problem. Figure 8.2 assumes that the decision frame influences some people
heavily and some people not at all. The former group attends closely to the frame;
when the problem presents losses, they gamble, when the problem presents gains,
they embrace certainty. They vary in terms of the degree to which they like the
choice they make, but the framing effect is determinative. The latter group of subjects, by contrast, is completely indifferent to frame. They have different reactions
to the choice, but these reactions do not depend on the frame. The frame has no
hold on them.

Summing the distributions of the preferences of the two types would yield a
graph that looks exactly like Figure 8.1. That is to say, it would produce two distributions of responses to the problem—one in the loss frame and one in the gain
frame. But Figure 8.2 suggests that the data masks an important distinction. Half
of the subjects resist the cognitive trap that Tversky and Kahneman have laid and
half are so vulnerable to the trap that their vulnerability completely dictates their
choice.

The data that the Asian disease study produced does not distinguish between the
nomothetic and ideographic models of human cognition. The binary choice that
the problem demands is too clumsy. But measuring the strength of the preferences
would not help either. Such a measure would be likely to produce something like
Figure 8.1 above. If the continuous measures dovetail with the binary choice, they
would simply confirm that the frames shift preferences. As noted above, a summa-
tion of the two types of populations of subjects (those affected by frame and those
unaffected by frame) would also produce the distribution in Figure 8.1. Hence,
results consistent with Figure 8.1 do not indicate whether the subjects can be distinguished into two subtypes.

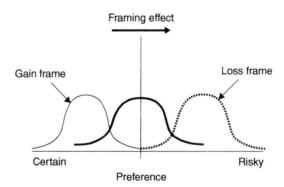

Figure 8.2. Ideographic interpretation of vaccine problem

A within-subjects design (exposing subjects to both frames and simply asking the question twice) also provides no way of distinguishing the two models. In within-subjects studies, roughly 30 per cent of the subjects express inconsistent preferences.[11] As discussed, the between-subject study suggests that half of the subjects will switch preferences. The results do not, however, suggest that 70 per cent (or even 20 per cent) of the subjects are immune from framing effects. Rather, the within-subjects problem presents a different question than the between-subjects problem. The within-subject design provides more clues to the arbitrary, and potentially misleading, aspects of the decision frame. Some of the subjects identify these clues and respond consistently. These people might well have been influenced by the decision frame had they reviewed only one of the two problems.

Distinguishing between the two approaches requires identifying some ideographic parameter that divides people into those who are affected by frame and those who are not. For example, suppose that those who are highly experienced with making public-health decisions are unaffected by frame. Such experts might each choose different vaccines, but they might be able to ignore the features of the problem that give rise to a frame. Dividing up the experts and laypersons might reveal that the frame had a decisive effect on lay judgement, but no effect on the judgment of the experts. If so, then the nomothetic model would have to be rejected as failing to recognize an important factor in the decision making process. A policy proposal founded upon data on framing gathered from laypersons but directed towards experts might be misleading.

The binary nature of the Asian disease problem makes an ideographic parameter particularly difficult to identify, and can lead to easy misinterpretation. For example, suppose that laypersons exhibit the pattern of data that Tversky and Kahneman originally documented, but that experts all embraced the certain outcome regardless of the frame. Such results could mean that experts are simply trained to embrace the certain outcome, and hence the frame has no effect on them. But such results could also indicate that experts are much more risk averse than lay persons. The distribution of expert preferences might lie so far to the left of the cut-off point that the problem would not provide an adequate test of the impact of framing on experts.

This analysis is not unique to framing. Many of the cognitive processes on which BLE scholars rely could be similarly assessed. Studies of the hindsight bias, endowment effect, contrast effects, and anchoring, typically present two variations on binary decisions. In these studies, rational choice theory makes no prediction as to the appropriate decision, other than that the answer people select should not vary by condition. By showing that people make different decisions in the two frames, the researchers reveal the influence of these psychological

[11] *See* KE Stanovich & RF West, *Individual Differences in Framing and Conjunction Effects*, 4 THINKING AND REASONING, 289, 295 (1998) (reporting that 69.2% of the subjects in a within-subjects presentation of the Asian disease problem expressed consistent preferences in the two frames).

phenomena. This methodology makes it particularly difficult to identify an individual difference.

Researchers use slightly different methods to identify phenomena such as overconfidence, representativeness, availability, hyperbolic discounting, and reciprocity. In these studies, rational choice (or deductive logic) dictates a particular answer. Deviations from that answer therefore produce the demonstration of the erroneous influence of the psychological process. Distinguishing between the two models is somewhat easier in studies in which rational choice implies a correct answer. Although such studies commonly demonstrate that a large percentage of people deviate from the predictions of rational choice theory, some people get the correct answer in these studies. This fact presents the greatest empirical challenge for the nomothetic model, particularly if the percentage of people who get the correct answer is large. The identification of a variable that predicts who gets the right answer and who does not provides simple, direct support for the ideographic model.

Individual Differences in Cognition

The nomothetic model is a sitting duck. People are likely to express enormous variation in ability to make accurate judgements and any variable that differentiates how people make judgements undermines the nomothetic model. But an identification of an ideographic parameter provides better support for the ideographic approach if the parameter arises from a coherent theory as to how it affects cognitive processes. In the absence of some theory, a scattershot of variables that sometimes predict who commits errors or interacts with the conditions in a psychological study are apt to be too spurious to be of value to legal analysis. Given the present state of research, the most likely sources of sensible theoretical parameters that might affect cognitive processes are intelligence (or cognitive ability), experience and training, or demographic factors.

Variations in Cognitive Ability

The most intuitive source of vulnerability to cognitive error is intelligence. Psychologists who study judgement and choice frequently assert that cognitive limitations force people to rely on heuristics, which in turn produce errors in judgement. If so, then people with greater cognitive abilities have less need to rely on simple heuristics and therefore might make fewer errors.[12] Deviations from the principles of deductive logic and rational choice that require the intervention of

---

[12] *See* KE Stanovich & RF West, *Individual Differences in Reasoning: Implications for the Rationality Debate?* 23 BEHAVIORAL & BRAIN SCI. 645 (2000).

the legal system might therefore only be useful for those who lack the cognitive capacity to make reasoned decisions.

Psychologists Stanovich and West have provided most of the research relating cognitive ability to cognitive error.[13] Their work suggests that people with greater cognitive ability make fewer mistakes on many kinds of problems that produce straightforward departures from deductive logic. For example, people with greater cognitive ability are less likely to commit the conjunctive fallacy (eg concluding that a severe earthquake in the United States is less likely than an earthquake in California) and are more able to solve complex problems like the Wason card-selection task (which is thought to be related to the confirmation bias—the tendency to seek out only confirmatory evidence in hypothesis testing, even when the presence or absence of disconfirming evidence would be more useful). Lower cognitive capacity thereby implicates a cognitive error that marketers commonly try to trigger. Marketers, particularly of pharmaceuticals, often present confirmatory evidence as to the benefits of their product. For example, pain reliever advertisements routinely feature testimonials by those who consumed an analgesic and reported that their pain disappeared. Such evidence is only half of the story, because it reveals nothing about the relative benefits of the product to other analgesics or to taking nothing.

The data on base rate neglect, however, reveals the relationship between cognitive capacity and cognitive errors to be ambiguous. Smarter people are a little more likely to attend to statistical base rates in favor of vivid, salient exemplars (eg using Consumer Reports as opposed to an anecdote by a friend), but only when the base rates identify a causal connection between the information and the category. Intelligence has no effect on performance on problems involving non-causal, or diagnostic, base rates (such as the rare disease problem). The logical structure of Bayesian problems does not depend on whether the evidence is causal or merely diagnostic, and so it is unclear why intelligence should matter in some circumstances but not others.

These results suggest that the influence of cognitive capacity on ability to avoid error will be highly contextual and hard to explain. Stanovich and West have offered a rough account of the mixed evidence on base rates. They argue that when approaching decision making problems that involve base rates, people first try to identify the logical structure, and if they cannot, they follow instincts, which might be misleading. A decision maker with greater cognitive abilities is more likely to identify cues embedded within the problem that reveal the deductive structure. Diagnostic, non-causal base rates present an extremely difficult problem with few internal cues as to the correct resolution, and so greater cognitive capacity is of no help. Determining which problems embed cues that would be useful to smarter people is a messy empirical task. Even if smarter people

---

[13] *See id.* (This article summarizes the results I discuss in this section).

sometimes avoid mistakes of deductive logic in some settings, policy makers might be unable to identify these settings.

Furthermore, greater cognitive capacity seems to produce greater overconfidence in judgement. Theoretically, this makes some sense because of the way that the cognitive mechanism underlying overconfidence operates. After making a judgement, people generally try mentally to generate justifications for their judgement. Reasons that the judgement might be wrong seem to fade after a choice has been made. It is thus a faulty decision making style that produces overconfidence. People with better memory, or who can process information more quickly, will be better able to marshal support for their beliefs. Even as greater cognitive capacity allows people to identify clues to the logical structures of some problems, it promotes too much faith in one's abilities. Having intelligence is not the same as having the wisdom to recognize that one's greater abilities have been put in the service of a defective decision making style.

Other cognitive phenomena are unlikely to be affected by cognitive capacity. Although some evidence suggests that greater cognitive capacity immunizes people against framing effects, the evidence is all from within-subject experimental designs.[14] In the within-subject design, people with greater cognitive capacity are better able to identify the similarities of the two versions. In between-subject designs, it is unclear how cognitive capacity would be helpful. In the examples that illustrate framing effects, no correct decision can be identified; the certain outcome is usually as defensible a choice as the uncertain outcome. The effect arises from psychometric and associational aspects of risky decisions. Just as people are more sensitive to changes in physical properties of the world than to absolute levels of physical stimuli (illumination, sound, smell), so too are people more sensitive to changes in wealth or risk than to absolute levels of wealth. Losses also trigger different associations than gains. Because cognitive limitations do not produce framing effects, cognitive abilities should not correlate with the expression of framing effects.[15]

Cognitive ability is thus no panacea for avoiding cognitive errors. Smart people seem to have greater ability to identify cues to the underling structure of some logical problems, but they remain vulnerable to errors. The positive correlation between intelligence and overconfidence also suggests that smart people are even more vulnerable to cognitive errors outside the lab because they will be less aware of the need to be cautious in trusting their own judgement. Cognitive capacity also seems completely irrelevant to other cognitive phenomena. Given the erratic nature of the limited protection from cognitive error that cognitive capacity provides, it presents a poor basis for legal policy.

---

[14] Stanovich & West, n 11 above, 295–6.

[15] *See also* AF Simon, NS Fagley & J Hallern, *Decision Framing: Moderating Effects of Individual Differences and Cognitive Process*, 17 J. BEHAVIORAL DECISION MAKING 77 (2004) (demonstrating that those who are both high in a personality measure that psychologists refer to as 'need for cognition' and have high mathematical abilities show no framing effects).

Variations in Training or Education

People can be taught to make better decisions. Research on judgement and choice has always included a large number of studies devoted to identifying 'debiasing' techniques or ways of avoiding bad judgement. Self-serving biases can be eliminated by forcing individuals to identify the weaknesses in their own arguments.[16] Imagining that alternative outcomes could have occurred and identifying explanations for how these outcomes might have occurred can reduce the hindsight bias and related phenomena.[17] Highly invasive strategies such as drawing out 'fault trees' or identifying and assigning probabilities to causal pathways can sharpen probability estimates.[18] Overconfidence can likewise be overcome by thinking about the problem in a frequentist (eg, 7 out of 10) rather than a subjective (eg 70 per cent), probability format.[19]

Learning a debiasing strategy, however, is not sufficient to ensure that people will make good judgements. Training people to use a debiasing technique will not improve judgement unless people learn, either through training or experience, when to rely on these techniques. Indeed, research on experienced decision makers provides numerous instances in which experienced professionals exhibit a range of vulnerability to cognitive errors. Studies of accountants, lawyers, judges, real-estate brokers, securities analysts, mental health professionals, and futures traders have revealed them all to be vulnerable to committing cognitive errors, even on questions within the domain of their expertise.[20] Thus, experience and training, by themselves, do not constitute an ideographic parameter that insulates people from cognitive error. But certain kinds of experience and training might produce people who avoid cognitive errors in judgement. Meteorologists, for example, give well-calibrated estimates for the likelihood of rain and snow.[21] A recent study of insurance claims adjusters also finds them to be able to avoid framing effects.[22]

Some characteristics of certain experience demonstrates why it does not produce unbiased decision making. The cost of cognitive errors is often low, or hard

---

[16] *See eg*, L Babcock, G Loewenstein & S Issacharoff, *Creating Convergence: Debiasing Biased Litigants*, 22 LAW & SOCIAL INQUIRY 913 (1998) (describing debiasing procedures against self-serving biases).

[17] *See eg*, P Slovic & B Fischhoff, *On the Psychology of Experimental Surprises*, 3 J. EXPERIMENTAL PSYCHOL.: HUM. PERCEPTION & PERFORMANCE 544, 549 (1977).

[18] *See eg*, B. Fischhoff *et al*, *Fault Trees: Sensitivity of Estimated Failure Probabilities to Performance Representation*, 4 J. EXPERIMENTAL PSYCHOL.: HUM. PERCEPTION & PERFORMANCE 349 (1978).

[19] *See eg*, G Gigerenzer, *How to Make Cognitive Illusions Disappear: Beyond 'Heuristics and Biases'*, 2 EUR. REV. SOC. PSYCHOL. 83 (1991).

[20] *See* C Guthrie, JJ Rachlinski & AJ Wistrich, *Inside the Judicial Mind*, 86 CORNELL L. REV. 777, 782–3 (2001) (summarizing this literature).

[21] *See* AH Murphy & RL Winkler, *Probability Forecasting in Meteorology*, 79 J. AM. STATISTICAL ASS'N, 489 (1984).

[22] JJ Rachlinski & C Guthrie, Heuristics and Biases Among Expert Negotiators (Draft available).

to identify. Lawyers who are influenced by framing effects in evaluating settlement offers, for example, will often give their clients advice that will hurt the clients, but further the goals of the attorney. Specifically, if defence attorneys, with clients who face losses, give risk-seeking advice about settlement, then the client will spend more on billable hours than if the advice is risk neutral. Although one might expect the market to drive out errors among experienced participants (or drive out participants who make errors), the marketplace for professional services is apt to be quite inefficient at doing so. The feedback necessary for individuals to identify mistakes is often lacking. Continuing with the example of attorneys and settling civil litigation, they almost always settle cases, thereby only rarely getting a true indication of how a judge and jury would have decided the case. Because no attorney gets such feedback, it is hard to see how market forces would drive erroneous judgement out of the profession.

Training is also an unreliable means of avoiding cognitive errors in judgement. In most professions, people are trained in the jargon and skill necessary to understand the profession, but are not necessarily given training specifically in making the kind of decisions that members of the profession have to make. Thus, even though some psychologists have argued that certain types of reasoning can be taught quickly and easily,[23] such training is extremely rare. Generalized training that allows people to avoid a wide range of cognitive errors also seems unavailable. One study of the effects of graduate-level training in various disciplines revealed that medical training and training in the hard sciences conferred no immunity to common errors of statistical reasoning.[24] Although training in social sciences (and ironically in law) produced some improvement in reasoning, the benefits were limited.

Even when training and experience improve judgement, the improvement might be exceptionally context specific. One study of insurance executives demonstrated that although they demonstrated some resistance to the conjunction fallacy, the resistance depended upon direct experience with a precise context.[25] Thus, reinsurance executives resisted the conjunction fallacy when estimating the likelihood that the United States would be hit by a damaging hurricane (an event with which they had tremendous experience), but they fell prey to the error when estimating the likelihood that the United States would be hit by a devastating terrorist attack (the study was conducted before 9/11). Insurance executives (from Missouri) studied over a year after 9/11 displayed the opposite pattern, presumably because they lacked experience with hurricanes, but had given enormous thought to the experience of 9/11. Even though the structure of the logical error is identical in all four parts of the study, the ability to avoid the conjunction fallacy depended upon having had direct experience with the risk. The results do not show a general ability to avoid the error.

[23] P Sedlmeier & G Gigerenzer, *Teaching Bayesian Reasoning in Less Than Two Hours*, 130 J. Exper. Psychol. General 380 (2001).
[24] DR Lehman, RO Lempert & RE Nisbett, *The Effects of Graduate Training on Reasoning*, 43 Am. Psychologist 431, 440 (1988).   [25] Rachlinski & Guthrie, n 22 above.

The task-specific nature of the effects of training and experience make it unlikely that these variables represent ideographic parameters that would easily mark those who are immune from cognitive error. Successful debiasing procedures are incredibly invasive and often only partly successful, good feedback is rare, overconfidence hides the awareness that debiasing is necessary, biases are often costless and sometimes even economically beneficial, and debiasing strategies seem highly context specific.

Demographic Factors

Easily identifiable demographic parameters, such as race, sex, and age might all correlate with cognitive error. Large differences in cognitive vulnerabilities along race or gender lines would have significant implications for legal analysis. Marketers would be able to target these sub-groups and policy makers would have to consider carefully how to address these differences. Demographic differences in cognitive ability are also among the most highly studied and highly contested areas of social science inquiry. But, as noted above, variations in cognitive ability do not readily translate into differential vulnerability to cognitive errors. Studies of differential vulnerability to cognitive error by demographic factors are extremely rare.

The research on sex differences in judgement is typical of the state of scholarship. Several studies suggest that women make more risk-averse choices than men.[26] While these results suggest that men and women view risk differently, they do not indicate a differential susceptibility to cognitive error. In reference to Figures 8.1 and 8.2, gender might give some indication as to where on the continuum an individual falls, but does not help to distinguish the two different models that the figures represent. Much the same can be said for the research on cultural differences. The research indicates that people from collectivist cultures are more willing to undertake risky gambles.[27] Researchers believe this tendency results because people from collective cultures have a strong norm of sharing benefits and risks, thereby allowing them to behave in a fashion that more closely approximates risk neutrality. As with gender, however, even though people from different cultures express different risk preferences, they do not necessarily express any real differential vulnerability to cognitive error.

Research on collective versus individualist cultures has produced some limited evidence of differential vulnerability to cognitive errors. Whereas people in Western, individualistic cultures excessively attribute human behaviour to stable personality traits—a phenomenon known as the fundamental attribution error—people

---

[26] *See* VL Bajtelsmit, A Bernasek & N Jianakopolos, *Gender Differences in Defined Contribution Pension Decisions*, 8 FINANCIAL SERVICES REV. 1 (1999); R Schubert *et al*, *Financial Decision-Making: Are Women Really More Risk-Averse?* 89 AMERICAN ECON. REV. 381 (1999).

[27] EU Weber & C Hsee, *Cross-Cultural Differences in Risk Perception, But Cross-Cultural Similarities in Attitudes Towards Perceived Risk*, 44 MANAGEMENT SCI. 1205 (1999).

from more collective societies avoid this error.[28] Self-esteem among people from collective cultures is also more closely bound up with group, rather than individual, achievement. Collectivism is no panacea for good judgement, however. Curiously, people from collective cultures exhibit greater overconfidence in judgement.[29]

Taken together, this research suggests that people from different cultures have different risk preferences. Further research in the United States echoes this conclusion. People in the United States who are white and male tend to be less concerned about environmental risks than people who are black and female.[30] The groups are reversed on other kinds of risks, such as those posed by abortions, thereby suggesting that deeper cultural beliefs underlie these differences. These demographic variations do not correspond to differential vulnerability to cognitive error; at least, not without knowing which groups are over- or under-reacting to risk (or whether they truly face different risks). Still, these results represent significant individual variation that might be of importance to law and policy. People who believe they face more serious risks are apt to demand different programmes from the government, behave differently as jurors (or judges), and respond differently to legal rules governing the allocation of risk. Furthermore, marketers might be able to take advantage of differential risk preferences. Advertising and marketing strategies that concern risky behaviour (including financial decisions) are commonly directed carefully at specific demographic segments.

Individual variations in vulnerability to cognitive errors in smaller groups might also be common. Although researchers in judgement and choice often do not study social behaviour, imitation of trusted peers is one of the most common responses to uncertain situations. People who are uncertain about how to assess the complexities of such choices as how to finance the purchase of an automobile (lease or buy), the choice of a health-care plan (HMO or PPO), or whether to take social security benefits early are apt to rely heavily on the choices made by trusted others. One might describe this in terms of an imitation heuristic. Such a heuristic might leave whole communities vulnerable to certain kinds of cognitive mistakes. Indeed, marketers target particular communities for costly financing schemes such as rent to own or tax rebate advances in large measure because some communities seem willing to embrace such schemes. Choices about flood insurance likewise are more sensitive to social contagion effects than to rational perception of actual risk (or even to informational campaigns or subsidies).[31]

---

[28] MW Morris & K Peng, *Culture and Cause: American and Chinese Attributions for Social and Physical Events*, 67 J. PERSONALITY & SOC. PSYCHOL. 949 (1994).

[29] *See* JF Yates, J-W Lee & JG Bush, *General Knowledge Overconfidence: Cross-National Variations, Response Style, and 'Reality'*, 70 ORGANIZATIONAL BEHAVIOR & HUMAN DECISION PROCESSES 87 (1997) (reviewing evidence of greater overconfidence among Asians).

[30] *See* D Kahan *et al*, Gender, Race & Risk Perception: The Influence of Cultural Status Anxiety (unpublished manuscript) (reviewing this literature).

[31] *See* J Gerson, Strategy and Cognition: Regulating Catastrophic Risk (unpublished manuscript).

Conclusion

Supporters of the nomothetic model face real challenges from the evidence of individual variation in vulnerability to cognitive error. It is clear that individual variations exist. Nevertheless, for the purposes of law and policy, the nomothetic model might well be sufficiently accurate that it should be accepted as a reasonable approximation. The circumstances in which intelligence, experience, and training matter seem too contextual to represent a solid foundation for policy making. Ironically, this is much the same argument that is often made by devoted proponents of rational choice theory in response to evidence of cognitive errors in judgment—that they are erratic, undetectable, and sufficiently small that they can be neglected. Demographic factors, however, might represent a notable exception, even though most of the data reflects different underlying preferences and not differential vulnerability to cognitive error.

Implications of the Ideographic Model for Law

Replacing the nomothetic assumption with an ideographic model of cognitive errors has two basic implications for law. First, it somewhat alters several common arguments that cognitive psychology supports paternalism. The presence of significant individual variation in vulnerability to cognitive error suggests that the law needs to attend more closely to individual variations in cognitive ability, and perhaps craft legal rules that sort individuals more carefully. Secondly, it casts new light on how marketers behave, and casts suspicion on marketing practices that are designed to play on the cognitive errors of individuals.

The Costs of Paternalism

The most common use of cognitive psychology in legal scholarship is to support paternalistic legal interventions. It stands to reason that if individuals make predictable cognitive errors, then they can be protected from the consequences of these errors. Such arguments have been made to support: an expansion of strict liability in tort, more aggressive use of the unconscionability doctrine in contract law, tighter restrictions on the marketing of securities, mandatory health and safety rules in the workplace, the imposition of non-waivable (or difficult to waive) contract terms, and greater restrictions on access to credit (among others). Inevitably, paternalism comes at a price. It creates costly enforcement regimes and imposes choices on people who, even holding the influence of cognitive error aside, would prefer a different alternative than the one that the law mandates.

Take the framing problem as an example. Suppose that the choice being made were an individual choice about a treatment, rather than a collective one as a public-health official concerning a vaccine. (Maybe the treatment choices involve years of life added for sure or a probability of more years or no years.) Suppose also that unbiased officials believed that most people would be better off with the certain treatment, although some could sensibly prefer the risky treatment. In effect, the 'correct' distribution of choice might reflect the distribution of the gains frame in Figure 8.1. But further suppose that people often see the choice from the perspective of losses. Most choose the risky treatment, even though an unbiased observer would conclude that most should prefer the safe treatment. Framing can be blamed for the mistaken choice, rather than this being a true reflection of unbiased preferences. Hence, public-health officials might consider refusing to allow anyone to choose the risky treatment. Because most unbiased patients would choose the safe treatment, this mandate might improve social welfare. Under the mandate only one-quarter of patients get the 'wrong' treatment, while under the loss frame, fully half of the patients choose the wrong treatment.

The ideographic model does not change this analysis—not yet. If Figure 8.2 accurately depicts how the choice is being made, then the mandate still has the same effect. In the absence of the mandate, half of the patients are immune from framing and they choose treatments appropriate for them. The other half are affected heavily by framing (more so than in the nomothetic model) and half of them choose the wrong option, solely because of the frame. These people can be saved from their unwise choice by the mandate, but only by imposing the wrong choice on the quarter of patients who properly choose the risky treatment and who are not affected by frame.

The ideographic approach raises the possibility that those who are not being affected by frame can be identified and offered free reign to select their own treatment options. If the ideographic parameter that marks them can be easily observed, then there is little reason to impose the wrong choice on those who are immune from the cognitive error. Examples of sorting methods like this in law are rare. Securities regulation includes a few examples in which 'qualified' investors are offered choices that others are not. Tort law contains a few examples involving experienced parties who assume risk. The law of unconscionability in contract also gives weight to the experience of the contracting party.

Even though the law thus seems to recognize that ideographic parameters should be used to limit paternalistic inclinations, the law relies on the wrong variables. The key ideographic parameter the law uses is experience. Those who have experience with an activity are said to assume the risks of the activity—those with experience in an industry are thought to be less vulnerable to unconscionable contractual terms. As noted above, however, experience is an unreliable indicator of good judgment. The common law has seized upon an intuitive, but unreliable, ideographic factor.

Arguably, an ideographic model supports weak paternalism in which the law does not prohibit choice, but alters the context in which people make decisions. In the framing example, the dominant solution would perhaps entail inducing everyone to see the problem from a gains perspective (assuming the risk-aversion it induces to be sensible). Altering the default rule would be one way of accomplishing this. Under the nomothetic model, such a change eliminates the unwanted influence of framing that induces half of the patients to make the risky choice when they should make the certain choice. Under the ideographic model, all of those affected by the frame switch to the safe choice and those who are not affected are, well, not affected. This is the analysis that leads Camerer and his colleagues to argue forcefully for this soft form of paternalism.[32] It makes no one worse off and some better off. To the extent that switching the default rule is costly, this cost is needlessly imposed on those who are not vulnerable to the cognitive error.

Targeted Marketing

The ideographic model casts a new light on the behaviour of marketers. Although efforts by marketers to segregate consumers can have legitimate and socially useful ends, the ideographic model also suggests that marketing might be designed to identify consumers who are vulnerable to committing cognitive errors.

Legal scholars who rely on psychology have largely argued that marketing has socially undesirable properties. Led largely by Professor Jon Hanson, many legal scholars contend that marketing represents an effort to dupe consumers into ignoring undesirable aspects of products.[33] According to this work, marketing targets cognitive vulnerabilities. The theory has conceptual and many pragmatic problems,[34] but is appealing in its simplicity. Marketers face a bewildering array of cognitive biases in consumers that point in many directions, but marketers need not sort them out. All they need to do is tinker with their advertising until they sell more product. In Professor Hanson's view, this will occur when the marketing hits upon a strategy that hides dangers that the product poses. Marketers thus need not understand the psychological research in order to take advantage of cognitive vulnerabilities in consumers.

Hanson's model is basically nomothetic, but an ideographic approach provides another dimension supporting his argument. Marketers need not truly understand whether the cognitive vulnerabilities that sell their products affect all or some of their potential customers, although they should be sensitive to the variations in consumer cognition. Observable ideographic parameters that mark highly vulnerable individuals can help marketers to direct their campaigns. Just as they need not understand the basic cognitive mechanisms that induce consumers

---

[32] Camerer *et al*, n 1 above.

[33] JD Hanson & DA Kysar, *Taking Behavioralism Seriously: The Problem of Market Manipulation*, 74 N.Y.U. L. REV. 630, 715 (1999); JD Hanson & DA Kysar, *Taking Behavioralism Seriously: Some Evidence of Market Manipulation*, 112 HARV. L. REV. 1420 (1999).

[34] *See* JA Henderson, Jr & JJ Rachlinski, *Product-Related Risk and Cognitive Biases: The Shortcomings of Enterprise Liability*, 6 ROGER WILLIAMS U. L. REV. 213 (2000).

to misunderstand the risks of products, they need not understand the theoretical underpinnings of why certain individuals are vulnerable to cognitive errors while others are not. All that marketers need do is monitor the demographics of who is exposed to their advertisements and who buys their products.

Efforts to exploit the cognitive vulnerabilities of certain sub-groups of consumers differ in character from other efforts to segregate markets through price discrimination. Price discrimination usually consists of an effort to identify consumers who value a product more highly than other consumers. Identifying cognitive vulnerabilities, however, consists of an effort to find consumers who probably should not engage in the transaction and induce them to do so by exploiting cognitive errors that they are apt to make. As one example, a recent paper by Jonathan Klick argues that many businesses use standard-form contracts as a way of price discriminating.[35] He contends that those consumers most interested in the terms covered by the forms negotiate these terms, while most consumers do not. However plausible this story,[36] it is not clear whether the small minority of consumers are really those who value variations from the boilerplate more than the rest or whether those consumers are just the minority who are not affected by cognitive errors that plague the rest of the population. Similarly, the variations in the financing of home appliances in different communities might well reflect cognitive vulnerabilities, rather than fixed preferences or variations in the creditworthiness of people in the communities.

Price discrimination might well be a benign, or even socially useful aspect of the economy. But the ideographic model suggests that it might instead constitute evidence of efforts to exploit cognitive vulnerability. The difficulty of distinguishing sensible price discrimination from cognitive exploitation might make regulatory intervention to curtail segmented marketing strategies challenging, or even unwise. An ideographic perspective might, at least, cast suspicion on segmented marketing efforts.

Distinguishing between the nomothetic and ideographic models of cognitive error is methodologically challenging. Evidence that identifies clear ideographic parameters that identify cognitive vulnerability are sufficiently rare that it is not surprising that most legal scholars who consume psychological research have embraced the nomothetic model. Still, an ideographic model is apt to be superior in some circumstances. Marketers will identify ideographic parameters, even if law-makers do not. Individual differences in cognitive error cannot be wholly ignored.

---

[35] J Klick, *The Micro Foundations of Standard Form Contracts: Price Discrimination vs. Behavioral Bias*, 32 FLA. ST. L. REV. (forthcoming, 2005).

[36] *See* R Korobkin, *Possibility and Plausibility in Law and Economics*, 32 FLA. ST. L. REV. (forthcoming, 2005) (suggesting that it is implausible).

9

Developmentally Appropriate Interview Techniques

Michael E Lamb and Anneli S Larsson[1]

Alleged victims of child abuse are often the only sources of information about the crimes by which they have been victimized. This places them in the role of experts when conversing about their experiences. Although there are clear developmental deficiencies in memory, communication skills, and social style that have long fed scepticism about the reliability or accuracy of child witnesses, a considerable body of research now demonstrates that children's informativeness in such conversations is profoundly shaped not only by the children's capacity but also by the behaviours and practices of their interviewers. Specifically, when interviewers conduct developmentally appropriate interviews with children, they help children to become competent informants about their experiences. Because young children tend to remember less information and provide briefer accounts of their experiences than older children do, it is particularly (but not exclusively) important for interviewers to recognize children's strengths and limitations when interviewing them (see Lamb, Orbach, Warren, Esplin, and Hershkowitz, 2006; Pipe, Lamb, Orbach, and Esplin, 2004). Our goal in this paper is to summarize current understanding of developmental factors that affect children's ability to provide accurate information about events they have experienced. Specifically, we will discuss what can be remembered about such experiences, how this information can be retrieved, and how it can be communicated or conveyed more effectively. Communicative success depends on how well children understand their role in the interviews and how effectively interviewers can take advantage of children's competences and abilities to help them recount past experiences accurately and maximize their performances.

[1] Correspondence should be addressed to Professor Michael Lamb at the Faculty of Social and Political Sciences, University of Cambridge, Free School Lane, Cambridge CB2 3RQ, United Kingdom. Phone: +44(0)1223 334523. Fax: +44(0)1223 334550. E-mail: mel37@cam.ac.uk

Memory

In the late 1970s and early 1980s, researchers began to focus on children's memory for events in which they had been participants or witnesses. The general finding was that, as children grow older, the length, informativeness, and complexity of their recall increase (see Fivush, 1997, 1998; Poole and Lamb, 1998; Saywitz and Camparo, 1998; Schneider and Pressley, 1997). It is also well established that even very young children can provide temporally organized and coherent narratives (eg Flin, Boon, Knox, and Bull, 1992). Although young children tend to provide briefer free narrative accounts of their experiences than do older children and adults, these accounts are generally quite accurate (eg Goodman and Reed, 1986; Lamb *et al*, 2006). As time passes, both children and adults forget, however. Making errors of omission is much more common than errors of commission among both adults and children. These errors are a special problem where children are concerned because their accounts, especially their recall narratives, are often so brief.

Early research on memory development also highlighted the tendency for children to form general event representations, or scripts, of typical events instead of remembering particular incidents when similar events were repeatedly experienced. Memories serve to facilitate predictions about the future and, as a rule, repeated experiences permit better predictions than experiences that happened only once. As a result, children are particularly attuned from an early age to 'what usually happens' (see Pipe *et al*, 2004). Several researchers have examined factors affecting the ability to report specific single experiences from a sequence of repeated similar experiences without confusing them (see Roberts, 2002; Roberts and Powell, 2001). Findings from such studies indicate that children can maintain accurate memories of what happened even though they may confuse episodes and not remember accurately when or as part of which specific occasion something happened. Such migration of details across episodes and confusion regarding source are more likely among younger than older children, particularly over time. Also, the tendency to make script-related confusions generally declines with age and children are less likely to make source errors when asked for open-ended, free recall accounts than when asked specific questions (Roberts and Powell, 2001).

Results from analogue studies indicate that, with older children, but not with three- to four-year-olds, it can be helpful to ask explicitly whether they are describing something they saw (or experienced) as opposed to something that someone told them about (see Roberts, 2002; Roberts and Powell, 2001). Several researchers have attempted to improve children's source monitoring performance and their ability to recall specific experienced events accurately and without intrusion of information from other similar experiences. Moreover, repeatedly recalling seen and imagined objects without regard to their source leads adults to be more confused and to make more source monitoring errors in subsequent memory tests. This appears to be true of children, too (see Pipe *et al*, 2004).

In memory, the distinction between recall and recognition is crucial. When adults and children are asked to describe events from free recall ('Tell me everything you remember . . .'), their accounts may be brief and sketchy, but are more likely to be accurate. When asked for more details using open-ended free-recall (eg 'Tell me more about that' or 'And then what happened?') or recall (eg 'When did that happen?') prompts, children often recall additional details, although younger children often retrieve relatively few. When interviewers prompt with focused questions such as 'Did he have a beard?' or 'Did this happen in the day or in the night?' however, they shift from recall to recognition testing, and the probability of error rises. Recall memories are not always accurate, of course, especially when children feel pressure to provide information of which they are unsure. Nonetheless, accounts based on open-ended questions are much more likely to be accurate than those elicited from the child using recognition cues or prompts, because they activate recall memory. Most focused questions, in contrast, activate recognition memory, focus respondents on domains of interest to the investigator, and exert greater pressure to respond or agree with the interviewer, whether or not the respondents are sure of the response. Recognition probes are also more likely to elicit erroneous responses in eyewitness contexts because of response biases (ie tendencies to say 'yes' or 'no' without reflection) and false recognition of details that were only mentioned in previous interviews or are inferred from the gist of the experienced events (eg Brainerd and Reyna, 1996).

Young children, especially pre-schoolers, are more likely than older children to respond erroneously to suggestive questions about their experiences and to select erroneous options when responding to forced choice questions. Regardless of age, responses to open-ended questions are more likely to be accurate than responses to more focused questions. The risk for interviewer contamination during children's recall thus increases the more specific the questions that the interviewer asks. This was considered when researchers at the National Institute of Child Health and Human Development (NICHD) sought to categorize types of interviewer utterances: open-ended invitations, cued invitations, directives, option-posing prompts, and suggestive prompts (Lamb *et al*, 1996). Open-ended invitations are defined as memory prompts that elicit free-recall responses from children using very general invitations (eg 'Tell me what happened'; 'Then what happened?'). Cued invitations are more specific invitations that prompt children's free recall by referring to details already mentioned by the child (eg 'Tell me about the touching', when touching was previously mentioned by the child). Directives prompt children to provide more information about previously mentioned details using 'wh'- questions (eg 'Where did he touch you?' when the child had mentioned that he/she was touched). Option-posing questions, such as yes-no and forced-choice questions, prompt children for information not previously mentioned by them in ways that did not imply expected responses (eg 'Did he touch you?'). Suggestive questions presuppose information not mentioned by the child (eg 'Did he touch you over or under your clothes?' when the child had not mentioned any touching), imply expected responses (eg He forced you to do that, didn't he?'), or invite the child to speculate about what could have happened (Thierry, Lamb, Orbach, and Pipe, 2005).

Although long delays in memory are typically associated with forgetting, this is not always the case. Just how well children remember and recount particular experiences depends on a number of interacting variables. In the past, forensic professionals often dismissed the relevance of experimental research on children's memory by arguing that, for example, the stressful nature of sexual abuse makes memories thereof distinctly different. Considerable controversy persists in the literature concerning the effects of increased arousal or stress on the accuracy of children's memory. It is unclear whether memories for traumatic experiences involve unique mechanisms or can be accounted for by the same mechanisms that affect memories of other events (ie salience) (eg Cordon, Pipe, Sayfan, Melinder, and Goodman, 2004). It is well established that traumatic experiences often are distinctive, however, so memories thereof might be retained over time better than memories of less distinctive or meaningful events (see Howe, 1997, 2000).

Whether or not special mechanisms are involved, however, real-world events such as child abuse may not necessarily be better remembered than memories of events or stimuli studied in the laboratory. First of all, not all incidents of sexual abuse are painful or traumatic, and thus the potentially facilitative effects of arousal and salience cannot be assumed. Relatedly, children's ignorance or misunderstanding of sexual events may make some abusive experiences even less memorable. Secondly, stress may affect different types of memory encoding and retrieval (eg recall, recognition, and reconstructive memory) in different ways. The context in which children are asked to retrieve information about the experienced event— during interviews with child protection service workers, policemen, attorneys, or judges—may be stressful regardless of whether or not the target events were (Goodman *et al*, 1992). Thirdly, whether the event involves shame, perceived responsibility, embarrassment, or guilt, and whether, in turn, it is talked about, reflected on, kept secret, or even negated, may all affect how experiences of abuse or trauma are remembered and recalled over time. Overall, although salience generally affects the memorability of experienced events, we cannot presume that instances of abuse will always be salient and thus easy to remember.

In summary, children can remember and recall experiences, sometimes over long time periods, and this is especially likely when the experience was highly distinctive, as is frequently (although not always) the case with distressing and traumatic experiences. Recalling one of several similar experiences may be particularly difficult, however, and details are likely to be confused across episodes. Accuracy can be enhanced when children successfully focus on individual events, although confusions among episodes do not necessarily cast doubt on the accuracy or credibility of child witnesses.

Communication

Young children often do not articulate individual sounds consistently even after they seem to have mastered them, so it is not uncommon for interviewers to misunderstand children, especially pre-schoolers. The vocabularies of young children are also much more limited and less descriptive than those of adults (eg de Villiers and de Villiers, 1999), although they are clearly able to describe their experiences well when given the chance to do so. Misunderstandings also occur because children's rapid vocabulary growth often leads adults to overestimate their linguistic capacities. Despite their apparent maturity, young children, especially pre-schoolers, frequently use words before they know their conventional adult meaning, they may even use words that they do not understand at all, and they may understand poorly some apparently simple concepts, such as 'any', 'some', 'touch', 'yesterday', and 'before' (eg Walker, 1994).

In the process of learning words and the rules for combining words into sentences, children are also learning how to participate in conversations. They must learn how to stay on topic, how to adapt their speech appropriately to different audiences (eg a 'strange' interviewer who does not know their family members and was not present for the event in question), and how to structure coherent narratives about past events (Warren and McCloskey, 1997). The challenge confronting investigators is to encourage and help children to provide organized accounts that are rich in descriptive detail.

Unfortunately, systematic analyses show that inappropriate questioning strategies characterize the vast majority of forensic interviews (eg Lamb *et al*, 1996; Sternberg, Lamb, Davies, and Westcott, 2001; Warren *et al*, 1996). Indeed, years of analysing forensic interviews have led many researchers to question widespread assumptions about children's linguistic inabilities and to focus more on the competence, perspective-taking abilities, and linguistic styles of investigators (Pipe *et al*, 2004). The more impoverished the children's language, the greater the likelihood that their statements will be misinterpreted or that children will misinterpret the interviewers' questions and purposes. When interviewers misrepresent what children say, furthermore, they are seldom corrected, and thus the mistakes, rather than the correct information, may be reported later in the interview (Roberts and Lamb, 1999). Moreover, children are often asked to negate adult statements or to confirm multifaceted 'summaries' of their accounts (eg 'Is it not true that . . . ?'), and expected to understand unfamiliar words and syntactically complex or ambiguous compound sentences (eg Saywitz, 1988).

Children's accounts of abusive experiences are also influenced by social or pragmatic aspects of communication. For example, when asked questions such as 'Do you remember his name?' or 'Do you know why you are here today?', 'Can you show me where he touched you?', older children usually read between the lines and provide the desired information, whereas younger children may simply answer 'Yes' or 'No' (Walker and Warren, 1995, Warren *et al*, 1996). Young witnesses are typically unaware of the amount and type of information being sought by forensic investigators and are thus unaccustomed to being viewed as informants rather than novices being tested about the quality of their knowledge. The richness of children's accounts of experienced incidents of abuse is also influenced by the interrogatory style modelled in brief introductory segments of the interview, and a single carefully worded prompt could elicit so much information from children (Lamb *et al*, 2006). As a result, interviewers need to communicate their needs and expectations clearly, motivating children to provide as much information as they can.

Findings reported by Sternberg, Lamb, Hershkowitz, Yudilevitch, Orbach, Esplin, and Hovav (1997) are consistent with the results of laboratory analogue studies suggesting that motivational and contextual factors play an important role in shaping children's reports of experienced events. Specifically, Sternberg *et al* showed that children provided many more details in response to an initial open-ended prompt about the event being investigated when previously 'trained' to produce detailed responses to the interviewers' questions. They thus showed that, even in authentic forensic interviews, it is possible to entrain response styles that enhance the richness of information provided by children by affording them an opportunity to practise providing detailed narrative accounts of experienced events and by reinforcing this style in the pre-substantive portion of the interviews. Richly detailed accounts of abusive events facilitate the more effective investigation of crimes and provide child protection workers with more information upon which to base their evaluations. The results of this study also highlight the value of having interviewers clearly communicate their expectations concerning the child's role. Indeed, it is crucial for adults to recognize the effects of perceived roles in an interview situation. A successful interviewer should also understand children's communicative powers and acknowledge the unambiguous difference between children's *abilities* and their *performances*. In fact, the interviewer can affect the child's level of performance by changing her or his own behaviour—despite the child's abilities.

One technique that has been designed to overcome children's cognitive limitations and help them to recount past experiences more fully is the Narrative Elaboration Technique (NET) (Saywitz and Snyder, 1996; Saywitz, Snyder, and Lamphear, 1996). This technique involves pre-interview modelling, practice, and feedback about the kinds of information needed by the listener. Children are also trained to use cue cards as reminders of what to talk about (the participants, the setting, actions, conversation and affect associated with the event). In analog contexts, the NET has been found to help children provide more complete and equivalently accurate event reports (eg Brown and Pipe, 2003a, 2003b; Dorado and Saywitz, 2001).

Most adults are aware that children are often quiet with strangers and recognize the need to establish rapport when initiating interaction with an unfamiliar child, especially when the topics are stressful or embarrassing. Although it seems intuitively obvious that rapport-building is critically important, we actually know very little about how much and what kind of rapport-building is necessary or effective, and almost nothing about how rapport-building needs may differ depending on the age and other characteristics of the children interviewed. Surprisingly, few researchers have examined different kinds of rapport-building techniques or compared interviews with and without attempts to build rapport. Field research has found that rapport-building using open-ended questions (invitations) about the child's everyday life and a particular past event (such as a recent birthday or holiday) helped interviewers to elicit more abuse-relevant information than did closed-ended specific rapport-building questions (Sternberg *et al*, 1997).

Forensic interviewers are routinely encouraged to establish rapport with alleged victims before seeking to elicit information about the suspected incidents of abuse. Despite this consensus, many forensic interviewers fail to make more than perfunctory efforts to establish rapport before broaching the substantive issue under investigation (Sternberg, Lamb, Esplin, and Baradaran, 1999; Warren, Woodall, Hunt, and Perry, 1996). We thus recommend future research to investigate the relationship between type and amount of rapport-building and the quality of children's accounts. We strongly encourage interviewers to build rapport with children by asking open-ended questions about neutral, everyday events before questioning them about sensitive topics. In addition, we support interviewers' engagement in pre-interview practice where the child gets feedback about the kinds of information needed by the questioner.

Sternberg *et al* (1997) found open-ended training influenced the children's responses but often had little effect on the interviewers' style of questioning. In other words, even when children provided lengthy responses to the first open-ended substantive question, interviewers did not continue to ask open-ended questions but rather shifted to more focused questions. This unexpected finding suggested that it might be valuable to specify additional open-ended questions to be asked throughout the substantive phase of the interview. Interviewers clearly have difficulty internalizing recommended interview techniques and may need more explicit guidelines than those typically provided in training sessions or manuals, however intensive. Increasingly detailed scripts have thus been developed by researchers at the National Institute of Child Health and Human Development (NICHD) for the entire interview (including substantive and non-substantive sections).

The NICHD Protocol

The NICHD investigative interview protocol covers all phases of the investigative interview and is designed to translate research-based recommendations into operational guidelines in order to enhance the retrieval of informative, complete, and accurate accounts of alleged incidents of abuse by young victim-witnesses (Orbach, Hershkowitz, Lamb, Sternberg, Esplin, and Horowitz, 2000; Sternberg, Lamb, Orbach, Esplin, and Mitchell, 2001). This is accomplished by creating a supportive interview environment (before substantive rapport build-ing), adapting interview practices to children's developmental levels and capabil-ities (eg minimizing linguistic complexity and avoiding interruptions), preparing children for their tasks as information providers (by clarifying the rules of com-munication and training children to report event-specific episodic memories), and maximizing the interviewers' reliance on utterance types (eg invitations) that tap children's free recall. When following the protocol, interviewers maximize the use of open-ended questions and probes, introduce focused questions only after exhausting open-ended questioning modes, use option-posing questions (including Yes/No questions) only to obtain essential information later in the interview, and eliminate suggestive practices. Interviewers are also encouraged to use information provided by the children themselves as cues to promote further free-recall retrieval. In essence, the protocol is thus designed to maximize the amount of information elicited using recall prompts because information elicited in this way is more likely to be accurate. In addition, the structured inter-view protocol minimizes opportunities for contamination of the children's accounts. The use of the NICHD protocol has been shown to increase dramatic-ally the amount of information obtained from alleged victims using recall rather than recognition prompts (Orbach *et al*, 2000; Sternberg *et al*, 2001).

Because forensic interviewers seldom know what actually happened in the incidents described by interviewees, they have largely had to rely on generaliza-tion from laboratory analogue research when assuming that recalled information was more likely to be accurate than information retrieved in other ways. There have been, however, few attempts to explore the effects of prompt type on accur-acy in actual forensic contexts. Using an alternative approach to the estimation of accuracy, Lamb and Fauchier (2001) and Orbach and Lamb (2001) identified self-contradictions in forensic interviews of nine and one alleged victims, respect-ively. Details elicited using suggestive prompts were most likely to be contra-dicted by the same informants, followed by those elicited using option-posing prompts, whereas those elicited using open-ended prompts were never contra-dicted. Such findings add support to recommendations by professional and expert groups emphasizing that forensic interviewers should rely as much as pos-sible on open-ended questions when obtaining information from alleged victims of child sexual abuse and take special care to avoid risky questions when inter-viewing young children (American Professional Society on the Abuse of Children, 1990, 1997; Home Office, 1992, 2002). These principles are, of course, central to the NICHD protocol discussed here.

Summary

Even young children can be valuable informants when interviewers recognize their strengths and limitations. Specifically, children often can remember important details of incidents that they have observed or experienced when the interviewer recognizes the power of children's communicative powers and acknowledges the difference between children's abilities and their performances. That is, the interviewer might not be able to change the child's abilities, but she or he can affect the child's level of performance by changing her or his own behaviour. Interviewers should take advantage of developmentally appropriate strategies for motivating children to be informative and provide the child with the cognitive support that helps them to retrieve as much information as possible, uncontaminated by the interviewers' beliefs and expectations.

References

American Professional Society on the Abuse of Children (1990). *Guidelines for psychosocial evaluation of suspected sexual abuse in young children*. Chicago, Ill.

—— (1997). *Guidelines for psychosocial evaluation of suspected sexual abuse in young children (Revised)*. Chicago, Ill.

Brainerd, CJ and Reyna, VF (1996). 'Mere testing creates false memories in children'. *Developmental Psychology* 32: 467–76.

Brown, D and Pipe, M-E (2003a). 'Individual differences in children's event memory reports and the narrative elaboration technique'. *Journal of Applied Psychology* 88: 195–206.

——and —— (2003b). 'Variations on a technique: Enhancing children's recall using narrative elaboration training'. *Applied Cognitive Psychology* 17: 377–99.

Cordon, IM, Pipe, M-E, Sayfan, L, Melinder, A, and Goodman, GS (2004). 'Memory for traumatic experiences in early childhood'. *Developmental Review* 24: 101–132.

de Villiers, J and de Villiers, P (1999). 'Language development'. In MH Bornstein and ME Lamb (eds) *Developmental psychology: An advanced textbook* (4th edn). Mahwah, NJ.

Dorado, JS and Saywitz, KJ (2001). 'Interviewing preschoolers from low- and middle-SES communities: A test of the Narrative Elaboration Recall Improvement technique'. *Journal of Clinical Child Psychology* 30: 568–80.

Fivush, R (1997). 'Event memory in early childhood. Studies in developmental psychology'. In C Nelson (ed) *The development of memory in childhood*. Hove, England.

—— (1998). 'Children's recollections of traumatic and nontraumatic events. Trauma, memory, and suggestibility in children'. *Development and Psychopathology* 10: 699–716.

Flin, R, Boon, J, Knox, A, and Bull, R (1992). 'The effect of a five month delay on children's and adults' eyewitness memory'. *British Journal of Psychology* 83: 323–36.

Goodman, G and Reed, RS (1986). 'Age differences in eyewitness testimony'. *Law and Human Behavior* 10: 317–32.

——Taub, EP, Jones, DPH, England, P, Port, LK, Rudy, L, and Prado, L (1992). *Testifying in criminal court. Monographs of the Society for Research in Child Development* 57 (5, Serial No 229).

Home Office. (1992). *Memorandum of good practice on video recorded interviews with child witnesses for criminal proceedings*. London: Home Office.

——(2002). *Achieving best evidence in criminal proceedings: Guidance for vulnerable and intimidated witnesses including children*. London: Home Office.

Howe, ML (1997). 'Children's memory for traumatic experiences'. *Learning and Individual Differences* 9: 153–74.

——(2000). *The fate of early memories: Developmental science and the retention of childhood experiences*. Washington, DC.

Lamb, ME, Hershkovitz, I, Sternberg, KJ, Esplin, PW, Hovav, M, Manor, T, and Yudilevich, L. (1996). 'Effects of investigative utterance types on Israeli children's responses'. *International Journal of Behavioral Development* 19: 627–37.

——and Fauchier, A (2001). 'The effects of question type on self-contradictions by children in the course of forensic interviews'. *Applied Cognitive Psychology* 15: 483–91.

——Orbach, Y, Warren, AR, Esplin, PW, and Hershkowitz, I (2006). 'Getting the most out of children: Factors affecting the informativeness of young witnesses'. In MP Toglia, JD Read, DF Ross, and RCL Lindsay (eds) *Handbook of eyewitness psychology. Vol 1: Memory for events*. Mahwah, NJ.

Orbach, Y, Hershkowitz, I, Lamb, ME, Sternberg, KJ, Esplin, PW, and Horowitz, D (2000). 'Assessing the value of structured protocols for forensic interviews of alleged abuse victims'. *Child Abuse and Neglect* 24: 733–52.

——and Lamb, ME (2001). 'The relationship between within-interview contradictions and eliciting interviewer utterances'. *Child Abuse and Neglect* 25: 323–33.

Pipe, ME, Lamb, ME, Orbach, Y, and Esplin, PW (2004). 'Recent research on children's testimony about experienced and witnessed events'. *Developmental Review* 24: 440–68.

Poole, DA and Lamb, ME (1998). *Investigative interviews of children: A guide for helping professionals*. Washington, DC.

Roberts, KP (2002). 'Children's ability to distinguish between memories from multiple sources: Implications for the quality and accuracy of eyewitness statements'. *Developmental Review* 22: 403–35.

——and Lamb, ME (1999). 'Children's responses when interviewers distort details during investigative interviews'. *Legal and Criminological Psychology* 4: 23–31.

——and Powell, MB (2001). 'Describing individual incidents of sexual abuse: A review of research on the effects of multiple sources of information on children's reports'. *Child Abuse and Neglect* 25: 1643–59.

Saywitz, KJ (1988). 'The credibility of the child witness'. *Family Advocate* 10: 38.

——and Camparo, L (1998). 'Interviewing child witnesses: A developmental perspective'. *Child Abuse and Neglect* 22: 825–43.

——and Snyder, L (1996). 'Narrative elaboration: Test of a new procedure for interviewing children'. *Journal of Consulting and Clinical Psychology* 64: 1347–57.

——Snyder, L, and Lamphear, V (1996). 'Helping children tell what happened: A follow-up study of the narrative elaboration procedure'. *Child Maltreatment* 1: 200–12.

Schneider, W and Pressley, M (1997). *Memory development between two and twenty* (2nd edn). Mahwah, NJ.

Sternberg, KJ, Lamb, ME, Hershkowitz, I, Yudilevitch, L, Orbach, Y, Esplin, PW, and Hovav, M (1997). 'Effects of introductory style on children's abilities to describe experiences of sexual abuse'. *Child Abuse and Neglect* 21: 1133–46.

——Lamb, ME, Esplin, PW, and Baradaran, LP (1999). 'Using a scripted protocol in investigative interviews: A pilot study'. *Applied Developmental Science* 3: 70–6.

———, ——— Orbach, Y, Esplin, PW, and Mitchell, S (2001). 'Use of a structured investigative protocol enhances young children's responses to free-recall prompts in the course of forensic interviews'. *Journal of Applied Psychology* 86: 997–1005.

———, ——— Davies, GA, and Westcott, HL (2001). 'The Memorandum of Good Practice: Theory versus application'. *Child Abuse and Neglect* 25: 669–81.

Thierry, KL, Lamb, ME, Orbach, Y, and Pipe, M-E (2005). 'Developmental differences in the function and use of anatomical dolls during interviews with alleged sexual abuse victims'. *Journal of Consulting and Clinical Psychology*, 13, 1125–34.

Walker, AG (1994). *Handbook on questioning children: A linguistic perspective*. Washington, DC.

——and Warren, AR (1995). 'The language of the child abuse interview: Asking the questions, understanding the answers'. In T Ney (ed) *True and false allegations of child sexual abuse: Assessment and case management*. New York.

Warren, AR, Woodall, CC, Hunt, JS, and Perry, NW (1996). 'It sounds good in theory, but . . .': Do investigative interviewers follow guidelines based on memory research? *Child Maltreatment* 1: 231–45.

——and McCloskey, LA (1997). 'Language in social contexts'. In SB Gleason (ed) *The development of language* (4th edn). New York.

10

Nothing But the Truth: Achieving Best Evidence Through Interviewing in the Forensic Setting

Sarah Henderson and Linda Taylor

Within the legal system a great deal of emphasis is placed upon the veracity of eyewitness testimony with little regard to how external stimuli, namely inappropriate questioning, can affect individual recall. This is particularly true of the preliminary legal interview and court process, both of which, in their current form, may compromise recollection of an event. The authors consider the impact of the use of various questioning styles, including complex syntax and vocabulary, on individual recall and critically evaluate the most commonly used forensic interview techniques.

Memory may be broadly defined as the retention of previous events and experiences (Crowder, 1976). It is an exceedingly important process as it allows individuals to function in their environment, since it is through memory that humans and other organisms learn. Tulving (1995, 285) defines memory as . . . 'a trick that evolution has invented to allow creatures to compress physical time. Owners of biological memory systems are capable of behaving more appropriately at a later time because of their experiences at an earlier time, a feat not possible for organisms without memory'.

The word 'memory' is itself an umbrella term for the three main interrelated processes that allow individuals to convert episodes they have experienced into cognitive information that can be recalled at a later date; these processes are termed encoding (or acquisition), storage (or retention), and retrieval (Loftus, 1979). The initial stage, encoding, is the process by which information is inputted to the brain, to be remembered at a later stage. Once it is in the individual's short-term memory it is then defined via the individual's previous experience and knowledge, during which the process is moved into long-term memory. Any memory is therefore reliant upon individual context. When this input has been encoded, it has to be retained, until such time as it is retrieved or remembered.

Despite this, the memory process does not recall events with perfect clarity; rather, memory seems to be an easily distorted medium. This occurs not least because memory appears to summarize the gist of the events, and then uses conjecture to estimate what else could have happened to fill in the missing information (Sachs, 1967; Bransford and Franks, 1971; Loftus, 1979; Spanos, 1996). Bartlett (1932) dubbed memory a reconstructive process, and theorized that individuals, in part, construct memory from information gathered from past experiences and other schemata. It could be argued that the memory process as described above may be affected by the individual's prior experiences, emotional or physical well-being, and personality. It is considered that this may explain why central details of a traumatic occurrence can be remembered better than peripheral information (Memon and Young, 1997; Safer, Christianson, Autry, and Osterland, 1998). In such cases, the individual is focusing on the important information, and then using their own self-knowledge to fill in the less important peripheral circumstances. Therefore with repeated retrieval, recall may become less accurate and increasingly confused. A number of different factors can influence memory (as well as affect an individual's perception and judgement), and also contribute to erroneous recall; for example, the majority view can influence memory (Betz, Skowronski, and Ostrom, 1996). This has been highlighted by numerous experiments in the area of conformity which have found that individuals subtly change their beliefs in response to a real or merely perceived peer pressure, even when the group has not explicitly asked them to change their views (Zimbardo and Leippe, 1991). Additionally, in an interview situation the status and authority of the questioner, the style of questioning/question types asked, and the suggestibility of the subject (for example, individuals with low IQ, low self-esteem, and high levels of compliance who may be easily influenced) could also influence memory.

Despite the obvious and well-documented fallibility of memory, eyewitness testimony remains a fundamental tenet of the criminal justice system. It is perhaps the most highly regarded of all non-scientific evidence, and as a result it is vitally important that this evidence is as clear and accurate as possible. Any confusion or doubt on a witness's part could have serious ramifications, such as an innocent individual being falsely convicted, a guilty individual being acquitted, or, in rare cases, the witness (or more likely a potential suspect) implicating themselves through falsely confessing to a crime. It follows therefore that the interview style is imperative. The police have had their interviewing styles assessed and recommendations made to refine and improve technique. However, the legal interviews and the oral examination procedures commonly used in court have never been assessed in this way, despite the fact that these 'interviews' (in the broadest sense) are often just as important as the interviews conducted by the police.

Language plays a particularly important role in law. Unfortunately, lawyers often use a traditional, archaic form of questioning characterized by long complex sentences, complicated jargon and sentence structure, and high usage of negatives and double negatives which can often make it difficult for non-lawyers to understand the proceedings (Trosberg, 1994; Han Teck, 2004). As Kebbell and Johnston (2000) discuss, there has been a great deal of research into how individuals should be interviewed when in police custody. However, there has been little research done into the effects of lawyers' interviews on witness and suspect recall of events. A number of question types and styles typically used by lawyers have been identified (Brennan, 1995; Kebbell *et al*, 2000). These include:

- negatives
- double negatives
- leading questions
- complex vocabulary
- complex syntax
- multipart.

This is especially troubling in the instance of child testimony. Courts generally wish to avoid causing children unnecessary trauma, and a number of recommendations have been implemented to put children at their ease when giving evidence. These include the removal of wigs and gowns by judges, counsel, and solicitors, and the physical removal of anyone not having a direct interest in the proceedings. Additionally the Vulnerable Witnesses (Scotland) Act 2004 allows certain categories of persons, including children, to give their evidence via live television link or videoed interview. While such efforts are laudable, the child is still questioned by the prosecuting lawyer, and then cross-examined by the defence lawyer, or vice versa. This cross-examination often causes confusion and may cause the child to contradict their previous statements, especially if these initial statements were taken a significant period of time prior to the court appearance.

The only way a witness, whether they are child or adult, can provide an accurate recount of any situation is if they are asked questions they can understand. An individual may very well have the knowledge that the question requires, however, if they do not understand the meaning of the question they will be unable to provide the appropriate answer for it. In order to minimize this, lawyers need to take individual circumstances into account (Perry and Wrightsman, 1991). In particular, during cross-examination, lawyers often change the order of questions, unwittingly or deliberately to confuse witnesses (Brennan, 1995).

So, how does interviewing currently work in the forensic setting? It is clear that interviewing is a fundamental part of the investigative process. Interviews themselves have a number of distinct and important stages. The first stage establishes the relationship between the interviewer and the interviewee and the tone taken at this point tends to dictate how the encounter will progress. Interviews that start in an easy, conversational style will probably continue in that vein. An interviewer who begins the interview by being aggressive or dominant will unsettle the interviewee, who might then become distressed and forget points or be unwilling to divulge details (Sherr, 1986). The purpose of the interview is to find out information about an event, and the interviewer is responsible for controlling the interview in order to cover all the pertinent points. This is done through the types of questions employed and careful consideration of non-verbal behaviours. Ease of communication is also an important consideration; the language used in the interview room should be readily understood by the interviewee. There should also be a final stage of closure, for the interviewer to review what has been expressed in the interview, and for the interviewee to ask any questions they may have (Shepherd, 1990). This stage is often overlooked due to inexperience or (less forgivably) pressure of time, but is particularly important in the taking of precognitions or affidavits, another form of legal interview.

In police interviews with witnesses and suspects, one of the objectives is to maximize the quantity and accuracy of recalled information. In addition to the standard legal interview, the police have tended to concentrate on selective review where the officer will focus on the salient details as they are provided and later ask for repetition/clarification of these details. Before the advent of the Cognitive Interview, the police used structured interviews. Various studies have assessed this interviewing style and found it wanting. Structured interviewing was typically run by domineering interviewers, asking inappropriate question types. In addition, the interviewers were often biased and displayed poor conversational skills; they may have interrupted the interviewee and were inattentive to things they were saying. The interviewer was traditionally encouraged to gain confessions whenever possible when dealing with suspects, and allay suspicions when interviewing witnesses (Fisher, Geiselman, and Raymond, 1987; Stephenson and Moston, 1990; Clifford and George, 1996).

In addition, the interviewer often displayed a limited understanding of the interviewee's personal details (for example, personality, emotional state, or socio-economic status) which increased the suspect's vulnerability and threw doubt on the confession's reliability (Loftus, Levidow, and Duensing, 1992). As Walkley (1988) states, the police conducting a simple background check can displace these effects and improve the interview situation. The interviewer's background knowledge of the interviewee is just one of many areas that need to be improved.

This type of interviewing style, the structured interview, is unproductive for many reasons. By assuming a dominant role, the interviewer can influence (consciously or unconsciously) the interview and impose his own biases on the witnesses or suspects. If there is a more balanced relationship between the interviewer and the interviewee there is more likely to be a more truthful exchange of information rather than just having the more submissive interviewee acquiescing to the dominant interviewer's version of events (Brandon and Davies, 1973; Gudjonsson and Mackeith, 1988; Shepherd, 1990).

The suspect is, naturally, charged if there is a large body of evidence against him or if he confesses to the crime. Obviously if there is substantial amount of corroborating evidence against the individual, a confession does not unduly affect the decision to charge him. However, if there is little evidence, then the confession is usually the strongest evidence against him or her (Stephenson and Moston, 1990). Unfortunately in this case, the need for corroboration is relaxed as a confession is considered to be contrary to self-interest (Field and Raitt, 1998; Walker, Walker *et al*, 2000). As a result, interviews are primarily geared towards eliciting confessions from suspects. If the interviewer was less determined to secure a confession (and by association assuming guilt) then they would be more open to the idea of a balanced dynamic in the interview situation and therefore be able to establish an account of the events that would reveal the true guilt or innocence of the suspect (Stephenson and Moston, 1990).

As a result of these inadequacies in interviewing, psychologists were charged with developing an alternative interviewing style. The Cognitive Interview uses a number of techniques to improve communication and recall within the interview situation. First the interviewee must mentally reinstate the physical and mental contexts that occurred at the time of the event. The individual must then try to recall as many details as possible (no matter how irrelevant they may seem) which will hopefully lead to the remembrance of additional information. They are also asked to recount the events in a variety of different orders and from a number of different perspectives (Memon, Holley, Milne, Koehnken, and Bull, 1994). These techniques are thought to help the individual to recall information that may be otherwise inaccessible (Memon, Walk, Bull, and Koehnken, 1997). In addition, there are a number of tasks the interviewer has to do before, during, and after the interview. He must first plan a strategy before the interview starts, then introduce himself to the interviewee and explain the purpose of the interview. This allows for a level of rapport to be built. When the interview is concluded there must also be a period of closure where the interviewer thanks the interviewee and answers any questions they may have about the process. It should be remembered that suspects or witnesses may be bewildered by the process they have just undergone and may not understand what will happen next. Before the Cognitive Interview the interviewer used just to end the interview as soon as the confession was obtained with little concern about the suspect's well-being or rights (Stephenson and Moston, 1990). After the interview, any information received should be reviewed. This also gives an opportunity for the interviewer's performance to be evaluated by the other members of the team.

Notwithstanding this, however, there have been some criticisms of the Cognitive Interview. It has sometimes been seen as too time-consuming and logistically inappropriate; also, for some crimes the police are understandably loath to reinstate the context in case the witness is subject to further unnecessary trauma. Despite these objections the literature does state that police officers generally find it a useful tool that appears to enhance recall.

So far, we have primarily concentrated on the chambers interview or precognition. Little should be made of this different setting. In the courtroom the *de minimis* evidential etiquette tends to disallow leading or suggestive questioning styles. It is thereafter for the judge or opposing counsel to object to what could broadly be termed 'inappropriate questioning'. Comparisons can be drawn between the techniques employed during examination in chief and cross-examinations. The purpose of the examination in chief is to lay before the court all that the witness knows that is relevant and material. It is paramount that the lawyer should be in control of his witness from opening question to closing statement, without being seen to lead the witness on any material issue. In practice, closed and leading questions are often asked. It is a well-known principle that during examination in chief, no question should be asked to which the questioner does not know the answer. The experienced advocate will give the impression that the witness has given his own account of events without prompting.

The purpose of cross-examination, by contrast, is to destroy or weaken the evidence of your opponent's witnesses or undermine their credibility. The focus therefore shifts to adversarial advocacy. In addition, cross-examination may be used to elicit favourable evidence by means of discrete and tactical questioning. This is particularly dangerous. The inexperienced advocate will frequently confuse tactical questioning with complex questioning: herein lies the problem, as the credibility of the witness may be lessened by subsequent inconsistencies in the recounting of facts. However, it is wise to remember that different interviewers may elicit different information due to varying approaches to questioning.

Ultimately, the importance of clarity of thought in the framing of questions cannot be overstated. If witnesses can be put at their ease, and respond to simple, well-structured questions, their evidence will be clearer and more accurate, and miscarriages of justice may more easily be avoided.

References

Bartlett, FC (1932). *Remembering: A Study in experimental and social psychology*. Cambridge.

Betz, AL, Skowronski, JJ, *et al* (1996). 'Shared realities: Social influence and stimulus memory'. *Social Cognition* 14(2): 113–40.

Brandon, R and Davies, C (1973). *Wrongful Imprisonment*. London.

Bransford, JD and Franks, JJ (1971). 'The abstraction of linguistic ideas'. *Cognitive Psychology* 2: 331–50.

Brennan, M (1995). 'The discourse of denial: Cross-examining child victim witnesses. Special issue: Laying down the law: Discourse analysis of legal institutions'. *Journal of Pragmatics* 23: 71–91.

Clifford, BR and George, R (1996). 'A field investigation of training in three methods of witness/victim investigative interviewing'. *Psychology, Crime and Law* 2: 231–48.

Crowder, RG (1976). *Principles of Learning and Memory*. New Jersey.

Field, D and Raitt, F (1998). *The Law of Evidence in Scotland*. Edinburgh: W Green and Sons.

Fisher, RP, Geiselman, RE, and Raymond, DS (1987). 'Critical analysis of police interviewing techniques'. *Journal of Police Science and Administration* 15: 177–85.

Gudjonsson, GH and Mackeith, JAC (1988). 'Retracted Confessions: Legal, Psychological and Psychiatric Aspects'. *Medical Science and Law* 28: 187–94.

Han Teck, C (2004) 'On Speaking Terms'. *Inter Se* 149: 3–7.

Kebbell, MR and Johnson, SD (2000). 'Lawyers' Questioning: The Effect of Confusing Questions on Witness Confidence and Accuracy'. *Law and Human Behavior* 24(6): 629–41.

Loftus, EF (1979). 'The malleability of human memory'. *American Scientist* 67: 312–20.

——Levidow, B, and Duensing, S (1992). 'Who remembers best? Individual differences in memory for events that occurred in a science museum'. *Applied Cognitive Psychology* 6: 93–108.

Memon, A, Holley, A, Milne, R, Koehnken, G, and Bull, R (1994). 'Towards Understanding the Effects of Interviewer Training in Evaluating the Cognitive Interview'. *Applied Cognitive Psychology* 8: 641–59.

——Wark, L, Bull, R, and Koehnken, G (1997). 'Isolating the effects of the cognitive interview'. *British Journal of Psychology* 88: 187–98.

——and Young, M (1997). 'Desperately Seeking Evidence: The Recovered Memory Debate'. *Legal and Criminological Psychology* 2: 131–54.

Perry, NW and Wrightsman, LS (1991). *The child witness: Legal issues and dilemmas*. California.

Sachs, JS (1967). 'Recognition memory for syntactic and semantic aspects of connected discourse'. *Perception and Psychophysics* 2: 437–42.

Safer, M, Christianson, SA, *et al* (1998). 'Tunnel Memory for Traumatic Events'. *Applied Cognitive Psychology* 12(2): 99–117.

Shepherd, E (1990). 'Ethical Interviewing. Paper presented at the Aspects of Police Interviewing Symposium, Conference of the Division of Criminological and Legal Psychology'. In E Shepherd (ed) *Aspects of police interviewing. Issues in Criminological and Legal Psychology* No 18. Leicester.

Sherr, A (1986). *Client interviewing for lawyers: an analysis and guide*. London.

Spanos, NP (1996). *Multiple identities & false memories: A sociocognitive perspective*. Washington, DC.

Stephenson, GM, and Moston, SJ (1990). Attitudes and Assumptions of Police-officers When Questioning Criminal Subjects. Paper presented at the Aspects of Police Interviewing Symposium, Conference of the Division of Criminological and Legal Psychology. In E Shepherd (ed) *Aspects of police interviewing. Issues in Criminological and Legal Psychology* No 18. Leicester.

Trosborg, A (1995). 'Statutes and contracts: An analysis of legal speech acts in the English language of the law'. *Journal of Pragmatics* 23: 31–53.

Tulving, E (1995). 'Introduction to the Section on Memory'. *The Cognitive Neurosciences*. MS Gazzaniga. Cambridge, Mass. 751–3.

Walker, AG, Walker, NML, *et al* (2000). *The law of evidence in Scotland*. Edinburgh.

Walkley, J (1988). *Police Interrogation: A Handbook for Investigators*. Letchworth, Herts.

Zimbardo, PG and Leippe MR (1991). *The psychology of attitude change and social influence*. New York.

11

Lie Detection Assessments as Evidence in Criminal Courts

Aldert Vrij and Samantha Mann[1]

Lie Detection Tests

In principle, lies could be detected in three different ways: by measuring people's physiological responses, by analysing their speech content, or by observing their behaviour. Several physiological lie detection tests exist, such as the Relevant–Irrelevant Test, Directed Lie Test, and Guilty Knowledge Test, but the Control Question Test is the most widely used (Gallai, 1999; Raskin and Honts, 2002). Several verbal lie detection methods exist, including Scientific Content Analysis (SCAN), but Statement Validity Analysis (SVA) is the most widely used test. To our knowledge, official non-verbal lie detection tools do not exist, with the exception of the Behaviour Analysis Interview (Inbau, Reid, Buckley, and Jayne, 2001). The success of this method in differentiating between truths and lies is far from promising (Kassin and Fong, 1999; Mann, Vrij, and Bull, 2004; Vrij, Mann, and Fisher, 2005). In this paper we will discuss the Control Question Test and Statement Validity Analysis. We will discuss how those tests work, which problems are associated with them, and how accurate they are in distinguishing between liars and truth tellers. We will also discuss whether these tests meet the criteria that are required for admitting expert scientific evidence in criminal courts according to the US Supreme Court *Daubert* decision.

Main Problems in Lie Detection

The main problem lie detectors face is that there is no cue uniquely related to deception. That is, lying per se does not result in a particular physiological response or in particular speech. In other words, cues akin to Pinocchio's growing

[1] Correspondence should be addressed to: Aldert Vrij, University of Portsmouth, Psychology Department, King Henry Building, King Henry 1 Street, Portsmouth, PO1 2DY, United Kingdom or via e-mail: aldert.vrij@port.ac.uk.

nose do not exist, and there is no cue a lie detector could truly rely upon. A second problem lie detectors face is that there are large individual differences in people's responses. Some people show stronger physiological responses to certain questions than others, and some people are more eloquent than others. Consequently, a single physiological response or statement cannot be used for lie detection purposes because the lie detector would not know whether it is a natural response or a sign of deceit.

Physiological lie detectors try to address these problems by comparing the physiological responses of a single examinee when he or she answers a series of questions. The rationale behind the test is that when the responses to the individual questions are compared, deceptive examinees will show a different pattern of responses to innocent examinees: deceptive examinees will show the strongest responses to so-called relevant questions and innocent examinees will show the strongest responses to so-called control questions. We will argue that this rationale is theoretically invalid.

Verbal lie detectors attempt to get around the above-mentioned problems in a different way. Their analyses of a person's speech content will result in a 'quality of the statement score', a so-called CBCA-score. They will then try to determine whether factors other than veracity could have influenced the examinee's CBCA score, such as the age and cognitive ability of the examinee. We will argue that checking for these alternative outcomes is a hazardous exercise.

How Do the Two Methods Work?

Control Question Test

Physiological activity is measured with a polygraph (from two Greek words, 'poly'—many, and 'grapho'—to write). This is a scientific measuring device which can display, via ink pens on to charts or via a computer's visual display unit, a direct and valid representation of various types of bodily activity (Bull, 1988). The most commonly measured activities are sweating of the fingers, blood pressure, and respiration. The polygraph accurately records even very small differences by amplifying signals picked up from sensors attached to different parts of the body.

The Control Question Test (CQT, also labelled the Comparison Question Test) compares responses to relevant questions with responses to control questions. *Relevant questions* are specific questions about the crime. A relevant question in a murder investigation could be: 'On March 12, did you shoot Scott Fisbee?' (Iacono and Patrick, 1997). *Control questions* deal with acts that are indirectly related to the crime under investigation, and do not refer to the crime in question. They are general in nature, deliberately vague, and cover long periods of time. They are meant to embarrass the suspects (both guilty and innocent) and to evoke arousal. This is accomplished by giving the suspect no choice but to lie when answering the control questions. Examiners formulate control questions for which, in their view, denials are deceptive. The exact formulation of these questions will depend on the examinee's circumstances, but a control question in an examination regarding a murder might be: 'Have you ever tried to hurt someone to get revenge?' (Iacono and Patrick, 1997), where the examiner believes that the examinee has indeed hurt someone in his life. Under normal circumstances, some examinees might admit this (control) wrongdoing. However, during a polygraph examination they will not do this because the examiner will tell the examinee that admitting this would cause the examiner to conclude that the examinee is the type of person who would commit the crime in question and would therefore be considered guilty. Thus, the examinee has no choice but to deny this (earlier) wrongdoing and thus to be untruthful in answering the control questions. Obviously, an examinee cannot be found guilty for having committed the crime under investigation by answering control questions untruthfully, as the control questions are not directly related to the crime. The examiner knows this and in that respect they are purposely misleading the examinee.

CQT is based on the assumption that in the *innocent suspect* control questions will generate more arousal than the relevant questions. This pattern will emerge because the innocent examinee will become more concerned with regard to his or her answers to the control questions, because (1) the examiner puts so much emphasis on the control questions, and (2) the examinee knows he or she is lying to the control questions but is answering the relevant questions truthfully. However, the same control questions are expected to elicit less arousal in *guilty suspects* than the relevant questions. A guilty suspect gives deceptive responses to both types of question, which in principle should lead to similar physiological responses to both types of question. However, relevant questions represent the most immediate and serious threat to the examinee, which are expected to lead to a stronger physiological response than the control questions.

Problems with the CQT Polygraph Test

Several problems have been identified with the CQT polygraph test (see Ben-Shakhar, 2002; Vrij, 2000), including the following four problems. First, the theoretical assumption underpinning the test is invalid. Theoretically, innocent suspects could also exhibit stronger responses to the relevant questions. One should keep in mind that polygraph tests are typically conducted when there is no conclusive evidence available. This means that innocent examinees have been unable so far to convince the investigators that they are innocent. Meanwhile, they may well be in a very unfortunate situation. Despite being innocent, they have probably undergone stressful police interrogations, may have been locked up in a cell, and perhaps friends, relatives, neighbours, and colleagues have started to doubt their innocence (thinking 'no smoke without fire'). For them the relevant questions are threatening too, as they realize that failing the test would mean that their unfortunate situation continues. Also, strong responses could be elicited due to the nature of the question. Suppose that an innocent man, suspected of murdering his beloved wife, is asked the question 'Did you murder your wife?' in a polygraph test. The memory of his late wife might reawaken his strong feelings about her.

Secondly, the examiner purposely misleads the examinee. This misleading aspect is essential in the test, as creating arousal while answering control questions is necessary for innocent examinees to pass the test. However, misleading suspects might be considered unethical and may be contrary to law in many countries.

Thirdly, the test is not standardized, because the control questions which could be asked depend on the type of crime under investigation. Different control questions need to be asked when investigating a theft than when investigating a murder. Also, control questions such as 'Have you ever tried to hurt someone to get revenge?' can only be asked of examinees who are known to have hurt someone in the past. The lack of standardization means that much depends on the skills of the individual polygraph examiner who formulates the questions.

Fourthly, examinees may attempt to influence their responses so that they will appear truthful. Examinees who are trained to do this can do so successfully without being noticed by the examiner (Honts and Amato, 2002), for example by pressing their toes to the soles of their shoes at the appropriate moments.

Statement Validity Analysis: Criteria-based Content Analysis

Statement Validity Analysis (SVA) is a tool to assess the veracity of written statements (Steller and Köhnken, 1989). SVA was developed to evaluate statements from children who are witnesses or alleged victims in sexual abuse cases. Many authors still describe CBCA as a technique solely developed to evaluate statements made by children in sexual offence trials (Honts, 1994; Horowitz, Lamb, Esplin, Boychuk, Krispin, and Reiter-Lavery, 1997). Others, however, advocate expanding the use of the technique to evaluate the testimonies of adults who talk about issues other than sexual abuse (Köhnken, Schimossek, Aschermann, and Höfer, 1995; Porter and Yuille, 1996; Ruby and Brigham, 1997; Steller and Köhnken, 1989). The core component of SVA is Criteria-Based Content Analysis (CBCA). CBCA comprises 19 different criteria (see the Appendix below). CBCA-trained evaluators judge the absence or presence of each of these 19 criteria in a written transcript. The presence of each criterion strengthens the hypothesis that the account is based on genuine personal experience. In other words, truthful statements will have more of the elements measured by CBCA than false statements. According to Köhnken (1996, 1999) both cognitive and motivational factors explain why truth tellers will have higher CBCA scores than liars. With regard to cognitive factors, it is assumed that the presence of several criteria (criteria 1 to 13, see also the Appendix) are likely to indicate genuine experiences as they are typically too difficult to fabricate. Therefore, statements which are coherent and consistent (*logical structure*), whereby the information is not provided in a chronological time sequence (*unstructured production*) and which contain a significant amount of detail (*quantity of detail*) are more likely to be true. Regarding details, accounts are more likely to be truthful if they include *contextual embeddings* (references to time and space: 'He approached me for the first time in the garden during the summer holidays'), *descriptions of interactions* ('The moment my mother came into the room, he stopped smiling'), *reproduction of speech* (speech in its original form: 'And then he asked: Is that your coat?'), *unexpected complications* (elements incorporated in the statement which are somewhat unexpected, eg the child mentions that the perpetrator had difficulty with starting the engine of his car), *unusual details* (details which are uncommon but meaningful, eg a witness who describes that the man she met had a stutter), and *superfluous details* (descriptions which are not essential to the allegation, eg a witness who describes that the perpetrator was allergic to cats). Another criterion that might indicate truthfulness is when a witness speaks of details that are beyond the horizon of his or her comprehension, eg when he or she describes the adult's sexual behaviour but attributes it to a sneeze or to pain (*accurately reported details misunderstood*). Finally, possible indicators of truthfulness are if the child reports details which are not part of the allegation but are related to it (*related external associations*, eg a witness who describes that the perpetrator talked about various women he had slept with and the differences between them), when the witness describes his or her feelings or thoughts experienced at the time of the incident (*accounts of subjective mental state*), or describes their interpretation of the perpetrator's feelings, thoughts, or motives during the incident (*attribution of perpetrator's mental state*: 'He was nervous, his hands were shaking').

Other criteria (criteria 14 to 18) are more likely to occur in truthful statements for motivational reasons. Truthful persons will not be as concerned with impression management as deceivers. Compared to truth tellers, deceivers will be more keen to try to construct a report which they believe will make a credible impression on others, and will leave out information which, in their view, will damage their image of being a sincere person (Köhnken, 1999). As a result, a truthful statement is more likely to contain information that is inconsistent with the stereotypes of truthfulness. The CBCA list includes five of these so-called 'contrary-to-truthfulness-stereotype' criteria (Ruby and Brigham, 1998): *spontaneous corrections* (corrections made without prompting from the interviewer ('He wore black trousers, no sorry, they were blue'), *admitting lack of memory* (expressing concern that some parts of the statement might be incorrect: 'I think', 'Maybe', 'I am not sure', etc), *raising doubts about one's own testimony* (anticipated objections against the veracity of one's own testimony: 'I know this all sounds really odd'), *self-deprecation* (mentioning personally unfavourable, self-incriminating details: 'Obviously it was stupid of me to leave my door wide open because my wallet was clearly visible on my desk'), and *pardoning the perpetrator* (making excuses for the perpetrator or failing to blame him or her, such as a girl who says she now feels sympathy for the defendant who possibly faces imprisonment).

The final criterion relates to *details characteristic of the offence*. This criterion is present if a description of events is typical for the type of crime under investigation (for example, a witness describing feelings that professionals know are typical for victims of, for example, incestuous relationships). It is difficult to see how this criterion fits into the cognitive and motivational theoretical framework. Raskin and Esplin (1991) pointed out that this criterion is not related to the statement itself but to the particular crime to which the statement refers. They therefore argue that this criterion should not be included in the CBCA criteria list.

Statement Validity Analysis: The Validity Checklist

CBCA scores may be affected by factors other than the veracity of the statement. Take, for example, the age of the interviewee. Cognitive abilities and command of language develop throughout childhood, making it gradually easier to give detailed accounts of what has been witnessed (Davies, 1991). Therefore, all sorts of details are less likely to occur in the statements of young children. Also, children under eight years old may have difficulty in viewing the world from somebody else's perspective (Flavell, Botkin, Fry, Wright, and Jarvis, 1968), thus criterion 13 (accounts of perpetrator's mental state) is unlikely to occur in the statements of young children. Finally, younger children have less developed metacognitive and metamemorial capabilities (ie knowing whether or not they know or remember an answer (Walker and Warren, 1995)), so they are less likely to be aware of gaps in their memories (criterion 15). The result is that CBCA scores of older children are likely to be higher compared to CBCA scores of younger children.

A validity checklist has been developed consisting of issues that are thought to be relevant and hence worth examining, as they might affect CBCA scores. SVA evaluators consider the following issues (Steller, 1989; Steller and Boychuk, 1992): (1) appropriateness of language and knowledge (mental capability/age of the child); (2) appropriateness of effect shown by the interviewee; (3) interviewee's susceptibility to suggestion; (4) evidence of suggestive, leading, or coercive questioning; (5) overall adequacy of the interview; (6) motives to report: Does the interviewee's relationship with the accused, or other people involved, suggest possible motives for a false allegation?; (7) context of the original disclosure or report: Are there questionable elements in the context of the original disclosure?; (8) pressures to report falsely: Are there indications that others suggested, coached, pressured, or coerced the interviewee to make a false report?; (9) consistency with the law of nature: Are the described events unrealistic?; (10) consistency with other statements: Are there major elements of the statement that are inconsistent or contradicted by another statement made by this interviewee?; and (11) consistency with other evidence: Are there major elements in the statement that are contradicted by reliable physical evidence or other concrete evidence? Henceforth we will call such issues 'external factors'. In another stage of the SVA procedure, 'evaluation of the CBCA outcome', the evaluator systematically addresses each of the external factors mentioned in the checklist, and explores and considers alternative interpretations of the CBCA outcomes.

To date, validity checklist research has concentrated on the impact of three external factors included in the validity checklist (age of the interviewee, interviewer's style, and coaching of the interviewee) on CBCA scores (see Vrij, 2005, for a review of SVA research). Research has convincingly demonstrated that, as predicted, CBCA scores are positively correlated with age (ibid). CBCA scores are also related to the interview style of the interviewer. For example, open-ended questions, and facilitators (non-suggestive words of encouragement) yielded more CBCA criteria than other more direct forms of questioning; positive correlations were also found between CBCA scores and verbal affirmations ('Yes, I see', etc) and confirming comments (ie the interviewer summarizing what the child has said); and statements obtained from interviewees who were interviewed with the cognitive interview technique, which facilitates the retrieval of information from memory, received higher CBCA scores than statements obtained using a standard interview technique (ibid). Finally, research has demonstrated that CBCA scores are related to 'coaching': examinees who are given some guidelines on 'how to tell a convincing story' (in fact, they were taught several CBCA criteria) obtained higher CBCA scores than untrained participants. Given that some external factors influence CBCA scores, do SVA experts take these factors into account when making their final judgements? Research about how the validity checklist is used in daily life is rare, but several issues could be raised on the basis of the available psychological principles and research (ibid).

Problems with the Validity Checklist

There are numerous problems with the validity checklist (Vrij, 2005), and we will discuss here some of the main difficulties. First, some factors on the validity checklist may be difficult to identify. SVA experts look for evidence that an adult might have coached the child in order to enhance the perceived credibility of statements. For example, in a bitter divorce settlement, one parent might use dubious tactics of falsely exposing their ex-spouse as a child-abuser in order to enhance their chances of winning custody of the children. Experimental research regarding coaching, where some participants were coached about the CBCA criteria and others were not coached, has shown that CBCA experts have considerable difficulty in spotting which participants have been coached (ibid).

Secondly, at least one external factor, 'susceptibility to suggestion' (criterion 3, Steller, 1989), is difficult to measure. Some witnesses are more prone to suggestions made by interviewers than others, and a suggestible child may be more inclined to provide information that confirms the interviewer's expectations but is, in fact, inaccurate. Yuille (1988) therefore recommends asking the witness a few leading questions at the end of the interview in order to assess the witness's susceptibility to suggestion. He recommends asking some questions about peripheral information rather than central information, as asking leading questions may distort the interviewee's memory and may therefore harm the case (Loftus and Palmer, 1974). The fact that questions can only be asked about peripheral information is problematic, as it may say little about the witness's suggestibility regarding core issues of his or her statement. Children show more resistance to suggestibility for central parts than peripheral parts of an event (Goodman, Rudy, Bottoms, and Aman, 1990). They are also more resistant to suggestibility for stressful events, most likely to be the central events, than for events which are less stressful, most likely to be peripheral events (Davies, 1991). Moreover, this criterion also seems to assume that suggestion is more the result of individual differences than of circumstances. This may not be a valid assumption (Milne and Bull, 1999).

Thirdly, some factors that influence CBCA scores are not present in the validity checklist. Research has shown that CBCA scores are related to verbal and social skills (Vrij, 2005). For example, Vrij, Akehurst, Soukara, and Bull (2002) found that CBCA scores were, in some age groups, positively correlated with social adroitness (being experienced in verbally manipulating others) and self-monitoring (naturally engaging in impression management) and negatively correlated with social anxiety (feeling uncomfortable in the presence of others). However, this is not taken into account by SVA experts when they rely on the validity checklist.

Fourthly, it is possible to question the justification of some of the external factors listed on the validity checklist, such as: criterion 2 'inappropriateness of affect' (Steller, 1989); criterion 10 'inconsistency with other statements' (ibid); criterion 9 'consistency with the law of nature' (ibid); and criterion 11 'consistency with other evidence' (ibid). Criterion 2 refers to whether the child displayed an absence of affect or inappropriate affect during the interview. It suggests that if a child reports details of abuse without showing any signs of emotion or showing inappropriate signs of emotion, the story might be less trustworthy. This view on emotional displays is too rigid, as the notion of an 'appropriate affect' does not exist. For example, some rape victims exhibit an 'expressed' self-presentation style in which their distress is clearly visible to outsiders, whereas others display a more controlled 'numbed' style, whereby cues of distress are not clearly visible (Burgess, 1985). These styles represent a personality factor and are not related to deceit (Littman and Szewczyk, 1983).

Criterion 10 deals with inconsistencies between different statements from the same witness. It suggests that one statement may in fact be fabricated when interviewees contradict themselves in two different statements. However, Granhag and Strömwall (1999, 2002) have demonstrated that inconsistency between different statements is not a valid indicator of deception in adults.

In their review of child research, Fivush, Peterson, and Schwarzmueller (2002) also conclude that inconsistency, in itself, is not an indication of inaccuracy. Neither is it the case, as these authors point out, that consistency necessarily means accuracy.

Criteria 9 and 11 deal with the realism of the statement. Dalenberg, Hyland, and Cuevas (2002) report that for a small group of children that each made initial allegations of abuse and for whom there was a 'gold standard' of proof that abuse has occurred (ie the injuries were judged medically consistent with the allegations), bizarre and improbable material was included in their statements (reference to fantasy figures, impossible or extremely implausible features of the story, and descriptions of extreme abusive acts that should have been (but were not) supported by external evidence if they had genuinely occurred).

Fifthly, even when an SVA expert knows that an external factor that appears on the Validity Checklist is present, it is still difficult to determine the exact impact of that factor on CBCA scores. In Lamers-Winkelman and Buffing's (1996) field study, CBCA-raters were instructed to take the age of the child into account while calculating their CBCA scores. Nevertheless, six criteria positively correlated with age.

Given these difficulties in identifying the relevant external factors and examining the exact impact of these factors on CBCA scores, it is clear that the validity checklist procedure is more subjective and less formalized than the CBCA procedure (Steller, 1989; Steller and Köhnken, 1989). It is therefore not surprising that if two experts disagree about the truthfulness of a statement in German criminal cases, they often disagree about the likely impact of some external factors on that statement (Gumpert and Lindblad, 1999; Vrij, 2005).

Moreover, Gumpert and Lindblad's (1999) field study with SVA experts in Sweden revealed that SVA experts may use the validity checklist incorrectly. First, although SVA experts sometimes highlighted the influence of external factors on children's statements in general, they did not always discuss how this factor may have influenced the statement of the particular child they were asked to assess. Secondly, although experts sometimes indicated possible external influence on statements, they tended to rely upon the CBCA outcome, and tended to judge high-quality statements as truthful and low-quality statements as fabricated. Gumpert and Lindblad (1999) only examined a limited number of cases, and to draw convincing conclusions is perhaps premature, but their findings are worrying. It implies that SVA decisions are no more likely to be accurate than CBCA assessments, as the final decision based upon CBCA outcomes, together with the validity checklist procedure, will often be the same as the decision based upon CBCA outcomes alone. It also implies that interviewees who will naturally produce low-quality statements and therefore are likely to obtain low CBCA scores (ie young children, interviewees with poor verbal skills, and so on) might well be in a disadvantageous position.

Legal Implications

What are the implications for the use of the CQT polygraph test and CBCA/SVA assessments as scientific evidence in legal systems? A possible way to answer this question is by examining the extent to which CQT polygraph tests and CBCA/SVA assessments meet the criteria that are required for admitting expert scientific evidence in criminal courts. In *Daubert v Merrel Dow Pharmaceuticals, Inc.* (1993), the US Supreme Court set out a set of guidelines for admitting expert scientific evidence in the federal (American) courts. The following guidelines are provided by the Supreme Court, and reported and discussed by Honts (1994): (a) Is the scientific hypothesis testable?; (b) Has the proposition been tested?; (c) Is there a known error rate?; (d) Has the hypothesis and/or technique been subjected to peer review and publication?; and (e) Is the theory upon which the hypothesis and/or technique is based generally accepted in the appropriate scientific community? Table 11.1 summarizes our answers to each of these five questions.

Is the Scientific Hypothesis Testable?

The prediction that truthful statements will have more of the elements measured by CBCA than false statements can be tested in scientific research, although this is not an easy task. It can easily be tested in experimental laboratory-based research, where participants lie or tell the truth for the sake of the experiment. For CBCA laboratory research the answer to this question is thus 'yes'. However, the findings might not be ecologically valid, given the artificial nature of such studies. Conducting field studies, where the decisions made by SVA experts in real life criminal cases are evaluated, is possible in principle, but in practice it is sometimes difficult. The problem is how to establish the truth/innocence status of the examinee beyond doubt (so-called ground truth). SVA assessments take place in sexual abuse cases. It is often difficult to determine the facts of a sexual abuse case, since often there is no medical or physical evidence. Frequently the alleged victim and the defendant give contradictory testimonies and often there are no independent witnesses to give an objective version of events. Therefore, in CBCA field studies confessions are often used as a criterion. This is problematic as confessions are not independent from CBCA veracity judgments. For example, if the only evidence against the guilty defendant is the incriminating statement of the child, which is often the situation in sexual abuse cases, it is unlikely that the perpetrator will confess to the crime if the incriminating statement is of poor quality. On the other hand, if a false incriminating statement is persuasive and judged to be truthful by a CBCA expert, the chances for the innocent defendant obtaining an acquittal decrease dramatically, and, if there is no chance of avoiding a guilty verdict, it may be beneficial to plead guilty in order to obtain a reduced penalty (Steller and Köhnken, 1989). In summary, poor quality (eg unconvincing) statements decrease

Table 11.1. Answers to the five Daubert questions

	CBCA laboratory	CBCA field	Validity Checklist	SVA	CQT laboratory	CQT field
(1) Is the scientific hypothesis testable?	yes	problematic	problematic	problematic	yes	problematic
(2) Has the proposition been tested?	yes	no	no	no	yes	possibly
(3) Is there a known error rate?	yes, too high	no	no	no	yes	yes, too high
(4) Has the hypothesis and/or technique been subjected to peer review and publication?	yes	no	no	no	yes	yes
(5) Is the theory upon which the hypothesis and/or technique is based generally accepted in the appropriate scientific community?	no	no	no	no	no	no

the likelihood of obtaining a confession and high-quality (eg convincing) statements increase the likelihood of obtaining a confession, regardless of whether a statement is truthful or fabricated.

A further complication in testing CBCA in field research is some problems associated with the validity checklist. Several of the hypotheses underpinning the validity checklist (the second part of SVA) are testable, for example the premise that CBCA scores are correlated with cognitive ability. We also saw, however, that other issues are more difficult to test, for example the extent to which the child has been suggestible during the interview. Other issues are difficult to spot, for example whether or not the child has been coached. In our view, this puts enough questions as to the testability of CBCA in field studies and the validity checklist, and, subsequently, for the SVA procedure as a whole. We therefore cannot answer the first *Daubert* question with an unequivocal 'yes' but believe that the answer is 'problematic' for CBCA in field studies, the validity checklist, and SVA as a whole.

CQT polygraph tests can be conducted in laboratory studies and in such studies the underlying rationale is testable. However, as with CBCA laboratory research, the findings may lack ecological validity. Conducting CQT field studies is as problematic as conducting CBCA field studies. As mentioned before, CQT polygraph tests are carried out when there is no other conclusive evidence available. This makes obtaining ground truth just as difficult as in CBCA research. Also in CQT research, confessions are used as ground truth, but, like CBCA assessments, confessions are not independent from CQT outcomes either. For example, a guilty suspect who passes the test is unlikely to confess as there is no further evidence against him or her. Since that suspect is the culprit, it is unlikely that someone else will confess to that crime. In other words, in this case a confession will typically not occur. This, however, implies that the case will not be included in the field study as only cases where a confession has been made will be included. The incorrect polygraph decision will therefore not be noted, and the result is that accuracy percentages reported in field studies which are based on confessions (almost all field studies) are likely to be inflated.

A further obstacle preventing CQT from fulfilling this first *Daubert* criterion is that CQT testing is not based on a valid theoretical premise (see above). The question than arises, as phrased by Gallai (1999, 96): 'How can the underlying science be tested when it has been conceded that no adequate explanation exists as to how the underlying science operates?' Further, we saw earlier that trained examinees can influence CQT outcomes without being noticed by the examiner. The answer to the first *Daubert* question is thus 'problematic' regarding CQT polygraph testing in field studies.

Has the Proposition been Tested?

The answer to this second question is affirmative for CBCA laboratory research. A substantial number of CBCA laboratory studies have been carried out, and provide empirical support for the underlying CBCA hypothesis. In eight out of nine laboratory studies where a total CBCA score was calculated (in most studies adults participated), the CBCA score was significantly higher for truth tellers than for liars (Vrij, 2005). This is a rather impressive result. Deception research outcomes are typically erratic with different studies showing different outcomes. Vrij (2000) reviewed studies regarding fifty-one verbal and non-verbal cues to deceit, and none of them showed a pattern as consistent as the CBCA results pattern. The most consistent findings regarding non-verbal behaviour were that liars have a higher-pitched voice and make fewer movements with their hands and fingers than truth tellers. However, these findings only emerged in seven out of twelve studies where pitch of voice was measured and in seven out of ten studies where hand and finger studies were examined. (In the remaining studies no difference emerged between liars and truth tellers.) Also, when the individual CBCA criteria were taken into account, a more erratic and less consistent pattern occurred (Vrij, 2005). The most consistent finding was that truth tellers include more details in their stories than liars, and this was found in thirteen out of seventeen studies where it was investigated, whereas no differences were found in the remaining four studies.

There is a scarce number of properly conducted field studies testing CBCA (Vrij, 2005) and insufficient to allow us to conclude that the proposition has been properly tested in field situations. As already mentioned, proper testing of the Validity Checklist in real life situations has not taken place to date, although some of the issues covered by the validity checklist have been dealt with in experimental research. The answer to the second *Daubert* question is therefore 'no' for CBCA field research, the validity checklist, and SVA research.

A substantial number of laboratory CQT polygraph tests have been carried out (Granhag and Vrij, 2005), and these studies generally show favourable results for polygraph testing (see Raskin and Honts, 2002; and Vrij, 2000, for recent reviews of laboratory-based polygraph studies). However, they are fiercely attacked by polygraph opponents. Amongst other things, they argue that the guilty participants have little incentive to try to beat the test, and that innocent participants are unlikely to be concerned about the relevant questions (Iacono and Patrick, 1997).

Numerous field studies have been published to date, but they are subject to debate. The problem is that the quality of these published polygraph field studies is low (National Research Council, 2003), and most problems are related to establishing a ground truth that meets scientific standards. Regarding CQT tests, the answer to the second *Daubert* question is therefore 'possibly'.

Is there a Known Error Rate?

There is a known error rate of CBCA judgments made in experimental laboratory research. A review of that research (Vrij, 2005) revealed that in such studies, on average, 73 per cent of the truths and 72 per cent of the lies were correctly classified, resulting in a known error rate of almost 30 per cent for both truths and lies.

This is relatively high and implies that CBCA assessments are not made 'beyond reasonable doubt', which is the standard of proof often set in criminal courts. A known error rate in CBCA field research, however, does not exist. Accuracy rates of CBCA field studies have been calculated in two CBCA field studies (Esplin, Boychuk, and Raskin, 1988; Parker and Brown, 2000) but both studies were flawed (Vrij, 2005). Amongst others, there were problems with how the ground truth was established. Error rates regarding the validity checklist and the SVA method as a whole have been reported in only one study (Parker and Brown, 2000), which was flawed (Vrij, 2005). The answer is therefore 'no' regarding CBCA field research, the validity checklist, and SVA research.

Raskin and Honts (2002), two supporters of control question polygraph testing, reviewed eight 'high-quality' CQT laboratory polygraph tests and found high accuracy rates: 80 per cent of the guilty participants were correctly classified as guilty and 8 per cent were incorrectly classified as innocent. The test scores for the remaining 12 per cent of the participants were inconclusive. Of the innocent participants, 84 per cent were correctly classified as innocent, 8 per cent were incorrectly classified as guilty, and the results for 8 per cent of the participants were inconclusive. This results in a known error rate of 8 per cent. Other reviews, analysed in Vrij (2000), revealed somewhat lower accuracy rates, but still show positive results for CQT polygraph testing. On average, the error rates in those reviews were 9 per cent for guilty participants and 13 per cent for innocent participants.

Several reviews have been published to date regarding the accuracy of CQT field research, and the BPS Working Party (2004) analysed the seven reviews regarding the scientific status of the polygraph that they were aware of. Different reviews showed different outcomes because different researchers included different field studies in their reviews. Because the quality of the published field studies was generally low, researchers often left out some field studies which they felt did not meet minimum quality criteria. However, different researchers left out different field studies. Taking all seven CQT reviews into account, results showed that there is some agreement amongst the reviews regarding guilty suspects. Correct guilty classifications were made in 83 per cent to 89 per cent of the cases, and incorrect innocent classifications were made in 1 per cent to 17 per cent of the cases. There is less agreement regarding innocent suspects. Also, the findings for innocent suspects are less positive than for guilty suspects. Depending on the review, between 53 per cent and 78 per cent of innocent suspects were correctly classified as innocent, and between 12 per cent and 47 per cent of innocent suspects were incorrectly classified as guilty. These relatively high error rates for innocent suspects imply that, despite being innocent, they nevertheless may have been aroused when answering the relevant questions. We have already identified this potential problem above. The accuracy scores thus reveal that CQT polygraph examiners are not able to present the accuracy of their CQT assessments as being 'beyond reasonable doubt', hence CQT assessments are not accurate enough to be presented as scientific evidence in criminal courts.

Has the Hypothesis and/or Technique been subjected to Peer Review and Publication?

The answer to the fourth question has already been touched upon above. A growing number of CBCA studies have now been published in peer reviewed journals, although most studies were laboratory based where the participants were often adults rather than children. Validity checklist studies and SVA studies are lacking. The answer to the fourth *Daubert* question is thus 'yes' regarding CBCA laboratory research, 'yes' regarding CBCA field research, but 'no' regarding validity checklist research and SVA research. As already discussed above, the answer is 'yes' regarding both CQT laboratory and field research, although the number of high-quality field studies testing the accuracy of CQT testing is relatively low.

Is the Theory upon which the Hypothesis and/or Technique is based Generally Accepted in the Appropriate Scientific Community?

The answer to the fifth and final question is 'no' for CBCA research, the validity checklist research, SVA research and CQT polygraph testing. Regarding the latter, Iacono and Lykken (1997) published a survey where the scientific opinion concerning the polygraph was examined. They asked members of the American Society of Psychophysiological Research (who can be considered as experts) and fellows of the American Psychological Association (Division 1, General Psychology) for their opinions regarding CQT polygraph tests. The findings revealed that the opinions of both groups of psychologists were very similar. A minority of interviewees (about 33 per cent) considered the Control Question Test to be based on scientifically sound psychological principles. Moreover, only 22 per cent would advocate that courts admit into evidence the outcome of control question polygraph tests.

A similar survey concerning CBCA and the validity checklist is lacking. However, several authors have expressed serious doubts about the CBCA method (Brigham, 1999; Davies, 2001; Lamb, Sternberg, Esplin, Hershkowitz, Orbach, and Hovav, 1997; Rassin, 1999; Ruby and Brigham, 1997; Wells and Loftus, 1991). The discussion above concerning the validity checklist makes clear that this part of SVA is not without its critics either.

Conclusion

CQT tests and SVA evaluations do not meet the *Daubert* guidelines for admitting expert scientific evidence in criminal courts. The error rate is unknown for SVA assessments and too high for CQT polygraph testing, and the two methods are not undisputed in the relevant scientific community. We also raised doubts about whether the scientific hypotheses underlying both methods are actually testable.

We therefore believe that both methods should not be allowed as evidence in criminal courts. Saxe and Ben-Shakhar (1999, 204) pointed out that 'courts have almost universally rejected polygraph evidence', but they also noticed that this status 'continues to be litigated' (ibid). At present, SVA evaluations are accepted as evidence in criminal courts in several European countries, including Austria, Germany, the Netherlands, Sweden, and Switzerland (Köhnken, 2004).

We are aware that our firm standpoint will be challenged by those who propose to allow CQT and SVA analyses as evidence in court. Their main argument is that these methods need to be compared with other methods used in court procedures that yield even lower accuracy rates (Daniels, 2002; Köhnken, 2004). We expect that more people working in the criminal justice system will be sensitive to this argument. If, against our wishes, it is decided to allow CQT and SVA assessments as evidence in court then, at the very least, SVA and CQT experts should present the problems and limitations of their assessments in court so that judges, jurors, prosecutors, and solicitors can give thoughtful consideration to the validity of their decisions. In addition, because of the subjective nature of both assessments (ie involving human interpretation rather than fact-finding), more than one expert should judge each statement in order to establish inter-rater reliability between evaluators. Our impression is that, to date, assessments made by single experts have typically been used.

Because true and fabricated stories can be detected above the level of chance with CBCA assessments in both children and adults, and in contexts other than sexual abuse incidents (Vrij, 2005), we believe that CBCA/SVA judgments could be a valuable tool for police investigations. This may be useful, for example, in the initial stage of investigation for forming rough indications of the veracity of statements in cases where there are multiple suspects or where police detectives have different opinions about the veracity of a statement, and so on. However, thorough training in how to conduct CBCA/SVA assessments is desirable, given the erratic effects obtained in previous studies when trainees were exposed to less thorough training programmes (see Vrij, 2005, for a review of these studies).

In police investigations, alternative verbal detection tools may be used to obtain an indication of the veracity of statements. For example, 'reality monitoring' has been presented as an alternative in recent years (Sporer, 1997; Vrij, 2000), and this method yields accuracy rates in laboratory studies similar to those in CBCA laboratory studies (Granhag and Vrij, 2005; Masip, Sporer, Garrido, and Herrero, 2005; Vrij, 2000). The advantage is that reality monitoring assessments are easier to conduct than CBCA assessments (Sporer, 1997; Vrij, 2000).

We are hesitant to promote CQT polygraph tests even in police investigations. Our main concern is that such a test is not based on sound theoretical assumptions. In that respect, another polygraph test, the Guilty Knowledge Test (GKT), may be a better alternative, because it is based on sound theoretical grounds and is more accepted by the scientific community (Iacono and Patrick, 1997).

Ben-Shakhar, Bar-Hillel, and Kremnitzer (2002) believe that GKT tests even meet the *Daubert* criteria, and argue for considering their admissibility as evidence in court. We believe that this is premature. The GKT technique has rarely been tested in real life situations, and in the incidental cases where it has been tested, it resulted in relatively high error rates that do not satisfy *Daubert* standards (Vrij, 2000). An additional issue is that it cannot be used in many cases, because formulating proper GKT questions requires factual knowledge of the case under investigation that is often not available. See Ben-Shakhar *et al* (2002) for a discussion of GKT tests.

Appendix

Content Criteria for Statement Analysis*

General Characteristics
1. Logical structure
2. Unstructured production
3. Quantity of details

Specific Contents
4. Contextual embedding
5. Descriptions of interactions
6. Reproduction of conversation
7. Unexpected complications during the incident
8. Unusual details
9. Superfluous details
10. Accurately reported details misunderstood
11. Related external associations
12. Accounts of subjective mental state
13. Attribution of perpetrator's mental state

Motivation-Related Contents
14. Spontaneous corrections
15. Admitting lack of memory
16. Raising doubts about one's own testimony
17. Self-deprecation
18. Pardoning the perpetrator

Offence-Specific Elements
19. Details characteristic of the offence

* Adapted from Steller and Köhnken (1989).

References

Ben-Shakhar, G (2002). 'A critical review of the control questions test (CQT)'. In M Kleiner (ed) *Handbook of polygraph testing* 103–26. London.

—— Bar-Hillel, M and Kremnitzer, M (2002). 'Trial by polygraph: Reconsidering the use of the guilty knowledge technique in court'. *Law and Human Behavior* 26: 527–41.

BPS Working Party (2004). *A review of the current scientific status and fields of application of polygraphic deception detection*. Leicester.

Brigham, JC (1999). 'What is forensic psychology, anyway?' *Law and Human Behavior* 23: 273–98.

Bull, R (1988). 'What is the lie-detection test?' In A Gale (ed) *The polygraph test: Lies, truth and science* 10–19. London.

Burgess, AW (1985). *Rape and sexual assault: A research book*. London.

Daubert v Merrell Dow Pharmaceuticals, Inc 113 S Ct 2786, 1993.

Dalenberg, CJ, Hyland, KZ, and Cuevas, CA (2002). 'Sources of fantastic elements in allegations of abuse by adults and children'. In ML Eisen, JA Quas, and GS Goodman (eds) *Memory and suggestibility in the forensic interview* 185–204. Mahwah, NJ.

Daniels, CW (2002). 'Legal aspects of polygraph admissibility in the United States'. In M Kleiner (ed) *Handbook of polygraph testing* 327–38. London.

Davies, GM (1991). 'Research on children's testimony: Implications for interviewing practice'. In CR Hollin and K Howells (eds) *Clinical approaches to sex offenders and their victims* 177–91. New York.

—— (2001). 'Is it possible to discriminate true from false memories?' In GM Davies and T Dalgleish (eds) *Recovered memories: Seeking the middle ground* 153–76. Chichester, UK.

Esplin, PW, Boychuk, T, and Raskin, DC (1988, June). *A field validity study of Criteria-Based Content Analysis of children's statements in sexual abuse cases*. Paper presented at the NATO Advanced Study Institute on Credibility Assessment in Maratea, Italy.

Fivush, R, Peterson, C, and Schwarzmueller, A (2002). 'Questions and answers: The credibility of child witnesses in the context of specific questioning techniques'. In ML Eisen, JA Quas, and GS Goodman (eds) *Memory and suggestibility in the forensic interview* 331–54. Mahwah, NJ.

Flavell, JH, Botkin, PT, Fry, CK, Wright, JC, and Jarvis, PT (1968). *The development of role-taking and communication skills in children*. New York.

Gallai, D (1999). 'Polygraph evidence in federal courts: Should it be admissible?' *American Criminal Law Review* 36: 87–116.

Goodman, GS, Rudy, L, Bottoms, B, and Aman, C (1990). 'Children's concerns and memory: Issues of ecological validity in the study of children's eyewitness testimony'. In R Fivush and J Hudson (eds) *Knowing and remembering in young children* 249–84. New York.

Granhag, PA and Strömwall, LA (1999). 'Repeated interrogations: Stretching the deception detection paradigm'. *Expert Evidence: The International Journal of Behavioural Sciences in Legal Contexts* 7: 163–74.

—— and Strömwall, LA (2002). 'Repeated interrogations: Verbal and non-verbal cues to deception'. *Applied Cognitive Psychology* 16: 243–57.

—— and Vrij, A (2005). 'Deception detection'. In N Brewer and K Williams (eds) *Psychology and law: An empirical perspective* 43–92. New York.

Gumpert, CH and Lindblad, F (1999). 'Expert testimony on child sexual abuse: A qualitative study of the Swedish approach to statement analysis'. *Expert Evidence* 7: 279–314.

Honts, CR (1994). 'Assessing children's credibility: Scientific and legal issues in 1994'. *North Dakota Law Review* 70: 879–903.

—— and Amato, SL (2002). 'Countermeasures'. In M Kleiner (ed) *Handbook of polygraph testing* 251–64. London.

Horowitz, SW, Lamb, ME, Esplin, PW, Boychuk, TD, Krispin, O, and Reiter-Lavery, L (1997). 'Reliability of criteria-based content analysis of child witness statements'. *Legal and Criminological Psychology* 2: 11–21.

Iacono, WG, and Patrick, CJ (1997). 'Polygraphy and integrity testing'. In R Rogers (ed) *Clinical assessment of malingering and deception* 252–81. New York.

Inbau, FE, Reid, JE, Buckley, JP, and Jayne, BC (2001). *Criminal interrogation and confessions* (4th edn). Gaithersburg, Maryland.

Kassin, SM, and Fong, CT (1999). '"I'm innocent!": Effects of training on judgments of truth and deception in the interrogation room'. *Law and Human Behavior* 23: 499–516.

Köhnken, G (1996). 'Social psychology and the law'. In GR Semin and K Fiedler (eds) *Applied social psychology* 257–82. London.

—— (1999, July). *Statement Validity Analysis*. Paper presented at the pre-conference programme of applied courses 'Assessing credibility' organized by the European Association of Psychology and Law, Dublin, Ireland.

—— (2004). 'Statement Validity Analysis and the "detection of the truth"'. In PA Granhag and LA Strömwall (eds) *The detection of deception in forensic contexts* 41–63. Cambridge, UK.

—— Schimossek, E, Aschermann, E, and Höfer, E (1995). 'The cognitive interview and the assessment of the credibility of adults' statements'. *Journal of Applied Psychology* 80: 671–84.

Lamb, ME, Sternberg, KJ, Esplin, PW, Hershkowitz, I, Orbach, Y, and Hovav, M (1997). 'Criterion-based content analysis: A field validation study'. *Child Abuse and Neglect* 21: 255–64.

Lamers-Winkelman, F and Buffing, F (1996). 'Children's testimony in the Netherlands: A study of Statement Validity Analysis'. In BL Bottoms and GS Goodman (eds) *International perspectives on child abuse and children's testimony* 45–62. Thousand Oaks, Calif.

Littmann, E and Szewczyk, H (1983). 'Zu einigen Kriterien und Ergebnissen forensisch-psychologischer Glaubwürdigkeitsbegutachtung von sexuell misbrauchten Kindern und Jugendlichen'. *Forensia* 4: 55–72.

Loftus, EF, and Palmer, JC (1974). 'Reconstructions of automobile destruction: An example of the interaction between language and memory'. *Journal of Verbal Learning and Verbal Behavior* 13: 585–9.

Mann, S, Vrij, A, and Bull, R (2004). 'Detecting true lies: Police officers' ability to detect deceit'. *Journal of Applied Psychology* 89: 137–49.

Masip, J, Sporer, SL, Garrido, E, and Herrero, C (2005). 'The detection of deception with the Reality Monitoring approach: A review of the empirical evidence'. *Psychology, Crime, and Law* 11: 99–122.

Milne, R and Bull, R (1999). *Investigative interviewing: Psychology and practice*. Chichester, UK.

National Research Council (2003). *The polygraph and lie detection*. Committee to Review the Scientific Evidence on the Polygraph (2003). Washington, DC.

Parker, AD, and Brown, J (2000). 'Detection of deception: Statement validity analysis as a means of determining truthfulness or falsity of rape allegations'. *Legal and Criminological Psychology* 5: 237–59.

Porter, S and Yuille, JC (1996). 'The language of deceit: An investigation of the verbal clues to deception in the interrogation context'. *Law and Human Behavior* 20: 443–59.

Raskin, DC, and Esplin, PW (1991). 'Statement Validity Assessment: Interview procedures and content analysis of children's statements of sexual abuse'. *Behavioral Assessment* 13: 265–91.

—— and Honts, CR (2002). 'The comparison question test'. In M Kleiner (ed) *Handbook of polygraph testing* 1–48. London.

Rassin, E (1999). 'Criteria-Based Content Analysis: The less scientific road to truth'. *Expert Evidence* 7: 265–78.

Ruby, CL, and Brigham, JC (1997). 'The usefulness of the criteria-based content analysis technique in distinguishing between truthful and fabricated allegations'. *Psychology, Public Policy, and Law* 3: 705–37.

—— and —— (1998). 'Can Criteria-Based Content Analysis distinguish between true and false statements of African-American speakers?' *Law and Human Behavior* 22: 369–88.

Saxe, L and Ben-Shakhar, G (1999). 'Admissibility of polygraph tests: The application of scientific standards post-*Daubert*'. *Psychology, Public Police and Law* 5: 203–23.

Sporer, SL (1997). 'The less travelled road to truth: Verbal cues in deception detection in accounts of fabricated and self-experienced events'. *Applied Cognitive Psychology* 11: 373–97.

Steller, M (1989). 'Recent developments in statement analysis'. In JC Yuille (ed) *Credibility Assessment* 135–54. Deventer, the Netherlands.

—— and Köhnken, G (1989). 'Criteria-Based Content Analysis'. In DC Raskin (ed) *Psychological methods in criminal investigation and evidence* 217–45. New York.

—— and Boychuk, T (1992). 'Children as witnesses in sexual abuse cases: Investigative interview and assessment techniques'. In H Dent and R Flin (eds) *Children as witnesses* 47–73. New York.

Vrij, A (2000). *Detecting lies and deceit: The psychology of lying and its implications for professional practice*. Chichester, UK.

—— (2004). 'Why professionals fail to catch liars and how they can improve'. *Legal and Criminological Psychology* 9: 159–81.

—— (2005). 'Criteria-Based Content Analysis: A qualitative review of the first 37 studies'. *Psychology, Public Policy, and Law* 11: 3–41.

—— Akehurst, L, Soukara, S, and Bull, R (2002). 'Will the truth come out? The effect of deception, age, status, coaching, and social skills on CBCA scores'. *Law and Human Behavior* 26: 261–83.

—— Mann, S, and Fisher, R (2005). *An empirical test of the Behaviour Analysis Interview.* Manuscript submitted for publication.

Walker, AG, and Warren, AR (1995). 'The language of the child abuse interview: Asking the questions, understanding the answers'. In T Ney (ed) *True and false allegations in child sexual abuse: Assessment and case management* 153–62. New York.

Wells, GL, and Loftus, EF (1991). 'Commentary: Is this child fabricating? Reactions to a new assessment technique'. In J Doris (ed) *The suggestibility of children's recollections* 168–71. Washington, DC.

Yuille, JC (1988). 'The systematic assessment of children's testimony'. *Canadian Psychology* 29: 247–62.

12

Towards a Broader Perspective on the Problem of Mistaken Identification: Police Decision-Making and Identification Procedures

Andrew Roberts

The legal system has long acknowledged the dangers that attend attempts at identification by eyewitnesses. These dangers have been manifested in numerous miscarriages of justice which have attracted significant attention and concern, and the treatment of eyewitness identification evidence has been subject to review by law reform bodies in a number of jurisdictions.[1] These exercises have invariably drawn on a corpus of psychological research on the subject of the accuracy of eyewitness identification which is now substantial.[2] Although the volume of research concerning the phenomenon of mistaken identification is formidable, its scope is rather narrow and there remain many perspectives on the problem that offer fertile grounds for future research. It was suggested, some twenty years ago, that research and discourse concerning the problem of mistaken identification ought to be set in the context of a comprehensive model of legal processes, and of a clearly articulated theoretical framework.[3] Furthermore, this

---

[1] See Devlin Report; Law Commission of New Zealand, *Evidence: Total Recall? The Reliability of Witness Testimony*, Miscellaneous Paper 13 (1999: NZLC, Wellington); Australian Law Reform Commission, Report No 26, *Evidence* (Interim), vol 2 (1985: ALRC, Canberra) ch 11; Australian Law Reform Commission, Report No 38, *Evidence* (Final), (1987: ALRC, Canberra) ch 15; Scottish Home and Health Department, *Identification Procedure under Scottish Criminal Law* (1978: HMSO); N Brooks, Law Reform Commission of Canada Study Paper, *Pretrial Eyewitness Identification Procedures* (1983: LRCC, Ottawa); *Eyewitness Evidence: A Guide for Law Enforcement* (1999: US Dept of Justice, National Institute of Justice).

[2] See, eg M Kebbel and G Wagstaff, *Face Value? Evaluating the Accuracy of Eyewitness Information*, Police Research Series Paper 102 (1999: Home Office, Policing and Reducing Crime Unit), who noted that over 700 academic journal articles existed on the subject of eyewitness memory.

[3] W Twining, 'Identification and Misidentification in Legal Processes: Redefining the Problem' in S Lloyd-Bostock and B Clifford (eds) *Evaluating Witness Testimony: Recent Psychological Research and New Perspectives* (1983: Chichester) 255–6.

framework would be an elaborate one; one which would need to draw on the language of law and psychology,[4] integrate concepts from cognitive and social psychology, information theory, and from legal discourse.[5]

The fact that little progress appears to have been made in this respect is unsurprising. Such a project would be a daunting one, not least because it would require much foundational work to be done before it could be undertaken in earnest. Moreover, the development of such a theoretical framework would need to be a collaborative venture. Although research in the field of 'law and psychology' is, by definition, trans-disciplinary, examples of collaborative research, involving researchers from both disciplines, are rare—the result, it has been suggested, of a lack of communication between lawyers and psychologists.[6] Kapardis has commented generally, that results of psychological research might exert greater influence on law were psychologists to show greater familiarity with legal doctrine and theory, thereby avoiding the adoption of 'myopic perception[s] of . . . legal issue[s]'.[7]

This, of course, pre-supposes that academic lawyers have something of substance to contribute to any collaborative enterprise. In fact, notwithstanding empirical data which suggests that eyewitness identification is important evidence in a significant proportion of cases,[8] it is a matter that has failed to attract significant research attention among legal scholars. Consequently, the normative bases of eyewitness identification procedures which are used in the criminal process have not been adequately articulated.

In contrast, the degree of attention to which eyewitness testimony and identification has been subjected by forensic psychologists has been such that there have been appeals for the scope of the applied research agenda to be broadened.[9] However, although a review of research concerning eyewitness identification might disclose a considerable body of research, the scope of that research appears concentrated on a relatively narrow range of issues even within this field. Generally, studies have been concerned with the cognitive processes of the identifying witness and the reasoning processes of juries. Consequently, a great deal of that research has been directed towards developing more accurate identification

---

[4] ibid, 273.   [5] ibid.

[6] D Farrington, K Hawkins, and S Lloyd-Bostock, 'Introduction: Doing Psycholegal Research' in D Farrington, K Hawkins, and S Lloyd-Bostock (eds) *Psychology, Law and Legal Processes* (1979: Basingstoke). See also Ogloff, *Taking Psychology and Law into the Twenty-First Century* (2002: Dordrecht) 3, who notes that in 1971, 40% of all members of the American Psychology-Law Society were lawyers and that by 1999, this proportion of lawyer-members stood at only 7%.

[7] A Kapardis, *Psychology and Law*, 2nd edn (2003: Cambridge)14.

[8] See, eg C Phillips, and D Brown, (1998), *Entry into the Criminal Justice System: a survey of police arrests and their outcomes*, Home Office Research Study 185, (London; Home Office) 42; analysis of police arrests at 10 police stations across England and Wales disclosed that in 23% of all cases there was eyewitness identification evidence provided by an independent witness, with the victim providing it in 18% of all cases and security personnel in 10% of cases.

[9] See M Saks, 'The Law Does Not Live by Eyewitness Testimony Alone' (1986) 10 *Law and Human Behavior* 279.

parades/line-ups (or video identification procedures)[10] and demonstrating the need for expert testimony on the dangers of eyewitness identification evidence. Twining made the observation that such has been the focus on identification procedures in applied psychological research that, at times, it has appeared that the problem of mistaken identification has been perceived as being co-extensive with apparent defects of that procedure.[11] The problem, however, is one that extends beyond the fallibility of a witness's memory, the manner in which identification procedures are conducted, and the weight that juries attach to eyewitness testimony. The scope and complexity of the problem of mistaken identification becomes more apparent if we consider the procedural context in which identification procedures and jury decision-making occurs.

The Identification Process

An initial step towards establishing a broader perspective on the problem might be to elaborate the notion of an *identification process* and to distinguish it from the term *identification procedure*. The latter describes a discrete mechanism in which a witness attempts to identify a suspect. The former is a term which relates to a broad framework comprising a series of interrelated procedures, processes and decisions relating to eyewitness identification the components of which include *identification procedures*.

The validity of any suggestion as to the effect that increasing the accuracy of identification parades/line-ups (and video identification procedures) will have on reducing the risk of miscarriages of justice is contingent on the efficacy of the complex series of processes in which these particular procedures are embedded. There are various aspects of legal decision-making which might have a significant bearing on the risk of the occurrence of miscarriages of justice as a result of mistaken identification. While studies have been conducted to ascertain the extent of *knowledge* about factors that influence the reliability of eyewitness identifications, none appears to have investigated the *decision-making processes* of any group of decision-makers other than juries.

The trial provides a sub-optimal mechanism for inquiring into the reliability of identifications made by eyewitnesses. It has long been recognized that the traditional safeguards of cross-examination and witness demeanour do not satisfactorily indicate the weight that ought to be placed on any purported identification of the defendant. Memory is malleable and information about an event that witnesses acquire from third parties can be assimilated into the memory and later

---

[10] In England and Wales video identification is preferred to an identification parade/line-up, see Police and Criminal Evidence Act 1984, Codes of Practice, Code D, para 3.14. As to the advantages of video identification procedures, see Y Tinsley, 'Even Better than the Real Thing? The Case for Reform of Identification Procedures' (2001) 5 *International Journal of Evidence and Proof* 99.

[11] Twining, n 3 above, 265.

recalled as having been observed during observation of the original event.[12] Any additional information acquired from an interviewer, for example, might lead the witness to use general knowledge and fall back on social expectations to fill 'gaps' in his recollection of events.[13] Furthermore, a witness's confidence in the accuracy of those recollections can be inflated as a result of feedback and exchanges with others which might tend to reinforce the witness's belief in the accuracy of his or her memory. As the pre-trial stage of proceedings progresses, the opportunities for cross-pollination of inaccurate information will be manifold and the task of detecting whether a witness's recollection of events has been coloured by information (and misinformation) acquired from other parties becomes more difficult.[14] Identification procedures have been developed which mitigate the risks of error and any bias or suggestiveness inherent in police attempts to procure identifications from witnesses. If conducted at an early stage of pre-trial proceedings these procedures may provide not only valuable safeguards against the risk of error, but particularly cogent evidence where identity is an issue. However, the extent to which these do, in fact, offer safeguards and provide such evidence is contingent on legal decision-making.

The diagram in Figure 12.1 represents various legal decision-making processes that surround the use of identification procedures and which might occur in the period between a witness's observation of an offender and the point at which the issue of admissibility of identification evidence is considered at a trial or hearing. In a grand project to establish a comprehensive theoretical framework of the kind alluded to earlier, it constitutes a small but significant component. Notably it does not relate to any aspect of the cognitive processes of the witness. It applies only to the pre-trial stage of proceedings and the issue of the admissibility of identification evidence which will generally be determined at a pre-trial hearing or at the outset of a trial. It does not extend to the legal decision-making of defence and prosecution lawyers during the course of trials. Neither does it extend to the decision-making of judges, lay magistrates, and magistrates' legal advisers in this stage of proceedings, nor to the reasoning processes of the appellate courts in appeal proceedings in which an appellant submits that there has been some defect in the procedure relating to eyewitness identification evidence. It is, then, a rather limited representation of some of the processes that might occur in part of the identification process, but it provides a useful framework for discussion.

A number of decision-making processes are set out down the centre of the diagram (in the series of diamond shapes). In the light of the constraints on the

---

[12] See, eg G Mazzoni, M Vannucci, and E Loftus, 'Misremembering Story Material' (1999) 4 *Legal and Criminological Psychology* 93; see generally G Davies, 'Contamination of Witness Memory' in A Heaton-Armstrong, E Shepherd, and D Wolchover (eds) *Analysing Witness Testimony* (1999: London).

[13] See G Kohnken 'Interviewing Adults' in R Bull and D Carson (eds) *Handbook of Psychology in Legal Contexts*, 1st edn (1995: Chichester) 218.

[14] See generally A Roberts, 'The Problem of Mistaken Identification: Some Observations on Process' (2004) 8 *International Journal of Evidence and Proof* 100.

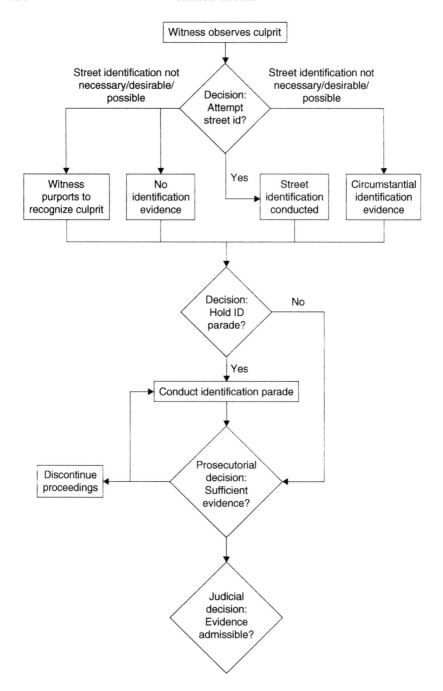

Figure 12.1. Legal decision-making processes concerning the use of identification procedures

length of this paper, its emphasis will be on the second of these decision-making processes, that is, police decisions as to whether an identification procedure ought to be conducted. The various decision-making processes in the diagram are inter-related. *Street identification* (or field show-up) procedures might take place in a relatively short period when the police are called following a criminal event. They may occur spontaneously, where a witness is taken around the area in which the offence took place in the hope that the culprit is nearby. They can also take place, more contentiously, where acting on a description of the culprit provided by the witness, the police discover close to the scene of the incident, someone who resembles the person described and arrange a confrontation between witness and suspect.[15] These procedures are inherently suggestive and do not provide the safeguards that are afforded by the more formal identification procedures. However, their attraction for the police is not difficult to perceive. They take place while the event remains fresh in the mind of the witness. They entail none of the resource implications and practical problems associated with arranging formal procedures. Such identifications often provide the cornerstone on which the prosecution case is built. In circumstances in which the police find a suspect in the vicinity soon after an offence is committed, who could be arrested and presented to the witness in formal procedures, a street identification is likely to be alluring. The police might take the view that the possibility of obtaining a positive identification outweighs the uncertainty of deferring to formal procedures arranged at some future time. This aspect of decision-making is deserving of far greater attention than can be afforded here.

Instances in which a witness has identified a suspect in a street identification provide one of a number of broad factual circumstances in which the second decision-making process—whether or not an identification procedure should be arranged—might occur. It may not be possible to conduct a street identification procedure, for example, either because no suspect is found after the police are called to the scene, or the crime is not immediately brought to the attention of the police. Alternatively, the witness might purport to recognize and name the person he or she saw committing the offence. Otherwise, there might be circumstantial evidence which could be tendered in order to prove identity, for example, a latent ear print at the scene or CCTV footage which could be subjected to facial mapping analysis. Finally, the police may have a suspect in respect of whom there is no evidence which could be tendered by the prosecution in order to establish identity where this is disputed.[16]

[15] See D Wolchover and A Heaton-Armstrong, 'Ending the Farce of Staged Street Identifications' [2004] 3 *Archbold News* 5; also A Levi and R Lindsay, 'Line-up and Photospread Procedures: Issues Concerning Policy Recommendations' (2002) 7 *Psychology, Public Policy and Law* 776, who suggest that street identifications should never occur.

[16] There are other variations which have been omitted from the diagram for the sake of clarity, eg circumstances in which a witness has examined an array of photographs including the suspect. It might also be that a number of eyewitnesses are available, one of whom has identified the suspect in an identification procedure; a decision must then be made as to whether further procedures ought to be conducted.

The second and third diamond shapes in the diagram represent prosecutorial and judicial decision-making on the issue of identification evidence. Relatively little attention has been directed towards such decisions made by these actors, and while a detailed examination cannot be conducted here, I will suggest that 'downstream' decision-making in the criminal process is likely to affect the decision-making processes of the police. Similarly, the merits of conducting identification procedures in any particular circumstances are beyond the scope of this paper. What we are concerned with here is the adoption of appropriate normative decision-making processes that ensure that identification procedures are conducted when they ought to be. This begs the question 'when ought procedures be conducted?'

All procedures are purposive insofar as they provide a means of achieving some ends or securing an objective. Any inquiry into the adequacy of legal (or official) decision-making on identification procedures and the adoption of appropriate procedures requires (1) articulation of the normative purposes served by identification procedures, and (2) an understanding of the manner in which the questions of whether or not identification procedures are to be held are determined. The evaluation of legal decision-making in the present context entails an inquiry in which normative and empirical analyses should be seen as necessary and complementary components rather than alternative perspectives. Empirical accounts of descriptive decision-making provide an insight into the peculiarities and shortcomings of decision-makers. Research of this nature might establish a rational basis for choosing between various normative decision-making models according to which provides the most effective means of ensuring that identification procedures are conducted when the purposes that they serve dictate that they should be held.[17]

The Purposes Served by Identification Procedures

It might be thought that it would be obvious when an identification procedure ought to be held. This, however, presupposes that there exists a consensus on the purposes served by such procedures. Perception of what these purposes are is likely to vary depending on the perspective from which the procedures are viewed.[18] Policy-makers, judges, lawyers, police officers, and suspects might all have different attitudes to them.[19] It appears implicit in much of the psychological research concerning identification parades/line-ups that the subject is approached from an official standpoint, particularly from the perspective of police officers. Indeed, there have been suggestions from psychologists that one approach that might

---

[17] See J Michon and F Pakes, 'Judicial Decision-making: A Theoretical Perspective' in Bull and Carson, n 13 above.

[18] For an exhaustive analysis, see D Galligan, *Due Process and Fair Procedures: A Study of Administrative Procedures* (1996: Oxford).   [19] ibid, 6.

bring 'success' in future eyewitness research would be to work with the law enforcement community.[20] It might be beneficial, it is claimed, to ascertain what this group perceive to be the problems in this area, and to develop and test procedures designed to resolve these concerns.[21]

The Police/Prosecutorial Perspective

Among the principal roles fulfilled by the police is that of evidence gatherer for the prosecuting authorities. From this perspective, identification procedures exist as a means of procuring admissible evidence for the prosecution case that will be admissible at trial. Consequently, the police might consider conducting such a procedure to be an imperative only where this is the sole means of establishing identity and thereby ensuring that matters progress to trial. This appears to be the paradigm that is adopted for much of the psychological research concerning identification procedures.

If sufficient evidence could be, or has been, secured to establish a *prima facie* case without having to resort to an identification procedure, on this narrow view, the underlying purpose served by the procedure is already fulfilled and there is no need to conduct one. One might assume, therefore, that in circumstances in which there already exists some evidence which could be tendered in order to prove identity in subsequent criminal proceedings—a street identification, a witness who purports to recognize the culprit as someone known to him or her—the police and prosecution authorities might be inherently biased towards a decision not to conduct identification procedures.

The Suspect's Perspective

The function of identification procedures appears rather different when viewed from the suspect's perspective. Where the police or prosecuting authorities seek to procure identification evidence from an eyewitness, the suspect is likely to view an identification procedure as a valuable safeguard against the risk of mistaken identification. However, where, for example, there is circumstantial evidence which the prosecution intend to adduce in order to prove identity, where an eyewitness has identified the suspect in a street identification, or the witness purports to know the suspect, the suspect might perceive an identification procedure to be a means of procuring evidence which could either assist his defence or lead to proceedings against him being discontinued.

An identification procedure might result in one of the following outcomes: (1) the witness identifies the suspect; (2) the witness wrongly identifies one of the foils; (3) the witness makes no identification; or (4) the witness states that the

---

[20] R Lindsay, J Brigham, E Brimmacombe, and G Wells, 'Eyewitness Research' in J Ogloff (ed) *Taking Psychology and Law into the Twenty-First Century* (2002: Dordrecht) 219.   [21] ibid.

person who committed the crime does not appear in the procedure.[22] Depending on the circumstances, any of those set out in (2)–(4) might provide evidence valuable to a suspect's claim of mistaken identity. Where the police have circumstantial evidence suggesting that the suspect committed the criminal act in question, the value of a procedure in which the witness states that he is not the culprit is obvious. Were the witness to make no identification, the jury may infer from this that the culprit did not appear in the procedure. The weight that they accord to this inference may be sufficient to tip the balance in favour of the accused and result in a finding that the prosecution has failed to prove guilt to the standard required in criminal trials. In other words the failure of a witness to make an identification might raise a reasonable doubt in the minds of the jury.

The usefulness to the suspect of an outcome whereby the witness identifies a foil might be limited to circumstances in which the witness has either (1) previously identified the suspect in a street identification, or (2) purports to know and has named the person he saw on the earlier relevant occasion. The value of an identification procedure in the former circumstance might lie in the extent to which the jury recognize any suggestiveness in the manner in which the street identification was carried out and accept the witness's selection of a foil as an indication of the unreliability of his or her ability to identify. In the latter circumstance, a failure to identify might undermine the assertion of recognition based on familiarity.

It is worth noting that relatively little research attention has been focused on negative outcomes of identification procedures.[23] Generally such outcomes are seen as the redundant product of police attempts to secure reliable prosecution evidence. However, advances in forensic technology have provided the police and prosecution authorities with more diverse means of obtaining evidence which might be adduced in order to prove identity. Where the police were once reliant on eyewitnesses for such proof of identity, modern technology now provides 'scientific' alternatives which might be perceived as more reliable. The traditional view that identification parades and video identification procedures are means of procuring prosecution evidence is inherent in the instructions that have to be given to witnesses prior to taking part in a procedure. In England and Wales a witness is invited only to make a positive identification. If he cannot do so he is simply required to state this fact. If one of the functions of an identification procedure is to procure evidence which might assist the defence, framing the instruction in these terms appears inappropriate and the witness ought also to be invited to state that the culprit does not appear in the procedure where he or she is sure that that is the case.

---

[22] These are discussed in *R v Donald* [2004] EWCA Crim 965; [2004] Crim LR 841.

[23] For examples of studies that do address this issue, see G Wells and A Olson, 'Eyewitness Identification: Information Gain from Incriminating and Exonerating Behaviors' (2002) 8 *Journal of Experimental Psychology: Applied* 155; G Wells and R Lindsay, 'On Estimating the Diagnosticity of Eyewitness Non-Identifications' (1980) 88 *Psychological Bulletin* 776.

It has been claimed that the right of parties to proceedings to bring all evidence relevant to the adjudication of their case is a fundamental principle in the administration of justice.[24] If identification procedures are capable of securing, for a defendant, evidence which is valuable to his defence, then we might start to think in terms of a suspect's moral, political, or legal right to identification procedures.[25] In common law jurisdictions it is the police who have physical control over the means of conducting identification procedures. Where a procedure might yield an outcome which undermines the prosecution case there is an obvious conflict. The primary function of the police is to secure evidence for the prosecution case. They are also custodians of apparatus which might generate evidence which could seriously undermine, if not provide a fatal blow to, the prosecution case. The concept of rights might be invoked as a justification for regulating decision-making to ensure that the preferences of the police and prosecution authorities do not influence decision-making in a way that jeopardizes the accuracy of the outcome of proceedings.

Legislative/Policy/Judicial Perspectives

While the police, prosecution, and defence are embroiled in the adversarial aspects of the criminal process, for those with overarching and more direct responsibility for the administration of the criminal justice system, considerations other than achieving accurate outcomes assume some importance. Ashworth and Redmayne[26] suggest that criminal procedure ought to have two main objectives. First, to determine accurately whether or not a person has committed an offence, and secondly, to do so fairly in a manner that respects a suspect's fundamental rights. While it is not possible to discuss the issues in any detail here, it is worth noting that the latter objective finds expression in instrumental values that act as side-constraints on decision-making processes. These values, sometimes referred to as *process values*, do not necessarily bear directly on the issue of accuracy, and might include respect for the suspect's privacy and dignity.[27] For example, in *Perry v United Kingdom*[28] the applicant successfully argued before the European Court of Human Rights, that by covertly recording visual images of him without statutory powers to do so, the police had violated his right to respect for private life under Article 8 of the European Convention on Human Rights. Notwithstanding this violation, the domestic courts found the identification procedure in which the images were used was reliable, and

---

[24] A Zuckerman, 'Privilege and Public Interest' in C Tapper (ed) *Crime, Proof and Punishment* (1981: London).
[25] See A Roberts, 'Procedural Rights and Identification Procedures' (forthcoming).
[26] See A Ashworth and M Redmayne, *The Criminal Process* 3rd edn (2005: Oxford) ch 2.
[27] See eg I Dennis, 'Fair Trials and Safe Convictions' (2003) 56 *Current Legal Problems* 211; N Taylor and D Ormerod, 'Mind the Gap: Safety, Fairness and Moral Legitimacy' [2004] *Crim LR* 266.   [28] [2003] Crim LR 281.

appeals against his conviction were unsuccessful. Questions concerning the point at which procedures so flagrantly violate instrumental values as to vitiate the moral legitimacy of the outcome of a process, notwithstanding its accuracy, raise difficult issues which cannot be explored here.[29]

Normative Decision-making Models

The substance of the decision as to whether to conduct identification procedures in particular circumstances involves determining whether the underlying purposes of those procedures would be served by doing so. This might be addressed by the adoption of differing normative models of decision-making.

The publication by the US Department of Justice of *Eyewitness Evidence: A Guide for Law Enforcement* (NIJ Guidelines)[30] was lauded as a significant achievement and development in that jurisdiction. The Guidelines contain, *inter alia*, recommendations for composing line-ups, instructing a witness prior to viewing a line-up, conducting identification procedures, and recording results. Notably they contain no provision regarding the circumstances in which identification procedures ought to be conducted.

In England and Wales pre-trial identification procedures are the subject of statutory regulation. This is found in Code D of Codes of Practice which are established by the Police and Criminal Evidence Act 1984. The Code comprises four broad sets of provisions: (1) those concerning the manner in which identification procedures are to be conducted, (2) those which establish a hierarchy among those procedures, (3) those concerning the manner in which street identifications (field show-ups) are to be conducted, and (4) those which set out the circumstances in which identification procedures should be conducted.

Let us assume that in the United States the lack of any provision in the NIJ Guidelines concerning such decisions leaves police officers to decide the issue as they think fit. Perceived in this way, Code D and the NIJ Guidelines provide useful practical examples of contrasting normative decision-making models, the former appears to impose a rule-governed, decision-making process and in the latter the absence of regulation provides for discretionary decision-making.

Rule-governed Decision-making

It has been suggested that *rule-governed* and *discretionary* decision-making processes cannot be distinguished conceptually and that whether a process is

---

[29] For a consideration of such issues, see A Zuckerman, 'Illegally Obtained Evidence: Discretion as the Guardian of Legitimacy' (1987) 40 *Current Legal Problems* 55.

[30] Technical Working Group for Eyewitness Evidence, *Eyewitness Evidence: A Guide for Law Enforcement* (NCJ No 178240/1999), (Washington, DC: US Department of Justice, Office of Justice Programs).

characterized as rule-governed or discretionary is a matter of degree.[31] It might be the case that the two processes lie at opposite ends of a continuum. However, for the purposes of the following analysis they can be distinguished in the extent to which the decision-maker is permitted to refer to the normative purposes or principles that ought to guide decision-making on the course of action being contemplated.

In a *rule-governed* decision-making process the decision-maker follows prescriptive rules. These rules embody relevant legal standards and are used to apply pressure to the world in order to 'guide, control or change the behaviour of agents with decision-making capacities'.[32] Such rules comprise two conceptually distinct parts: a statement of the conditions that trigger the application of the rule—what Schauer refers to as the *factual predicate*—and a prescription—the *consequent*. The *factual predicate* describes a set of facts standing in a relationship of probabilistic causation with the justification for the rule. The *consequent* sets out a prescribed course of conduct which is to be followed when the circumstances set out in the factual predicate are found. For example, we might perceive that risk of the consequences that we seek to avoid—mistaken identification—which provide the justification for conducting identification procedures is particularly acute where certain conditions x, y, and z occur in the circumstances of events that might be observed by witnesses. Accordingly, this might be reflected in a rule that: 'Where x, y and z occur (the factual predicate), identification procedure ϕ shall be held (the consequent)'.

The value of prescriptive rules is that, by virtue of their status as rules they provide the decision-maker with a reason for action which is independent of the subject matter of the rule. In other words, the decision-maker need not refer to the underlying objectives of the rule. It should be followed merely because it emanates from a body that has authority over the decision-maker. The basis of this claim is the assumption that the authority is generally better placed than the individual decision-maker to determine whether or not a specified course of action—the holding of identification procedures—is required.[33] We might assume that policy-makers (presumptively some arm of the executive/legislature) occupy such a position. The authority is able to draw on expert knowledge in various relevant fields. It is elevated from the case-by-case decision-making of the courts and the police, better able to perceive the issue from differing perspectives, and better placed to resolve any conflicts that arise in ensuring accurate outcomes and adhering to instrumental or process values. There are rule-utilitarian arguments which might be made in favour of following such rules. Doing so, it is said, leads to more

---

[31] This issue is addressed by Galligan, n18 above, 42–6.

[32] F Schauer, *Playing by the Rules: A Philosophical Examination of Rule-Based Decision-Making in Law and in Life*, (1991: Oxford) 1–2.

[33] On the nature of legal authority and its role in practical reasoning generally, see J Raz, 'Authority, Law and Morality' (1985) 68 *Monist* 295; J Raz, *The Morality of Freedom* (1985: Oxford).

efficient decision-making. It does not require the decision-maker to spend time determining what course of action is required in particular circumstances. Furthermore, it is likely that, across a range of decisions, the correct course of action will follow more frequently by following the rule than would be the case if decision-makers were left to determine what was required.

The Problem of Over- and Under-inclusiveness

The problem of framing a satisfactory rule is starkly illustrated by the metamorphosis of the provision of Code D, which concerns the circumstances in which the police should arrange identification procedures. The 1995 version of the Code contained a relatively simple rule:

Whenever a suspect disputes an identification, an identification parade shall be held if the suspect consents unless [it is not possible to arrange one on grounds of practicability].[34]

However, this rule was both over- and under-inclusive. For example, one manifestation of its over-inclusiveness is that it appears to have required an identification parade to be conducted where a father claimed to have seen his son committing a criminal act but the son asserted that he was elsewhere at the time. It was under-inclusive (presuming acceptance that one purpose of identification procedures is to procure evidence that might benefit the defence as well as the prosecution) in that it did not appear to require the police to conduct identification parades where there were eyewitnesses who had seen the culprit but not the suspect and therefore there was no act of 'identification' which could be the subject of dispute.

The various aspects of its over- and under-inclusiveness were addressed in a number of appellate proceedings, and in the version of the Code issued in 2003, it was reformulated as follows:

Whenever:
(i) a witness has identified a suspect or purported to identify them prior to [an identification procedure] having been held; or
(ii) there is a witness, who expresses an ability to identify the suspect, or where there is a reasonable chance of the witness being able to do so, and they have not been given an opportunity to identify the suspect in [an identification procedure];
and the suspect disputes being the person the witness claims to have seen, an identification procedure shall be held unless it is not practicable or it would serve no useful purpose in proving or disproving whether the suspect was involved in committing the offence. For example, when it is not disputed that the suspect is already well-known to the witness who claims to have seen them commit the crime.[35]

---

[34] Code D, 1995 version, para 2.3

[35] Code D, 2003 version, para 3.12. See also, for the proposed provision on which para D3.12 appears to have been based, A Roberts and S Clover, 'Managerialism and Myopia: The Government's Consultation Draft on PACE Code D' [2002] Crim LR 879.

The most obvious characteristic of this provision is that it is much more complex than the rule which it replaced. However, on a closer reading, questions might be raised as to whether it can be characterized as a rule in the way that its predecessor could. It uses prescriptive language insofar as it appears to demand that 'an identification procedure shall be held' in given circumstances. It then qualifies this by conferring a broad discretion enabling the decision-maker to decline to do so where he or she determines that it 'would serve no useful purpose in proving or disproving whether the suspect was involved in committing the offence'.

Furthermore, the provision remains over-inclusive insofar as it requires an identification procedure to be conducted unless 'it is not disputed that the suspect is already well-known to the witness'. This would appear to require an identification procedure to be conducted where the suspect's assertion, from the position of the objective bystander in possession of all of the facts, appears unreasonable. There have already been a number of appeal cases on the grounds that the police have failed to conduct an identification procedure where the witness claims to have known the suspect well but in which the suspect disputed this fact.[36] To the extent that under- and over-inclusiveness cannot be eliminated, it would be desirable that a rule which is designed to ensure that identification procedures are held where they might prevent a miscarriage of justice should be over- rather than under-inclusive. This would ensure that a suspect was always afforded safeguards when required. However, in a criminal justice system which has finite resources, the margin of over-inclusiveness will be an important consideration.

Discretionary Decision-making

Discretionary decision-making requires the decision-maker to ascertain and apply the purposes or principles that provide the justificatory basis for taking a course of action (in our case conducting identification procedures) and applying these directly to the factual matrix in the particular case. Pattenden[37] distinguishes two forms of discretion: *overt* and *concealed* discretion.[38] If a decision-maker is not bound by any governing statute or rule, the discretion that he or she enjoys is said to be *overt*. Where the decision-maker is subject to a provision containing open-textured language which when applied to a wide range of facts does not compel any particular result, he or she is said to possess *concealed* discretion. In the NIJ Guidelines, the absence of any provision relating to the circumstances in which identification procedures are to be conducted appears to confer on police officers overt discretion in determining the issue. While the relevant provision in the 1995 version of Code D can be characterized as a rule, the corresponding provision of the version of the Code issued in 2003 appears to confer on the decision-maker a

---

36 See eg *R v Harris* [2003] EWCA Crim 174.
37 R Pattenden, *Judicial Discretion and Criminal Litigation* 2nd edn (1990: Oxford).
38 ibid, 5–6.

concealed discretion. In the case of the latter, the duty to arrange identification procedures is subject to qualification where doing so 'would serve no useful purpose in proving or disproving whether the suspect was involved in committing the offence'. The starting position for the decision-maker is that procedures ought to be conducted in the circumstances set out in the first part of the provision. However, he or she is then permitted to resort to the purposes behind the procedures in making a determination on the facts.

Descriptive Decision-making: The Importance of Empirical Research

Given the inherent problems of framing sufficiently accurate rules, some form of discretionary decision-making might appear the most satisfactory normative decision-making process for determining when identification procedures ought to be conducted. This claim is, however, contingent on the capacity of police officers to: (1) ascertain and appropriately weigh the various purposes served, and process values to be respected by procedures; and (2) apply what emerges to the particular factual matrix. The latter entails the decision-maker identifying and attaching appropriate weight to facts which are relevant to the decision and ignoring those which are not relevant.

However, once we move away from the normative aspects of procedures to practical reasoning we encounter what Galligan has described as a 'rich and complex relationship' that exists between the framework of legal norms on which procedures are founded and the social environment in which decisions are made.[39] The adoption of appropriate normative procedures requires an understanding of the nature of this environment and the extent to which the social values, attitudes, and perceptions held by decision-makers are incorporated into and affect decision-making. This relationship provides significant scope for research on the descriptive decision-making processes employed by police officers in considering whether or not to conduct identification procedures.

In the light of long-standing and widespread concerns over the danger of mistaken identification it is perhaps surprising that there has been no significant debate surrounding appropriate normative decision-making mechanisms for determining when identification procedures ought to be conducted. Once analysis of the kind set out in the previous sections of this chapter is undertaken, the value of empirical research on decision-making in this context becomes obvious, as do the difficulties caused by the paucity of it. Normatively, a discretionary decision-making model appears to offer the optimal mechanism as it enables the problems of over- and under-inclusiveness that are inherent in a rule-governed decision-making process to be mitigated. However, it is not known whether

---

[39] Galligan, n 18 above, 15.

police officers possess the cognitive capacity required to reach appropriate decisions with a satisfactory degree of consistency. Any empirical inquiry along these lines would also need to take account of the adversarial context in which such decisions are made.

There is considerable ambivalence in the development of procedures relating to police decisions to conduct identification procedures. The courts have pointed out that the police cannot be expected to make 'impartial' decisions as to the need for identification procedures and the form which they might take. In *Alexander v R*[40] the High Court of Australia observed that the methods of identification that the police might choose to use, though well suited to the investigation and detection of crime, would probably not be calculated to yield evidence of high probative value in a criminal trial.[41] If this assumption is valid, does it follow that we should leave the question of whether or not identification procedures will be conducted to the discretion of the police? In an English appeal case, *R v Forbes*,[42] Lord Bingham expressed reservations over entrusting decisions concerning the important safeguard of an identification parade to police officers 'whose primary concern will (perfectly properly) be to promote the investigation and prosecution of crime rather than to protect the interest of suspects'.[43]

However, the absence in the NIJ Guidelines of any provision as to when the identification procedures that it prescribes should be conducted appears to leave such decisions to the discretion of the police. Furthermore, through various revisions of Code D, the provision concerning the circumstances in which such procedures ought to be arranged appears to have evolved from one which imposes a rule-governed decision-making process to one which confers a concealed discretion on the decision-maker. Moreover, a governmental review of the Codes of Practice carried out in 2002,[44] proposed a greater move towards discretionary decision-making. This, it was suggested, would be achieved through focusing on outcomes rather than processes and placing greater reliance on the professional judgment of police officers. While the trend towards discretionary decision-making under Code D has evaded any significant critical comment, the US Department of Justice Guidelines have been criticized by McKenzie[45] on the grounds that they do not 'force' the police to conduct the identification procedures set out in the document. The failure of the drafters of the Guidelines to encompass this aspect of procedural decision-making might be explained on the grounds of political expedience. It appears that the psychologists on the Technical Working Group which drafted the Guidelines encountered, from law enforcement representatives, considerable resistance to their proposals

---

[40] *Alexander v R* (1981) 34 ALR 289.   [41] ibid, *per* Mason J, at 312.

[42] *R v Forbes* [2001] 1 All ER 686.   [43] ibid, 696h.

[44] PACE Review: Joint Home Office/Cabinet Office Review of the Police and Criminal Evidence Act 1984 (2002) (London: Home Office).

[45] I McKenzie, 'Eyewitness Evidence: Will the United States Guide for Law Enforcement Make Any Difference?' (2003) 7 *International Journal of Evidence and Proof* 237.

concerning identification procedures.[46] Alternatively, the explanation might lie in a rather limited perception of the purposes served by identification procedures. Among the three objectives and goals of the study which led to the publication of the Guidelines was the desire to: 'Heighten the validity/accuracy of eyewitness evidence as police, prosecutors, and other criminal justice professionals [*sic*] work with witnesses to identify suspects.'[47] The basis of McKenzie's criticism of the NIJ Guidelines is that police culture leaves officers inimical to rules which are perceived to obstruct the conviction of the guilty. The implication being that the exercise of discretion would be inherently biased towards a course of action least likely to undermine the prosecution of a suspect.[48]

The persuasiveness of any argument drawn from police culture might be rather too thin to prove particularly persuasive in any discussion as to decision-making on identification procedures. Such arguments and the intuitive observations of the courts, based on behavioural assumptions as to the adverse influence that the social attitudes and values held by police officers might have on decision-making, provide a meagre basis for passing judgment on appropriate normative decision-making processes. It might be that such reservations are well-founded and discretionary decision-making is an inappropriate mechanism for determining whether or not identification procedures ought to be conducted. However, evaluation of the effectiveness of various decision-making processes is dependent on the availability of a sufficient amount of relevant empirical data. The findings of research, such as that on magistrates' discretionary decision-making on bail, might provide some indication as to the shortcomings of this kind of decision-making.[49] However, the decisions with which we are concerned involve partisan rather than notionally 'impartial' decision-makers and take place in a very different context. Descriptive research into decision-making in other contexts provides no substitute for context-specific empirical research.

Empirical research should not be seen as being confined to investigating any shortcomings in discretionary decision-making. The effectiveness of greater prescription in securing the purposive objectives of identification procedures might also be subject to empirical scrutiny. Insofar as appeal hearings provide a barometer of deficiencies in criminal procedure, appeals heard in English appellate courts which have been based on some alleged defect in pre-trial identification procedures are informative. There are numerous cases in which the courts, the police, and the prosecution authorities have accepted that Code D imposed an unambiguous duty to arrange identification procedures, yet none was held. This has been explained in some cases as an 'oversight'.[50] In the vast majority of cases no explanation is apparent, and occasionally failure to conduct a procedure appears to be the result of irrational decision-making.[51]

[46] See G Wells, 'Police Line-ups: Data, Theory and Policy' (2001) 7 *Psychology, Public Policy and Law* 791, 793.   [47] Technical Working Group for Eyewitness Evidence, n 30 above, 4.
[48] McKenzie, n 45 above.   [49] See Ch 4, by Mandeep Dhami, in this volume.
[50] See *R v Donald* [2004] Crim LR 841.
[51] On the purpose and importance of rationality in decision-making, see D Galligan, *Discretionary Powers* (1986: Oxford) 5–8, 65–72.

Rationality, in the sense in which it is used here, means a decision which is based on reasons which are either not related to the underlying purposes of identification procedures or insufficiently related to them to be considered relevant. *R v DPP*[52] provides an example of apparently irrational decision-making. In this case preliminary arrangements were made to conduct a video identification procedure but the process was abandoned after it was decided, by the police and prosecuting authorities, that the priority was to proceed to trial promptly. In an Australian case, *Wheeler v Police*,[53] a police officer purported to identify the defendant as the driver of a car which was being driven dangerously. The officer who made the identification had never before seen the defendant in person but had viewed police photographs of him. It was accepted that in such circumstances an identification parade ought to have been conducted, but none was held. Under cross-examination at trial, the officer responsible for conducting parades explained that he had decided not to hold one because of the risk that the officers concerned in the incident had access to photographs of the defendant and might have viewed them before there was an opportunity to conduct a parade.

Although a case relating to the rules concerning the manner in which identification procedures are to be conducted rather than the circumstances in which they are to be arranged, *R v Marcus*[54] provides a striking example of seemingly irrational decision-making. Here the police were proposing to conduct a video identification procedure. The suspect was a black male approaching middle-age with facial hair and greying hair. The police had an insufficient number of images of similar looking foils on the database of images. A number of foils were considerably younger than the suspect and few had any facial hair. It was proposed that the images be masked so as to hide greying hair around the temples and hair on the lower face. However, without the consent of the suspect the police compiled a second set of unmasked images which would be shown to the witness if she failed to identify the suspect from the masked images. It transpired that she could not identify anyone in the masked set of images but identified the suspect when shown the unmasked set. The trial judge allowed the evidence from the unmasked set of images to be adduced at trial, although the conviction was overturned by the Court of Appeal on the grounds that the suspect stood out to such an extent that the procedure was 'blatantly unfair'. For the purposes of issues under consideration here the case is interesting in two respects. The first is the decision-making of the trial judge as to the admissibility of the evidence. The second is that the report of the appeal hearing explains that the reason that the police prepared a set of unmasked images was their frustration about circumstances in which the witnesses had found it difficult to make identifications from obscured images. This tends to support the suggestion that the objective of the police is to obtain evidence to establish a prosecution case. It further suggests that they are willing to disregard well-established rules in order to do so.

---

[52] [2003] EWHC Admin 3074; (2004) 68 *Journal of Criminal Law* 183.
[53] [2005] SASC 156.   [54] [2005] Crim LR 384; *The Times*, 3 December 2004.

Research which reveals 'how, and under what conditions, officials come to perceive particular social goals as sufficiently pressing to justify bringing them into the legal process without clear authority'[55] would be particularly valuable. The utility of rule-governed decision-making is undermined in circumstances where the subjects of the rules decline to follow them. In this respect a particularly interesting question is the extent to which deviations from a rule can be explained by decision-making that occurs later in the identification process.

Judicial Decision-making: Admissibility of Evidence

In respect of normative decision-making processes, Schauer observes that the strength of any regulatory provision lies in the conditions surrounding its applicability, acceptance, and performance.[56] In other words, the strength of a rule derives from the sanctions that attach to any violation of it. In the context of descriptive decision-making processes, Michon and Pakes suggest that decision-makers will rely on frequency estimates; that is to say they use personal knowledge of the likelihood that a certain outcome will follow a particular action.[57] If the police perceive that the courts usually allow the prosecution to adduce identification evidence obtained in breach of the Code, the option of non-compliance becomes more available and attractive. Why should they spend the time and effort necessary to comply with the provisions if it is likely that no adverse consequences will flow from any failure to do so? Salembier observes that 'in such circumstances a participant's actions cease to be guided by the rules and instead become dependent on its knowledge of enforcement proclivities'.[58]

During the course of its comprehensive review of the rules of evidence operating in that jurisdiction, the Australian Law Reform Commission expressed concerns that the courts too readily allowed evidence of identification to be given where there had been no identification parade conducted. Consequently it recommended that decisions on the admissibility of eyewitness identification evidence be subject to an exclusionary presumption in circumstances in which no parade had been conducted. This was subsequently enacted in section 114 of the Evidence Act 1995. The provision establishes a general prohibition on the reception of identification evidence where there has been no identification parade in the pre-trial stage of proceedings. This general prohibition is subject to an inclusionary discretion which permits evidence to be received, notwithstanding failure to conduct an identification parade by reference to a number of

---

[55] Galligan, n 18 above, 17.
[56] See, F Schauer, *Playing by the Rules: A Philosophical Examination of Rule-Based Decision-Making in Law and in Life* (1991: Oxford) 122–34.   [57] Michon and Pakes, n 17 above, 515.
[58] JP Salembier, 'Designing Regulatory Systems: A Template for Regulatory Rule-Making' (2002) 23 *Statute Law Review* 165, 177.

specified factors. Interestingly this proposal was adopted even though the Commission appeared to base its recommendation on anecdotal evidence.

By way of contrast, in England, the admissibility of eyewitness identification evidence is considered under a general statutory discretion to exclude evidence in order to ensure the fairness of proceedings. This discretion has been subject to considerable criticism due to the lack of discernible principles which guide its application.[59] A cursory review of appellate cases in England leads one to conclude, as the Australian Law Reform Commission has done, that the courts will rarely exclude eyewitness identification evidence where the police fail to comply with the provisions of the regulatory code by omitting to conduct an identification procedure. Perhaps the most striking example of this is *R v Williams*,[60] a recent case heard by the Court of Appeal. Here a woman waiting at a bus stop became the victim of an attempted robbery during which the culprit struck up a conversation which became more menacing and culminated with a demand for cash and jewellery and a threat to stab her with a hypodermic needle. She managed to escape and call the police. She provided a description by telephone and then went to the house of a relative. That description was of a clean-shaven man with a London accent wearing black or dark blue trousers, a black jacket with black zip, and brown shoes. The police making their way to the scene saw and gave chase to a man who was eventually detained on the roof of a factory. This man spoke with a distinctly different Glasgow accent, had two to three days' stubble on his face, was wearing black trousers and a black jacket which had a brass zip, and black rather than brown shoes. The officers who detained the suspect were told of the culprit's threat to stab the victim with a hypodermic needle. As a result he was handcuffed. The victim was driven to the scene where she saw the handcuffed suspect standing by a police car surrounded by police officers. She observed him from a distance of about 10 metres and stated that she was positive that he was the culprit. The Court accepted that there had been a breach of the regulatory code either by virtue of the nature in which the street identification had been conducted or because no formal procedures were subsequently conducted. Moreover, the Court acknowledged the suggestiveness of the procedures adopted, stating that 'a clearer way of pointing out to her who it was that the police sought her to identify could not have been imagined'.[61] Notwithstanding the only evidence against the defendant was the identification by the victim, it was held that the trial judge's decision not to exclude the evidence was correct and the conviction was safe.

This case provides a vivid indication of the need for research into the manner in which judicial discretion is exercised in cases concerning eyewitness identification evidence. Legal decision-making in respect of decisions on the admissibility of eyewitness identification evidence, and use of the exclusionary discretion more generally, provide fertile research pasture. Little is known of the decision-making

---

[59] See generally, D Ormerod and D Birch, 'The Evolution of the Discretionary Exclusion of Evidence' [2004] Crim LR 767.   [60] [2003] EWCA Crim 3200.
[61] *Williams* [2003] EWCA Crim 3200, para 12.

processes employed by judges in considering the admissibility of such evidence. A useful starting point might be work which explores whether structuring decision-making in the way that the Australian legislation does—an exclusionary presumption with an inclusionary discretion—leads to decision-making outcomes that differ significantly from those made in conditions in which there is a presumption of admissibility which is subject to an exclusionary discretion. Another significant line of inquiry ought to be police and prosecutor perceptions of judicial decision-making on the admissibility of identification evidence and the effect of those perceptions on police and prosecutorial decisions.

Conclusion

Optimizing the accuracy of identification parades (and more recently, video identification procedures) remains the object of a significant proportion of the research activity in this field. Important though this endeavour might be, in terms of averting the risk of miscarriage of justice on the basis of mistaken identification, further efforts in this direction are likely to deliver increasingly marginal returns.

Twining characterized the approach to much law reform as following the way of the 'baffled medic' who substitutes one prescription for another without adequate diagnosis.[62] The 'baffled medic' analogy does not seem wholly appropriate in the context of the problem of mistaken identification. The efforts of psychologists have provided a considerable corpus of research on the potential causes of erroneous identification, and identification procedures have been developed on the basis of this knowledge.

Identification procedures, however, should be viewed as comprising only one part of a regimen for tackling the problem of mistaken eyewitness identification in the criminal process. Sophisticated and accurate identification procedures are effective in averting miscarriages of justice only to the extent that the anterior decision-making process on whether to conduct them ensures that they do, in fact, take place when they would serve that purpose. There is little point in striving to increase the accuracy of identification parades without devoting similar efforts to legislating carefully for their application and enforcing adherence to the scheme. Underlying the neglect of this issue of police decision-making might be uncritical fundamental assumptions about the purpose of identification procedures, the role of the police in an adversarial criminal justice system, and how the police perceive their role. Research and discussion of how the problem of mistaken identification ought to be addressed in the criminal justice system has been atomistic. Too much attention has been focused on particular aspects of procedure without any consideration of how these aspects relate to, and might be affected by, what precedes and what follows.

[62] *Williams* [2003] EWCA Crim 3200, 264–5.

13

Child Witness Testimony: What Do We Know and Where Are We Going?

Helen L Westcott[1]

As a legal psychologist immersed in child witness issues for many years now, I want to take the opportunity to step a few paces back and take stock of 'where we are at' with respect to psychological research on child witness testimony. Thus, I will present a personal view that has been shaped by my own journey through the myriad psychological and legal issues one encounters when considering children's evidence. In addition, I would like to use this paper to ask questions, or at least raise questions which I think need to be asked, without feeling obliged to be able to offer answers—I hope this is an opportunity to be more reflective than is often the case. In this spirit, where I may later be seen to criticize psychologists, I am including myself as a member of the psychological community in question.

In order to address the questions posed by this paper's title, I am going to structure it as follows. First, I will summarize some of what we know about child witnesses, adult interviewers, and the questioning environment. Secondly, I will highlight where I think psychological research is currently 'going' with reference to topics that tend to dominate the published literature. I will then suggest a number of 'blindspots' that psychologists and lawyers might consider. Finally, I will suggest some issues for further research or debate by psychologists and lawyers.

What Do we Know about Child Witnesses?

At the risk of stating the obvious, we know that child witnesses can be accurate and inaccurate, consistent and inconsistent, honest and dishonest.[2] None of these

[1] The author would like to thank Dr Clare Wilson for her helpful comments on an earlier draft of the paper that forms this chapter. A version of this chapter has appeared in *Child and Family Law Quarterly* (2006) 18(2) 175–90 and is reproduced here with permission.
[2] HL Westcott and DPH Jones, 'Are children reliable witnesses to their experiences?' in P Reder, S Duncan, and C Lucey (eds), *Studies in the Assessment of Parenting* (Hove, 2003) 105.

qualities is related to completeness or credibility of accounts. I think it is important to state the obvious here, because as soon as we start considering children as a
separate category from other witnesses, namely adults, then questions about accuracy, consistency, and honesty become somehow uniquely or peculiarly associated
with children's evidence. Historically, this has been evident in legal descriptions of
the particular weaknesses ascribed to child witnesses, such as beliefs that they are
ego-centric, prone to fantasy, or manipulative liars.[3] It has also been reflected in
psychological debates about suggestibility, which has come to be seen as a problem
inextricably linked with *children's* evidence.[4] In reality, of course, any individual,
irrespective of age, can be more or less accurate, consistent, or honest depending
on the circumstances. And my separate consideration of child witnesses, adult
interviewers, and the questioning environment in this paper can itself contribute
to an artificial decontextualization of particular issues.

Psychological research which has investigated the accuracy of children's statements typically reports very high levels of correct recall, and percentage accuracies
of over 80 or 90 per cent are not uncommon when children are questioned fairly
soon after an event in a supportive and appropriate manner. Long delays can have
a negative effect on children's memories, which is reflected in a drop in testimonial
accuracy.[5] However, some psychologists have demonstrated remarkable resilience
over time in children's memories for events,[6] a relationship which may be affected
by the salience of the event, and the type of questioning experienced. Similarly,
the effects of stress on children's memory continues to be debated, and there does
not appear to be a straightforward correlation between stress (at encoding or
retrieval of information) and accuracy.[7] I return to the effects of questioning and
support on children's accuracy below, when I consider interviewers and environment, but here note that, for the most part, children's 'untainted' accuracy, when
they are able to give their account in their own words (eg in the free narrative
phase of an interview) remains high. Unfortunately, even if a child's account is
accurate, it is very often limited in quantity, which poses difficulties for police
officers and others who are attempting to ascertain what may have happened to
the child. For this reason, questioning to obtain further information is almost
inevitably required, and it is in questioning that children's accuracy is most often
compromised.

---

[3] eg J Heydon, *Evidence, Cases and Materials* (London, 1984, 2nd edn).
   [4] eg SJ Ceci and M Bruck, 'Suggestibility of the child witness: A historical review and synthesis'
(1993) 113 *Psychological Bulletin* 403.
   [5] eg RH Flin, J Boon, A Knox, and R Bull, 'The effects of a five month delay on children's and
adults' eyewitness memory' (1992) 83 *British Journal of Psychology* 323.
   [6] eg R Fivush and A Schwarzmueller, 'Children remember childhood: Implications for childhood
amnesia' (1998) 12 *Applied Cognitive Psychology* 455.
   [7] eg R Fivush, 'The development of autobiographical memory' in HL Westcott, GM Davies, and
RHC Bull (eds), *Children's Testimony: A Handbook of Psychological Research and Forensic Practice*
(Chichester, 2002) 55 [hereinafter *Children's Testimony*].

Psychologists have demonstrated, in an extensive body of research, that for most children the most effective questions are those that are 'open', and do not proscribe the child's report in any way (eg 'What happened yesterday?').[8] Specific questions, which offer more support to the child's memory without leading the child or limiting their options in responding, are also of value, although they have been shown to lead to a decrease in overall accuracy (eg because the child may guess in order to respond to a question that they cannot answer). Other categories of questions are of less value, because they may suggest to the child what answer is required (eg 'You saw him touch it, didn't you?'), or may limit the child's answer to a number of different options (eg 'Were you lying on top of him, or he on top of you?'). Such leading or option-posing questions rely less on the child's memory, and more on the information provided in the question, and so can decrease the accuracy of the child's account.

Consistency in children's accounts is another perplexing issue, until one unpicks what is meant by 'consistency': for example, consistency within a single interview, or across different interviews; consistency about a single event; or consistency about a repeated event.[9] Further, psychological research has shown that, in fact, inconsistency in witness statements is to be expected when questioning takes place across a number of interviews, since it is a natural phenomenon of memory that we remember different aspects of events at different times.[10] Lawyers are fond of highlighting such discrepancies in accounts during cross-examination, a practice which psychological research would suggest is at best misleading.

In brief, when children are asked only open questions, then simple repetition of questions across interviews is beneficial (because the memory trace is strengthened).[11] If children are inconsistent in subsequent interviews only in response to specific questions, then the inconsistent details may be inaccurate.[12] Inconsistency within an interview (or examination at court) may suggest that the child is responding to social cues, for example, changing their answer to try and please the adult questioner.[13] To improve accuracy, interviewers should not repeat questions using the same form of words, for example, they should feign misunderstanding, or forgetfulness of the child's response and repeat a slightly different question. Inconsistencies across a child's description of a repeated event are likely, because of the difficulties children (and adults) have in identifying which unique aspects of

---

[8] eg DA Poole and ME Lamb, *Investigative Interviews of Children: A Guide for Helping Professionals* (Washington, DC, 1998). [9] Westcott and Jones, n 2 above.

[10] Fivush, n 7 above.

[11] L Baker-Ward and PA Ornstein, 'Cognitive underpinnings of children's testimony' in Westcott, Davies, and Bull, *Children's Testimony*, n 7 above, 21.

[12] M Powell and D Thomson, 'Children's memories for repeated events' in Westcott, Davies, and Bull, *Children's Testimony*, n 7 above, 69.

[13] S Moston, 'How children interpret and respond to questions: Situational sources of suggestibility in eyewitness interviews' (1990) 5 *Social Behaviour* 155.

an event were experienced on which occasion.[14] There is an increasing risk that children will acquiesce to misleading questions which require only a 'yes/no' answer about aspects of the event which vary across their experiences. This is particularly pertinent to questioning about repeated sexual abuse, and again challenges us to reflect on the effects of typical questioning practice, especially at court.

Finally, children's honesty as witnesses continues to be a controversial issue, especially in the context of sexual abuse. It is important to distinguish between children's deliberate lies, and their making an 'erroneous' statement honestly—a theme first highlighted by the Sterns at the beginning of the twentieth century in their discussion of outright lies and 'false belief'.[15] It may be that certain adult interventions, for example, sustained coaching or questioning, can lead children to report an event as if they genuinely believe it has occurred when it has not. To summarize, psychological research on deception has shown that children can be deliberately deceptive from around the age of four years, and before that they can mislead—by not answering a question, for example.[16] However, at this young age children are unlikely to be able to maintain elaborate verbal lies spontaneously. This is another reason why adults should avoid asking questions which require only 'yes/no' answers, since any deception will be easier to maintain in these circumstances. Psychologists and lawyers have been particularly concerned with lies in the context of false allegations of abuse (ie errors of commission in accounts). However, the extent to which children lie to minimize the extent of wrongdoing, or to deny abuse altogether (ie errors of omission), is a notable oversight in the experimental literature. I am now going to highlight some other 'gaps' in our knowledge about child witnesses.

What Don't we Know about Child Witnesses?

There are certain groups of children for whom psychological research, and law, has so far shown little consideration. For example, until recently, research on the testimony of children with learning impairments has been very limited. Contrary to historical stereotypes of such children as hopelessly suggestible,[17] psychological research has demonstrated that learning impaired children can provide useful and accurate information about events they have experienced if they are questioned appropriately, and without excessive use of closed questions.[18] The particular

---

[14] Powell and Thomson, n 12 above.

[15] C Stern and W Stern, *Recollection, Testimony and Lying in Early Childhood* (trans JT Lamiell, Washington, DC, 1999). See also Westcott and Jones, n 2 above.

[16] A Vrij, 'Deception in children: A literature review and implications for children's testimony' in Westcott, Davies, and Bull, *Children's Testimony*, n 7 above, 175.

[17] W Coles, 'Sexual abuse of persons with disabilities: A law enforcement perspective' (1990) 18 *Developmental Disabilities Bulletin* 35.

[18] eg SA Agnew and MB Powell, 'The effect of intellectual disability on children's recall of an event across different question types' (2004) 28 *Law and Human Behavior* 273.

difficulties facing bilingual children have also received scant attention,[19] as have those facing child witnesses from minority ethnic groups.[20] As psychologists we can anticipate issues for children from these different groups associated with memory, language, and socio-cultural factors, yet research into such issues has fully to develop. It is also the case that little psychological research has involved children known to have been abused as participants,[21] yet we know that abuse can have serious effects on children's development, which can in turn have implications for children's 'performance' (eg on an interviewing task). Psychologists, I would suggest, have a responsibility to consider these types of issues facing children from diverse backgrounds in their research, more than the routine reporting of age, sex, and 'socio-economic status' found in the experimental methods sections of published studies. We know that, in England and Wales, the developments in law and legal procedure following successive Criminal Justice Acts have galvanized a great deal of psychological research on child witnesses. Perhaps an optimistic view might be to hope that the Youth Justice and Criminal Evidence Act 1999, with its emphasis on a much wider group of vulnerable witnesses, will have a similar motivating effect.

We know surprisingly little about the effects on children of their participation in the criminal justice system. No doubt this is due in part to the enormous methodological difficulties researchers face when trying to carry out longitudinal studies which can disentangle the effects of different factors, such as effects of abuse versus effects of court appearance. The relatively few studies which do exist have suggested that: repeated interviews are detrimental to children's welfare; testifying more than once may have negative effects on child witnesses; lengthy and harsh cross-examination is harmful; maternal support promotes well-being; case resolution and the passage of time promotes recovery from the court experience; and, testifying in court for some children *who desire it* can have positive effects.[22] Cross-examination practice has provoked most concerns,[23] with many child witnesses continuing to report their unhappiness with this experience.[24] However, we do not know, and rarely consider, the impact of investigative

---

[19] But see M Aldridge and J Wood, *Interviewing Children: A Guide for Child Care and Forensic Practitioners* (Chichester, 1998).

[20] A Gupta, 'Black children and the Memorandum' in H Westcott and J Jones (eds), *Perspectives on the Memorandum: Policy, Practice and Research in Investigative Interviewing* (Aldershot, 1997) 81.

[21] But see TD Lyon and KJ Saywitz, 'Young maltreated children's competence to take the Oath' (1999) 3 *Applied Developmental Science* 16.

[22] eg GS Goodman, EP Pyle-Taub, DPH Jones, P England, LK Port, L Rudy, and L Prado, 'Testifying in court: Emotional effects of criminal court testimony on child sexual assault victims' (1992) 57 *Monographs of the Society for Research on Child Development*.

[23] eg M Brennan and R Brennan, *Strange Language* (Wagga Wagga, 1988, 2nd edn). N Perry, B McAuliff, P Tam, L Claycomb, C Dostal, and C Flanagan, 'When lawyers question children: Is justice served?' (1995) 19 *Law and Human Behavior* 609. R Zajac and H Hayne, 'I don't think that's what *really* happened: The effect of cross-examination on the accuracy of children's reports' (2003) 8 *Journal of Experimental Psychology: Applied* 187.

[24] eg J Plotnikoff and R Woolfson, *In Their Own Words: The Experiences of 50 Young Witnesses in Criminal Proceedings* (London, 2004).

interviews on child witnesses,[25] especially when, for example, no further action results. What is the impact of having one's account 'shaped' in particular ways for consumption by others in the criminal justice system? What is the effect of having certain parts of one's account challenged in detail, and other aspects overlooked or 'silenced'?[26]

This is one example of what I see as a lack of 'joined up' thinking in psychology's treatment of children and their evidence. Greater collaboration between psychologists from academic, legal, educational, and clinical backgrounds could afford us insights into the personal consequences of participation in the legal process, for example, on children's self-esteem, and their identity.[27] This issue itself highlights another group of children about whom psychologists working in the witness field have had little to say—children who are called as defence witnesses, and children who are defendants. One of the psychiatrists who interviewed Jon Venables, one of the ten-year-old killers of toddler James Bulger,[28] reported that:

When the trial was mentioned, the applicant [Venables] had described his sense of shock when he had seen the public being let in and his considerable distress when his name and photograph were published. He had been terrified of being looked at in court and had frequently found himself worrying what people were thinking about him. Most of the time he had not been able to participate in the proceedings and had spent time counting in his head or making shapes with his shoes because he could not pay attention or process the whole proceedings. He did not follow when he heard his and [Thompson's] interviews with the police being played in court and he recalled crying at that time.[29]

Surely, as psychologists, we should also be concerned with the implications for children's long-term development of participation in legal proceedings that they cannot understand?

What Do we Know about Adult Interviewers?

As with children, we know that adult interviewers can be accurate and inaccurate, consistent and inconsistent, honest and dishonest. I am talking here about adults who interview children early in an investigation, as well as those who interview them later in court. I have already alluded to the impact adults can have on children's accuracy above, through their use of different questioning techniques. To recap, if we want accurate, consistent, and honest child witness

---

[25] Nor on interviewers.

[26] R Fivush, 'Voice and silence: A feminist model of autobiographical memory' in JM Lucariello, JA Hudson, R Fivush, and PJ Bauer (eds), *The Development of the Mediated Mind: Sociocultural Context and Cognitive Development* (Mahwah, NJ, 2004).

[27] HL Westcott and M Page, 'Cross-examination, sexual abuse and child witness identity' (2002) 11 *Child Abuse Review* 137.

[28] A case in the UK in which two ten-year-old boys murdered a two-year-old child (eg B Morrison, *As If* (London, 1997)).   [29] <www.guardian.co.uk/bulger>, accessed 25 July 2002.

testimony, then we need to use open questions as much as possible, and closed (option-posing) and leading questions as little as possible. That is to say, adults need to be accurate in their selection and implementation of questioning techniques. Research has shown that police officers and social workers struggle, in particular, to ask children sufficient open questions; however, contrary to popular belief, they do not rely extensively on leading questions. For example, two recent studies reported the mean number of leading questions asked per interview to be just four and one.[30] Interestingly, while psychologists are in agreement about the advantages and disadvantages of different types of questions and their effects on children's accuracy, lawyers have developed a certain 'schizophrenia' in this regard. This is eloquently described by John Spencer, Professor of Law at Cambridge University:

British lawyers seem to be extremely concerned with the dangers of leading questions being posed by social workers, doctors or police officers during the early stages of a criminal investigation. Paradoxically, they do not seem to be the least bit concerned about their own use of leading questions in cross-examination and the effects this may have on the quality of a child's evidence. The characteristics of a typical interview conducted during cross-examination appear to violate all the principles of best practice, with the predicted outcome of maximizing the risk of contaminating the evidence.[31]

To promote accuracy in children's accounts we also need to adapt our language to that of the child, something police officers are getting much better at doing,[32] but which lawyers have been consistently shown to resist.[33] I would suggest that the use of formal, complex, and jargon-laden language with child witnesses is another way in which adult interviewers can be 'inaccurate', since at best it reveals a lack of awareness of child development and the needs of child witnesses, and at worst it can be seen as an abuse of power.[34]

Research has demonstrated that adults are inaccurate and inconsistent in interviews when they 'distort' children's responses, and incorporate their distortions into later questions or summary statements, for example, by changing the name of the perpetrator, or mis-describing the manner in which a child has said they were

---

[30] KJ Sternberg, ME Lamb, GM Davies, and HL Westcott, 'The Memorandum of Good Practice: Theory versus Application' (2001) 25 *Child Abuse and Neglect* 669. HL Westcott, S Kynan, and C Few, 'Improving the quality of investigative interviews for suspected child abuse: A case study' (2005) *Psychology, Crime and Law* 77–96.

[31] JR Spencer and RH Flin, *The Evidence of Children: The Law and the Psychology* (London, 1993, 2nd edn) 307.

[32] GM Davies, C Wilson, R Mitchell, and J Milsom, *Videotaping of Children's Evidence: An Evaluation* (London, 1995).

[33] eg Brennan and Brennan, n 23 above. V Kranat and HL Westcott, 'Under fire: Lawyers questioning children in criminal courts' (1994) 3 *Expert Evidence* 16. R Zajac, J Gross, and H Hayne, 'Asked and answered: Questioning children in the courtroom' (2003) 10 *Psychiatry, Psychology and Law* 199.

[34] HL Westcott, 'Children's experiences of being examined and cross-examined: The opportunity to be heard?' (1995) 4 *Expert Evidence* 13.

touched.[35] Children rarely challenge such distortions, with the danger that they go on to include the adult's misrepresentations into their later responses.

Finally, a comment on interviewer honesty or dishonesty. One of the leading psychological treatises on witness testimony, *Jeopardy in the Courtroom*,[36] gives a number of examples of early American pre-school cases where interviewers, arguably with the best of intentions, have employed dishonest questioning techniques—for example, by telling a child that they already know what happened because another child told them—as a method of getting a child to talk. This is linked to the supposition that investigative interviewers typically have a hypothesis about what has happened to the child which they seek only to confirm, not disconfirm, in the interview. (At court, of course, lawyers for the prosecution and defence do explicitly operate on the basis of such hypotheses.) This supposition is still frequently listed as a criticism of interviewers in publications I read. However, I see little evidence for this in my experience of working with investigative interviewers, and also I have not seen convincing empirical evidence in contemporary psychological research. My own research suggests that the situation is much more complex, and that interviewers themselves debate the 'pros and cons' of receiving more or less detailed referral information before interviewing a child.[37]

I think it is therefore more honest ourselves to say that we do *not* know the extent to which police officers, social workers, etc, really do operate on the basis of preconceived hypotheses when they interview children. Nor do we know how interviewers might effectively test different hypotheses in investigative interviews without confusing the child or compromising the value of the videotaped record as the child's examination-in-chief. I am now going to suggest a few other areas where I think we need to know more about adult interviewers.

What Don't we Know about Adult Interviewers?

It seems to me that the most obvious examples of our lack of knowledge relate to the role of experience, qualifications, and personal qualities in shaping an individual as a good interviewer. We really do not have information about how many child witnesses a police officer, or barrister, routinely questions each month, nor whether an increase in experience with children leads to improved questioning skills—although one would hope it does! Similarly, we do not know whether employing certain personality measures or psychological tests as part of the recruitment process for interviewers would result in better appointments—a state

---

[35] KP Roberts and ME Lamb, 'Children's responses when interviewers distort details during investigative interviews' (1999) 4 *Legal and Criminological Psychology* 23. HL Westcott and S Kynan, 'Interviewer practice in investigative interviews for suspected child sexual abuse' (2005) *Psychology, Crime and Law* (in press).

[36] SJ Ceci and M Bruck, *Jeopardy in the Courtroom: A Scientific Analysis of Children's Testimony* (Washington, DC, 1995).   [37] Westcott, Kynan and Few, n 30 above.

of affairs I am sure many occupational psychologists would like to comment upon (and I'm rather surprised they haven't done so extensively already).

Another big challenge is to understand why so many interviewers find it difficult to maintain skills and knowledge they have acquired during training. This particular finding has been demonstrated a number of times in evaluations of training interventions[38] but as yet no convincing solutions have been put forward, with the exception of the National Institute of Child Health and Human Development (NICHD) interviewing protocol, developed by Michael Lamb, Kathleen Sternberg, and associates.[39] Unfortunately, the NICHD protocol is resource intensive to a degree that makes it prohibitive for many interviewing authorities. Again this is an area in which forensic and occupational psychologists could collaborate fruitfully in the future.

What Do we Know about the Questioning Environment?

There are two different aspects of the questioning environment which can be considered: the 'social environment' which is created by the interviewer and the extent to which she or he creates a relationship or rapport with the child, and the 'physical environment' such as a videotape suite or courtroom. Psychologists have demonstrated that establishing a good social environment through rapport has beneficial effects on children's accounts. For example, providing social support through the provision of a friendly (but neutral) questioning manner, positive body posture, and the maintenance of eye contact can help children to resist misleading questions.[40] Good rapport also enables adults to clarify what is expected of children in the interview, such as detailed responses, no guessing, etc.[41]

Some early studies demonstrated that an overly formal physical environment had a negative impact on children's evidence,[42] and research which has evaluated changes designed to help children in formal court settings, such as through the

---

[38] J Aldridge and S Cameron, 'Interviewing child witnesses: Questioning techniques and the role of training' (1999) 3 *Applied Developmental Science* 136. AR Warren, CE Woodall, M Thomas, M Nunno, JM Keeney, and SM Larson, 'Assessing the effect of a training program for interviewing child witnessses' (1999) 3 *Applied Developmental Science* 128. JM Wood and S Garven, 'How sexual abuse interviews go astray: Implications for prosecutors, police and child protection services' (2000) 5 *Child Maltreatment* 109. Westcott, Kynan, and Few, n 30 above.

[39] Y Orbach, I Hershkowitz, ME Lamb, KJ Sternberg, PW Esplin, and D Horowitz, 'Assessing the value of structured protocols for forensic interviews of alleged child abuse victims' (2000) 24 *Child Abuse and Neglect* 733.

[40] eg GS Goodman, B Bottoms, B Schwartz-Kenney, and L Rudy, 'Children's testimony about a stressful event: Improving children's reports' (1991) 7 *Journal of Narrative and Life History* 69.

[41] MR Mulder and A Vrij, 'Explaining conversation rules to children: An intervention study to facilitate children's accurate responses' (1996) 20 *Child Abuse and Neglect* 623. Westcott, Kynan, and Few, n 30 above.

[42] For a review, GM Davies and HL Westcott, 'Videotechnology and the child witness' in H Dent and R Flin (eds), *Children as Witnesses* (Chichester, 1992) 211.

implementation of video technology, has reported generally favourable results.[43] Technological developments in the absence of a corresponding cultural shift are likely to have limited effects, however.[44] It is too simplistic to consider the impact of, say, livelinks or CCTV in courtrooms, if we don't simultaneously consider the attitudes of courtroom personnel towards the technology and child witnesses, nor other factors such as how child witnesses would prefer to give their evidence, or how they are otherwise looked after in the court buildings.[45]

Where are we Going in Child Witness Research?

Suggestibility seems certain to continue as a predominant topic. Suggestibility has been referred to as the 'act or process of impressing something (an idea, attitude or desired action) on the mind of another'.[46] However, psychologists have sometimes failed to address the different processes involved for different actors in their use of the global term 'suggestibility'—such as the activity of suggesting, and the predisposition to be suggestible, and the current experience of being under the influence of suggestion—in terms of implications of their findings.[47] Nevertheless, researchers have argued that suggestibility is made worse when young children are questioned by a biased interviewer, repeatedly asked misleading questions, or questioned in an over-authoritarian manner.[48]

Studies of individual differences, such as in children's temperament, family circumstances, and cognitive abilities, and their relationship to child witness behaviour (eg performance on memory tests, in interviews) are also increasingly published. For example, introverted and socially anxious children (as many may be in the courtroom environment) are less likely to be believed by observers, irrespective of whether they are accurate or truthful.[49] A recent volume devoted to

---

[43] GM Davies and E Noon, *An Evaluation of the Live Link for Child Witnesses* (London, 1991). Davies, Wilson, Mitchell, and Milsom, n 32 above. Plotnikoff and Woolfson, n 24 above.

[44] J Plotnikoff and R Woolfson, *Prosecuting Child Abuse: An Evaluation of the Government's Speedy Progress Policy* (London, 1995). Plotnikoff and Woolfson, n 24 above.

[45] J Cashmore and N de Haas, *The Use of Closed Circuit Television for Child Witnesses in the ACT* (Sydney, 1992). Plotnikoff and Woolfson, n 24 above. A Wade, 'New measures and new challenges: Children's experiences of the court process' in Westcott, Davies, and Bull, *Children's Testimony*, n 7 above, 219.

[46] T Fundudis, 'Young children's memory: How good is it? How much do we know about it?' (1997) 2 *Child Psychology and Psychiatry Review* 151.

[47] For a critique, J Motzkau, 'Cross-examining suggestibility: Memory, childhood, expertise. Children's testimony between psychological research and juridicial practice' in A Czeredecka, T Jaskiewicz-Obydzinska, R Roesch, and J Wojcikiewicz (eds), *Forensic Psychology and Law: Facing the Challenges of a Changing World* (Krakow, 2005).

[48] SJ Ceci, AM Crossman, MH Scullin, L Gilsrap, and ML Huffman, 'Children's suggestibility research: Implications for the courtroom and the forensic interview' in Westcott, Davies, and Bull, *Children's Testimony*, n 7 above, 117.

[49] A Vrij and JJ van Wijngaarden, 'Will truth come out? Two studies about the detection of false statements expressed by children' (1994) 3 *Expert Evidence* 78.

individual and developmental differences in suggestibility,[50] suggested that the following cognitive and psycho-social factors were related to suggestibility: language ability; creativity; self-efficacy; maternal attachment; and the parent-child relationship.[51] However, despite a general caution about the use of suggestive interviewing techniques, especially with children who are learning disabled, the authors concluded that 'the scientific evidence suggests that one cannot, at present, identify individual children who are most at risk for heightened suggestibility'.[52] Thus, echoing Binet,[53] who at the beginning of the twentieth century, doubted that it was possible or useful to conceptualize suggestion in general terms, or to search for personality traits that would correlate with suggestibility.[54]

Finally, the concept of source-monitoring appears to be becoming increasingly important. Children can sometimes find it particularly difficult to identify the 'source' of information in their memories, for example whether someone really said something, or whether they imagined someone saying it.[55] This concept is also related to the concept of suggestibility, since suggestive or leading questions increase source-monitoring difficulties. Children who understand that knowledge may have different origins (sources) produce more information in their free-recall accounts than children who are less aware of source knowledge.[56] They are also more likely to recall source information,[57] which suggests that we need to find ways of prompting non-suggestively for source information in the early stages of an interview, to model the type of information that is required.

Child Witness 'Blindspots'

I would like to suggest that one child witness blindspot relates to the way in which psychologists and lawyers conceptualize children and their testimony. I am concerned that we may, in fact, set certain children up to fail (especially those who are very young, or very traumatized). For example, traditional experimental approaches to child witness testimony seem to suggest that if only we can get the questions right then children will give us the correct, and accurate answers. I believe this adds to the pressures acting upon child witnesses, and also upon interviewers. It also overlooks the host of motivational issues that children caught up in

---

[50] AM Crossman, MH Scullin, and L Melnyk (eds), (2004) 18 *Applied Cognitive Psychology*.

[51] M Bruck and L Melnyk, 'Individual differences in children's suggestibility: A review and synthesis' (2004) 18 *Applied Cognitive Psychology* 947.　　[52] Bruck and Melnyk, n 51 above, 990.

[53] A Binet, *La Suggestibilité* (Paris, 1900).　　[54] See review by Motzkau, n 47 above.

[55] DS Lindsay, 'Children's source monitoring' in Westcott, Davies, and Bull, *Children's Testimony*, n 7 above, 83.

[56] KL Thierry, ME Lamb, and Y Orbach, 'Awareness of the origin of knowledge predicts child witnesses' recall of alleged sexual and physical abuse' (2003) 17 *Applied Cognitive Psychology* 953.

[57] ibid.

investigations experience, as well as minimizing the potential influence of other traumas or life events on a child's willingness or ability to talk. Social constructionist approaches to interactions emphasize the degree to which narratives are co-constructed, and pay particular attention to power dynamics and the management of ambiguity.[58] It seems to me that they might offer valuable insights into the peculiar dynamics of investigative interviews, where power issues and ambiguity are key features,[59] especially with younger and traumatized children, and the 'normal' rules of conversation with adult authority figures do not apply. We can also learn from the growing numbers of studies which have endeavoured to document children's experiences as witnesses, and which demonstrate the complex nature of the process from their perspective.[60]

This is linked to a further point, that I have made recently elsewhere with my colleague Karen Littleton; namely, that we may be in danger of 'theorizing incompetent children' when we underestimate their role in investigative or research interviews.[61] If we create interview situations which become interrogations where children are not viewed as equal and active participants, and where well-intentioned guidance is implemented as a list of chores to be adhered to, then the chances are that we will be reducing children's competence to participate. Earlier in this paper I cautioned about the dangers of unthinkingly treating child witnesses differently from adults, and I think we do have a duty to question whether our research and/or practice is contributing to perceptions of children as so different from adults that we are creating further difficulties for them and for ourselves. A balanced view of strengths and vulnerabilities is required, not an over-riding focus on children's 'inadequacies' in interview situations.

A second blindspot relates to the degree to which we scrutinize our own practice as psychologists and as lawyers. Ethics is an obvious issue, and one I have raised a number of times previously in relation to psychological research.[62] For example, if we permanently alter a child's autobiographical memory, perhaps through attempts to create a 'false memory' which we can later probe through different questioning techniques, is that ethical?[63] I have also previously questioned

[58] J Potter and MS Wetherell, *Discourse and Social Psychology: Beyond Attitudes and Behaviour* (London, 1987).

[59] HL Westcott and S Kynan, 'The application of a "story-telling framework" to investigative interviews for suspected child sexual abuse' (2004) 9 *Legal and Criminological Psychology* 37.

[60] Plotnikoff and Woolfson, n 24 above. Wade, n 45 above. A Wade and HL Westcott, 'No easy answers: Children's perspectives on investigative interviews' in HL Westcott and J Jones (eds), *Perspectives on the Memorandum: Policy, Practice and Research in Investigative Interviewing* (Aldershot, 1997) 51.

[61] HL Westcott and KS Littleton, 'Exploring meaning in interviews with children' in S Greene and D Hogan (eds), *Researching Children's Experience: Approaches and Methods* (London, 2005) 141.

[62] HL Westcott, 'On sensitivity and ethical issues in child witness research' (1994) 18 *Child Abuse and Neglect* 287. HL Westcott, 'Ethical considerations in studies with children' in B Hopkins (ed), *The Cambridge Enclyclopedia of Child Development* (Cambridge, 2005) 153.

[63] HL Westcott, 'Commentary on Herrmann and Yoder "The potential effects of the implanted memory paradigm on child subjects"' (1998) 12 *Applied Cognitive Psychology* 225.

the ethics of extreme cross-examination tactics, including behaviours towards children that would not be tolerated in any other modern day context.[64] I do not believe that *all* psychologists or lawyers necessarily intend to act unethically; rather, pressures can lead inevitably to a question of priorities, and little time to question later whether our priorities were misplaced.

As a psychologist, another issue which I feel deserves more scrutiny, is the relationship between statistical significance, and real-world significance, in experimental research. Increasing sophistication in research designs, together with complex statistical interpretations, can sometimes make it difficult to judge how much weight should be accorded to psychological investigations. This is particularly true for multi-disciplinary audiences, and practitioners who are unfamiliar with formal psychological terminology and statistical designs. Thus, I would argue that a further blindspot relates to the degree to which we continually question the extent to which our research is truly useful and accessible: are we, as researchers, accurate, consistent, and honest in our interpretations? As academics, we must strive to increase the validity of our findings, especially when they are derived from experimental situations, and we need to examine how we permit our findings to be presented by interested parties and the media.[65] Lawyers might also question how the construction of expert evidence in courts, especially within adversarial systems, impacts on the validity of research, when the necessary qualifications, explanations, and contextualizing of research findings are generally restricted by lawyers for purposes of maintaining control. Are lawyers accurate, consistent, and honest in their interpretations?

Where Might We Go Next?

I have already hinted at opportunities for better interdisciplinary and multi-disciplinary links within and outside psychology, and indeed this volume represents one such opportunity. Clinical and forensic psychologists, and lawyers, could together explore concerns around the impact of criminal justice interventions on child witnesses. Occupational and forensic psychologists, police officers, and lawyers, could review the training and supervision requirements of investigative interviewers and barristers. There are also opportunities for us to review the kinds of research we conduct, and to be receptive to alternative approaches (eg social constructionist/discourse analytic approaches to interviews, which I mentioned earlier), and to small-scale research projects which are rooted in practice.

---

[64] Westcott, n 34 above.

[65] TD Lyon, 'The new wave in children's suggestibility research: A critique' (1999) 84 *Cornell Law Review* 1004. HL Westcott, 'Book review: Jeopardy in the Courtroom: A Scientific Analysis of Children's Testimony, by Stephen Ceci and Maggie Bruck' (1998) 89 *British Journal of Psychology* 525.

I would suggest that psychologists and lawyers need to engage in more reflective debate around the 'bigger picture' and continuing 'thorny questions' surrounding criminal justice and child protection investigations. The past two decades have seen a host of relatively minor reforms, such as those included in the Criminal Justice Act 1988, as well as more major reforms, such as those within the Youth Justice and Criminal Evidence Act 1999. It is no surprise, indeed it is very telling, that the most child-centred of the latest reforms—the introduction of intermediaries, and videotaped cross-examination, have yet to be implemented fully, if at all. This reflects the point I made earlier about the need for cultural shifts in the way child witnesses and their evidence are regarded. Should we be debating more seriously other possibilities for these most difficult of cases—for example, the creation of family courts that could deal with civil and criminal proceedings related to a child and offender simultaneously; or a possible role for more expert evidence to the court in criminal cases, in a way that preserves the spirit of the *Turner* ruling—for example, having such evidence presented independently and directly to the court, rather than via defence or prosecution expert witnesses?

We do need constantly to review reforms and legislative changes that have been enacted. The lack of central, systematic data recording and collection is lamentable, and reflected in the difficulties researchers face in tracking cases through the system, even those concerning child witnesses which are supposed to be flagged, for example for fast-tracking.[66] The available evidence regarding attrition of cases involving vulnerable witnesses must be a cause for concern, given the spirit of reforms aimed to facilitate their testimony in courts. Approximately 70 to 80 per cent of such cases are 'No Further Action-ed' or do not otherwise progress past the police stage of an investigation.[67] The introduction of videotaped evidence-in-chief apparently led to no statistically significant increase in the number of convictions nor guilty pleas in cases involving child witnesses.[68] Delays remain endemic in the system, and time taken to progress child witness cases has not improved despite specific reforms.[69] Such findings must surely make psychologists and lawyers question what our objectives are concerning children (and other vulnerable witnesses), and their participation in the criminal justice system, as well as to what extent we can truly say we are meeting our objectives. Sanders and colleagues, following a study of learning disabled victims in the criminal justice system, have commented: 'It is important to recognise that normal procedures which create formal equality between defendant and victim often create substantive inequality when the victim is vulnerable.'[70]

[66] Plotnikoff and Woolfson, n 44 above.

[67] B Gallagher and K Pease, *Understanding the Attrition of Child Abuse and Neglect Cases in the Criminal Justice System* (Unpublished ESRC report, 2000). L Kelly, J Lovett, and L Regan, *A Gap or a Chasm? Attrition in Reported Rape Cases* (London, 2005).

[68] Davies, Wilson, Mitchell, and Milsom, n 32 above.

[69] Plotnikoff and Woolfson, n 44 above.

[70] A Sanders, J Creaton, S Bird, and L Weber, *Victims with Learning Disabilities: Negotiating the Criminal Justice System* (Oxford, 1997).

If psychologists want substantive equality for children and vulnerable witnesses (as I do), then I suspect this must take us out of our 'comfort zone' in our research and practice, and into some uncomfortable discussions with colleagues from law. It requires discussions at another higher level as to the possible influence of psychology, or other disciplines, within law.[71] It also requires honesty about the integrity of the law as it is practised in relation to children's testimony, and the position of vulnerable witnesses. In this paper I have discussed much psychological research which has had, and can have, a positive impact upon professional practice within legal contexts. However, it is also clear that this impact has been curtailed in many instances by existing structural relations and power dynamics within law, and it is to such relations and dynamics we must inevitably turn.

[71] eg M King, *Psychology In and Out of Court: A Critical Examination of Legal Psychology* (Oxford, 1986). M King and C Piper, *How the Law Thinks About Children* (Aldershot, 1995, 2nd edn).

14

The Controversy over Psychological Evidence in Family Law Cases

Nicholas Bala and Katherine Duvall Antonacopoulos

Best Interests Decisions and Mental Health Professionals

In the latter half of the twentieth century, courts and legislatures abandoned presumptive rules for the resolution of disputes about the care of children and adopted the best interests of the child principle (or welfare principle), requiring individualized determinations of what arrangements best meet the needs of the children involved in a specific case. The best interests of the child principle is now used to resolve disputes between separated parents, and has an important role in the resolution of cases in which the state is intervening in the family to respond to allegations of parental abuse or neglect. With the increase in family breakdown has come an increase in family law litigation, and a growing involvement of psychologists, psychiatrists, and social workers to help determine what arrangements are in the best interests of children. When mental health professionals were first involved in these cases, it was as party-retained experts, but it has become increasingly common for there to be a court-appointed assessor[1] who investigates the circumstances of a case, and makes a recommendation about what arrangements are in the best interests of the children involved. While these recommendations are not binding on the courts, they are often influential if a case goes to trial, and are frequently the basis for a settlement. Although now in family law cases mental health professionals are frequently involved and the use of psychological concepts is widespread, there is controversy over the use of psychological research and witnesses in these cases.

The controversy over the use of psychological evidence is related to the nature of best interests decisions, and the relationship of these decisions to psychological knowledge and research. Despite the growing body of literature on conducting

---

[1] In this paper the term 'assessment' is used in a generic sense, and includes involvement of court-appointed social workers, psychologists, psychiatrists, and multi-disciplinary teams in child-related litigation. In different jurisdictions or contexts, such terms as 'evaluation', 'clinical investigation', and 'family study' are also used.

assessments, it is often impossible for a mental health professional to make accurate, research-based predictions about the effects of different child care arrangements on an individual child. Recommendations about which arrangements will be in the 'best interests' of a child are inevitably based, at least in part, on the values and clinical judgement of the assessor.

This paper considers the assessment process and involvement of mental health professionals in the resolution of disputes about the care of children, both private cases between separated parents (or other individuals like grandparents) and public cases that involve a state agency seeking to protect children.[2] It discusses the emerging critique of the role of these professionals and the applicability of the general legal rules about expert witnesses to assessments. It is argued that mental health professionals, and in particular court-appointed assessors, have a unique and important role in the resolution of family law cases, and accordingly should be able to express their opinions about best interests issues, even if this type of evidence does not meet the legal requirements for the admission of expert evidence that are applied by the courts to other cases.

While there are significant variations in the legal rules and institutional arrangements concerning assessments and the involvement of mental health professionals in the family law process in different jurisdictions, this chapter focuses on some of the common themes and issues that apply across jurisdictions, with some discussion of differences, primarily in the context of Canada, the United States and England.

Court-appointed Assessors

Starting in the 1960s, courts and legislatures in North America and England began to adopt legal rules that required decisions about the care of children to be based on the best interests of children, rather than on presumptions or parental rights. As litigation over children became more frequent in the middle of the twentieth century, it was increasingly common for parties to retain mental health professionals to testify in court. There were significant concerns about resolving child-related disputes with the only psychological evidence being provided by party-retained professionals. Party-retained experts generally only have access to one party to the dispute, and have an incomplete picture of the case, limiting the value of their opinions.[3] There are also concerns that, while expert witnesses are

---

[2] In the public cases, involving child protection and possible termination of parental rights, there is an onus on the child welfare agency to justify removal of a child from parental care. In many jurisdictions there is some reference to the 'best interests of the child' in child protection legislation, but the term has a different meaning from its use in private disputes. While there are significant differences between public and private child-related disputes, the issues related to assessments are similar.

[3] AI Schepard, *Children, Courts and Custody: Interdisciplinary Models for Divorcing Families* (Cambridge, Mass, 2004) 152.

expected to maintain objectivity, parties are likely to retain experts who have predispositions that will tend to favour the position of the party who has retained them. Further, it is very expensive for parents separately to retain their own experts. For these reasons, legislation and rules of court have been adopted which provide for a single mental health professional (or a team of professionals working collaboratively) to conduct an assessment for the parties and the court. Assessors become involved in family law cases with the consent of the parties to the litigation, or as a result of a court order. The assessment may be general, or may be focused, for example, solely on the issue of visitation.

In many jurisdictions, the parents are required to pay for assessments, dividing the costs equally, or in portions determined by the court, usually reflecting their incomes. In a number of jurisdictions the costs of an assessment may be covered by the government for low income parents. The use of court-appointed assessors has reduced, but not eliminated, the involvement of privately retained mental health professionals in child-related disputes.

In a few jurisdictions, there are publicly funded programmes which provide court-ordered assessments without charge to the parents, regardless of their financial means.[4] In Ontario, the Office of the Children's Lawyer has been providing social work assessments since the 1960s. In England, the Children and Family Court Advisory and Support Service (CAFCASS) is an independent public body which provides social work assessments in different types of family proceedings. These government programmes generally employ social workers; higher income parents in these jurisdictions may choose also to have a court-appointed psychologist conduct an assessment, with the parties paying the costs.

There is wide variation, even within one jurisdiction, in the types of assessments that are carried out by court order, and even greater variation between jurisdictions. Many assessments are conducted by social workers, especially in jurisdictions where the government funds assessments, but psychologists and to a lesser extent psychiatrists also do assessments. Some assessors have taken courses on conducting forensic family law assessments and have had supervised clinical experience in this work; they may have extensive professional experience in conducting assessments for court, and conduct many assessments in a year. Other assessments, however, may be done by professionals who have little or no academic background or supervised experience in conducting assessments, and who may do only a few assessments a year as a 'sideline' to a therapeutically-oriented practice. As a generalization, assessments performed by social workers tend to be more 'factual', while assessments conducted by psychologists or psychiatrists are more likely to be 'clinical', analysing personalities and

---

[4] L Martin, 'To Recommend or Not to Recommend: That is not the Question' (2005) 43 *Family Court Review* 246; Schepard, n 3 above, 152; LS Horvath, TK Logan, and R Walker, 'Child Custody Cases: A Content Analysis of Evaluations in Practice' (2002) 44(2) *Professional Psychology: Research and Practice* 557.

relationships. Social workers are more likely to do home visits, while only psychologists are qualified to give certain tests to reveal personality traits.

The amount of time that is devoted to an assessment may vary from as little as 5 to 10 hours, to 60 hours or more. The time and resources devoted to the assessment will reflect the funding available, the complexity of the case, the orientation of the assessor, and any special directions given by the referring source. Some of the most sophisticated (and expensive) assessments are conducted by professional teams that include social workers and psychologists or psychiatrists, and might in appropriate cases include other professionals like an educational specialist or a physician.

Despite the varying nature and complexity of individual assessments, there is a common core of elements for most assessments. There is a significant body of literature to guide assessors and to help lawyers and judges understand their work.[5] There are, for example, the guidelines created by the American Psychiatric Association, the American Psychological Association, and the American Association of Family and Conciliation Courts.[6] Assessors who are members of a regulated profession may have professional standards within their jurisdiction that govern ethical issues or the conduct of assessments. Assessors who are employed by a state agency, like the Ontario Office of the Children's Lawyer, may have government policies to guide their work.

While there is not a single, standardized protocol for conducting assessments, the guidelines of different professional organizations and assessment literature share common themes. Because of concerns that the information from any one source may potentially be unreliable, it is widely accepted that good assessments should be 'multi-modal', using a number of different methods to obtain as much reliable information as possible about a child and parents. Generally an assessment will include:

- interviews with each parent and any new partners;
- interviews with the child, and observation of interaction between parents and children;
- contact with adults who have had involvement with the parents or children, such as teachers and family doctors, as well as relatives who have a significant role in the lives of the children, such as grandparents;

---

[5] See eg P Reder, S Duncan, and C Lucey, *Studies in the Assessment of Parenting* (Hove, East Sussex, 2003); TD Pezzot-Pearce and J Pearce, *Parenting Assessments in Child Welfare Cases: A Practical Guide* (Toronto, 2005); R Galatzer-Levy and L Kratz (eds), *The Scientific Basis for Child Custody Decisions* (New York, 1999); LO Condie, *Parenting Evaluations for Court in Care and Protection Matters* (New York, 2003). For a short summary on parenting capacity assessments, see R Kennedy, 'Assessment of Families' [2002] *Family Law* 843.

[6] For disputes between parents, there are guidelines of the American Psychiatric Association Task Force on Clinical Assessment in Child Custody (1981); the American Psychological Association (1994) 49 *American Psychologist* 677 (under revision in 2006); and the American Association of Family and Conciliation Courts (revised 2006). The American Psychological Association also has *Guidelines for Psychological Evaluations in Child Protection Matters* (1998). See also S Herman *et al*,

- a review of significant records or reports about the children or parents;
- psychological tests on parents and perhaps children, if a registered psychologist is the assessor, and perhaps use of other assessment inventories or instruments.

Interviews with each adult party are critical to the assessment process. Topics to be covered include a personal and marital history, parental understanding of the children's personalities and needs, and parental plans for the child.

The assessor requires the parents, and sometimes the children, to complete questionnaires and perhaps have psychological testing. Some tests used in the assessment process can only be administered by qualified psychologists, such as personality and intelligence tests. These standardized psychological tests have a demonstrated reliability for their intended purposes (eg determining intelligence), and can provide useful information. However, there is a lack of empirical research to establish the validity of these tests for determining parenting capacity or predicting outcomes for children in child-related disputes.[7]

Over twenty-five tests have been developed specifically for use in parental disputes and child protection cases, such the Ackerman-Schoendorf Scales for Parenting Evaluation of Custody (given to parents in custody cases).[8] Some of these instruments are relatively straightforward, asking parents to identify their behaviours and attitudes towards parenting, and can be administered by social workers with appropriate training in the use of the instruments. There should be caution in relying on results from tests, considering, for example, what validity the test has for the parents, given their cultural, social, and linguistic background. Further, while these tests may provide some insights into the parents and there is quite a strong correlation between the results of some widely used tests and judicial decision-making, the scientific validity of these tests for predicting outcomes for children has not been established through empirical research.[9]

Meeting with the child is an important part of the assessment process. The assessor should normally meet with the child alone on at least two occasions, with the child being brought in by a different parent for different meetings. Young children, in particular, may be difficult to interview directly, and the meetings may consist partially of observing children playing or drawing. While

---

'Practice Parameters for Child Custody Evaluations' (1997) 36 *Journal of the American Academy of Child and Adolescent Psychology* 57S.

[7] For a good review of many of the psychological tests used in child-related disputes, including the limitations of various tests, see R Otto and J Edens, 'Parenting Capacity' in T Grisso (ed), *Evaluating Competencies: Forensic Assessments and Instruments* (2nd edn, New York, 2003) 229.

[8] See eg B Bricklin, 'The Contribution of Psychological Tests to Custody-Relevant Evaluations' in R Galatzer-Levy and L Kratz (eds), *The Scientific Basis for Child Custody Decisions* (New York, 1999) 120.

[9] See eg D Schuman, 'The Role of Mental Health Experts in Custody Decisions: Science, Psychological Tests, and Clinical Judgement' (2002) 36 *Family Law Quarterly* 135.

these observations can be useful as children may reveal much in these activities, there is no sound empirical research to relate children's play or drawings to determinations about optimal parenting arrangements.

Assessors should avoid directly asking children with which parent they want to live, as this may place undue stress on a child who may be suffering from loyalty conflicts. The views and preferences of children can usually be determined through indirect questioning about their relationships with their parents. Children with definite preferences will make clear to an assessor what they want. Assessors should be sensitive to parental pressure on a child; a child's feelings of guilt, loyalty or fear may affect what a child will tell an assessor. Children may be reluctant to express negative attitudes about a parent due to feelings of loyalty, even if the children are in fact apprehensive about living with that parent.

The assessor should also interview each parent with the child, and observe their interactions. New partners should also be interviewed and, if possible, also observed interacting with the children.

Some psychologists conducting assessments will administer general personality or relationship perception tests to children. There are also tests which have been developed specifically for use with children involved in the family law litigation process. While there is a literature about these child-directed tests, as with the tests administered to parents involved in litigation, there is a lack of empirical research to establish the predictive validity of these tests for determining optimal arrangements for the care of children.[10]

An important aspect of many assessments is the contacting of 'collaterals' or 'third parties', such as the children's teachers, coaches, and doctors, and the review of available records or reports about the children and parents. Independent professionals who know the parents and children, such as teachers, may be able to provide important information. It can also be useful for an assessor to contact friends and relatives, like grandparents, though they may to be biased and caution should be used in relying on their information.

The assessment process involves not just observation and interpretation, but also an element of fact finding. Inevitably, in a dispute between parents, there will be differences in the histories that the parents provide; usually each will be putting themselves in the most favourable light, and sometimes there will be concerns about fabrication. In some cases, there will be differences concerning important issues. One parent may, for example, allege that the other has been an abusive spouse or has a drug addiction problem, while the other parent may deny this allegation. The assessor may feel obliged to resolve this type of factual dispute, though if a judge concludes that the factual finding of the assessor is wrong, the assessment may be disregarded by the judge.

After conducting interviews and formulating opinions about a case, the assessor will prepare a report for the court and the parties. The report should describe

---

10 ibid.

what the assessor did, and set out the assessor's information and conclusions about the parents and children. Assessment reports generally include the assessor's recommendation or opinion about what arrangements will be in the best interests of the child. As discussed below, these recommendations are often very influential with the courts, but the practice of making recommendations is controversial. Not infrequently, after receiving an assessor's report the parties will settle their case based on the recommendations in the report. If the case proceeds to trial, the assessor is very likely to be a key witness. Both parties will have an opportunity to cross-examine the assessor.

The Influence of Assessors

There is a significant body of jurisprudence and empirical research which establishes that court-appointed assessors are very influential in the resolution of child-related disputes. While the parties may challenge any of the factual findings or conclusions of an assessor, and the judge is free to disregard any of the assessor's recommendations, parties often settle their dispute based on the assessor's recommendations, and if a case goes to trial, the assessor's views are likely to be influential.[11] One recent American study found that over 80 per cent of family law judges and lawyers wanted court-appointed assessors to make recommendations, and they considered these assessments to be one of the most important sources of information for the courts.[12]

There are many judicial statements recognizing the value of an assessor's recommendations. For example, writing more than two decades ago, Justice Abella, now on the Supreme Court of Canada, observed:

... since the evidence required must necessarily go beyond materially demonstrable perceptions, it is difficult to see how informed judgements can be made about the best interests of children without at least the assistance of a non-partisan expert who can better attempt to evaluate the competing emotional claims that underlie the pursuit of legal remedies ... This is not usurpation of the judicial function—it is an indispensable contribution to its proper exercise.[13]

---

[11] See eg D Schuman, 'The Role of Mental Health Experts in Custody Decisions: Science, Psychological Tests, and Clinical Judgement' (2002) 36 *Family Law Quarterly* 135.

[12] See eg J Bow and F Quinnell, 'Critique of Child Custody Evaluations by the Legal Profession' (2004) 42 *Family Court Review* 115–27, reporting on a study of family law practitioners in Michigan. They found that 84% of judges and 86% of attorneys want assessors to provide a recommendation about custody. R Joyal and A Quéniart, 'Enhancing the Child's Point of View in Custody and Access Cases in Quebec: Preliminary Results of a Study Conducted in Quebec' (2002) 19 *Canadian Journal of Family Law* 173, report that 87% of the superior court judges in a survey in Quebec considered family evaluations to be 'of great assistance in making more accurate decisions'.

[13] RS Abella, 'Procedural Aspects of Arrangements for Children Upon Divorce in Canada' (1983) 61 *Canadian Bar Review* 443.

English judges have gone the furthest, creating a legal requirement for trial judges to explain their reasons for departing from the recommendations of an assessor. In the 1999 English decision in *Re W*, Thorpe LJ reversed the decision of a trial judge who had ignored the assessor's recommendation that the child's residence should be with his mother, without offering a clear explanation, observing:

> . . . it cannot be too strongly emphasised that . . . the court welfare service is the principal support service available to the judge in the determination of these difficult cases. It is of the utmost importance that there should be free co-operation between the skilled investigator, with the primary task of assessing not only factual situations but also attachments, and the judge with the ultimate responsibility of making the decision. Judges are hugely dependent upon the contribution that can be made by the welfare officer, who has the opportunity to visit the home and to see the grown-ups and the children in much less artificial circumstances than the judge can ever do. It is for that very good practical reason that authority has established clearly . . . that judges are not entitled to depart from the recommendation of an experienced court welfare officer without at least reasoning that departure.[14]

Reflecting their influence in court, assessments frequently result in settlements based on the assessor's recommendations.

The settlement promotion function of an assessment reflects the fact that in *some respects* an assessor may be regarded as an initial, legally mandated decision-maker for resolving child-related disputes. Attempting to challenge the assessor's recommendations has *some* of the characteristics of an appeal. While judges are not bound by the recommendations of an assessor, in most cases the ultimate decision at a trial is broadly consistent with the recommendations of the assessor. In practice, the party seeking to challenge an assessor's recommendations has an onus to show why the assessor was wrong, and this may be analogized to the onus that a party has on an appeal. Indeed, some of the ways of challenging an assessment before a judge may be analogized to the standard grounds for an appeal of the decision of a trial judge, such as demonstrating bias or unfairness by the original decision-maker. Challenging an assessor is, however, quite different from an appeal of a trial judgment in two critical respects. First, the party challenging the assessor has complete latitude to establish that the assessor made a factual error which was central to the recommendations proffered and, hence, that the recommendations should be rejected. Secondly, the assessor can be called as a witness who is subject to cross-examination in court, and the weaknesses and limitations of the report can be fully explored before the trial judge.

There may be a tendency to give more weight to an assessment prepared by a professional with 'higher status', like a psychologist or psychiatrist, than one

---

14 [1999] 2 FLR 390, [1999] Fam Law 454.

prepared by a social worker. George Thomson, at the time an Ontario Family Court judge, observed:

For a host of reasons, there is a tendency to want to draw lines based upon the expert's profession and level of training, and yet there is little to suggest that such lines can validly be drawn. Within this inexact science of prediction, no one profession seems to have claim to any superiority . . . There may be much better potential in an approach that focuses upon the individual's demonstrated capability in the past, regardless of professional affiliation, and particularly upon the work undertaken by the witness to merit 'expert' status in the particular case before the court. [15]

There should be caution in giving preference to the opinions of experts with higher academic qualifications as there is no empirical evidence that they provide better family assessments, or are better at interviewing children.[16]

Controversy over Assessments

Although mental health professionals are frequently asked to assist in the resolution of child-related disputes, their involvement in these cases has been criticized on two related grounds. First, it is argued that an assessor's analysis and recommendations about a specific case are based more on personal judgement rather than on the application of objective scientific criteria. Secondly, it is argued that the consideration of this type of evidence violates the legal rules for the admission of expert evidence.

Lack of Scientific Basis for Assessments

Although there are some assessment practices that are clearly not appropriate, and there is some research on the reliability of different psychological tests and assessment methodologies, there is no standardized protocol for conducting assessments or determining what recommendations to make in child-related disputes.[17] Critics argue that the lack of a widely accepted methodology, protocol, or tests for the assessment process means that the personal judgement and values of the assessor, not objective expert criteria, determine the recommendations. In all but the most obvious cases, a best interests recommendation is a matter of 'clinical judgement,' not an application of scientific methodology and knowledge.

---

[15] GM Thomson, 'Judging Judiciously in Child Protection Cases' in R Abella and C L'Heureux-Dubé (eds), *Family Law: Dimensions of Justice* (Toronto, 1983) 220–1.

[16] See eg TM Horner and MJ Guyer, 'Prediction, Prevention and Clinical Expertise in Child Custody Cases in Which Allegations of Sexual Abuse Have Been Made' (1990) 25 *Family Law Quarterly* 217.

[17] See eg RA Nicholson and S Norwood, 'The Quality of Forensic Psychological Assessments, Reports and Testimony: Acknowledging the Gap Between Promise and Practice' (2000) 24 *Law and Human Behavior* 9.

In any individual case there are multiple interacting factors in terms of parent characteristics, child characteristics, and family circumstances (such as new partners) that make it very difficult to apply existing research with any degree of precision to predict child outcomes from different possible parenting arrangements. Further, even if a clear link can be established between particular parental conduct or characteristics and likely child outcomes, there is often no objective basis for establishing whether one type of outcome is 'best' for a child. An assessor's recommendation about a child's 'best interests' is set in a particular legal context and involves an application of a legal standard, which ultimately involves the making of value judgements about what is 'best' for a child.

American psychologists O'Donohue and Bradley observe that 'beyond extremes such as severe physical abuse, without empirical research regarding the effects of relevant events on children, it is still difficult to comprehensively assess which variables will "hurt" a child', and even if that empirical research was available, recommendations about best interests decisions would still in large measure be a question of values.[18] Accordingly, O'Donohue and Bradley propose 'a moratorium of mental health professionals' participation in child custody evaluations, as it appears that the mental health profession currently cannot ethically conduct these evaluations'.[19]

American psychologist Jeffrey Wittmann and lawyer Timothy Tippins provide an important analysis of the limitations of forensic child-related assessments in a recently published article.[20] While they support the continued involvement of mental health professionals as assessors, they argue that these professionals should not make recommendations about what child care arrangements would be in the best interests of children. They argue that there is insufficient empirical knowledge to allow accurate predictions to be made about the effect of different parenting arrangements. Further, there is often not an objective basis for establishing whether one type of outcome is 'best' for a child:

> . . . such socio-moral constructs as 'best interest' or 'best custodian' . . . represent an attempt to measure the incalculable (partially because such value-laden constructs can reasonably be given different definitional contours by legal and mental health professionals who have different preferences/values, yielding little consensual agreement about what is important to a child and to the definition of the construct).[21]

While many judges recognize the value of involving court-appointed assessors in child-related disputes, some judges have significant reservations about the influence of these professionals. For example, in 1993 L'Heureux-Dubé J of the Supreme

---

[18] W O'Donohue and AR Bradley, 'Conceptual and empirical issues in child custody evaluations' (1999) 6 *Clinical Psychology: Science and Practice* 310, 312.   [19] ibid, 320.
[20] TM Tippins and JP Wittmann, 'Empirical and Ethical Problems with Custody Recommendations: A Call for Clinical Humility and Judicial Vigilance' (2005) 43(2) *Family Court Review* 193.   [21] ibid, 201–2.

Court of Canada, suggested that experts should be used sparingly in cases where the best interests of a child are in dispute:

Expert evidence should not be routinely required to establish the best interests of the child. In my view, it is a modern-day myth that experts are always better placed than parents to assess the needs of the child . . . judges have increasingly come to rely on the recommendations of experts . . . believing that such experts possess objective, scientific knowledge and can in fact 'know' what is in the best interests of the child. However, expert testimony, while helpful in some and perhaps many circumstances, is often inconclusive and contradictory . . . such assessments are both speculative and may be affected by the professional values and biases of the assessors themselves.[22]

It is interesting to observe that despite these general, cautious comments, in the specific case before the Court, L'Heureux-Dubé J placed significant weight on the testimony of a family court counsellor and a court-appointed psychologist.

Best Interests Recommendations and the Expert Evidence Rule

Related to the concerns about the lack of a sound scientific basis for the recommendations of assessors is an argument that their opinions are not legally admissible as 'expert evidence' and hence should not be communicated to the courts. Although there is some variation in the details, the courts in England, Canada and the United States have developed relatively narrow rules governing the admission of expert evidence, emphasizing the role of the trial judge as a 'gatekeeper' who is responsible for excluding evidence not considered sufficiently reliable to be used in court.

In 1993, the US Supreme Court, in the tort case of *Daubert v Merrell Dow Pharmaceuticals*, articulated a rule which requires the trial judge to determine 'whether the reasoning or methodology underlying the testimony is scientifically valid and whether that reasoning or methodology properly can be applied to the facts in issue'.[23] In determining admissibility under *Daubert*, factors which the trial judge should consider include whether the theory or technique has been tested, whether it has been subject to peer review and publication, whether the rate of error is known, and whether it is generally accepted within the scientific community. While the *Daubert* rule applies to proceedings in the federal courts, at least some state courts, where family law cases are heard, have retained the older, broader test of *Frye v United States*, which requires judges to consider the evidence of an expert if it is based on a procedure that is 'sufficiently established to have gained general acceptance in the particular field in which it belongs'.[24]

The Supreme Court of Canada in a 1994 criminal case involving allegations of child sexual abuse, *R v Mohan*,[25] held that a psychiatrist called by the defence

---

[22] *Young v Young* (1993), 49 RFL (3d) 117, 212–3.   [23] 509 US 579 (1993) 592–3.
[24] 293 F 1013, 1014.   [25] *R v Mohan* [1994] 2 SCR 9.

could not testify based on his 'personal opinion'. Justice Sopinka stated that there
is a 'basic threshold of reliability' that must be established before expert evidence
can be admitted, expressing concern that a criminal trial should not become
'nothing more than a battle of experts'. While a qualified expert is not automatically precluded from expressing an opinion on the 'ultimate issue' before the court,
the 'closer the evidence approaches an opinion on an ultimate issue, the stricter
the application' of the principle that the evidence must be necessary and reliable.[26]
Justice Sopinka considered some of the 'dangers' of admitting expert evidence:

There is a danger that expert evidence will be misused and will distort the fact-finding
process. Dressed up in scientific language which the jury does not easily understand and
submitted through a witness of impressive antecedents, this evidence is apt to be
accepted by the jury as being virtually infallible and as having more weight than it
deserves. [27]

In 2001, the English Court of Appeal held in *R v Gilfoyle* that, in the context of a
criminal trial, testimony from a psychologist called by the accused will only be
admissible if it meets the *Frye v United States* standard of being a result of the use
of procedures 'accepted by the scientific community as being able to provide
accurate and reliable opinion'.[28] The Court emphasized that the opinion of an
expert is only admissible if he is in a 'better position to draw an inference on these
facts than the jury'.[29]

   Although there is some variation in the rules about the admission of expert
testimony, it is clear that significant portions of the evidence that assessors normally give in family law cases, in particular their opinions about the best interests of
a child, would not be admissible under any of these tests. While traditionally
judges dealing with family law cases have *not* applied the general rules about the
admission of expert evidence when dealing with assessors, recently some judges
and commentators have favoured the application of the narrow expert evidence
rule to assessors.

   The adoption of a narrow approach to assessors' evidence is clearly favoured by
the American commentators Tippins and Wittmann, who recently wrote an article to advocate use of the *Daubert* standard in family law cases to restrict significantly the scope of assessors' evidence. They argue that, while mental health
professionals may be accepted as qualified experts to give evidence on certain
issues in family law cases, under the *Daubert* test for the admissibility of expert
witnesses, they are not qualified to answer the question of which arrangement
would be in the best interests of the child. Tippins and Wittmann find it troubling
that judges permit assessors to address the 'ultimate issues' in child-related
disputes as this 'blurs critically important boundaries between the person

---

[26] ibid, paras 24–28.   [27] ibid, para 19.
[28] *R v Gilfoyle* [2001] EWJ No 7209; [2001] 2 Cr App R 57, para 25.   [29] ibid.

invested with the power to make socio-moral and social-control decisions (the judge) and the expert witness who is hired to assist the court'.[30] The analysis offered by Tippins and Wittmann has been cited by some courts in New York state to restrict use of experts,[31] though a commission in that state recently proposed that forensic experts should continue to make recommendations on custody and visitation.[32]

In Canada, family law judges have generally *not* applied the expert evidence standard articulated by *R v Mohan* for the admission of evidence in child-related disputes, but there have been a few recent cases where this narrow approach was adopted, such as the 2001 Ontario decision in *Mayfield*. At issue in that case was the admissibility of the evidence of an experienced custody assessor who was retained by one party to critique the assessment report prepared by a court-appointed social worker. While the original assessment report was prepared with the consent of both parties, it was the first custody assessment prepared by this social worker. The judge ruled that the critique was not admissible as it did not satisfy the *Mohan* standard of being 'necessary' to assist the trier of fact, observing:

Prior to the decision in *Mohan*, the general standard for admissibility of expert evidence was the relatively low threshold of 'helpfulness.' . . . Subsequent to *Mohan*, the Court in effect had been asked to function as a 'gatekeeper', keeping out novel scientific evidence. The standard of helpfulness was explicitly rejected as being too low a threshold . . .

. . . it must not be forgotten that expert evidence is time consuming and expensive. The practice of calling unnecessary evidence of experts which does not meet the test of necessity should be discouraged for the benefit of the parties to litigation.[33]

A central argument of this paper is that courts should not use the legal rules that apply to party-retained experts in ordinary litigation when making decisions about court-appointed assessors in child-related litigation; these rules were developed to deal with the testimony of experts who were retained by one party to testify in criminal or tort litigation, a very different context from the child-related family law case. While the *Frye* and *Gilfoyle* standard of 'general acceptance' in the scientific community may be useful in terms of considering the methodology used by an assessor, in most cases it is not possible for an assessor who is making a best interests recommendation to meet this standard. The complex nature of most contested cases makes it impossible to use existing research to make 'scientifically-based' predictions for child outcomes with different parenting arrangements with a high degree of confidence.

[30] TM Tippins and JP Wittmann, 'Empirical and Ethical Problems with Custody Recommendations: A Call for Clinical Humility and Judicial Vigilance' (2005) 43(2) *Family Court Review* 193, 203.
[31] See eg *SM v GM, New York Law Journal*, 4 May 2005, 20, col 1 (Suffolk Cty Sup Ct); *John A v Bridget M*, 16 AD 3d 324, 791 NYS 2d 421(App Div, 1st Dept, 2005).
[32] *Matrimonial Commission: Report to the Chief Judge of New York State* (February 2006, New York State Office of Court Administration).   [33] (2001) 18 RFL (5th) 328, at 337(Ont Sup Ct).

Recognizing the Value and Limitations of Assessments

Lawyers, judges, and mental health professionals should be aware of the limitations of assessments, including concerns about the cost and delay caused by the assessment process. While some assessments are of poor quality, this does not justify questioning the value of *most* assessments. Court-appointed assessors in child-related disputes have some unique functions in the litigation process which justify different legal treatment from that afforded experts in other cases.[34] The distinctive treatment of court-appointed assessors is justified by the special obligations that the state has to children who are the subject of litigation to ensure that decisions are made with as much information as possible, and in a way that promotes the interests of the children involved. Assessors are important not only for cases that go to trial, but also play a central role in helping to resolve the much larger number of cases which are settled. However, assessments are not appropriate for all cases.

Uniqueness of Child-related Cases

Child-related family law cases may be distinguished from other types of cases on a number of grounds. It is not the qualifications of the court-appointed assessor or even the nature of the matters in dispute that requires a difference in approach, rather, it is the nature of the proceedings and the role of the assessor. Some of the issues that arise in family law cases, for example, related to child abuse or domestic violence, may also be the subject of other proceedings. A judge in the family law case may receive and rely on evidence from a court-appointed assessor that might not be admissible if the same person were called as a party-retained expert witness in the criminal or tort case dealing with the same factual issues.

One reason to distinguish child-related cases is their prospective nature. In most other cases the focus is retrospective, with the court trying to *determine what happened*. In child-related cases, the focus of inquiry is prospective; the role of the court is to *affect what will happen*. A prospective inquiry inevitably has a speculative quality, as no one can testify about what will occur without expressing 'opinions'. As Australian Family Court judge Linda Dessau observes, courts dealing with child-related disputes are not in search of an 'ultimate truth'.[35] There is inherently more need for the assistance of experts when the court is trying to predict and affect the future. It is interesting to observe that at the stage of the

---

[34] For a fuller version of the arguments about the value of assessments in family law cases, see N Bala, 'Tippins and Wittmann Are Wrong: Evaluators May Not be "Experts" But They Can Express Best Interests Opinions' (2005) 43(4) *Family Court Review* 554–62.

[35] L Dessau, 'A Short Commentary on Timothy M Tippins and Jeffrey P Wittmann's "Empirical and Ethical Problems with Custody Recommendations: A Call for Clinical Humility and Judicial Vigilance"' (2005) 43(2) *Family Court Review* 266.

criminal process that is prospective, the sentencing stage, the rules of evidence about hearsay, character evidence, and opinion evidence are not strictly applied.[36]

A second difference is that child-related cases are relationship and personality oriented, while other kinds of cases tend to be event focused. Many of the rules of evidence are intended to focus the trier of fact on the events, and to preclude consideration of the character or propensity of an individual to do something. There are strict rules in criminal cases that generally exclude consideration of the past conduct of the parties. It is inherent in child-related family law proceedings that the focus of inquiry is on personalities, character, relationships, and feelings. These are ephemeral; almost all witnesses in a child-related proceeding express opinions about human relationships.

The third difference is that the general legal rules restricting the admission of expert evidence developed in a context in which there is the possibility, or likelihood, that the case will be determined by a jury. There is a concern that jurors may be more easily misled by an expert witness, and may unduly rely on the expert's testimony. Child-related family law cases are never decided by a jury (except in Texas), and hence there is less need for restrictive rules about the admission of expert evidence.

Fourthly, unlike in an ordinary civil case and even more so a criminal trial, in a child-related case, the judge does not have the luxury of being able to rely on the presumptions and burdens of proof to resolve situations of uncertainty. The family law judge is faced with awesome decisions about the future of the child, and is understandably likely to 'err on the side' of receiving more information, and discounting the evidence as appropriate, rather than placing a premium on having a decision that is perceived to be the result of 'due process'.[37]

Assessments as a Source of Information for Judges

An assessment is a potentially important source of factual information for the judge about the specific child and parents before the court. It is often the most effective and least intrusive way to bring information before the court about the child's wishes and perspectives, as well as about the personality and needs of the child. An assessor can provide the court with relatively objective information about the parents' personalities and relationships with the children.

Assessors can also provide the judge with their analysis and opinions, relating social science research to the specific family before the court. It is inevitable that a judge dealing with a case involving a child will rely on some theories, information, or opinions about children and parents. If expert testimony is not permitted, judges will use their own beliefs about human behaviour, child development, and family life, acquired over a lifetime from their personal experience, formal and

---

36 *R v Gardiner* [1982] 2 SCR 368.
37 See the comments of Herold J in *Krieger v Krieger* [2002] OJ 339 (Sup Ct).

informal education, legal practice and judging. As Canadian legal scholar Professor Paciocco points out, the 'uncomfortable reality' is that judges must rely on their personal experience and education to understand and analyse the cases with which they deal.[38] This judicial use of 'background knowledge' is inevitable, especially in family law cases. It can, however, be problematic to the extent that a judge may unconsciously be basing decisions on misconceptions, stereotypes, or personal experiences that are very different from those of the individuals in the case before the court. Having an assessment prepared for the court is often the best way in which to 'educate' the judge about relevant knowledge in the social sciences, and relate it to the specific case before the court. An independent assessment can provide a court with relatively objective and insightful information about the parents and children. While there may be limits to an assessor's knowledge or disputes about the research, these may be tested through cross-examination or even by calling other expert evidence. If the assessor does not establish a social science knowledge context for a case, it may be impossible for the parties to know or challenge the basis of the judge's understanding of the social context of their case.

Settlement Promotion Function

Although some family law disputes are decided by judges, many more cases are settled by lawyers, mediators, or the parties themselves through negotiations that occur 'in the shadow of the law'. The recommendations of assessors frequently play a critical role in facilitating settlement; the settlement promotion function is an important reason for judges to take a flexible approach to ordering assessments. Some commentators argue that the reason that an assessment often results in a settlement based on the recommendations of the assessor is that parents are advised by their lawyers that a judge is likely to follow those recommendations, and taking the matter to trial is unlikely to result in a different outcome.[39] There is some validity to this argument, but this is essentially another way of saying that judges respect the opinions of assessors. Further, in many cases, it is not simply the expectation that a judge is likely to follow the recommendation that leads to a settlement, but rather it is the assessment process and the information which it provides to the parents that produces the settlement. The assessment process may provide important information, about the children, of which their parents were previously unaware, regarding their needs, perspectives, and wishes, and this too may help to promote a settlement.

As a result of the assessment, parents may feel that they and their children were 'heard' by a neutral party who has their children's interests at heart, and they may

---

[38] D Paciocco, 'The Promise of *R. D. S.*: Integrating the Law of Judicial Notice and Apprehension of Bias' (1998) 3 *Canadian Criminal Law Review* 319, 327.

[39] TM Tippins and JP Wittmann, 'Empirical and Ethical Problems with Custody Recommendations: A Call for Clinical Humility and Judicial Vigilance', (2005) 43 *Family Court Review* 193, 217.

be ready to accept a settlement based on the recommendation of that professional. Good assessors often develop a rapport with parents; they make an effort to write their reports with sensitivity to each parent's strengths and weaknesses, and they are prepared to meet with the parents to explain their recommendations. It is understandable that parents are often prepared to accept these recommendations as the basis for a settlement.

The settlement promotion function of the court-appointed assessor has no direct analogue with the function of the party-retained expert. This settlement promoting function would be significantly reduced if an assessment does not offer a 'best interests' recommendation. The facilitation of settlements is a valuable function for the overburdened judicial system. Further, while an assessment can be costly for parents, it is inevitably less expensive than a trial. Perhaps most importantly, unless there are abuse or violence issues that have been improperly resolved, a settlement which the parents are prepared to accept is almost always preferable for a child than the emotional trauma resulting from continuing litigation.

Court-appointed Assessor versus Party-retained Expert

In Canada and the United States, one of the important distinguishing aspects of the involvement of mental health professionals in child-related cases is that an assessor is appointed by the court (often with the consent of both parties), whereas in other legal contexts, an expert (including a mental health professional) is only involved in litigation when retained by one party. By enacting laws to allow for court-appointed assessors, law-makers have made a substantial modification to the ordinary rules governing the litigation process which justifies a significant difference in the treatment of the court-appointed assessors' evidence in a trial. (It is interesting to note that in England, where the use of a single court-appointed expert is a not uncommon feature of all kinds of litigation, there seems to have been less controversy over the issue of whether CAFCASS reporters should make best interests recommendations, as it seems to be accepted that court-appointed experts are to have a relatively broad role.)

One of the concerns with party-retained experts in the litigation process is that they tend to be viewed as 'hired guns', retained by one party to advance their case.[40] The party-retained expert is involved in litigation by one party in the belief that the expert will advance the position of that party. While it is unfair to conclude that party-retained experts are biased because they are being paid by just one side, there is often an expectation by the party who retains an expert that the expert will have an opinion favourable to that party. By way of contrast, a court-appointed assessor is selected in the expectation that he or she is an

---

[40] See eg remarks of Major J in *R v DD* [2000] 2 SCR 275, para 52.

unbiased professional. Further, being a court-appointed expert gives a mental health professional access to all of the parties to the litigation.

The laws about the appointment of an assessor by the court reflect a recognition that the justice system has a unique responsibility when making a best interests decision about a child's future. By having a court-appointed expert, a best interests case is different not only from non-family litigation, but even from a family law case (or portion of a case) that deals with the economic issues and which is governed by the ordinary rules of civil litigation and expert evidence.

Concerns about Assessments

While assessment reports have an important role in the resolution of child-related cases, lawyers, judges, and mental health professionals must be aware of the concerns about the assessment process. There are limitations even to the best assessments, and some assessments are done poorly.

One fundamental concern is that some judges, faced with very difficult decisions about the future of children, may rely too heavily on 'experts' who profess to have knowledge about what is in the best interests of children. There is a natural human tendency, when faced with uncertainty and a difficult choice, to want to rely on an external expert who appears to possess objective knowledge. The courts should be cautious about placing too much reliance on a mental health professional's opinion about what disposition is in a child's 'best interests', for such opinions inevitably have aspects that are speculative and value based. The application of psychological research to an individual case is never a matter of pure science, but always involves clinical judgement and some degree of prediction. Different assessors can have different opinions about the same case (just as different judges might make different 'best interests' decisions about the same case).

Another concern about the assessment process is that it is intrusive. For parents, the process of feeling that they are 'under a microscope' can be stressful. The final report may reveal details of a parent's personal history that the parent feels uncomfortable having disclosed. The assessment process is also intrusive for the child. While assessors should have training and sensitivity in interviewing children, the child is subjected to questioning about highly personal matters, with the answers ultimately revealed to the child's parents. The glare of professional attention may cause a strain on the relationship between estranged parents, or between a parent and child. However, while assessments can be more intrusive than a mediated or negotiated settlement, they are rarely more intrusive than a trial.

The assessor role is very different from the therapeutic role played by many mental health professionals, including some of those who do assessments. Those being assessed have a tendency to want to 'put their best foot forward'. Assessors need to be able to deal effectively with manipulation, distorted perceptions, and dishonesty. Mental health professionals conducting assessments must also always consider both positive and negative 'counter-transference' issues; they must be aware of the effect of their own values and emotional reactions on the persons whom they are assessing. The personality, values, and life experiences of assessors inevitably affect their assessments, and the recommendations may, at least to some extent, be based on speculation or unproven theory. Nevertheless, a good assessment should not merely reflect the personal opinions of the assessor, but the opinion expressed should be informed by available research.

The assessment process will usually be time consuming, especially if the assessor has a busy agenda. If an assessment is not ordered at a relatively early stage in the process, there will be cases in which it should not be ordered. Delays while awaiting an assessment can be upsetting to the child, and if the trial is significantly delayed, this may tactically work to the advantage of the party with the care of the child during the assessment process.

Finally, it must be recognized that in those jurisdictions and cases in which the parties are to bear the cost of the assessment, an assessment can be expensive. In some cases, the parties simply will not be able to afford an assessment. However, while an assessment can be costly for parents (though in some jurisdictions it may be paid for by the government), it is inevitably less expensive than a trial. If an evaluation results in a settlement, the cost of the assessment is clearly money well spent by the parties. If the case goes to trial, the assessment may help to narrow the issues at trial and reduce the cost of litigation, as well as provide the court with information not otherwise available.

Judicial Decisions about Assessments

Judges making decisions about assessments must keep in mind both their value and their limitations. The first set of decisions is whether an assessment will be ordered, if so, who will be the assessor, and if there will be any specific directions or limitations on the scope of the assessment. The second set of decisions deals with the admission into evidence of the assessment. Finally the judge must decide what weight to place on the assessor's factual findings and opinions

Appointing an Assessor

The first, and perhaps most useful, point at which to exercise a judicial gate-keeping function is when consideration is being given to the appointment of an assessor, if for no other reason than to limit the time and expense of the proceedings, both for the parties and the court system. In jurisdictions without a government mandated assessment scheme, the court must identify a specific professional to undertake the assessment. Judges should only appoint an assessor with appropriate education and training for dealing with the issues in the case before the court. While in some jurisdictions there is government funding to retain psychologists or social workers to perform assessments, in many places there are few professionals who are willing and able to do this type of work, or the parents may not be able to afford to have an assessment. A lack of appropriate qualifications is, for example, a particular concern when sexual abuse allegations arise, as these cases require special knowledge and sensitivity.

In some cases, the judge appointing the assessor, based on the submissions of the parties or the judge's own reading of the materials filed, should limit the scope of the assessment to one or more specific issues. This may be done due to concerns about cost, delay, or the assessor's qualifications, or because the parties have narrowed the range of outstanding issues.

Standard for Admission of Assessor's Evidence

The recommendations provided by assessors in most child-related disputes would not meet the relatively restrictive standards for admittance of expert testimony established by the courts in other types of cases. However, since the context in which these rules developed is very different from a child-related family law dispute, it is submitted that these general rules for expert evidence should not apply to child-related family law cases, and in particular should not apply to the testimony of the court-appointed assessor. By enacting laws to allow for court-appointed assessors, the legislators have made important modifications to the ordinary rules governing the litigation process. This requires different treatment of the court-appointed assessor's evidence in a trial.

While it is submitted that judges, as 'gatekeepers', should use a more flexible approach to determine whether to admit the evidence of an assessor, there may still be cases in which part, or even all, of the report may be ruled inadmissible. Judicial supervision is needed to ensure that the assessor's opinion is within the terms of the original appointment. Further, the evidence should be ruled inadmissible if the assessor failed to follow the generally accepted procedures or standards of his or her discipline or of the assessment field, or if the assessor expresses an opinion that is clearly beyond his or her education or training. The testimony of an assessor may be ruled inadmissible on grounds other than lack of expertise, such as an opinion being formed in violation of ethical codes, for example, through reliance on illegally obtained materials. Most of the deficiencies in an assessor's report, however, will go to its weight, not its admissibility.

What Weight should be Given to the Assessor's Opinion?

There are a range of different concerns that may limit the value of the report of an assessor or other expert witness in a child-related case. While it is impossible to catalogue all of the factors that might lead a judge to discount an assessment, it is useful briefly to discuss a few of the most common situations.

A mental health professional should have appropriate qualifications and experience to deal with the issues before the court. For an assessment in a child-related dispute, this requires appropriate child-related professional education, as well as some form of supervised training or experience with this type of forensic work. A lack of specific qualifications is, for example, a particular concern in regard to sexual abuse allegations, which require special care, knowledge, and sensitivity. There are also cases that require an assessor to have the knowledge and sensitivity to deal with children (or parents) who have disabilities or different cultural backgrounds. When dealing with issues that arise relatively infrequently or are novel, doing independent reading, attending a short course, or discussing the particular test or approach with experienced colleagues may be sufficient to admit the testimony about that issue, provided that the professional already has an appropriate background in the assessment field. Limited experience with the issues that are before the court may, however, affect the weight that the court will give that evidence.

A judge may discount the testimony of a court-appointed assessor if he or she has manifested an institutional or professional bias,[41] which may be reflected in the selective collection, presentation, or interpretation of data. This may, for example, occur in cases where sexual abuse allegations are made because the assessor starts with strong preconceived notions about how a particular case should be viewed, such as treating any situation where abuse is alleged as likely to be a true allegation.[42] There may also be an actual, or at least apprehended, bias if an assessor treats the parties differently and, for example, chooses to consult more fully with the informants or relatives put forward by one party than the other.[43]

In some cases an assessor's recommendations may be attacked because the methodology or analysis is unsound, or because the assessor failed to support the recommendations adequately by reference to published research. Perhaps the most common challenge is that the assessor failed to correctly ascertain all of the relevant facts, or relied on inaccurate sources of information.[44] Judges are willing to disregard an assessor's recommendation if it is based on a factual finding that a judge concludes is erroneous.[45] Further, family breakdown is a dynamic process, and parents and their children may change over time. As a result, a person may be under considerable stress at the time of the assessment as a result of the family breakdown. If there has been a significant change in circumstances between the

---

[41] See *Miglin v Miglin* (2001) 16 RFL (5th) 106 (Ont CA).

[42] See eg *Jarrett v Jarrett* (1994) 10 RFL (4th) 24 (Ont Gen Div). However, an assessor may, in the exercise of professional judgement, conclude that it is not necessary to interview *all* persons nominated by one party for interview, provided that both parties are treated in a similar fashion: *Irwin/Halfacree v Halfacree* [1995] OJ 749 (Ont Gen Div).

[43] See eg *Weir-Bersette v Bersette* [1995] OJ 1528 (Gen Div).

[44] See eg *Richardson v Gardner* (1995), 11 RFL (4th) 292 (Ont Prov Div).

[45] See eg *Mulligan v Mowat* [2002] OJ 1270 (Ont Sup Ct); *Haider v Malach* (1999) 48 RFL (4th) 314 (Sask CA).

time of assessment and the time at which a judicial decision is made, this may affect the weight that should be placed on an opinion based on an earlier assessment.[46] There may, for example, be significant new relationships formed, or there may have been an improvement (or deterioration) in the mental health of one of the parents.

While it is necessary to be aware of the potential problems with assessments, an important corollary is that if an assessment is carried out by a competent, unbiased assessor, with access to the relevant facts, there is a strong tendency for the assessor's views to have considerable weight with the court.

Party-retained Experts

In addition to child-related assessments prepared by mental health professionals appointed with the consent of both parties or by order of the court, it is also possible for an individual litigant to retain a mental health expert to testify. This may be done in cases where the court has not appointed an assessor, or if one party wants the court to receive a 'second opinion' after an assessment.

An expert retained by one party usually does not have access to all of those involved in the litigation, so some mental health experts are unwilling to act unless they are appointed with the consent of all the parties.[47] Judges tend to scrutinize the evidence of a party-retained expert more closely than the evidence of a court-appointed assessor, as that expert has typically only met with one parent, and hence has a limited view of the case.[48] Further, there may be a suspicion that the lawyer who selected and retained the expert did so with some expectations about the assessor's favourite theories and predispositions.[49] Nevertheless, party-retained experts can provide valuable and persuasive testimony.

In England, there are restrictions on the involvement of party-retained experts in child-related cases. Under rule 4.18 of the Family Proceeding Rules, before a child is medically or psychiatrically examined for the purpose of the preparation of expert evidence, the court's permission is required. If it is not obtained, the evidence arising out of the examination or assessment cannot be used during the proceeding.[50] The approach used in Canada and the United States towards party-retained experts in child-related family law cases is more flexible than that used in England.

---

[46] *Johnson v Cleroux* (2002) 23 RFL (5th) 176 (Ont CA).

[47] Some critics go further, referring to *some* expert witnesses as 'hired guns' ('money talks'), or at least as 'advocates' ('I am on your team'), rather than 'impartial experts' ('let the chips fall where they may'). Often, the manner in which an expert is retained may influence the role assumed, though professional orientation and values will play a crucial role. See Canadian psychologist D Wolfe, 'The Right Expert—Qualifications, Training and Education' (1994) 11 *Canadian Family Law Quarterly* 1, 2.

[48] See eg Canadian psychologist Dona Blum, 'The Psychologist As Inexpert Witness' (1980) 15 RFL (2d) 24, 31. [49] See eg *Mitchell v Price* [1995] SJ 70 (UFC).

[50] *Re A (Family Proceedings: Expert Witnesses)* [2001] 1 FLR 723, [2001] Fam Law 343.

It is submitted that there should be some flexibility in admitting evidence that challenges the opinion of a mental health professional appointed by the court, especially if that professional was not jointly nominated by the parties, but was rather specifically selected by the court or by the state agency responsible for arranging assessments. While in some cases counsel may be able to challenge the original report by means of cross-examination and submissions, some assessors are quite resistant to cross-examination and a critique by an experienced professional is more likely to explore fully any deficiencies of the original report. Further, without calling an expert to critique the original assessment report, it may not be possible for counsel to establish through cross-examination alone what is an appropriate methodology for conducting an assessment.

Conclusion: The Need to Assess the Assessment

It is submitted that a court-appointed assessor in a child-related family law case should be permitted to express an opinion on the 'ultimate issue', what type of child care arrangement is in the 'best interests of the child', even though such evidence might not be admissible under the ordinary standard for the admission of expert testimony in other civil and criminal cases. Such an approach will tend to prevent judges from relying on their personal beliefs, however ill-informed, about optimal parenting arrangements. This approach will also tend to facilitate and encourage settlements. However, it is also important for mental health professionals to be aware of the limitations of the assessment process, and for judges and lawyers to be ready to scrutinize and assess the opinions of assessors.

Justice Linda Dessau of the Family Court of Australia observed that in dealing with the 'excruciatingly difficult' issues related to the future care of a child, the 'combination' of a good assessment and a good judge is 'probably as good as it gets in the present system'.[51] She concludes that judges should have the benefit of receiving 'all the relevant evidence', including the opinions and recommendations of the assessors about the 'ultimate issue'. This is a sound analysis.

In practice, there is great variation in the experience and expertise of assessors, but there is also great variation in the experience and interests of judges who make best interests decisions. While ideally both the assessor and judge will have the requisite skills, knowledge, and sensitivity to promote effectively the best interests of the children who are the subject of family law litigation, in practice if one of these professionals should have less knowledge, it is to be hoped that the child's interests will be protected by having the other professional involved in the process. It is a reality that some judges lack the expertise and experience to deal effectively

---

[51] L Dessau, 'A Short Commentary on Timothy M Tippins and Jeffrey Wittmann, "Empirical and Ethical Problems with Custody Recommendations: A Call for Clinical Humility and Judicial Vigilance"' (2005) 43 *Family Court Review* 266, 268.

and appropriately with family law cases; in these cases, the children will be fortunate if there has been a good assessor involved, as the judge, aware of his or her limitations, may rely on that professional's opinion. Resources for the resolution of family law cases are limited; if too high a standard is set for the admission of evidence from a court-appointed assessor in a child-related case, this will usually not result in better evidence being introduced. It will simply result in the court making a decision with less evidence and, inevitably, more reliance on the values and sometimes ill-informed opinions of judges.

While assessors generally perform an important function in the resolution of family law cases, there are legitimate concerns about the assessment process. Some of the measures which would enhance the utility of assessments include:

- clearer statements by assessors in their reports on the limitations of existing research and about the limitations on their abilities to make reliable predictions about the future;

- better training and clearer qualification standards for those who perform assessments;

- the development of clearer standards, to guide the assessment process, by professional organizations whose members undertake evaluations;

- further research to develop valid and reliable instruments for measuring the effects of separation and making predictions about the effects of future child care arrangements on children; and

- better education for judges and lawyers on psychological evidence and social science research and their limitations.

15

Domestic Violence and Child Protection: Can Psychology Inform Legal Decisions?

Elizabeth Gilchrist

Introduction

Recently the effects of domestic violence on children, and the links between domestic violence and child abuse, have become more widely recognized (Stanley, 1997). Research with adult victims and survivors, and with professionals working in both child protection and domestic violence, suggests that a good understanding of both is necessary to act in the best interests of children without re-victimizing women. This chapter briefly reviews this area, then describes data from research with perpetrators and their partners, looking particularly at typologies of perpetrators (Gilchrist, Johnson, Takriti, Weston, Beech, and Kebbell, 2003) and research from a separate study with children (Gilchrist and Letherby, 2004), to explore issues related to risk and implications for practice in the area of child protection.

Legal Context and Child Protection

Current legislation in England and Wales (the Children Act 1989) requires that the child's interests are paramount in any decisions relating to children. This, and later guidance and legislation, also instituted a 'duty to investigate . . . if they have reasonable cause to suspect that a child who lives, or is found, in their area is suffering, or is likely to suffer, significant harm' (section 47 of the Children Act 1989). This has meant that any professional who is made aware of ongoing risk to a child is seen as having a duty to inform appropriate authorities. If a child discloses they have witnessed domestic violence at home, that in itself can be a reason to register them as being 'at risk'. A parent or guardian who is not directly involved in either abuse or neglect of children can be held responsible for failing to protect a child. In addition the Domestic Violence, Crime and Victims Act 2004 has created an offence of causing or allowing the death of a child or vulnerable adult and also established a new responsibility for a member of a household, where they know a child or vulnerable adult is at risk of significant harm (Domestic Violence, Crime and Victims Act 2004). There is a duty to intervene and most professional bodies, including schools, have set 'child protection' procedures which identify the disclosure processes. One of the fundamental tenets of the Children Act 1989 is that decisions will be made 'in the best interests of the child'. Often this is interpreted to mean that the physical safety of the child overrides any other consideration, for example, emotional attachment to a non-abusive parent, and that uncertainty regarding safety cannot be tolerated.

Domestic Violence Context

We know that domestic violence is widespread; it is the second largest type of violence in the United Kingdom, assaults on wives accounting for 25 per cent of victim-reported offences (Mirlees-Black, 1999). We also know that the majority of domestic violence in the United Kingdom tends to be perpetrated by men against a female partner or ex-partner. Figures of 67 per cent, 76 per cent, and 88 per cent of victim-reported incidents of violence in the home have been identified as male perpetrated violence or 'wife beating', as opposed to 1.2 per cent being identified as 'husband beating' (Mirlees-Black, 1999; MPS, 2001). This is the most common type of violence against women, accounting for 56 per cent of all assaults on women (British Crime Survey, 2004). Research in London suggested a prevalence rate of 30 per cent (Mooney, 1993) and research from the United States suggested that physical or sexual abuse occurred in up to 31 per cent of all marriages over a lifetime (Collins, Schoen, Joseph *et al*, 1999).

Data shows that the level of violence is high and can result in fatalities, with two women per week being killed by current or former partners (Home Office, 1999). Thirty five per cent of murders investigated nationally by the police are domestic violence related (MPS, 2001). Research also indicates that many children are affected by this type of offending. The British Crime Survey suggests that in at least 25 per cent of cases children were aware of the abuse (Mirlees-Black, 1999), and a recent study of perpetrators of domestic violence on probation, suggested that in 37 per cent of cases, children witnessed the offence, and in 10 per cent of cases, children were directly involved in the incident (Gilchrist, Johnson, Takriti, Weston, Beech, and Kebbell, 2003).

A further feature of domestic violence in relation to children is that exposure to domestic violence in childhood can have a long-lasting negative effect in later life. Many studies have found some empirical data to support the notion of intergenerational transmission of violence. Recent data from England and Wales supports this, with 50 per cent of men convicted of an offence of domestic violence having experienced domestic violence in their family of origin (Gilchrist *et al*, 2003). There are negative effects on females also; Foa, Cascardi, Zoellener, and Feeny (2000) identified having experienced domestic violence in family of origin as being one of the factors which decreased a woman's ability to leave an abusive relationship; child care was also influential in the ability to make such decisions. Studies of women who have accessed refuge services suggest that the services available to women greatly affect their ability to make decisions to keep themselves and their children safe (McKay, 1994). Earlier research also identified issues around child care and fear of losing their children as greatly affecting a woman's ability to disclose and discuss abuse (Mooney, 1993).

The philosophies, policies, and practices of those engaged in promoting the needs of adult female victim/survivors of domestic violence and those focusing more on the needs of children and child protection issues, have often been seen as conflicting (Humphreys, 1998). Research in the child welfare arena suggests that social workers have failed to recognize the links between child abuse and domestic violence (Stark and Flitcraft, 1988) and often those working within a child protection agenda have held women responsible for the safety of their children, even in situations where they are clearly victims too (Fleck-Henderson, 2000). Women victim/survivors of domestic violence have been accused of engaging in risky behaviour by, for example, continuing to meet with an abusive partner post-violence in the process of ending a relationship. Also, women have been seen almost as negligent, in cases where they have remained with an abusive partner, despite professionals' concerns about their and their children's safety (Humphreys, 1998).

Critiques of these approaches have suggested that rather than seeing the needs of women and the needs of children as clashing, if we enable women to make themselves safe, whilst recognizing some of the realities of domestic violence, then this is more appropriate. Kelly (1994) suggested that 'one simple key principle from which we can begin is that protection of women is frequently the most effective form of child protection (Kelly, 1994, 54). Some of the realities that need to be recognized are, for example, that ending an abusive relationship is a process, not a single stage; that women often want the abuse to end but are equivocal about ending the relationship; that many women are physically, economically, and socially bound to their abusing partners; that provision for women and children does not always meet their needs. If this occurs, then we can more effectively ensure that children are also safe (Magen, 1999). It is vitally important that the safety and needs of women and children affected by domestic violence are recognized and dealt with appropriately so that neither is neglected, but nor should the needs of one group take precedence or be treated as reflecting any 'truth' more than any other (Featherstone and Trinder, 1997). It is suggested that a lack of clarity in this area is a problem for all professionals and that more integrated knowledge is required.

To achieve this, in addition to researching adult and child victim/survivors, we also need to know more about perpetrators, particularly different sub-groups of offenders with differing patterns of abuse and risks of ongoing violence. It is suggested that by marrying the knowledge from research with perpetrators, research with adult victim/survivors and specifically including the wishes of children, we can start to identify key areas for development and change.

Range of Abuses and Risk

Research with victim/survivors has identified that domestic violence incorporates a far wider range of abusive behaviours than merely violence. The 'power and control' wheel was developed from victim data from the United States and it identifies eight dimensions of abuse: intimidation, threats, emotional abuse, isolation, economic abuse, minimizing, denying and blaming; indirect abuse: using the children and entitlement, with core attitudes of power and control at the centre of the wheel, to explain domestic violence (Pence and Paymar, 1986). Current work with perpetrators suggests that, in addition to this, different types of perpetrator exist and they are likely to pose different levels of risk and to perpetrate abuse in different ways (Holtzworth-Munroe and Stuart, 1994). Current research in the United Kingdom suggests that the risk of intimate partner *murder* appears to be related to tenuous relationships; those in which the couple are cohabiting (32 per cent) or dating (25 per cent) were large groups within the study. Also, lethality appeared to be related to particular views of the relationship: there was often conflict about the man's possessiveness and jealousy (26 per cent) (Dobash, Dobash, Cavanagh, and Lewis, 2005). In addition, previous violence within that relationship, violence within a previous relationship, and, critically for those working in all areas of child protection and domestic violence, for whom the question 'Why doesn't she leave and protect the children?' might appear pertinent, the ending of a relationship linked with lethality, as 36 per cent of the women had been killed when they tried to leave an intimate relationship or were in the process of leaving (Dobash *et al*, 2005). These findings replicate previous work which identified that more than one-third of women experienced post-separation violence (Humphreys and Thiara, 2003) and that the risk to women as opposed to men is far greater post-separation (Wilson and Daly, 1993).

Types of Perpetrators

Violence can have different aetiologies. It is suggested that, whilst not being mutually exclusive, violence can be seen as being primarily goal-orientated (instrumental) or as being emotionally driven (expressive). Within domestic violence, the notion of emotionally driven violence was influential very early on, but then rejected as not truly reflecting the purposeful nature of the violence. However, research in the United States and in the United Kingdom has identified that there is a great deal of heterogeneity among perpetrators of domestic violence. One key issue within these typologies is the link between the different types of offender and the notion of instrumental violence and expressive violence.

Various researchers have identified sub-groups of offender within domestically abusive groups. For example, Hamberger, Lohr, Bonge, and Tollin (1996) identified three groups: antisocial/narcissistic, schizoid/borderline and dependent/compulsive; Holzworth-Munroe and Stuart (1994) identified three (and then four) groups: generally violent/antisocial, (low level antisocial, identified in 2000), dysphoric/borderline passive, and dependent (family only); Saunders (1992) identified three groups: generally violent, emotionally volatile, and emotionally suppressed; and Tweed and Dutton (1998) identified two groups: impulsive and instrumental offenders.

Generally the dimensions along which the perpetrators are described as varying include a dimension of generality of violence—general or only against partner; one of severity of violence—low level violence to severe violence; and an aspect of psychopathology—including anger, personality dysfunction, and alcohol use. The various typologies tend to identify one, two, or three groups of violent offenders for whom the violence serves some goal, often linked to power and control (instrumental); and one group of offenders whose violence tends to be more linked to poor emotional regulation, high arousal, and dysphoria (expressive).

Work from the United States also suggests that these different types of perpetrator suffer from different underlying problems and pose different levels of risk (Sonkin, 2005). Sonkin (2004) identified three sub-groups of offender and suggested that there were differences in terms of behaviour, personality, and attachment. For example, he suggested that 'psychopathic' offenders would tend to use violence inside and outside home, would have a history of antisocial behaviour, show negative attitudes and a high acceptance of violence, and tend to have a dismissing attachment. 'Over-controlled' batterers were reported as tending to have a history of violence and alcohol, displaying a constantly cheerful persona, trying to avoid conflict, and as having preoccupied and avoidant attachment. 'Borderline' batterers were reported as using violence predominantly or exclusively in an intimate relationship, as showing the cyclical phases of abusive behaviour (linked with the cycle of violence (Sonkin, Martin, and Walker, 1985)), as showing high levels of jealousy, depression, and anxiety-based rage, having ambivalence to their wife/partner, and being assessed as having fearful/angry attachment.

'Borderline' offenders were identified as having a higher rate of re-offending, linked in with their poor emotional regulation; 'psychopathic' and 'over-controlled' offenders were seen as likely to perpetrate the most severe violence, linked to psychopathic tendencies and low empathy for the 'psychopathic' group and to 'over-controlled' offenders compensating for inadequacy (Sonkin, 2004).

Recent UK work replicates the finding of heterogeneity with domestic violence offenders and identifies a four-group typology of domestic violence perpetrator but suggests that in terms of nature of violence (as opposed to generality or severity) it may be more helpful to apply a two-group typology, splitting the perpetrators into 'antisocial/narcissistic' and 'borderline/emotionally volatile' groups; the first group being more closely linked with instrumental violence and the second group being more closely linked with expressive offending (Gilchrist *et al*, 2003). This research suggests that 'anti-social/narcissistic' offenders constitute the larger group (72 per cent) and that the borderline/emotionally volatile group is the smaller one (28 per cent). The groups differed in terms of general anti-social behaviour, with those in the first groups evidencing more macho attitudes, lower empathy, higher numbers of previous convictions, narcissism, and anti-social attitudes, whilst the second group evidenced more traits of borderline personality disorder, high interpersonal dependency, high anger, depression, anxiety, low self-esteem, external locus of control, physical and sexual abuse as children, fearful attachment, and suicidal ideation (Johnson *et al*, 2006). Linking this work with the previous work, it might be suggested that the 'borderline/emotionally volatile' offender identified in this study might evidence the higher risk of re-offences and the 'anti-social/generally violent' might be seen as at greater risk of perpetrating more serious violence.

These differential patterns of abuse and of risk need to be taken into account when assessing men as fathers and when considering the reality of the abuse for the partners and the impact of the violence on the children. Further work within the same study, with partners of domestically abusive men, suggests that in addition to evidencing different characteristics, these men also show different patterns of abuse as reported by their (ex-) partners.

Impact of Abuse on Women

We know that there is no one typical victim of domestic violence, and domestic violence occurs across all sub-groups of society. However, a victim study conducted in the 1990s provides some data which is of interest as it reinforces the length of time over which victimization tends to be experienced, the number of children involved, and the typical help-seeking behaviour of victims. In this study, 81 per cent of the women were aged twenty to thirty-four, and on average there were two to three children within the family. The average length of suffering violence was seven years, with 59 per cent of the sample having been abused for over three years. In 90 per cent of the cases in this study there was a child under the age of five in the family. In 36 per cent of cases the violence had started during pregnancy (Browne and Herbert, 1997).

Counselling and psychological research would identify that many domestic violence victims are likely not to be easy clients. The experiences of abuse leave many women with trauma symptoms, poor emotional regulation, and limited and often inappropriate coping strategies. Many women resort to drink and other unhelpful strategies in response to their abuse. Many appear to lead chaotic lives and to make poor choices regarding themselves, their relationships, and their children.

These problematic behaviours and limited coping strategies can be understood with reference to psychological research. Research with victim/survivors of domestic violence indicates that leaving is a process, not a one-off decision; women have often made at least eight attempts to leave prior to a final separation and have generally accessed information and asked for help and support from a number of agencies in order to plan and effect this move (Browne and Herbert, 1997) Typical effects of intimate partner violence include: ambivalent loyalty and distorted attributions; internalized blame and compliant behaviour; passive and avoidant coping; and social isolation (Browne and Herbert, 1997). For example, in terms of amibivalent loyalty and distortions, women often want the violence to end but the relationship to continue, and see the positives as well as the negatives in their partners, identifying the perpetrators as good fathers or good providers and often feeling that they have a social duty to ensure their children do have a father figure within the family. Adult victims often blame themselves (believing they 'cause' the violence, as they argue with/defy the abuser, which tends to be reinforced by the abusive partner's tendency to blame the victim also) or other external factors for the abuse, citing alcohol and stress as reasons for the abuse, which reinforces ambivalence. Unhelpful coping strategies, such as denial or use of drink and drugs, and high levels of mental health issues, for example, minimal reactivity, depression, low self-esteem, and 'learned helplessness' exacerbate feelings of blame and isolation, leading to dependence on partners and placing limits on safe access to professional services. It is clear that the effects of abuse can make adult victims difficult to work with.

Additonally, an implicit belief that the ending of a relationship is a possible and appropriate method of making victims safe persists among professionals. This does not reflect the realities of the impact of abuse, nor the realities of risk. Research in this area shows there are many reasons cited by women to explain why they found it hard to leave the relationship: a large proportion of women were fearful for themselves (afraid, 63 per cent) and an even larger proportion were fearful of losing their children (74 per cent). Over half of the women were fearful of upsetting their children (54 per cent). Structural factors were identified by many women: 58 per cent of women did not want to leave their homes; 49 per cent reported that they had nowhere to go; and 44 per cent could not afford to leave. More relationship-focused explanations were provided by respondents too, with 31 per cent of women identifying the fact that they did not want the relationship to end, 37 per cent suggesting that they did not leave as they were in love, and 22 per cent saying that there was family pressure for them not to leave. Unstable attributions influenced a large proportion of women, with 72 per cent of women indicating that they stayed as they thought their partner would change and a small but significant proportion of women suggesting that they saw the abusive incident as a one-off (23 per cent) (Browne and Herbert, 1997). Also, the recent work on the links between separation and risk of lethality and the high level of continuation of abuse post-separation (Dobash *et al*, 2004) calls into question whether leaving is an appropriate, or safe, goal.

A further important point is that, given that male perpetrators show heterogeneity in offending patterns, it is suggested that looking at how different types of offender are experienced by their partners and what this means in terms of risk to adults and to children should also be addressed. The study by Gilchrist *et al* (2003), used data from partners of men post-conviction for a domestic violence-related offence, to explore whether there were differences between the experiences of partners of 'antisocial/generally violent' perpetrators and 'borderline/emotionally volatile' offenders. The men were classified and then qualitative data from the partner who had been the victim of this abuse was thematically analysed along the

Table 15.1. Range of abusive behaviours by category of perpetrator

Abuse/incidence	Antisocial/narcissistic	Borderline/emotion volatile
Economic abuse N = 20 (53%)	No—more jealousy wife working with men	Very controlling with money
Emotional abuse N = 25 (66%)	Very	Only at time of assault
Male privilege N = 23 (61%)	No housework, expects gratitude	When helpful—to control partner, eg shop not let her out
Isolation N = 27 (71%)	Not unless affects him (eg childcare)	Stops partner, going out, friends, family
Coercion/threats N = 21 (55%)	Threat/try suicide	Threats to kill kids, family, smash property
Minimizing N = 30 (79%)	Blame, deny	Apologize
Intimidation N = 12 (32%)	Looks smash property, children	Limited
Using children N = 12 (32%)	Direct use of children to hurt partner	Argue, emotional abuse irrespective of children

dimensions of abuse as identified by previous victim-based research (Pence and Paymar, 1986).

Table 15.1 summarizes the different ways in which partners of abusive men described how these men used the various abusive tactics (Gilchrist *et al*, 2003b) as identified from previous victim samples (Pence and Paymar, 1986).

Examination of the qualitative data from this study clarifies how the abuse differed. An example of this, showing the way in which the perpetrators used children differently, is given below.

The partners of the borderline/emotionally abusive men reported that their partners tended to be violent, irrespective of the children:

He just kept punching me, punching me, my head was killing me. My son come downstairs, he was crying 'don't hit me Mum', he said he wouldn't hit me again, at which point he did hit me again.

He had the baby in his arms, but he had a knife as well, he started stabbing the wall in the living room.

Partners of the anti-social/narcissistic perpetrators tended to report that their partners tended to use the children more directly in their abuse.

He'd say I wasn't a good mother and things like that.

I had hold of the baby at the time and he was only, what, six weeks old, and he floored me for it [attending to child], he really did, and I fell off the bed and I had a split lip.

Differences also emerged across many of the areas, and interestingly in terms of working with victim/survivors, in terms of where women attributed the blame/responsibility for the abuse. Women whose partners were 'borderline/emotionally volatile' offenders tended to be more likely to blame themselves for the violence, believing that they had provoked their partner in some way or that the violence had occurred due to their partner's jealousy. These attributions were not given by the 'antisocial/narcissistic' offenders who were more likely to attribute the violence to alcohol abuse. The statements below demonstrate this.

It's just every time he's had a drink that's it. Like if he has spirits then I know, you know . . . if he just has lager he's okay, but when he starts hitting the thing you know, especially when he has whisky that's the worst, you know. He's alright if he has like just a couple of vodkas, I know, if he has vodka I know he'll just come home and go to sleep, but when he has whisky then it sends him, you know. (Antisocial/Narcissistic)

There's always drink involved, when he's sober there's no problem whatsoever, I never actually saw him being violent when he wasn't drunk. (Antisocial/Narcissistic)

Just jealousy, he didn't want me to go out. (Borderline/Emotionally Volatile)

It's all jealousy with him you see, it's about other men and me, that's what, that's what G's got a temper about, it's always about other men. (Borderline/Emotionally Volatile)

I think maybe I made my husband both feel insecure and it came out in violence. (Borderline/Emotionally Volatile)

I sort of like said that he was like his Dad and that upset him 'cos his Dad was violent when he was younger and abusive towards him, so maybe I had contributed to it a little bit by saying that, that might have like triggered him off a little bit. (Borderline/Emotionally Volatile)

Partners of both types of offenders tended to attribute violence to life events, noting that violence tended to escalate around times of upheaval such as marriage, moving in together, or pregnancy and birth (Gilchrist *et al*, 2003b, Home Office, 1999).

It is possible that further exploration of this type might lead us to be able to identify that a victim who has experienced high levels of controlling behaviours in relation to money and to contact with friends would be at more risk of further assault, but that those who had experienced a greater degree of intimidating behaviours might be at greater risk of highel levels of violence. It is clear that information about the type and range of abuse suffered might indicate the type of batterer involved and potentially inform professionals as to likely triggers, and levels of risk and changes in risk. This type of work, where the type of abuse that might be experienced by partners of different types of abuser could feed into safety planning, is extremely useful for professionals to include in their assessments and planning in domestic violence cases.

Children's Knowledge and Experiences

The information above was very much focused on the experiences of adult victims. Historically, the knowledge and impact of domestic violence on children has been minimized, but recent research specifically focusing on children challenges some of the assumptions and reinforces the fact that children are significantly affected by domestic violence, similarly to adult victims. Data does show that violence between adults is likely to co-exist with violence towards children: 53 per cent of those showing violence towards a partner also abused their children and 52 per cent of child-abusing families show other forms of family violence. Also, forms of abuse co-exist: in 23 per cent of reported cases parents both abuse and neglect their children, and 33 per cent of sexually abused children had also been physically abused by their parents (Browne and Herbert, 1997). NCH Action for Children (1994) reported that in 62 per cent of cases children had overheard at least one attack, and in 73 per cent of cases children had witnessed the violence. The children were also aware of the effects of the abuse: in 99 per cent of cases children had seen their mothers upset or crying, and 52 per cent of children had seen the injuries resulting from an attack (NCH Action for Children 1994).

Women in this study reported that domestic violence had a significant effect on the children. In the study conducted for NCH Action for Children (1994) 86 per cent of mothers reported that children had experienced long-lasting effects from the abuse. Some of the more common longer-term effects were: children were frightened (72 per cent), clung to their mothers (63 per cent), and around a third of children tried to protect their mothers (32 per cent). Thirty-three per cent of children were reported as being violent or aggressive and experienced bitterness and anger, 25 per cent of children were protective and defensive, but 20 per cent of children were reported as no longer having any respect for their mothers, and as being sad and withdrawn. More than one in eight of the children were not living with their mother, due directly to the domestic violence.

In a more recent study, children's experiences of domestic violence were explored qualitatively, and their thoughts about what type of help and services they would require were sought (Gilchrist and Letherby, 2004). This study reported the experiences of eighteen children, from one location in the Midlands, so should not be over-generalized. All the children had been referred to one of the local services due to issues of domestic violence so it is a selected group, and perhaps atypical: their experiences may be more extreme as they have come to the notice of the authorities, or less extreme as they have been able to access service. Unfortunately, given the usefulness of the application of typologies in exploring detailed patterns within adult victim experiences, there was not enough data available on abusive behaviour and personal characteristics of the perpetrator to explore typologies within this project. Despite these caveats, the work does provide some insight into the range of experiences, linking perhaps with the heterogeneity of perpetrators and the diversity of families within a multi-cultural society, and does raise some interesting questions as to how to serve the interests of the child, and whether children do not report to avoid overly intrusive intervention. The data was collected 'second-hand' via professionals working with the young people, to avoid them having to discuss emotional and personal information with unknown researchers. The data is presented in the passive as this is how it was reported to the researchers.

Range of Experiences

The young people reported a wider range of experiences from witnessing the violence. One respondent reported having watched:

. . . her dad breaking her mum's arm and then had to go to the hospital and watch her mum lie about what had happened (Girl, aged 10).

Another respondent described how she had watched:

. . . her Dad try to murder her mum and due to the level of risk had been taken away from everything she knew and was under police protection (Girl, aged 12).

Other respondents discussed how they were used as a target instead of their mother, one respondent spoke about:

. . . being a 'punch bag' for his Dad when he could not hit his Mum and how his father would tell his mother it was her fault (Boy, aged 13).

Another talked about:

. . . the ways that he would physically assault his mother because his Dad told him to (Boy, aged 13).

Another respondent:

. . . described his father finding the panic alarms in their house (installed to protect the family) and how his father ripped out the wires (Boy, aged 10).

The points to note here are that the children were very aware of the abuse, at whatever level, and often actively involved in the victimization, the abuse, or in dealing with the results of the abuse themselves. Many of the children described post-separation abuse and certainly described ongoing effects long after the perpetrator had separated from the family. Finally, the complexity of the situation they described and the conflicting loyalties and emotions they felt were clear. These situations are difficult for adult professionals to understand and respond to appropriately, and it did appear to be overwhelmingly difficult for the children to deal with the issues raised.

Within this study the children were asked to produce drawings of themselves and their families and to describe themselves as animals and explain why. The drawings are not reproduced here but some of the comments are and they are telling in their clarity.

Jennifer, aged 9, wanted her '*Dad to be an ant so he couldn't pick on us*' and for the rest of her family to '*be tortoises as they would be around for a long time*'.

Jamie, aged 11, wanted to be '*like an eagle so I can fly away*'.

David, aged 7, wanted to be '*like a cat 'cos they can run fast*'.

Kalin, aged 7, wanted to be '*a big dog so I could look after my family and baby Rhiannon*'.

It was clear that many of the children wanted to escape, but also that many of the children were taking on 'adult level' responsibilities in terms of their families. They felt responsibility for the violence and for intervening to protect their mother. This seemed to apply to the authorities as well as to the perpetrator.

What the Children Wanted

As a final part of this study, the children were asked what they felt would help then, or would have helped them and their situation. The children identified a number of practical and more psychological or emotional supports and services they could be offered. For example:

> Jenny, aged 9, suggested 'My mum drinks so I can't live with her' and says 'Nan doesn't believe us', 'if my Nan could have been on my mum's side . . . the refuge could have been closer to school . . . I wanted to see my counsellor more often'.

> Chelsea, aged 6, was 'sad' at being apart from her half-siblings, she would like there to be 'someone who could tell people when I am upset' and said it was 'difficult to get help for someone like me'.

> Jamie, aged 11, says 'the police could have taken Dad away quicker' and would like 'summer clubs where I could meet people with sad things happening to them'.

> Stacey, aged 8, wanted 'there to be a refuge for the men so we wouldn't have to move'.

Overall the children had a good understanding that positive intervention with the perpetrator would help, that a safe place to talk would be useful for them, they did not want to feel as isolated and they wanted people to understand their situation. A point that was clear from the children's reports of their experiences and the help they would like is clearly stated by Jennifer, aged 9, who wanted 'my teachers to help me, but not try to save me'.

In summary, the children wanted to be able to talk to their teachers, for other children to understand them, not to feel lonely, to be able to share their feelings, somewhere for them to go, for people to listen to them and understand them but not try to save them. This study concluded that pre-crisis intervention and education around domestic violence was a priority, and that schools should be involved, but also suggested that a specialist and perhaps local, safe, confidential telephone listening service might be made available for children (Gilchrist and Letherby, 2004).

It is clear that we need to allow children to disclose their situation and discuss their fears and practical problems at school, without judgements being made of their mothers. We need to encourage professionals to listen to children, but this needs to be confidential. Service provision needs to be within the mainstream to respond to the children's desire for those they interact with normally to understand them and to reduce isolation. Perhaps most crucially we need to respond to the children's fears about their mother being blamed for the abuse and also, given the experience of ongoing abuse post-separation, work to manage the risk within the context of an ongoing relationship, of whatever nature.

Summary and Conclusions

It is clear from this brief review of a selection of the literature and research exploring issues around domestic violence and child abuse, that this is a difficult and complex area and one in which multi-disciplinary approaches are perhaps more necessary than ever. Research into the practice of child protection and domestic violence has identified that often the interests of the mother and those of the child are seen as conflicting, but that many of the expectations that professionals have regarding appropriate behaviour in terms of protecting children do need to be (re-)viewed through an understanding of the effects of abuse on adult women and the lack of protection, in fact the increased risk faced at the point of separation.

Research with perpetrators of domestic violence alerts us to the fact that there are sub-groupings of offender, who may abuse differently and pose differential risk. This type of knowledge and the differential impact on women and children needs to be integrated into practice to enable professionals to be better informed in their assessments and practice. Professionals need to include psychological knowledge of effects of abuse and potential differences in patterns of abuse and then identify how to work with the victims within the realities of their situation, recognizing both structural and psychological barriers to engagement. Professionals need to consider active management of abuse within the limits of a dangerous relationship and recognize the danger associated with leaving and the likelihood of ongoing violence post-separation. We might consider developments in places such as Canada (Haskell, 2002), where the psychological impact of the abuse is recognized and specifically addressed within women's support provision, and start to focus and improve our psychological provision for women victim/survivors of domestic violence.

Finally, work with children suggests that, despite the rhetoric of making the child's interests paramount, their voices and concerns are being ignored. The children want to be listened to and helped but are conscious of the likely blame which would attach to their mother if abuse is disclosed; they do not want to be removed but for professionals to work within current settings to help them to manage their safety. Professionals need to provide service to children and respond to children in such a way as to allow them to disclose without fear of overly intrusive intervention.

It is clear that there is a need to develop a co-ordinated system where work with perpetrators and adult and child victim/survivors are informed by all perspectives. It is also clear that further work is required to educate legal professionals so that they do not inadvertently collude in abuse or inadvertently increase risk. These are difficult tasks but further interdisciplinary research, theory integration, and dissemination of research to practitioners in addition to academics should provide a good foundation.

References

Browne, K and Herbert, M (1997). *Preventing Family Violence*. Chichester.

Buchbinder, E and Eisikovits, Z (2004). 'Reporting bad results: The ethical responsibilities of presenting abused women's parenting practices in a negative light'. *Child and Family Social Work* 9: 359–67.

Collins, K, Schoen, C, Joseph, S *et al* (1997). 'Health Concerns Across a Woman's Lifetime: 1998 Survey of Women's Health'. New York.

Dobash, R, Cavanagh, K, and Lewis, R (2005). *Homicide in the Family—New Findings Revealed*. Manchester: University of Manchester website, <http://news.man.ac.uk>.

Fagan, J (1993). Social Structure and Spouse Assault in B Forst (ed) *The Socio-Economics of Crime and Justice*. Toronto.

Featherstone, B and Trinder, L (1997). 'Familiar Subjects? Domestic Violence and Child Welfare'. *Child and Family Social Work* 2: 147–59.

Fleck-Henderson, A (2000). 'Domestic Violence in the Child Protection System: Seeing Double'. *Children & Youth Services Review* 22(5): 333–54.

Gilchrist, E, Johnson, R, Takriti, R, Weston, S, Beech, AR, and Kebbell, M (2003a). *Domestic Violence Offenders: Characteristics and Offending Related Needs. Findings No 217*. London.

—— —— —— and ——(2003b). *Domestic Violence Offenders: Characteristics and Offending Related Needs, Final Report*. London: Home Office.

——and Letherby, G (2004). Someone to Listen: Children's Experiences of Domestic Violence. *Centre for Social Justice Annual Conference Abstracts*. Coventry.

Hamberger, LK, Lohr, JM, Bonge, D, and Tollin, DF (1996). 'A large sample empirical typology of male spouse abusers and its relationship to dimensions of abuse'. *Violence and Victims* 11(4): 277–91.

Haskell, L (2002). Key findings from new research and development in psychology—Assaulted women's experience and trauma. Amsterdam: Paper presented at XXVIIth International Congress on Law and Mental Health.

Holtzworth-Munroe, A and Stuart, GL (1994). 'Typologies of male batterers: Three subtypes and the differences among them'. *Psychological Bulletin* 116(3): 476–97.

——Meeham, JC, Herron, K, Rehman, U, and Stuart, GL (2000). 'Testing the batterer typology'. *Journal of Consulting and Clinical Psychology* 68(6): 1000–19.

Home Office (1999). *Living Without Fear*. London: Home Office.

Humphreys, C (1999). 'Avoidance and confrontation: social work practice in relation to domestic violence'. *Child and Family Social Work* 4: 77–87.

——and Thiara, R (2003). 'Neither Justice nor Protection: Women's Experiences of Post-separation violence'. *Journal of Social Welfare and Family Law* 25(3): 195–214.

Johnson, R, Gilchrist, E, Beech, T, Weston, S, Takriti, R, and Freeman RPJ (2006). 'A Psychometric Typology of U.K. Domestic Violence Offenders'. *Journal of Interpersonal Violence* (forthcoming).

Kelly, L (1994). 'The interconnectedness of domestic violence and child abuse: challenges for research policy and practice', in A Mullender and R Morley (eds) *Children Living with Domestic Violence: Putting Men's Abuse of Women on the Child Care Agenda.* London.

Magan, R (1999). 'In the Best Interests of Battered Women: Reconceptualising Allegations of Failure to Protect'. *Child Maltreatment* 4(2): 127–35.

McGee, C (1997). 'Children's Experiences of Domestic Violence'. *Child and Family Social Work* 2: 13–23.

McKay, MM (1994). 'The link between domestic violence and child abuse: assessment and treatment considerations'. *Child Welfare* 73: 29–39.

Metropolitan Police (2001). Enough is Enough. *Domestic Violence Strategy.* London: MPS.

Mirlees-Black, C (1999). *Domestic Violence: Findings from the British Crime Survey Self complete Questionnaire.* London: Home Office

Mooney, J (1993). *The Hidden Figure: Domestic Violence in North London.* London: Centre for Criminology, Middlesex University.

Mullins, A (1997). *Making a Difference.* London.

NCH Action for Children (1994). *The Hidden Victims: Children and Domestic Violence.* London.

Pence, E and Paymar, M (1986). Power and Control Tactics of Men Who Batter. *Minnesota Program Development.* Duluth.

—— and —— (1993). *Education groups for men who batter: The Duluth Model.* New York.

Radford, L, Hester, M, Humphries, J, and Woodfield, KS (1997). 'For the Sake of the Children: The law, domestic violence and child contact in England'. *Women's Studies International Forum* 20(4): 471–82.

Saunders, DG (1992). 'A typology of men who batter: Three types derived from cluster analysis'. *American Journal of Orthopsychiatry* 62: 264–75.

Sonkin, DJ (2004). The assessment and treatment of interpersonal violence and unresolved trauma. Accessed at <http://www.daniel-sonkin.com/>.

——Martin, D, and Auerbach Walker, LE (1985). *The male batterer: A treatment approach.* New York.

Stanley, N (1997). 'Domestic Violence and Child Abuse: Developing Social Work Practice'. *Child and Family Social Work* 2: 135–45.

Stark, E and Flitcraft, A (1988). 'Women and Children at Risk: A Feminist Perspective on Child Abuse'. *International Journal of Health Services* 18: 97–118.

Stith, S, Williams, M, and Rosen, K (1990). *'Violence Hits Home'.* New York.

Tweed, RG and Dutton, DG (1998). 'A comparison of impulsive and instrumental subgroups of batterers'. *Violence and Victims* 13(3): 217–30.

Waugh, F and Bonner, M (2002). 'Domestic Violence and Child Protection: issues in safety planning'. *Child Abuse Review* 11(5): 282–95.

Wilson, M and Daly, M (1993). 'Spousal Homicide Risk and Estrangement'. *Violence and Victims* 8: 3–14.

16

Legal and Psychological Approaches to Understanding Domestic Violence for American Indian Women

Cynthia Willis Esqueda and Melissa Tehee[1]

> It has been said that the position of woman is the test of civilization, and that
> of our women was secure. Before this calamity came upon us [colonization]
> you could not find anywhere a happier home than that created by the Indian
> woman.[2]

In order to recognize the legal and psychological approaches for understanding the domestic violence issue for American Indian communities,[3] basic facts concerning American Indians must be acknowledged. Currently, there are 562 American Indian Nations that are recognized by the US government,[4] and several hundred more tribal entities and thousands more individual American Indians that are not federally recognized as such. Thus, numerous tribal histories, traditions, and colonization experiences create great diversity among American Indian tribal nations and among American Indian people within the United States.

[1] Appreciation is extended to the Indian Center, Inc in Lincoln, Nebraska, Lori Hack, Mona Bearskin, JD, and John Wunder, PhD, JD. This research was partially funded by a grant from UCARE and a grant from Human Rights and Human Diversity at University of Nebraska-Lincoln.

[2] C Eastman, *The Soul of the Indian* (Lincoln, Nebraska, 1911) 42–3.

[3] American Indian, Native American, Indian, and indigenous people are used interchangeably throughout this paper. Although it is recognized that there are conceptual and political issues tied to these labels, this usage is not meant to offend any individual or group. These terms reflect the numerous labels that are currently used in and among American Indian communities, and within the social sciences. Furthermore, it is recognized that such terms can apply to all indigenous people within the Americas; however, the focus here is on North American Indians.

[4] The US Bureau of Indian Affairs (BIA) was established in 1824 and maintains a listing of all current federally recognized tribes within the US. Those tribes wishing to reclaim or gain federal recognition must provide documentation and petition for such status through the BIA. See Barry T Hill, Natural Resources and Environment, Bureau of Indian Affairs, Department of the Interior, Testimony to the General Accounting Office Before the Committee on Indian Affairs, US Senate, *Indian Issues: Basis for the BIA's Tribal Recognition Decisions Is Not Always Clear* (17 September 2002) Washington, DC: GAO 0296T. See also Federal Register (12 July 2002) Vol 67, 134. Department of the Interior, Bureau of Indian Affairs, *Indian Entities Recognized and Eligible To Receive Services From the United States Bureau of Indian Affairs*, 46327.

At the same time, there are commonalities among tribes. For example, most of the federally recognized tribal nations possess nation-to-nation treaty rights, and tribal nations and their members receive federal benefits based on those rights. Indeed, the majority of these treaty rights (for example, the Fort Laramie Treaty of 1868) predate the late 1880s arrival of the bulk of ancestors of European Americans in the United States today.[5]

Another commonality among tribal nations concerns the actions of tribal governments. Like other nation states, most tribal governments expend a great deal of energy in generating, regulating, and maintaining subsistence levels for tribal members who live on reservations. These governments must demand and supervise fulfillment on a constant basis of treaty rights[6] that include a vast array of legal, resource, and land issues, such as education,[7] employment,[8] poverty,[9] housing,[10] environment,[11] health,[12] and justice.[13]

Moreover, today most of these nations have legal systems that are sanctioned by the United States.[14] Such legal systems are self contained and include law enforcement, prosecution, jails, and tribal courts for adjudication.[15] At the same time, the United States has not provided resources to develop fully effective legal systems, including tribal courts,[16] even while it demands incursions into the

---

[5] SD McLemore, HD Romo, and S Gonzalez Baker, *Racial and Ethnic Relations in America* (Boston, Mass, 2001).

[6] US Commission on Civil Rights, *A Quiet Crisis: Federal Funding and Unmet Needs in Indian Country* (Washington, DC, 2003).

[7] C Freeman and MA Fox, *Status and Trends in the Education of American Indian and Alaska Natives*, United States Department of Education. NCES 2005–108 (Washington, DC, 2005).

[8] Employment discrimination litigation occurs at both the local and national levels. See US Department of Justice, *Justice Department Reaches Settlement with the City of Gallup, New Mexico Regarding Employment Opportunities for American Indian Applicants* (Washington, DC, 2004) #04–660, or *Tribes file civil rights complaint against Nebraska County* (19 March 2004) <http://www.Indianz.com>.

[9] *Poverty in Indian Country still higher than average* (31 August 2005) <http://www.Indianz.com>.

[10] M Kelley, Indian Health Service Has Doctors Who Were Disciplined for Sexual Misconduct, Medical Errors, *National Indian Health Board* (5 March 2002) <http://www.nihb.org>. R Seldon, *Families sicken and die in mold-plagued HUD housing* (2 April 2002) <http:www.Indiancountry.com>.

[11] See the *Indigenous Environmental Network* at <http://www.ienearth.org/>. B Norrell, *Navajos receive award for banning uranium mining* (5 September 2004) <http://www.indiancountry.com>.

[12] For information on American Indian Health see the Native American Health Database from the University of New Mexico Health Sciences Center, <http://hsc.unm.edu/library/nhd/>.

[13] WC Bradford, 'Another Such Victory and We Are Undone: A Call to An American Indian Declaration of Independence' (2004–2005) 40 *Tulsa Law Review* 71.

[14] *National Tribal Justice Resource Center*, <http://www.tribalresourcecenter.org/tribalcourts/directory>.

[15] See *Cabazon Band of Mission Indians v Smith* 388 F 3d 691 (CD Ca 2004) and also *Tribal Court Clearinghouse* (2005) <http://www.tribal-institute.org/>. S Wakeling, M Jorgensen, S Michaelson, and M Begay, 'Policing On American Indian Reservations' *National Institute of Justice*, Washington, DC: NCJ 188095 (2001). K Washburn, 'Reconsidering the Commission's Treatment of Tribal Courts' (2005) 17 *Federal Sentencing Reporter* 209–14. T Minton, *Jails in Indian Country, 2001*, US Department of Justice, Bureau of Justice Statistics, NCJ 1934000 (Washington, DC: 2002).

[16] K Baca, 'The Changing Federal Role in Indian Country' (April 2002) *National Institute of Justice Journal* 8, 13. *BIA: Law enforcement head offered to be reassigned* (3 June 2004) <http://Indianz. com>. J Snyder, 'Convicts Go Free Because of Deteriorating Shiprock Jail' *Farmington Daily Times*

functioning of such systems.[17] Nevertheless, tribal courts are a viable means of providing indigenous-based justice within Indian country.[18]

Unfortunately, another commonality among tribes concerns the explosion of domestic violence in the last several decades. Some have argued that domestic violence may be one of the most significant health and psychological issues facing American Indians in the future.[19] Historically, American Indians' domestic violence was almost non-existent.[20] America's Indigenous women held cultural, political, spiritual, and economic power.[21] Tribal histories and our own family information tell us that this was so. The earliest written accounts by American Indian women confirm that they possessed power and respect within their communities. For example, Pretty Shield (Crow), Waheenee (Hidatsa), Zitkala-Sa (Oglala Lakota), and Nancy Ward (Cherokee) came from different tribes, but all demonstrated the power inherent in women's tribal gender roles and participation.[22] Among the Haudenosaunee (Iroquois), women held rights that inspired

30 June 2004 <http://www.daily-times.com>. Wakeling, Jorgenson, Michaelson, and Begay, NIJ, n 15 above, 9–10, 26. Although tribal legal systems, including tribal courts, are characterized by too few personnel, inadequate detention facilities, and lack of resources for tribal attorneys and courts, the federal government has initiated the Office of Tribal Justice to ensure the continued growth and integrity of tribally based legal systems.

[17] WC Canby, Jr, 'The Status of Indian Tribes in American Law Today' (1987) 62 *Washington Law Review* 1. MLM Fletcher, 'The Insidious Colonialism of the Conqueror: The Federal Government in Modern Tribal Affairs' (2005) 19 *Washington University Journal of Law and Policy* 273.

[18] RD Cooter and W Fikentscher, 'Indian Common Law: The Role of Custom in American Indian Tribal Courts, Part I' (1998) 46 *American Journal of Comparative Law* 287, 338. K Washburn, 'Reconsidering the Commission's Treatment of Tribal Courts' (2005) 17 *Federal Sentencing Reporter* 209, 214.

[19] P Jumper Thurman, R Bubar, B Plested, R Edwards, P LeMaster, E Bystrom, M Hardy, D Tahe, M Burnside, and ER Oetting, *Violence Against Indian Women, Final Revised Report* National Institute of Justice (Washington, DC, 2003). LA Williams, *Family Violence and American Indian and Alaska Natives: A Report to the Indian Health Service Office of Women's Health* (Washington, DC, 2002), 9.

[20] P Gunn Allen, 'Violence and the American Indian Woman' in P Gunn Allen (ed), *The Speaking Profits Us: Violence in the Lives of Women of Color*, Center for the Prevention of Sexual and Domestic Violence (Seattle, Washington, 1986), 5–7. B Chester, RW Robin, MP Koss, J Lopez, and D Goldman, 'Grandmother Dishonored: Violence Against Women by Male Partners in American Indian Communities' (1994) 9 *Violence and Victims* 249–58. S Hamby, 'The Importance of Community in a Feminist Analysis of Domestic Violence Among American Indians' (2000) 28 *American Journal of Community Psychology* 649–69. G Valencia-Weber and CP Zuni, 'Domestic Violence and Tribal Protection of Indigenous Women in the United States' (1995) 69 *St John's Law Review* 69. Williams, n 19 above, introductory comments on page 2. JW Zion and EB Zion, 'Hozho' Sokee'—Stay Together Nicely: Domestic Violence Under Navajo Common Law' (1993) 25 *Arizona State Law Journal* 407.

[21] K Anderson, *Changing Woman: A History of Racial Ethnic Women in Modern America* (New York, 1996). BR Berger, 'Indian Policy and the Imagined Indian Woman' (2004) 14 *Kansas Journal of Law and Public Policy* 103–20. LE Murphy, 'Autonomy and the Economic Roles of Indian Women of the Fox-Wisconsin Riverway Region' in N Shoemaker (ed), *Negotiators of Change: Historical Perspectives on Native American Women*, (New York, 1995) 1763–832. T Perdue, *Cherokee Women: Gender and Culture Change, 1700–1835* (Lincoln, Nebraska, 1998).

[22] FB Linderman, *Pretty Shield* (Lincoln, Nebraska, 1932/1972). N Lurie, *Mountain Wolf Woman: Sister of Crashing Thunder* (Ann Arbor, Mich, 1961). GL Wilson, *Waheenee: An Indian Girl's Story* (Lincoln, Nebraska, 1981). Zitkala Sa, 'Impressions of an Indian Childhood, The School Days of an Indian Girl, An Indian Teacher Among Indians' (1900) 85 *Atlantic Monthly*. A biography of

their non-Indian sisters to seek equality and early male colonists to organize a democratic form of government.[23]

Colonization produced changes in women's status and power. After colonization and the introduction of European political and religious systems, American Indian women's power and status diminished.[24] After colonization, stereotypes concerning American Indian women led to the demise of their inherent powers, both within tribal communities and with European American contact. Out of this colonization, two main stereotypes of American Indian women emerged. The 'Indian maid' or princess is one such icon, as represented in the internationally known Disney Pocahontas character.[25] Numerous examples exist of this woman, who is young and seductive.[26] The other icon is the drudge or slave-like minion, as represented in numerous accounts of the life that American Indian women were reported to lead.[27] Both of these images are depicted as historical figures, and both

Zitkala Sa (Gertrude Bonnin) is available from <http://www.ipl.org/div/natam/>. She was an author, educator, and activist during the early part of the 20th century. CS Kidwell, 'Indian Women as Cultural Mediators' (1992) 39 *Ethnohistory* 97–107, provides information on the life of Nancy Ward.

[23] See eg the Haudenosaunee website, under the Culture link at <http://www.sixnations.org>. Also, for early American suffragists' notions of Haudenosaunee women, see S Roesch Wagner, 'Iroquois women inspire 19th century feminists' (1999) 31 *National NOW Times* 11. DA Grinde, Jr, 'The Iroquois and the Nature of American Government' (1993) 17 *American Indian Culture and Research Journal* 153–73.

[24] Gunn Allen, n 20 above, 5–6. P. Gunn Allen, 'Angry Women are Building: Issues and Struggles Facing Native American Women' in J Cole (ed), *All American Women* (New York, 1986) 407–9. Berger, n 21 above. CA Eastman, *The Soul of the Indian: An Interpretation* (Boston, Mass, 1911) 42–3. D Mihesuah, *Indigenous American Women* (Lincoln, Nebraska, 2003) 41–61.

[25] Berger, n 21 above. BR Berger, 'After Pocahontas: Indian Women and the Law' (1997) 21 *American Indian Law Review* 1830–934. Kidwell, n 22 above, 97. LF Klein and LA Ackerman, *Woman and Power in Native North America* (Norman, Okla, 1995) 5–6. D Mihesuah, *American Indians: Stereotypes and Realities* (Atlanta, Georgia, 1996) 61. The American Indian princess image came to be a popular icon. Although American Indians had no royalty or 'princess' titles or positions, many European Americans allude to their grandmothers who they describe as American Indian Princesses. This affinity for an indigenous root in American soil is in contrast to the lack of ancestral claims for an American Indian male relative. The popular Indian princess image was epitomized in the story of Pocahontas, who married an Englishman, became assimilated into English culture, was presented to the English sovereign at court, and is even buried in Gravesend, outside London. See G Riley, *Women and Indians on the Frontier, 1825–1915* (Albuquerque, New Mexico, 1984) 33, 34, 35.

[26] See the numerous items sold through the Bradford Exchange at <http://www. collectiblestoday.com> or Paradise Galleries at <http://www.paradisegalleries.com> which depict American Indian women as young, seductive, historical figures. We were unable to find one item being sold that depicts American Indian women as modern day figures.

[27] Anderson, *Changing Women*, n 21 above, 19. Gunn Allen, n 20 above, 5. Kidwell, n 22 above, 97. Annual Report of the Commissioner of Indian Affairs (1848) H Exec Doc No 1, 30th Congress, 2d Sess, in FP Prucha (ed), *Documents of United States Indian Policy* (Lincoln, Nebraska, 2000) 77. Klein and Ackerman, n 25 above, 6. Thomas Jefferson Morgan, Commissioner of Indian Affairs 1889–93, spoke of Indian women and their degraded status, as well. See FP Prucha, *The Great Father: The United States Government and the American Indians* (Lincoln, Nebraska, 1986) 239. Information on early 19th-century descriptions of the slave-like status of American Indian women can be found through University of Virginia, <http://xroads. virginia.edu/~HYPER/DETOC/ FEM/indian.htm>.

are found in film, literature, and advertising. Moreover, these images are broadcast within the Americas and globally as representatives of real American Indian women.

These stereotypes have left the dominant culture with a restricted notion of what real American Indians are like, particularly American Indian women. Dominant culture images of American Indian women differ significantly from the traditional indigenous view of women and their cultural status.[28] For example, although there is great variability among American Indian women,[29] traditionally, they are revered for achieving advanced age rather than maintaining youthfulness, because wisdom, gained from experience and learning, is valued and passed down to younger generations. American Indian women are celebrated for their spirituality, economic resourcefulness, and tribal knowledge and connections. More importantly, they are educators, business owners, law enforcement personnel, governmental officials, physicians, health care personnel, spiritual advisors, parents, grandparents, and even attorneys and psychologists. We know of no recognizable, dominant culture icon in the media that represents American Indian women as a modern person, although there are certainly such women that could be represented.[30]

The diminished status of American Indian women has coincided with increased violence against them. Although no historical written records exist for domestic violence rates, today American Indians experience domestic violence at higher rates in comparison to other ethnic groups.[31] In addition, unlike other ethnic groups where interpersonal violence is intra-racial, for American Indians,

---

[28] HC Rountree, 'Powhatan Indian Women: The People Captain John Smith Barely Saw' (1998) 45 *Ethnohistory* 1–29.

[29] D Mihesuah, 'Commonality of Difference: American Indian Women and History' (1996) 20 *American Indian Quarterly* 15.

[30] Although not an exhaustive list, several women come to mind as potential modern day images or icons that could represent the best of indigenous womanhood. Women such as Wilma Mankiller, Winona LaDuke, Cecilia Fire Thunder, Karen Gayton Swisher, Bea Medicine, Elizabeth Cook-Lynn, Louise Erdrich, Tantoo Cardinal, Buffy Sainte Marie, and Mary Wynne, are fine examples of the diversity of modern Indian women. We conducted an informal survey of undergraduate student office workers at the University of Nebraska-Lincoln and found that none could mention a nationally known modern American Indian woman, and certainly none could mention an Indian woman who could serve as a nationally known role model for both Indians and non-Indians.

[31] Numerous studies have consistently found a high prevalence of domestic violence in the American Indian population. Chester *et al*, n 20 above. DG Fairchild, M Wilson Fairchild, and S Stoner, 'Prevalence of Adult Domestic Violence Among Women Seeking Routine Care in a Native American Health Care Facility' (1998) 88 *American Journal of Public Health* 1515, 1517. SL Hamby, 'The Importance of Community in a Feminist Analysis of Domestic Violence Among American Indians' (2000) 28 *American Journal of Community Psychology* 650. L Halinka Malcoe and BM Duran, *Intimate Partner Violence and Injury in the Lives of Low-Income Native American Women*, US Department of Justice, National Institute of Justice, National Institute on Drug Abuse, National Institutes of Health (Washington, DC, 2004), NCJ 199703. L Halinka Malcoe, BM Duran, and JM Montgomery, 'Socioeconomic Disparities in Intimate Partner Violence Against Native American Women: A Cross-Sectional Study' (2004) *BMC Medicine*, <http://www.biomedcentral.com/1741-7015/2/20>. SB Murphy, C Risley-Curtiss, and K Gerdes, 'American Indian Women and Domestic Violence: The Lived Experience' (2003) 7 *Journal of Human Behavior and the Social*

domestic violence (eg between victims and former or current spouses, boyfriends, and girlfriends) is most often inter-racial in nature.[32] It has been estimated that 70 per cent of domestic violence among American Indians occurs between people of different races (ie American Indian and non-Indian).[33]

Considering the prevalence of domestic violence in the lives of American Indians, a legal approach is important for several reasons. Among these reasons are: (1) the enforcement of peace; (2) the prosecution and sentencing of offenders; (3) the passage of new laws to protect abuse victims; (4) the implementation of social policies; and (5) a community understanding of women's social status.

While domestic violence is prevalent in Indian country, and while such violence has enhanced negative consequences for a population already at risk, the legal approach to domestic violence intervention for American Indians is complicated. American Indian law can be considered in terms of three separate entities of law: tribal law, federal law, and state law.[34] Tribal Nations possess limited sovereignty, including criminal jurisdiction for most Indian on Indian minor offences on reservations.[35] Thus, tribes hold their own set of laws and methods for case management and dispensing justice. The federal government is responsible for major crimes investigation and litigation and can change the range and content of Tribal Nations' self-governance and legal power.[36] States battle tribal governments and the federal government over jurisdiction and the limits of state authority over tribes and their members.[37]

Environment 159–81. P Tjaden and N Thoennes, *Extent, Nature, and Consequences of Intimate Partner Violence: Findings from the National Violence Against Women Survey*, US Department of Justice, National Institute of Justice, Centers for Disease Control and Prevention (Washington, DC, July 2000), NCJ 181867.

[32] Halinka Malcoe and Duran, *Intimate Partner Violence*, n 31 above, I-2-7. LA Greenfield and SK Smith, *American Indians and Crime*, US Department of Justice, Bureau of Justice Statistics (Washington, DC, 1999) NCJ 173386.   [33] Greenfield and Smith, n 32 above.

[34] V Deloria, Jr and CM Lytle, *American Indians, American Justice* (Austin, Texas, 1983) 110. DH Getches, CF Wilkinson, and RA Williams, Jr, *Federal Indian Law* (4th edn, American Casebook Series, St Paul, Minnesota, 1998) 2–7. It should be noted that although the current orientation to American Indian law incorporates tribal law, state law, and federal law, American indigenous systems of justice predate colonial and US legal systems.

[35] WC Canby, JR, *American Indian Law In a Nutshell* (St Paul, Minnesota, 1998) 123, 168. *Ex p Crow Dog* 109 US 556 (1883). Getches *et al*, n 34 above. *US v Lara* No 03-107 (8th Cir April 19, 2004) <http://www.supremecourtus.gov/opinions/03slipopinion.html>.

[36] B Clark, *Lone Wolf v Hitchcock: Treaty Rights and Indian Law at the End of the Nineteenth Century* (Lincoln, Nebraska, 1999). DE Wilkins, *American Indian Sovereignty and the U. S. Supreme Court* (Austin, Texas, 1997). David Wilkins provides a definition of the plenary power of the US Congress over tribal affairs, such that 'in federal Indian policy and law, this term has three distinct meanings: a) exclusive—Congress, under the commerce clause is vested with sole authority to regulate the federal government's affairs with Indian tribes; b) preemptive—Congress may enact legislation which effectively precludes state government's acting in Indian related matters; c) unlimited or absolute—this judicially created definition maintains that the federal government has virtually boundless governmental authority and jurisdiction over Indian tribes, their lands, and their resources' (374).

[37] See K Abourezk, *Border dispute sign of deeper problem*, 23 October 2003, <http://www.journalstar.com/>, for review of a case involving a state and tribal nation border dispute. *Judge bars Kansas from*

Historically, under US federal law, American Indians held no legal right to protection against violence, unless by tribal law and custom.[38] Two Acts were passed by the US Congress to assert jurisdiction in Indian country when non-Indians were involved in crime (as either perpetrator or victim) and to assert criminal jurisdiction over specified major crimes by both Indians and non-Indians.[39] The General Crimes Act of 1817 and the Major Crimes Act of 1885 were intended to take control of crimes within Indian country in order (1) to assert authority over crime involving Indians and non-Indians and (2) to manage the type of crimes that would be litigated and the type of punishment certain offenses would incur. Neither of these acts addressed domestic violence specifically. Consequently, violence in Indian country was allowed to flourish,[40] even as tribes

action in dispute with Winnebagos, 21 May 2002, <http://www.omaha.com>. See K Abourezk, *Tribes allege county is biased*, 19 March 2004, <http://www.journalstar.com>, for case involving alleged discrimination against Omaha and Winnebago tribal members in employment hiring by county. See R Boczkiewicz, *State loses fight to tax tribal gasoline*, 29 August 2003, <http://www. capitaljournal.com/>, for the 10th Circuit Court of Appeals unanimous decision barring the State of Kansas from taxing gasoline sold by the Winnebago Tribe in Nebraska to the Kickapoo Tribe in Kansas. See *Cabazon Band of Mission Indians*, n 15 above. See D Melmer, *Judge supports Yankton Sioux*, 18 June 2002, <http://Indiancountry.com/>, for review of case involving Yankton Sioux and the state of South Dakota in dispute over reservation boundaries and burial sites. *Winnebago executive to appear in Kansas*, 27 August 2002, <http://www.Indianz.com/>.

Public Law 280 was passed in 1953 to relinquish federal criminal jurisdiction with mandatory passage of such jurisdiction to several states (California, Minnesota, Nebraska, Oregon, and Wisconsin), including Alaska in 1958. A state could assume such jurisdiction over tribes residing within the state. Some did so, but assumed jurisdiction over some, but not all, subject areas. The purpose of Public Law 280 was to reduce federal responsibility for law enforcement and criminal and civil jurisdictions on reservations and trust lands and address states' complaints of lawlessness. States and tribes found the arrangement untenable, due to lack of increased funding and the lack of tribal consent to such jurisdictional arrangements. In fact, the Omaha Nation and Winnebago Tribe of Nebraska were left without any law enforcement at all. The Civil Rights Act of 1968 made arrangements for states to retrocede their jurisdiction back to the tribes and federal government. However, the Secretary of the Interior was responsible for approving such retrocession. Consequently, such approval could mean that two tribes with adjoining reservations had different jurisdictional arrangements. For example, the Omaha Nation's jurisdiction was retroceded, but the Winnebago Tribe of Nebraska's jurisdiction was not. This created a plethora of jurisdictional problems between tribes, state, and federal law enforcement systems. For a full discussion see Canby, n 35 above, 216, 239. Getches, Wilkinson, and Williams, n 34 above, 488, 493. Wilkins, n 36 above, 166.

[38] K Peak, 'Criminal Justice, Law, and Policy in Indian Country: A Historical Perspective' (1989) 17 *Journal of Criminal Justice* 393–407. The US organized, developed, and maintained Indian police forces as early as 1869. These forces handled domestic violence between Indians. However, their main function was to repress insurgency and provide swift punishment to outlaws, murderers, and persons who threatened official federal Indian policy.

[39] General Crimes Act 18 USCA §1152. This Act was passed in 1817 and has been revised many times. It can be reviewed at <http://www.usdoj.gov/usao/eousa/foia_reading_room/usam/title9/crm00678.htm>. The Act provided for federal jurisdiction over crime involving non-Indians, as part of the federal government's responsibility to protect American Indians from non-Indians and maintain peace. Major Crimes Act 18 USC §1153. The Act extended the federal jurisdiction for major crimes involving either Indians or non-Indians. The act can be viewed at <http://www.usdoj.gov/usao/eousa/foia_reading_room/usam/title9/crm00679.htm>. Although the Major Crimes Act has been modified, it contains provisions for the federal government to assert jurisdiction over major crimes, like murder or severe crimes, but domestic violence is not seen as serious enough to list, unless a murder occurs.   [40] Greenfield and Smith, n 32 above.

grappled with ways to maintain traditional culture and social institutions that did not sanction familial violence.

This has intensified conflict between tribal, state, and federal law enforcement systems over jurisdiction for domestic violence, particularly when non-Indians are involved.[41] Tribal courts cannot prosecute non-Indians, but there is a lack of federal intervention when the domestic violence abuser is non-Indian.[42] This has produced situations where non-Indians commit intimate partner violence against Indian women and are never prosecuted, or even identified, by state or federal authorities.

Recently, a question over whether tribal courts could prosecute Indian non-tribal members existed. Prior to contact, Tribal Nations held absolute authority to handle criminal actions by anyone within tribal lands. Since the beginnings of contact, Tribal Nations held the inherent authority to arrest, detain, and prosecute Indians from other tribes. However, in *Duro v Reina*[43] the Supreme Court held that tribes only had jurisdiction over tribal members. This led to confusion and chaos with regard to the prosecution of domestic violence. Reservations are often contiguous and Indians from different tribes frequently enter relationships. In fact, a number of Indians can claim ancestry from two or more tribes.[44] Inter-tribal relationships are fairly common, as the large number of children of mixed tribal ancestry demonstrates. Subsequently, the US Congress passed a statute known as the 'Duro fix' to reaffirm tribal jurisdiction over all Indians committing crimes in Indian country. Thus, in *United States v Lara*[45] the US Supreme Court found that tribal governments have criminal jurisdiction over tribal member *and* non-member Indians. This decision has allowed tribal police to arrest, and tribal courts to prosecute, non-tribal member Indians for domestic violence in Indian country,[46] but there is still no comprehensive, effective policy to address arrest and prosecution of non-Indian abusers on reservations.

[41] J Adams, 'Cousin's Arrest Puzzles Councilman' 18 June 2001, <http://Indiancountry.com>. VH Holcomb, 'Prosecution of Non-Indians for Non-Serious Offenses Committed Against Indians in Indian Country' (1999) 75 *North Dakota Law Review* 761. J Rave, *Jurisdictional Disputes Are Increasing Tensions Around Native Lands*, 23 February 2003, <http://www.journalstar.com>. J Rave, *Power to Enforce Restraining Orders Often an Obstacle in Fight Against Domestic Violence*, 23 February 2003, <http://journalstar.com>.

[42] J Adams, *Patchwork Jurisdiction Hampers Tribal Police: Cross Deputization Eases Enforcement Problems*, 1 November 2001, <http://www.indiancountry.com>. *Federal Prosecutor Seeks To Change 'National Shame'*, 19 April 2004, <http://www.indianz.com/>. *Oliphant v Suquamish Indian Tribe* 435 US 191 (1978). D Marrero, *Groups Seek Protections for Women*, 8 September 2005 <http://www.greatfallstribune.com>. Rave, *Power To Enforce*, n 41 above.

[43] *Duro v Reina*, 495 US 676 (1990). Historically, tribes held jurisdiction over all crimes involving Indians on reservations, whether members of the tribe or not. This case changed the historical power of tribes to adjudicate such crimes by holding that tribes had no such jurisdiction. Tribes only had jurisdiction over tribal members. In 1994, the US Congress passed a statute, 25 USC §1301(2), which stated that tribes hold jurisdiction over all Indians, whether tribal members or not.

[44] See the US Census Bureau at <http://www.census.gov/population/cen2000/phc-t18/tab001.pdf>.   [45] See *US v Lara* 541 US 193 (2004).

[46] See eg *Means v Navajo Nation* No 17489 (9th Cir August 23, 2005). Means, an enrolled tribal member of the Oglala Lakota, had appealed Navajo Nation tribal jurisdiction over his case to the US

Based on the fact that the majority of domestic violence cases for American Indian women involve a non-Indian abuser, and the current problematic issues of criminal jurisdiction involving non-Indians, we were interested in determining if biases exist against American Indians in domestic violence cases, in comparison to European Americans involved in such cases. This is important, given the need for federal intervention with non-Indian abusers and for allocation of resources for American Indian legal systems and domestic violence shelters.

Study 1

Consequently, in one study we examined the influence of anti-American Indian attitudes on culpability decisions for domestic violence when the man's and woman's race (American Indian/European American) and alcohol use (intoxicated or not) were varied. Alcohol use is a significant factor in domestic violence involving American Indians,[47] and American Indians are thought more culpable for an alleged crime when intoxicated, compared to European Americans.[48] Part of the enduring stereotypes of American Indians is that of a drunk.[49]

From responses gathered in an earlier project, we developed an Anti-Indian Attitude Scale which measured biases against American Indians. This 17-item scale included questions that related to resource allocations, fulfillment of treaty rights (eg education, health care, legal systems), and personal trait ratings (eg spiritual, drunk, lazy, trustworthy).[50] With non-American Indian research participants, we predicted that those higher in bias would also rate American Indians as more culpable for domestic violence, and be more punitive toward them, compared to European Americans involved in such violence. In addition, we predicted that American Indian couples who were intoxicated at the time of the violent incident would be found more culpable, particularly by those who held anti-American Indian attitudes. After reading a bogus trial transcript that manipulated

Court of Appeals. That court had withdrawn the submission subsequent to the *US v Lara* decision, n 45 above. However, the US intervened because Means raised a constitutional issue with the Congressional statute that made the *US v Lara* decision possible. See the Native American Rights Fund website at <http://www.narf.org/sct/meansvnavajonation/Answering%20Brief%20of%20US.pdf>.

[47] T Black Bear, 'Native American Clients' in AL Horton and JA Williamson (eds), *Abuse and Religion: When Praying Isn't Enough* (Lexington, Mass, 1988) 136. Chester *et al*, n 20 above. Greenfield and Smith, n 32 above.

[48] C Willis Esqueda and K Swanson, 'The effects of stereotypical crime and alcohol use on criminal culpability attributions for Native Americans and European Americans' (1997) 21 *American Indian Culture and Research Journal* 229.

[49] For a discussion of enduring stereotypes of the American Indian and alcohol, see RF Berkhofer, Jr, *The White Man's Indian* (New York, 1979) 30. JE Trimble, 'Stereotypical Images, American Indians, and Prejudice' in PA Katz and DA Taylor (eds), *Eliminating Racism* (New York, 1988) 181–202. J Westermeyer, 'The Drunken Indian: Myths and Realities' (1974) 4 *Psychiatric Annals* 29. Willis Esqueda and Swanson, n 48 above.

[50] Copies of this scale can be obtained from the first author.

the man's race (American Indian/European American), the woman's race (American Indian/European American) and the presence of alcohol (intoxicated or not) participants were provided with culpability ratings. In general, we found those high in anti-Indian attitudes were biased against American Indian women on culpability decisions. Those low in anti-Indian attitudes were biased in favour of American Indian women on culpability decisions. Thus, attitudes about American Indians made a difference in perceptions of domestic violence culpability. In contrast to the European American women, when the woman was American Indian, those high in bias thought it more likely that other men would respond the same way with her, that the man would respond this way with her in future, and that the man's response would only have occurred with her, in comparison to those low in bias. In addition, the European American man who abused an American Indian woman received the lowest recommended sentence.

Regardless of anti-American Indian attitudes, our non-Indian participants were less likely to report that they would call the police if a drunken Indian man was involved in the violence, compared to a drunken European American man. No differences emerged for culpability ratings when no alcohol was involved.

These biased culpability decisions for American Indian women involved in domestic violence have ramifications for intervention, arrest, prosecution, and treatment. Indeed, such biased notions may have implications for legal outcomes at each stage of the system, given that most police, attorneys, and judges are European American men.[51] Moreover, based on these findings, intervention for domestic violence may be compromised when the couple has been drinking and the man is Indian.

After determining that biases do exist in culpability decisions by European American participants, we thought it prudent to determine empirically if American Indian and European American women conceptualized domestic violence in the same way. Although research has focused on approaches to understanding domestic violence, treatment for domestic violence, and prevention of such violence, there is virtually no research that considers the definitions, appropriate treatments, and methods of prevention from women of color's perspectives in the United States.[52] Consequently, we conducted a qualitative study concerning the conceptualization of domestic violence for American Indigenous women and European American women. We predicted that American Indian women would focus on actions and external explanations, whereas European American

[51] American Bar Association, *Facts About Women and the Law* (1998) <http: www/abanet.org>. BA Reaves and MJ Hickman, *Law enforcement management and administrative statistics, 2000: Data for individual state and local agencies with 100 or more officers*, Bureau of Justice Statistics (Washington, DC, 2004), NCJ 203350.This report can be found at <http://www.ojp.usdoj.gov/bjs/pub/pdf/lemas00.pdf>.
[52] O Barnett, CL Miller-Perrin, and RD Perrin, *Family Violence Across the Lifespan* (Thousand Oaks, California, 2005). CM West (ed), *Violence in the Lives of Black Women* (New York, 2002). C Willis Esqueda and LA Harrison, 'The Influence of Sex Role Stereotypes, the Woman's Race, and Level of Provocation and Resistance for Domestic Violence Culpability Attributions' (2005) 53 *Sex Roles* 821.

women would focus on internal issues and traits as explanations. We made these predictions based on attribution styles, whereby those from western, individualistic cultures tend to use dispositional attributions concerning behaviour, while those from communal cultures tend to use more situational attributions.[53] American Indians have traditionally included environmental and social contexts to understand behaviour, while European Americans have relied on internally driven traits to explain behaviour. [54]

Study 2

Although several studies have examined the prevalence of domestic violence for American Indian women,[55] we wanted spontaneous descriptions of what constitutes such violence from both American Indian and European American women from the same geographic region. Toward this end, we conducted semi-structured interviews with twenty American Indian women and twenty European American women from the local community.[56] The mean age for both groups was 36 years. Both ratings scales and open-ended questions were used. The women wrote their own responses to the questions, and the interviewer facilitated discussion of the topics. Some of the questions included:

- How does domestic violence begin?
- Who starts domestic violence?
- What actions occur with domestic violence (for the man and the woman)?
- What is the history of domestic violence within your ethnic group?
- What percentage of men and women are abused?
- What actions would occur so you would call police?
- Is the legal system fair?

[53] HC Triandis, 'Individualism, Collectivism and Personality' (2001) 69 *Journal of Personality* 907. MA Zárate, JS Uleman, and CI Voils, 'Effects of Culture and Processing Goals on the Activation and Binding of Trait Concepts' (2001) 19 *Social Cognition* 295.

[54] Fritz Heider, personal communication, 16 October 1984. See also F Heider, *The Psychology of Interpersonal Relations* (Hillsdale, NJ, 1958).   [55] n 31 above.

[56] M Tehee and C Willis Esqueda, *American Indian and European American Women's Perceptions of Domestic Violence* (2005) in press. The interviews were conducted with some ratings scales and some open-ended questions. All the interviews were conducted in Lincoln, Nebraska, which is located in the Northern Plains. Although the city of Lincoln's population is overwhelmingly European American, there are 5 reservations located within the state. The Omaha Nation, Winnebago Tribe of Nebraska, Santee Sioux Tribe of Nebraska, the Ioway, Sauk, and Fox Nation, and Oglala Lakota Nation at Pine Ridge Reservation are located in Nebraska. The Pine Ridge reservation tribal agency is located in South Dakota and part of the reservation lies within the boundaries of Nebraska. See VE Velarde Tiller, *American Indian Reservations and Trust Areas,* US Department of Commerce (Washington, DC, 1996). The Rosebud Sioux Tribe is located in South Dakota, but is contiguous with Nebraska's northern border, as well. Within Nebraska, reservations are geographically close enough that tribal members often travel back and forth to their homelands if they live in urban areas or off the reservation.

- Does the legal system work?
- Who should be punished for domestic violence, the man, woman, or both?
- What causes domestic violence?

Responses to open-ended questions were categorized by two raters who were blind to the participants' race. Overall, inter-rater reliability was 97 per cent. Any disagreements between raters were resolved by a third party who was also blind to the ethnic group of the respondent.

The American Indian sample was obtained by posting flyers at the local Indian Center and through voluntary recruitment by participants. A total of sixteen different tribes were represented within the sample, from a variety of regions around the United States. The European American sample was obtained via flyers and voluntary recruitment by participants as well. Participants contacted a researcher who arranged for data collection. In order to accommodate the respondents, the interviewer (an American Indian woman) went to a designated place to conduct interviews and have the ratings scales completed. This precluded the necessity for the women to have a telephone in their residence. At the end of all interviews, participants were encouraged to contact the interviewers should they have questions regarding the research content, process, or results.

The responses to the questions indicated several significant differences between the two groups of women. American Indian women estimated that almost 69 per cent of women in their community experienced domestic violence, while European American women estimated that 47 per cent of women in their community experienced such violence. Both groups of women believed approximately 20 per cent of men in their communities were involved in abuse as victims. Moreover, significant differences occurred between the two groups of women on a variety of questions involving what constitutes domestic violence.

According to the Indian women, domestic violence did not exist for the ancestors, historically. However, European American women believed domestic violence always existed, it was just hidden. This difference in perceived socio-cultural history is important, because it confirms empirically what early American Indian women writers, current writers and scholars, and family information has told us. Domestic violence is perceived to be a product of more recent origin within American Indian communities.

American Indian women believed domestic violence begins with an argument and then physical violence follows, while European American women did not mention an argument. For American Indian women domestic violence is synonymous with physical violence, even extreme physical abuse. This response was given to almost all questions related to conceptualizations of violence, including what women did as part of domestic violence and what men did as part of such violence. American Indian women also mentioned retaliation as part of women's role in domestic violence. European American women tended to view domestic violence as verbal aggression, insults, and emotional abuse, along with physical violence. Moreover, verbal aggression, insults, emotional abuse, and physical violence were thought to be performed by both men and women. Thus, our predictions were confirmed. American Indian women's notions of domestic violence include actions and external, observable behaviour, while European American women viewed verbal and emotional actions that emanate from internally generated effect as part of domestic violence.

According to both groups of women, men are the instigators of abuse. However, they differed in terms of what causes domestic violence. American Indian women viewed the cause of such violence to be factors such as poverty, unemployment, and lack of mobility due to geographic isolation. European American women viewed the cause as the abuser's personal dysfunctions (eg anger control issues). Again, our predictions were confirmed. American Indian women viewed the cause of domestic violence to be external in origin, while European American women focused on internal issues such as men's anger management, personal traits, and lack of control.

In terms of what actions would occur so that the police would be summoned, differences emerged between the two groups of women. American Indian women reported that the police should only be called if threats, physical action, or extreme injury occurred (the latter being reported by 50 per cent of the respondents), but European American women said the police should be called if threats (reported by almost 90 per cent of respondents) or any form of physical violence occurred.

As would be expected, then, there were differences in perceptions of whether the legal system worked in handling domestic violence. Almost all American Indian women reported that the legal system did not work, but the majority of European American women stated the system did work, at least sometimes. These ethnic differences in perceptions highlight fundamental contrasts in the psychological environments from which these women operate in terms of intimate partner violence.

The women did not differ in what they believe domestic violence does to children. All the women mentioned that it was traumatic for children and that it had inter-generational effects. There were also no differences in what they believed was the most effective way to end it. Most of the women mentioned leaving the relationship through a variety of means, although some of the American Indian women stated that abuse victims should come back to traditional spirituality. Finally, there were no differences in their reported personal experiences as victims of domestic violence. Neither group reported significant personal experience with violence.

The results of this study indicate that American Indigenous women and European American women do not view domestic violence in the same way, nor do they have the same orientation to the legal system as a method of intervention.[57] These research findings have ramifications for several legal and

---

[57] In a study conducted with 'tribal leaders' who acted as representatives for their communities, it was conveyed that the legal system is inadequate for dealing with American Indian domestic violence in both reservation and urban areas. See Jumper Thurman *et al*, n 19 above.

psychological issues, such as: (1) self identification as a victim; (2) seeking out legal interventions and prosecution; (3) participation in counter-violence or retaliation; (4) participation in court proceedings; (5) ability to identify and report others' victimizations; and (6) preference for community-based resolutions. All of these issues are ones that require further study, based on the findings of the research reported here.

General Discussion

We believe that the research we have undertaken has implications for a number of issues facing Indian country in the fight to end domestic violence. For example, biases in culpability decision making when American Indian women are involved in domestic abuse have implications for federal intervention and prosecution of non-Indian abusers on reservations and for urban cases as well. In Nebraska, the HoChunk (Winnebago Tribe of Nebraska) and the Umo^{n}ho^n (Omaha Nation) have demanded increased federal intervention in cases involving non-Indian abusers and the federal prosecutor agreed to pay more attention to the prosecution of abusers.[58] Perhaps those federal prosecutors who are high in bias will be less likely to prosecute when the abused is an Indian woman, and if they do prosecute and convict the non-Indian abuser will receive a lighter sentence compared to situations where the abuser is an Indian. Data from actual law enforcement calls from tribal, state, and federal interventions has yet to be analysed for arrests and later prosecutions with comparisons between American Indian and non-Indian actors. This would be an important contribution to the growing literature on racial disparities in the US legal system and to an understanding of the intricacies and practical implications of American Indian criminal jurisdiction.

One new approach that may alleviate problem issues regarding intervention, prosecution, and sentencing of non-Indian abusers committing domestic violence in Indian country, concerns cross-deputization of officers between tribal, local, state, and federal authorities. Such an approach has been advocated by the International Association of Chiefs of Police.[59] This approach brought cross-deputization agreements between the Oneida Nation and Oneida and Madison counties of the state of New York. Recently, the governor of Nebraska signed cross-deputization agreements with the Omaha Nation, the Winnebago Tribe of Nebraska, and the Oglala Lakota Nation that allows tribal officers to arrest offenders on and near reservation lands, regardless of tribal membership or whether one is Indian. After arrest, non-Indians will be tried in state court and Indians will be tried in tribal courts.[60] However, both the Omaha Nation and the

---

[58] Rave, *Power to Enforce*, n 41 above.   [59] Adams, n 42 above.
[60] The Nebraska State Attorney signed a letter recommending cross-deputization; however, it should be noted that Omaha Tribal officers were going to receive federal cross-deputization,

Winnebago Tribe of Nebraska reside in Thurston County, Nebraska where 52 per cent of the population is American Indian. Non-Indian, local government officials are already concerned about increased tribal authority and may file a lawsuit in court to have the state agreements overturned.[61]

Another issue concerns the fragmented court system involved in the seeking of protection orders for abused women and for adjudication of domestic abuse cases in Indian country. It can be the case that an Indian woman must seek a protection order from a non-Indian abuser with a local, off reservation court, state court, or federal court, rather than a tribal court, but if the man violates the protection order, there is no means of enforcement of the order.[62] This becomes a central issue when no mechanism is in place to allow tribal and state courts access to information regarding the respective protection orders.[63] This means that Indian women are left with little or no legally sanctioned protection against non-Indian abusers. If the non-Indian abuser is prosecuted, the woman (and presumably tribal law enforcement) must provide the local off reservation or state court with evidence and participate in court proceedings. Again, if the results from our research are indicative of a general bias among European Americans (which anecdotal information suggests is the case) then this process is untenable for promoting a legal approach to addressing violence in Indian country.

Of course, if cross-deputization and community-based partnerships between tribal, local, state, and federal law enforcement systems are successful, ammunition

---

regardless of the state's decision. The authorization letter can be seen at <http://gov.nol.org/news/pdf/2005_08_12_AttyGenOpinion.pdf>. In addition, information on the Nebraska agreements can be found at N Jenkins, *Pine Ridge Tribal Officers Soon to Patrol Village*, 31 August 2005, <http://journalstar.com>. *Tribes Sign Cross-Deputization Agreements with State*, 15 August 2005, <http://www.Indianz.com>. *Tribe, State Sign Whiteclay Policing Agreement*, 31 August 2005, <http://Indianz.com>. Lincoln Journal Star On-line, 31 August 2005. The National Tribal Justice Resource Center also provides an overview of the Nebraska cross-deputization agreement at <http://www.tribalresourcecenter.org/news/newsdetails.asp?138>.

Other states hold agreements as well. The state of Oklahoma has numerous agreements between the state and tribal law enforcement agencies. A list of the agreements can be found at <http://www.state.ok.us/~oiac/crossdep.htm>. The State of New Mexico has agreements on cross-deputization which can be found at <http://www.ago.state.nm.us/cia/cia_intergovagree_gcrs.htm>.

[61] *Non-Indians Question Omaha Tribe's Jurisdiction*, 21 January 2004, <http://www.Indianz.com>. *Tribes Sign Cross-Deputization Agreements*, n 60 above.

[62] This is true even though the Violence Against Women Act of 1994 (and the amended 2005 version) contains provisions for tribal, local, and state courts to give 'full faith and credit' to protection orders issued by another court. See BJ Jones, 'Welcoming Tribal Courts Into The Judicial Fraternity: Emerging Issues In Tribal-State and Tribal-Federal Court Relations' (1998) 24 *William Mitchell Law Review* 457, and also ML Tatum, 'Establishing Penalties for Violations of Protection Orders: What Tribal Governments Need to Know' (2003) 13 *Kansas Journal of Law and Public Policy* 123. One of the problems concerns the lack of clear jurisdiction, particularly given the complexity of Public Law 280 states and the limits of the Major Crimes Act.

[63] The recently extended and amended Violence Against Women Act of 2005 allows for tribal law enforcement to have access to federal criminal databanks. This will enable tribal law enforcement to have better control over suspected and/or arrested domestic violence abusers. The Act does not allow for tribal courts to arrest and prosecute non-Indian abusers, however, making cross-deputization the best possible remedy at the present time.

may be given to those seeking to empower tribal legal systems and return criminal jurisdiction over all people committing crimes in American Indian Nations. This may facilitate the legal approach to elimination of domestic violence in Indian country for both Indians and non-Indians, and promote the enforcement of peace and the implementation of social policies, which can signal the value placed on American Indian domestic life.

The results from the qualitative interviews indicated that American Indian women and European American women look to different sources in determining if domestic violence has taken place. As predicted, American Indian women indicated that such violence emanates from actual physical acts by both men and women, while European American women mentioned emotional, verbal, and physical actions from men and women are necessary. The cause of such violence derives from different sources as well. Again, as predicted, American Indian women reported that issues that are external to the abuser caused violence, while European American women mentioned issues that were internal to the abuser. We believe this occurs from differences in attribution styles, whereby American Indians put more emphasis on situational influences for behaviour, but European Americans favour dispositional explanations. More research is needed to determine if attribution styles are different or whether these differences emerge for domestic violence scenarios, because the causes of abuse are truly different between the two populations.

In addition, the findings here indicate American Indian women and European American women conceptualize domestic violence in markedly different ways, with different historical and cultural views of its place within their communities, and different orientations to the legal system as an appropriate means to respond to such violence. Consequently, we believe development and implementation of tribally controlled and culturally appropriate domestic violence shelters is imperative. Calls for such shelters occurred almost twenty years ago.[64] Several tribal entities have undertaken the arduous task of developing, maintaining, and monitoring domestic violence shelters and counselling centres on reservations. Although not an exhaustive list, the Cangleska Inc (Pine Ridge Reservation), White Buffalo Calf Women's Society (Rose Bud Reservation), and Ama Doo Alchini Bighan, Inc (Navajo Nation) are such organizations, and the US Department of Justice continues to promote the development of programs throughout Indian country. There is also an indication that American Indian women prefer domestic violence shelters and counseling centers be implemented by Indian women, as well.[65]

Will reservation based, tribally controlled domestic violence shelters be enough to end domestic violence in Indian Country? It is unlikely. The majority of

[64] Gunn Allen, n 20 above.
[65] Black Bear, n 47 above. Halinka Malcoe, and Duran, *Intimate Partner Violence and Injury*, n 31 above.

American Indians now live in urban settings,[66] or at least travel back and forth from reservations to urban settings. Consequently, tribally controlled and implemented shelters, counselling centres, and tribal law enforcement and courts will need to be supplemented with other, non-reservation social service agencies that are responsive to American Indians and their unique psychological needs. Pamela Jumper Thurman and her colleagues have advocated a community preparedness approach in response to American Indian domestic violence that includes both reservation and non-reservation communities.[67] In this approach, a community's readiness to provide culturally appropriate services is determined, and educational programs can then be geared toward correction if preparedness is lacking. The assessment of a community includes areas such as: (1) available resources, (2) community knowledge, (3) authority and willingness of the leadership to address the issues, and (4) community commitment to participate. In addition to Indian-centred services, this assessment should include state and federal law enforcement and health care systems, in order to best meet the needs of American Indians involved in such violence. In light of the research findings reported here, communities should monitor their preparedness to serve American Indians involved in domestic violence, and state and federal courts must listen to the voices from Indian country that demand an improved response to American Indian domestic violence issues, particularly with regard to improved authority from tribal law enforcement and courts.

From each understanding of history the judge provides, comes a shaping of history. By articulating assumptions and rules regarding the relationships of Indian women to their partners and children, the judges transform those relationships.[68]

Such judicial transformations of relationships should produce a healthier domestic life among American Indians and not result in additional trauma to American Indian women.

---

[66] See the US Census Bureau's information on total populations and populations by reservations at <http://www.census.gov/statab/www/sa04aian.pdf>.
[67] Jumper Thurman *et al*, n 19 above.   [68] Berger, n 21 above, 5.

17

Worlds Colliding: Legal Regulation and Psychologists' Evidence about Workplace Bullying

Lizzie Barmes[1]

Introduction

The language of workplace bullying is increasingly encountered in a range of contexts: from human resources departments to trade unions; victim campaigns to media reports; government funded taskforces to academic writings.[2] One consequence is that lawyers are being called upon to advise on the legal consequences of conduct that has been characterized by the victims in this way. Yet workplace bullying has no distinctive legal meaning. As a result, both inside[3] and outside[4] courtrooms, the law is being mapped onto a construct that is, in essence, foreign to it.

There is an obvious parallel to be drawn with inception since the late 1970s into various legal systems of the idea (or ideas) of sexual harassment. Usage of this term outside the courtroom[5] came over time to be reproduced in legal discourse, notably

---

[1] I am grateful to Hugh Collins, Hazel Genn, Claire Kilpatrick, Nicola Lacey, David Robertson, and Joanne Scott for insightful comments on an earlier draft of the paper that now forms this paper. Remaining errors are my own.

[2] See the project, 'Working Together for Dignity at Work', jointly funded by Amicus and the DTI. Some recent press reports on the subject are: D Turner, 'Top companies sign up to drive against bullying', *Financial Times*, 25 October 2004; J Hirschkorn, 'Union and government gang up on the bullies', *The Daily Telegraph*, 28 October 2004 (both referring to the Amicus/DTI project); L Glendinning, 'Bullying rife at work, says study', *Guardian*, 28 September 2004 (citing research done with the magazine, *Personnel Today*); M. Skapinker, 'Be cheered: the workplace bully has a soft underbelly', *Financial Times*, 23 March 2005; and C Hall, 'Bosses are victims of bullying in workplace', *The Daily Telegraph*, 1 April 2005.

[3] Prominent examples are *Horkulak v Cantor FitzGerald International* [2003] EWHC 1918, [2004] ICR 697 (in the High Court) and [2004] EWCA Civ 1287, [2005] ICR 402 (in the Court of Appeal); *Dunnachie v Kingston-upon-Hull City Council* [2004] UKHL 36, [2005] 1 AC 226; and *Majrowski v Guy's and St Thomas' NHS Trust* [2005] EWCA Civ 251, [2005] QB 848.

[4] This occurs in the many cases that never get to court but in which lawyers have advised.

[5] See L Farley, *Sexual Shakedown: The Sexual Harassment of Women on the Job* (New York, 1978).

through novel judicial interpretations of existing wrongs of sex discrimination.[6] This happened in the UK in the 1980s, when the notion of direct sex discrimination was, with some strain, adapted to proscribe sexual harassment.[7] This had parallel implications for interpretation of the law on direct race discrimination. That way of dealing with racial and sexual harassment endured for many years, before the enactment recently of dedicated laws regarding various forms of this wrong.[8]

The route into legal reasoning of the idea of workplace bullying is harder to track. This is not because there is no law to which claimants may make appeal. Rather there is a bewildering array of legal instruments that are potentially implicated in a given instance of workplace bullying. These range from the laws now directly prohibiting discriminatory harassment to personal injury law and the common law of the contract of employment. A general statute of particular significance is the Protection from Harassment Act 1997, much as it was the social problem of stalking that prompted it.

A particular difficulty is that navigating this fractured and fragmentary legal framework is creating significant conceptual and practical confusion in the law's response to bullying at work. This is perhaps most noticeable at the boundaries between different legal sources. But it goes more deeply to the internal consistency, and defensibility in policy terms, of specific interventions and of the complex as a whole. This is to be expected in circumstances where none of the laws in question were designed with workplace bullying in mind. But it is of no less pressing concern for that.

This context makes it curious that academic lawyers in the UK and elsewhere have remained relatively silent about the legal regulation of workplace bullying. The contents of this chapter form part of a larger project that will contribute to filling that gap. One aspect of the overall project involves detailed, internal analysis of the UK law relevant to bullying conduct at work. The other draws on research by non-legal scholars to inform external appraisal of the law. This is possible because the relative silence on workplace bullying in the legal academy has not been replicated elsewhere, with organizational psychologists being especially active.

---

[6] C MacKinnon, *Sexual Harassment of Working Women: A Case of Sex Discrimination* (New Haven, 1979) was particularly influential in this regard.

[7] The reasoning in *Porcelli v Strathclyde RC* [1986] ICR 564 was especially important. But note that subsequent interpretations of that case were disapproved by the House of Lords in the now leading case on harassment as direct discrimination, *MacDonald v Advocate General for Scotland and Pearce v Governing Body of Mayfield School* [2003] UKHL 34, [2003] ICR 937. See L Barmes, 'Constitutional and Conceptual Complexities of the UK's Uniform Approach to Discriminatory Harassment' (unpublished paper, 2005) for a full account of the law.

[8] Prohibition on discriminatory harassment currently extends to harassment related to disability, gender re-assignment, race, religion (and similar philosophical beliefs), sex, and sexual orientation. From October 2006, there will also be legislation proscribing age-related harassment.

This second dimension of my project has raised challenging questions about how learning deriving from other disciplines may validly be used to appraise the legal response to workplace bullying. What quickly became clear is that it would not be a case of unproblematically extracting knowledge from the psychological literature and injecting it into an evaluation of the law. It became necessary rather to theorize about how two complexes of doubt and insight, themselves in a far from straightforward relationship to one another and to their (allegedly) common subject matter, might inter-relate. This paper explores that terrain.

There are three different ways in which I have concluded that psychologists' evidence about workplace bullying can deepen and enhance evaluation of the relevant law. First, it is significant that, on the one hand, those carrying out empirical investigations have grappled with many of the same problems as are confronted by lawyers and, on the other hand, that they have approached them from quite different premises. These contrasts create a foil against which to test and develop insights about legal intervention. Secondly, adverting to the psychological literature enables lawyers better to appreciate what is behind the shift towards understanding some workplace interactions in terms of bullying. Some of the larger social, economic, and political forces at play can be discerned, and consideration given to their consequences for an effective legal response. Thirdly, empirical research has uncovered some highly interesting features of workers' reports of their experiences of bullying, shedding new light on the aptness of the existing law or of proposed reforms. The next section of this paper exposes the puzzles internal to the psychological literature of which these suggestions seek to be cognizant, while the final part contains a fuller explanation of what lies behind them.

Before proceeding, however, I need explicitly to dissociate myself from any claim that my conclusions are rooted in some 'view from nowhere'. It is inevitable that my take is coloured, not only by the fact that I am not a psychologist, but also by my being a lawyer. Aside from the practical constraints derived from my disciplinary background, discussed further below, it is inevitable that my perception of the assumptions, concerns, and methodologies associated with the two disciplines[9] is structured by that outsider/insider status. I have drawn some comfort in that regard from the fact that my concern is ultimately with ways that the law might be more fully understood. At the same time, a central ambition for this project is that it will stimulate dialogue across subject boundaries about the issues raised by this kind of inter-disciplinary work.[10]

---

[9] This should not be taken as implying that it is easy to define either discipline or its subject matter. Definitions of law, as well as attempts to distinguish the entity from the discipline, are, of course, highly contested. I maintain, however, that there are methodologies, common both to the social practices of law and to its academic study, that are foundational whatever one's conception of where the definitional lines should be drawn.

[10] It is of interest that my arguments indicate scope for influence in both directions. So it may be that law can at times assist in the resolution of dilemmas faced by psychologists. This feature of the analysis provides further tantalizing glimpses of the scope for productive mutual exchange.

Conceptual and Methodological Issues in the Psychological Literature

The fact that I am not a psychologist had two main practical effects on my approach to the literature from that discipline. First, it led me to concentrate on more determinate empirical findings and, secondly, to be most tentative in deploying scholarship that sought to explain or account for workplace bullying. My premise was that empirical evidence about the practice of workplace bullying is accessible to a general audience in a way that work whose aim is to give a causal account is not.[11]

Thankfully, my over-arching project was able to retain integrity while accommodating this restriction. This is because my primary concern in turning to non-legal scholarship is that my legal analysis should have regard to what is known about the experience of workplace bullying. This reflects my theoretical starting point that law should be evaluated, not merely in abstract, internal terms, but as it interacts with its subject matter.[12]

But the detailed and open discussion in the psychological literature about conceptual and methodological issues inherent in experimental investigation of workplace bullying presented an immediate challenge. These demonstrated that there were as many controversies and uncertainties internal to non-legal commentary on workplace bullying as there are within relevant legal discourse. Less like legal discourse, however, these epistemological problems were faced head on and their consequences probed. The result was a range of cautionary tales about what could and could not be drawn from the data produced, for example about the incidence or characteristics of workplace bullying. I set out below the most critical warnings that I derived from my immersion in the psychological literature.

Problems with Defining Workplace Bullying

It seems uncontroversial that whether or not behaviour is properly classed as bullying depends, at least in part, on how it is experienced by those immediately involved. If no participant perceives conduct as bullying it is hard to see how it could be characterized as such. By the same token, if a victim or perpetrator believes bullying to have occurred, it is hard to see how their perception could appropriately be ignored.

---

[11] I also concentrated on work from the UK, seeing as this is the focus of my study, drawing only selectively on that from the rest of Europe and further afield.

[12] I remain regretful, however, at not having been able more fully to engage particularly with psychological theorizing and hypothesizing about how systems, within workplaces and beyond, produce, sustain and perpetuate workplace bullying. This is a further area in which there is potential for continued inter-disciplinary exchange.

Yet a dispassionate outsider is bound not always to agree with the characterizations of participants in an interaction, and certainly not one that is conflictual. On
the one hand, such an outsider is likely to regard some conduct as so 'beyond the
pale' that it should count as bullying whatever the view of the participants. On the
other hand, some actions are equally likely to be seen as acceptable irrespective of
the reaction they elicit. This raises a number of difficulties. First, whose characterization, ultimately, should prevail? Secondly, if it is conceded that the subjective
attitudes of the participants should not be determinative of whether workplace
bullying has occurred, what role should be played by the outsider point of view?

The spectres of 'the accidental bully' and 'the accidental non-bully' haunt these
enquiries. The former is easy to picture in that it is not unusual for a person to see
nothing wrong with behaviour that is nonetheless badly received. The question in
such circumstances is how far the recipient's subjective experience should be
sufficient for the behaviour to be categorized as bullying. At what point, if at all,
should an outside standard prevent the bullying label being applied?

The idea of 'the accidental non-bully' is more difficult to conjure with. By this
I mean a person who is subjectively aware that their behaviour is bullying, but
who is not seen by their 'victims' as a bully. This might happen in the context of
particular working relationships in which bad behaviour was regarded as appropriate and unproblematic. Fast-moving, stressful workplaces, like City trading
floors, might be thought to fall into this category.[13]

Interestingly, it does not follow that the existence of such attitudes must be
indicative of a generally abusive environment. It is at least possible for conventional
standards of conduct to be dispensed with because there is such a high level of trust
that they are no longer required. In any event, even if an environment were generally abusive, would that mean that conduct was properly classed as bullying even if
a recipient was untroubled by it? If so, again, at what point should the outside
standard be permitted to override the subjective attitudes of the participants?

The situation is made more complex by the fact that subjective perceptions are
liable to change over time. With hindsight a person may come to perceive actions
as unacceptable which at the time they regarded as appropriate. Equally, someone
might become uncomfortable with a class of behaviour that they previously had
no problem with. Should subjective perceptions of this kind carry the same
weight as ones that are stable over time? If not, what is it about these attitudes that
renders them less worthy of influence than others?

The same behaviour by different people may also not be viewed in the same
way. There are actions that, quite rationally, individuals find acceptable from some

---

[13] The facts and analysis in *Horkulak v Cantor Fitzgerald International* [2003] EWHC 1918,
[2004] ICR 697 (in the High Court) were of particular interest. The judge accepted (at para 17) that
'foul and abusive expressions' were in 'general currency' in the workplace in question. But he found
(at 80) that: 'The frequent use of foul and abusive language did not sanitise its effect. By remaining in
employment . . . and resorting to it himself on occasions, the claimant nevertheless remained entitled
to proper treatment in accordance with his contract.'

and not from others. For example, behaviour that is found appropriate from someone of the same gender may well be regarded as unacceptable across genders. Equally, a person's professional or hierarchical position may make a difference. A Tasmanian study, for example, showed that nurses were more disturbed by negative behaviour from nursing colleagues than from doctors and others.[14]

All of these factors mean that the task of defining workplace bullying is far from simple. If a purely subjective approach is taken, situations will be both included and excluded in ways that are out of step with widely accepted standards of conduct. This is highly problematic. If subjects may dictate when the bullying label applies, it ceases reliably to denote conduct that is transgressive in a way that is meaningful for more than the immediate participants to a given interaction. The vocabulary of bullying is rendered no more, at root, than a way of describing behaviour that a person, for whatever reason, dislikes.

If a purely objective approach is taken, there will be the opposite problem. Situations will be included and excluded out of step with the subjective understandings of the participants. This is unsatisfactory for failing to acknowledge the genuine complexity of human relations. Definitional stability is bought at the cost of realism. In other words, contending that the concept of bullying should embody standards of conduct that are meaningful in some general sense, is not inconsistent with recognizing that it may be fiendishly difficult to determine what those standards require in a given situation.

These issues are plainly of concern for the law. Versions of the questions raised are also familiar to legal reasoning from other contexts, particularly the attempt to define discriminatory harassment.[15] But the question for present purposes is not how law confronts the problems inherent in defining bullying, but how psychologists do so. What is immediately clear is that, albeit for different reasons, the task is as significant for them. Most importantly, defining workplace bullying is central to any research exploring its incidence. Different approaches to measuring the incidence of workplace bullying in fact often lie behind different definitions. But independently of the uses to which definitions are put, it is necessary to have a clear sense of their theoretical underpinnings. Without this, the impact of conceptual features on the results of surveys and experiments may be overlooked.

One approach, pioneered by Leymann, involved identifying a series of behaviours that were judged, particularly using qualitative research, to be typical

---

[14] See G Farrell, 'Aggression in Clinical Setting: Nurses' Views' (1999) 29(3) *Journal of Advanced Nursing* 532, 534, 538, 540.
[15] See Barmes, n 7 above, for a full account of legal struggles with analogous issues in the context of discriminatory harassment. The latest legislative formulations of different forms of such harassment are especially notable. In particular, where it is necessary to determine if conduct has either violated a victim's dignity or created an intimidating, hostile, degrading, humiliating, or offensive environment for them, it is provided that this is to be judged according to whether it is reasonable so to view the conduct in all the circumstances. But it is specifically stated that the circumstances to be taken into account include the complainant's perception.

of bullying.[16] As a result, several different lists of bullying behaviours are now available to researchers. For example, the largest-scale UK study to date ('the UMIST study') adapted Einarsen and Raknes' Negative Acts Questionnaire[17] for use in the UK.

A variety of frequency and duration elements are used in connection with such lists. Leymann's view was that a person must experience one of the bullying behaviours on a weekly or more frequent basis, over a period of at least six months, before they could properly be classified as bullied.[18] This approach continues to be influential. But, as discussion below of the UK evidence on prevalence demonstrates, it has not been universally adopted.

The range of behaviours typically included is large, ranging from obviously work-related activities to more personal communications and even violence. The UMIST study listed twenty-nine negative behaviours. The following are some examples: 'persistent criticism of work and effort', 'excessive monitoring of your work', 'having insulting or offensive remarks made about your person (ie habits and background), your attitudes or your private life', 'being the subject of excessive teasing and sarcasm', 'being given tasks with unreasonable or impossible targets or deadlines', 'someone withholding information which affects your performance', and 'being shouted at or being the target of spontaneous anger (or rage)'.[19] Quine developed slightly shorter lists of bullying behaviours, drawing on earlier approaches of this kind.[20]

Three conceptual features stand out. First, it is notable that account is taken of a range of views about what conduct is potentially bullying. This introduces a valuable collective dimension to the process of definition. Of course, the significance in practice of any group input depends on the precise methodology used. But this remains a striking aspect. Secondly, subjective beliefs about conduct will be reflected in responses in that many of the listed behaviours include an evaluative stance. This is apparent from the examples included above, which speak, for instance, of persistent criticism, excessive monitoring, and unreasonable targets.

Thirdly, the use of any particular frequency or duration criteria can appear somewhat arbitrary.[21] In particular, it is not obvious that it is impossible to bully

[16] See the Leymann Inventory of Psychological Terror (Stockholm: Violen, 1990), discussed in H Leymann, 'The Content and Development of Mobbing at Work' (1996) 5 *European Journal of Work and Organizational Psychology* 165, 170–1.

[17] See S Einarsen and BI Raknes, 'Harassment in the Workplace and the Victimisation of Men' (1997) 12 *Violence and Victims* 247.

[18] See, eg H Leymann, 'Mobbing and Psychological Terror at Workplaces' (1990) 5 *Violence and Victims* 119, 120.

[19] H Hoel and CL Cooper, *Destructive Conflict and Bullying at Work* (2000) Manchester, UK: School of Management, University of Manchester, Institute of Science and Technology (unpublished report) 27.

[20] L Quine, 'Workplace Bullying in NHS Community Trust: Staff Questionnaire Survey' (1999) 318 *British Medical Journal* 228, 229 and L Quine, 'Workplace Bullying, Psychological Distress and Job Satisfaction in Junior Doctors' (2003) 12 *Cambridge Quarterly of Healthcare Ethics* 91, 94.

[21] See Leymann, n 18 above, 120, in which a link was made between the nature of workplace bullying and the circumstances in which deleterious health consequences were to be anticipated: 'This definition eliminates temporary conflicts and focuses on the transition zone where the psychosocial

someone for a short period, or even only once. There are even reasons to anticipate short-lived or isolated events being of especial seriousness, in that the worse the incident the more quickly a victim might take steps to get away. Equally, as Einarsen *et al* point out, one act may have ongoing consequences, for example, in the spreading of a nasty rumour.[22]

Definitions in the second category adopt a narrative approach. The UMIST study, aside from adapting the Negative Acts Questionnaire, also used a narrative account of workplace bullying, again adapted from the Scandinavian literature:

> We define bullying as a situation where one or several individuals persistently over a period of time perceive themselves to be on the receiving end of negative actions from one or several persons, in a situation where the target of bullying has difficulty in defending him or herself against these actions. We will not refer to a one-off incident as bullying.[23] ('the UMIST definition')

The target's *perception* is here put at the centre. This definition might even be read to say that conduct should be classed as bullying on the basis of the target's perceptions alone. But it may be that it was meant to be understood as requiring in fact more than one incident[24] and for the target actually to have difficulty defending him- or herself.

Even so, it is again not self-evident that bullying cannot occur only once. The requirement that a target should have difficulty defending him- or herself also raises questions. This would be questionable if it meant a target must be in a formally inferior position to be a potential victim of bullying. Targeting a person on the basis of their membership of a traditionally disadvantaged or subordinated group, for example as a female or homosexual, is one way that people, even the apparently powerful, can be attacked. This does not, however, seem to be how this

---

situation starts to result in psychiatric and/or psychosomatic pathological states.' See also H Leymann, 'The Content and Development of Mobbing at Work' (1996) 5 *European Journal of Work and Organizational Psychology* 165, 168.

[22] S Einarsen, H Hoel, D Zapf, and CL Cooper, 'The Concept of Bullying at Work' in S Einarsen, H Hoel, D Zapf, and CL Cooper (eds), *Bullying and Emotional Abuse in the Workplace, International Perspectives in Research and Practice* (London, 2003) 7. They also point out that bullying may consist in an ongoing state of affairs rather than being episodic, eg if it takes the form of poor physical conditions of work.

[23] H Hoel, CL Cooper, and B Faragher, 'The Experience of Bullying in Great Britain: The Impact of Organisational Status' (2001) 10(4) *European Journal of Work and Organisational Psychology* 443, 447. This was derived from the Scandinavian literature. See S Einarsen and A Skogstad, 'Bullying at Work: Epidemiological Findings in Public and Private Organisations' (1996) 5(2) *European Journal of Work and Organizational Psychology* 185, 191, in which the following definition was set out: 'Bullying (harassment, badgering, niggling, freezing out, offending someone) is a problem in some workplaces and for some workers. To label something bullying it has to occur repeatedly over a period of time, and the person confronted has to have difficulties defending himself/herself. It is not bullying if two parties of approximately equal "strength" are in conflict or the incident is an isolated event.'

[24] Note that Einarsen and Skogstad's definition above made this requirement clear, which reinforces that it was intended to be read into the UMIST definition.

requirement is meant to be read, in that relative defencelessness may be present irrespective of a person's structural position.[25]

Note that the need to focus on real, rather than formal, power relations is made even clearer in the equivalent aspect of the following definition, used by the authors in a recent review of the state of international research on the topic:

Bullying at work means harassing, offending, socially excluding someone or negatively affecting someone's work tasks. In order for the label bullying (or mobbing) to be applied to a particular activity, interaction or process it has to occur repeatedly and regularly (eg weekly) and over a period of time (eg about six months). Bullying is an escalating process in the course of which the person confronted ends up in an inferior position and becomes the target of systematic negative social acts. A conflict cannot be called bullying if the incident is an isolated event or if two parties of approximately equal 'strength' are in conflict.[26] ('the international definition')

Subjectivity remains important in that bullying is described in terms of its effects on targets. It is true that some of the effects listed, namely socially excluding a person or negatively affecting their work tasks, will often—perhaps normally—be observable. Offending or harassing a person might also be. But whether the given effect is produced will ultimately depend on how conduct is subjectively experienced. Note also that it is again not entirely clear if it would be sufficient for victims to perceive themselves to have 'ended up' in an inferior position and to be of unequal 'strength'. But this version does make plain that the persistence, regularity, and duration features included set objective limits. This is despite, as we have seen, the possibility of contention about such criteria.

Perhaps the most inclusive of the three narrative accounts included here is that developed by UK trade unions and deployed in a number of recent UK studies. According to this, workplace bullying is: 'Persistent, offensive, abusive, intimidating, malicious or insulting behaviour, abuse of power or unfair penal sanctions, which makes the recipient feel upset, threatened, humiliated or vulnerable, which undermines their self-confidence and which may cause them to suffer stress.'[27] This time, concentration on the target's subjective perception of, and response to, behaviour is not combined with additional requirements in terms of frequency, duration, or inequality. It is especially noticeable that the persistency element in this definition seems to be listed alternatively rather than cumulatively.

Each of the definitions considered, then, embodies a particular attitude to the subjectivity/objectivity dilemmas inherent in defining workplace bullying. For the most part, the definitions combine requirements for both subjective perceptions and observable phenomena. In each, therefore, there is implicit acceptance

[25] See in this regard, eg Einarsen, Hoel, Zapf, and Cooper, n 22 above, 10–11.
[26] See in various of the essays included in Einarsen, Hoel, Zapf, and Cooper, n 22 above, 15, 103,166–7.
[27] R Lyons, H Tivey, C Ball, *Bullying at Work: How to Tackle It. A Guide for MSF Representatives and Members* (London: MSF, 1995) and Fire Brigades Union, *Bullying at work: How to tackle it* (Kingston Upon Thames, UK: FBU, 1997).

to some extent that even unjustifiable subjective beliefs should be influential. Except in respect of the last definition, also, objective features are included that some might regard as overly rigid. The question becomes whether such definitional premises have an impact on the results of surveys which make use of them. It is crucial for this to be carefully tracked to avoid inappropriate conclusions being extracted.

Problems with Determining the Incidence of Workplace Bullying

The major source of empirical evidence on the incidence of workplace bullying is questionnaire surveys of various populations of workers, ranging from single workplace, or 'captive audience', investigations to much larger studies like the one undertaken by the UMIST researchers. The two main approaches to discovering the frequency of workplace bullying focus on investigating, on the one hand, the prevalence of bullying behaviours and, on the other hand, whether people see themselves as bullied. These two methods are, however, quite often combined in a single study for comparative purposes. Development and innovation is also ongoing, including in the design of experiments to test for variations in results according to methodology.

The first main approach uses what may be called an 'inventory method'. It is in connection with this methodology that lists of negative behaviours were developed. Survey questionnaires then ask about experience of each behaviour. Categorization of a respondent as bullied or not depends on whether their answers bring them within the researchers' working definition, whether this incorporates Leymann's position on frequency and duration or some other set of criteria.

The second main approach uses what may be called a 'labelling method'. In short, questionnaires ask respondents if they have been bullied. It is usual, although not invariable, for respondents to be presented with a definition of bullying on the basis of which they are asked to categorize their own experience. This is an important function served by narrative definitions already encountered. Verifiable features of researchers' working definitions might also be probed with questions regarding, for example, the frequency of the conduct.

The problems with these two methodologies mirror the problems identified above with objective and subjective definitions of bullying. On the one hand, the inventory method seeks to factor out respondents' subjective understandings, at least of what bullying is, while, on the other hand, the labelling method gives primacy to victims' perceptions. Hence the inventory method results in people being categorized as bullied when they do not see themselves in this way and leaves out respondents whose sense of victimhood relates to behaviour that wouldn't usually be seen as bullying.[28] In fully acknowledging the subjective nature of the

---

[28] APD Liefooghe and R Olafsson, 'Scientists and Amateurs: Mapping the Bullying Domain' (1999) 20(1/2) *International Journal of Manpower* 39, 40.

bullying experience, however, the labelling method results in people being categorized as bullied when others would not regard them in this way and leaves out those
who put up uncomplainingly with mistreatment that is obviously bullying.[29] It is
unsurprising, therefore, that the two methods typically result in different findings,
with inventory methods tending to deliver higher prevalence rates.[30]

It is also noteworthy that difficulties potentially flow from differences in how
people read or interpret language. Take, for example, the definition used in the
labelling, as opposed to the inventory, aspect of the UMIST study. My own
doubts about how this was intended to be read show that it leaves room for interpretation, making it unlikely that the definition was always understood by
respondents as it was meant. This makes it difficult to be confident that people
were always labelling themselves as bullied according to a common conception, or
that their understanding equated with that of the researchers. Analogous points
could be made with regard to different elements in lists of bullying behaviours.
One person's understanding of 'persistent' or 'unreasonable' may not be another's.

Also, any arbitrariness in objective elements in a given definition will be
reflected in evidence so far as these requirements are stringently adhered to. This is
a particular issue for the inventory method because a respondent is given no
opportunity to communicate that they regard themselves as bullied even though
their experience does not fit the researchers' definition. The problem is less acute,
although not entirely absent, for the labelling method. With that approach,
respondents' perceptions will still be revealed even if, for example, follow-up
answers prevent them from being categorized by the researchers as bullied.[31]

In respect of both methodologies, the use of self-reports is a further important
limitation.[32] The question here is whether there are inherent biases because of
quirks in how people respond to surveys about bullying. Such effects can be
produced in many ways, including from sample selection, question design, or

---

[29] Liefooghe and Olafsson, n 28 above, 39, 40.

[30] See for an overview and discussion of international findings on prevalence, D Zapf, S Einarsen,
H Hoel and M Vartia, 'Empirical Findings on Bullying in the Workplace' in Einarsen, Hoel, Zapf,
and Cooper, n 22 above, 104–9. For a comparative investigation and discussion of the two main
methodologies, see, eg E Mikkelsen and S Einarsen, 'Bullying in Danish Work-life: Prevalence and
Health Correlates' (2001) 10(4) *European Journal of Work and Organisational Psychology* 393, 405–6
and D Salin (same volume) 'Prevalence and Forms of Bullying Among Business Professionals:
A Comparison of Two Different Strategies for Measuring Bullying', 425, 436–7.

[31] This issue came up in the results in the UMIST study in that some respondents labelled
themselves as bullied but indicated that this had happened 'very rarely'. Arguably, therefore, these
individuals did not fall within the definition of bullying used in the study. The researchers nonetheless included them in the bullied group, again emphasizing the subjective conception of workplace
bullying underlying the research. Note also that this well exemplifies the point above that the
labelling method leaves room for respondents' understandings of the definition presented to differ
from that of the researchers.

[32] See Einarsen, Hoel, Zapf, and Cooper, n 22 above, 11, where they said: 'Although most studies
theoretically seem to regard bullying as an objective and observable phenomenon, which is not
entirely in the "eye of the beholder", with only a few exceptions the empirical data have so far been
gathered by the use of self-report from victims... So far, little is known about the "inter-rater reliability" with regard to bullying, that is the agreement of the victim with some external observers.'

mode of data collection. Researchers have put forward a range of hypotheses about the likelihood or not of questionnaire data thereby being skewed towards over- or under-reporting of bullying.[33] But the critical point for present purposes is that little is yet clear about the existence or systematic impact of such effects.

Note that this is important not only in respect of whether people label themselves as bullied or not. It also matters with regard to what they say about particular elements in a given definition, when either follow-up questions are asked in a labelling study or the inventory method is employed. In other words, the possibility of inherent bias is common both to methodologies that give primacy to subjective beliefs about whether bullying has occurred and to ones that seek to exclude these. It is just that the issue presents itself in different ways. For example, the follow-up questions in a labelling study will be addressed only to those who see themselves as bullied.

The difficulties have been graphically demonstrated in a recent study by Coyne, Chong, Seigne, and Randall.[34] Given the delicacy of collecting data about whether people have experienced bullying, or themselves bullied, almost no demographic information was obtained from participants. The organization in question was, however, reported to be male-dominated. Two hundred and eighty-eight respondents were studied in thirty-six teams. Participants were asked, having been presented with the trade union definition, to indicate how often they had been a target of such behaviour in their team, with what frequency, and over what period. They were also asked to say if they had acted in this way in their current position. Finally, respondents were requested to identify targets or perpetrators of bullying in their teams according to an anonymous coding system.

There were self-reports of having been bullied from nearly 40 per cent of respondents and admissions of bullying from nearly one-fifth (19.3 per cent). Around 10 per cent (twenty-eight people) in fact identified themselves as both victims and bullies. Note, however, that the proportion in the category of self-reported victims fell dramatically (to 3.9 per cent) on inclusion of a requirement of a weekly occurrence over at least six months.

So far as peer nominations went, the researchers required two or more nominations to classify a person as a 'victim' or 'perpetrator'. This was 'to control for possible idiosyncratic views and to obtain some level of agreement between peers'.

---

[33] See eg the discussion in Zapf, Einarsen, Hoel, and Vartia, n 30 above, 109. See also L Quine, 'Workplace Bullying, Psychological Distress and Job Satisfaction in Junior Doctors', n 20 above, 92, 95, 98, which is of particular interest regarding the possibility that 'negative affectivity' influences whether people label themselves as bullied. She concluded that negative affectivity accounted for 6% of the variation in self-reports of bullying in that study. Also, she found no significant differences in negative affectivity between men and women or between white doctors and those from minority ethnic groups, while female and ethnic minority respondents were over-represented in those labelling themselves as bullied.

[34] See I Coyne, P Smith-Lee Chong, E Seigne, and P Randall, 'Self and peer nominations of bullying: An analysis of incident rates, individual differences and perceptions of the working environment' (2003) 12 *European Journal of Work and Organizational Psychology* 209, from which the following account is drawn.

On this approach the proportion of victims and perpetrators fell significantly from the overall self-report numbers, to 11.3 per cent of victims and 7.9 per cent of perpetrators. No-one was now identified as a victim/bully. The numbers fell again when the self and peer reports were combined: so only 7.4 per cent were identified as victims and 2.7 per cent as perpetrators under both measurement systems. Clearly, therefore, self-understandings, whether that a person had been, or had, bullied, often did not coincide with the views of others.

Aside from reinforcing the need carefully to deconstruct empirical evidence about the incidence of workplace bullying, this study illustrated that evidence about links between personality or organizational environment and experience of workplace bullying needs to be treated with caution. If different methodologies place different people in victim or perpetrator categories, evidence about associations will necessarily have different meanings according to the system of categorization. These points were highlighted by the researchers' findings that there were differences in personality, as well as perceptions of their working environment, as between different classifications of victims and perpetrators and a control group.

Problems with Learning about Workplace Bullying

Questions also arise about reliance exclusively on questionnaires in order to find out about the circumstances surrounding workplace bullying. The problem is again that knowledge about the circumstances of bullying is generally obtained from those who identify themselves as victims.

This matters because it is known that subjective narratives should not be treated as necessarily determinative of what really happened. For example, an experiment concerning narrative accounts of being angry, or being the target of anger, found differences depending on the role adopted, with 'targets' giving less resolved narratives than 'perpetrators'.[35] In essence, people are liable to attribute reasons for events that are contestable. The suggestion is that those who perceive themselves as the object of negative acts tend to blame factors external to themselves, like the alleged bully or their organizational environment, rather than to enquire into their own conduct. On the other hand, those in the bullying role are motivated to find external explanations for what happened.[36]

---

[35] RF Baumeister, A Stillwell, and SR Wotman, 'Victim and Perpetrator Accounts of Interpersonal Conflict: Autobiographical Narratives About Anger' (1990) 59(5) *Journal of Personality and Social Psychology* 994. But note that it was not the same incidents being described from two points of view, although it was the same narrators adopting different roles. Accordingly the researchers concluded that 'there appears to be a broad tendency for perpetrators to regard the incident as a closed, isolated episode, whereas victims tend to describe lasting consequences and implications. Whether these discrepancies arise from distorting the events or from choosing which events to describe is impossible to determine from our data. Either way, however, these discrepancies reflect how roles determine the structure of personal narratives'.

[36] See, eg the discussions at: H Hoel, C Rayner, and CL Cooper, 'Workplace Bullying' (1999) 14 *International Review of Industrial and Organizational Psychology* 195, 207–9 and D Zapf and

The most obvious strategy for verifying accounts given by those who self-report as victims would be to investigate the points of view of those they regard as having bullied them. Yet there are particular methodological obstacles to designing effective research of this kind. It would be challenging to obtain the participation in research of pairs or groups of self-reported victims and 'their bullies'. Devising effective experiments amongst groups of bullies would present analogous problems. Equally there are ethical objections to re-creating bullying situations for experimental purposes.

Solutions to these difficulties may very well be found with time. But for now their effect is that there is a dearth of evidence deriving directly from bullies. This points to further reasons for caution in drawing on evidence about the circumstances in which workplace bullying takes place.

Problems with Establishing Causal Links

Finally, it is vital to notice that 'snapshot' studies do not disclose cause and effect relationships. This matters because the empirical work that has been done on workplace bullying is almost exclusively of this kind, being cross-sectional rather than longitudinal. This means that the study of workplace bullying to date has disclosed associations between it and various phenomena, not the causal relationships behind these associations. In other words, research has explored the links between workplace bullying and several features of working life in the sense of showing how these coincide. It has not demonstrated what workplace bullying results in, nor how it is itself caused. It is possible, in fact, for two associated phenomena to be caused by something else entirely.

This is relevant both for data regarding the consequences of bullying[37] and about the possible causes of workplace bullying.[38] For example, an association between workplace bullying and poor mental or physical health does not establish that the workplace bullying caused the health problems. In theory, the health problems could have caused the workplace bullying, or both the bullying and the health issues might have been caused by something else. Equally, an association between a particular personality profile and workplace bullying does not mean that having that personality causes workplace bullying. The workplace bullying could have caused the personality profile to develop, or both might be the result of something else. While, therefore, evidence of associations may be suggestive of particular hypotheses, it should not be treated as probative of them.

S Einarsen, 'Individual Antecedents of Bullying' in Einarsen, Hoel, Zapf, and Cooper, n 22 above, 165, 173.

[37] See, eg Zapf and Einarsen, ibid, 167.

[38] See, eg H Hoel and D Salin, 'Organisational Antecedents of Workplace Bullying' in Einarsen, Hoel, Zapf, and Cooper, n 22 above, 203, 215.

Conclusion

The overall message is that careful account needs to be taken of the impact on evidence about workplace bullying of these conceptual and methodological issues. To draw meaningfully on this work requires entry into the detail of how results were produced, and, as importantly, why a particular approach was chosen. But the interesting side-effect is that insight emerges, not only about appropriate uses of the data, but also about the significance for law of ideas underlying their production. It is this creative interplay which is perhaps the unexpected element in the arguments that follow.

How Psychologists' Evidence Can Help Legal Analysis

Learning from the Different Premises Behind Law and Psychology

It is certainly striking that psychologists and others carrying out empirical investigations of workplace bullying have grappled with many of the same problems as confront law and lawyers. A prime example, as we have seen, is that a workable, meaningful definition of workplace bullying is central to quantitative empirical research. But the similarities do not rest there. Work in other disciplines is also vitally concerned with, for example, attributing responsibility for bullying conduct and examining causal relationships between workplace bullying and its possible outcomes.

   Equally significant is that psychologists come at these questions with quite different ideas, influences, and assumptions about workplace bullying and, more fundamentally, knowledge itself.[39] This makes it necessary to engage with those differences before making use of psychological data. But beyond this, it is possible to learn from the different premises underlying legal and psychological perspectives. Probing why psychologists take a particular approach elicits ideas against which to test lawyers' differing viewpoint. This type of analysis is capable both of exposing weaknesses in the legal framework and of suggesting fruitful possibilities

---

[39] cf Quine, 'Workplace Bullying in NHS Community Trust: Staff Questionnaire Survey', n 20 above, where the contention was made that: 'Most definitions of workplace bullying share three elements that are influenced by case law definitions in the related areas of racial and sexual harassment.' The three elements identified were: first, defining bullying in terms of its effect on the recipient, not the intention of the bully; secondly, requiring a negative effect on the victim; and thirdly, requiring persistence. The influence of Scandinavian research on definitions of workplace bullying in UK (and other) studies seems to undermine this thesis. It is also worth noting that the three elements mentioned could not accurately have been derived from harassment case law (although that would not preclude a faulty translation process). A straightforward example is that case law established early on that a single incident could constitute harassment (*Bracebridge Engineering Ltd v Darby* [1990] IRLR 3 (EAT) and *Insitu Cleaning Co Ltd v Heads* [1995] IRLR 4 (EAT)) (and see further more generally in Barmes, n 7 above).

for development. The existence of careful enquiry elsewhere into workplace bullying thereby provides an external perspective against which to measure, and hence to develop, the law relating to workplace bullying.

Defining Workplace Bullying

Consideration of what lies behind psychologists' definitions of workplace bullying illustrates the possibilities. There is a paramount, functional need, for the purposes of quantitative research at least, to coin a recognizable category of behaviour that is well adapted to survey studies. Not least this enables a field of study to be identified.[40] Equally it gives some hope of appropriate comparisons being made across experiments over time. It is unsurprising then to find an emphasis on definitions that seek to capture the distinctive, visible elements of workplace bullying. In theory one would also expect insistent pressure towards uniformity, especially to maximize the potential for survey findings to be compared and even aggregated. As we have seen, however, in practice convergence seems quite far from being achieved.

Where quantitative empirical investigation is not at stake, quite different needs and constraints are involved in defining workplace bullying.[41] So far as legal discourse is concerned, one important functional requirement is for a concept that is workable in the hands of judges deciding individual cases. Yet, the variety of legal tools at issue means that the legal meaning (or meanings) of workplace bullying necessarily derives from the interplay between different interventions and actors. The picture is further complicated by justice concerns with striking a balance over time, between, on the one hand, internal consistency and coherence in widely differing fact situations and, on the other hand, capturing the essence of the wrong.

The question becomes whether there is something to be learned from the emphasis in the psychological literature on isolating the essential features of a bullying situation, in contrast to the recurrent legal methodology of analysing individual fact situations, often by analogy with others, in the light of a rule coined at a high level of abstraction. Viewed in this light, the arbitrariness that lawyers perceive in various definitions of workplace bullying might be understood as resistance to categorization according to the 'best' example, or paradigm case.

It is true that such an approach is unlikely to work well in 'hard' cases, for example the single bad incident of bullying or harassment, nor to deliver the

---

[40] See, eg the discussion in Hoel, Rayner, and Cooper, n 36 above, 196–7.

[41] Interestingly, Einarsen, Hoel, Zapf, and Cooper analyse whether an objective or subjective conception of workplace bullying should be used in terms of the function to be served. See note 22 above, 12: 'On the whole, we tend to agree . . . that an objective conceptualisation is of course, necessary in connection with legal issues and cases of internal disciplinary hearings. However, subjective conceptualisations will be a better prediction of victims' responses and reactions, organisational outcomes such as turnover and absenteeism, as well as organisational responses. Also, subjective conceptualisations must suffice to evoke organisational interventions and attempts at problem-solving and mediation.' Note also that qualitative work internal to the psychological literature has very helpfully problematized the task of defining workplace bullying, as the discussion below demonstrates.

unifying concept that explains all eventualities, however extreme. But it surely has strengths in concentrating the mind on what is quintessential about the practice of bullying. Aside from making unified, consistent development more straightforward, it requires that choices be made between theoretical approaches so far as these conflict. As such, the psychological approach to defining workplace bullying provides a useful perspective against which to evaluate the law. It becomes pertinent to enquire whether legal discourse, in courts or elsewhere, is underpinned by a vision of the paradigm case of workplace bullying and, so far as it is not, whether it should be.

More substantively, it seems obvious that legal notions of workplace bullying should be evaluated in the light of psychologists' conclusions about what is central to this conduct. Particularly striking in this regard are the emphases, first, on workplace bullying as more than a one-off experience and, secondly, on investigating the range of negative actions that may constitute bullying.

In relation to the former, inclusion in psychological definitions of ideas like persistence, repetition, or escalation places the spotlight on workplace bullying as a relational or iterative process. It is depicted as fundamentally about ongoing, complex, developing, bad relations between work-mates, rather than discrete, isolated incidents of discord. An important implication is that preventative or remedial measures must be appropriate to such encounters. It is not necessary to agree that workplace bullying cannot be a one-off event to see the significant challenge that this vision presents for legal regulation. A whole series of questions arise about whether law has either appreciated the dynamic aspect to workplace bullying or has adapted its liability and remedial rules to this reality.

In relation to the substance of bullying conduct, psychologists have again not been satisfied with identifying the abstract notion that bullying comprises negative actions. Rather, they have attempted to enumerate the forms that such behaviour can take. It is again not necessary to believe that all the ways that a person might be bullied can exhaustively be identified, nor to agree with any given catalogue, to see that there may be value in elaborating the forms it is likely to take. A number of questions are again raised for law. Is it able to perceive and respond appropriately to a range of bullying behaviours? Is there scope for it to resolve subjectivity/objectivity dilemmas by using some form of listing technique?

Investigating the Causes and Consequences of Workplace Bullying

The differing premises between the psychological literature on workplace bullying and legal analyses is again significant in this context. Most importantly, legal intervention is so often designed to culminate in adjudication of individualized, fact-specific disputes. Yet the detailed scrutiny of events that takes place in the course of litigation is an important instance of law's processes being ill-adapted to unravelling a long-running, changeable, complex conflict. Certainly, so far as this sort of procedure investigates the causes or consequences of bullying, it does so within a carefully circumscribed frame of reference. The only cause investigated is almost always the individual fault of the alleged bully as understood by the liability rules in issue. The only consequences attributed are the costs, including in health terms, to the victim.

It is true that this close attention to individual cases enables some victims to prove that workplace bullying has had serious deleterious consequences to their health and well-being. But such legal process is rarely interested in whether this might be part of a larger pattern, nor in where it might fit into a general set of causal relationships.

This is not to deny that there are legal technologies that in some sense 'collectivize' problems. For example, workplace health and safety regulation plays this sort of role even if its impact on workplace bullying seems especially indirect. Vicarious liability of employers for the conduct of their employees also frequently locates responsibility at the organizational level. It is notable that both the common law and statute have in recent times imaginatively developed this form of liability to encourage more sophisticated attitudes to employer responsibility for individual bad behaviour and its prevention.[42] Despite such interventions, however, it remains individual wrong-doing that is both at the conceptual heart of the main relevant constructions of unlawfulness and the primary subject matter of minute forensic dissection in court-rooms and beyond.

Again, the challenge posed by the empirical methodologies pursued by psychologists is important. It may be that there is not yet conclusive proof of what systematically causes workplace bullying, nor of what it results in. But the work done has brought into the frame a whole range of possible causal influences that are frequently invisible to law. By collectivizing the causal questions at stake, it becomes obvious that there may be a wide spectrum of explanations for workplace bullying other than ones which concentrate on individual fault or agency. At the same time, the scope of possible outcomes beyond the individual can more easily be discerned.

It is also worth noting that, notwithstanding the methodological limitations of snapshot studies, the data that has emerged reinforces these lessons. So the evidence on personality,[43] and organizational evidence,[44] has suggested a highly complex pattern of causal relationships, whereas that on outcomes has suggested a

---

[42] See the reformulation of the common law test for vicarious liability in *Lister and ors v Hesley Hall Ltd* [2002] 1 AC 215 (HL), the purposive approach taken to interpreting provisions on vicarious liability in the Race Relations Act 1976 in *Jones v Tower Boot Co Ltd* [1997] ICR 254 (CA), and the interesting design of the vicarious liability provisions in the UK anti-discrimination statutes. These adopt a formula whereby, first, anything done by an employee will be treated 'as done by his employer as well as by him, whether or not it was done with the employer's knowledge or approval' and, secondly, employers have a potential defence to liability. This enables an employer to escape vicarious liability in circumstances where it is able to show that it 'took such steps as were reasonably practicable' to prevent the employee from doing the prohibited act, or from doing acts of that description in the course of employment.   [43] For an overview see Zapf and Einarsen, n 36 above.

[44] For an overview see Hoel and Salin, n 38 above.

wide range of negative outcomes.[45] The latter comprise health and other costs for those reporting bullying, as well as 'ripple effects' for witnesses, families, and friends. There are also suggestions of negative organizational consequences on workplaces more generally.

Quite a number of associations have been found between aspects of personality and organizational environment and workplace bullying (as measured) suggesting that it is the interplay of factors that matters.[46] It is true that the evidence leaves open whether there is one dominant cause of workplace bullying that is yet to be investigated. But given the variety of ways that a person might be bullied, it seems much more likely that it is the combination of elements that is crucial.

This provides some empirical grounding to the notion that interventions which theorize workplace bullying as quintessentially a matter of individual responsibility do not reflect reality. The question becomes how far this larger picture is cognizable to the law. It becomes plain that it is not enough to concentrate on law's post-hoc verdicts about particular entanglements, nor to ignore the possibility that forces are at stake beyond the immediate causes and effects of individualized squabbles. Careful thought is shown to be necessary about the balance between law as a tool for calling individuals to account and as a mechanism for structuring working environments. Apart from anything else, if law partially constructs that environment, it should be possible for it to assist in reconstructing it in ways that are useful to preventing, minimizing, or remedying workplace disputes.

Associations between workplace bullying and a range of bad consequences also support the view that this behaviour imposes a variety of costs beyond the individual participants in a conflict. It is significant that the research comprises accounts of what a person believes the consequences of workplace bullying to have been. In several studies individuals have reported their perception that workplace bullying caused a particular outcome, for example, that they left their job, reduced their commitment to work, or suffered deleterious health effects. Such perceptions are potentially damaging in themselves.

Studies amongst populations of victims of workplace bullying are also revealing. It may not yet be known what systematic effects workplace bullying has, but this work is highly suggestive that, in some cases at least, health consequences are severe. This further supports the need to evaluate the impact of law in larger perspective. In particular, are legal interventions sufficiently attentive to the actual

---

[45] For an overview see S Einarsen and E Gemzoe Mikkelsen, 'Individual Effects of Exposure to Bullying at Work' in Einarsen, Hoel, Zapf, and Cooper, n 22 above, 127 and H Hoel, S Einarsen, and CL Cooper, 'Organisational Effects of Bullying', ibid, 145.

[46] See, eg Zapf and Einarsen, n 36 above, 180: 'To summarise: so far there are few "hard facts" regarding the causes of bullying. However, taking all the existing empirical data together, there is sufficient evidence that there are many possible causes and probably often multiple causes of bullying, be it causes within the organisation, within the perpetrator, within the social system or within the victim. One-sided and simplistic discussions are in this respect usually misleading. One should consider carefully the circumstances of each bullying case as in our experience they can be extremely different.'

and potential costs of workplace bullying? Or is there more that legal process could do to aid streamlined and efficient resolution of disputes at work, or, indeed, to stop them coming about?

Learning from the Interplay Between Psychological and Legal Discourse

Psychologists' evidence is also helpful to legal analysis in the information it provides about what lies behind the shift towards disputes being presented to courts in terms of workplace bullying. It is unmistakable that there has been a change in this direction, but not at all clear where it has come from nor what it has been inspired by. Yet understanding this process would be of enormous value in evaluating the relevance and potential impact of existing and possible legal interventions.

Psychological research has much to offer in this regard, in the clues it has uncovered about the forces behind emergence of the language of workplace bullying. It is notable that focusing on what has been learned about the appearance of a discourse, rather than about the conduct it describes, converts methodological concentration on subjective characterizations and self-reports into something of a virtue. This approach seems well-fitted to determining how the idea of workplace bullying is being deployed outside the courtroom, which is in turn instructive regarding its translation into legal discourse. Beyond this there has been interesting qualitative research specifically probing understandings of bullying amongst various working populations.

The Scale of the Challenge to Law

Data about the incidence of workplace bullying is a good example of the usefulness of the psychological literature in this regard. The striking fact is that it has been consistently demonstrated that very significant proportions amongst each of the populations surveyed view themselves as victims of workplace bullying. In addition, this has repeatedly been supported by even larger numbers reporting having witnessed bullying at work. This evidence matters because it suggests that the demands being made of the law are underpinned by a widespread perception amongst working people that ordinary standards of conduct are not being respected. So it can be extrapolated, not only that the trend towards invoking law in relation to workplace bullying has deep and wide roots, but that it may be expected to gather pace. Equally, difficult qualitative questions arise as to why this perception exists and, hence, what legal interventions might be capable of altering it.

To summarize the evidence,[47] the starting point must be the UMIST study undertaken in 1999.[48] The sample was drawn from seventy organizations in the

---

[47] The account that follows draws particularly on the writing up of this research in Hoel, Cooper, and Faragher, n 23 above, and in C Rayner, H Hoel, and CL Cooper, *Workplace Bullying: What we know, who is to blame, and what can we do?* (London, 2002).

[48] Hoel and Cooper, n 19 above.

private, public, and voluntary sectors, with a combined workforce of just under 1,000,000.[49] The researchers received 5,288 completed questionnaires, a response rate of 42.8 per cent. The sample had a broadly even gender split.[50] Of respondents, 97.1 per cent defined themselves as white; 85 per cent worked full time; 47.5 per cent categorized their jobs as professional or managerial; 43.6 per cent defined themselves as workers; and 43.3 per cent said they had some managerial responsibility.

It was found that 10.6 per cent of respondents (or 553 individuals) labelled themselves as having been bullied in the last six months, while quite close to 50 per cent reported having witnessed bullying within the last five years. Of those reporting bullying in the last six months, 1.4 per cent indicated that this had happened on a weekly or more frequent basis, while 9.2 per cent reported that it had happened either 'very rarely', 'now and then', or 'several times a month'. The 1.9 per cent who said they had been bullied 'very rarely' arguably did not fall within the definition of bullying proffered because of the frequency criterion. Nonetheless the researchers counted these individuals in the 'bullied' group because they perceived themselves in this way.[51]

Very strikingly, however, significantly different numbers were disclosed by application of a Leymann-type inventory approach. As discussed above, this involved counting as bullied anyone who answered questions about typically bullying behaviours to the effect that they had experienced at least one such act on a weekly or more frequent basis for the previous six months. The startling effect of applying this methodology was that up to 38 per cent of respondents fell into the 'bullied' category.[52]

Smaller scale UK studies, with a range of methodologies, have also yielded a variety of figures. For example, 53 per cent of respondents to a questionnaire study of part-time students at Staffordshire University labelled themselves as having been bullied at some time in their working lives and 77 per cent as having witnessed bullying at work.[53] In a study by Lewis in the further and higher education sector in Wales, 18 per cent indicated that they had directly suffered from workplace bullying, 25 per cent that they had been told by colleagues that they had been bullied, 22 per cent that they had witnessed bullying, and 21 per cent that there had been cases of bullying in their organization.[54]

---

[49] The researchers excluded Northern Ireland from the survey because of the potentially distorting effect of sectarian harassment.   [50] 52.4% men and 47.6% women.

[51] See Hoel, Cooper, and Faragher, n 23 above, 457: 'With 10.6% of respondents reporting having been bullied within the last 6 months, a figure which rises to 24.7% for bullying within the last 5 years, the present study confirms that workplace bullying is a major social problem in Great Britain. Taking into account that 46.5% reported having witnessed bullying in the last 5 years, it is possible to conclude that a majority of employees will have some experience of bullying either directly or indirectly as a witness or observer of bullying.'   [52] Hoel and Cooper, n 19 above, 25.

[53] See C Rayner, 'The Incidence of Workplace Bullying' (1997) 7 *Journal of Community and Applied Social Psychology* 199.

[54] D Lewis, 'Workplace Bullying—Interim Findings of Study in Further and Higher Education in Wales' (1999) *International Journal of Manpower* 106, 112.

Quine's 1996 study of employees of an NHS community trust employed an inventory type methodology. Staff were asked in a postal questionnaire to indicate by a yes/no response whether they had been persistently subjected to any of twenty bullying behaviours derived from previous literature about bullying at work. Of the 1,100 respondents, 38 per cent answered yes in relation to one or more of these behaviours and 42 per cent reported having witnessed the bullying of others.[55]

Quine's later study of junior hospital doctors also disclosed very large prevalence figures. Labelling and inventory methods were combined. Respondents were presented with the trade union definition and asked to indicate if they had been subjected to this conduct in the past twelve months, and whether they had witnessed others being bullied. They were also asked about experience of twenty-one bullying behaviours in the same time period: 37 per cent labelled themselves as having been bullied, 69 per cent reported having witnessed bullying, and 84 per cent reported that they had experienced one or more of the bullying behaviours within the previous year.[56]

The conclusion that the psychological research has uncovered a large shadow of people who characterize themselves as bullied at work is interestingly reinforced by the figures resulting from labelling methodologies based on subjective perceptions. Equally it does not matter that the prevalence data disclosed by such studies might in part be based on perceptions that are not defensible[57] nor that it may be distorted in the other direction by people not characterizing themselves as bullied when they have been. Finally, the conclusion remains valid even though the actual numbers that emerge from the UK evidence are rather variable. The common denominator between all the data is that significant proportions of those surveyed classify themselves as bullied, and that their view is supported by that of witnesses.

The Meaning of the Challenge to Law

It is difficult to know what lies behind the encapsulation of discontent in the idea of workplace bullying. How far does it reflect a new sense of grievance and how far is it just the vocabulary that is new? Indeed, is there a sense in which it is the psychological research itself that has, wholly or partly, prompted that which it has then recorded? Amid the myriad possibilities, one thing seems clear, which is that the emergence of the discourse of workplace bullying has not been importantly influenced by the legal sources relevant to it. This would be implausible in circumstances where workplace bullying is a notion without distinctive legal meaning.[58]

---

[55] Quine, 'Workplace Bullying in NHS Community Trust: Staff Questionnaire Survey', n 20 above, 230. See also L Quine, 'Workplace Bullying in Nurses' (2001) 6 *Journal of Health Psychology* 73, about the findings of this research regarding nurses.

[56] Quine, 'Workplace Bullying, Psychological Distress and Job Satisfaction in Junior Doctors', n 20 above, 94–5.

[57] It is even possible, although perhaps unlikely, that some respondents are deliberately misleading.

[58] But this is not to say that ideas about law more generally are necessarily irrelevant. For example, it is possible that ideas, including misconceptions, about the availability of compensation might have

This strongly suggests that we are witnessing law being forced to adapt to people conceptualizing their working lives in a novel way. Yet it is in the nature of law and legal process that translation of experience into a set of legal outcomes entails the vindication of some accounts and the denial of others. As these two interpretative worlds collide, therefore, namely that of workers conceiving of their lives in terms of workplace bullying and of law accommodating that change, we may expect law increasingly to shape how workplace bullying is understood. It follows that insight now into what is behind the shift in language holds out the promise of law's influence being purposely directed towards coherent, valuable ends.[59]

Against this background, the repeated findings, in keeping with international experience, that many more people in the UK report significant negative behaviour at work than label their experience as bullying are highly interesting. These substantiate at a general level that workers engage in a complex evaluative process in ascribing the bullying label or not. Usefully, qualitative work by psychologists has probed what is behind these characterizations.

First, the meaning of workplace bullying has been found to be highly contested, with workers deploying a variety of frameworks to make sense of the concept. The language of workplace bullying has been shown to be mutable and adaptable, evidenced by its application to a quite stunning range of situations and behaviours.[60]

In a study amongst university staff and students, for example, focus group participants were asked to discuss their understanding of workplace bullying and to describe an incident they considered to be bullying. They were probed by the researchers to identify the salient features of these events. The researchers observed the malleability of the idea of workplace bullying, in that participants made choices between possible explanatory models in accounting for their experiences. At the same time, the discussions revealed the importance of theories about bullying being shared. If they were not, individuals were liable to be deterred from relying on what they had initially perceived. Conversely, the sense that their ideas were shared reinforced individual convictions.[61]

---

had an impact. The narrower point being made here is that it is, in essence, inconceivable that the law relevant to workplace bullying has had a significant impact.

[59] Comparison with emergence of the concept of sexual harassment, and its reception into law, is again of interest. Consider, for example, the account given, focusing on the US, in MA Crouch, *Thinking about Sexual Harassment, A Guide for the Perplexed* (New York, 2001) 25–100, as well as the sceptical analysis at 101–38 of the capacity of empirical evidence to assist in resolving key questions.

[60] This observation is reflected in the large range of behaviours researchers found should be included in the negative acts questionnaires developed for use in measuring workplace bullying according to the 'inventory' methodology discussed above.

[61] See Liefooghe and Olafsson, n 28 above. The writers extrapolated that organizations could constructively influence what was perceived as bullying and not. For example, see their comment at 47: 'It is important for organisations to cultivate a social representation, shared by the whole organization, which clearly delineates acceptable and unacceptable behaviour at work. In other words, rather than

Liefooghe and Mackenzie Davey again observed considerable flexibility in the language of workplace bullying when studying its use in three call centres in the North and Midlands of England.[62] Twenty-five focus groups were conducted amongst 113 staff. No definition of bullying was offered, but participants were asked to comment on whether they would apply the term to describe any relationship in their workplace, and how they would define it. A very broad range of behaviours were encompassed within workplace bullying, with appeal being made to a variety of ideas in accounting for the attributions made.

The same authors reported on a study commissioned by a UK high street bank because of worrying results in the bank's annual employee survey:[63] 53 per cent of the workforce had reported that they had been bullied at work on the first occasion that a question had been included about this. Notably perhaps, these results were somewhat in the order of the very high reported rates of workplace bullying in some UK studies.

Liefooghe and Mackenzie Davey this time drew participants in focus groups from two departments. Sessions were kept as unstructured as possible, with initial introductions, assurances that only generic information would be given to the bank, followed by mention of the survey results and the group being asked what the term 'bullying' meant to them. No definition of bullying was offered. In reporting their findings, the researchers particularly commented on the ambiguity in the proffered definitions. Instead of a homogenous or clear meaning of bullying emerging, participants again drew on a range of ideas in striving to define the term.

Secondly, the last two studies also observed workers moving easily between individualistic and organizational accounts of bullying. In a sense this was merely further evidence that the idea of workplace bullying is highly adaptable. But it is important in itself that this language routinely encompassed actions that did not target workers as individuals, nor for which responsibility could easily be ascribed to individuals. Rather, the concept was applied to measures that workers experienced as oppressive to them as a group, and that were organizational in nature. Significantly, this was the case even in respect of matters that were the subject of negotiation pursuant to formal collective arrangements.

In Liefooghe and Mackenzie Davey's call centre study, therefore, it was found that participants shifted between individual and organizational bullying in their accounts. Organizational practices such as the use of statistics, call handling times, and sickness policy were all described as bullying. The researchers also recorded bullying behaviours by managers, or lack of cooperation by colleagues, being

"allowing" the existing implicit representations to guide employees' actions, the organisation can take an active role in introducing a new representation in the form of a shared policy or code of conduct.'

[62] APD Liefooghe and K Mackenzie Davey, 'Accounts of Workplace Bullying: The Role of the Organisation' (2001) 10(4) *European Journal of Work and Organisational Psychology* 375.

[63] APD Liefooghe and K Mackenzie Davey, 'Explaining Bullying at Work: Why Should We Listen to Employee Accounts?' in Einarsen, Hoel, Zapf, and Cooper, n 22 above, 219.

accounted for by the incentives created by work systems. Finally, bullying was used to describe several threats to employees, including that of dismissal, being replaced by machines, and being superfluous to requirements.

The bank study produced analogous findings. Negotiations between the union and human resources over pay were given as an example of bullying. The researchers made the following interesting point: 'The lack of negotiation, being told what to do, forms the core of bullying here . . . . This use of the term "bullying" as not being heard was very common in our sample. It was discussed both in traditional union-management negotiations and in individuals' daily experiences of work . . .'.[64] The system of appraisal and performance-related pay was also regarded as bullying, for example, in targets being tightened in response to pressure to cut costs. Yet it was the system that was blamed rather than individual managers, who were seen as operating within organizational constraints. The researchers' conclusion overall was that the use of 'bullying' to denote organizational practices was the explanation for the large incidence of reported bullying in the employee survey.

A unifying factor in these findings seems to be that the language of bullying gives workers one label for any conduct that they regard as having 'crossed the line'. It seems to be a way of condemning all behaviour that is perceived as going too far in asserting, on the one hand, the dominance, power, and control of employers and, on the other hand, the subordination of employees. Moreover, this holds true even where bullying is alleged to be by a co-worker. The point remains that it is the employee's subordinate status that entails that the demands of work should trump resistance to negative behaviours. The crucial point is that the idea of bullying enables people to distinguish coercive, negative behaviour at work that should be condoned, and that which should not be. Different people may draw the line in different places, using different justifications or frames of reference in doing so, but it is this function that the language of workplace bullying seems consistently to perform.[65]

The point has also been made that the idea of bullying is regarded as having purchase at work in ways that other modes of expressing dissent do not. Alleging workplace bullying is seen as a way that discontent, even if amorphous, wide-ranging, and collective, may be voiced with the expectation at least of eliciting a reaction.[66]

It may be speculated that the presentation of all manner of battles in terms of bullying is to some extent a response to a working world in which it is increasingly difficult to articulate concerns in non-individualistic terms. In such circumstances, it seems quite rational, even inspired, for workers to recast their difficulties in language that superficially accepts an individualistic construction of the

[64] Liefooghe and Mackenzie Davey, n 63 above, 226.
[65] See the highly interesting discussion along these lines in Liefooghe and Mackenzie Davey, n 62 above, 387–9.   [66] See ibid, 389. See also Hoel and Salin, n 38 above, 203.

employment relationship while being capable nonetheless of subverting that point of view.

Be that as it may, this discussion has confirmed what is fundamentally at stake for the law in regulating workplace bullying and the magnitude of the challenge involved. The demand is that law adjudicate between the manifold versions in circulation of how legitimate and illegitimate exercises of workplace power should be distinguished and, in so doing, articulate clear standards for judging the acceptability or otherwise of all and any workplace conduct. At the same time, in showing that preoccupation with workplace bullying in part reflects a deeper, more systemic malaise than is evident from the circumstances of any particular workplace conflict, this evidence further reinforces the case for departing from a resolutely individualistic focus.

Perhaps more esoterically, it is also arguable that the terms in which the law responds to the challenge to it are significant. There are many reasons, for example, to do with internal coherence or the limitations of legal process, why the law, and especially judicial discourse, is frequently unable substantively to address deeper societal concerns or trends that lie behind a given legal conundrum. But there is no reason why law, and especially judicial decision-making, should ignore this context, nor any reason for the rationales behind law's evolutions to be inscrutable to the outside world. In other words, irrespective of what the law does directly about workplace bullying, the discourse of law could be framed mindfully so as to enrich, rather than to elide, wider discussion on that topic.

Learning from Psychologists' Evidence About Workplace Bullying

The third way in which the law might usefully draw on psychologists' evidence is perhaps the most straightforward, in that researchers have made empirical findings about the circumstances attending workplace bullying that are of great potential relevance to legal interventions. Two features of the evidence are of particular interest: first, that rates of reported bullying have generally not differed as between men and women, although the UMIST study found disparities once organizational status was taken into account;[67] and secondly, that large numbers of respondents have consistently reported being bullied with others.

---

[67] While male workers and supervisors were more likely to report bullying, the position was reversed with regard to middle and senior managers. Indeed, in respect of the senior management group, 15.5% of the women reporting bullying as opposed to 6.4% of the men. There were also interesting gender differences in the inventory aspect of the study once organizational status was taken into account. Hoel, Cooper, and Faragher, n 23 above, 449, 461. See also the non-UK support for this in Salin, n 30 above, 432, 435. Interestingly, also, Quine's study of junior doctors found that women were more likely both to label themselves as bullied and to report experience of some of the bullying behaviours investigated. See Quine, 'Workplace Bullying, Psychological Distress and Job Satisfaction in Junior Doctors', n 20 above, 95, 98.

The Gender Dimension

It is necessary still to reflect on the implications of the methodological issues identified earlier. Reliance is again being placed on questionnaire studies. It follows that the possibility of in-built distortions cannot be excluded. In other words, it may be that gender patterns in the way people label themselves as bullied or not, and in the way they report experience of negative behaviours, reflect some form of gender bias in the way people respond to surveys about bullying rather than in their perceptions of their working lives.

For present purposes, however, the findings remain informative. Even if the gender patterns in the evidence were not to map precisely onto experience, much of what is striking is what has been discovered rather than what might have been left out. If it turned out that there was a shadow of women, or of men, who were not labelling themselves as bullied when they had been, or perceived that they had been, this would not gainsay the discovery that sizeable proportions of both men and women perceive themselves to have been victimized. In other words, workplace bullying cannot be regarded as gendered to the degree that one or other sex is excluded from seeing themselves as targets.

The burning question is whether the wrongfulness of workplace bullying, disconnected from mistreatment based on group membership, is sufficiently recognized in law. Space does not allow me to explore this question in detail here. But that the psychological literature reveals a particular issue about mistreatment of lower status men presents the issues in a novel light.[68] It is important also to see that a general prohibition of workplace bullying would not in any sense require that identity-based bullying be viewed as less serious than general bullying. All it would imply is that general workplace bullying should not be seen as so much less serious that it should not attract legal sanction. It would remain possible for the particular egregiousness of identity-based bullying to be recognized in other ways, for example at the remedial level. On this approach, sexual harassment, for example, would become one especially problematic form of workplace bullying rather than a thing wholly apart.

The Group Dimension

In relation to questions about whether a person was victimized alone or with others, it must be remembered that these would be posed only to those who self-identified as bullied. In addition to possible distortions arising from the way people generally answer questionnaires, therefore, there might be specific distortions related to that group only. For example, it is conceivable that the findings reflect a tendency amongst people who label themselves as bullied to report that others were victimized at the same time.[69]

---

[68] Hoel, Cooper, and Faragher, n 23 above, 461.
[69] See, eg the discussion in Hoel, Rayner, and Cooper, n 36 above, 201.

But would it matter if those saying they had shared their experiences were found in fact often to have been on their own or if those victimized alone tended not to own up to this? Much as, in any event, this seems unlikely, the fact would remain that many of the respondents conceived of bullying as a shared experience. They did not see their experience as individualized and isolated. On any analysis, this casts the phenomenon of workplace bullying in an interesting perspective.

Not only does this finding fit very neatly with the qualitative evidence discussed above, in itself it suggests that there is an important collective dimension to workplace bullying. Apart from anything else, this raises doubts about the appropriateness of highly individualistic definitions of workplace bullying by suggesting that the perception of being oppressed as a member of a group may be a salient feature of the experience. This would surely give a very distinctive quality to a target's sense of victimization.

Not least, perhaps especially in these individualistic days, it might engender a sharp sense of the collective, communal side to working life. There is perhaps no more powerless position than to be part of a group that is unable to resist mistreatment. The implication is that the ill-treatment is simply part of the way things are, that it is intrinsic to the experience of being a worker, that it is embedded in the structure of working life. This feature of the evidence again shows how the idea of workplace bullying seems to bring into play larger dilemmas about the distribution of power at work.

The more technical issue for legal analysis is whether cognizance of a group dimension to workplace bullying might helpfully inform legal regulation. There are a number of ways that this might be imagined. For example, could workgroups assist to give specificity and meaning for particular workplaces to over-arching definitions of workplace bullying (thereby incidentally also contributing to the resolution of subjectivity/objectivity puzzles)? Could incentives be built into regulation for employers to take preventive measures that engaged with relevant groups in their workforces? Could procedures for resolving conflicts be devised that recognized the potential for whole groups to be bullied?

Conclusion

The recurring motif has been that the emergence of a discourse on workplace bullying is requiring that law take a stance on the most basic conflicts at work. In defining and adjudicating on workplace bullying, it is being required to determine the circumstances in which negative conduct at work, whatever its incarnation, should be condoned or condemned. In a new way, therefore, law is being drawn into setting ground rules for the distribution of power and authority at work. The contention of this paper is that it will do a far better job at meeting this challenge the more it is responsive to insights from beyond its own discipline.

18

Psychology, Law, and Murders of Gay Men: Responding to Homosexual Advances

Peter Bartlett[1]

The text of this paper forms part of a larger project examining homicides of gay men occurring in the context of casual sexual contact. The larger project is based on the files of the Crown Prosecution Service (CPS), for the years 1976–2000, and includes consideration of the psychiatric records and dispositions in those cases. This paper considers the psychological issues raised by the cases.

It will argue that the existing theoretical context has been shaped by the interface between psychological and legal history. That has led to a focus on whether and in what circumstances a partial defence to murder may arise based on a homosexual advance by the deceased to the accused. The psychological literature has offered little to this debate beyond the concept of 'homosexual panic', a diagnosis considered but argued to be largely unhelpful. Nonetheless, I will argue that male-on-male murders in the context of a casual sexual encounter constitutes a coherent subject for research. The focus on the legal question of whether a partial defence lies has obscured the different but equally important question of the role of psychology in understanding why these deaths occur.

[1] Address for correspondence: School of Law, University of Nottingham, Nottingham, NG7 2RD, or <peter.bartlett@nottingham.ac.uk>. I would acknowledge with thanks the assistance of the Home Office for allowing me to make use of the Homicide Index to identify relevant cases. I would further acknowledge the assistance of the CPS in allowing me access to their files and providing a congenial working environment during the collection of the empirical data in this paper. The good-natured cooperation of the CPS made a variety of practical problems disappear, and I am very grateful for the assistance of their staff. During the rather long gestation of this project, I was fortunate to receive academic residency at the Wellcome Trust Centre for the History of Medicine at University College London and the School of Law at Birkbeck College, London. I am grateful to both for the collegiality offered during my time there. Last, and certainly not least, I am grateful to the Small Grants programme of the British Academy for funding much of the data collection costs of this research.

Methodology

The larger project focuses on homicides of men occurring in the context of relatively casual sexual contact with other men. The paper refers to these as 'gay' homicides. The use of the term 'gay' should not be taken to imply that the participants adopted a specific political or psychological identity. Indeed, many of the participants do not appear to have identified themselves as 'gay'. The term 'gay' is instead used as a linguistic convenience from refer to homicides related to casual sexual contact between men, whether the participants defined themselves as gay, homosexual, heterosexual, some other label, or no relevant label.

The study focuses on deaths occurring during casual sexual activity. Deaths occurring in the context of established domestic arrangements were excluded from the study, on the assumption that they would resemble heterosexual domestic killings, or at any rate would be different enough from those in a casual context to warrant a different study. Similarly, cases where the deceased was under the age of 16 were excluded, as paedophiliac killing was considered likely to have its own different characteristics. Further, as the detailed study would be based on the archive of the Crown Prosecution Service, cases from Scotland and Northern Ireland were excluded.

The empirical aspects of this paper are based on the files of the CPS. The relevant files were identified primarily through a search of Homicide Index maintained by the Home Office, searching for cases where the relationship between the accused and deceased was coded as 'homosexual: casual' or where accused and deceased were both men and the circumstances were identified as sexual. This initial data set was extended by the inclusion of relevant cases identified through law reports and the press. Finally, the staff of the Records Office of the CPS occasionally became aware of relevant cases, and kindly passed those references on. From this list, the CPS was able to locate files for seventy-seven deceased, resulting in the conviction of seventy-eight accused.

This is a significantly larger set of cases than in other empirical studies.[2] Nonetheless, it does not represent a complete set of such homicides for the period.

---

[2] See eg J Mouzos and S Thompson, 'Gay-Hate Related Homicides: An Overview of Major Findings in New South Wales' in *Trends and Issues in Crime and Criminal Justice*, Paper No 155 (Canberra: Australian Institute of Criminology, 2000) which relies on 29 cases; New South Wales, Attorney General's Department, Criminal Law Review Division, 'Homosexual Advance Defence: Final Report of the Working Party' (Sydney: 1998) which uses 13 cases; F Gemert, 'Chicken kills hawk: Gay murders during the eighties in Amsterdam' (1994) 26(4) *Journal of Homosexuality* 149, which uses 18 cases. Stephen Thomsen's study from New South Wales is most comparable. He considers 74 deaths, of which 54 were solved and of which 38 he subjected to close scrutiny. His study is not precisely overlapping with the current one, as his concern is with an express or implied anti-gay animus in homicides, so a significant proportion of his data set concern deaths outside the context of immediate sexual behaviour: see *Hatred, Murder and Male Honour: Anti-Homosexual Homicides in New South Wales, 1980–2000*, Research and Public Policy Series No 43 (Canberra: Australian Institute of Criminology, 2002).

While the Homicide Index is generally well-regarded, indexing inevitably requires coders to make decisions. Some relevant cases may have been excluded for that reason. For some cases, the files at the CPS had disappeared. Perforce, they were excluded from the study. More important, however, is that the case papers only exist, and the case is only entered in the Homicide Index when an accused is identified and charged. If the case was unsolved, therefore, it is absent from the study. The use of newspaper reports to buttress the Homicide Index results does not necessarily correct the potential for sampling bias, as it may be subject to statistical biases of its own. The statistics in the following discussion therefore should be read as descriptive. No claim is made that they meet the standards of formal statistical rigour.

The case files themselves generally contained reports by police officers and junior counsel summarizing the case, a correspondence file, full copies of statements by potential witnesses and the accused, psychiatric and similar expert reports, a note of the verdict, and, generally, some account of the trial. While the material contained in the file is rich, it is not unproblematic for the purposes of this study. First, it is designed for the purpose of identifying the perpetrator of the homicide, and determining how the trial should be conducted.[3] While this is the case for all of the CPS file, it is for current purposes particularly an issue for the psychiatric reports. These are directed to the question of whether a psychiatric defence or partial defence exists. They are not directed to the presence or absence of psychological conditions or psychiatric disorders outside that specific context.

Secondly, the statements contained in the files record conversations made in the context of a police investigation to find the killer. There may be a wide variety of reasons why the witnesses, particularly if they may be suspects in the death, may wish to portray their actions in certain ways, if not lie completely. The statement of the accused person, if he chooses to make a statement at all, is unlikely to be disinterested reflections on the events of the death. This is a particularly difficult issue, as for sixty of the seventy-seven deaths in the study, a single accused and the deceased were the only persons present at the time of the death, and the deceased *ex hypothesi* does not make a statement. A broader range of evidence may be available as to the general circumstances of the accused and the crime, but the only direct account of the death itself is therefore provided by the accused, and then only if the accused makes a statement.

A similar problem relates to the psychiatric reports themselves, as often they are premised on facts that may well be controversial in the overall evidence. The professionals in question may not meet the accused until well on in the pre-trial

---

[3] Regarding the active role of the police in construction of cases, see A Sanders, 'From Suspect to Trial' in Maguire, Morgan and Reiner (eds) *The Oxford Handbook of Criminology*, 2nd edn (Oxford, 1997) ch. 29; M McConville, A Sanders, and R Leng, *The Case for the Prosecution: Police Suspects and the Construction of Criminality* (London, 1991); A Sanders, 'Constructing the Case for the Prosecution' (1987) 14 *Journal of Law and Society* 229.

process, at a time when the accused may have become wiser as to the ways of the legal system.

Finally, until relatively recently, defence psychiatric reports did not need to be served on the Crown in advance. The case files contain medical reports for sixty-two (79 per cent) of the accused persons, but for only twenty-one (27 per cent) was there a medical report that clearly was commissioned by the defence. That may be a significant limitation to the study. That said, in the nineteen cases where diminished responsibility appears to have been an issue at trial, there were defence reports on file for at least fourteen. In two other cases, reports were on file in addition to reports of prison psychiatrists, but it was unclear who had commissioned them. Diminished responsibility was successfully pleaded at trial in twelve cases, of which between nine and eleven have defence medical reports. The fact that reports exist in most cases where diminished responsibility was an issue suggests that the methodological limitation may be less significant than might at first appear.

The Psycho-legal Context

The legal issues surrounding gay murder have centred on the question of 'homosexual advance'. Essentially, these homicides involve the deceased making a sexual advance—usually a grope, but occasionally merely a salacious invitation—to his killer. The killer responded with violence, killing the deceased. Pleas of this sort appear to have been used for many years. A proper study of the historical origins of the plea, known colloquially as the 'Portsmouth defence', has not been done, but historian Angus McLaren[4] discusses cases of this sort in early twentieth-century Canada, and there are some hints in the histories of homosexuality that the origins may be much older. Until well into the middle of the twentieth century, such cases appear to constitute part of the legal landscape. The author of *Russell on Crime*, writing in 1964, for example, provides an extended footnote to question the basis of the plea, but the inclusion of this footnote suggests that such verdicts were a part of legal experience at that time.[5]

Several things happen in the middle years of the twentieth century to alter the psycho-legal landscape. One is the rise of the gay liberation movement, with its consequent effects in social attitudes, psychological and psychiatric attitudes, and law. The Wolfenden Report[6] had recommended the decriminalization of consen-

---

[4] A McLaren, *The Trials of Masculinity: Policing Sexual Boundaries 1870–1930* (Chicago,1997) 124–6. While his overall point is credible, the specifics of Angus McLaren's discussion are problematic, as he perceives the defences as failing because, he presumes, the juries were not convinced of the fact of the advances. In fact, the accused he discusses were given prison sentences, suggesting that the provocation defences were successful at reducing murder to manslaughter. Otherwise, the accused would have been hanged.

[5] C Turner, *Russell on Crime*, 12th edn (London. 1964) 531–2.

[6] *Report of the Departmental Committee on Homosexual Offences and Prostitution*, Cmnd 247 (London: HMSO, 1957).

sual homosexual activity between men in 1957, a result finally achieved in England and Wales by the Sexual Offences Act 1967. In America, similar decriminalization was occurring in much of the country, and in 1972, the American Psychiatric Association (APA) declared that homosexuality was no longer to be considered a mental disorder. Homosexuality and homosexuals became politically visible as never before.

The effect of this increased visibility is complex. Insofar as the provocation defence was based on male concepts of honour, it does not follow that potential killers changed their self-definition as an immediate result of the Wolfenden Committee or the APA decision. Nonetheless, there are indications that a jury might not react uncritically to a provocation defence based simply on a homosexual advance. In *R v McCarthy* in 1954,[7] the accused had apparently gone up a road to urinate following a night's drinking. He was apparently accompanied by the deceased, Rees, who allegedly made an indecent assault on McCarthy, and invited him to engage in sodomy. McCarthy then 'went raging', and apparently beat Rees's head on the roadway, resulting in the latter's death. The jury returned a verdict of murder; and McCarthy's appeal was unsuccessful. Lord Goddard CJ further held that as a matter of law, the provocation alleged could not have justified the injuries inflicted.

That legal position would have put paid to the provocation defence in most homosexual advance cases in England and Wales, but for the Homicide Act 1957. That Act specifically provided that the sufficiency of provocation was a matter for the jury, not for the judge. While the formal bar to homosexual advance *simpliciter* as a ground for provocation was thus removed, the *McCarthy* verdict nevertheless suggests that attitudes were changing. Some juries changed more slowly than others. Indeed, cases where an alleged non-violent homosexual advance without medical evidence successfully grounded a provocation plea occur in the CPS files consulted as late as 1999. Nonetheless, well before that time it must have been no longer obvious that juries would uncritically return a manslaughter verdict simply on the allegation, proven or not, of a homosexual advance.

Partial defences to murder, pleas which reduce murder to manslaughter, were also undergoing revision starting in the middle years of the twentieth century. For provocation, the significant alteration comes not through statute, but via the common law glosses on the defence. Provocation requires both that the 'reasonable man' would be provoked to violence by the conduct of the deceased, and that the accused before the court was so provoked on the occasion in question. The case of *DPP v Camplin*[8] in 1978 is particularly pivotal. Up to that time, the reasonable man was considered to have no particular characteristics of the accused: for example, youth or developmental handicap of the accused could not be taken into account in determining whether the 'reasonable man' would have been provoked.

---

[7] *R v McCarthy* [1954] 2 QB 105.   [8] [1978] AC 705.

That began to change with the *Camplin* case. While the reasonable man was still not permitted to be exceptionally pugnacious or excitable, other factors of the accused, such as age in the *Camplin* case, could be attributed to the reasonable man: would the reasonable man aged 15 (in that case) have behaved as the accused did?

The *Camplin* decision in this context can be seen to open up new space for medical discourse, in that it addresses two developing problems with the use of the provocation defence in homosexual killings. First, and following on from *Camplin* directly, it allowed the defendant to be portrayed as having an unusual condition. This was arguably significant, since this was a time when homosexuality was entering increasingly into the mainstream of culture. Gone (or at least going) were the arguments that gay people were ill, or morally degenerate; the risk was that the perception would be that the 'reasonable man' would not respond with aggression to a homosexual pass. The use of a more specific medicalized discourse would allow the claim that 'perhaps not in general; but this man would—and it is his particular characteristics that are taken to inform the view of the reasonable man'. To put it another way, the law had never allowed the defence to justify mere quick-temperedness; a medicalized discourse around responses of the accused to homosexual advances allowed the possibility of a claim that the accused was not merely quick-tempered but also clinically ill. Secondly, for analogous reasons, it provided the possibility of escaping the problem that the violence of the accused had to be proportionate to the gravity of the provocation: certainly, for most men this response might be out of all proportion; but not for this particular accused. In this context, there is an obvious set of parallels with cases such as the much more recent *R v Thornton (No 2)*,[9] where battered wife syndrome is taken into account in determining provocation.

The other place where new space for psychiatric testimony was opened at a roughly similar period was in the area of diminished responsibility. This was an innovation introduced by section 2 of the Homicide Act 1957. It allowed the reduction of murder to manslaughter in cases where the accused 'was suffering from such abnormality of mind ... as substantially impaired his mental responsibility for his acts and omissions in ... being a party to a killing'. Where there was no tradition of medical evidence in provocation cases, here, medical evidence was the norm from the beginning. It was less desirable for an accused than a provocation defence, in that it resulted in the accused, if convicted, being placed in the system of criminal psychiatric detentions; nonetheless, it once again provided a way to get medical evidence in front of the jury.

The two defences can be run concurrently; indeed, as soon as there is evidence that could raise a question of provocation, the judge is obliged to instruct the jury on this matter, even if the defence has not raised it. The result is a somewhat peculiar dynamic in a trial situation: even if the medical evidence may not be

---

[9] [1996] 1 WLR 1174.

introduced with the provocation defence in mind, but instead for diminished responsibility, who is to know how it will influence the jury, which is not necessarily as savvy about the use of expert evidence as legal academics would like to think?

New judicial spaces were therefore opening up for testimony relating to the psychological state of the accused. This may explain why homosexual panic enters the theoretical lexicon for homicides in situations of homosexual advances. This happened originally in the United States.[10] Homosexual panic was first identified by Edward J Kempf, an American clinical psychiatrist, in his 1920 book, *Psychopathology*.[11] The intellectual background to the diagnosis is Freudian, based most obviously on the Schreber Case.[12] Kempf defines 'acute homosexual panic' as 'a panic due to the pressure of uncontrollable sexual perverse cravings'. The condition is identified in cases of repressed homosexuality. When the individual is placed in an all-male environment, an army barracks being perhaps the classic example, the cravings become more difficult to control. The subject is both in terror of the homosexual feelings, but also afraid of the heterosexual relations required by the role the subject is at least ostensibly attempting to lead. In the result, the subject feels he is losing control of himself—feelings of hypnotism were typical, or feelings of being controlled by others, or even psychotic symptoms:

A patient might complain that 'someone is "throwing voices"' into his head, making him hear voices or have visions, making him have a peculiar taste in his mouth, putting poison in his food, shooting electricity into his body, hypnotizing him, going to kill, crucify, initiate him, or make him join a society or religion, or steal his manhood, etc.[13]

The subject's defence measures were typically self-punishing: self-inflicted injury, occasional suicidal tendencies, or depression. While Kempf mentions the possibility of violence against persons perceived to be making a sexual advance, his case studies do not actually provide instances of this. The non-violent nature of the disorder is further reflected in a 1947 paper by Robert E James, where subjects are described as responding by weeping and fear of persecution, helplessness, lacking social confidence, and in similar relatively passive terms.[14]

---

[10] The first case would appear to be *R v Rodrigues* 256 Cal App 2d 663, 64 Cal Reptr 253 (1967). Other significant cases include *People v Parisie* 287 NE 2d 310 (Ill App Ct, 1972); *Parisie v Greer*, 705 F 2d 882 (7th Cir, 1983); *State v Oliver* No 49613, (Ohio Ct App, 1985).

[11] FE Kempf, *Psychopathology* (St Louis, 1920).

[12] S Freud, 'Psycho-Analytic Notes upon an Autobiographical Account of a Case of Paranoia (*Dementia Paranoides*)' in J Strachey (ed) *Standard Edition of the Complete Psychological Works of Sigmund Freud* (London, 1911) vol 12, 1–84.

[13] Kempf, n 11 above, 479.

[14] RE James, 'Precipitating factors in acute homosexual panic (Kempf's Disease) with a case presentation' (1947) 2 *Quarterly Review of Psychiatry and Neurology* 530. For a similar characterization of those affected as lacking social confidence and being passive, see B Karpman, 'Mediate Psychotherapy and the Acute Homosexual Panic (Kempf's Disease)' (1943) 98 *Journal of Nervous and Mental Disease* 493–506.

The triggering factors in the classic definition do not involve sexual advances. Such was not a factor in any of Kempf's original nineteen cases; and James reports the triggering events to be (as with Kempf) sequestration in an all-male environment, or the loss of a man to whom the subject is particularly attached.

From the 1950s, these factors, the triggering event and the response, become less narrowly defined. Burton Glick, writing in 1959 about homosexual panic in the *Journal of Nervous and Mental Diseases*,[15] suggests that a distinction may be drawn between acute homosexual panic and acute aggression panic, triggered by a homosexual advance. While Glick seems to argue for a distinction in cases of violence, the association between aggression and homosexual panic does seem to move into the medical mindset. The condition begins to show up fairly routinely in the sections of textbooks devoted to psychiatric emergencies. The tenth edition of Henderson and Gillespie's *Textbook on Psychiatry*, for example, describes paranoia, suspicion, and aggression as the result of a belief that the subject has discovered in himself, or that others perceive in him, homosexual feelings.[16] In 1985, Walter[17] showed how far this line of argument had moved. Gone is any discussion of all-male environments, or quiet depression. Walter states:

Given a situation where repressed ego needs are thwarted by [a] disparate and convoluted network of barriers which prohibit accommodation, the sudden recognition of the emergent repressed needs can cause a panic reaction in the service of denial. Defensively, the panic reaction allows an emotional catharsis of repressed internal demands via a hostile transference onto an external scapegoat. Although there are varying forms of homosexual panic reactions, the key elements of homosexual panic and acted-out violence consist of a recognition of repressed needs; and the hostile assignment of those needs onto an external source.[18]

In this case, the accused had met the deceased in a pub, drunk with him all day, been treated to a meal, and then invited back to the deceased's hotel room. He stated that there, the deceased had groped him. He strangled the deceased with his hands, mutilated the genital organs of the deceased, and placed the body in the bath. He then pilfered the room of money and valuables, and left (returning later to pick up a knife he had apparently forgotten). Forensic evidence showed that he had ejaculated on the body, after it was placed in the bath. This is a long way from Kempf's paradigm: the panic was not brought about by an all-male environment, or the loss of a loved one. The accused (aged 30) still lived with his parents, not in any all-male institutional environment, and the result of the panic is not passive despair, but a rather violent murder.

---

[15] BS Glick, 'Homosexual Panic: Clinical and Theoretical Considerations' (1957) 129 *Journal of Nervous and Mental Disease* 20.

[16] I Batchelor, *Henderson and Gillespie's Textbook of Psychiatry*, 10th edn (Oxford, 1969) 445.

[17] R Walter, 'Homosexual panic and murder' (1985) 6(1) *American Journal of Forensic Medicine and Pathology* 49–51.   [18] ibid, 49.

Walter's 1985 paper does continue to view the case in Freudian terms of repressed homosexuality. While that does not seem to have disappeared entirely, we can see something of a move away from a particularly tight Freudian straitjacket. This can perhaps be identified, for example, between the first two editions of Freedman *et al's Comprehensive Textbook of Psychiatry.* The first, 1967, edition reflects Kempf's initial, Freudian approach.[19] The second, 1975, edition begins by referring to 'delusions and hallucinations that accuse the patient, in derisive and contemptuous terms, of a variety of homosexual practices'[20] without particular reference to repression, ids, and egos. Again, that is consistent with a move in psychiatric discourse of this period away from a fixation on Freud.

Consistent with that progression, and at about the same time, issues relating to both homosexuality and to neurotic disorders, under which homosexual panic was still classified, were increasingly open to dispute in psychiatric circles. Homosexual panic had been contained expressly as such a disorder in DSM-II. Under DSM-III, it disappears, along with other neuroses. As discussed above, though, it remains in standard medical texts as a type of psychiatric emergency.

Consistent with the fracturing of psychological literature on the subject, the American case law suggests a variety of theoretical frameworks for homosexual panic.[21] The first theory grows from Kempf's original conception: a repressed homosexual man, confronted with sexual advance, 'panics' due to a combination of revulsion and desire.[22] The second theory or group of theories perceives homosexual panic in terms of personal disturbance or personality type, rather than pathology. This sort of theory may parallel Kempf's model, insisting that the individual affected must be homosexual; but declines to pathologize the condition. Alternatively, this sort of theory may instead associate the condition not with repressed homosexuality, but with an overly aggressive personality.[23] A third theory denies the separate identity of homosexual panic at all, but instead theorizes it as a manifestation of another mental illness, generally schizophrenia, it would seem.[24]

The legal system should be understood as an active player in this development. It seems that criminal proceedings have been the most significant recent use of the homosexual panic classification. In a trial situation, defence lawyers ask specific questions of psychiatric experts, initially in written reports and then in the witness

[19] A Freedman and H Kaplan (eds) *Comprehensive Textbook of Psychiatry* (Baltimore, 1967) ch 26.3, regarding homosexuality in general, and ibid, 1181 regarding homosexual panic in particular.

[20] A Freedman, H Kaplan, and B Sadock (eds) *Comprehensive Textbook of Psychiatry,* 2nd edn, 1975. See also ch 24.15a, where the Freudian approach is much less central to the analysis of homosexuality generally.

[21] See H Chuang and D Addington, 'Homosexual Panic: A Review of its Concept' (1988) 33 *Canadian Journal of Psychiatry* 613–17.

[22] This theory is evident, eg, in *State v Thornton* 532 SW 2d 37 (Mo Ct App, 1975) and *State v Oliver,* No 49613 (Ohio Ct App, 1985).   [23] See ibid.

[24] See, eg *People v Parisie* 287 NE 2d 310 (Ill App Ct, 1972), *Parisie v Greer* 705 F 2d 882 (7th Cir, 1983).

box. Those questions will be directed specifically to the criteria for provocation or diminished responsibility, and less to the generalities of diagnostic criteria. It is thus not surprising to see the diagnostic structures develop as a result of the inter-action with the legal system.

This contextualization of homosexual panic within the legal system places the disorder in a particularly volatile political space. Critics of the case law complain that the resulting courtroom dynamic places the deceased on trial, portraying him as a predator of a vulnerable younger man. They complain that the existence of partial defences in these cases trivializes the murder of gay men in social terms.[25] These are serious criticisms, and should not be dismissed lightly. There are con-cerns about the legal ramifications of homosexual panic, however. If homosexual panic were not associated with a partial defence to murder, it is difficult to see that its most vocal critics would be much concerned about it.

Nonetheless, as things have developed, it is difficult to see that homosexual panic as a concept progresses the understanding of gay sexual homicides very far. Of the three theories identified above, the first requires an uncritical acceptance of Freud, a view that now appears unusual. The second would not cloak the events in pathological terms. For the third, it is fair to wonder whether homosexual panic adds much to the schizophrenia or other disorder with which the individual is affected. Homosexual panic seems to lead to a dead end in furthering the analysis.

There is a broader psychological literature related to sexual homicide,[26] but it is difficult to apply in a gay context. It is uniformly assumed in this literature that the assailant is male, and the deceased female. While this may represent the statistical prevalences,[27] it does import a set of gender-related dynamics into the analysis. Sometimes, misogyny is taken to be central to the analysis, with the crimes theorized as displaced matricides.[28] It is not obvious how such Oedipal

---

[25] See, eg K Banks, 'The "Homosexual Panic" Defence in Canadian Criminal Law' (1997), CR (5th) 371; G Comstock, 'Dismantling The Homosexual Panic Defense' (1992) 2 *Law and Sexuality* 81; Editors of the *Harvard Law Review*, 'Recent Developments: Sexual Orientation and the Law' (1989) 102 *Harvard Law Review* 1508; A Lunny, 'Provocation and "Homosexual" Advance: Masculinized Subjects As Threat, Masculinized Subjects Under Threat' (2003) 12(3) *Social and Legal Studies* 311–33; R Mison, 'Homophobia in Manslaughter: The Homosexual Advance as Insufficient Provocation' (1992) 80 *California Law Review* 133; New South Wales, Attorney General's Department, Criminal Law Review Division, 'Homosexual Advance Defence: Final Report of the Working Party' (Sydney: 1998); S Oliver, 'Provocation and Non-violent Homosexual Advances' (1999) 63(6) *Journal of Criminal Law* 586. For a partial defence of the use of provocation in these cases, see J Dressler, 'When "Heterosexual" Men kill "Homosexual" Men: Reflections on Provocation Law, Sexual Advances, and the "Reasonable Man" Standard' (1995) 85 *Journal of Criminal Law and Criminology* 726–63.
[26] See, eg R Meloy, 'The Nature and Dynamics of Sexual Homicide: An Integrative Review' (2000) 5(1) *Aggression and Violent Behavior* 1; E Beauregard and J Proulx, 'Profiles in the Offending Process of Nonserial Sexual Murderers' (2002) 46(4) *International Journal of Offender Therapy and Comparative Criminology* 386; S Porter, M Woodworth, J Earle, J Drugge, and D Boer, 'Characteristics of Sexual Homicides Committed by Psychopathic and Nonpsychopathic Offenders' (2003) (27)5 *Law and Human Behavior* 459; L Schlesinger, *Sexual Murder: Catathymic and Compulsive Homicides* (Boca Raton, 2004).
[27] ibid, 8, and sources cited therein.   [28] Meloy, n 26 above, 14.

dynamics can be translated into the gay context. While this broader literature may yield some general approaches of relevance in the gay context, as the section below will show, gay homicides seem to be noticeably different.

At the same time, it will be argued below that there appears to be little distinguishing the cases of homosexual advance from other gay homicides. It will thus be argued that while psychology has an important role to play in understanding why gay murders occur, it is not obviously productive to focus on the fact of the alleged homosexual advance in understanding these events. Psychology must look more broadly to gay murders as a whole.

The Cases

The basic demographics of the cases in the CPS sample already suggest differences from heterosexual sexual homicides. Perpetrators in the gay cases appear in general to be considerably younger than in heterosexual murders—a median age of 23 years in the CPS sample, compared to a mean of 30 in Grubin's[29] study of heterosexual sexual murder. Victims are also older in gay murders—a median of 43 years in the current study, compared to 38 years in Grubin's.

Intent appears to work very differently. In the heterosexual cases, it would seem that the intent to commit a crime of violence, and perhaps the intent to kill, is often formulated in advance. The victim is frequently stalked, or her house is broken into, apparently with the intent of committing sexual violence. Sadistic sexual fantasy is often part of the way these are understood. Power relations in these cases are in that way unambiguous: these heterosexual cases are about intent to harm, often for sexual gratification. Certainly there are some serial murders. Three murderers in the current study killed someone else in the study, and two others someone outside the study. In these cases, the pattern identified above fits to a greater or lesser degree.

These are the exceptions, however. Much more frequently, power relations between the accused and the deceased are much more ambiguous. The fact that the accused and the deceased are the same sex removes the male/female dynamic to the power relations. There is not necessarily a dynamic introduced by different sexual orientations. Sexuality, is of course, a very difficult category to code empirically, but if 'gay' is understood to refer to a man who has had sex with another man previously as an adult for fun rather than profit, somewhere between half and two-thirds of the killers in the sample can be considered gay. An anti-gay animus is conspicuously absent even from the cases where the assailant is apparently heterosexual. In only a few of the cases in the sample—something like three—is there an articulated homophobic intent. 'Queer-bashing' in any direct or simplistic sense is thus not a useful framework for analysis here.

---

[29] D Grubin, 'Sexual Murder' (1994) 165 *British Journal of Psychiatry* 624.

Power dynamics are nonetheless an inescapable factor in the homicides. Of the killers, 78 per cent were on benefits at the time of the killing, as compared to 45 per cent of the deceased. As noted, the perpetrators in the gay homicides were on average 20 years younger than their victims. The age and class differentials raise a different range of potential questions about the power dynamics between the key actors. In some ways, the increased age may bring a perception of increased experience, which, particularly when combined with increased socio-economic power, may suggest a position of power or authority. That said, youth has its attractions in a sexual context, and may imply a higher level of physical strength. Power relations are thus not clear-cut in these cases. Certainly, though, the killers frequently describe themselves in terms suggesting disempowerment or betrayal of trust. That may, for example, involve the older man serving as confidante to the younger, with the subsequent sexual advance being perceived as betrayal. It may alternatively be that the violence is perceived by the accused as the only way to terminate an unwanted sexual encounter. In one case, for example, the accused met the deceased in a gay bar, and understood that sex would be likely to occur when they went home together. The accused had just broken up with a boyfriend, and had nowhere else to go. He states that he considered the sexual come-ons by the deceased to be within the realm of expected behaviour: it seems that it did not occur to the accused, or that the accused did not see it as appropriate, simply to say no. The violence resulted.

The power issues are complicated by the fact that it is relatively uncommon that there is any indication that violence, let alone murder, is planned in advance. Gay killings seem much more likely to be impulsive than their heterosexual counterparts.

The professional testimony in the files, almost always by a psychiatrist rather than a psychologist, raises as many questions as it answers. Diagnoses were made for thirty patients. Homosexual panic was given as a diagnosis for two accused persons in the sample, once in 1993 being cited by a prison psychiatrist and once in 1992 by a defence psychiatrist. In neither case was it successful to ground a provocation defence. In the former case, the accused eventually pleaded to murder, and in the latter, received a diminished responsibility conviction. In the latter case, there were multiple psychiatrists, and as personality disorder was the most frequent diagnosis, it seems reasonable to question how relevant the homosexual panic diagnosis in fact was. Since thirty-nine of the seventy-eight killers in the study alleged that they had responded violently to an unwelcome sexual advance by the deceased, this low frequency of homosexual panic diagnosis is notable. It does not appear that these accused necessarily did not receive other diagnoses. Indeed, seventeen of them, including the two diagnosed with homosexual panic, were diagnosed with a psychiatric disorder. For nine of these, the disorder was sufficiently serious that the author of the report supported a plea of diminished responsibility, and in six cases that plea was successful. It is significant that here, as in the sample more generally, the primary diagnosis was personality disorder, ascribed to ten accused. This may perhaps be unsurprising, as the behaviour patterns of these individuals tends to disclose the hallmarks of personality disorder: eight had been sent to special schools or placed in care in their youth; eight had a history of violence, all had criminal records, and five had criminal records of violent offending.

This focus on personality disorder is not unique to those who stated they were responding to homosexual advances. In the sample as a whole, nineteen of the thirty accused who were given diagnoses were identified as personality disordered. By comparison, only three people were diagnosed as having a psychotic disorder associated with schizophrenia, and four had mental impairments (two of whom were also identified as having personality disorder). That gives some cause for pause, as the academic literature would suggest that diagnoses of personality disorder have in the past not been statistically very reliable.[30] Certainly, a number of other accused appear to have long histories of disruptive behaviour which might be expected to justify a personality disorder diagnosis. Overall, roughly half of the sample had either been sent to a special school or taken into care in childhood, two-thirds had a history of violence, 95 per cent had criminal records at the time of their arrest for the homicide, and about half had a criminal record for a violent offence. It is fair to wonder if there is an element of luck of the draw about who received diagnoses of personality disorder.

The medical reports in the sample are relevant primarily to pleas of diminished responsibility. For twenty-one accused, at least one psychiatrist considered the disorder diagnosed sufficiently severe to raise an issue of diminished responsibility. In roughly half of these cases, there was agreement between at least one defence and one Crown psychiatrist. Diminished responsibility was pleaded nineteen times, and was successful in thirteen of those cases. In all six cases where it was not successful, the diagnosis in question was personality disorder, suggesting some scepticism on the part of juries. In the eight personality disorder cases where it was successful in bringing about a diminished responsibility result, the Crown or prison psychiatrist concurred in the diagnosis. Such concurrence was not necessarily sufficient to convince juries, however: in four of the six unsuccessful personality disorder pleas for diminished responsibility, the Crown or prison psychiatrist was also in agreement with the diagnosis.

A few of the medical reports do not speak to diminished responsibility, but instead to provocation. Among the seventy-eight killers, provocation was pleaded by thirty-one, of whom thirteen were successful at trial and an additional three on appeal. Of these thirty-one cases, all but five alleged provocation based on homosexual advance. Interestingly, in five of the unsuccessful provocation pleas and in five of the successful ones, medical diagnoses were present. In some of these, the diagnosis appears to have been peripheral to the provocation question,

[30] See, eg J Gunn, 'Personality Disorders' in J Gunn and P Taylor (eds) *Forensic Psychiatry: Clinical, Legal and Ethical Issues* (Oxford, 1993) 373, 377.

but in others, medical evidence seems to be addressing the provocation question directly. It is not always clear how medical these matters are. Consider, for example, the following portion of a medical report:

It appears to me that this killing was the result of [assailant's] being touched by [deceased], which he hated, and he warned [deceased] to leave him alone. [Deceased's] advances did not stop and [assailant's] reaction of uncontrollable rage, being under the influence of alcohol, resulted in the killing of [deceased].

The doctor does not find a medical diagnosis in this case, but instead sets the scene for a provocation plea, which was successful in this case. There is a question here of the appropriateness of the testimony. If the doctor's view is that the pivotal factors were outside the medical arena, then that doctor was not testifying about matters that were necessarily in his area of expertise.

The similarities between the homosexual advance cases and the other sexual homicides is considerably broader than the overlapping diagnostic categories. The demographic profiles are similar between the two groups. Further, characteristics of the homicides themselves have some similarities. It is often very difficult to ascribe convincing motives to the homicides. They do not generally appear to be planned in advance; indeed, in only twenty cases did the accused bring the weapon to the scene of the homicide, apart from cases where the accused used his own clothing to effect the death. Notwithstanding the lack of planning and the lack of obvious motive, the homicides tend to be committed with exceptional violence. There are shades here of the early homosexual panic discourse, which referred to bodily mutilation. While mutilation per se was rare in the sample, exceptional violence against the deceased was commonplace. While it was common that the accused would have been drinking, relevance of other drugs was very uncommon. Again with shades of the early homosexual panic discourse, roughly half the men in the homosexual advance group had been sexually active with men in the past, a proportion only slightly less than the non-homosexual advance group.

It is difficult to see that the continuation of a focus distinguishing between homosexual advance and other gay sexual murder cases is sustainable. The psychological literature seems to have been focused as a result of the trial process into boxes relating to legal defences, and the structure of the older provocation defence still seems to control the dynamic of the professional thinking in this area. That may be inevitable for courtroom reports, although the recent decision in *AG for Jersey v Holley*,[31] re-asserting a stronger objective test to the reasonableness of the 'reasonable man' of provocation, may reduce the relevance of psychiatric testimony in that area. The similarity overall of the gay homicide cases does suggest that the current approach, based on the behaviour of the accused as flowing implicitly from the behaviour of the deceased, may not tell us much about the nature of the

---

[31] [2005] UKPC 23.

homicides, however. It would seem that instead of an implied focus in part on the actions of the deceased, the relevant issue is the psychological state of the accused. Part of that will no doubt involve his attitudes to homosexuality, and his feelings at involvement in such activity; but it is not obvious that this is the only criterion.

As a somewhat different approach, Revitch and Schlesinger[32] offer a motivational model for understanding sexual homicide. They place homicide on a continuum, from those homicides instigated by external factors, to those precipitated by internal or psychogenic factors. Their spectrum has five categories, three towards the former end of the scale, and two towards the latter. They categorize homicides as environmental, situational, impulsive, catathymic, or compulsive.[33] When applied to sexual homicide, these categories suffer from the gendered articulation discussed above: the assumption is that this is about men killing women. Nonetheless, the categories do provide some assistance.

These seem to fit best into the impulsive and acute catathymic categories. Schlesinger provides the following characteristics of impulsive offenders who commit homicide:

- a history of multiple anti-social acts;
- offences are poorly structured, committed without planning;
- frequent involvement in amateurish and semi-professional crime;
- lifestyle characterized by lack of direction, random actions, and unpredictability;
- offenders are passive, easily led, and overreact to environmental circumstances;
- personality is loosely integrated, with strong feelings of inadequacy;
- frequent history of developmental disabilities (eg ADHD, learning and speech problems, minor physical handicaps);
- chronic feelings of hostility and anger, and a non-specific need for revenge;
- may not have impulse control disorder per se.[34]

There is a considerable overlap here with the offenders in the current sample. Much of this speaks directly to the questions of alienation shown above to be prevalent in the current sample of offenders: they have histories of anti-social acts and crime, lives with little direction, and histories of violence suggesting hostility and anger. A further advantage of this approach is that it re-focuses the analysis back onto the assailant. At the very least, it provides some sort of a fresh starting point for psychological analysis of murderers of gay men.

---

[32] L Schlesinger, *Sexual Murder: Catathymic and Compulsive Homicides* (Boca Raton, 2004).
[33] ibid, 91.   [34] ibid, 102.

Conclusion

The empirical study of the CPS records suggests that sexual murders of gay men are sufficiently similar as to form a coherent object of study. The existing psychological literature is sparse, and has focused on the concept of homosexual panic. It is difficult to see that this takes the understanding of the murders very far. Nonetheless, psychologists should have a role in furthering the understanding of these deaths. It is an important set of problems waiting for serious study.

19

Trial by Jury Involving Persons Accused of Terrorism or Supporting Terrorism

Neil Vidmar

Introduction

This paper explores issues in jury trials involving persons accused of committing acts of international terrorism or financially or otherwise supporting those who do or may commit such acts. The jury is a unique institution that draws upon laypersons to decide whether a person charged with a crime is guilty or innocent. Although the jury is instructed and guided by a trial judge and procedural rules shape what the jury is allowed to hear, ultimately the laypersons deliberate alone and render their verdict.[1] A basic principle of the jury system is that at the start of trial the jurors should have open minds and regard the accused as innocent until proven guilty.

The paper raises issues about jurors' assumptions of innocence in the aftermath of terrorist bombings in the United States, England, Bali, Spain, and elsewhere when persons are persons accused of committing acts of terrorism or indirectly supporting terrorists through financing organizations associated with terrorism. A study of a US trial involving charges of supporting terrorism is used to illustrate the problem, but the thesis of this chapter is that the basic issues apply to trials that might be held in England, Australia, Canada, or other countries with jury systems.

Contemporary International Terrorism and its Public Perception

While recognizing that terrorism can take many forms and may be driven by different ideologies, the paper is concerned with the era following al-Qaeda-inspired attacks on New York City's World Trade Center and the US Military's Pentagon Building in

---

[1] N Vidmar, 'A Historical and Comparative Perspective on the Common Law Jury' in N Vidmar (ed), *World Jury Systems* (Oxford, 2000).

Washington on September 11, 2001,[2] the 2002 bombings in Bali that killed many Australians,[3] the 2004 bombings in Madrid,[4] the 2005 bombings in the centre of London and ongoing fears in each country about future attacks.[5] The perpetrators of these attacks have been associated with al-Qaeda's hostility to the United States and its allies because of their hegemony in political, military, and cultural spheres in the Middle East and other parts of the world. The perpetrators have been members of the Muslim faith or linked in some way to that faith. Most are of Middle Eastern or Pakistani ethnic descent. Many were citizens or legal residents of the countries that were the targets of terrorism.

The threat is ongoing. Government leaders have informed their publics that the dangers stem not just from those associated directly with al-Qaeda but organizations that share roughly similar goals with that organization. Western-oriented governments have passed measures that are directed toward not just the terrorists themselves, but also any persons who support those organizations through financing or other means. Government-sponsored websites give detailed accounts of terrorist threats and the steps that are being taken to counter the threats.[6] Public leaders in the United States, England, and Australia, among others, have continually emphasized the threat of terrorist organizations to Western life-styles and political structures. This is not to claim that these concerns and warnings are unwarranted, but the result is that whole citizenries consider themselves to be victims.[7] This sense of being a victim goes beyond just the threat of physical harm to themselves, loved ones, or acquaintances, but also threats to their deeply held personal values, national membership, and culture. Some of these attitudes have been expressed in racial and religious slurs or violence against persons identified as Muslim or Arab.[8]

These attitudes have serious implications for the right to trial by a fair and impartial jury because they may influence the way that jurors perceive and evaluate trial evidence. Not everyone accused of acts of terrorism or of indirectly supporting terrorists is necessarily guilty. The central issue is whether ordinary procedural safeguards of the jury system will be sufficient to ensure a fair trial or

---

[2] Archives of the September 11, 2001 terrorist attack on America at the World Trade Center Towers in New York City and The Pentagon in Washington, DC <http://www.september11news.com/>.

[3] <http://en.wikipedia.org/wiki/2005_Bali_bombings>; <http://edition.cnn.com/SPECIALS/2002/bali/>.

[4] <http://en.wikipedia.org/wiki/March_11,_2004_Madrid_attacks>; BBC News Online readers react to the Madrid bombings, <http://news.bbc.co.uk/1/hi/in_depth/europe/2004/madrid_train_attacks/default.stm>.

[5] <http://www.cnn.com/SPECIALS/2005/london.bombing>; <http://news.bbc.co.uk/1/hi/uk/4661059.stm>.

[6] For the US, <http://www.dhs.gov/dhspublic/index.jsp>; for the UK, <http://www.mi5.gov.uk>; for Australia, <http://www.nationalsecurity.gov.au>.

[7] For the UK, <http://www.cpcr.org.uk/eventreport.html>.

[8] For the US, <http://unisci.com/stories/20014/1129014.htm>; for the UK, <http://www.jihadwatch.org/dhimmiwatch/archives/004325.php>; for Australia, <http://www.hreoc.gov.au/racial_discrimination/isma/consultations/launch_speech.html>.

whether additional steps might be necessary. Because trial procedures—and their underlying presumptions—differ from country to country, a first step is to consider these differences.

Comparative Perspective on Trial Prejudice and Legal Remedies

Procedural Perspective

Among the more than fifty common law countries and territories that still retain trial by jury[9] the United States is unique in a number of important ways. The mass media have almost unfettered ability to cover all phases related to a trial, including pre-trial hearings, as well as the trial itself.[10] In some state courts proceedings are televised live. This access of the media relates to the US Constitution's First Amendment providing for freedom of the press and that amendment's interpretation by the US Supreme Court. However, even before the age of mass media, indeed, even before the American Revolution, trial procedures had begun to shift from their English origins, in that jurors were questioned about their biases by the two sides involved in the criminal or civil dispute.[11]

Today, in the process known as *voir dire*, jurors in the United States are questioned about their biases and subject to challenges for cause or peremptory challenges before being seated on the jury. In some high profile trials, particularly in state courts, the process of jury selection may take days or weeks of questioning by the lawyers for the contending sides before a jury is seated. Often the judge, with input from the two contending sides, will send the members of the selected jury pool a lengthy questionnaire to be filled out before their court appearance and their answers are used as a basis of *voir dire* questioning. Attention needs to be drawn to differences between federal court trial procedures in comparison to many state courts. In most cases today the federal trial judge, rather than the contending lawyers, conducts the *voir dire* questioning. The *voir dire* is truncated, usually involving only a few questions about impartiality, although as I will describe below, there are exceptions to this general rule. Additionally, federal courts prohibit cameras of any kind in the courtroom.

Finally, despite the remedial procedure of *voir dire*, a change of venue is possible when one of the parties can convince a judge that *voir dire* will be insufficient to obtain a fair and impartial jury. In other instances lawyers in federal courts have persuaded judges to expand *voir dire* questioning and allow the parties to participate in the process.[12]

---

[9] N Vidmar (ed), *World Jury Systems* (Oxford, 2000); N Vidmar, 'Juries and Law Assessors in the Commonwealth: A Contemporary Survey' (2002) 13 *Criminal Law Forum* 385–407.

[10] N King, 'The American Criminal Jury' in N Vidmar (ed), *World Jury Systems* (Oxford, 2000).

[11] N Vidmar and V Hans, ch 3 in *American Juries*, book manuscript in preparation.

[12] A 'continuance' to allow prejudice to dissipate is an alternative measure to change of venue, but is seldom used.

For our purposes here, it is also important to draw attention to another fact, namely that American judges do not engage in 'summing up' the evidence during their charge to the jury. In fact some state constitutions forbid the practice.[13]

In contrast to American practices, other common law countries place strong emphasis on pre-trial, mid-trial and post-trial restraints on media.[14] The contempt power of judges is used to attempt to constrain media publicity that might affect jurors. In some instances post-trial reporting may be controlled if it is believed that it would jeopardize future proceedings against a defendant or co-defendants, or if it would otherwise bring the administration of justice into disrepute. Going still further, jurors in these countries are either proscribed or strongly discouraged from discussing jury room deliberations with representatives from mass media sources. In most of these other countries jurors are forbidden from discussing jury deliberations with anyone.

Prior restraint is not a perfect remedy for trial prejudice. In an article in the *Criminal Law Review* Corker and Levi have noted a shift in case law in England and Wales wherein courts have recognized that pre-trial publicity can cause substantial prejudice, in part because the policing mechanisms are limited.[15] Sometimes prejudicial publicity is generated before charges are laid and sometimes afterwards. In addition, focusing solely on media coverage does not take into account potential prejudice arising from pre-existing prejudices against accused persons because of their ethnic or religious identities or prejudice that can arise from widespread community gossip about the alleged crime or the accused person.[16]

Concomitantly, these other common law countries rely heavily on the presumptions that, first, jurors as called remain 'impartial between the Queen [or State] and the accused' and secondly, that judicial instructions on their oath to be impartial plus guidance, including 'summing up,' will off-set any biases. Finally, remedies such as a temporary stay of proceedings, or in extreme cases, a permanent stay, may be made. In others a change of venue is considered as a remedy.

Australia and New Zealand have a similar approach to the criminal trial.[17] There are proscriptions about mass media reporting of substantive matters disclosed in pre-trial proceedings and the press or other persons may not query jurors after trial with the intent of publishing anything about jury deliberations. The jurors are chosen as randomly called from the jury panel. After a limited number of peremptory challenges for each side are exercised, the surviving jurors

---

[13] King, n 10 above.   [14] Vidmar, n 1 above.

[15] D Corker and M Levi, 'Pretrial Publicity and Its Treatment in the English Courts' (1996) *Criminal Law Review* 622.

[16] N Vidmar, 'Case Studies of Pre- and Mid-trial Prejudice in Criminal and Civil Litigation' (2002) 26 *Law and Human Behavior* 73.

[17] M Chesterman, 'Criminal Trial Juries in Australia: From Penal Colonies to a Federal Democracy' in N Vidmar (ed), *World Jury Systems* (Oxford, 2000); N Cameron, S Potter, and W Young, 'The New Zealand Jury: Towards Reform' in N Vidmar (ed), *World Jury Systems* (Oxford, 2000).

are seated. While theoretically available, the challenge for cause process is almost never used. Change of venue is a remedy when there is a concern about strong prejudice tainting the community. In England and Wales, even peremptory challenges have been abolished.[18]

Pre-trial Prejudice Issues

The issue of pre-trial prejudice in the United States arising from media coverage has been explored in great detail by both courts and academics.[19] This coverage includes the trial of Timothy McVeigh for bombing the federal courthouse in Oklahoma,[20] and John Walker Lindh, the 'American Taliban,' captured when the United States invaded Afghanistan.[21] The problem, however, arises in other countries as well.

English courts have struggled with a number of cases infected with potential pre-trial prejudice.[22] These are reviewed by Corker and Levi[23] and by Naylor.[24] The 'Maxwell' trial for fraud in the administration of pension schemes posed major problems of prejudice because of the massive negative media coverage throughout England and Wales and due to the fact that pensioners scattered throughout the country were affected when it was discovered that the pension funds were insolvent.[25] As a consequence, Justice Phillips, deviating from contemporary English practice, took the extraordinary step of interviewing prospective jurors in chambers in an attempt to seat an impartial jury. More recently, in *R v Bowyer* extensive media coverage of a Leeds United football player resulted in a mistrial due to media-generated publicity and difficulties when a second trial was attempted.[26]

Canada has struggled with issues of pre-trial publicity in a number of cases.[27] These include, but are far from limited to, the Mount Cashel cases, involving

[18] S Lloyd-Bostock and C Thomas, 'The Continuing Decline of the English Jury' in N Vidmar (ed), *World Jury Systems* (Oxford, 2000); The Auld Report at <http://www.criminal-courts-review.org.uk>.

[19] Vidmar, n 16 above, 73; C Studebaker and S Penrod, 'Pre-trial Publicity: The Media, the Law, and Common Sense' (1997) 3 *Psychology Public Policy and Law* 428; N Steblay *et al*, 'The Effects of Pretrial Publicity on Juror Verdicts: A Meta-analytic Review' (1999) 23 *Law and Human Behavior* 219.

[20] S Jones and H Hillerman, 'McVeigh, McJustice, McMedia' (1998) *Chicago Legal Forum* 53.

[21] N Vidmar, 'When All of Us Are Victims: Juror Prejudice and "Terrorist" Trials' (2003) 78 *Chicago-Kent Law Review* 1143.

[22] Naylor, 'Fair Trial or Free Press: Legal Responses to Media Reports of Criminal Trials' (1994) 53 *Cambridge Law Review* 492; Corker and Levi, n 15 above, 622; T Honess, S Barker, EA Charman, and Michael Levi, 'Empirical and Legal Perspectives on the Impact of Pretrial Publicity' (2002) *Criminal Law Review* 719.   [23] Corker and Levi, n 15 above, 622.

[24] Naylor, n 22 above, 492.

[25] *R v Maxwell* unreported 25 May 1995; F Gibb, 'The Result of the Maxwell Brothers' Case Has Put the System Under the Spotlight' *The Times*, January 30, 1996, at 31.

[26] <http://www.soccergaming.tv/archive/index.php/t-21015.html>; <http://www.portal.telegraph.co.uk/news/main.jhtml?xml=/news/2003/06/03/nposh103.xml>.

[27] In Canada, the judge may proscribe mass media publication of pre-trial proceedings if such publication might jeopardize the right to a fair trial; in fact the accused has the right to request that

sexual assaults by lay Catholic priests on boys under their care in the Mount Cashel Orphanage in St John's, Newfoundland, and the Bernardo trial involving the abduction, rape, and killing of teenage girls by Paul Bernardo and his wife, Karla Homulka.[28]

Analysing the Potential Effects of Prejudice: A Social and Psychological Perspective

Dimensions of Prejudice

Psychological research has shown that prejudicial attitudes and beliefs can affect the way in which trial evidence is perceived and evaluated, with the juror tending to accept evidence consistent with his or her prior beliefs and rejecting evidence inconsistent with those beliefs. In turn, the juror constructs narratives or stories of causation and guilt based around those beliefs.[29] Issues that have high emotional elements appear to be harder to overcome than factual material.[30] There is a substantial body of research investigating the effects of media articles on juror attitudes and beliefs. This research on mass media effects is critical but incomplete. It has not substantially addressed the effects of access to internet sites that often provide many details, correct or incorrect, about upcoming trials. More important, however, the focus on mass media ignores the sociological dimensions of trial prejudice. Prejudice is often embedded in a broader personal and community

---

the judge enter such an order. The proscription might even apply to the trial itself if publication might jeopardize a future trial of the accused or a co-accused. Jurors are proscribed from discussing their verdict under threat of a hefty fine and up to six months in jail. In typical trials jurors are randomly chosen from the venue and not questioned. Except for a limited number of peremptory challenges allowed to each side, the jurors are sworn and seated. Canada does allow exceptions to the pre-trial questioning process if one of the parties, usually the accused, convinces the judge that there is a likelihood of some jurors not being impartial due to pre-trial publicity. In these instances a limited number of questions may be put to potential jurors in what is called a 'challenge for cause'. Two 'triers' chosen from the jury pool then determine if the potential juror is impartial. A change of venue is available if the judge concludes that the community is sufficiently tainted that a challenge for cause proceeding, combined with juror instructions about the responsibility of their oath to remain impartial, would be insufficient to eliminate bias. See N Vidmar, 'The Canadian Criminal Jury: Searching for a Middle Ground', in N Vidmar (ed), *World Jury Systems* (Oxford, 2000).

[28] Vidmar, ibid.

[29] eg N Pennington and R Hastie, 'A Cognitive Theory of Juror Decision Making: The Story Model' (1991) 13 *Cardozo Law Review* 519, and 'Explaining the Evidence: Tests of the Story Model for Juror Decision Making' (1982) 62 *Journal of Personality and Social Psychology* 189; J Holstein, 'Juror's Interpretation and Jury Decision Making' (1985) 9 *Law and Human Behavior* 83; J Casper *et al*, 'Juror Decision Making, Attitudes and Hindsight Bias' (1989) 13 *Law and Human Behavior* 291; V Smith and C Studebaker, 'What Do You Expect?: The Effect of People's Knowledge of Crime Categories on Fact Finding' (1996) 20 *Law and Human Behavior* 517.

[30] T Honess, E Charman, and M Levi, 'Factual and Affective/Evaluative Recall of Pretrial Publicity: Their Relative Influence on Juror Reasoning and Verdict in a Simulated Fraud Trial' (2003) 33 *Journal of Applied Social Psychology* 1404.

context and may have powerful effects on juror attitudes and beliefs. This broader context is especially important in considering trials of accused terrorists and their supporters.

In previous articles I have described an intellectual framework for thinking about juror prejudice.[31] It contains four categories: interest prejudice, specific prejudice, generic prejudice and conformity prejudice.

Interest prejudice involves prejudices arising from a juror having a direct or indirect stake in the outcome of the trial. Case law has recognized, for example, that someone being affiliated with an accused may be deemed to be not impartial. In an article based on the John Walker Lindh case, I drew attention to the terrorist attacks of September 11 and its aftermath and argued that the attacks created fears not only about future physical attacks, but also perceived threats to American values and culture.[32] Research has demonstrated that when deep-rooted cultural and personal values are threatened, people respond with hostility to persons who are perceived as outsiders or otherwise different.[33]

Specific prejudice exists when the juror holds attitudes or beliefs about specific issues in the case at trial that prevent the juror from evaluating the trial evidence with an open mind. These attitudes and beliefs may result from many life experiences, including media coverage of issues. Mass media coverage of events both helps to create public perceptions and reflects community interests and attitudes. Rumour and gossip may generate prejudicial beliefs to jurors. Research with actual trials has shown that the information on which these beliefs are formulated is often erroneous and misleading.

Generic prejudice involves the transferring of pre-existing prejudices about categories of persons or other entities to the trial setting. Generic prejudices come into play in the terrorist trials by means of prejudicial attitudes toward Palestinians, Arabs and people of the Muslim faith or perceived Muslim faith. In short, the category of persons to which an accused is perceived to belong, such as an Arab or Muslim, may invoke assumptions of guilt in addition to the specific prejudice arising out of the long history of negative publicity leading up to and including the charges against the defendant.

---

[31] Vidmar, n 16 above, 73.

[32] Vidmar, n 21 above; N Gertner and J Mizner, *The Law of Juries* (San Francisco, 1970) 5.

[33] eg Greenberg *et al*, 'Terror Management Theory of Self Esteem and Cultural Worldviews: Empirical Assessments and Conceptual Refinements' in M Zanna (ed), *Advances in Experimental Social Psychology*, Vol. 29 (New York 1997) 61; Fishfader *et al*, 'Evidential and Extralegal Factors in Juror Decisions: Presentation Mode, Retention and Level of Emotionality' (1966) 20 *Law and Human Behavior* 565; Kerr *et al*, 'On the Effectiveness of *Voir Dire* In Criminal Cases With Prejudicial Pretrial Publicity: An Empirical Study' (1991) 40 *American University Law Review* 665; Kramer *et al*, 'Pretrial Publicity, Judicial Remedies and Jury Bias' (1990) 14 *Law and Human Behavior* 409; J Ogloff and N Vidmar, 'The Impact of Pretrial Publicity On Jurors: A Study to Compare the Effects of Television and Print Media In a Child Sex Abuse Case' (1994) 18 *Law and Human Behavior* 507. On the other hand, there is evidence that strong emotional sympathies for victims also adversely affect rational decision making in verdicts, see N Feigenson, 'Sympathy and Legal Judgment: A Psychological Analysis' (1997) 65 *Tennessee Law Review* 1 for a review.

Conformity prejudice exists when the juror perceives that there is such strong community reaction in favor of a particular trial outcome that he or she is inclined to reach a verdict consistent with that perceived consensus rather than an impartial evaluation of the evidence. This is one of the most important factors and deserves greater elaboration.

One of the founders of modern sociology, Emile Durkheim, observed in 1893:

As for the social character of [penal] reaction, it comes from the social nature of the offended sentiments. Because they are found in all consciences, the infraction committed arouses in those who have evidence of it or who learn of its existence the same indignation. Everybody is attacked; consequently, everybody opposes the attack. Not only is the reaction general, but it is collective . . . It is not produced isolatedly in each one but with a totality and a unity of purpose . . . [34]

In a Canadian case involving the killing of a young child, a great deal of prejudice developed in the community even though a defence lawyer had obtained an order proscribing any media coverage.[35] People gossiped because they saw the killing as an odious event relevant to and reflecting on their community. The bombing of the Murrah Federal Building in Oklahoma in April 1995 with the loss of so many lives also caused discussion, rumour and gossip throughout the United States. It threatened community values and evoked calls for the death penalty as punishment. Importantly, citizens of Oklahoma City, where the bombing occurred, were strongest in their reactions and calls for justice but the prejudice was widespread throughout the state of Oklahoma. After reviewing testimony and survey data trial Judge Maitch of the US District Court concluded that 'the entire state had become a unified community, sharing the emotional trauma of those who had become directly victimized.'[36] In the decision to move the trial from Oklahoma, Judge Maitch reviewed various evidence and concluded that Oklahomans were 'united as a family,' that there was 'extraordinary provocation of their emotions of anger and vengeance,' that there was 'a prevailing belief that some action must be taken to make things right again,' and that the common reference in articulating these feelings was 'seeing that justice is done.'

Psychological research on trial prejudice has distinguished between potentially biasing factual beliefs and beliefs that have high negative affective content.[37] Beliefs involving negative affect are most likely to have effects on jury decision-making. For example, Honess, Charman and Levi conducted a study involving

[34] E Durkheim, *The Division of Labor in Society* (George Simpson, trans.) (1893/1967).

[35] N Vidmar and J Melnitzer, 'Juror Prejudice: An Empirical Study of a Challenge for Cause' (1984) 22 *Osgoode Hall Law Journal* 487.

[36] *US v McVeigh*, 955 Federal Supplement 1281 (US District Court, District of Colorado 1997); *see also US v McVeigh* Federal Supplement 1467, 1473 (US District Court, Western District of Oklahoma 1996).

[37] For reviews of this research, *see* N Steblay *et al*, 'The Effects of Pretrial Publicity on Juror Verdicts: A Meta-analytic Review' (1999) 23 *Law and Human Behavior* 219; C Studebaker and S Penrod, 'Pre-trial Publicity: The Media, the Law and Common Sense' (1997) 3 *Psychology, Public Policy and Law* 428; Vidmar, n 16 above.

a simulation of the *Maxwell* fraud trial, mentioned above.[38] The case involved four defendants accused of conspiring to defraud the beneficiaries of company retirement funds. In the actual trial the defendants were acquitted, but many persons were dissatisfied with the verdict.

The research was carried out some time after the trial had taken place and was intended to explore the effects of attitudes on juror reasoning processes. Jury-eligible participants were interviewed to determine their recall of the case and then asked to participate as jurors in an experiment involving a six-hour video simulation of the trial using actors working from verbatim transcripts and documents from the actual trial. The jurors were interviewed at four time periods throughout the trial presentation.

The results showed that the degree of jurors' factual recall of details about the *Maxwell* case had minimal influence on juror judgments about the trial evidence. In contrast, negative attitudes associated with the case did have an effect, but in a complicated and unexpected way. In the first interview period conducted during the simulation, jurors with greater degrees of negative effect about the *Maxwell* case were not significantly different than those with lesser negative effect. However, jurors with negative affective responses began to express reasoning favouring guilt at the end of the prosecution's case. This reasoning about guilt was maintained during and after the defence presentation. The authors of the research hypothesized that these jurors had withheld judgment at the early stages of evidence presentation because they were waiting for more evidence before reaching a decision, suggesting that the jurors were not pre-emptively deciding guilt but rather the negative attitudes had led them to interpret the evidence using a prosecutorial mental framework.

The Honess *et al* study is consistent with previous research and is highlighted here because it shows the subtle effects that negative attitudes can have on jurors' reasoning processes.

There is not space to further review additional research in this paper, but the basic findings lead to the conclusion that prejudice can be manifested at various points in the trial process and jeopardize an impartial evaluation of the evidence against an accused.[39] Specifically,

(1) it can prejudice jurors' initial assumptions about a defendant's guilt;

(2) it can improperly influence the evaluation of evidence through selective attention and weighting of evidence consistent with pre-existing biases;

(3) it can influence pre-deliberation preferences of verdicts;

(4) it can influence the initial distribution of juror verdicts that lead to the final verdict;

[38] T Honess, E Charman and M Levi, 'Factual and Affective/Evaluative Recall of Pretrial Publicity: Their Relative Influence on Juror Reasoning and Verdict in a Simulated Fraud Trial' (2003) 33 *Journal of Applied Social Psychology* 1404.   [39] Vidmar, n 16 above.

(5) it can promote jury deliberations that enhance the initial biases of the jurors;

(6) it can instigate a 'rotten apple' effect whereby one or more tainted jurors infect other jurors with emotional appeals during deliberation; and

(7) in the event that the evidence of guilt is near equipoise at the end of trial, the deliberations pre-existing juror attitudes can improperly tilt the jury toward a guilty verdict.

There is an important caveat to the implications of this research. Prejudicial attitudes are most likely to have their impact when the evidence supporting guilt or innocence is near equipoise. If the prosecution's case is very strong or very weak, the fact that some of the jurors hold prejudicial attitudes will not be of as much importance as when the evidence is close. Prejudicial attitudes come into play when there is ambiguity that allows jurors to justify their reasoning about evidence in a manner that is consistent with their pre-existing beliefs.

Al-Qaeda-linked Trials are Different than Routine Criminal Trials

As already indicated, after September 11, 2001 and the subsequent bombings in Bali, Spain and London, trials involving persons accused of al-Qaeda-linked terrorism are different in complexity and magnitude. All of the types of potential prejudice may be at play. There may be extensive media coverage of related events well before charges are laid. Statements by authority figures such as politicians and police, informal gossip, prejudicial racial and ethnic stereotypes of the accused, fears of personal harm for oneself and for loved ones and widely shared feelings of cultural victimization may all be present. A mere focus on mass media-based publicity deflects attention from these other factors that can improperly influence jury outcomes.

Jurors Sometimes Lack Self-awareness of their Prejudice

Sometimes judges address the whole panel of assembled jurors about the need to be impartial in deciding the case. They invite any jurors who believe they may not be impartial to identify themselves and then excuse them. The assumption is that the remaining panel members have open minds. A case study involving a Canadian couple accused of killing their child raised serious questions about this assumption.[40] Although the defence lawyers were successful in obtaining a ban against pre-trial media coverage, the death of the child aroused considerable community gossip, including very strong feelings against the two accused. At trial the judge addressed the whole panel of 125 jurors and asked any persons who could not be fair in judging the case to excuse themselves. Only a few persons did so. The judge

---

[40] N Vidmar and J Melnitzer, 'Juror Prejudice: An Empirical Study of a Challenge for Cause' (1984) 22 *Osgoode Hall Law Journal* 487; see also G Mize, 'On Better Jury Selection: Spotting Unfavorable Jurors Before They Enter The Jury Room' (1999) 36 *Court Review* 10.

then allowed a challenge for cause in which jurors were randomly called and questioned individually. Many of the persons who were questioned under this procedure admitted biases that they had not disclosed in response to the judge's original request to step forward. (Most were subsequently excused from the panel.)

There are different reasons for not disclosing bias, including simple unwillingness to admit bias in front of other jurors, but survey research in high profile criminal cases has shown that a major reason for some jurors, often substantial numbers of them, may be that these jurors are not self-cognizant of their biases. Another reason involves the tendency to give socially desirable responses, that is, say what they believe is expected of them.[41]

Telephone survey research for the expected trial of John Walker Lindh, the so-called 'American Taliban,' serves as a particular example. Mr Lindh, an American citizen, was captured along with Taliban fighters during the American invasion of Afghanistan.[42] He was brought back to the United States and faced numerous charges. In advance of trial, surveys of jury-eligible persons were conducted in the northern Virginia venue in which he was scheduled to be tried, as well as four other venues across the country: Chicago, Minneapolis, San Francisco and Seattle.

Citizens in Virginia were more likely to have been exposed to greater amounts of media publicity than other areas of the country[43] and the surveys revealed that Virginians were more likely to have known persons killed in the attacks. Nevertheless, levels of hostility toward Mr Lindh, as expressed in the surveys, were generally similar across all five locations.

The survey first asked the respondent a lengthy series of questions about Mr Lindh before asking if he or she could be a fair and impartial juror for his trial. While some persons said they could not be fair and impartial jurors, a substantial number said they could and explained why. However, among the self-professed impartial persons many had just offered responses to other questions that were in sharp contradiction to their professions of impartiality. These responses are documented in detail elsewhere,[44] but several examples help to illustrate the inconsistencies and raise serious questions about the jurors professed ability to be an impartial juror.

Respondent # 165 asserted she could be impartial in deciding Mr Lindh's guilt or innocence and explained why by saying 'It must be proven with facts.' Yet her just expressed responses to other questions on the survey indicated that she had a 'strongly unfavourable' impression of the accused and had said that 'he is a traitor,' that he was 'definitely guilty,' 'he killed Americans and should be shot.' That a jury's not guilty verdict would be 'very unacceptable,' that he should experience 'death by hanging' for the reason that 'I want him to feel pain.'

[41] Mize, n 40 above and Vidmar, n 16 above.   [42] Vidmar, n 21 above.
[43] Declaration of Steven Penrod in Support of Defendant John Walker Lindh's Motion to Dismiss, or in the Alternative, for Change of Venue, *United States v Lindh* (US District Court, Eastern District Virginia No 02-37-A).   [44] Vidmar, n 32 above.

Respondent # 506 also said he could be an impartial juror by explaining, 'I believe in the system and that everyone should have a fair trial.' But similar to Respondent # 165 other interview responses raise questions about his openness of mind. He said Mr Lindh was 'Punk-a traitor' who was 'definitely guilty' because 'they captured him with a gun in his hand where [a] CIA agent was killed.' This respondent further stated that if a trial by judge and jury found the accused not guilty, he would find the verdict 'very unacceptable.'

Respondent # 514 explained that she could be an impartial juror because 'I feel like it's my Christian duty to be fair, and listen to all of the things set forth in the courtroom; to me that's the most important thing—my responsibility as a citizen and my Christian duty to be fair.' Yet, like other respondents documented above, her earlier answers directly contradicted this profession of ability to be impartial. She had just said, 'I feel that he was a traitor to our country. And now that he's been caught, he's trying to reverse his decision in order to avoid paying the price;' 'It's because I feel he was a traitor who embraced the life of terrorism;' 'He has to be tried first but he was with them. He was training with them and didn't have a very good attitude when he was captured.'

In short, as these examples illustrate, there can be a substantial disjuncture between professions of having an open mind as a juror and expressed feelings and beliefs about an accused.

Case Study: The Trial of Dr Sami Al-Arian

Background: *United States v Sami Al-Arian*

Professor Sami Al-Arian, a Palestinian legal resident in the United States, holding a doctorate from an American university, was a professor of computer science at the University of Southern Florida.[45] Since the 1990s Professor Al-Arian had been an outspoken and harsh critic of US policies toward Israel and the Palestinians. Since 1995 he had been the subject of negative news coverage by the Tampa and St Petersburg, Florida newspapers. In 2003 Al-Arian and others were charged with supporting the Palestinian Islamic Jihad movement. Shortly after, Al-Arian was fired from his tenured university position on the grounds that he had improperly used his university position in support of Palestinian causes.

In 2005 Professor Al-Arian and three other men were scheduled for trial on multiple charges, including conspiracy to commit murder abroad, money laundering and obstruction of justice associated with other charges that the men had helped to organize and finance the Palestinian Islamic Jihad, a designated terrorist group that was responsible for more than a hundred deaths in Israel and the occupied territories. The Attorney General of the United States declared in front of

---

[45] For details of the case, including a copy of the indictment and other legal documents *see* <http://reports.tbo.com/reports/alarian> or <http://en.wikipedia.org/wiki/Sami_Al-Arian>.

national television cameras that the charges were an important strike against terrorism. Local and national newspapers carried many stories on the background leading up to the trial. Almost 1,000 articles related to Al-Arian in the *Tampa Bay Tribune* and *St Petersburg Times* between January 2001 and mid-April 2005. No systematic data was available for newspaper coverage in the decade before 2001, but the number of articles would number in the hundreds, perhaps higher. Al-Arian's notoriety played a prominent role in the 2004 primary elections for a US Senate seat when the former University of South Florida president, Betty Castor, running for that seat, was heavily criticized in advertisements for not firing Al-Arian much earlier than she did, and this probably contributed to her defeat. In those advertisements Al-Arian was described as a 'suspected terrorist.' Local television coverage of the arrest and charges was intense, including detailed television coverage of Al-Arian being led off in handcuffs after his arrest. Commentary characterizing him as a terrorist and alleging his guilt was featured on the nationally syndicated Fox network's 'O'Reilley Factor' television programme both before and after his arrest.

Al-Arian and the co-defendants denied that they condoned violent activities, and that any promotion of Islamic Jihad was protected by political speech permitted under the First Amendment of the US Constitution. They further contended that their money-raising efforts were to support Palestinian charities. If convicted, Al-Arian and his associates each faced several life sentences.

Concerns about Trial Prejudice

With this background as context, a series of questions arose about the ability to obtain a fair and impartial jury. Had the community been tainted by the long controversy involving Dr Al-Arian and the relevance of the controversy to the Tampa Bay area from which the jurors would be drawn? To be sure, the case received nationwide attention and was taking place in the still-resounding aftermath of the September 11, 2001 attacks, but the saturation of and relevance to the Tampa Bay community was extremely high. The Tampa Bay area has a large Jewish population that, some speculated, would be especially offended by Al-Arian's verbal attacks on Israel and Jews. In addition, the Tampa Bay area has a sizeable population of persons of Arab background and Muslim religion, many of whom are not American citizens. There was indirect evidence of endemic prejudice in the area against Arabs and persons of the Islamic religion.

Juror Questionnaires

As noted above, in contrast to common perceptions about the American trial process, jurors in most federal courts, as opposed to state courts, are subject to limited pre-trial questioning. Questioning is usually conducted only by the trial judge.

The defence teams for all of the accused were concerned about whether they should seek a change of venue or a lesser remedy, such as an extended *voir dire* with lawyer participation in the process. At minimum there was a need to provide evidence that, if extraordinary prejudice existed, there was a need for an extraordinary remedy. On prima facie grounds the trial judge was persuaded to send prospective jurors a lengthy questionnaire developed in conjunction with the lawyers for the prosecution as well as the defense. The questionnaire contained eighty-three questions with the additional instruction that the juror should explain answers in their own words on the questionnaire and not consult with anyone else about how to respond to the questions.[46]

A letter accompanied the questionnaire from the court. The juror was instructed to omit his or her name and simply use an assigned juror number. The final page of the questionnaire required the juror to declare as follows: 'I declare under penalty of perjury that the information which I have provided in this juror questionnaire and any attachments is true and correct. I further declare that I have completed this questionnaire without anyone's assistance.' The questionnaire was sent to 500 randomly selected names using the court's normal procedures for drawing a jury panel.

Responses on the Questionnaires

As a first matter in considering the data, the court's juror survey raises questions about response rates. Of the 500 hundred questionnaires only 328 were returned.

---

[46] The questionnaire and the data reported in this paper are based upon, N Vidmar, Declaration in *United States v Al-Arian and Hatem Fariz*, Case No 8:03-CR-77-t-30TBM, US District Court, Middle District of Florida, Tampa Division (April 28, 2005). The jury questionnaire offered many opportunities for the juror to express in his or her own words impressions and any biases about the case that arose from media coverage and from discussions about the case with family members, co-workers, friends and acquaintances. The responses offered by the jurors provided important insights into the degree of community attitudes and beliefs about Mr Al-Arian and his likely guilt on the charges that had been laid against him. They also provided an opportunity to examine inconsistencies in the attitudes and beliefs of jurors who stated that they could be fair and impartial. For example, Question 40c asked whether the juror had any connection with the defendants in the case and/or whether they had heard or read about it. This question also allowed the juror an opportunity to express his or her opinion. Question 41 offered a similar opportunity and so did Question 42a, which asked, 'What were your reactions or impressions based on what you saw, read or heard?' Question 43b offered a similar opportunity for self-expression. Questions 44 and 45 asked about the Senatorial Primary Race controversy about Mr Al-Arian and again offered the opportunity for jurors to state their impressions and feelings in their own words. Question 44d specifically asked the juror: 'Based on this opinion, would it make it difficult for you to sit as a fair and impartial juror in this type of case?' and allowed space to express the reason(s) for the opinion. Question 48 asked: 'Is there anything you have seen, heard or read about that would interfere with your ability to render a fair verdict in this case solely on the evidence presented in court?' Question 49 asked: 'Have you formed an opinion as to the innocence or guilt of any of the defendants in this case before hearing the evidence?' and offered the options of 'Guilty,' 'Innocent' and 'No Decision' followed by 'Please explain what led to your position.' Question 50 asked about opinions on pre-trial rulings and asked for an explanation. Question 52 which asked about the conflict between Israel and the Palestinians also allowed another opportunity for self-expression. Q81 asked 'Is there any reason that you could not be completely fair and impartial to the defendants in this case?' Question 82 asked the same question about being fair and impartial to the government and then asked the juror to explain 'yes' answers to either of these two questions.

Sixty-eight surveys were returned because the person had moved. Discounting those persons, the sample would be 432, but 104 questionnaires were unanswered, yielding a response rate of only 76 per cent. This is surprising since the survey was an official command of the Federal Court. Possibly many persons ignored the command because they did not want to serve in a trial that might last as long as six months. But there is another possible reason, namely fear for personal safety. Fear of serving as a juror may have been a significant factor in the low response rate. This issue is discussed in more detail later in this paper.

The juror questionnaire contained open-ended questions that required the potential jurors to explain in their own words reasons behind their beliefs. It concluded with three crucial questions. Question 81 asked, 'Is there any reason that you could not be completely fair and impartial to the defendants in this case?' Question 82 asked the same question about being fair and impartial to the government. Question 83 then asked the juror to explain affirmative answers to either of these two questions. In response to the question about being impartial to the accused, 34 per cent of jurors declared themselves to be biased. No respondents said they were biased against the government.

What were the bases of this lack of impartiality? In the limited space available for this paper I offer several edited examples. Some statements are in italics to draw especial attention to what the prospective jurors said.

Juror 009: [I have] read newspapers, O'Reilley's Spin Zone TV Newscasts and CNN News, O'Reilley said he believed Al-Arian was guilty and he would spy on him everywhere he went in order to get evidence; I heard that *while Al-Arian was a Professor at University of South Florida he was also raising money to sponsor terrorist groups.* I have discussed the case with my husband and sister-in-law. I was angry; *I feel he is guilty and should be punished.* Yes, it [election controversy] would [bias me]; Mr. Martinez accused Mrs. Castor of doing nothing when the accusations about Al-Arian were made public; I feel he is guilty. Yes [I would be biased]. *[Al-Arian is] guilty. Government [law officials] found evidence which incriminates him.*

Juror 204: I wondered why it took so long to build a case against Dr. Al-Arian. *It seems like the evidence was there a long time before they arrested him.* I wondered how he could stay and live in this country without being asked to leave. I believe on what I have seen on TV, he should have been arrested a long time before he was. *Yes, I think he is 99.9% likely to be guilty of what he is charged with* based on what I have seen heard, and read on TV and in the newspaper; I believe that *Dr. Al-Arian along with his partners helped to raise money and funnel that money to organizations that are against the U.S.* Yes, *having lived with the hate that Arabs and Palestinians have for the U.S. makes me wonder why we would give assistance to these types of individuals or countries.* Yes [I am biased] [Al-Arian is] guilty. Everything that I have read and heard about this case has led me to believe that he and his group are guilty. *I would have a hard time being fair and impartial to people who take life for granted.*

Juror 124: If Sami Al-Arian is on record for supporting these 'charitable' groups that are actually terrorist groups, then I believe that he is someone who supports/incites terrorist attacks or activities against the United States. Right now I think he is guilty. *There would have to be overwhelming evidence to convince me of his innocence.* I don't know if that labels me impartial or not; Guilty. Footage aired on TV news allegedly shows Sami Al-Arian speaking in support of terrorist groups and activities. *Sami Al-Arian has ties directly or indirectly to Qaida or other terrorist groups.* I already think he is guilty based on news and publicity. I am assuming that it means that I am not impartial.

Juror 316: I feel they are both guilty of terrorism acts against the U.S.; I feel Al-Arian is a threat either directly or indirectly to the U.S. citizens, and that he is guilty of the crimes as charged. Yes, my opinions are formed and extremely unlikely to change. What I've read/heard points to Al-Arian's guilt when he's labelled a terrorist. Yes, very difficult to be impartial. Reports on the defendant's connection to terrorist organizations, money laundering charges, monies paid to individuals to carry out suicide attacks; Terrorism charges are hard to swallow after 9/11; if you live in America you should not be involved in activities that are harmful to American citizens.

Juror 480: Too much to state here—read and followed everything I could. I have a daughter attending USF in Tampa and the jerk was a professor there. *Sami Al-Arian looks like a Moslem Radical to me*; Sami is probably one of those 'kill the infidels;' He's probably had a hand in fund raising for terror organizations. . . . *What do you think! I saw him all sweaty and screaming with laundry wrapped on his head on those films clips.* Looked obvious to me. I think he's guilty of fund raising for terrorists. What I've read and seen in the media *you can take my vote now and save all that taxpayer money. Remember 911?* I think Sami is guilty!

However, questions like Question 81 frequently evoke socially desirable responses about being impartial that may be inconsistent with actual attitudes and beliefs. Therefore, I examined the total responses to the juror questionnaire of persons who declared themselves not biased and found seventeen additional jurors who were inconsistent. Consider some edited examples from persons who professed ability to be impartial:

Juror 120: They are accused of funding terrorist activities and plots and make out like ordinary people; it has been going on so long, most of the facts are forgotten by all, [I have] *outrage that he's at least somewhat behind this*; I'm not sure (it would be difficult to sit as fair and impartial juror). [He is] *guilty. The government has tons of evidence of at least some acts and has been shown these people could pull a 9/11 on us.* They were in Tampa.

Juror 139: [I have seen] TV news reports, newspaper articles, comments from my parents. I feel that Sami Al-Arian and his supporters are liars and terrorists and that they use our freedoms in the U.S. as a cover for their terrorist activities. I think he is a terrorist. Yes [it would be difficult to sit as fair and impartial juror]. He is Guilty. [I base my feelings on] What I have read and heard from the newspapers and my parents.

Juror 320: [I have seen] newspaper and TV stories leave me to believe they are all guilty. They had the funds and opportunity to do these things. [I am] upset that others can come to America and get away with anything. The man and all of his co-defendants are guilty! Yes, [it would be difficult to sit as fair and impartial juror]. I feel that the group had been planning some terrorist activities for a long time. They had been spreading the word to others around the country for more support and were never stopped. Yes, [it would be difficult to sit as fair and impartial juror]. Yes [from what I have heard] he is guilty. [I have formed an opinion that he is] guilty. As stated before, the group . . . had plenty of papers, etc. which proved what they were doing. I feel the government will have enough evidence to prove their case before coming to court. . . .

Classifying these additional respondents as 'not impartial' leads to an estimate of 129 of 328 persons with very strong biases, or 39 per cent of the sample.

Interest Prejudice in the Community: The Effects of September 11, 2001

Research for the John Walker Lindh ('American Taliban') case, as described above, documented the strong reactions that the attacks of 9/11 had on the American public. The attacks were seen not only in terms of physical fear, but also feelings of hostility arising from strong emotional reactions that American values and culture were being attacked. Similarly, in the *Al-Arian* case many jurors mentioned the September 11, 2001 attacks on various questions in the lengthy survey. One question asked jurors if they believed Palestinians were involved in the 2001 attacks. Consider these examples: Juror 004; 'Sept.11;' Juror 008: 'I have family and friends living in New York and are still suffering from 9/11 attack;' Juror 018, 'The events of 2001 and subsequent involvement impact on entire society . . . ;' Juror 025: 'As with 9/11, these people demonstrate the ability to live amongst us unnoticed . . . ;' Juror 038: 'Every American was affected by 9/11 & I wonder and fear what could be next;' Juror 362: 'Friends and family associates murdered on 9-11-01.'

Interest Prejudice: Fear of Being a Juror in the *Al-Arian* Case

Consider Juror 280's answer to a question about serving on the Al-Arian jury: 'Due to the nature of the case, I would potentially fear for the safety of self and family.' Juror 414 said: 'It is important my identity be kept secret from the defendants and from the media.' Juror 343 asked: 'What if these defendants are found guilty? What about retaliation against the jurors? What's to stop their terrorist affiliants from coming after us? Or bombing the courthouse, etc.(?).' Similarly, Juror 367 wrote: 'I think the biggest fear of people to serve on this jury will be reprisal. How do you know if you are in harm's way from these people? I feel intimidated.' Juror 422 said: 'If these men are guilty and associated with terrorists how safe will it be for myself and family?' Juror 178 expressed a similar concern: 'I am worried that my fear of terrorists would affect me to be fair and impartial.'

Generic Prejudice Regarding Muslims, Arabs/Palestinians and Non-citizens

A number of items in the lengthy questionnaire gave respondents the specific opportunity to express any attitudes or beliefs that they had about Palestinians and other Arabs and toward Muslims. One set of questions asked whether non-citizens were entitled to the same constitutional protections that citizens are accorded. Both jurors who declared that they could not be impartial and those who either did not answer questions or who declared themselves to be impartial on the matter of Mr Al-Arian's guilt expressed many beliefs and attitudes that show negative stereotyping of Arabs and Muslims. Fully 50 per cent of jurors expressed a view that Arabs/Palestinians or Muslims were more violent than other ethnic groups or were responsible in some way for the September 11 attacks on the United States. Many jurors would not accord non-citizens the same rights of free speech that citizens have, particularly when it is seen as, 'espousing terrorism' or 'degrading the USA.' Some were even more explicit such as juror 480 reported above who said, '[I saw] him all sweaty and screaming with laundry wrapped on his head on those films clips.'

Community/Conformity Prejudice

It is clear from juror responses, both those admitting bias and those who did not express opinions on guilt, that extensive Tampa Bay area television, radio and newspaper accounts about Mr Al-Arian had been watched and read by the whole community. Many of these opinions apparently developed prior to the charges being laid against the accused, although they were further exacerbated by subsequent media coverage. Mr Al-Arian's residence, employment, and publicized speeches and alleged terrorist-supporting activities occurred in the community in which he was being tried. Some respondents drew attention to this fact with a sense of concern or even of outrage. As a group, the jurors who answered the questionnaire appeared very aware of many details about Mr Al-Arian. The jurors were cognizant that a not guilty verdict might be met with outrage by some of their friends, family and co-workers. This raised a reasonable concern that a juror or jurors might be influenced by community feeling about the proper verdict in the trial.

The Trial and Its Outcome

Based on the juror questionnaire responses and survey research findings tendered by other defendants, the trial judge deviated from customary procedures. He conducted some preliminary questioning of prospective jurors himself and then allowed both defence and prosecution lawyers to conduct further questioning. A number of jurors were dismissed on hardship grounds because of the expected length of the trial and other jurors were dismissed by the judge 'for cause' based upon their questionnaire answers and their in-court examination. Other jurors were dismissed through peremptory challenges. The final jury consisted of twelve persons plus four alternate jurors, who would replace any jurors that, for illness or other reasons, would be dismissed before the jury reached its verdict.

The trial lasted six months. The government produced over a hundred witnesses, many flown in from Israel specifically for the trial. Other evidence consisted of hours of surreptitious Federal Bureau of Investigation wiretaps of conversations involving Mr Al-Arian and other defendants. After the prosecution closed its case, Mr Al-Arian's defence counsel concluded the prosecution's case was so weak that there was no need to call defence evidence. After final arguments and judicial instructions the case was placed in the hands of the jury. After thirteen days of deliberations the jury rejected the charges that Mr Al-Arian and the three co-defendants operated a North American cell for Palestinian Islamic Jihad. The jury unanimously found Mr Al-Arian not guilty of conspiring to commit murder abroad, money laundering and obstruction of justice; it could not reach consensus on other counts. Two of the other defendants were acquitted of all charges and a third was found not guilty of the main charges and the jury could not reach consensus on the remaining charges.[47]

Reflections on Jury Trials involving Charges of Terrorism

Each case has unique characteristics and must be evaluated on its own terms. Prior to trial, public opinion surveys were also undertaken for the *Al-Arian* case.[48] The results suggested that if the trial were held in Atlanta, Georgia, a city in the same federal judicial district as Tampa, some of the problems of media publicity would have been much less. Possibly fears of jurors about retaliation expressed in the Tampa area would have been less. Possibly prejudice against persons associated with Islam or Arab culture would have been less.

Conceivably there was still some prejudice among the Al-Arian jurors who rendered the not guilty verdicts. If the government's case had been stronger, those prejudices may have come into play. Prejudices are likely to have their strongest influence in instances when the evidence is ambiguous. The Honess *et al* study, described earlier, and related research indicates that strong negative attitudes and beliefs have a subtle and invidious impact on the way that jurors interpret trial evidence.

Post-charge media coverage in the *Al-Arian* case greatly added to the problems of the defence. Because of contempt laws, accused persons tried in England, Australia, or Canada would not have been subject to the same media coverage. On the other hand, negatively toned media coverage of events prior to the laying of charges might occur in these other countries, just as occurred in the *Maxwell* trial. At least for the near future, the prior bombings and terrorist threats have created an atmosphere of fear of and hostility toward terrorism that may lie in the minds of prospective jurors. Problems of community gossip, generic prejudices against

[47] M Fechter, E Silvestrini, and L Savino, 'No Guilty Verdicts in the Al-Arian Trial', *The Tampa Tribune*, December 6, 2005.
[48] E Bronson, Declaration in *US v Al-Arian and Hatem Fariz*, Case No 8:03-CR-77-t-30TBM, US District Court, Middle District of Florida, Tampa Division (April 28, 2005).

Muslims and Arabs, and juror fears of retaliation after a conviction might well be present, possibly in even greater degrees than were present in the *Al-Arian* case. Research on the Al-Arian jurors' response to the pre-trial questionnaire as well as research involving other cases indicates that jurors may hold strong prejudices but still profess an ability to be an impartial juror in deciding guilt or innocence. A jury randomly selected from a population holding such prejudices would not produce a fair and impartial hearing of the charges. It would seem that, similar to the steps taken in England's *Maxwell* case, a trial judge should consider extraorsdinary problems that may accompany terrorism trials and be willing to take extraordinary steps to ensure that the jury consists of persons who can weigh the evidence fairly and impartially. The nature of these procedures will, of course, have to be sensitive to the common law procedural practices of the particular country.

20

Illuminating or Blurring the Truth:[1] Jurors, Juries, and Expert Evidence

Judith Fordham[2]

Introduction

The jury is central to the Australian criminal justice system. In spite of this, little research has been undertaken with real juries into how juries process evidence and make decisions based upon it. The difficulty for juries is thought to be most acute with expert evidence, especially where there is disagreement among the experts themselves. Research in Australia has been constrained by legislative barriers[3] and the reluctance of justice administrators to interfere in any way with jurors.

Rare permission has been given by the Attorney-General of Western Australia for this researcher to interview jurors after criminal trials in which expert evidence was presented. Without this permission, soliciting, disclosing, obtaining or publishing 'protected information'[4] is an offence. 'Protected information' includes, significantly for this research, 'statements made, opinions expressed, arguments advanced or votes cast by members of a jury in the course of their deliberations, other than anything said or done in open court'.

While the project is not yet complete, this paper explores some of the preliminary findings.

---

[1] Comment by anonymous juror: experts can either illuminate or blur the truth.

[2] The support and assistance of the Attorney-General of Western Australia, the Chief Justice of Western Australia, the Chief Judge of the District Court of Western Australia and the Department of the Attorney General is gratefully acknowledged, as is the financial support of the University of Western Australia and the Law Society of Western Australia Public Purposes Trust.

[3] Juries Act 1957 (WA). Similar restrictions exist in Canada, England and New Zealand (see N Vidmar, 'When Jurors Talk About Their Verdict' in J Kleinig and JP Levine (eds), *Jury Ethics: Juror Conduct and Jury Dynamics* (Boulder, 2005) 237–245).

[4] Juries Act 1957 (WA), s 56A.

Expert Evidence

Expert evidence has always been a special issue in the law. Fears are expressed, usually without anything other than anecdotal evidence that jurors will:

- be unduly influenced by such testimony;
- uncritically give it proportionately more weight than other evidence;
- accept it unquestioningly;
- be unable to understand it;
- be influenced by the most articulate expert; and
- be unable to critically evaluate it.[5,6]

Others consider the jury sadly underestimated.[7]

Evidence given in technical fields such as blood spatter or fingerprinting, which (arguably) might not fall into the category of scientific evidence, and in areas of expertise such as engineering, accountancy, and architecture are said to be attended by the same challenges for jurors. Hence, the term 'expert evidence' is used in preference to the narrower term 'scientific' evidence.

Jurors without technical training are frequently required to consider complex expert evidence. That consideration is not just a matter of understanding the expert evidence: in the case of 'opposing' experts called by defence and prosecution, the juror is expected to discriminate between and critically evaluate different interpretations of a particular set of data. Crucially, a juror must then integrate that consideration into their assessment of the rest of the evidence at trial, giving the expert evidence appropriate weight.

In the United Kingdom, the Roskill Committee[8] recommended that in some complex fraud cases trial by judge and jury should be abolished. The randomly selected jury was considered to be an inappropriate tribunal for the trial of complex fraud cases as:

... in almost every area of the law, society has accepted that just verdicts are best delivered by persons qualified by training, knowledge, experience, integrity or by a combination of these four qualifications. Only in a minority of cases [i]s the delivery of a verdict left in the hands of jurors deliberately selected at random without any regard for their qualifications.

... In our opinion the absence from the jury box in a complex fraud case, except by chance, of persons with the qualities described *in the preceding paragraph seriously impairs the prospect of a fair trial.*

---

[5] DI Lehman, RO Lempert, *et al*, 'The Effects of Graduate Training on Reasoning: Formal Discipline and Thinking about Everyday-Life Events' (1988) 43 *American Psychologist* 431–432.

[6] MB Kovera and BD McAuliff, 'The Effects of Peer Review and Evidence Quality on Judge Evaluations of Psychological Science: Are Judges Effective Gatekeepers?' (2000) 85(4) *Journal of Applied Psychology* 574–586.

[7] G Edmond and D Mercer, 'The Politics of Jury Competence' in B Martin (ed), *Technology and Public Participation* (Wollongong, 1999) 85–112.

[8] Lord Roskill, *Fraud Trials Committee Report* (London, 1986) 147.

However, the New South Wales Law Reform Commission,[9] referring to the comment above, noted that:

We consider that the argument which has been put forward in support of the abolition of trial by jury in complex cases, particularly commercial and 'white collar' crimes, is not compelling. It is invariably based on the assertion that jurors are incapable of understanding the evidence upon which prosecutions of this kind depend. We question the validity of that assertion. There is in fact very little evidence to show that jurors, or more accurately juries, do not have an adequate grasp of the relevant material on which their verdicts should be based. There is a strong body of opinion which holds that juries generally reach acceptable verdicts in these cases.

... it appears to us that the collective wisdom and experience of juries has enabled the jury system to adapt and meet the demands placed on it by trials involving complicated evidence.

It should be noted that neither the Committee nor the Commission were able to rely upon research data to support the opinions referred to. We simply do not know.

Most jury research has been undertaken in the United States. This work has been published elsewhere, and this paper does not purport to provide a survey. Briefly, in respect of expert evidence, Penrod, Heuer and others [10] [11] have published widely on such topics as decision making in complex trials[12] [13] and giving written or preliminary instructions.[14] Margaret Bull Kovera has concentrated on the impact expert testimony has on jurors' decisions and the methods of presentation and degree of understanding, asking whether cross-examination helps jurors become more sensitive to flaws in methodology.[15] Hans and Ivkovic[16] have carried out qualitative analyses of interviews with jurors in civil trials, developing a model of the factors jurors incorporate into their evaluation of expert testimony. A rare *in vivo* study was conducted by Vidmar and Diamond[17] in Arizona where deliberations were audio- and video-recorded. Innovations in that state such as allowing jurors to

[9] New South Wales Law Reform Commission, *Report 48 Criminal Procedure: The Jury in a Criminal Trial: Promoting Satisfactory Verdicts*, The Jury In Complex Cases: Evidence of a Complex, Scientific or Technical Nature (Sydney, 1986).

[10] SD Penrod and B Cutler, 'Witness Confidence and Witness Accuracy: Assessing their Forensic Relation' (1995) 4 *Psychology, Public Policy and Law* 1.

[11] SD Penrod and L Heuer, *Improving Group Performance: the Case of the Jury. Theory and Research on Small Groups* (New York, 1998).

[12] L Heuer and SD Penrod, 'Jury Decision Making in Complex Trials' in R Bull and D Carson (eds), *Handbook of Psychology in Legal Contexts* (New York, 2003).

[13] BD McAuliff, RJ Nemeth, *et al*, 'Juror Decision-Making in the 21st Century: Confronting Science and Technology in Court' in R Bull and D Carson (eds), *Handbook of Psychology in Legal Contexts* (New York, 2003).

[14] L Heuer and SD Penrod 'Instructing Jurors: a Field Experiment with Written and Preliminary Instructions' (1989) 13 *Law and Human Behavior* 409.

[15] MB Kovera, BD McAuliff *et al*, 'Reasoning About Scientific Evidence: Effects of Juror Gender And Evidence Quality on Juror Decisions in a Hostile Work Environment Case' (1999) 84(3) *Journal of Applied Psychology* 362–375.

[16] SK Ivkovic and V Hans, 'Jurors' Evaluations of Expert Testimony: Judging the Messenger and the Message' (2003) *American Bar Foundation* 441–482.

[17] SS Diamond, N Vidmar *et al*, 'Juror Discussions During Civil Trials: a Study of Arizona's Rule 39 (f) Innovation, Arizona Superior Court in Pima County' (2002) *State Justice Institute* 21–30.

discuss evidence with each other during the trial, and allowing jurors to ask questions during a trial have been introduced, partly as a consequence of this work.[18]

In Australia, expert evidence is coming under increasing scrutiny, largely due to the increasing importance of forensic evidence in the detection and prosecution of crime, including the advent of DNA testimony. Expert testimony has sometimes determined the outcome of trials without any real understanding of the scientific issues by judge, counsel and therefore, one would expect, jury.[19]

General statements have been made about improvements in presentation, until recently with little justification other than a 'gut' feeling.[20] In the course of his 1984 report, the Royal Commissioner who inquired into the *Splatt*[21] conviction (which followed poorly investigated and poorly presented forensic evidence) placed responsibility for presentation and testing of scientific evidence with lawyers and scientists:

> The vital obligation which lies upon the testifying scientists is that they spell out to the jury, in non-ambiguous and precisely clear terms, the degree of weight and substance and significance which is or ought properly to be attached to the scientific tests and analyses and examinations as to which they depose; and specifically the nature and degree of any limitations or provisos which are properly appended thereto .... [T]he critical responsibility which rests upon legal persons is to ask such detailed and probing questions of the scientists as are most likely to elicit the type of evidence just mentioned.[22]

Gary Edmond, in a recent publication discussing experts in the legal system[23] notes in conclusion:

> What then can we say about the state of our legal system and the roles played by experts within it? Unfortunately, we are not in a position to say a great deal ... Perhaps more than ever the issue of expertise warrants immediate and sustained empirical investigation.

The Jury Trial System in Western Australia[24]

Criminal trials in Western Australia take place in one of three courts in a hierarchy. Minor offences are dealt with in the Magistrates Court, without a jury. Serious offences including assault occasioning grievous bodily harm and sexual assault are

---

[18] BM Dann, VP Hans, and DH Kaye, *Testing the Effects Of Selected Jury Trial Innovations On Juror Comprehension of Contested mtDNA Evidence, Final Technical Report* (2005), <http://www.ncjrs.gov/pdffiles1/nij/grants/211000.pdf>, accessed 10 November 2005.

[19] *R v Keir* [2002] New South Wales Court of Criminal Appeal (NSW CCA) 30 (28 February 2002).

[20] B Selinger, 'Science in the Witness Box' (1984) (June) *Legal Service Bulletin* 108.

[21] *R v Splatt*, unreported, Court of Criminal Appeal, Supreme Court of South Australia (28 February 1979).

[22] *Report of the Royal Commission of Inquiry into the Conviction of Edward Charles Splatt*, Royal Commission of Inquiry, Government of South Australia (Adelaide, 1984).

[23] G Edmond, 'Judging Surveys: Experts, Empirical Evidence and Law Reform' (2005) 33 *Federal Law Review* 1, 95–139.

[24] See generally the Juries Act 1957 (WA) and M Chesterman, *Criminal Trial Juries in Australia: From Penal Colonies to a Federal Democracy* (1999) 62(2) *Law and Contemporary Problems* 69–102.

tried in the District Court. All offences punishable by life imprisonment (such as wilful murder and armed robbery) are tried in the Supreme Court.

In Western Australia, jurors who are aged between 18 and 70 are randomly selected by computer from Electoral Commission rolls. The Sheriff summons approximately 700 people every week for jury service in the Perth (state capital) metropolitan area.

Some citizens are either exempt or ineligible for jury service. In a masterpiece of drafting, the Act exempts those who 'have been convicted of an offence and sentenced to death (and the sentence was not carried out)'. In addition to those lucky souls, others exempt or ineligible include those who:

- have been sentenced to imprisonment;
- have disability which will affect their ability to discharge their duty;
- are police;
- are lawyers.

Many others may be excused as of right, including:

- emergency services workers;
- doctors;
- dentists;
- veterinarians;
- psychologists;
- chiropractors;
- priests;
- people over the age of 65.

Still others may ask to be excused if they have sufficient reason, including illness or recent jury service.

The day before the trial, jury lists are made available to lawyers. The defence is made aware of names, addresses and occupations, and in addition the prosecution is told whether the juror has a criminal record. Some 'pop psychological' judgments are made by lawyers at this stage as to which jurors might be favourable (or not). For example, a defence lawyer would try to avoid selecting a bank manager in a case involving a bank robbery.

When potential jurors arrive at the jury assembly area, they are given individual identifying numbers. Panels of at least twenty-six persons (more in the case of a long or complex trial) are randomly selected and sent to each courtroom where a trial is to commence.

In the courtroom, the accused person is identified, the indictment read and a plea of not guilty is entered. The jury is then empanelled. Juror numbers are randomly drawn until a jury of twelve to eighteen persons is selected, the number depending on the expected length of the trial. During the selection process, the prosecution or the defence lawyer may exercise up to five peremptory challenges. Jurors may ask the judge if they may be excused, offering reasons which may or may not be considered sufficient.

Once the jury is empanelled, a list of witnesses is read out by the prosecutor (and defence if they choose), and the judge asks the jurors to say whether there is any reason in light of the witness list they could not render a fair verdict. If so, they may be excused and a further juror selected to take their place.

The accused then has the charge(s) read to him or her and pleads guilty or not guilty. The prosecutor opens the State case, outlining the allegations against the accused and the evidence which will be called. The defence then makes an opening address to the jury, in a similar fashion to the prosecutor.

Jurors may take notes,[25] and are frequently given documents or folders of documents such as the indictment, summaries of transactions or call charge records, and sometimes expert reports to assist them during the trial. The jurors are permitted (even encouraged) to discuss the evidence among themselves during the trial, but not to come to any conclusion until the end.[26] They are instructed not to discuss the evidence with anyone outside the jury, and to base their verdict only on the evidence led in the case. They are permitted to go home each evening, but are kept together during the day.

Once all the evidence has been given, both lawyers make a closing address to the jury, with the defence following the prosecution. The judge then instructs the jury on the applicable law and comments on the evidence to whatever extent he or she thinks is appropriate. A ballot is then held (from which the foreperson is exempt) to reduce the jury to twelve.

The jury then retires to consider its verdict, taking with it the exhibits which were tendered during the trial. The jurors' task is to decide the facts and then apply the law (as instructed by the judge) to those facts and to reach a verdict. A unanimous verdict is required in wilful murder, murder, and manslaughter cases. In other cases, juries are initially told a unanimous verdict is required, but after extended deliberations, a majority of at least ten is accepted.

Jurors, Juries and Expert Evidence

Research into jurors and juries has been conducted by various means, each of which carries its own advantages and disadvantages:[27]

- Mock juries are commonly used, with mock trials ranging from a written outline of evidence to a scripted trial conducted by actors; with student

---

[25] Note-taking is common in Australia and New Zealand. See JRP Ogloff, J Clough, and J Goodman-Delahunty, *The Jury Project: Stage 1—A Survey of Australian and New Zealand Judges* (Melbourne, 2006).

[26] Unlike in some other jurisdictions. See PL Hannaford, VP Hans, GT Munsterman, 'Permitting Jury Discussions During Trial: Impact of the Arizona Reform' (2000) 24(3) *Law and Human Behavior* 359–382.

[27] See generally DJ Devine, LD Clayton *et al*, 'Jury Decision Making—45 Years of Empirical Research on Deliberating Groups' (2001) 7(3) *Psychology, Public Policy and Law* 622–727 and BH Bornstein, 'The Ecological Validity of Jury Simulations: Is the Jury Out?' (1999) 23(1) *Law and Human Behavior* 75–91.

jurors or more demographically representative juries. Such studies are often criticized due to the non-representative sample and the fact that the decision making (to the knowledge of the participants) is simulated, not real, resulting, it is said, in limited external validity.

- Judge-juror verdict agreement studies have been undertaken, with the predictable criticism being: 'Who is to say the Judge got the verdict right?'
- Post-trial questionnaires have been administered, gleaning information about jurors' perceptions of their own level of understanding, and much less frequently, post-trial interviews with jurors have been carried out. Qualitative data analysis software now permits detailed consideration of the actual individual and group deliberations. One question, however, is whether jurors can or will accurately report their thought processes.

The United States legal system is very different from that which exists in Australia, Canada and the United Kingdom. In particular there is a different and more extensive *voir dire* process to select jurors, and much of the research has been carried out on civil trial juries. Some practices such as note-taking, which are routine in Western Australia, are not usual in some of the US states.[28] It is unlikely, given cultural differences and differing systems of justice, that the results from the United States are capable of direct application to criminal trials within 'British' justice systems.

There is a paucity of jury research using real juries and real trials in Australia, New Zealand, Canada and the United Kingdom, whether generally or about expert evidence, largely due to the legislative barriers noted above. Hence, very little is known in these jurisdictions about the manner in which jurors evaluate expert testimony. In respect of expert evidence, there is only a modest amount of research even in the United States.[29] In 1999, Young and others[30] [31] carried out a survey of jurors in New Zealand following a series of criminal trials. The questions were wide-ranging and as a result the conclusions were necessarily somewhat broadly expressed. A brief (unpublished) pilot study took place in the Australian Capital Territory in 2001.[32] Freckelton and others have carried out two surveys of judges'[33] and magistrates'[34] perspectives on expert evidence.

---

[28] BM Dann and V Hans, 'Recent Evaluative Research on Jury Trial Innovations' (2004) 41 *Court Review* 12.   [29] Ivkovic and Hans, n 16 above, 449.

[30] W Young, N Cameron *et al, Juries in Criminal Trials—a Summary of the Research Findings*, New Zealand Law Commission, vol 2 (Wellington, 1999) 41–50; Y Tinsley, 'Juror Decision-Making: A Look Inside the Jury Room' in R Tarling (ed), *The British Criminology Conference: Selected Proceedings*, vol 4 (Leicester, 2000).

[31] W Young, Y Tinsley *et al*, 'The Effectiveness & Efficiency of Jury Decision-Making' (2000) 24 *Criminal Law Journal* 89.

[32] E Magnusson and R Wheate, *Expert Evidence and Jury Comprehension in Australian Courts. The ADNIFSJA project* (2001, unpublished).

[33] I Freckelton, P Reddy *et al, Australian Judicial Perspectives on Expert Evidence: An Empirical Study* (Carlton, 2000).

[34] I Freckelton, P Reddy *et al, Australian Magistrates' Perspectives on Expert Evidence: a Comparative Study; Summary of Key Findings and Outcomes* (Carlton, 2001).

There is a strong school of thought[35] suggesting jurors are incapable of understanding such evidence or of giving it appropriate weight in relation to other non-expert evidence and that no matter what resources are devoted to assisting jurors with this task, they will be unable to accomplish it with any degree of fairness.

However, as Mark Cowie, who contributed the comprehensive chapter 'Juries and Complex Trials'[36] in the Victorian Parliament's Law Reform Committee Final Report, *Jury Service in Victoria,* noted:

In a survey of jurors in New South Wales by the Law Foundation, it was found that over 90% of the jurors said they found the evidence and proceedings understandable .... However, this question is a rather moot point given that the jury's understanding of the issues in either of these two jurisdictions cannot be measured and nor can the basis for the verdict be analysed because the jury room is sacrosanct.

... in trying to formulate some sort of conclusion as to the nebulous issue of juror comprehension of complex matters, the best that can be said at this point is that the lack of understanding of jurors has not been adequately defined or empirically demonstrated.

This Study

The purpose of the present research is to learn more about how real jurors and real juries assimilate, evaluate and use expert testimony. This will provide a basis for practical, sound proposals about ways to improve the manner in which expert testimony is communicated to juries in Australia. It is proposed to identify variables which may inhibit or assist juror comprehension and to consider whether the view that jurors are 'bedazzled' and/or 'incompetent' in the face of expert evidence reflects reality. A distinction is drawn between 'jurors' and 'juries' as it is postulated that there are valid distinctions in practice to be drawn between the processes used by the individual and the group.

Particularly in light of the minimal data available from the real jury research, the nature of the inquiry has demanded a qualitative approach. Not only is it close to impossible to test hypotheses within a trial situation (although the Arizona civil jury study[37] could be seen as a rare attempt to do so), but even the process of formulating hypotheses without sufficient observational data being available carries with it the risk of preconceived notions influencing the research design and so contaminating the content of the data derived.

This study incorporates qualitative and quantitative approaches examining the manner in which jurors deal with expert evidence: how they perceive it, process it,

---

[35] G Edmond and D Mercer, 'Scientific Literacy and the Jury: Reconsidering Jury "Competence"' (1997) 6 *Public Understanding of Science* 329–357.

[36] MT Cowie, 'Jury Service in Victoria' (1997) 3 *Law Reform Committee* 39–125.

[37] N Vidmar, S Diamond *et al*, 'Juror Discussions During Civil Trials: Studying an Arizona Innovation' (2003) 45 *Arizona Law Review* 1–82.

tackle understanding it individually and collectively, apply it to the facts of the case, integrate it with and weigh it in relation to other evidence. In the absence of recording devices in the jury room the individual jurors' approaches and the jury process must be gleaned from the reports of the individual jurors, in the context of what is publicly known about the trials.

Methodology[38]

Crucial portions of a series of jury trials involving complex expert evidence as an important component are attended. The transcript of the remainder of the trial is perused. The jurors are not told that anyone is conducting research until after the verdict is returned, when the trial judge tells them something about the project and invites their participation.

The jurors, jury officer and researcher then retire to the jury room where a ten-to-fifteen-minute written survey instrument is administered. Topics canvassed in the initial written instrument include non-identifying demographic details, subjective impressions of the expert evidence, ease of comprehension and general comments about the juror's experience. Respondents are invited to take part in a later semi-structured interview as soon as is convenient for them. The same researcher contacts all willing jurors and carries out the interviews at a time and place suitable to the juror.

At the interview approximately forty-five questions are explored. The interviews are recorded and transcribed. The questions are directed to issues such as:

- the manner of presentation of the evidence and the effect this had on individual understanding;
- what presentation methods are most effective;
- alternative methods of presentation;
- the individual and group deliberative process as it related to understanding, integrating, evaluating, weighing and applying the evidence; and
- the effect of the introduction of an opposing expert.

Themes

There has been a high degree of co-operation from individual jurors. So far, sixty-two jurors from seven trials have completed the brief questionnaire and in excess of half of these have agreed to be interviewed. The interviews last on average 1.5 hours longer than initially anticipated.

A preliminary analysis of the questionnaires and interviews completed so far has been undertaken. The following portion of this paper canvasses some of the

---

[38] A full explanation of the methodology and analytical approach will be given in a future publication when the study is complete and data fully analysed.

interview data, and is accompanied by the *caveat* that the data gathering and analysis is incomplete and that what follows are simply comments about questions which have been posed in the past and themes which seem to be emerging.

Notably, almost half the respondents were educated to tertiary level and even assuming those who chose not to take part were educated to below this level, jurors are significantly more highly educated than the general population.[39] The material gleaned to date is both surprising and somewhat reassuring in terms of the sophistication of jurors' and juries' approaches to expert evidence.

In addition to the material relating to expert evidence, valuable additional information is being volunteered, providing a fruitful source of further research directions. Most of the jurors who agreed to be interviewed seemed to welcome the opportunity to debrief and to share their ideas.

It should be noted that some factual details have been altered to prevent identification of particular trials and therefore risk identifying jurors.

Is there a CSI Effect?

The media, and to some extent, academic commentators, are starting to discuss the existence of a supposed 'CSI effect'. The 'CSI effect' is supposed to result in the jurors acquitting in trials where there is no scientific evidence, even though the evidence against the accused is strong and scientific evidence is neither required nor expected. It is also said to result in jurors uncritically accepting whatever an expert tells them simply because the expert is an expert. Jurors are said to fail to integrate expert evidence with other evidence and to give that expert evidence more importance than it perhaps deserves. The following excerpt from a recent newspaper article[40] demonstrates the effect the popular media is said to have upon jurors and their expectations:

TELEVISION crime shows were giving Australians an unrealistic understanding of forensic science that could influence future juries, a Sydney academic has warned.

In Phoenix last month, jurors in a murder trial noticed that a bloody coat introduced as evidence had not been tested for DNA. They alerted the judge. The tests hadn't been needed because the defendant had acknowledged being at the murder scene. The judge decided that TV had taught jurors about DNA tests, but not enough about when to use them.

In Arizona, Illinois and California, prosecutors now use 'negative evidence witnesses' to try to assure jurors that it is not unusual for real crime-scene investigators to fail to find DNA, fingerprints and other evidence at crime scenes.

The preliminary findings of this study would suggest that jurors are more sophisticated than they are often given credit for, and do consider such issues as bias,

---

[39] C Nagle, *Selected Social and Housing Characteristics for statistical local areas: Western Australia, Cocos (Keeling) and Christmas Islands 2001*, Australian Bureau of Statistics, Canberra (2002) Cat No 2015.5.   [40] S Neufeld, *CSI 'not real life'* (14 June 2005) AAP.

congruence of the expert evidence with other evidence in the trial, and the expert's basis for his or her opinion, including an evaluation of their reasoning process.

Thus far, this study is producing mixed messages about the so-called 'CSI effect'. One juror in this study commented on the absence of DNA evidence in a murder trial:

- We were so upset that . . . they never did the nail scrapings. It leaves us jurors thinking 'why not?' . . . on TV they say that they can get DNA . . . There was all these questions that we asked. Even though we know we're not meant to, we still ask ourselves that in the juror's room . . . it was such a hard case anyhow, but we thought 'oh well, if they've got DNA we'll be fine. It will just give us the answers,' . . . if he had DNA under his fingernails because of the fighting . . . belonging to someone else, then we're going to know . . . .

So what they probably should do is really present the thing on how it is you get DNA and that it's not that easy and maybe show the jurors that first, before you don't give them any evidence otherwise they're really disappointed because we just expect it . . . and really explain it because they explain so many other things and I think 'why didn't they explain that' . . . [A]ll they said to us was 'it's not like it is on TV' but that isn't really explaining . . . On TV they show us that you can get DNA out of that bit of blood. Can you? Can't you? Do you need this, do you need that? Really explain how you get the problem and why didn't you get it. [T]he police obviously knew what they were doing . . . they didn't get the DNA just because they couldn't be bothered not because they couldn't get it. That's how we all took it. [They should have] [t]horoughly explained why it was absent. Not just 'we haven't got it, don't worry about that' because we do worry about that.

. . . To me it was like a lot of it was circumstantial and if I was in that position and it was based on that evidence and then I was charged it is not enough . . . . Whereas if they did have the DNA, that's just 100% and the other wasn't concrete enough.

. . . [M]y husband says I'm crazy for watching those shows . . . CSI . . . Law and Order . . . I've stopped watching them since I've done jury duty [b]ecause I was disappointed. I got in there and they didn't give me the evidence—oh those shows are a load of rubbish. I don't want to watch them anymore . . . They had no results at all for any of the DNA stuff and on CSI they always get results. They can always see the blood too with their shiny lights and they couldn't do that here. . . . Look at reality instead of what the movies are saying. [T]he movies are wrong. I've always had a problem with a lot of the detail that they used to pull out. I thought I wish I had that program on my PC.

Do Jurors Consider Bias?

Jurors were alive to the possibility of unconscious or conscious bias. Consider the following remarks:

- They're not there to help sides. That has nothing to do with it, they're just there to do their job, and to put it as they see, whether it helps the opposition or prosecution or defence is immaterial . . . . They have been called to give evidence by the goodies and baddies because it leans in their direction anyway. So it is not the person leaning in the direction, it's their facts that do anyway.

- Now the first guy that was up there covered his backside. He was for prosecution but he did actually state that he gave his opinion. Now I appreciated that, because he wasn't going to be swayed by the prosecutor saying this is what's going on, because the prosecutor just stopped asking the questions after he wasn't getting the answers that he wanted... [H]e didn't give the answers that the lawyer was wanting, because if he'd have done that then he wouldn't have been an expert witness. He would've been working for the lawyer....

- He could have been really easily shaken and pushed around and he could have got fumbled easily by these guys. He didn't, he stuck his ground and knew exactly what he was there to say. He knew how to say it and he wasn't going to be pushed into another direction or distracted by them into saying something that wasn't necessary, that would make things sound a little bit funny.

- ... [A]nyone that's acting on behalf of the state has to be impartial.... If a person's being paid by the state and by the taxpayer's money in my mind I believe it's their job description and their duty to be impartial because they can't take sides. It's just not right.... [A defence expert is there] to help the defence because why else would you engage them... [I]t wouldn't have been cheap. If it was me I'd be getting the guy to try and clear me... I would say whatever he said would be favourable to the defence. I don't think being a person of science; I don't think he would be able to bend the truth. He would try and minimise the impact [of what the other expert] had to say and then I think he tried to cast doubt... It comes down to pure human nature. If I say to you Judith, here's $1,000, I want you to go and do... you're going to think jeez, Fred paid me $1,000. You will just automatically, no matter who you are, you think I've got to earn my $1,000. Now oh jeez, if I say that he'll want his money back and he's not going to pay me. So... I'll make it look like something totally different and I won't be telling lies. You're coming from a different angle. It's like a tree. You've got a tree in the middle of a paddock and you've got a camera and you take a picture of it at a certain distance away and you present that photograph. Now the photo is... postcard size,... if I tell you that that tree is 60 foot tall and you see it in the back, that's never 60 foot, but it is, but because of the way I have portrayed the situation, the way I've portrayed it, your first impression, oh it's only a small tree. But if you go and stand next to it and you nearly fall over backwards looking up it, but I haven't told a lie because I've just presented you with it.

- ... I think he knew his role. I think he knew his duty was to just be concise... But I think, you know, in the end it's that he is a prosecution witness, and... where they get their expert witnesses from, whether they're friends of friends,... there's always going to be a little issue there, you know, as to whether or not he's completely fair. It's a human thing, isn't it?... You're there to do a job, in the end... he did his role, but that's not to say that a juror is 100%, you know, convinced. I think that's what a juror's for, isn't it? Like... that's a part of it, you've got to decide, because it is objectivity...

Experts Who Admit Error

Experts who admitted they had made a mistake or were willing to alter their position in the face of new information enhanced their credibility in the eyes of many jurors. Those who resisted the attempts of the party calling them to give a particular answer also favourably impressed jurors. Experts who acquiesced when they should not have were also noticed.

- ... [H]e also referred to a mistake that he made that the other person had picked up on and then he then looked at that as well ... I guess it proved that he wasn't closed to ideas.

- I quite liked the ... biochemist, then again, that's his consistency. He was given quite a hard time with his cross examination, and again, it was either deliberately or he was just useless at adding up. Was confusing the issue with how you get that level [with] how much blood he was given. It didn't shake him, he was consistent, he was happy to say that was wrong, he put a wrong proposition and be corrected. And that all helped.

- He agreed when he shouldn't and I really don't, I expect if he's not sure or if he needs to work something out, well he should say it shouldn't he? [It's wrong to] agree to get out of there.

Jurors Generally Correctly Appreciated their Role vis-à-vis the Expert Witness

Courts have often been reluctant to admit expert opinion evidence for fear that the expert will somehow usurp the jury's role. This fear may be unjustified.[41]

- [T]hey basically left it to the jury to make that final decision. Several of them said nothing was absolutely 100% watertight, but this was their best guess. Then it was really a matter for the jury looking at all the various evidence presented by all the witnesses to then say in the total picture what is the best outcome.

- I think an expert witness is there to just put a perspective ... If a juror takes guidance, complete guidance off him, I don't think they're doing the job, because ... there's two sides to the story, and ... [his evidence was] just a part of the process.

- To provide a scientific or technical or a knowledgeable ... explanation of a circumstance that occurred and why it occurred and how it occurred and probabilities about it, but not to actually pinpoint something. It's not their job to say that's what did it without a reasonable doubt.

- ... [H]e didn't want to be led up the garden path which is what I believe an expert should be. He should be a guy that has actually got an opinion and has formed that opinion by being learned. He's actually got the ability to say 'this is what I believe happened' ... He didn't say 'this is what happened'. It's only the lawyer that says 'this is what happened'.

- We listening to them have got to make up our minds and give an accurate version of what we feel happened, not what they think or what they say happened.

- [She] more or less left it up to the jury ... 'this is what I've seen. You are the people who make the final decision. Was it the ... accused that caused these things?' Never did she

---

[41] See, eg, *R v C(G)* (1995) 110 CCC (3d) 233, 259.

in any way allow herself to get drawn into saying 'look the accused caused this'. She just presented the facts and it was the jury's decision to use those facts in making their ultimate decision.

On the other hand, some jurors were frustrated with the inability of an expert to give a definitive answer rather than an opinion.

- [O]ne of the big issues is when they use words like 'most likely' because a lot of people took that as 'anything could have happened' and that added to confusion. Particularly when you've got people who don't want to decide on guilty anyway, as soon as they are given an out on 'this is the most likely cause' or 'that is not very likely' that creates a whole heap of doubts in people's minds...Using words like 'is consistent with'... made it very difficult to get to a decision at the end.

- I would have thought, had they thought it was murder, that they would have been on the side of proving that it was murder. They didn't do that and they didn't prove it wasn't. Everything was just open ended. I suppose I thought that they could have been a bit more precise...Nothing about the whole case ever became concrete. Everything was just so open ended because whatever one person said there was somebody there to counteract that. You as the juror were left somewhere in between trying to decipher what you could take from each side of it.

Others were aware that this was not possible, and appreciated the expert's limitations:

- [A]s much as you're hoping for a definite answer you generally understand that you're not really going to get one.

- [T]hey basically left it to the jury to make that final decision. Several of them said nothing was absolutely 100% watertight, but this was their best guess. Then it was really a matter for the jury looking at all the various evidence presented by all the witnesses to then say in the total picture what is the best outcome?

- She had it all organised. She knew the answers or she knew when she didn't know the answer as well. I think it was very important, she didn't make a story to fit the question.

Congruence of the Expert Evidence with Other Evidence in the Trial

A strong theme emerging is that jurors are very careful not to just accept expert evidence at face value, but to look to see what other aspects of the evidence supported or contradicted the expert evidence, and assess evidence on that basis. They were also conscious of which witnesses were independent and ascribed more weight to their evidence, all other things being equal. This was a powerful factor in assessing expert testimony.

- ... Mr X's evidence was basically supported by witnesses as to actually what took place.

- Well the evidence that was presented to us in the form of the video and also the photos of the tyre marks seemed to support his conclusions as to the course that the vehicle took...

- [Y]ou would expect them to be there for a reason and you respect their opinion because of all of the other evidence. The witnesses are too close to the action. They're all emotionally involved. Even bypassers, that's important. Everyone external to the situation is important... you do weight the expert evidence heavily because they're emotionally uninvolved.

The 'Story' Model, Primacy and Recency Effects

One of the foremost explanations of the process of jury decision making is the 'story' model stemming from the original theories of Hastie and Pennington.[42] It is said that jurors construct narratives or explanations (stories) which fit with or explain the evidence during the course of the trial, and that these stories determine the jurors' decisions.[43] The present study has offered mixed support for the view that the expert who gives evidence first enjoys a bias in favour of whoever goes first, 'primacy' effect.[44] It should be noted that there is also said to be a 'recency' effect, namely that material presented last is better remembered and more favourably viewed.[45]

- ... [I]t's really the guy who goes first... That was our first impression of the story, of why we were all there. To me that was... it's a like a book with a picture on the front and you might say I remember reading a book and it had a such and such on the front. I can't remember the details of the book but it had a such and such. I clearly remember [the prosecutor] was from here to there, from me to you, he was right there and it was a big impact on me. It settled me down and I thought gee wiz, this is something and then obviously the defence did their bit, but I think I was already on the side of the prosecution at that point. He made me look at his side of the fence, his side of the play.... [A]s the defence were doing theirs, I kept saying: 'No, that can't be right. That's a red herring or that's a smoke screen.'

- It made quite a bit of sense to me... being the first one, and I didn't realise there was going to be a second one, that I took all of it in and pretty much... accepted it and if there was an amount of time between the two witnesses, then that information that

---

[42] R Hastie, SD Penrod *et al*, *Inside the Jury* (Cambridge, 1983); N Pennington and R Hastie, 'Juror Decision Making Models: the Generalization Gap' (1981) 89 *Psychological Bulletin* 246–287; N Pennington and R Hastie, 'Evidence Evaluation in Complex Decision Making' (1986) 51 *Journal of Personality and Social Psychology* 242–258; N Pennington and R Hastie, 'Explanation Based Decision Making; Effects of Memory Structure on Judgement' (1988) 14 *Journal of Experimental Psychology: Learning, Memory, and Cognition* 521–533; N Pennington and R Hastie, 'Explaining the Evidence: Tests of the Story Model for Juror Decision Making' (1992) 62 *Journal of Personality and Social Psychology* 189–206; N Pennington and R Hastie, 'A Cognitive Theory of Juror Decision Making: the Story Model' (1991) 13 *Cardozo Law Review* 519–517.

[43] N Pennington and R Hastie, 'Reasoning in Explanation-Based Decision Making' (1993) 49 *Cognition* 123–163.

[44] KA Carlson and JE Russo, 'Biased Interpretation of Evidence by Mock Jurors' (2001) 7(2) *Journal of Experimental Psychology* 91–103.

[45] N Miller and DT Campbell, 'Recency and Primacy in Persuasion as a Function of the Timing of Speeches and Measurements' (1959) 59(1) *Journal of Abnormal and Social Psychology* 1–9.

I received from [the first expert] just implanted itself even further into my picture of the whole event and I think again, when [the second expert] got up there, I thought 'no, that's not right, [the first expert] said otherwise, what are you on about?'...It was almost as though he is coming along with evidence as a bit of an after thought...I just felt 'well, hang on, we've done that. Now he is contradicting, this isn't right'.

- You've had all that time to think about it and as other witnesses come up you're still thinking of how that fits in. Rather than taking the last evidence in with an open mind you're comparing it to the first, so I think it's an advantage to go first.

On the other hand, other jurors commented as follows:

- I took everything they said in with the same context...We assessed the first one. Like I said there was a bit of break before the next one. I suppose I did make partial judgment but then the other guy came in with the doubt...You put all the evidence together to try and get in your head what is a plausible concept of what was happening, you know.

- ...[A]fter the prosecution has delivered what they deliver you think 'Guilty.' Pretty black and white. Then the defence lawyer does his bit and you think 'Okay now it's back to grey.' So it seems to work out pretty well. You go away the first day thinking guilty and the next day you're thinking okay now I'm 50:50 again...I think it evens up. You've got a very short term advantage for the first day but...I think people wait to hear both sides before they make a judgment.

- I kept an open mind right from the start because the evidence given by...the prosecution, their witnesses, certain aspects didn't make full sense to me and it wasn't until the defence was heard that certain things seem to fall into place and his version of events made more sense to me after that.

Jurors assigned weight to the evidence of 'opposing' experts by considering both content and the manner of presentation:

- I rejected [the second expert's] because what he was saying didn't make a lot of sense...I actually watched the video tape again and looked at the photos...I think the way that [the first expert] gave his evidence was a lot better and a lot more to the point and as far as I am aware, a lot more unbiased, because the other guy was—the concept that he came up with was I suppose, it was a plausible thing that could have happened but for it to happen, would have been an extreme, I think.

- We just looked at all the evidence and the maps and tried to sort of trace it, re-trace and imagine what was going on. And then I think it was pointed out that [the second expert] didn't actually get to the scene till quite some time after, so therefore certain things weren't going to be evident because time had passed and also the fact that [the second expert] had swayed [the first expert] on that one point. I think once all that was kind of pointed out, not so much that we tended to believe [the second expert] over [the first expert]; it's putting the big picture together.

- What would have been really helpful there was if he could have given us an idea as to how many simulations he had done...and if he could have assigned some level of probability to them but he was asked and said he couldn't really answer that. It would have been nice if he could have put a number on it.

- I didn't take [the first expert's] evidence as . . . gospel sort of thing, but certainly what he said and the things that we could see supported what he said . . . His line of reasoning was better supported than [the second expert's] really.

One proposal designed to counter the unfairness of the primacy effect is to hear the experts 'back to back'. Jurors considered the merit of this proposal:

- I think it would've been helpful if they were both close together. . . . You could get all the information at once and you can weigh it up together rather than . . . I had to flick back through my notes while I was listening to him to try and see how it came up against hers.

- . . . probably better that [the experts] are separated [as] I think you get a chance to sort of reflect on what the first expert said before you hear the otherwise . . . I think it could lead to more confusion to sort of have one point of view presented and then have someone completely opposite against it . . . [It would have been useful to bring the first expert back] . . . In fact either commenting on the others . . . Not that you want them to get into arguments.

Should Jurors be Allowed to Take Notes?

Note-taking by jurors in Western Australian courts is now commonplace, as opposed to some other jurisdictions.[46] This was positively viewed by jurors, however, they consistently volunteered that they would have liked clear guidance early in the trial, particularly as to the law,[47] but also as to the factual issues. Instruction as to the law applying to the particular trial (as opposed to general instructions about such matters as burden of proof) is rarely given in Australia.[48] A partial solution at least in relation to the facts may lie in advocates appreciating this concern and dealing with it in their opening addresses.

- I wish I had taken more [notes] . . . I wish that had been stressed to us more because when they say you've got, I think they had 72 witnesses—you don't think about it at the beginning but when we got to about witness 4 or 5 and we were having a hard time remembering what number 1 said, I went 'Oh my gosh, I'd better start writing' and that's when I started writing. Then when we got to the juror's room and we needed to know things, it was like 'please did someone write out those first few?' That's when we realised how important it was. . . . [W]e all got our notes together. There was a couple that just wrote absolutely everything—like books. A couple of pads one guy, I couldn't believe it. . . . We couldn't believe how much they came in handy.

- . . . [U]p front you don't know what's important . . . so it was hard to follow some of the questioning in the beginning and to take relevant notes. So I found certainly probably the first three or four weeks of notes weren't that interesting.

[46] IA Horowitz and L ForsterLee, 'The Effects of Note-Taking and Trial Transcript Access on Mock Jury Decisions in a Complex Civil Trial' (2001) 25(4) *Law and Human Behavior* 373–391.

[47] In this regard, see MJ Bourgeois, IA Horowitz *et al*, 'Nominal and Interactive Groups: Effects of pre-instruction and deliberations and evidence recall in complex trials' (1995) 80 *Journal of Applied Psychology* 58–67.   [48] Ogloff, Clough, and Goodman-Delahunty, n 25 above.

- There was one person in particular who had very good notes. But again, he had the same problem that most of us had. When you are taking notes, you don't know the relevant ones of what people are saying. You are not taking a transcript, you just trying to take relevant points. You don't know where the evidence fits in.

- [The opening addresses] sort of give you a broad outline of what it's all going to be about. But . . . it's like looking for gold in the desert. You know what I mean? There's a lot of mineral out there but where's the nugget?

Should Jurors be Allowed to Ask Questions of Experts?

Judges do not encourage jurors to ask questions generally, and to the author's knowledge never of expert witnesses, during the trial.[49] Several US researchers have considered the issue of whether jurors should be permitted to ask questions of witnesses during trials.[50]

- [We] are not professional and know the finer details of things. It would take up an awful lot of court time. Then one thing would trigger another and I think it could quite easily get out of control. Whereas a lawyer would stick to the facts and he would stick to the facts of answering that. Whereas if it was a jury person to the pathologist I think it could get a bit messy.

- . . . [I]t was quite hard to sit there and think you're quite invisible because you can't say anything, you can't talk and you don't ask questions. . . . You are just there with what could be a wall between you. Knowing that you don't ask questions at all . . . You're thinking 'I wonder what they meant by that?' when the witness answered something. Or you're saying 'Take it easy, take it slow' . . . You're important but you're not at the time.

- . . . [W]e had, just a particular question just wasn't answered . . . We actually raised it couple of times, 'can we pass a note to the judge to get him to ask the questions' and we were told 'no.'

- Say . . . the first day of a six week trial . . . the jury gets fully informed . . . and at that time if the person running that says, 'Now there is an opportunity for the jury to put questions to certain key people, being [the experts] and you will be given an opportunity to ask them questions after the prosecution and defence have finished their cross examinations, . . . related to information they've provided . . . the Judge may say, 'No, you can't ask that question or you don't have to answer it or the Judge may answer it on their behalf,' . . . and the thing about that is what that will do is it will make the jury more involved . . . [T]hey will then automatically want to participate more because you feel almost not an outcast, but you're sitting there, you have to make a judgment but you can't say anything really.

[49] Ogloff, Clough, and Goodman-Delahunty, n 25 above.
[50] See, eg SD Penrod and L Heuer, 'Tweaking Commonsense; Assessing Aids to Jury Decision Making' (1997) 3 *Psychology, Public Policy and the Law* 259–285; Dann, Hans and Kaye, n 18 above, 14; M Dodge, *Should Jurors Ask Questions in Criminal Cases: a Report Submitted to the Colorado Supreme Court's Jury System Committee*, 2002, at <http://www.courts.state.co.us/supct/committees/juryreformdocs/dodgereport.pdf>, accessed 22 March 2006.

Should Jurors have Copies of Expert Reports in the Jury Room?

In the author's experience, expert reports rarely go to the jury room. Jurors are expected to rely on what has been said in the witness box, with the aid of their notes, if any. Mock jury research using a civil trial scenario has suggested that provision of such statements would improve the quality of juror decision making.[51] Jurors were asked whether they thought access to the reports would have assisted them.

- There was also another part of his report that wasn't publicly in the court room which was a diagram he had on the last page which indicated the point at which the hammer left the hand ... and ... showed where the vehicle would've been at that point which was about twenty metres away. It then gave as both the vehicle and the hammer move towards each other, the closing distances and the point of impact. I found that that was a really important thing to think about ...

- I found there was more supporting evidence for the defence when you looked into that report than the defence brought up.

- I think it would be good because to go back over it. It's long days and it was quite long. . . . I think sometimes you do forget things they say.

What do Experts do to Help the Jurors?[52]

Presentation style[53] was an important factor for jurors in understanding the expert evidence:

- I was so happy I was there. . . . It's like a breath of fresh air in the whole court because the way she approached it and the crucial thing she would say ... that's a very good question. And we all went wow, why would you say that, because by then you've sussed a few things, what you say and you don't say and she would go and explain it and she would do a scientific explanation, then she'd explain it for the plebs like me and say this is that and this is a patella and this will happen in that case and I thought that was great. I revelled in that because it was like being in medical school. I've never been but I could imagine that's what it would be like and you're not going to get that education anywhere else. In my life I'd never be exposed to that ... and you were seeing a real live happening of an occurrence that happened to someone and how she explained what happened to ... his body, his internal parts and ... because of the way that she explained the scientific reasoning behind everything.

- It all fitted together what she said. It just flowed on and it was logical. She explained it both in scientific terms and in layman's terms. ... [S]ome people can ... in a way belittle you. Patronising, yeah and she didn't. She just looked at you. She gave all the body language ... said hey guys, I'm telling you this; this is how it is. I know you

[51] L ForsterLee, I Horowitz *et al*, 'The Bottom Line: the Effect of Written Expert Witness Statements on Juror Verdict and Information Processing' (2000) 24 *Law and Human Behaviour* 259–270.   [52] Ivkovic and Hans, n 16 above.
[53] ibid.

haven't been to university and none of you are doctors of science at all, but this is how it is. And you went yeah, I can understand that, yep. And we all went back and we all talked about it with our little biscuits and whatever we were given and that was good stuff . . . and she smiled at everybody when she could. When she spoke to you she looked at you, made connection with you and she just didn't look at one of us, she scanned the whole lot of us.

What Could Experts Do Better?[54]

Jurors commented not just on presentation styles, but on the need to provide a basis for an opinion. This attitude echoes the 'basis' rule in the law of evidences, where an opinion may be excluded if the basis for it is not made clear.[55]

- I think he needed to explain it a couple of more times . . . [W]e all learn differently, we all listen differently so he had to put it in a few different scenarios for us to understand where he was coming from.
- [The expert] didn't really relate to us, I don't think. He didn't look at us at any stage, he just looked straight at the prosecutor and to me that's rude, would you say? I think it's rude because we're the ones that are there to say yes or no and I think he should be looking at you as well, you know.
- I would've expected more from him. In more detail. I would've expected some sheets from him to show some calculations and if an object that weight is ejected and actually done some experiments with an object that weight and we discussed that, . . . I wasn't convinced by him at all actually, come to think of it now. I was disappointed for a person who was supposed to be very learned and I even got the impression he didn't want to say one way or the other. He could've done more I think. Maybe I'm wrong, I'm no person with a huge degree, but I would've thought some more experimentation could've gone on and have been detailed that experimentation.

How did the Lawyers and Judges Help or Hinder Understanding of the Expert Evidence?

The presentation of expert evidence in the courtroom depends not just on the expert, but also on the manner in which the expert is questioned by the lawyers, and presented by the lawyers and judge in addressing the jury directly.

- It did get confusing. It got straightened out in the end but there were some points where he just got into calculating and bits and pieces where it got confusing because we were all trying to write it down and stuff like that. It would have been better on the whiteboard. [The lawyer] did it later on the whiteboard and it made perfect sense.
- Well the baddie's side definitely tried to confuse the issue. That was their main intent. I think that their main point was to discredit this guy and confuse the issue. The guy wouldn't put up with that. That was good because we were all sort of rooting for him by that time. They have got to know that if they are nasty that people aren't going to

[54] ibid.   [55] See *R v Turner* [1975] 1 QB 834.

like them for it. They were rude and sarcastic and they were really detrimental to their own case in that way. You could see that they were being deliberately negative to try and put a negative light on the guy. But the guy was standing still on his belief and it was almost like watching a bully in the primary schoolyard to a certain extent. It was like 'I've lost all respect for you; you're just silly, aren't you?'

- ... [T]he lawyer for the goodie's side was very good and made sure that he explained everything the way that he should so we'd all understand it. We could ask a few just basic meaning questions like 'What does that word mean?'... And the judge was a funny little old man and he kept on coming back to points too, just making sure that if he understood it that hopefully we did. .... [H]e made him redefine some things that were a bit vague and stuff like that.

Some jurors carry out their own investigations, despite often[56] receiving judicial instructions to the contrary:

- ... I didn't come to any conclusion until I'd actually sat down with a model. I had a little car and I actually saw what would happen with the wheels and trying to depict when everybody's saying... I did it at home. Next morning, I explained to [the other jurors] what happened and it was logic....

- I did go home and ask my husband to look up something because he is a student in uni. 'You've got all the business books, could you look it up?' and he couldn't find it for me so I think we just gave up....

- I actually pulled my street directory out... that night I think, I had a look at the streets and location because things come up. That isn't to make a decision on obviously, it was just an idea to see where it was.

- I know that one person did go out and they said that it was a lot closer than they expected. I think she was told she shouldn't have gone out there.

The Deliberation Process

The foreperson is usually selected by the jurors early on the first day of the trial, upon the judge's request. The role of the foreperson has been said to be crucial.[57] The choice of foreperson was often regretted, depending on their competence in running meetings. Members of the jury other than the foreperson would frequently facilitate the deliberations. Jurors commented:

- A foreperson needs to be able to run a meeting.
- We need to pick the foreperson later when we know each other.
- Our [foreperson] was useless. Useless as tits on a bull. It was one of the other lasses who actually was writing the things down and calling the shots and I felt that this was sad.

Jury deliberations have been described as evidence-driven or verdict-driven.[58] That is, the former commence with a review of the evidence and issues in the case

---

[56] Ogloff, Clough, and Goodman-Delahunty, n 25 above.
[57] Young, Tinsley *et al*, n 31 above.
[58] PC Ellsworth, 'Are Twelve Heads Better than One?' (1989) 52 *Law and Contemporary Problems* 247.

before voting, whereas the latter poll early, and then work on the perceived minority to attempt to reach a verdict. Research in New Zealand suggests this distinction may be artificial.[59] Jurors interviewed thus far have reported each approach, sometimes within the one deliberation. Compromise verdicts (discussion of which is beyond the scope of this paper) were disturbingly evident.

- I think we started off on the points of law. I thought 'Did he cause the death?' and the answer's 'Yes' so that's a tick. Then we went onto the second part 'Was the death unlawful?' and then went through the sub points of that and there was a lot of discussion about that. Then after that we went back to get that point clarified. Some people had trouble focusing on just that sub point and not jumping towards another one because they basically intertwined a bit. Then from there that's when we started looking at the experts . . .

- It went around the table. That was just to get a rough idea of what people were looking at and then we went round the table and people spoke and if someone said 'Move on' and they didn't want to talk just yet we'd move on. People just let people have their say . . . when you listen to other people then you start to think. It was changed a few times. People got more evidence and then they read the [indictment] and we went through the papers . . . .Then we'd go through and vote again. Then we'd have another say . . . 'Why did you change your mind? What do you think now?' . . .

[A]t the beginning of the process when we were deciding what the rules of engagement were really, you know, for the meeting . . . It started with a vote. Just so that people could hear what it was, and it was very clear at that initial vote that this doesn't mean anything. This is just so we know this is our gut feeling . . . The vote was taken. The 'don't knows' kind of stayed in the middle because they didn't know. The people who were either guilty or not guilty actually put their arguments forward as to why they would arrive at a decision like that. So you had to justify your reasoning . . . We certainly started with the elements of murder . . . We got all the evidence. We pretty much reviewed the scene and we went over . . .

. . . [T]oo often when we went back to the jury room during the actual court proceedings, we never really sat down and discussed the evidence . . . people were just using it as a break to have a cup of coffee and I thought in some cases almost have a bloody holiday from work.

- . . . the girl that was doing the whiteboard was brilliant. She ended up saying that 'okay, in the end whoever is going for guilty, we'll go around—you give your reasons as to why you think they're guilty,' (so we noted them all up there) and us that thought they were innocent could then ask them questions on why they felt that and then okay, can you try and show us why'. She did it brilliantly. I swear. And you really need a system like that. If we didn't have them to come up with that, and we even said that in there actually, like 'how are we meant to do this' and we just figured it out.

- We dealt with it in the order of theories or propositions and evaluated the evidence associated with that particular proposition.

---

[59] Young, Cameron *et al* n 30 above; Young, Tinsley *et al*, n 30 above.

One Juror's Suggestions

Jurors are well equipped to make suggestions for change in the way expert evidence is presented, but rarely consulted:

- ... [T]he prosecution and defence, everybody knows who's going to come as a witness and roughly what they're going to talk about and I would think the first day of any case, especially eight weeks long, which involves some 80 plus people, that first day should be spent giving an overview to say that there's going to be this gentleman from the police forensic unit and he's going to tell you about the tests he's conducted and scenarios he's conducted and his presentation is going to be done this way. It doesn't mean that what he's saying is what actually happened or here's the implement, for argument's sake, but you'll have to make your mind up about that, but he'll tell you what he did right down as an independent type ... with the information he's got and you'll have a forensic pathologist get up and talk to you. Now some people will say, 'what's a forensic pathologist? I thought pathologists test blood,' and we can be told that you will have someone and they will go into very detailed account as to what they found. And you also have the defence bring their forensic pathologist ... in so we get an overview of who we're going to see and what we can expect from them and especially in a long case where you've got to absorb a lot.

The courts have to have someone that can do that. ... 'You're going to see video evidence. Do you all understand what time lapse videos are because you're going to see some time lapse video? If you don't understand it, ok, I'll explain what it is', maybe put it in a book that they get when they hand back at the finish. The reason I say that is because people came on and I had no idea ... why they were there ... and I said 'what the heck was that about. Why are we wasting time?' ... I think that they need to say the prosecution will be presenting these guys, the defence will have theirs and there'll be cross examination by both parties and the reason they do that is for such and such.

Conclusion

This study is due for completion in early 2007. Reports will be published at that time both as to the expert evidence aspects of the study, and the rich mine of additional data volunteered. Strong evidence is emerging suggesting that jurors and juries are better equipped to deal with expert evidence than popularly thought, and that though they may be forensically aware, they may not be bedazzled by the so-called 'CSI effect'.

21

Conflicts over Territory: Anti-Social Behaviour Legislation and Young People

Julia Fionda, Robert Jago, and Rachel Manning

Introduction

One of the hallmarks of New Labour's campaign on crime and its causes has been their attempt to crack down on what they call 'anti-social behaviour'. This catch all phrase lit up the statute books in 1998 when section 1 of the Crime and Disorder Act created a new order (the Anti-Social Behaviour Order (ASBO)) which was designed to deal with the relatively trivial but persistent problem of anti-social behaviour; that is, behaviour which may fall short of criminality but is nevertheless a social nuisance. The hallmark of the order was its 'catch all' status and the vague definition of 'anti-social'. This new form of 'delinquency' is victim-defined, and the order applies to any behaviour which a victim finds harassing, alarming or distressing. Indeed, Rutherford[1] suggested that the order's ambiguous definition was aimed at 'the elephant on the doorstep': behaviour which cannot be specifically detailed but which we know when we witness it. What is anti-social to one person may not be anti-social to another but if two people find it so then a court can, using the ASBO, adjudicate to remove or attempt to restrain that 'anti-social' behaviour. In the seven years since its inception, the order has been used to manage the prostitute, the troublesome delinquent, the elderly busybody and even the autistic teenager.[2] The ASBO's authority lies in civil law and its application therefore requires only the civil standard of proof, although sanctions for its breach are criminal, giving it a legally hybrid status which the government themselves have previously called 'sub-criminal' law.[3]

---

[1] A Rutherford 'An Elephant on the Doorstep: Criminal Policy without Crime in New Labour's Britain' in P Green and A Rutherford (eds), *Criminal Policy in Transition* (Oxford, 2000).

[2] See <www.statewatch.org> where these and numerous other examples are detailed.

[3] HC Standing Committee B, 28 April 1998, col 37.

In opposition in the early 1990s, New Labour had claimed that everyone was entitled to 'a quiet life'[4] and the ASBO sought to deliver on that commitment. Whilst the Home Office anticipated that these orders would relate to a wide range of social nuisance,[5] a further discussion of the problem in 2003 revealed their disappointment with the success of the ASBO and a determination to 'take a stand against' anti-social behaviour.[6] The Anti-Social Behaviour Act 2003 extends provisions in this area to tackle a greater range of more specific behaviours, including the running of crack houses, difficult tenants, errant parenting, the carrying of real or imitation firearms, noise, rowdy behaviour in public, graffiti and fly-posting and even failure to prune a high hedge.

This paper focuses on a measure aimed specifically at young people. Part 4 of the Act deals with the dispersal of groups of any age whose behaviour in public places is harassing, alarming or distressing. However, section 30(6) of the Anti-Social Behaviour Act 2003 applies more widely, giving the police officers (or their civil counterparts—community support officers—section 33 of the Act 2003) the power to remove from any public place people under the age of 16 if they are out and not under the control of an adult between the hours of 9pm and 6am, *regardless* of whether their behaviour is causing concern to members of the pubic.

This measure is controversial not least because it effectively enforces a curfew for young people in public places. There appears to be a conflict over territory. Young people have historically formed groups which enjoy 'hanging around' the streets. The police and the community at large believe that 'hanging around' is anti-social, intimidating and not to be tolerated. This latest measure is aimed at dealing with the perceived problem of young people in public places and resolving at least one side of this conflict. As soon as groups are dispersed and young people escorted home it is felt that other sections of the community who have long been afraid of using the streets will feel safe once more. Whether the impact of this provision on the young people so removed is conciliatory or inclusive is rather more uncertain.

In this paper we aim to explore the nature of this conflict over territory and we will challenge some of the manifestly outdated presumptions about the nature of groups and the impact of their behaviour on others. This will allow us to explore how governmental and media rhetoric often reinforces the fear of groups that has influenced the passing of this latest provision. Having explored concerns about the legislation, we will consider how criminological theory has viewed conflict between young people and other social groups as well as how psychology helps us to understand and challenge many of the assumptions made about

[4] Labour Party, *Safer communities, safer Britain: Labour's proposals for tough action on crime* (London, 1995).

[5] Home Office, *Tackling Anti-Social Behaviour Together: The one day count of anti-social behaviour* (London, 2003).

[6] Home Office, *Respect and Responsibility—Taking a Stand Against Anti-Social Behaviour* Cm 5778 (London, 2003).

groups and their place in human development. Concepts such as place attachment, for example, may help us to explain why sweeping powers of dispersal can have a detrimental effect on young people. Finally we shall investigate another conflict over territory: and ask whether the law ought to listen and respond more readily to psychological discourse which has much to contribute to understanding and preventing delinquency in young people rather than simply displacing it from one area to another. Removal to the home sounds suitably protectionist, but for many young people home may be more criminogenic than the public sphere.[7]

The Legislation and Its Concerns

The journey of the Anti-Social Behaviour Act 2003 through Parliament was suitably perilous in that a number of key commentators voiced concerns in both the House of Commons and the House of Lords. Their concerns centred on the potential of the provision for dispersal of young people to alienate young people from the mainstream of society and reinforce long-standing stereotypical perceptions of young people as threatening and unruly.[8] While the Bill's supporters were keen to point out that the dispersal provision was not just aimed at young people and their bad behaviour, it nevertheless became clear that the presence of young people in public places at night often caused distress regardless of their actions. Baroness Scotland of Asthal suggested that:

It is not only the behaviour of groups that makes people feel threatened in their communities. The presence of the group, and the fear of what it might do, prevents people from using the open spaces and facilities within communities ... The provisions are not limited to children. Groups can be dispersed, regardless of age.[9]

Whilst that may or may not be true, this was not justification enough for some in opposition to the Bill: 'we accept that the Bill is not just about young people [but] for the sake of young people, it [anti-social behaviour] must be addressed by measures that do not alienate and demonise them.'[10] The tension in the Parliamentary debates between the themes of maintaining the safety of public areas at night on the one hand and preserving the freedom of young people to act according to their own social norms on the other is symbolic of the conflict over territory that the provision appears to have created.

The provision to disperse is difficult to justify for four reasons: the subjectivity of the need to disperse; the location of the problem in terms of safety; the questionable need for the provision in the light of existing legislation; and difficulties with monitoring the implementation of the provision. First, the provision hinges

---

[7] J Graham and B Bowling, *Young People and Crime* HORS 145 (London, 1995).
[8] G Pearson, *Hooligans: A History of Respectable Fears* (Basingstoke, 1983).
[9] HL Debates, 23 October 2003, vol 653, col 1833.
[10] Baroness Walmsley, HL Debates, 17 September 2003, vol 652, col 1011.

on the *perception* of members of the public that young people's presence in public places is harmful. If someone perceives there to be a problem then they can request of an authorized person the dispersal of a group of young people, whether or not any harm has materialized. Baroness Walmsley voiced real concerns at this power:

> If someone who for no good reason, does not like people hanging around, he can make a complaint and the group can be dispersed. They may be children on their bikes or scooters around a village pond or a group at the bottom of the stairwell of an urban block of flats...they just have to be there. What kind of police state does it make us when it becomes a criminal offence to walk down the street?[11]

This is problematic because commentators on youth justice have asserted that people more readily perceive young people's behaviour as harmful or threatening[12] and that this is often borne out by surveys of public opinion on young people and crime.[13] Furthermore, few would deny that the behaviour targeted by the provision (that is, hanging around in groups) is inherently normal behaviour for young people. Perceptions that it is problematic stem from a fundamental misunderstanding by adults of the cultural norms for youth as a social group rather than from any real danger. Like a status offence young people may be demonized for what they commonly do and for who they are. Baroness Linklater suggested that this is in part due to 'a regrettable aspect of our British culture, which is an innate suspicion of the young...that generates the sort of fear of what a group of even two people might do just by their presence on a street corner, and which then actually fosters distrust, promotes more alienation of the young and feeds the fear of them'.[14] Baroness Sharp further claims that section 30(1) is 'antagonistic to young people. There is perhaps a failure to understand why they gather together in groups. Young adolescents are gregarious and they want to get together.'[15]

Secondly, the risk posed by the existence of young people out at night without supervision is presumed to be a vague and undefined risk to the safety of others. However, it could conversely be perceived as a risk to the safety of the young people themselves. Where other provisions have been enacted for the protection of unsupervised youngsters (such as local child curfews or child safety orders under the Crime and Disorder Act 1998): 'The new measures in the Bill reverse the presumption; they view children and young people as primarily a problem rather than in need of protection.'[16] Indeed, the Joint Committee on Human Rights voiced concerns that as there was a lack of evidence of a social need for this particular provision and any sufficient justification for it in terms of protecting children, it was likely to breach articles 5, 8 and 11 of the European Convention on Human Rights as a disproportionate and discriminatory provision simply aimed at preventing the

---

[11] HL Debates 17 September 2003, vol 652, col 1013.

[12] Pearson, n 8 above, and J Fionda, *Devils and Angels: Youth, Policy and Crime* (Oxford, 2005).

[13] M Hough and J Roberts, *Youth crime and youth justice: Public opinion in England and Wales* (Bristol, 2004).   [14] HL Debates, 18 July 2003, vol 651, col 1097.

[15] HL Debates, 18 July 2003, vol 651, col 1131.

[16] Baroness Walmsley, HL Debates, 17 September 2003, vol 652, col 1012.

free social association of young people.[17] It is also unlikely to be compliant with the United Nations Convention on the Rights of the Child which promotes the right to free assembly and recreational activities. Furthermore, a dispersal provision is unlikely to tackle any underlying social problems which result in the public association of youths, such as problems at home or a lack of social facilities for them: 'It is like giving an Aspirin to someone who complains of a headache rather than arranging a brain scan to find out whether they have a brain tumour, then operating to remove it.'[18] The provision tackles presence on the streets as the perceived, but possibly irrational, problem rather than its deeper social aetiology.

Thirdly, these dispersal powers are a replication of provisions already in existence in previously enacted public order legislation. The Public Order Act 1986, sections 4 and 5 criminalize threatening, abusive or insulting words or behaviour, or disorderly behaviour. The government therefore already has a tool to deal with this perceived problem. However, the same can be said for most aspects of anti-social behaviour legislation. The value of these civil, rather than criminal, procedures though, is that the criminal standard of proof can be dispensed with in responding to more trivial forms of problematic behaviour, as the authors of the Broken Windows theory, from which the legislation borrows heavily, behove in any strategy to combat problems of social nuisance which lie on the margins of criminal behaviour.[19] The political capital in measures which promise to protect us from fearful elements in our social environment cannot be underestimated and Baroness Linklater identified such a political agenda in these provisions: 'There is a real danger of employing politically attractive strategies which are simple, speedy and visible in the hope that they will reassure the electorate that action is being taken, regardless of whether a problem has really been addressed or has simply been moved on elsewhere.'[20]

Finally, there is concern about monitoring the implementation of this provision. Unlike the use of stop and search powers under the Police and Criminal Evidence Act 1984, which requires recording and documentation, section 30(6) does not appear to require any authorization, evidence of harm or official documentation. In common with informal, discretionary police cautions (a stern word from a police officer on the beat) it will be difficult to know not only how much it is being used, but in respect of whom. Lord Thomas worried about the impact with ethnic minority communities where racial tensions are already high.[21] Widespread and unmonitored powers to target young people whose behaviour may be perceived as problematic in a vague and undefined way, could be misused in way which further demonizes an already socially marginalized group.

---

[17] Joint Committee on Human Rights, *Anti-social Behaviour Bill*, Thirteenth Report, HC 766/HL 120 (London, 2002).
    [18] Baroness Walmsley, HL Debates, 23 October 2003, vol 653, col 1830.
    [19] JQ Wilson and G Kelling 'Broken Windows: The Police and Neighbourhood Safety' (1982) 249 *The Atlantic Monthly* 29.   [20] HL Debates, 17 September 2003, vol 652, col 1031.
    [21] HL Debates, 17 September 2003, vol 652, col 1014.

In policy terms, therefore, concerns over the efficacy and ethics of the dispersal powers have been expressed at an early stage through discussion on the Bill as it progressed through the Parliamentary process. This paper, however, suggests that both the disciplines of criminology and psychology offer evidence that the provisions are likely to be ineffective or even counter-productive, if their purpose is to prevent public disorder and youth crime. The empirical and theoretical discourse of each of these disciplines can, in its own way, inform an appraisal of the dispersal powers. However, policy makers have singularly failed to take into account these discourses in their perceptions of a problem that they claim to be solving and in making law to that end. Indeed, criminological theory suggests that such legislation may not necessarily have a problem-oriented slant, but rather a more complex function in reinforcing the cultural norms of powerful groups that make that law, thereby exacerbating conflicts between subcultures and maintaining the powerlessness and exclusion of young people from mainstream society.

Youth and Deviant Behaviour

Young people are undoubtedly a criminogenic group. Home Office statistics suggest that they commit a large proportion of all known crimes. Research would also suggest that young people are more prone to deviance, because their environment and transition into adulthood propels them into it.[22] Perceptions of deviant youth may therefore reflect reality to some extent, although the measurement of youth crime has become increasingly victim-focused in recent years, which means that the statistics may reflect perceptions of young people as deviant rather than those perceptions being formed from objectively gathered statistical information from the police and the courts. The British Crime Survey, a victim report survey, now forms an integral part of the picture of crime presented by the Home Office,[23] and the police have been encouraged to present more 'honest' statistics on victim 'calls for assistance' rather than numbers of incidents that, in their discretion, they view as criminal.[24] Moreover, theoretical criminology informs us that perceptions of young people as deviant can exacerbate deviant behaviour through labelling and the creation of cultural conflict.

Explanations and Perceptions

Historically the youth crime problem has been seen to stem principally from problems at home and a lack of attachment and positive relationships between

[22] Graham and Bowling, n 7 above; C Flood-Page, S Campbell, V Harrington, and J Miller, *Youth Crime: Findings from the 1998/99 Youth Lifestyles Survey* HORS 209 (London, 2000).
[23] See eg J Mattinson and C Mirlees-Black, *Attitudes to Crime and Criminal Justice: Findings from the 1998 British Crime Survey* HORS 200 (London, 2000).
[24] J Simmons, *Review of Crime Statistics: A Discussion Document* (London, 2000).

parents and their children, as well as disaffection from school; lack of educational achievement there resulting in truancy and exclusion.[25] Both factors compromise the extent to which young people can be nurtured, supervised or, in the most benevolent sense, socially controlled. The statistical evidence portrays a problem which is low key in terms of the seriousness of the offending behaviour, largely a transient problem as desistance sets in upon maturity (even though this may be much later than previously thought) and overall the level of crime is gently falling.[26]

Despite this 'reality' of youth crime, the perception of youth crime as dangerous, violent and increasing persists both in policy circles and popular discourse (including the media). The Home Affairs Committee in 1993 received a great deal of evidence from policy makers and practitioner representatives which smacked of a disbelief that the problem of youth crime could possibly be understated. Despite evidence to the contrary from pressure groups and organizations representing the welfare agencies, the Committee were told by representatives of the judiciary and the police that the problem was escalating and needed urgent control: '... there is plenty of evidence that the number of offences committed by juveniles is going up substantially and ... it is nonsense to say that the picture is media created.'[27]

Muncie[28] reviews media reporting of youth crime, which reveals a rather different picture. Indeed, we are all too familiar with headlines which portray young offenders as threatening, violent and persistent and which suggests that the youth crime problem is serious and increasing, a view diametrically opposed to the reality. This is not surprising given that Steve Chibnall[29] has identified that the selection of crime news tends to reflect the commercial concerns of newspaper editors rather than a concern to 'inform' readers of the true nature of youth crime. However, the perceptions of the public who consume media reports demonstrate that they often believe the essence of the headlines that confront them. Hough and Roberts conducted a survey of 1,800 people aged over 16 about their views on the nature of the youth crime problem and young offenders. The survey revealed a sense that youth crime was increasing (75 per cent of respondents reported this) and that young people were responsible for a disproportionate amount of recorded crime (74 per cent believed that young offenders committed more than 30 per cent of known crime, when the true figure is around 12 per cent). There were also (false) perceptions that drug crime among young people was increasing faster than other types of offences, and that over 40 per cent of youth crime involves violence.[30]

[25] Graham and Bowling, n 7 above; Flood-Page, Campbell, Harrington, and Miller, n 22 above.

[26] K East and S Campbell, *Aspects of Crime: Young Offenders 1999* (London, 1999).

[27] Home Affairs Committee, *Juvenile Offenders*, Sixth Report HAC 441-I (London, 1993) viii.

[28] J Muncie, *Youth and Crime* (2nd edn, London, 2002) 39–41.

[29] S Chibnall, *Law and Order News* (London, 1977).

[30] Hough and Roberts, n 13 above, 9–13.

The important question is, which view informs policy, the rhetoric or the reality? This is important, because a policy which seeks to provide a solution to a problem which is misconceived sets itself up for failure and, more significantly, could cause damage to the young people who find themselves subject to misguided intervention. The latest of these enactments has been the Anti-Social Behaviour Act 2003. We understand why young people may commit crime and we understand the extent to which the media and those in government seek to embellish the reality of crime as it becomes increasingly popular to target young people as the root of social ills. Theoretical criminology provides evidence that such interventions may exacerbate general crime levels and an individual's propensity to offend, but at societal level, these interventions can generate hostility towards youth as a social group, excessive social control of their behaviour and social exclusion, which pushes them further towards the margins of citizenship from where their proven social disadvantages and lack of opportunities are compounded. The theoretical evidence points to youth crime emanating from the behaviour of a sub-culture which is neither valued nor tolerated and is perceived as threatening to the social identity of the mainstream of society. The problem may be further escalated by the media, policy makers and authorities through the labelling process.

Cultural Conflict

Criminological theorists in the 1960s and 1970s developed a new radical explanation for crime which, departing from individualistic, positivist and pathological theoretical explanations, centred on the structure of power in society and the inequalities it produces. Collectively these theories, some based on the work of Karl Marx, argued that society's norms are not only established by the powerful groups in that society, but are also enforced by the powerful ruling groups in a way that maintains their power and represses challenges to it. The enforcement of a dominant culture in society creates conflict between that culture and other, less powerful sub-cultural groups, which are marginalized and socially excluded from mainstream society in the name of repressing their alternative culture and their perceived threat to the dominant group. These interactionist theories are, therefore, based on class structure and the use of power to control minority groups through the application of notions of deviance.

Thorsten Sellin's 1938 work, *Culture Conflict and Crime*,[31] argued that as each society or culture established its own norms, rules of behaviour were enacted in criminal laws, defined according to the moral code of those norms. Individuals within that culture are socialized to uphold and abide by those laws, which represent a social consensus. Where this consensus is truly present in any society, crime rates will be low. However, more realistically, where that consensus is not shared

---

[31] (New York, 1938).

by all, a conflict arises between two groups holding different cultural values and acting according to a different set of norms. Inter-cultural conflicts are the 'primary' conflicts identified by Sellin, where in neighbouring societies conflict arises, as a dominant society invades the territory of another and attempts to impose its cultural norms. We witness many such primary conflicts on a global scale. However, secondary conflicts are intra-cultural and arise between a dominant culture and sub-cultures within a particular society. Through a similar process, the dominant culture 'invades' and attempts to impose its norms, through the criminal law and deviant labels, on the accepted behaviour of sub-cultural groups. Youth may be one of a number of such sub-cultures within a society. Indeed, Vold[32] argued that social identity determines that human beings will inevitably congregate in like-minded groups, even if only transiently and for a specific purpose, to respond to crisis or challenge (such as a Trade Union or political pressure group). Therefore, while youth may be a transient state, young people may share cultural norms, which differ from those of the adult world. Where the balance of power between different cultural groups is relatively equal, Vold argues they may resolve their conflict through compromise and discussion. However, where the power imbalance is great, as between youth and adults, revolution occurs in which the more powerful group use the criminal law to suppress the interests of the less powerful culture.

In the context of anti-social behaviour, the legislation provides a tool to the dominant cultural interests in society with which to suppress the cultural norms of a perceived deviant sub-group. The norms of that sub-group may involve activities such as hanging around, socializing in public places and apparently 'doing nothing'. However, these behaviours may be perceived as threatening, not in the sense of any immediate danger, but rather more in the sense of a risk to the social identity of the dominant group. The social cohesion of the dominant group may depend on marginalizing the sub-cultural norms and psychology may take our understanding of this process further (as discussed below). However, legislation which essentially creates a form of deviance out of the 'normal' or habitual behaviour of a sub-group, creates a social conflict which young people lack the power to either resolve or win.

Labelling, Outsiders, and Deviance Amplification

In a similar vein, Howard Becker[33] and Stanley Cohen[34] have developed theories of crime which emphasize the role of society's response to deviance, rather than the role of the individual's psychology, physiology or reaction to their social circumstances. A process of social exclusion of deviant groups to the margins of

[32] *Theoretical Criminology* (New York, 1958).
[33] H Becker, *Outsiders: Studies in the Sociology of Deviance* (New York, 1966).
[34] S Cohen, *Folk Devils and Moral Panics: The Creation of the Mods and Rockers* (London, 1972).

society (either physically or rather more esoterically) prompts a vicious circle in which their behaviour, thus marginalized, is regarded with greater suspicion and the law is more heavily enforced against them. It is the labelling by society of certain acts or groups as deviant, that creates a crime problem. Since no act is intrinsically criminal, its deviant status rests on society's perception of either an act or those committing it as deviant. Put simply, the law enforcement apparatus creates crime by labelling it at such.

Howard Becker, a sociologist from the Chicago School in the 1960s, studied both dance musicians and the use of marijuana as examples of activities which foster cultural identities, complete with behavioural codes, belief systems and moral values. Their values and norms differ from those of mainstream society, who cast them in the role of deviants or 'outsiders'. Whether an act is deviant, therefore, depends on how other people perceive it, and whether an individual is a deviant depends on how others react to their behaviour. Perceptions of young people and crime will be discussed below, but it is significant that the legislation on anti-social behaviour takes Becker's view to its logical extreme in creating a form of deviance out of any behaviour perceived as such, whether or not it infringes any code of norms or causes any greater harm than annoyance or hatred.

Cohen studied this labelling theory in relation to public perceptions of youth sub-culture in Britain in the 1960s, and in particular the impact that the media have on the labelling process. His work, *Folk Devils and Moral Panics*, related the moral panic that ensued in response to the behaviour of groups of Mods and Rockers, who had descended upon Clacton for a Bank Holiday weekend in 1964. Inclement weather restricted the activities of these youths and, as they became bored, they committed minor acts of vandalism and became involved in minor skirmishes between rival groups. As the media reported this behaviour as threatening and out of control, so the police responded with a more authoritarian and controlling approach. As they arrested further young people behaving suspiciously, the media's fears were confirmed, a moral panic ensued and the vicious circle of more authoritarian policing continued. In this way, the groups of youths had been demonized as 'folk devils' who threatened social order, and social anxiety increased through the intensified response of the police and the hysterical reaction of the media. Here again, the response of institutions to deviant behaviour can manufacture or 'amplify' deviance rather than reduce it.

Psychological Explanations

There are a number of parallels between the criminological literature and the social psychological study of groups. The inclusion of a group level of analysis has implications for how we conceptualize young people's behaviour and evaluate the potential effects of the use of these dispersal powers in the context of intergroup relations. In addition, it is the spatialized nature of the behaviour and legislation that is also pertinent to a psychological analysis. To this end the relevant psychological approaches that will be drawn on stem from work in social and environmental psychology. More specifically it is primarily the social identity approach to crowd behaviour, pioneered by the work of Reicher *et al*,[35] which will be used to conceptualize the intergroup nature of the anti-social behaviour legislation. Moreover, the spatialized nature of the legislation prompts consideration of notions of place, identity and territoriality from environmental psychology.

The Social Identity Approach

The social identity approach proposes that our group memberships form an integral part of our self-concept. It is suggested that, depending on the social context, behaviour can be determined by either personal or social identities. The social identity (SI) approach has worked to counter the traditional view of groups as posing danger to individual responsibility and control, and instead sees social identities as equally meaningful as personal identities, and additionally as a means through which individuals can seek to maintain positive self-esteem. As Tajfel argued, social identity is 'the individual's knowledge that he [or she] belongs to certain social groups, together with some emotional and value significance ... of this group membership'.[36] The group thus becomes a key part of meaningful subjective experience, rather than a dangerous entity that acts as a dehumanizing force.

Self-categorization theory (SCT),[37] an offshoot of SI theory (and part of the 'social identity approach' more generally) constitutes a more recent development in the analysis of group processes, and enables a more developed focus on the dynamic nature of self and group/intergroup interaction. The key suggestion here is that the basic psychological process underlying group behaviour is the categorization of the self at the social category level. Where people define themselves in terms of a shared category, self-perception becomes depersonalized and people see themselves as similar, prototypical representatives of their ingroup category.[38] Other members of the group ('ingroup members') are perceived as sharing needs, goals and motives, and are seen as interchangeable. The dynamic nature of social identity is central to SCT, in that changes in social context lead to changes in

[35] SD Reicher, R Spears, and T Postmes, 'A Social Identity Model of Deindividuation Phenomena' in W Stroebe and M Hewstone (eds), *European Review of Social Psychology*, 6 vols (New York, 1995).

[36] H Tajfel, *Differentiation between social groups: Studies in the social psychology of intergroup relations* (London, 1978) 292.

[37] JC Turner, MA Hogg, PJ Oakes, S. Reicher, and M Wetherell, *Rediscovering the social group: A self-categorization theory* (Oxford, 1987).

[38] JC Turner, 'Some current issues in research on social identity and self-categorization theories' in N Ellemers, R Spears and B Doosje (eds), *Social Identity* (Oxford, 1999).

self-categorization.[39] The particular self-categorizations that are salient at any one time become important for understanding and explaining perception and behaviour.

Taken as a whole, the social identity approach offers a contemporary critique of traditional conceptualizations of crowd/group behaviour, and poses a number of practical implications relevant to the dispersal powers. This will be demonstrated through one of the areas in which the social identity approach has been applied: crowd psychology. The reconceptualization of the social group—as a meaningful entity that has implications for identity and behaviour—provides a group level of analysis that treats group behaviour as an important entity in its own right, as well as providing an articulation of group- and individual-levels of explanation. A key point is that while social identity is something that has important personal implications, it is also not reducible to the individual, being seen instead as a cultural and historical construct.[40]

Crowd Psychology

Traditional approaches to crowd psychology impact on the way in which groups are conceptualized—both within psychology, but also more widely. One of the key figures in the development of crowd psychology is Le Bon.[41] Although now largely discounted, Le Bon's work had an important impact on social psychology, and the context of the development of this approach parallels the development of legislation on anti-social behaviour. Le Bon suggested that, when in a crowd, members lose their sense of self and personal responsibility. Their behaviour shifts under the control of a primitive racial unconscious or 'group mind', and lacks the control of 'civilization'. While Le Bon's work is largely concerned with crowd behaviour, Le Bon himself suggested that all forms of collective assembly— including juries and parliamentary assemblies—could demonstrate the operation of this racial unconscious. Reicher's later critique of Le Bon's work[42] emphasized the way in which crowd psychology grew out of nineteenth-century thought: the fear among the propertied classes of 'the mob'. Reicher argues that the process of industrialization led to the increased separation of owner and worker, where a mass urban proletariat became an unknown quantity, exacerbating the fears of the ruling classes. The development of crowd psychology thus centred on a hostility to crowd action and—importantly—what Reicher terms a 'bias of perspective';[43] commentators were never participants of the crowd and therefore did not understand the experience of protest. These biases were built into early crowd

---

[39] MA Hogg, DJ Terry, and KM White 'A Tale of Two Theories: A Critical Comparison of Identity Theory with Social Identity Theory' (1995) 58(4) *Social Psychology Quarterly* 255.

[40] S Reicher, 'The context of social identity: domination, resistance, and change' (2004) 25(6) *Political Psychology* 921.   [41] G Le Bon, *The Crowd* (Dunwoody, Ga, 1895/1968).

[42] S Reicher, 'Crowd Behaviour as Social Action' in JC Turner, MA Hogg, PJ Oakes, S Reicher, and M Wetherell (eds), *Rediscovering the social group: A self-categorization theory* (Oxford, 1987).

[43] ibid, 173.

psychologies, which 'started from ideological premises and used theory to give these substance'.[44]

Reicher's critique of Le Bon's approach is formed of three key claims. First, Reicher asserts that Le Bon ignores the role of authority in crowd events, both in terms of the distal social background and the proximal involvement of the police or army. Secondly, through the elision of the context of crowd action, crowd behaviour becomes pathologized. Removing the intergroup context of conflict locates it in the crowd itself. Thirdly, the individual is presented as the preserve of reason—whereas all collective behaviour includes some degree of pathology. Social behaviour is therefore constructed as the antithesis of the rational individual. While further alternative approaches have at times taken more individualistic perspectives (for example, Allport)[45] the study of crowd psychology—and group behaviour more generally—tends to revolve around the concept of 'deindividuation', which, as Cannevale, Scarr, and Pepitone[46] have indicated, is derived from the Le Bonian concept of submergence and is concerned with the decreased self-evaluation, causing anti-normative and disinhibited behaviour that arises from presence in a crowd.

The SI critique of social psychological approaches to crowd behaviour more generally rests on two key observations: they conceptualize deindividuation as a loss or blocking of the self (and therefore that a unique personal self is the basis for rational action), and that the presence of a group is an antecedent of the deindividuated state (ie the group serves to hinder the operation of such selfhood).[47] Therefore the SI approach offers an alternative conceptualization of the self in order to challenge the assumption that the self is lost in the presence of a group. In addition, it challenges the assumption of the danger of the group for behavioural control. As Reicher *et al* have argued, explanations of deviance tend to invoke group processes, and in particular tend to rely on 'the logic of deindividuation theory: individuals, especially those with unformed or damaged selves, lose all sense of standards in the group and become liable to negative and dangerous influences'.[48] Moreover, they go on to argue that while 'delinquency' tends to be a group phenomenon, 'non-delinquents have a rich collective life' and that 'the assumption that individuals are deindividuated in the group and hence become at best volatile and at worst anti-social is in opposition to what we know about group processes'.[49] Group membership, therefore, does not necessitate involvement in conflict or violence—the group effect is not generic.

However, the SI approach to collective behaviour further suggests that what might be considered 'anti-social' can in fact be reconceptualized as highly social in its own right. As Reicher and Emler[50] have argued, membership of particular

[44] ibid, 173.   [45] Allport, F. *Social Psychology*. (Boston, 1924)
[46] Cannevale, F., Scarr H. & Pepitone A. 'Deindividuation in the small group: further evidence'. *Journal of Personality and Social Psychology*, 16, 141–147.
[47] SD Reicher, R Spears, and T Postmes, 'A Social Identity Model of Deindividuation Phenomena' in W Stroebe and M Hewstone (eds), *European Review of Social Psychology*, 6 vols (New York, 1995).
[48] ibid, 173.   [49] ibid.
[50] S Reicher, and N Emler, 'Managing reputations in adolescence: The pursuit of delinquent and non-delinquent identities' in H Beloff (ed), *Young People in Society* (London, 1987).

'delinquent' groups can serve an important function in terms of the maintenance of self-esteem, the need to belong and the management of reputations. Moreover, the developmental aspect of group membership points to the shifting nature of identity, and ultimately leads us to a consideration of the way in which the use of practices such as dispersal powers can impact on identity, and therefore behaviour. The behaviour of group members is not merely an expression of identity, but rather an active strategy to ground and convey that identity. Ignoring the developmental aspects of group membership loses this key dimension of behaviour.

The dynamic way in which identities are taken up, conveyed, and, most importantly, change over time leads us on to the particular theoretical and empirical contribution that the SI approach has provided. Reicher's work in this area stems from the study of the St Paul's riots in Bristol. Reicher has shown how accounts of crowd behaviour, when analysed in detail, paint a different picture to the 'irrationalist accounts of politicians and in the media'.[51] First, Reicher's work has suggested that there are clear limits to crowd action: in the first phase of the St Paul's rioting the police were targeted. In a second phase, once the police had gone, financial institutions and shops owned by outsiders were targeted. Moreover, in this account we begin to see the importance of the spatialized nature of collective action, in the sense that there were clear geographical boundaries to the action—with rioters chasing the police out to particular points and then staying there, subsequently controlling access to this area. Secondly, Reicher suggests that participants talked about themselves in terms of shared social identities: as members of the St Paul's community, and their relations to others on a categorical level. Thirdly, Reicher claims that there was a clear match between crowd action and self-definition as crowd members. A St Paul's identity was defined in terms of oppression by institutions such as the police, exploitation by financial institutions, and poverty in an affluent society—which Reicher claims derived from the black experience of group members (although only a minority were themselves black—this became the definition of the St Paul's group membership itself). Here again Reicher emphasizes the geographical limits to the attacks, and in so doing points towards the geographical characteristics of identity.

Reicher notes the sense of power that crowds can facilitate in people, allowing them to express identities that they might not otherwise feel able to, mirroring Phillips' claims regarding the instrumental nature of riots.[52] This might be translated to the realm of youth behaviour, whereby collective behaviour can give rise to identity expression that might not otherwise be possible. Indeed, it is perhaps the negation of this important role of the group in the lives of young people—and their more general psychological well-being (given the argument that groups do not necessarily lead to 'deviance' and the self-esteem functions that social

---

[51] S Reicher, 'The Psychology of Crowd Dynamics' in MA Hogg and RS Tinsdale (eds), *Blackwell Handbook of Social Psychology: Group Processes* (Oxford, 2001) 196.

[52] S Phillips, 'Social Issues and Policing: Politics or Psychology?' in R Cochrane and D Carroll (eds), *Psychology and Social Issues: A Tutorial Text* (London, 1991).

identities serve)—that is in part at issue in the employment of dispersal powers. However, the power of the police to enforce a displacement of young people through the use of these powers suggests that the power facilitated in the group may not necessarily be realized by young people who happen to be in places where they are not wanted by more powerful sections of society, particularly as their groupings may be on smaller scales.

Elaborated Social Identity Model

The elaborated social identity model (ESIM)[53] represents a more recent development in the SI approach to collective behaviour. This work has generally focused on the study of political protest and football matches to suggest a reconceptualization of some of the key features of the SI approach. In order to provide a more developed understanding of the dynamic and changing nature of crowd behaviour, the ESIM suggests that the context of particular groups is constituted by the actions of other groups. The implications of this in relation the anti-social behaviour legislation will be illustrated through an example of empirical research in this area.

The emphasis of the ESIM is on crowd behaviour as an intergroup phenomenon. Thus the way in which groups other than those perceived as deviant are implicated in the phenomenon in question (in this case anti-social behaviour) must be considered. Intergroup relations themselves change the nature of social relations as they redefine social identities and the associated norms of behaviour. Thus, while a particular group may perceive itself in a particular way, the actions of another group may lead them to redefine themselves. As Reicher suggests: 'When the outgroup has the power to privilege its interpretations this may lead actors into unimagined positions.'[54] Thus actions may have unintended consequences, due to these actions being interpreted by others.

Stott, Hutchison and Drury's field study of collective 'disorder' in the 1998 football World Cup finals in France illustrates this process.[55] Through an analysis of interviews, (participant) observation, and media-related resources, Stott *et al* constructed a 'consensual account' of behaviour which focused on the experience of English and Scottish football fans, in order to challenge explanations of the presence or absence of disorder in terms of the presence or absence of 'hooligan' fans. Essentially their analysis demonstrates how the treatment by other groups of English fans in particular led to a change in the behaviour of the fans

[53] J Drury and S Reicher, 'Collective Action and Psychological Change: The emergence of new social identities' (2000) 39 *British Journal of Social Psychology* 579; S Reicher, ' "The Battle of Westminster": Developing the social identity model of crowd behaviour in order to explain the initiation and development of collective conflict' (1996) 26 *European Journal of Social Psychology* 115; C Stott and S Reicher, 'How conflict escalates: The inter-group dynamics of collective football crowd "violence" ' (1998) 32 *Sociology* 353.   [54] Reicher, n 51 above, 201.

[55] C Stott, P Hutchison, and J Drury, ' "Hooligans" abroad? Inter-group dynamics, social identity and participation in collective "disorder" at the 1998 World Cup Finals' (2001) 40 *British Journal of Social Psychology* 359.

(and subsequent violence). Thus, both English and Scottish fans initially saw their respective groups in similar terms—as non-violent. English fans, like Scottish fans, therefore initially perceived the normative dimensions of their identity as 'boisterous but legitimate'. However, the intergroup context that English fans found themselves in, unlike the Scottish fans, was 'hostile'. Marseilles youths in particular were understood to be carrying out unprovoked and indiscriminately violent attacks on category members. In the absence of police intervention to prevent these attacks (and sometimes targeting English supporters rather than the local youths), English fans thus came to feel vulnerable to attack and therefore to perceive their own violence as legitimate—as a 'defensive activity on the part of ordinary category members'.[56] Moreover, in the context of a history of similar experiences, the English fan identity for some came to intensify its antagonistic nature, resulting in the 'no one likes us and we don't care' attitude when travelling aboard.

In contrast, the Scottish supporters found themselves in a non-hostile intergroup context, where the behaviour of other groups was seen as legitimate. Moreover, they achieved positive differentiation from English fans through the contrast between their own perceived identities and their perception of the stereotypical characteristics of English fans. While there was a general adherence to non-violence, violence was seen as legitimate in particular contexts, particularly in the regulation of ingroup members' behaviour (ie to stop transgressional ingroup violence and maintain non-violent norms). Finally, the historical context of positive intergroup relations between Scottish and other fans regenerated positive intergroup relations in new social contexts, and therefore positive behaviour of this group would effectively be self-policed.

This analysis thus illustrates the way in which outgroup activity perceived as illegitimate can lead to the redefinition of identity and thus behaviour—ultimately positioning violence as a legitimate activity in a particular intergroup context. The ESIM therefore suggests that social identities are in part determined by the way in which a group is reacted to by other groups, and the legitimacy of this action. Whether young people themselves perceive the actions of authorities towards them in the form of dispersal powers as legitimate is therefore highly significant. If they do not, according to the ESIM, this may have important implications for the behaviour of groups of young people in future.

The Spatialized Nature of Identity

While the application of the SI approach to collective behaviour has potentially important implications for the way in which anti-social behaviour is both conceptualized and policed, there is a general absence in this work of the consideration of

---

[56] Stott, Hutchison, and Drury, n 55 above, 369.

the spatialized nature of both conflict and violence. It has been argued above that the use of dispersal powers hinges on the conflict over appropriate locations for youth. Dispersal powers effectively regulate space, as they determine who can legitimately be where. Reicher's work explains how identities can be seen to have important geographical bases and that the places where particular groups are, may form important parts of particular identities. In moving particular groups from particular places, the police reinforce the notion that those places are not legitimately part of these particular identities.

Just as from an ESIM perspective other groups can be seen to play a defining role in the nature of social identity, so, it is argued, can place. Indeed, there is an increasing range of psychological research which underscores Relph's suggestion that attachment to places is a defining feature of human existence,[57] and examines the claim that places can form a significant component of a person's self concept, particularly in the form of 'place identity'.[58] The notion of place identity offers one possible route through which the spatial dimension of social identity might be explored in relation to anti-social behaviour. According to Proshansky *et al*, place identity is 'a sub-structure of the self-identity of the person consisting of, broadly conceived, cognitions about the physical world in which the individual lives which concern the physical settings that 'define day-to-day existence'.[59] This field of research suggests that 'place-belongingness' (a 'narrower conception of place identity')[60] is an important part of place identity, and thus important for processes of self-definition, mirroring the SCT approach, which points to the importance of self-definition in terms of group memberships. The place identity construct thus offers a possible route through which to theorize the links between the physical environment and social identity.

Of particular relevance here is Proshansky *et al*'s discussion of 'discrepancies between a person's place-identity and the characteristics of an immediate physical setting'.[61] They suggest that such discrepancies arouse cognitions for reducing or eliminating these discrepancies, which involve knowing what is 'right' and 'wrong' in a physical setting, and how this discrepancy might be overcome. Place identity cognitions are also claimed to function as 'anxiety and defense (sic) mechanisms', which may signal threat or danger.[62] While they point out that such cognitions are distinct from actual behaviour, their suggestion that it is only when 'a physical setting becomes dysfunctional'[63] that a person becomes aware of their expectations for that setting points to the way in which the disruption of routine experience can inform us about existing, albeit largely unattended to, place identifications. This work on place identity suggests that cognitions relating to the

[57] E Relph, *Place and Placelessness* (London, 1976).
[58] H Proshansky, A Fabian, and R Kaminoff, 'Place Identity: Physical World Socialisation of the Self' (1983) 3 *Journal of Environmental Psychology* 57.   [59] ibid, 59.
[60] ibid, 76; KM Korpela, 'Place-Identity as a product of environmental self-regulation' (1989) 9 *Journal of Environmental Psychology* 241.   [61] Proshansky *et al*, n 58 above, 70.
[62] ibid, 73.   [63] ibid, 75.

physical environment also contain the 'social norms, behaviours and rules associated with the environment'[64] and as such includes an explicitly social dimension.
It would appear that it is the place identity of particular groups that is being
attended to in the anti-social behaviour legislation—and, importantly, that these
groups do not include young people.

Territoriality

An alternative conceptualization of the importance of the spatial dimension of
behaviour comes in the form of territoriality. Although Gillis and Hagan suggest
that the concept of territoriality does not enjoy much popularity in the social sciences due to its common perception as instinctive,[65] its important psychological
dimension has meant that the concept has become of interest to psychologists.[66]
However, the definition of territoriality is not necessarily straightforward,[67] and
several accounts appear to rely on the features of animal territoriality prior to
attempting a 'human' analysis.[68] Brown's 'clustering' of a series of definitions leads
to a general consensus on territoriality as involving the endurance of territories
over time, owners not perpetually involved in demarcation and defence, and,
most importantly here, a focus on identification with places. Moreover, Brown
claims that some accounts suggest that the possession of territory decreases the
likelihood of aggression.

With regard to the specific qualities of human territoriality, Brown points to
the increased importance of social and cultural concerns, manifesting itself in, for
example, greater territorial behaviour towards objects than with animals.
Moreover, human territoriality is unlike the survival-orientated responses of
animals, focusing instead on the 'higher' needs of status, recognition by others,
and achievement or self-image.[69] Sack defines human territoriality as 'the attempt
to affect, influence, or control actions and interactions (of people, things and relationships) by asserting and attempting to enforce control over a geographic
area'.[70] It therefore appears to be the conflict between different groups' claims to
territory that is at issue in dispersal.

Altman has additionally suggested that territory serves an important role in the
maintenance of privacy, whereby people can close or open the self to contact with
others. Altman suggests that territories differ with respect to motives or needs,

---

[64] C Twigger-Ross, M Bonaiuto, and G Breakwell, 'Identity Theories and Environmental
Psychology' in M Bonnes, T Lee, and M Bonaiuto (eds), *Psychological Theories for Environmental
Issues* (Aldershot, 2003) 215.
[65] AR Gillis and J Hagan, 'Bystander Apathy and the Territorial Imperative' (1983) 53 *Sociological
Inquiry* 449.   [66] I Altman, *The Environment and Social Behavior* (Monterey, Calif, 1975).
[67] See eg RB Bechtel, *Environment and Behavior* (London, 1997).
[68] BB Brown, 'Territoriality' in D Stokols and I Altman (eds), *Handbook of Environmental
Psychology* (New York, 1987).
[69] JR Gold, 'Territoriality and human spatial behaviour' (1982) 6 *Progress in Human Geography* 44.
[70] RD Sack, 'Human Territoriality: A Theory' (1983) 73 *Annals of the Association of Human
Geographers* 55.

geographical features, social units, and temporal duration of occupancy. As a result he proposes a classification of human territories to highlight these distinctions: primary, secondary, and public.[71] The distinction between these different territories is made on the basis of the centrality of the territory to the person or group, its pervasiveness, and its personal involvement. As such, Altman proposes that the violation of a primary territory can be a 'serious affront to a person's self-identity'[72] with a lack of primary territory potentially leading to a lack of self-esteem and of identity itself. Primary territories are thus the most central to identity, and provide a sense of control.

Public territories, on the other hand, are owned by no one: 'almost anyone has free access and occupancy rights'.[73] Altman suggests that public territories are 'heavily' dependent on institutions, norms and customs, as rules are not commonly enforced by any particular user. Secondary territories are characterized as semi-public and are 'less central, and exclusive', and have a certain regularity of use. Due to their 'intermediate' status between primary and public territory, Altman suggests that 'the possibility exists for considerable conflict as boundaries are established, tested, and violated'.[74] It would seem that through the use of this particular form of anti-social behaviour legislation we are witnessing an example of this considerable conflict, perhaps suggesting the growing spatial scale of secondary territory claims.

Bonnes and Secchiaroli suggest that the majority of research on territoriality, along with personal space and privacy, has too often concerned itself with the psychological function of 'control' or personal 'defence'. In terms of territory in particular, Bonnes and Secchiaroli suggest that 'the central role played by the physical-geographical dimension in the definition of territoriality cannot be separated from that of the meanings which environmental spaces can variously assume for individuals' behaviours'.[75] They suggest that, rather than focus, for example, on the study of territorial markers, we should instead direct our attention towards examining 'the ways in which places and things become part of both the identity of persons and the social processes they more or less directly participate in'.[76] While Bonnes and Secchiaroli point to the lack of empirical studies in this area, a more social perspective on territoriality appears to necessitate a consideration of the identity-related implications of spatial regulation—both for legislators and those who become regulated by the dispersal provision.

Contemporary research is beginning to look at the interrelationships between place and social identity, in the form of 'socio-environmental identity', 'place-related social identity' and 'social urban identity'.[77] Valera *et al*, for example, elaborate the concept of social urban identity to suggest that it has

---

[71] Altman, n 66 above, 111.   [72] ibid, 112.   [73] ibid, 118.   [74] ibid, 114.

[75] M Bonnes and G Secchiaroli, *Environmental Psychology: A psycho-social introduction* (London, 1995) 83–84.   [76] ibid, 85.

[77] E Pol, 'The Theoretical Background of the City-Identity-Sustainability Network' (2002) 34 *Environment and Behavior* 8; D Uzzell and E Pol, 'Place Identification, Social Cohesion and

territorial, psycho-social, temporal, behavioural, social and ideological dimensions that underpin it. Most notably, Valera and Guàrdia suggest that an increase in shared values, and a greater spatial appropriation of a given (residential) area, will lead to greater care of the surroundings by residents, and an increase in 'solidarity attitudes'.[78] However, such approaches have a tendency to ignore the young person's perspective, and particularly those young people who may predominantly be subject to dispersal. Are young people to become marginalized, only being allowed to occupy those places where 'we' do not wish to be or do not care about? The interaction with police, and with the more general notion that their behaviour is illegitimate in particular places will have inevitable consequences for the ways in which groups of young people define themselves, as they are denied what they might perceive as a legitimate right to be in a particular place. The arguments used in the context of crowd psychology would appear to be instructive in terms of the possible effects of the use of dispersal powers, particularly in terms of the danger of oppression of particular groups. A conflict therefore arises over our need to control public space and our need in a civil society to allow different social groups to co-exist in public places to which they have formed an attachment. There is an evident need, in the light of the legislation, to look specifically at the attachments that young people themselves have with places. For example, where young people are attached to those places from which they have been excluded under the Anti-Social Behaviour Act 2003, or where such places form part of their personal or collective identities, there is a need to understand the potential impact this may have on their self-concept and behaviour.

Conclusion: Conflicts Explored

By identifying the hallmarks of the power to disperse groups we can see that the government, in its crackdown on what it perceives to be anti-social behaviour, is living up to the general perceptions of youth and crime. These perceptions are not without merit and we do not condone crime or anti-social behaviour. Neither do we condone the draconian nature of these powers, though, which, when considered alongside the psychological literature, can have a detrimental affect on young people, in terms of their attachment to place and their own social identities. To decide groups are automatically bad is to make an unwarranted presumption. If we did as Baroness Massey suggested listen to youth who 'want additional recreational facilities where they can meet friends and enjoy themselves'[79] then we may

---

Environmental Sustainability' (2002) 34 *Environment and Behavior* 26; S Valera and J Guàrdia, 'Urban Social Identity and Sustainability' (2002) 34 *Environment and Behavior* 34, 54; S Valera, J Guàrdia, and E Pol, 'A Study of the Symbolic Aspects of Space Using Nonqualitative Techniques of Analysis' (1998) 32 *Quality and Quantity* 367.

[78] Valera and Guàrdia, n 77 above, 64.
[79] HL Debates 17 September 2003, vol 652, col 997.

discover that our failure to provide alternative facilities punishes young people for their need to congregate, to assemble. Baroness Walmsley concludes that 'if asked why they are there they will say that they are too broke to go to the cinema... nowhere else to meet their mates... there is nothing'.[80] We are compounding what Baroness Linklater warned against, which is the notion of 'sanction creeping': 'we include younger people whose lives and lifestyles betray all sorts of inadequacies, the measures will increase the likelihood of them being drawn further into youth offending and the criminal justice system'.[81]

A final point of interest is that this conflict over territory may also be one for the disciplines themselves to resolve. Policy makers should look at this latest psychological literature which does suggest that group activity can be an important part of young people's social experience. Ignorance of this simply supports an approach blinded by penal populism and targeting an easy group. The triumph of clearing the streets or simply dispersing young people to other areas in this conflict cannot, it is argued, be rewarding when the price is so very high.

[80] ibid, vol 652, col 1012.   [81] ibid, vol 652, col 1030.

22

Psychology as Reconstituted by Education and Law: The Case of Children with Autism

Michael King and Diane King

Introduction

In this paper we examine the way that legal decisions concerning the education of children with autism (and other special educational needs) are able to overcome any shortfalls in existing psychological understanding by giving the impression that these decisions are underpinned by a sound body of knowledge. This enables courts and tribunals to claim that they are doing justice, while at the same time conveying the impression that *the right educational decision* has been made for the child. By applying a theoretical approach that concentrates on the interfaces between different social systems, we raise difficult questions concerning both law's claim to 'do justice' for children with autism and their parents and the assertion that courts and tribunals are capable of meeting the educational needs of these children.

Our particular concern is autism or, to be more precise, those psychological impairments which are given the label of 'autistic spectrum disorders'. These impairments may take on legal relevance and affect the outcome of court decisions in a number of different contexts. In criminal law, for example, an adolescent boy suffering from Asperger's syndrome (high-functioning autism) who killed a young girl was recently found guilty of murder, while Anti-Social Behaviour Orders have been imposed on autistic children who have exhibited odd and disturbing behaviour. The focus of this paper, however, is on 'special educational needs' and the ways in which paediatricians', developmental psychologists' and child psychiatrists' accounts of autistic spectrum disorders and descriptions of children suffering from these disorders are reproduced within education and subsequently within law and incorporated within educational and legal decisions.

Theoretical Approach

Until recently, both academics and practitioners have tended to conceptualize the relationship between law and those areas of science concerned with childhood disorders as one of symbiosis. According to this conceptualization, while the knowledge and treatment of childhood disorders on the one side and the knowledge and practice of law on the other are clearly very different, information between these two disciplines could be freely exchanged. Scientific knowledge could enter the legal system directly, mainly through the device of expert evidence and such evidence could be incorporated in legal decisions. Similarly, within medical and psychological practice, law, whether in the form of statute or case law, has been seen primarily as a body of knowledge which informs practitioners about their legal duties, what constitutes unlawful activity and, in particular, how to avoid claims for negligence, breach of contract and failure to report child abuse. We shall call this approach *the input-output model.*

Sociology has produced many theoretical accounts of law and the sciences of childhood disorders. There is the notion that both are engaged in creating and disseminating power gained from specialist forms of knowledge to be interpreted and applied only by professionals or experts.[1] Alternatively, these forms of knowledge have been seen as providing the information necessary to allow society to conceptualize and operationalize notions of risk and safety.[2] More recently, the ideology of children's rights has been reformulated as a social theoretical way of understanding the relationship between adults and children in different social settings, including those of education, health and law.[3] This approach offers a critique of a developmental psychology which portrays children as incompetent and unable to make decisions for themselves. All relationships involving adults and children are thus analysed in terms of the ways that power is exercised by adults over children through the pervasive notion of childhood incompetence.

None of these theories, however, begins to provide a satisfactory operational model of the complex manner in which information is transferred between the different institutions or professional bodies which exist side by side in modern

---

[1] See eg M Foucault, *The Order of Things: An Archaeology of the Human Sciences* (London, 1974). M Foucault, 'Disciplinary Power and Subjection' in C Gordon (ed), *Power/Knowledge: Selected Interviews and Other Writings* (New York, 1976) and M Douglas, *Risk and Blame. Essays in Cultural Theory* (London, 1994).

[2] U Beck, *Risk Society. Towards a New Modernity* (London, 1992); A Giddens, 'Risk and Responsibility' (1999) 62 *Modern Law Review* 1; and B Hudson, *Justice in the Risk Society* (London, 2003).

[3] A James and A Prout (eds), *Constructing and Reconstructing Childhood* (2nd edn) (Basingstoke, 1997). A Prout, 'Childhood Bodies: Construction, Agency and Hybridity' in A Prout (ed), *The Body, Childhood and Society* (London, 2000) 1. For a sociological critique of this model, see N Lee, 'Towards an immature sociology' (1998) *The Sociological Review* 458.

society. The *input-output model*, with its implicit assumption that information is freely transferable and may be reproduced unchanged in different social contexts, still prevails among practising lawyers and scientists who work together in different areas of the law. At the same time, there has been an increasing recognition of the defects in law's attempts to control 'expertise' and make it more reliable for the purpose of legal decision-making. This recognition has found expression in the ever-continuing quest among judges and law reformers for the perfect test for identifying what is and what is not scientific knowledge and for the 'philosopher's stone', through which such knowledge may be transformed into reliable expert evidence.[4] The relentless pursuit of this quest has resulted in frustration and disappointment as all efforts fail to prevent cases being decided on 'scientific' information which subsequently turns out to be wrong, biased or incomplete.[5]

On the 'scientific side', the intrusion of law into ever-wider areas of social activity (accelerated recently through the evolution of human rights law) has produced an increasing reliance on specialist scientific information. This in turn has provoked strong criticisms of the courtroom process and the demands made of expert witnesses.[6] Within some scientific disciplines it has even resulted in a general reluctance to take on the role of expert.[7] Although the belief among lawyers and scientists remains that these problems are solvable within the general framework provided by the *input-output model*, there has been a gradual but increasing awareness that the issue of making scientific knowledge available for legal decision makers is not nearly as simple as previously appeared to be the case.

Within the last twenty years a new theoretical model has emerged within sociology which totally reconceptualizes the relationship between what it describes as different systems of communication. This is *autopoietic theory* or *the theory of closed systems*. It was the late German social theorist, Niklas Luhmann who was responsible for developing this theory as a sociological account of the way in

---

[4] Examples of the search for 'the right formula' for distinguishing reliable scientific evidence from 'junk science' are the US Supreme Court cases of *Frye v US* 293 F 1013, 1014 Dc Cir 1923; *Daubert v Merrell Dow Pharmaceuticals* (1993) 113 SCt 2786; *Kumho Tire Co v Carmichael* (1999) 119 SCt 1167. In England, expert scientific evidence may be discounted by the courts because of the witness's lack of qualifications or experience or because the evidence is based on incomplete facts or research or represents an unorthodox position. *Manchester City Council v B* [1996] 1 FLR 324; *Re AB (Child Abuse: Expert Witnesses)* [1995] 1 FLR 181.

[5] The obvious example is the recent controversy concerning Sir Roy Meadow's expert evidence in the Sally Clark murder trial and his subsequent striking off by the British Medical Association for serious misconduct in misleading the jury over the statistical likelihood of two children in the same family dying from 'cot death'. The discrediting of expert diagnosis of Munchausen's syndrome by proxy is another, more general, recent example.

[6] See eg T Furniss, *The Multi-Professional Handbook of Child Sexual Abuse: Integrated Management, Therapy and Legal Intervention* (London, 1991) and The Honourable Mr Justice Wall and I Hamilton, *A Handbook for Expert Witnesses in Children Act Cases* (London, 2000).

[7] Carole Kaplan, a consultant child psychiatrist, wrote recently: 'A major challenge is how to encourage junior colleagues to work as experts.' C Kaplan, 'Children and the Law: The Place of Health Professionals' (2002) 7 *Child and Adolescent Mental Health* 181,185.

which modern society operates. Luhmann's general approach is counter-intuitive. It portrays society as consisting, not of individuals, but of communications which are organized socially within societal systems. Society therefore, becomes, the sum total of all meaningful communications.[8] According to Luhmann, the essential feature of the organization of modern society is its differentiation into separate and distinct social communication systems. Certain of these systems have become functional to the organization of meaningful communications *for society*. These include science, law, politics, economy and education. Each of these sub-systems has its own unique, non-replicable function which determines the form and nature which its communications take.

The essential point for our purposes is that each of these 'function systems' constructs, through its understanding (or coding) of the external world, a version of that world which is limited by its blinkered vision. The world 'in the eyes of law' consists, therefore, of a world which is divided into what is recognized as pertaining to law (*Recht*) and thus belonging to the legal system in a broad sense, and what is not law (*Unrecht*). Everything within that world-constructed-by law is seen, therefore, in terms of its relevance to legal issues. Moreover, everything that the legal system recognizes as belonging to law is reducible by the legal system to fit its code of lawful/unlawful; it becomes, in other words, amenable to legal decision-making.

Law's world (or law's environment) includes not only its self-identity (how law sees itself) but also law's version of all of society's other systems, such as economics, morality politics, science and education. This means that, although the legal system may give the appearance of importing information directly from these other systems, what it is in fact doing is invoking information from its own pre-constructed version of these systems, so that this information will always depend on the vision of the world that the legal system has itself created. This is equally true for all other systems, which, like law, have no way of relating to the external except by referring to the version of that world which one of them has constructed. They are all self-referring systems.[9]

The theory does not deny the existence of reality. Rather, it sees reality as in-accessible from within society except through the medium of social communication systems. Relationships between two systems are based, therefore, upon each reconstituting the other on its own terms, with each system generating its own version of what reality consists of. Thus, when communications produced by psychology—whether theories, research reports or assessments based on psychometric testing, enter the legal system, they do so as reconstructions of psychology within law. Similarly, when psychology concerns itself with legal communications,

---

[8] 'The system of society consists of communications. There are no other elements; there is no further substance but communications.' N Luhmann, *Essays on Self Reference* (New York, 1990) 100.

[9] M King and C Thornhill, *Niklas Luhmann's Theory of Politics and Law* (Basingstoke, 2003) 3–12. For a general account of Luhmann's theory, see King and Thornhill, ch 1.

such as courtroom processes, issues of legal guilt or children's best interests, it does so necessarily by applying its own scientific coding of psychologically true/ psychologically false. Within the terms of the theory, it would be impossible to do otherwise, since, as we have explained, the only reality that psychology recognizes is that constructed through its own operations.

The final point that we wish to make in this brief summary of the theory, is that its implications for the operations of the legal system in its relations with other social systems is not limited to concerns over the reliability of expert witnesses. It permeates, rather, all aspects of legal decision-making where law invokes information from extra-legal sources. In other words, it applies wherever legal communications go beyond a reiteration and interpretation of the law itself. In the particular area of special educational needs which we shall be examining in this chapter, there is usually no formal distinction between experts and other witnesses, and no special rules (other than time limits) governing the presentation of professionals' reports or oral evidence or criteria for testing the reliability of the information presented in evidence. Yet professional or expert witnesses' accounts of children's developmental disorders and educational impairments are nevertheless treated as if they represent facts or the truth and, as such, as knowledge on which to base decisions on how children's special educational needs will effectively be met.

The issue as to how scientific knowledge about developmental disorders and their implications for education finds its way into legal decisions is complicated by the fact that there are three distinct social communication systems involved: science in the form of psychology (or in some cases, psychiatry and paediatrics), education, and law. As we shall demonstrate, by the time that issues fall to be resolved by law, what started as accounts of children's impairments, as originally formulated within the system of science, have already been reconstructed in such a way as to make sense for educational purposes. Let us start, therefore, with the psychological account of 'autism' as a way of describing and diagnosing certain impairments in cognitive and affective functioning.

Psychology's Incomplete Understanding of Autism

Autism is a developmental disorder characterized by social and communication impairments and often accompanied by restricted interests and activities. Prevalence is estimated to be 5 per 1,000,[10] although this includes the full range of autistic spectrum disorders and not just 'classic' autism. Four times more boys than girls are thought to be affected. Diagnosis, under International Classification of Diseases (ICD) 10th Revision[11] and Diagnostic and Statistical Manual of

---

[10] C Gillberg and L Wing, 'Autism: not an extremely rare disorder' (1999) *Acta Psychiatrica Scandinavia* 399.   [11] World Health Organization 1994.

Mental Disorders (DSM) IV,[12] focuses on three areas of impairment:

- impairment in reciprocal social interaction;
- impairment in communication (verbal and non-verbal); and
- restricted repetitive and stereotyped patterns of behaviour, interests and activities.

There is considerable agreement over these behavioural criteria of autism and they have come to be known as the 'triad of impairment'.[13]

Autism was first recognized by Kanner[14] and later by Asperger,[15] who were working independently of each other in Baltimore and Vienna. A division is now commonly made between Kanner's autism (classic autism) and Asperger's syndrome (high functioning autism). In 1969 the concept of an autistic continuum was identified, according to which autism can be found with various degrees of impairment and functioning but with all autistic individuals showing impairment in reciprocal social interaction.[16] At the lower end of the spectrum, children may be severely impaired, have little or no language, low cognitive abilities and often other accompanying disabilities. Inevitably, they will require very specialist provision and care continuing into adulthood. Higher functioning children with autism have cognitive scores within the average or above average range, relatively good (but not unimpaired) language ability and are less likely to have accompanying disabilities. Although these children also need good care and provision to progress, they are less likely to need the level of care in adulthood needed by the child with classic autism.

The exact causes of autism are unknown, although there is strong evidence to show that it is due to brain dysfunction which is biological in origin.[17] Genetic factors are clearly important[18] but it is unlikely that one single gene is implicated. There are a number of cognitive theories which attempt to explain the link between brain and behaviour and these have generated a great deal of research which has furthered understanding of this disabling syndrome. Although a range of therapies and treatments are employed to help in the management of autism, as yet there is no real consensus on the most effective way to treat the disorder. This is in part due to the wide variability existing among individuals with autism. Among those psychologists specializing in the field, the need to assess each child and to develop an individual treatment and management plan for them is universally

---

[12] American Psychiatric Association, *The Diagnostic and Statistical Manual of Mental Disorders—Fourth Edition (DSM-IV)* (Washington, DC, 1994).

[13] L Wing and J Gould, 'Severe impairments of social interaction and associated abnormalities in children: epidemiology and classification' (1979) 9 *Journal of Autism and Developmental Disorders* 11.

[14] L Kanner, 'Autistic disturbance of affective contact' (1943) 2 *Nervous Child* 217.

[15] H Asperger, 'Die autistischen Psychpathen im Kindesalter' (1944) 117 *Archiv für Psychiatrie und Nervenkrankheiten* 245.   [16] Wing and Gould, n 13 above.

[17] J Morton, *Understanding Developmental Disorders* (Oxford, 2004).

[18] M Connor, 'Children on the autistic spectrum: Guidelines for mainstream practice' (1999) 14 *Support for Learning* 80.

accepted. Yet there is no cure for autism—it is a lifelong disorder, although individuals often make progress and develop coping strategies.

Children can be diagnosed with autism at various ages. Even those with severe impairments are often not diagnosed until over two years of age when they start to fail to reach the same social and communication developmental milestones as other children. A delay in language development is often the first obvious sign that something is wrong, but many parents will maintain that they had no concerns about their child until they entered pre-school or school. At this stage, when a child becomes part of a group situation, social and communication difficulties become more obvious. There is evidence to show that early diagnosis and intervention are beneficial,[19] but there is an obvious tension between early diagnosis and premature labelling of children who may exhibit difficulties which could disappear with maturity.

Psychology's Identification of the 'Educational Needs' of Children with Autism

Many children with autism do not look any different from other children and it can be difficult, therefore, for those around them to appreciate that they are nevertheless suffering from and struggling with the 'triad of impairment'. As they grow older, social situations, including those related to attending school, are likely to prove challenging for them. Their difficulties in making sense of the world can lead to increased anxiety levels and may result in behaviour which appears bizarre and antisocial. Although every child with autism is different and the behavioural manifestations of the cognitive impairments variable, there are certain key issues which make the education of these children within mainstream schooling a particular challenge. The 'triad of impairment' summarizes the difficulties of the autistic child, but the actual manifestation of these in the dynamics of the classroom can vary from situation to situation and child to child. For example:

Impairment with Reciprocal Social Interaction

A deficit in 'theory of mind',[20] that is a lack of understanding of how others think about and understand the world, means that children with autism fail to appreciate the feelings, beliefs and viewpoints of others. Understandably this leads to social difficulties and misunderstandings. Although all children with autism will have this impairment, some may react by withdrawing totally from social interaction whilst others attempt to interact but may upset, bore and irritate by their lack

---

[19] T Charman, 'Theory of Mind and the early diagnosis of autism' in S Baron-Cohen, H Tager-Flusberg, and DJ Cohen (eds), *Understanding Other Minds* (Oxford, 2001) ch 16.

[20] S Baron-Cohen, 'The autistic child's theory of mind: A case of specific developmental delay' (1989) 30 *Journal of Child Psychology and Psychiatry* 285.

of sensitivity for the feelings of others. Group activities, including games and play, will all present difficulties. The child with autism will often 'say what they think' without any heed to social conventions. In certain situations this can be amusing and refreshing but in the school system this will inevitably cause problems. The classroom teacher may not appreciate being told that the lesson is boring and stupid—even if it is! Specific teaching of social rules and skills is needed if the child with autism is to develop strategies to enable them to cope in the social world.

Impairment in Communication

As we previously mentioned, children with autism range from those with no language at all to, at the higher functioning end of the spectrum, those with adequate verbal expression. However, even these children are likely to have difficulties with non-verbal communication and with the pragmatic aspects of language, that is, the appropriate use of language to carry on a conversation. They will need to be taught explicitly aspects of communication, such as turn taking, intonation and eye contact and gestures, all of which come naturally to other children. Children with autism also have difficulties with receptive language (comprehension of language), and may either completely misunderstand what is being said to them or interpret literally language which is metaphorical or ambiguous, for example: 'It's raining cats and dogs.' A teacher cannot assume that instructions given to a child with autism have been fully understood.

Restricted, Repetitive and Stereotyped Patterns of Behaviour, Interests and Activities

Children with autism find change very difficult. They can become very set in their routines and resist any alteration. Often they develop obsessive interests which they are capable of concentrating on for long periods of time. The school day is full of changes, many sudden and without warning, and the child with autism lacks the flexibility of thought needed to deal with this. They respond best to an environment which is consistent and has an established routine. Without this they may become very anxious and distressed and behaviour problems can ensue.

How does Education Deal with Children with Autism?

All aspects of the triad of impairment associated with autism are potential barriers to learning in the conventional school. The problems for education, posed by the need to show that it is attempting to fulfil the potential of children diagnosed by psychology as suffering from 'autistic spectrum disorders', have been compounded in recent years by a widely held belief that children with disabilities should not be educated separately from 'normal' children. Based upon the political ideologies of human rights and equality, this belief had led to declarations to the effect that every child suffering from a disability has the right be educated with 'normal' children and not 'segregated' by having to attend a special school reserved for disabled children.[21]

In the United Kingdom, as in all post-industrial nations, this concern for equality for children with disabilities has inspired concerted campaigns for 'inclusive education' for such children. More recently, the English Education Act 1996 consolidated a legal framework for the implementation of a general policy of inclusive education and it is now estimated that over 66 per cent of pupils officially identified as having special educational needs[22] are educated in mainstream schools.[23]

The way in which the education system implements this policy in respect of children with autism is not uniform. This depends, first, upon the effects of the individual child's particular psychological impairment upon the *education system* and secondly upon the way in which the policy of inclusive education is interpreted by the different institutions responsible for education, whether schools or (in England and Wales) local education authorities (LEAs).[24] Not surprisingly those children who exhibit 'behavioural difficulties' are seen as more difficult to include within mainstream schools. Some commentators have questioned whether it is possible at all to meet the 'educational needs' of these children through inclusion and have pointed out the particular difficulties faced by schools in containing them and involving them in school activities.[25] Nevertheless, these concerns have not prevented some educational bodies from pursuing a policy of inclusion even in the case of severely autistic children, who have serious and multiple impairments, including little or no language, and severe behavioural problems.[26]

It is generally admitted within education, however, that children with autistic spectrum disorders (ASD) do present a major challenge, not so much for politics, which simply has to lay down a general policy for all school-age children with disabilities, but for education, which has to interpret this policy in respect of each

---

[21] This policy has obtained international endorsement in the Salamanca statement of 1994 UNESCO, *The Salamanca Statement and Framework on Special Needs Education* (Paris, 1994).

[22] This includes children with all manner of disabilities, physical as well as psychological.

[23] See DfES Statistics of Education: Special Educational Needs in England, January 2005 Issue No 24/2005, 2.

[24] The Education Act 1981 provided a legal imperative for the 'inclusion' of children classed as having special educational needs.

[25] S Shearman, 'What is the reality of "inclusion" for children with emotional and behavioural difficulties in the primary classroom?' (2003) 8 *Emotional and Behavioural Difficulties* 53. See also M Warnock, *Special Educational Needs: A New Look* (London, 2005).

[26] eg the London Borough of Newham, set out a policy statement in 1988 which contained the following: 'The ultimate goal for Newham council's inclusive education strategy is to make it possible for every child, *whatever special educational needs they may have*, to attend their neighbourhood school, to have full access to the national curriculum, to be able to participate in every aspect of mainstream life and achieve their full potential' (emphasis added). In a Tribunal case in which one of the authors of this article appeared as an advocate, Newham argued that they were able to meet the needs of a child with severe autism in a mainstream school.

individual child and for law which is required to determine whether these interpretations comply with the procedural criteria and rules of natural justice.

Since autism affects the way children understand and react to the world around them, this can lead to social, emotional and behavioural difficulties, as noted above. Often, within the school setting, the behaviour of these children can be unpredictable and difficult for others to understand. Because of this variety and unpredictability in the behaviour of children with autism, there are no easy solutions to the problems that they present to the education system. The challenge for education is how to provide schooling that can be seen to allow them to fulfil their potential or, in the terms of the English legislation, meet their 'special educational needs' whilst at the same time having regard to the 'educational needs' of the other children in the school.

In addition, the education system has to cope with a prevalent political ideology of individual rights which, when translated into educational terms, means that parents' views about the kind of education that they want for their children should, at the very least, be taken into account in educational decisions. At one point, English legislation insists that these parental views should be followed, unless there are specific reasons for not doing so.[27] Some parents of autistic children, for example, express a preference for 'mainstream provision', that is, education in a mainstream school; others choose specialist provision (a school that takes only children with disabilities).[28]

The purpose of this paper is not to offer solutions to these problems confronting the educational system, but rather to observe how law reconstructs them within its own communication system—a system which sees 'justice' as its objective, but is able to achieve this only by coding its environment in terms of what is lawful and what is unlawful. Once reconstituted in this way, highly complex issues which appeared intractable for education become simplified to the point that—always with the help of expert opinions—they emerge as amenable to legal decision-making. This, as we shall show, may create its own problems, but they are of a very different kind to those experienced by education or the scientific knowledge that supposedly informs the educational system.

Special Educational Needs Within Law

The same political ideology of individual rights that allowed parents to choose (within certain limits) the kind of school in which they wish their autistic child to

---

[27] Under Sch 27, para 3(3) to the Education Act 1996 the LEA is obliged to name in the statement the maintained school of the parent's choice, unless (a) the school is unsuitable to the child's age or aptitude or to his special educational needs, or (b) the attendance of the child at the school would be incompatible with the provision of efficient education for the children with whom he would be educated or the efficient use of resources.

[28] G Lindsay and JE Dockrell, 'Whose Job Is It? Parents' Concerns About The Needs Of Their Children With Language Problems' (2004) 37 *The Journal of Special Education* 225.

be educated has also, in England and Wales, offered these parents a legal process through which they may appeal against educational decisions made by an LEA. Since 1994 these appeals have been decided by an independent tribunal, recently renamed the Special Educational Needs and Disability Tribunal (SENDIST). It consists of a legally qualified chair flanked by two lay members, both experienced in children's education. Tribunal decisions are open to challenge by appeals on a point of law to the High Court and from there to the Court of Appeal and, with leave, to the House of Lords, the highest judicial authority in the United Kingdom. Appeals against the initial LEA's decisions are not confined to choice of school, but extend to every stage in the process of the educational system's assessment of an autistic child's special educational needs and the educational provision that should be put in place to meet those needs. A parent may, for example, appeal to a SENDIST against the LEA's decision not to assess a child who the parents claim has special educational needs.[29] Parents may also challenge the LEA's decision, following an assessment, that a statement of special educational needs is unnecessary.[30] Once a statement has been made, the parent may argue that the resources that the LEA proposes to put in place are not appropriate or sufficient to meet their child's needs, as set out in the statement, or may propose a different school to that which the LEA has chosen to meet the child's special educational needs.[31]

The introduction of these tribunals needless to say, has created within the legal system a whole vast new area for its communicative operations. In Luhmann's terms 'special educational needs law' has emerged as a programme within the legal system where law's lawful/unlawful coding of its environment may be applied to issues defined initially by other social systems, but reconstituted as legal problems requiring legal decisions. As a measure of the rapidity of the expansion of 'special education law' one needs only to contrast the number of recorded cases on special educational needs in the last twelve months with the incidence of cases in the year before the arrival of the independent lawyer-chaired tribunals. A search on LEXIS-NEXIS which compared the number of special educational needs cases reaching the courts annually (from 1 August to 31 July) revealed an eight-fold increase between the year 1991–2 and the year 1999–2000 (see Figure 22.1 below). Although there has been a decline in the number of cases over the last five years, the figure still stands at over four times that for 1991–2.

We have already drawn attention to Luhmann's general theoretical model of autopoietic social systems and the operation of the law as one of society's function systems. Indeed, much has been written in recent years about autopoietic law as a system of communication.[32] For the present purposes of examining how the legal system is able to transform psychological accounts of autism in a way that

---

[29] Education Act 1996, ss 329 and 329A.   [30] ibid, s 325.   [31] ibid, s 326.
[32] See eg King and Thornhill, n 8 above; N Luhmann, *Law as a Social System* (Oxford, 2004); and G Teubner, *Law as an Autopoietic System* (Oxford, 1993).

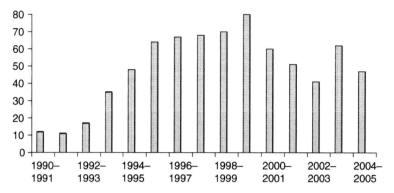

Figure 22.1. The number of 'special educational needs' cases recorded in Lexis/Nexis Professional

makes them useful for legal decision-making, however, we may legitimately distil these accounts of the complex nature of legal operations and apply them to special educational needs to extract the following:

(1) The self-referential nature of the legal system means that law invariably operates in a paradoxical way.[33] On the one hand it presents itself as doing justice by invoking 'the truth', 'facts', moral principles, common sense or rationality to justify its decisions. On the other hand, law has no way of knowing what these consist of, except through the optic which it itself has generated. The legal system, therefore, is involved in a continual process of concealing the paradoxical nature of its decisions by claiming that they are underpinned by values external to its own operations. It is only observers of the legal system who are able to see that these values are in fact the creation of law itself, fabricated out of a version of reality that exists only within the legal system. This applies equally to rational, moral, economic, scientific or educational justifications for legal decisions, as well as to those which invoke children's welfare or best interests.[34]

(2) Law's crude code lawful/unlawful does not enable it to perform the task of determining issues relating to special educational needs. The existence of these needs and the help needed to meet them are in themselves neither lawful nor unlawful. If law is to make decisions concerning special educational needs, therefore, there has to exist within the legal system a programme specialized for that purpose. This involves not only reconstituting 'the facts' in ways that made it possible for the code to be applied and for

---

[33] N Luhmann, 'Tautology and Paradox in the Self-Description of Modern Society' (1988) *Sociological Theory* 21; N Luhmann, 'The Paradox of Observing Systems' (1995) 31 *Cultural Critique* 37.

[34] M King, *A Better World for Children? Explorations in Morality and Authority* (London, 1997).

legal decisions to emerge. It is also necessary to introduce 'interpreters' into the system whose task would be to 'translate' communications from other systems so as to make them amenable to legal decision-making. Nevertheless, for law to be lawful, what emerges as 'legal communications' has to be a product of law itself and cannot simply endorse the communications of other systems without subjecting them to legal principles and values. Only law, and not education or psychology, may produce legal communications.

(3) Since law exists within an environment which is the product of its own operations, its binary code applies not only to events outside the legal system, but to legal decisions and legal operations themselves. If 'justice is to be done', these decisions too need to be coded as either lawful or unlawful.[35] They must conform to all the procedural requirements laid down by law and, where they take the form of legal judgments, they must correspond to what law recognizes as acceptable legal reasoning. This will usually, though not always, mean following the path laid down in cases of similar kind, or at least not deviating too far from that path. Once special educational needs becomes a programme within law, therefore, it should be anticipated that the issues that present themselves for legal decisions will involve not only those directly concerning the education of children with 'learning difficulties', but also procedural matters and challenges to the way that tribunals and courts dealing with special educational needs arrived at their decisions.

(4) Unlike most other social systems, law's performance does not depend upon the results of its decisions, it is not 'purpose-orientated'.[36] Where, for example, a tribunal rejects a parent's appeal against the refusal of the LEA to pay for education in a small private school, it cannot subsequently be held legally (or educationally) responsible for that child's failure to make satisfactory progress in the large state school. Only if the tribunal failed to follow the correct procedures or if its reasoning was faulty would the decision be wrong in law. Assuming there was no such transgression, the decision stands as legal and valid, both for law and for all other social systems. All legal programmes, therefore, take the form of *conditional programmes*, that is, of 'if...then' programmes.[37] In special educational needs law this could take the form of such conditional statements as '*if* the tribunal failed to take into account in its decision the educational psychologist's evidence of the child's needs, *then* the decision was faulty and the case must be reheard'. While conditional programmes may take the future into account, they do so always within the limits of what is known in

---

[35] King and Thornhill, n 9 above, 57.
[36] N Luhmann, *Das Recht der Gesellschaft* (Frankfurt am Main, 1993) 230–2.
[37] ibid, 182 and 231–3. See also King and Thornhill, n 9 above, 61.

the present, that is, at the time that the decision is made. They cannot be made provisional upon the occurrence of some future event, such as the child's examination performance. They avoid judgement by results.

'Autism' within 'Special Educational Needs Law'

Attaching the Autistic Label

The form that autism takes when it enters legal communications and the meaning attached to it will depend, according to our theoretical perspective, upon the particular programme that the legal system applies to filter 'noise' from the environment and so make it amenable to its code of lawful/unlawful.[38] Within the Education Act 1996 the law sees autism as relevant to special educational needs only (a) if it gives rise to a 'learning difficulty' and (b) if this learning difficulty requires special needs provision. Once these conditions are fulfilled, the question arises as to whether making a formal statement of special educational needs is necessary for determining and putting in place the special educational provision required[39]—a clear example of law's conditional mode of operating. In systems using a purpose-orientated mode of operation, the method for determining whether the needs of the child with autism are being met, would be one of continual monitoring and adjusting of different therapies and teaching methods. This may still be possible through 'informal' measures put into practice by the school through School Action or School Action Plus.[40] Once the issue goes to tribunal, however, any decision on how to meet the child's *future* needs must take place in the *present* on the basis of what the tribunal accepts as *present* knowledge of these needs and how these needs may be met by *future* provision.

A diagnosis of 'autism' by a psychiatrist or paediatrician in a child of school age will almost always be sufficient to satisfy that part of the conditional programme that requires proof of the child's 'learning difficulty' and so set in motion the first stage in the process—the 'statutory assessment'—during which a range of experts examine and produce a report on the child's problems and their implications for education. It is clear from reported cases that, so far as education and law are concerned, autism or 'autistic spectrum disorders' represents a category of disability which gives rise to learning difficulties. Despite the difficulties and controversies within developmental psychology concerning imposition of the autistic label on children with a wide range of abilities and behavioural symptoms, within law autism clearly exists as a medical condition which is readily available to diagnosis.

[38] See King and Thornhill, n 9 above, 23.   [39] Education Act 1996, s 324.
[40] These are programmes through which schools offer special educational help to pupils through the resources normally available to the school (including advisory and assessment services offered to schools by the LEA). This does not involve the LEA in providing specialist individual provision such as a learning (or teaching) assistant or regular therapy from a speech and language therapist. The LEA is obliged to make such provision only when they have been specified in an SEN statement.

396 Michael King and Diane King

While within psychology, psychiatry and paediatrics, diagnosing a child as 'autistic', rather than as suffering from some other disability, often involves considerable difficulties and may be open to controversy, within education and law, no such problems exist. Once the autistic label has been attached, they may simply assume the validity of the diagnosis and treat the child as having special educational needs of a particular kind. As extracts from reported cases illustrate, within law, children 'with autism' or 'on the autistic spectrum' may be distinguished from those who do not suffer from this disability.

C, aged 14, *was autistic*[41]

O has an *autistic spectrum disorder (ASD)*[42]

G is 6. He has an *autistic spectrum disorder*...[43]

J was diagnosed in December 2000 as *functioning at the high end of the autistic spectrum*[44]

Only in one reported case was there a hint of the tentative nature of some diagnoses of autism and this involved child who was too young for a clear diagnosis to be made.

At the age of 19 months, A had been diagnosed as *'probably' autistic*[45]

Even though medically and psychologically the diagnosis of autism is of far less importance than identifying the particular and specific disabilities of the individual child, for education and for special educational needs law this diagnosis operates as a passport to some specialist educational provision. In other words, it is the label or classification itself which is of major importance for obtaining educational help. It is true that children, who have not been diagnosed as 'autistic', may obtain the label as a result of the statutory assessment. However, the initial problem for these children, or rather for their parents, is how to convince LEAs, all of whom are on a tight budget, that the problems revealed by the child's school performance are sufficiently serious to justify such an assessment. The children may look 'normal' and have no obvious disabilities. Their deviant behaviour could well be interpreted as boisterousness, poor concentration, 'hyperactivity', aggression resulting from adverse home conditions or a poor teaching environment. Others may present no obvious behavioural problems for the teacher, but are withdrawn and uncommunicative. Without a diagnosis of autism, children, whose behaviour does not cause problems in the classroom, usually have extreme difficulty in

---

[41] *Oxfordshire County Council v M And Special Educational Needs Tribunal* [2003] ELR 718.

[42] *T v Hertfordshire County Council and anor* [2004] EWCA Civ 927 CA (Civil Division) C3/2003/1517.

[43] *R (on the application of L) v London Borough of Waltham Forest and anor* [2003] EWHC 2907 (Admin) 161, [2004] ELR.

[44] *T v Special Educational Needs Tribunal and Wiltshire County Council* [2002] EWHC 1474 (Admin), [2002] ELR 704.

[45] *R (A) v Cambridgeshire County Council and Lom* [2002] EWHC 2391 (Admin), [2003] ELR 464.

obtaining special educational needs provision, unless perhaps their performance on school tests falls far below average.

Fragmenting the Autistic Child

Once a statutory assessment has been put in place and the reports of the various experts filed, LEAs have to decide what provision is appropriate to meet the child's needs, whether to make and maintain a statement of special educational needs and, if so, what should go into the statement.[46] The preconditions that most LEAs impose before they are willing to undertake a statutory assessment are set out above. When the LEA decides that it is necessary to 'statement' a child, it is then under a duty to identify and make provision to meet the autistic child's *special educational needs*. So far as the law is concerned these needs are entirely separate and distinct from other needs of the child, such as health needs or social welfare needs. As a general rule, neither SENDISTs nor courts hearing appeals from these tribunals have any power to order area health authorities or social service departments to make any provision for the child. According to the law, the needs of autistic children are divided among these three agencies[47] and if parents wish to take steps to oblige health or social services to fulfil their statutory duties, they need to start an entirely different legal process. This division of labour reflects the organization of administrative agencies in the United Kingdom. As a result, one of the tasks that SENDISTs and the courts frequently face is that of determining what are 'educational' and what 'non-educational' needs. In terms of law's conditional formula, if the need is 'educational', only then is the LEA acting unlawfully by failing to provide for that need.

The courts have, in their decisions on this issue, tried to mitigate the obvious absurdity arising from this distinction by determining that not all therapy provided by clinics should be classified as non-educational. According to the judge in one case, although speech and language therapy was provided by health, 'to teach a child who has never been able to speak . . . seems to us as much educational provision as to teach a child to communicate in writing'.[48] It was, therefore, capable of being 'a special educational provision', although this does not mean that all speech and language therapy would be regarded in this way. The SEN Code of Practice,[49] which was published after this decision, states that 'speech and language impairment should normally be recorded as educational provision, unless there are exceptional reasons for not doing so'.[50]

[46] Education Act 1996, s 324.

[47] The Education Act 1996, and all previous SEN legislation, leaves open to interpretation what precisely is meant by the term 'education', although s 322 refers to help being given to the LEA by 'any Health Authority or local authority . . . in the exercise of any of their functions', this making a distinction between the LEA's functions and those of health and social services.

[48] *R v Lancashire County Council ex p M* [1989] 2 FLR 279 per Balcombe LJ in Headnote.

[49] The Code of Practice (2001) DfES 581/2001 is published pursuant to the Education Act 1993.

[50] para 8:49.

However, the matter does not rest here. Psychological and educational complexity has been transformed and reconstituted as legal complexity. Within law there is a constant battle going on between LEAs who frequently place speech and language therapy in that part of the statement which falls beyond their direct responsibility and parents (and their advisers) who insist that it should appear as an educational provision. Nor is this all. As the law stands, it is open to the LEA to determine in the statement what level of speech and language therapy is appropriate. The common practice is to provide for a visit once or twice a term by a therapist who will monitor the child's progress and give teachers and classroom assistants advice on what exercises will help the child. Those parents who have obtained legal advice, on the other hand, will frequently press for 'hands on' therapy at regular intervals by the therapist him- or herself. In this way, the amount and form of speech and language therapy becomes a bone of contention to be fought over in the negotiations between parents and LEAs and/or an issue to be decided by the tribunal. We should add here that there is absolutely no evidence that children who receive therapy from a therapist make any greater progress than those who take part in group interventions or who obtain the therapy 'second-hand' from teaching assistants or parents.[51]

While the status of speech and language therapy as a 'special educational provision' has now been largely settled in law, albeit with unintended consequences, the same is not true of other therapies. In *London Borough of Bromley v Special Educational Needs Tribunal and ors*[52] the Court of Appeal decided: 'It was open to a Special Educational Needs Tribunal to conclude that the needs of a severely disabled child for physiotherapy [and] occupational therapy [as well as] speech and language therapy formed part of his special educational needs for which his local educational authority was obliged to make provision.' Any decision in cases of controversy was best left to the judgment of the specialist tribunal. So in the case of children with autism it is up to the law to decide between *educational* and *non-educational*, between provision that the LEA is lawfully obliged to provide and that which it is not. The test appears to be that if the therapy or other intervention can be provided within a school setting, then it can be 'education'. This, however, begs the questions: 'What kind of school?' Some residential special schools, for example, are able to provide an extensive range of therapies for children with autism, while those offered by mainstream state schools may be very limited. The law's reconstitution of the child with autism, therefore adopts the circular proposition that responsibility for meeting the child's particular disabilities is divided up according to which social agency is legally responsible. There is no attempt by law to overcome the problem of splitting children's needs between different branches of local government and to treat the child holistically.

We should add that the distinction between education and social services is even more fraught with legal issues than that between education and health. The

---

[51] J Law and Z Garrett, 'Speech and Language Therapy: Its Potential Role in CAMHS' (2004) 9 *Child and Adolescent Mental Health* 50.   [52] (1999) 2 ELR 260.

recent case of *W v Leeds City Council and anor*[53] exemplifies the problems. This concerned C, an autistic boy aged 9, who soiled himself, had considerable trouble with eating, communicated only by gestures or use of pictures and was aggressive and bit people. He had no sense of danger and needed constant supervision. The Tribunal rejected his mother's wishes for a 'full waking day' curriculum and decided that C's *special educational needs* could properly be met within the normal school day, stating that it was not up to the LEA to provide help and support that was not essentially educational. On appeal the judge[54] made the following, telling comment:

> ...the Tribunal were aware of the deficiency in the social service provision and indeed criticised it. While recognising the hazy line between social and educational support, the Tribunal had to decide what educational provision was required. It made that decision on the evidence as to C's educational needs, and...rightly decided that, having reached its conclusion...it was not its function to throw upon the educational authority the burden of providing what was properly social, rather than educational support.[55]

Unfortunately then, children with autism frequently fall between the three stools of education, health and social services and parents are left as helpless bystanders as local government bureaucrats argue amongst themselves as to whose responsibility it is to provide services and resources for the child.

The Programme of 'Special Educational Needs Law'

The task for law, as we spelt out earlier in this paper, is to transform perturbations or disturbances within its environment into communications which are understandable and recognizable as legal communications. In effect, this means converting them into conditional statements which are amenable to law's coding of lawful/unlawful. How then does the programme of 'special educational needs' undertake this task?

It would be a mistake to believe that the process starts only when cases reach the specialist tribunals. In this kind of technical legal programme it is more and more usual for this process of transformation to begin with the drafting of statutes followed by detailed regulations which the statutes enable. Throughout the drafting process, there is usually continual consultation with and lobbying by interest groups, who, if they wish to be taken seriously, are required to formulate their demands in terms that are amenable to legal coding. They are obliged, in practice, either to respond to the clauses that appear in the draft statutes (in the UK, 'Bills') by proposing new provisions (clauses) or amendments to those proposed by the government or arguing against the inclusion of certain provisions. From the theoretical perspective that we are applying, the purpose of these

---

[53] [2004] EWHC (Admin) CO/3199/94, QBD (Admin Court).
[54] McCombe J.   [55] At para 27.

requirements is not simply political—to conform with the demands of democracy, but simultaneously, within the legal system to create order out of 'noise', to convert scientific, educational and economic communications into law, to convert purpose-oriented statements into conditional statements which may be subjected to the coding, lawful/unlawful. There is insufficient space in this paper to offer a detailed account of the lengthy legislative process that precedes the introduction of any new legislation or codes of practice relating to special educational needs. Suffice it to state that there are, typically, representations by groups representing LEAs and scientific and educational bodies as well as groups acting on behalf of autistic children and their parents, such as the National Autistic Society, the Independent Panel for Special Educational Advice and the Advisory Centre for Education. All of these, as we have seen, are drawn into the legal system purely and simply by the need to transform the demands and interests of those that they represent into terms that are acceptable *as law*, into legal communications.

One further important matter affects legal decision-making involving children with autism. This is the existence of the Special Educational Needs Code of Practice. Although the many detailed paragraphs of this code are not strictly law, but merely guidance,[56] within the programme of special educational needs law, many of them have been and continue to be transformed into legal communications, with non-compliance by LEAs being treated as unlawfulness. An example given earlier in this paper is paragraph 8:49, which states that 'speech and language impairment should normally be recorded as educational provision [in the statement] unless there are exceptional reasons for not doing so'.

Moving onto the actual processing of cases, education is transformed into law by the programme of special educational needs law in a variety of ways. To begin with, there are two lay panel members who sit either side of the legal chair. Their role ostensibly is to make available their specialist educational knowledge and experience to the tribunal hearings and decision-making process. Again, however, all their knowledge and experience has to be framed within the specific legal questions that the panel has to decide. It is not a matter of 'What can we do to help this child with severe autism?' but, for example, 'Is it lawful for the LEA to refuse to name an independent special school for this child?' and 'Is the LEA acting lawfully by claiming that it is able to meet this child's educational needs in a mainstream school?'

Given the growing complexity of the special educational needs law, arising from statutes, statutory guidelines, regulations and codes of practice and the continual production of reported court decisions, it is not surprising that the representatives

---

[56] Increasingly government departments in the UK publish Codes of Practice and Guidelines in an attempt to assist legal decision makers in their interpretation of statutes and to direct them to the issues that they should be considering in their decisions and the weight to be given to arguments and evidence. Within special education needs the government has also published statutory guidance on *Inclusive Schooling—Children with Special Needs* DfES 0774/2001.

who appear on behalf of the LEA and parents have rapidly had to become special-ists in what has become special educational needs *law*.[57] They too operate as 'translators' or 'mediators',[58] who, in the promotion of their interests, have no alter-native but to transform communications which originated in science and law in ways that make them recognizable as relating to legal issues. Appearing before the SENDIST is as much about winning and losing cases as in any court of law. However, it is also about presenting difficult, technical information from a number of different 'expert' sources in ways which make it possible for the legal decision makers to reach a conclusion which stands up to legal scrutiny on the educational needs of children with autism and on how to meet them. Needless to say, this involves no small degree of selection and reductionism, but, more than this, it also involves reconstructing them in a way that makes it appear that the knowledge and understanding exist that permit right and wrong,[59] lawful and unlawful decisions to be made about a future that is, and will always remain, uncertain.

Educational Psychology

This leads us to the specialist educational experts themselves. As we observed early on in this paper, the transformation from scientific facts about autism and chil-dren with autism into communications which make sense within a programme of special educational needs law is a two-stage process. Scientific communications must become amenable to the education system's pass/fail code before they become visible to law, or rather to this particular programme of the legal system. Educational psychology plays a central role in this transformation process. The appendix of every statement of special educational needs refers to the report of at least one educational psychologist.[60] Most of these reports contain observations of the child's behaviour in the classroom and in interview, accounts of the concerns that the parents have expressed to the educational psychologist and the results of standardized tests designed to evaluate the child's performance against the norms for children of the same age.

Educational psychologists' reports almost invariably then go on to make a series of proposals or recommendations—often in very general terms—on ways of improving the child's educational performance. It is here that educational

[57] Many LEAs now have appointed tribunal officers or their equivalent whose job it is to spend their time representing the authority at SENDIST hearings. Similarly, parents' advice and assistance organizations, such as IPSEA, train and appoint volunteer tribunal representatives.

[58] See N Lee, 'Faith in the Body? Childhood, Subjecthood and Sociological Enquiry' in A Prout (ed), *The Body, Childhood and Society* (Basingstoke, 2000) 149.

[59] It is notable that a major empirical study of Special Educational Needs Tribunals has the title *Getting it Right*. J Evans, *Getting it Right* (Slough, 1998).

[60] Parents, as well as the LEA, are entitled to submit reports during the assessment process and some take the opportunity to have their child examined by an educational psychologist who is independent of the LEA.

psychologists achieve the task of transforming psychological disorders into 'special educational needs' and from there to educational methods designed to meet these needs. Here is an example from an educational psychologist's report on S, a severely autistic boy, aged 12.

Special Educational Needs
- to develop communication skills
- to develop social interaction skills
- to develop play skills
- to develop early basic skills (e.g. pre-literacy, pre-number)
- to develop self-help skills

Teaching Methods and Approaches

S will require access to a highly structured teaching environment which incorporates visual as well as verbal means for indicating what is expected, the sequence of the day's events and the progress he makes.

He will require a teaching environment that includes visual prompts to encourage communication in close consultation with a qualified speech and language therapist.

A second example comes from an educational psychologist's report on another autistic boy, aged 4 years, with severe learning and communication difficulties.

Suggested Methods and Approaches to Fulfil the Objectives
1. behavioural training to lessen autistic behaviours;
2. highly structured programme to develop co-ordination skills;
3. highly-structured programme for social and self-help skills;
4. regular and frequent access to sensory input, e.g. soft play and sensory room;
5. introduction of switch technology, especially via computer mediation;
6. use of sign assisted communication . . .

For children with autism to be eligible for special educational provision, it has to be shown that they are 'failing' in their education. Almost by definition, even those children with high-functioning autism present as 'failures' in educational terms, since their capacity to meet the demands of normal school life, such as sitting still in class and concentrating on their work, accepting the authority of the teacher, switching from teacher to teacher and from classroom to classroom, is likely to be impaired and these failures to conform, alone, are likely to result in difficulties which, if not addressed, are likely to affect adversely the children's performance on Standard Assessment Tests (SATS) or school exams. Educational psychology then serves to reconstruct the raw data of developmental psychology into terms that are recognizable as educational communications and amenable to educational decisions. It operates in such a way as to identify the child's educational 'failures' and propose educational methods through which these failures may be mitigated and even reversed so that education may live up to its self-image of fulfilling children's potential. In performing this task the complexities and uncertainties in diagnosing and understanding the causes of autism, the problems of subjectivity involved in observing children and the controversies surrounding many psychometric tests[61] tend to be forgotten or ignored in the quest for educational solutions to what have now been posed as educational problems. True, some of these uncertainties and complexities may reappear if and when the issue of the child's special educational needs enters the legal system, transformed into controversies between LEAs and parents as to the wording of the statement and as to what the LEA needs to do in law to meet the child's needs. Yet when this occurs, it is not psychology itself or education itself which is called upon to resolve such controversies (even if it were able to do so), but legal precedent or law's own version of the psychological issues and educational issues, a version that is constructed by law itself from what it regards as valid evidence and reliable information.

Conclusion

Special educational needs law, as it has evolved in England, provides ample evidence of the legal system's ability to extend its operations through the creation of new legal programmes. Once science and education have been reconstituted within law, it simply does not matter, from law's perspective, whether decisions about the education of children with autism have been based on a sound scientific diagnostic of autism. Nor does it matter whether psychological tests of cognitive ability are able to measure educational potential or whether therapeutic or educational interventions actually work. All that matters in law is that *legal decisions should be lawful* and, where a child's special educational needs are concerned, that they should be capable of validation through law's own construction of scientific and educational knowledge. Accordingly, conflicts between parents and LEAs over the choice of school, over teaching methods within schools, over the need for therapeutic interventions, or over what qualifies as an efficient use of resources to meet a child's special educational needs, may all be resolved without reference to the complexity of scientific and educational knowledge by the expedient of finding the right answer *in law*. Of course, the search for the right legal answer may be a complex one, but the complexities involved here are those generated by law itself, and concern not 'what is best for the child' but how to determine what is lawful and unlawful from the ever-increasing body of statutes, regulations, case law and codes of practice.

As we have demonstrated in our discussion of children with autism, this method of determining legal decisions can be achieved only once scientific and educational complexities have been constructively misinterpreted[62] so as to

---

[61] See, for example, Morton, n 17 above, ch 3.
[62] See G Teubner, 'How the Law Thinks: Toward a Constructivist Epistomology of Law' (1989) 23 *Law and Society Review* 727. Also M King, 'An Autopoietic Approach to the Problems presented

provide a clear indication for and within the legal system as to where the child's special educational needs lie and how these needs may be met. Any ambiguities or admissions of ignorance in law's reconstruction of scientific or educational knowledge, are likely to emerge as an opportunity for a contest between competing versions of where the child's special educational needs *really* lie and what is *the right way* of meeting them.

Finally, let us return to the prevailing rights ideology which inspired the granting of a right of the appeal to parents and the network of independent tribunals set up under the 1993 Act. It is not difficult to appreciate that from the perspective of liberally minded lawyers and politicians, these reforms were seen as a major advance in helping children with learning difficulties to secure the help needed to overcome these difficulties.[63] Yet from the sociological theory of autopoietic systems it is clear that the reliance on the expedient of rights enforceable through legal processes to redress what was seen as the imbalance of power between LEAs and parents would inevitably result in the evolution of a new programme within the legal system. Moreover, the only way that a programme of special educational needs law could operate was, on the one hand, to simplify, reduce, distort and filter psychological and educational information to make it amenable to law's operations and, on the other hand, to construct a legal complexity which reflected the complexity generated by these other systems.

This reliance on a legal process of decision-making might well have resulted in what passes for justice in the eyes of the law, but at the expense of creating or turning a blind eye to other injustices that the law is unable to remedy. There is no doubt, for example, that it operates to the detriment of parents who are unable to gain access to specialist legal advice and representation to help them navigate the legal complexities.[64] There is also no doubt that the availability of special educational needs provision for children with autism varies considerably from one educational area to another, leading to the accusation of 'injustice by postal code'. Of course, nothing we have written in this paper is able to remedy these problems. However, in concentrating on the way that social systems reconstruct one another in their own terms, we hope to have increased awareness that the problems confronting the provision of special educational needs for children with autism go far beyond the current inclusion/special schools debate.[65] We hope also to have cast some doubt on analyses of the problems of educating children with autism which rely upon the simplistic premise of a single, seamless, unified social system where information may be readily transferred from one social context to another and

by "Parental Alienation Syndrome" for Courts and Child Mental Health Experts' (2002) 13 *The Journal of Forensic Psychiatry* 609.

[63] Evans, n 59 above.

[64] S Capper, *Sent Ahead. The IPSEA guide to the Special Educational Needs Tribunal* (Woodbridge, 2002) and Evans, n 59 above.

[65] See Warnock, n 25 above, and also the House of Lords Debate on Special Schools of 14 July 2005.

then used to arrive at *the right decision.* Our paper also raises the wider social issue of the difficulties in using legal programmes to steer social policies and legal decisions or regulate those institutions set up to put these policies into effect. The decisions that emerge from legal programmes may make perfect sense in law—the 'right decision' has been made according to 'the best knowledge' available to the tribunal or court—but there is no guarantee that they will steer policies or regulate social institutions in the way that was originally intended by Parliament or by those groups that pressed for more rights, more resources, or other equally well-meant reforms.

23

The Construction of Memory through Law and Law's Responsiveness to Children[1]

Ya'ir Ronen

There were seventy of us in a forestry commando unit for Jewish prisoners of war in Nazi Germany...the French uniform still protected us from Hitlerian violence. But the other men, called free, who had dealings with us or gave us work or orders or even a smile—and the children and women who passed by and sometimes raised their eyes—stripped us of our human skins. We were subhuman, a gang of apes. A small inner murmur, the strength and wretchedness of persecuted people, reminded us of our essence as thinking creatures, but we were no longer part of the world. Our comings and goings, our sorrow and laughter, illnesses and distractions, the work of our hands and the anguish of our eyes, the letters we received from France and those accepted for our families—all that passed in parenthesis. We were beings entrapped in their species; despite their vocabulary, beings without language... Social aggression... shuts people away in a class, deprives them of expression and condemns them to being 'signifiers without a signified' and from there to violence and fighting. How can we deliver a message about our humanity which, from behind the bars of quotation marks, will come across as anything other than monkey talk?

And then, about halfway through our long captivity, for a few short weeks, before the sentinels chased him away, a wandering dog entered our lives. One day he came to meet this rabble as we returned under guard from work. He survives in some wild patch in the region of the camp. But we called him Bobby, an exotic name, as one does with a cherished dog. He would appear at morning assembly and was waiting for us as we returned, jumping up and down and barking in delight. For him there was no doubt that we were men....

This dog was the last Kantian in Nazi Germany, without the brain needed to universalize maxims and drives.

[1] For the sake of simplicity, the term children in this paper implies both children and youth unless a different intention is implied from the context. Indeed, such a choice of words is liable to infantilize youth, but arguably only if the choice is both unmindful and implicit. When mindful, it may challenge us to respond to the diversity of children's needs. Age-related needs are only one instance of such diversity.

Introduction

Society's unacknowledged conflict over its collective memory and the question of responsibility to the Other encourages the politicization of empathy towards children. What we fail to acknowledge is how dynamic and conflictual the process of remembering and othering is. This paper describes how professionals who fail to reflect on this conflict can also neglect to respond to individual suffering. The paper also argues that alienated doctrinal thinking, which cannot appreciate the value of face-to-face dialogue with the individual when constructing legal norms, in fact facilitates the rationalization of politicized empathy and abrogates our sense of injustice. Dangerously, from the author's perspective, such doctrinal thinking can also be couched in rights rhetoric.

Two partially overlapping issues illustrate this chapter's thesis:

(1) The protection of family life for children from disadvantaged homes.

(2) The public response to the past victimization of young offenders.

Drawing primarily on the autobiographical opening vignette, the chapter first attempts to explain how doctrinal thinking may perpetuate alienation from the Other and illustrates how the law is as an author of memory, tying this to the challenge of psychological-mindedness mainly presented in the last decade by the movement for Therapeutic Jurisprudence. It is also explained how law can be more than a rationalization of selective remembering and subsequent politicized empathy, and how we can struggle more mindfully over the law's construction of collective memory. The paper does not purport to offer a comprehensive discussion of the law in any one country, but draws rather on examples from different countries. The examples are not brought to prove the author's thesis but to allow the reader the opportunity to be convinced by the feasibility of the thesis.

Alienation, Children's Experience and Doctrinal Thinking

In the above vignette, Levinas[2] clearly exposes the risks of relating to the Other solely through the intellect. This may happen when humane emotional relatedness becomes delegitimized by legal culture, as happens so often either directly or by implication.[3]

---

[2] Levinas, E, 'The Name of a Dog, or Natural Rights' in *Difficult Freedom: Essays on Judaism* translated from the French by Sean Hand (Baltimore, 1997) 152–153.

[3] Ronen, Y, 'Redefining the Child's Right to Identity' (2004) 18(2) *International Journal of Law, Policy and the Family* (1986) 147–177. Minow, M, 'Rights for the Next Generation: A Feminist Approach to Children's Rights' (1986) 9 *Harvard Women's Law Journal* 1–24.

One must concede that feelings can be irrational. On the other hand, though, rationality can degenerate into rationalization justifying the dehumanization of the Other, which in the case of child law is at times: the child offender, the illegal immigrant's child, or the enemy's child. Legal intervention can also be traumatic to the child but the traumatizing, painful aspect of judicial decision making is often denied, ignored or underplayed.[4]

In the above quotation, Levinas I believe hints that we are ensnared by the psychological defense of rationalization. Despite being 'captive' to doctrinal thinking, which excuses our attitudes and behavior, we consider ourselves free of such thinking and delude ourselves that we are free because we can reason and rationalize our behavior. This is reasoning along the lines of 'I think and ethically rationalize my behavior towards the Other('s) child therefore I am acting ethically towards him'. Again and again Levinas alludes to the weaknesses of an alienated doctrinal rights discourse.[5]

How do developments in international child law, primarily the consolidation and universal ratification of the Convention on the Rights of the Child (hereinafter: the CRC) and operation of the UN Committee on the Rights of the Child, relate to the risk of dehumanizing the Other child?

To a large extent, international children's rights law may be no more than a new universal ethics. The Committee frightens no one; it interprets a document primarily comprising principles, and one wonders what societies in ratifying states will make of the CRC and the Committee's observations. I suspect that if they rationalize present practices they will make very little of both.

Levinas draws on his personal experience to explain how the capacity to respond humanely does not demand the capacity to reason, generalize or universalize as a *sine qua non*. What he is telling us is that he regained something of the human dignity denied to him by his captors and the German civilians he met through the responsiveness of a dog.

It is noteworthy to state that rationalization and not unconscious dehumanization is exemplified and addressed in this vignette. I suggest that this is a valuable insight of general implications in the field of child law: consider, for example, how a very thin, easily penetrable veneer of rationalization can suffice to justify phenomena like child labor—not only in eighteenth century England—but in India today.[6] In India, Indian public rhetoric and Indian human rights NGOs

---

[4] Cover, R, 'Violence and the Word' in Minow, M, Ryan, M and Sarat, A (eds) *Narrative, Violence and the Law—The Essays of Robert Cover* (Ann Arbor, Mich, 1998) 203–238.

[5] eg Levinas, E, 'Ethics and Spirit' in Levinas, n 2 above, 3–10; Levinas, E, 'Chapter 1: Towards the Other' in Levinas, E, *Nine Talmudic Readings* translated from the French by Daniel Epstein (Tel Aviv, 2001) 9–28. Hebrew. Levinas, E, 'Chapter 5: Judaism and Revolution', ibid, 117–146.

[6] Nandy, A, 'Reconstructing Childhood: A Critique of the Ideology of Childhood' in Nandy, A *Traditions, Tryranny and Utopias—Essays in the Politics of Awareness* (Oxford, 2004) 54, 62. Weiner, M, *The Child And The State in India: Child Labor and Education Policy in Comparative Perspective* (Delhi, 1991).

wrongly assumed that Indian children find formal education meaningless and wish to join the workforce to aid their parents.[7]

This paper suggests that in order better to understand children's worldview, hopes and dreams, we must face up to children in all their subjectivity and uniqueness. Until then, we may find only peace or refuge in half-truths patched together to avoid disturbing the status quo or our professed commitment to the CRC ethos.[8]

A construction of childhood alienated from children's suffering can degenerate into a refusal to admit available data and incongruent experiences if, and to the extent that it is genuine false consciousness, it has a built-in resistance to recognizing its own falsity.[9] Drawing inspiration from Levinas, we can envision a level of responsiveness to children's needs that leads to recognition of general and universal norms. Levinas should not be understood as dismissing the value of reason or the capacity to generalize or universalize. Rather, I believe that the 'twist' in his self-contradictory, bitter, pseudo-recognition of the dog as the last Kantian[10] does not stem from cynicism or disdain for Kant's vision of morality, but rather from a view of sad disillusionment with the high expectations of a man whose formative years as a young adult were spent as a philosophy student in Kant's homeland, pre-World War II Germany.

A general or universal norm need not be alienated from human experience. The subjective can lead to the inter-subjective, and the inter-subjective can legitimately lead to the construction of a general and universal human rights–children's rights norm.[11] A children's rights doctrine can be responsive to children's experience. However, it is the aloofness of an intellectual frame of mind, which draws satisfaction from its own ability to philosophize and rationalize, that creates the risk of alienation of human rights advocates and scholars alike from the actual experience of children.

The Construction of Memory

Personal and group memory is actively constructed. Actively, because memory involves perpetual activity: it does not simply exist, but is built and continually altered. Thus, remembering is a dynamic process of reinterpretation.[12]

---

[7] Weiner, ibid.   [8] See ibid.   [9] Nandy, n 6 above, 62.

[10] Levinas would undoubtedly agree that a dog cannot *stricto sensu* practise Kantian morality since he cannot reason. For Kant, rationalist wisdom is the ultimate source of moral behaviour. See eg Kant, I, *Critique Of Practical Reason* (Mineola, NY, 2004) 35, 70.

[11] Mui, CL and Murphy, JS, 'Enduring Freedom: Globalizing Children's Rights' (2003) 18(1) *Hypatia* 197–203. Hesford, WS, 'Documenting Violations: Rhetorical Witnessing And The Spectacle Of Distant Suffering' (2004) 27(1) *Biography* 104–145.

[12] Minow, M, *Between Vengeance and Forgiveness: Facing History after Genocide and Mass Violence* (Boston, 1998) 120.

On the personal level, if, say in psychotherapy, a violent adolescent recalls childhood abuse of which he was always partly conscious, his memory of who caused that abuse, the object of his anger and his own identity can radically change. By isolating him from society, a juvenile offender who is institutionalized and later incarcerated becomes relatively insignificant as a prospective agent for social change. If, however, he identifies his past abuse as a result of systemic injustice, he may harness his anger to fight for social change and challenge that injustice. Thus, a formative life experience such as psychotherapy can provide a powerful directed-ness to the dynamic process of reinterpretation.[13] Let me exemplify my point.

Israeli law differentiates between parents and other caretakers in relation to mandatory reporting of offences against children: it is the duty of all individuals to report the suspicion of abuse by a parent or legal guardian either to a child protection officer or to the police. In contrast, if an offence against a child is com-mitted by staff at an institution in which a child was placed for his own good, one is not duty bound to report the offence. Only if severe injury or a sex offence has been committed is there a duty to report the offence, and then only by the staff of the institution, who may be fired the next day as a result of fulfilling a statutory duty. Now let us imagine a violent, turbulent seventeen-year-old, we shall call him Tom, who was institutionalized between the ages of ten and twelve because of parental neglect. Tom gets involved in fights with his peers and even slapped his teacher once when he humiliated him in front of the class. Everyone around him sees Tom as an angry and violent adolescent. Tom between the ages of ten and twelve is gradually becoming violent. He initially blames mainly himself for his ongoing physical abuse by institutional staff and bullying by his peers at the insti-tution, though this abuse brought about a change in his behaviour patterns and aggravated his anger and aggression. Tom may discover through psychotherapy that the responsibility for his suffering and the violence he experienced, lies not only with the perpetrators and institutional staff who were silent bystanders, but also with the legislators, the policy makers and the child advocates who knowingly let his voice to be silenced by endorsing a system of selective mandatory reporting, trusting the system where biological kin are no longer trusted.

He may also come to see that his sense of humiliation and powerlessness at his removal from home because of neglect, only to fall prey to institutional abuse, and his deep bitterness at never being visited by the child protection officer who took him from his home, are only natural. He may question the skewed distribution of funds by Israeli child welfare, which channels most of its funds to institutions whose quality of care varies considerably and fails to allocate social rights to chil-dren within their families and communities, rights, which might have helped avoid the need for out of home placement.

---

[13] For reinterpretation of personal history as re-biography see Rotenberg, M, *Re-Biographing and Deviance: Psychotherapeutic Narrativism and The Midrash* (New York, 1987). Maruna, S, 'Concluding Remarks' in Maruna, S, *Making Good—How Ex-Convicts Reform and Rebuild Their Lives* (Washington, DC, 2001) 165–168.

It is not inconceivable that sooner or later Tom may play an important role in advocacy for the reform of child protection law through recourse to his own valuable personal experience, and push for the equalization of mandatory reporting between abuse at home and in institutions, for allocation of social rights for children within their families and communities and for mandatory periodic visits by child protection workers to children in institutions and for the accountability of these workers to the children. In such a case, the child has no memory in the sense of an intact picture to be retrieved. Rather, his mind contains elements of past and present that are linked and differentiated[14] in a very individual and unique way. However, Tom's personal testimony has unique power in the public discourse, and his reported experience is commonly perceived as 'the' truth or at least his personal truth.

The construction of memory through psychotherapy involves a relatively slow process of reinterpretation. At the societal level, precedential case law and new legislation, two mechanisms of the legal system, both express and facilitate the reinterpretation of memory.[15] These mechanisms are fast routes in bringing about reinterpretation of collective memory and have a large-scale effect, they are ultimately mobilized by individuals, both laymen who are social activists and professionals such as judges, academic scholars and child advocates, whose identities and direction in life are dynamically self-constructed and influenced by formative events such as parenthood, psychotherapy, close friendships or mentoring. Remembering, then, is a politically potent tool,[16] though it is not necessarily utilized to promote social change, as the next example demonstrates.

History is a projection in the sense that individuals in positions of influence can project onto it the meaning of their choice, so that these projections become objective 'history', an account of 'the facts', 'what really happened'. Thus, one can read meanings into history that relate to perceived personal and national needs and aspirations.[17]

Let us now imagine 17-year-old Tom as an army draftee. He endures great physical and emotional challenges during his training, while being constantly reminded of his country's heroic national heritage, which is presented to him as part of his identity. The way the challenges are packaged may thus affect the recruit's evolving, self-constructed national identity. It may change his memory of who he is, and change the perceived source of his personal strength. He may learn to see his heroic national past as a key source of strength and inspiration. In a democratic regime, the rhetoric Tom is exposed to as part of his training naturally and typically mirrors to an extent collective memory as portrayed in public discourse. The public discourse on a country's national past—whether concerning

---

[14] Minow, M, 'Chapter 6: Facing History' in Minow (ed), n 12 above, 120.
[15] ibid.   [16] ibid, 119.
[17] Harkabi, Y, *Vision, Not Fantasy. The Lessons of The Bar Kochba Revolt and Political Realism in Our Times* (Jerusalem, 1982) 12–13, in Hebrew.

images of reconciliation or conflict—can influence the lessons individuals learn from both their own and their national history. Tom's case as a recruit only exemplifies a widespread phenomenon: we not only shape public discourse, we are shaped by it too.

Law as an Author of Memory and the Challenge of Psychological Mindedness

Law as culture, as a set of meanings, is loaded with selective memories and understandings based on those memories. By engaging these memories and understandings, the law defines society's rights holders, victims and offenders. When conflict occurs in which memory is involved, the struggle is often between clashing ideologies or vastly differing worldviews.[18] One such struggle concerns how the law should respond to an offending, victimizing youth who himself has been victimized. Is this youth the victim or the aggressor? That is, at times, the most pressing question confronting the sentencing judge. Seldom, though, is the youth seen as both, and we now find growing recognition in the literature that society is becoming less and less able to contain such ambiguities and that law mirroring this difficulty can enslave helping professionals to its agenda of reconstructing reality in terms of binary divisions between innocence and culpability.[19]

In line with the argument that Western legal culture is a culture of critique, which often does not allow the Other the benefit of the doubt and sanctifies skepticism,[20] and that only a few decades ago clients and lawyers were relegated to a gladiatorial, psychologically-blind style of law that often wreaked emotional damage upon all those involved with or touched by the legal process,[21] this paper contends that psychological mindedness can gradually liberate law, jurists and helping professionals from some of the legal culture's shackling of our thinking and behavior. I use the term 'psychological mindedness' as an umbrella term to denote the capacity to reflect on ourselves, the Other, and the relationship between the Self and the Other. The term implies a curiosity about what moves people emotionally and why we behave as we do. It also concerns our ability to see

[18] Hom, SK and Yamamoto, EK, 'Collective Memory, History, and Social Justice (Race and the Law at the Turn of the Century)' 47 (2000). *UCLA Law Review* 1747–1802.

[19] King, M and Trowell, J, *Children's Welfare and the Law* (London, 1992) 91–93. Cooper, A *et al Positive Child Protection—A View From Abroad* (Dorset, 1995) 108–109.

[20] Wexler, D, 'Therapeutic Jurisprudence and the Culture of Critique' (1999) 10 *Journal of Contemporary Legal Issues* 263–277; Tannen, D, *The Argument Culture* (New York, 1998). House. Levinas, n 5 above, 38, 40–42.

[21] Daicoff, S, 'The Role of Therapeutic Jurisprudence within the Comprehensive Law Movement' in Stolle, D, Wexler, D, Winnick, BJ (eds), *Practicing Therapeutic Jurisprudence—Law as a Helping Profession* (Durham, N Carolina, 2000) 465–492.

the past in the present and to form links between current issues and past events.[22] Thus, psychological mindedness prods us to examine critically official stories, the official links between past and present, through the official construction of memory implicit in both case law and legislation. We are encouraged in this by our recognition that the shackles have loosened even before we begin: jurists' current disillusionment with a legal culture of rivalry and belligerence may be slowly transforming the legal system into a more humane, healing and psychologically sophisticated agent in people's lives.[23] On the whole, a more psychologically healing approach advocated by the Therapeutic Jurisprudence Movement for the past fifteen years is gaining momentum.[24] Given that this is so, we may hope for a greater commitment to examining critically the tie between law's construction of memory and its responsiveness to children. Law is not only constrained by history and memory. It uses them as tools for legal reasoning. It may be seen as natural for a child advocate to choose whichever elements of the child's history he believes support his case. Though unsettling for some to contemplate, judges do much the same thing in their construction of the past. Their choice of words in describing the past is reconstructive.

Let us imagine a child consistently scapegoated by his father and stepmother who becomes a 'throwaway'— 'runaway' street child. He is portrayed as an undisciplined menace by a child protection worker alarmed at his association with offenders on the street and confident that recommending sentencing to an institution mixing adolescent offenders and adolescents at risk is a reasonable course of action, though she did not succeed in meeting the adolescent due to his refusal. She sees nothing wrong with her failure to expose the child's past victimization as she is overworked and very diligent in her work. Because the child protection officer chooses not to explore past victimization, which may repeat itself, this adolescent at risk is not presented to the court as an abused, victimized child, but as a potential offender, a threat to the moral fibre of society, leaving the court ignorant of his victimization and affecting his sentence and his future. The judge may consequently choose to adopt unquestioningly this characterization of the adolescent offered by the child protection officer. In choosing not to doubt this characterization the judge reconstructs this adolescent's history in collective memory through his judgment, a pronouncement of official truth.

Let us critically explore the official reading of the adolescent's personal history: Who is the greater moral threat to society—are we allowed to contemplate that it is not the confused adolescent but rather a helping professional who may, through smugness and indifference, become an accomplice of unresponsive parents? Or expressed in more general terms, is a child who is humiliated because of the colour of his skin, his circumcision, or his ethnicity, who explodes

---

[22] Hall, JA, 'Psychological-mindedness: A conceptual model' (1992) 46(1) *American Journal of Psychotherapy* 131–140. Murdoch, L, 'Psychological Consequences of Adopting a Therapeutic Lawyering Approach: Pitfalls and Protective Strategies' (2000) 24 *Seattle University Law Review* 483–497.   [23] Daicoff, n 21 above, 490.

[24] ibid.

emotionally at an emotionally distant, unproductive teacher, a victim of an oppressive system as portrayed in Pink Floyd's 1982 film, 'The Wall',[25] or simply 'out of line'? How does and how should legal rhetoric relate to the type of painful adolescent memory of the school system sketched out in 'Teacher, Leave them Kids Alone'?

The law's rejection of the child's counter-story through the pathologization of its author,[26] and its willingness to integrate part of that story into the mainstream discourse, covertly takes place through the courts' decisions. In some cases, decisions carry tremendous weight by mirroring not only present public responsiveness to children, but by framing future responsiveness as well. It is not possible for courts to decide what norms to apply without choosing which facts to include in a legal decision and what meaning to award them. The common law fiction that judges relying solely on case law only declare law and never create it is founded on a covert and perpetual reinterpretation of the past: that the interpretation of legal precedents is the arena of legal controversy since different jurists reach conflicting conclusions concerning applicable norms based on the same case law. Indeed, each jurist has his own story, and what is constructed as legal history and compelling precedent is unavoidably a byproduct of active reinterpretation of collective memory.

The *Brown* case,[27] possibly the most significant court case of the last century, is essentially a child advocacy case: involving the social group most humiliated by segregation—children. Yet, the humiliation caused by segregation did not start in 1954, when a politically conscious court decided to ensure equality for African-Americans. The court dramatically changed its interpretation of the Fourteenth Amendment to the American Constitution, which had been the cornerstone for decisions affirming racial segregation. Indeed, the court in the *Brown* case found support in social science evidence, though it would be naive to conclude that what had delayed its decision was the lack of such evidence.[28] The court made a conscious decision to respond to African-American suffering and sense of injustice through reinterpreting the meaning of racial equality in American Constitutional Law. Thus, it radically reconstructed the African-American past and a false consciousness of fairness and decency alienated from the experience of the African-American. Many rebelled against the decision through violent resistance. A psychologically conscious court became an uninvited and disputed author-inventor of national memory.

---

[25] <http://www.pink-floyd-lyrics.com/html/the-wall-lyrics.html>.
[26] Ronen, Y, 'Protection For Whom And From What? Protection Proceedings And The Voice Of The Child At Risk' in Douglas, G and Sebba, L (eds), *Children's Rights And Traditional Values* (Aldershot, 1998) 249, 263.   [27] *Brown v Board of Education of Topeka* (1954) 347 US 483.
[28] Mody, S, 'Note: Brown Footnote Eleven in Historical Context: Social Science and the Supreme Court's Quest for Legitimacy' (2004) 54 *Stanford Law Review* 793–829. Siegel, RB, 'Equality Talk: Antisubordination and Anticlassification Values in Constitutional Struggles Over Brown' (2004) 117 *Harvard Law Review* 1470–1547.

Struggle Over Memory

Often when trying to bring about social change by exposing the suffering of children—by reconceptualizing racial segregation as discrimination, corporal punishment as child abuse, paternalistic child welfare practices as the silencing of children, or advertising, which implicitly sexualizes children's beauty and charm as a form of child abuse—we in fact challenge past memories. These challenges may be fought off as contradictory to common sense by those opposed to the recognition of suffering and to law's responsiveness to it through the recognition of new rights.[29]

Returning to the *Brown* case, its aftermath is perhaps the prime example of such a struggle and of active turbulent resistance to a judicial attempt to challenge the meaning of responsiveness to the Other. One could compare the opposition to law's responsiveness to the Other child to the opposition women and slaves faced when demanding human rights, being perceived by society as the property of white men. Similarly, the notion that gladiatorial combat is not a sport or that all children benefit from the right to schooling or from the right not to work even if work allows them to help their families, was commonly perceived as unacceptable and weird. Thus, what may seem commonsense at one time can at another time be regarded as absurd, cruel or unjust. Moreover, it is not easy to perceive the development of collective memory in real time as it occurs. Tomorrow's heroes are liable to become today's targets of abuse and ridicule.

Freud was the first to point out that children are a particularly vulnerable group and that psychological defences have been used by societies for centuries to deny cruelty and abuse towards children. It is useful to recall that at times, child abuse was widespread and socially acceptable. Greek philosophers endorsed sexually abusive behaviours towards adolescents the same way they endorsed slavery. These philosophers were not fundamentally evil. Simply their moral sensitivity, in the Levinasian sense, was not deep enough to encompass disempowered groups such as children and slaves, and the collective memory had no space to admit their suffering.[30]

On the one hand, we purposely revise our collective memory through legal discourse. On the other hand, though, for good examples of collective memory revision, we must step outside the legal sphere. In the past century, Mahatma Gandhi's struggles against indentured labour and segregation of the untouchables, Martin Luther King's struggle against segregation and Rabin's legitimization of Palestinian nationalism and national struggle are all examples of threatening attempts to change collective memory (attempts which may have contributed to

---

[29] Rogers, C, *Carl Rogers On Personal Power* (London, 1989) 285.
[30] Nandy, A, *At The Edge Of Psychology—Essays In Politics And Culture* (Delhi, 1990) 32–33, 47–50.

the motivation to murder the three men). All three sought to transform the collective and individual memory of their own and the wider community. Psychologically speaking, I suggest that their starting point was their own sense of self worth,[31] which allowed them to transform their worldview and memories of their own past without feeling insecure. The CRC regime now recognizes the inherent dignity of every child and aims to promote universally a sense of dignity and worth.[32]

In the literary world of child advocacy, a similar mechanism occurs in Alice Miller's controversial work 'Drama of the Gifted Child',[33] in which she revises not only the memory of her own childhood, but doubtless that of many of her readers. Her book portrays an archetypal, gifted, middle-class child, who may have every material advantage and much adult attention to his development and accomplishments, as a child who was emotionally abused. Again, in her later books on Hitler and Stalin,[34] Miller alters the slant on them in her reinterpretation of known texts, presenting them as deeply abused children and disturbingly challenging our collective memory of their inherently demonic nature.

Similarly, we should venture to ask whether we allow ourselves to respond empathically to the difficulties of a neglecting and herself abused mother or to the past victimization of a violent adolescent? These are politically loaded questions, which challenge the present allocation of power between the mother and the child protection system or between an offending adolescent and the juvenile justice system.

Case law contains many examples of empathy and antipathy towards different individuals. Reading the purported 'facts' of a case often leads unconsciously to an empathic stance toward the 'suffering parent' or 'humiliated child' or, conversely, to indignant disgust or rejection of the 'abusive parent' or 'disturbed child'. The choice of who receives our empathy is a political choice in the sense that it allocates power to those we deem worthy of empathy. Their story becomes the official story and part of the collective memory, and the story of the excluded is likely to be forgotten. We must also recall that legislators, judges and policy makers often caution themselves against yielding to empathy, and dichotomize between reason and emotion.[35] The result is a tendency to empathize only with what they remember as painful or unjust and, having decided which norms should apply retroactively, rationalize their politicized choices as stemming from

[31] See also Rogers, n 29 above, Erikson, E, *Gandhi's Truth. On The Origins of Militant Nonviolence* (London, 1970) and Ronen, n 3 above.

[32] See the CRC, especially the preamble and sections 29 and 40.

[33] Miller, A, *The Drama of The Gifted Child and The Search for The True Self.* Translated from the German by Ruth Ward. (London, 1983).

[34] Miller, A, *The Untouched Key: Tracing Childhood Trauma In Creativity And Destructiveness.* Translated from the German by Hildegarde and Hunter Hannum. (London, 1990); Miller, A, *Banished knowledge: facing childhood injuries.* Translated from the German by Leila Vennewitz. (London, 1991).

[35] Minow, M, 'Words and the Door to the Land of Change: Law, Language and Family Violence' (1990) 43 *Vanderbilt Law Review* 1665–1699.

legal theory. Reflective practice[36] can help to democratize the politics of empathy towards children both by making decision makers more sharply aware of their accountability for their choices and by exposing empathic choices to critical public analysis. Once the choices are made, we should suspend moral judgment to allow ourselves to comprehend the full personal meaning of the other's experience and articulate an empathic narrative. Thus, we may ensure what has been called 'narrative due process'.[37]

As noted earlier, one issue in child law that illustrates this paper's thesis is the protection of family life of children from disadvantaged homes.

The Protection of Family Life of Children from Disadvantaged Homes

A Language of Comprehensive Protection from all Harm

A child in need of state protection is often defined as any child who may suffer emotional or physical harm, and the aim of child protection law is often formulated as the prevention of all such harm to the child whether by action or inaction.[38] On the whole, legal systems do not adopt a narrow definition of child abuse with a conclusive list of factual situations of abuse. The given rationale is often that an open-ended definition of abuse enables responsiveness to different types of abuse.[39] Different clauses refer to different instances of abuse and neglect, but only a few explicitly mention the behaviour of the child's parents or the behavior of those responsible for her. Child protection law is primarily civil law. Strictly speaking, parents are not accused and not punished through child protection law. It is not their blameworthiness which determines the outcome of the proceedings but rather the child's wellbeing. Thus, when observing child law, whether as laymen exposed to the media, as legislators, or as jurists, we are often gently guided through the wording of the statutes and case law to remember that

---

[36] Schon, D, *The Reflective Practitioner: How Professionals Think In Action* (New York, 1983).

[37] Livnat, Y, 'Narrative Justice' (2002) 18 *Bar Ilan Studies in Law* 283–322, in Hebrew.

[38] Sutherland, E, *Child and Family Law* (Edinburgh, 1999) 293; Fortin, J, *Children's Rights and the Developing Law* (London, 1998) 368–371; Van Bueren, G, *The International Rights of the Child* (Dordrecht, 1998) 88; Kilkelly, U, *The Child and The European Convention of Human Rights* (Aldershot, 1999) 160. Meriwether, M, 'Child Abuse Reporting Laws: Time for a Change' (1986) 20 *Family Law Quarterly* 141, 149–150.

[39] For English Law see Fortin, n 38 above, 368–371; Lyon, C and De Cruz, P, *Child Abuse* (2nd edn) (Bristol, 1993) 2–5. For Scottish law see Sutherland, n 38 above, 292–293. For Israeli law see Sharon, E, *Minors at Risk—Judgment, Treatment and Supervision in the Juvenile Court* (Netanya, 1998) 323, 349–350. Hebrew; Reifen, D, *The Minor and the Juvenile Court* (Tel Aviv, 1978) 215. Hebrew. Van Bueren explains that the non-definition of abuse and neglect in international law aims to prevent basing definitions of abuse and neglect on ethnocentric or arbitrary assumptions. See Van Bueren, n 38 above, 88.

the state offers the child comprehensive protection from all abuse and neglect and does not target parents as prime subjects for reprisal.

Raising Children and State Protection of Children

However, laws often assume implicitly that the primary risk to children stems from those directly responsible for them, and that it is from these individuals that children should be chiefly protected by the law. This is particularly evident in the US and Israel, where child protection has become the focal point of child welfare practices for social workers and other child welfare professionals.[40]

In contrast to the comprehensive definition of the child who needs state protection, in practice, we often find that child welfare has become a social construct, and consistently excludes the larger, more pressing issues that affect children's wellbeing. The narrower picture of child welfare policy currently accepted in both Israel and the US focuses chiefly on children harmed by their own families, and the apparatus and policies of state action aim to find and protect such children. However, is the problem of children harmed by their parents the most pressing issue in child welfare? Is it the key to protecting children?

In Israel and the US, strategies that broaden the lens of problems facing children and maximize the chance of children being raised by their own willing families, are hardly ever used. Children are denied basic necessities. Not surprisingly, in Israel, children from socially marginalized groups such as Palestinian children, children of foreign workers, Arab minority children, and the children of immigrants from the former Soviet Union and Ethiopia, are the first to suffer from the resistance to broadening the lens of child protection. One would thus expect Israeli children's rights discourse to be tied to questions of social justice and social exclusion. Regretfully, selective empathy is exemplified by the relative neglect of the plight of children from excluded groups in Israeli public discourse. Thus, in Israeli collective memory the children's rights agenda is making progress, children are more visible and more audible.

In both the legal and public discourse, the tie between social exclusion and injustice and identification as at risk has not been made.[41] The law can protect children based on proof of need. However, it runs the risk of seeing parents as solely responsible for responding to the child's needs, and therefore may become preoccupied with evidential issues of parental wrongdoing to justify intervention.[42] Evidential preoccupation is neither inevitable nor derived from the law's fundamental nature.[43] However it is easy to fall into a formalistic,

---

[40] Guggenheim, M, 'Book Review: Somebody's Children: Sustaining The Family's Place In Child Welfare Policy (Nobody's Children: Abuse and Neglect, Foster Drift, and the Adoption Alternative, Elizabeth Bartholet)' (2000) 113 *Harvard Law Review* 1716, 1749–1750.

[41] Guggenheim, ibid.   [42] Cooper *et al*, n 19 above.

[43] Madden, RG and Wayne, RH, 'Social Work and the Law: A Therapeutic Jurisprudence Perspective' (2003) 48(3) *Social Work* 338–347.

soulless preoccupation with procedure and evidence. Thus, achieving recognition of the child's authentic needs as a whole person tied to family and community is still a real challenge, even for democracies ostensibly committed to the rights regime set out in the CRC.

Returning to the Israeli context for further exemplification: in Israel, a governmental committee authorized to propose a comprehensive reform of Israel's child law made detailed recommendations indeed worthy of thoughtful examination on a wide array of subjects. However, the committee found no need to ensure commitment to multiculturalism in a country troubled by conflicts between cultural communities in which negation of the Other's identity is commonplace, failed to write a final report concerning children at risk, as such—the very subject matter of child protection law, a population alarmingly growing as a result of regressive social policies—and did not recommend the appointment of a commissioner for children whose independent discretion, authority and funding would be guaranteed under law. Experience teaches that such a commissioner can empower socially excluded children and their families in relation to the welfare and educational establishments and respond to their sense of injustice. The committee was well aware of the experience in other countries and of the unmet needs highlighted by the comments of the UN Committee on the Rights of the Child, but chose not to make a clear and unequivocal recommendation in this respect. Thus, I suggest, we witness implications of not fully recognizing the tie between children's rights on the one hand and social injustice and social exclusion on the other hand.

To summarize, in terms of the collective memory, an open-ended definition of abuse, coupled with interventions solely focused on protecting the child from his family, creates a distorted picture of childhood, the hazards children face, and the state protection offered. The implications of this distortion can be diverse and far reaching.

The Meaning of Paramountcy of Children's Interests in Remedying Harm to the Child

Once harm to the child is identified, the child's interests are often paramount and he may receive remedy under child law—despite infringement of the interests of others, such as biological kin, foster parents or adoptive parents.

In the wake of the struggle between children's rights proponents and the proponents of family autonomy and parental rights, the present state of child protection law in Israel, as in West European and North American democracies, signifies, on the whole, clear progress for the child's interests in the post-World War II era. State protection from harm for children has widened in scope and now mandates greater intervention into family life, despite infringement of what used to be perceived in the past as parental rights.[44] Seeing this, one might be tempted to

---

[44] Ronen, n 26 above.

argue that comprehensive paramountcy of children's interests under law has been achieved. Moreover, commitment to the child's interests in specific situations of proven harm and a tone of compassion in discussing their suffering in case law, public inquiries and parliamentary debates, may naturally lead to the conclusion that this commitment reflects a policy of comprehensive state responsibility for the child. However, in taking this view, we are tempted to forget what is probably the most important insight in Goldstein, Solnit and Freud's trilogy on the best interests of the child. This insight, which has been incorporated into case law in different jurisdictions, posits that state action to protect the child is always only the least detrimental option, and is not therefore the equivalent of paramountcy of children's interests under law when state intervention becomes needless as a result of preventive policies. An example of this would be the relationship between adoption, foster care and poverty: in an ideal society, adoption would be an accepted but rare alternative for children whose parents are unable to take care of them or choose not to. An ideal society would radically decrease its need for adoption by combating poverty and its dangers to children.[45] Thus, in Israel, a state where the gap between rich and poor is the second highest in the western world, and where there are virtually no statutory social welfare rights, we nevertheless entertain the illusion of a commitment to children. To paraphrase Gary Melton, the question now is whether a system that developed from intrusion into the lives of the poor can be reconstituted to provide services that can nurture the quality of the lives of all children.[46] Melton's question assumes greater force when socially regressive child and family policies lead to poverty in a large proportion of families. When the poor are no longer a very small minority, exclusive emphasis on intrusive intervention in family life in the name of children's rights leads to what Mondlak calls a 'democratic deficit':[47] when a large segment of the population suffers from the policies that target it and becomes powerless through the politics of un-recognition, one cannot but conclude that democracy in its deeper more pervasive meaning has been compromised. The present international rights regime has not created effective mechanisms for combating the un-recognition of children's sense of belonging to a family and community and their suffering when subjected to outdated laissez-faire social policies built on spurious assumptions of equal opportunities.[48] Thus, the experiences of these children become invisible in the collective memory. Levinas would see it as only natural that his discussion of

[45] Roberts, D, 'Is There Justice in Children's Rights? The Critique Of Federal Family Preservation Policy' (1999) 2 *University of Pennsylvania Journal of Constitutional Law* 112, 126–127. See also Cahn, N, 'Children's Interests in a Familial Context: Poverty, Foster Care, and Adoption' (1999) 60 *Ohio State Law Journal* 1189–1223.
[46] Melton, G, 'Is There A Place For Children In The New World Order?' in Asquith, S and Hill, M (eds), *Justice for Children* (Dordrecht, 1994) 26, 38.
[47] Mudlak, G, 'Workers or Foreigners in Israel? The "Foundational Contract" and the Democratic Deficit' (2003) 27 *Tel Aviv University Law Review* 423–488, in Hebrew.
[48] eg Novoa, A, 'Count the Brown Faces: Where is the "Family" in the Family Law of Child Protective Services' (1999) *The Scholar—St Mary's Law Review on Minority Issues* 5, 43.

his own invisible humanity (buried under a constructed memory of the Jew) can be utilized to understand why the suffering of children from disadvantaged homes becomes invisible despite recourse to doctrinal rights discourse, since the human intellect is harnessed while neglecting to come to terms with the subjective, personal assault on our senses: the actual experience of children's suffering.

If we take the US as an example, we find that not only are a disproportionate number of foster care children from minority cultures, but they are also overwhelmingly poor.[49] These demographics hold true for many other societies, including Israel. In practice, our societies generally respect the privacy and autonomy of middle-class families, but we accede to coercive intervention and intrusion in low-income or otherwise excluded disempowered families, by convincing ourselves that such interventions are unavoidable from a child-centred perspective.[50] We discount and devalue the cultural backgrounds and solid parenting skills of many such disempowered parents. In trying to protect children, we often disregard their parents' needs and interests and their communities' cooperative values, and thus mainstream society evades the responsibility for the flawed development of children from these families. It is less painful psychologically to point an accusing finger at dysfunctional parents than to face our responsibility for the systemic factors causing the dysfunction.[51]

The American child welfare system has been castigated as a coercive system that thrives on punishment and blame of the poor. The 'othering' of poor families in the US context, particularly when they are of colour, makes it easy for the dominant culture to devalue them: to view them as dysfunctional and not families at all. Annette Appell, a proponent of openness in adoption, has criticized the 'growth industry' that has arisen from the state's 'protective' involvement with poor families and families of colour and the state's punitive treatment particularly of the mothers of these families. These mothers are outside norms and myths of white, middle-class mothering in a number of ways, including the simple fact that they are poor, but also because they depend upon informal kinship and community networks for child care. Similar observations have been made concerning the Israeli context.[52]

Many of the same families whose 'cultures' are marginalized and misunderstood by the child welfare system are also affected by domestic violence. The above discussion thus also applies with equal force to cases of domestic violence. The

[49] Roberts, n 45 above, Cahn, n 45 above.

[50] Brooks, S and Ronen, Y (forthcoming, 2006) 'On the Idea of Interdependence and its Implications for Child and Family Policy' *Journal of Feminist Family Therapy—An International Forum*. Ronen, Y and Ben Harush, Y, 'The Legal Treatment of Youth: Between Reality and Prevalent Conceptions' in Wozner, Y and Rahav, G (eds), *Youth in Israel* (Tel Aviv, 2005) 207–246, in Hebrew. Ronen, Y, 'On the Strengths of the Child and his Family in a Legal Context' in Cohen, B and Buchbinder, E (eds), *Maximizing Capacities Applications of the Strengths Perspective in Social Work* (Tel Aviv, 2005) 133–156, in Hebrew.   [51] Brooks and Ronen, n 50 above. Ronen, n 3 above.

[52] Brooks and Ronen, n 50 above. Ronen, n 3 above. Ronen and Ben Harush, n 50 above.

'othering' of victims/survivors makes it easier for us to condemn them for their choices and to fail to appreciate the complexities of their situations.

The Ethos of Liberal Individualism as Implied in Child Protection Law

The ethos of liberal individualism does not foster state responsibility for hunger, homelessness, violent educational environment, inadequate healthcare, or nonexistent counselling services for children whose working parents are at times physically absent and emotionally spent.[53] Children exposed to such hazards are often ignorant and apathetic regarding civil liberties such as freedom of expression, freedom of conscience or freedom of education, and have little chance of becoming the autonomous adults who widely exercise these liberties, as liberal theory imagines they do. Often, such individuals, even if they are cognizant of civil liberties, perceive them as irrelevant to their struggles and worries, which to a degree makes sense.

The liberal individualist ethos has led some, including the author of this paper, to utilize an economic rationale for justifying the allocation of social rights under child protection law. This approach, though not blameworthy if it achieves recognition of children's social rights, nevertheless highlights the public blindness to an instrumental approach to children's needs: if a society genuinely respects children it will invest in their social rights not because it is cheaper than investing in long-term institutionalization, but because it recognizes that their right to identity and to a family life stem from their fundamental human dignity as inter-dependent human beings[54]—there should be no need to turn to an economic rationale for justifying social rights. Children, we know, can develop complex identifications, which despite abuse or neglect by the family and community, often remain important to them. An atomistic or individualistic ethos does not foster authentic self-actualization in children nor recognize the importance of family and community ties to the formation of identity.

We must also remember that protecting the child's identity and autonomy is different from protecting the same in adults. To value a child's evolving capacities and partial autonomy is to respect her conceptions of others, even though she does not start with plans or conceptions.[55] Here, liberal individualism comes to our aid.

There is a danger, however, that liberal, individualistic rights discourse might aid the reconstruction of the social problem of harm to children as a question of private disputes between individuals. According to this reconstruction, the sole

---

[53] Cover, R, 'A Jewish Jurisprudence of the Social Order' in Minow, Ryan and Sarat, n 4 above, 239–248.   [54] Brooks and Ronen, n 50 above, Ronen, n 3 above.
[55] Appiah, A, 'Identity, Authenticity Survival: Multicultural Societies and Social Reproduction' in Taylor, C *et al*, *Multiculturalism: Examining The Politics of Recognition*. Edited and introduced by A Gutmann. Expanded Edition of Multiculturalism and 'the Politics of Recognition', (Princeton, 1994) 149, 158.

role of the state would be the advocacy of the child *vis-à-vis* those who are intimately responsible for her wellbeing. Furthermore, the absolute quality of individualistic 'rights talk' heightens social conflict and inhibits dialogue possibly leading toward consensus or at least the discovery of a common ground. Moreover, it contributes to the 'othering' of vulnerable populations, which fosters a climate that systematically disadvantages caretakers and is alienated from society's so-called 'losers'.[56]

In individualistic rights discourse, the traditional image of the state as one corner of a triangle and the parents and their children as the other two corners (an image of rivalry and competition) is one expression of this reconstruction. The state and parents may indeed compete sometimes and rival each other in the struggle to define what is best for the child and to uphold the child's interests. However, for children to develop their potential, the state should serve primarily as one of many resources open to the child and his family. I am hopeful that the distortion of children's needs implicit in the traditional liberal individualistic ethos is gaining greater recognition and that we shall be witnessing less emphasis on rigid unconstrained individualism and more emphasis on preserving relationships, connectedness and identity within a family and community in the development of children's rights.[57]

The preceding arguments may lead to important questions: For example: Do we empathically understand the narrative of a poor and neglectful mother who receives tax payers' support? From a genuinely child-centered perspective, can we morally afford not to offer her help? Is the price that children pay for the liberal individualistic ethos behind the legal rhetoric acceptable in as much as it is blind to social injustice and the lack of opportunities for the excluded poor? Is children's rights discourse naturally responsive to the suffering of the excluded, poor children?

Participation and the Non-appearance of Individual Suffering in the Collective Memory

The above discussion, leading to its concluding questions, highlights the pitfalls of *misusing* the terminology of individual rights[58] to frame child and family policy. However, international law, primarily in the form of the CRC, is an articulation of children's rights that demonstrates the potential for a rights-based framework to reflect an ethos of interdependence rather than rigid individualism. The CRC serves as a solid foundation on which to construct a children's rights regime based on interdependence. Specifically, the children's rights principles laid out in the

---

[56] Brooks and Ronen, n 50 above.
[57] See also Ronen, n 3 above, Daicoff, n 21 above, 468, Minow, n 3 above.
[58] See also Fortin, n 38 above, 30. Freeman, M, *The Moral Status of Children—Essays on the Rights of the Child* (The Hague, 1997) 391–394. Minow, M, *Making All The Difference: Inclusion, Exclusion and American Law* (Ithaca, 1990) 303.

CRC affirm the reciprocal attachments of the child and his/her family and community.[59]

The criticism of liberal individualism that often underlies children's rights rhetoric does not negate the value of the rights discourse which can be grounded in the CRC, and highlights the danger of its distortion and abuse. Allowing children's participation in decisions that affect them is indispensable if we are to achieve the genuine state responsibility for child protection envisaged here.

Alienated doctrinal thinking, which does not appreciate the value of face-to-face dialogue with the individual when constructing legal norms, actually facilitates the rationalization of politicized empathy and the abrogation of our sense of injustice. Dangerously, such doctrinal thinking can also be couched in either rights rhetoric or traditional child protection rhetoric. A language of needs implies an assessment of needs, but may lead to children's objectification. A widespread conception of professionalism in child protection, calls for children's needs assessment to be based on objectifiable factors. However, this may serve to disempower children, who may have difficulty expressing anger and frustration towards professionals who they feel have treated them unjustly. The individual child with no right to participate in defining her own abuse and neglect and what she believes can protect her against them under the law cannot effectively challenge those professionals who view children in need of protection simply as children with problems that must be assessed in order to identify needs objectively, and who disregard children's unique strengths and ignore their ability to overcome adversity. Only by acknowledging children's strengths in adversity can we genuinely respect the child's human dignity as an individual capable of self-actualization.[60]

Recognizing children's rights to participation will allow new stories constantly to be heard and help to expose the limitations of our understanding of the injustices and suffering they endure. Again, it is important to recognize that memory is actively constructed either through an unfounded assumption of objectifiable needs or by recognizing children's diverse experiences.

The Public Response to Past Victimization of Young Offenders

The murder of two-year-old James Bulger in 1993 by two ten-year-olds, Jon Venables and Robert Thompson, was a horrendous event. A child was horribly murdered. His parents and others who knew him and cared for him undoubtedly suffered painful trauma. It was this trauma, as will now be demonstrated, that both the court and key politicians chose to relate to and empathize with. For this reason, only twenty minutes of the seventeen-day public trial held in an adult court were devoted to the mental state of the two accused, who by then were eleven years

---

[59] Ronen, n 3 above, 147–177.   [60] Ronen, n 26 above.

old. I shall not dwell here on the possible victimization of offenders through legal proceedings blind to their special needs, an issue which has been widely discussed both by the courts and in the literature in this case[61] but rather on the public response to the *past* victimization, the victimization prior to offending.

Mr Justice Morland, presiding over the case, described the killing as a cunning and wicked act of 'unparalleled evil and barbarity'.[62] He continued by elegantly blocking the view to what might have been perceived as mitigating factors in the public's image of the boys: 'It is not for me to pass judgment on their upbringing, but I suspect exposure to violent video games may in part be an explanation.'[63] Nowhere is there any mention of the social and economic causes of the crime.[64]

The judge never explained why the court should not pass judgment on the children's upbringing, even though in this statement, he was indeed passing judgment. Note, however, that the question of responsibility for the children's upbringing was never explored. Implicitly, the boys' parents were responsible for their children's upbringing, but out of respect for family privacy and the parents' dignity, the court refrained from tarring them with a more explicit moral accusation. Shifting the focus to violent video games served to reposition the question of responsibility in an impersonal, asocial sphere. Dismissed by the court, it was left to post-trial academic research to clarify the children's family and social background.

How did the court's demonization of the two compare with other constructions affecting the collective British memory? Can we envision an alternative to demonization at one pole and complete innocence at the other when faced with such a terrible act? The then British Prime Minister, John Major, called for greater condemnation and less understanding. The politicization of empathy in this case involving professional politicians created an invisible barrier between the public and the murdering children. The Minister of State for probation services at the time lambasted the church for spending its time discussing social issues such as housing and leaving the politicians to debate right and wrong.[65]

---

[61] See eg Buckley, F [2002] 'One Murder, Three Victims: James Bulger, Robert Thompson and Jon Venables' *Cork Online Law Review*. <http://colr.ucc.ie/2002x.html>. The trial and later setting of tariff by the Home Secretary, vulnerable to influence by public opinion were held by the European Court of Human Rights to be in violation of the European Convention for the Protection of Human Rights and Fundamental Freedoms. More specifically, the court held that the two children could not participate effectively in the public, highly-publicized proceedings and were in consequence denied a fair hearing. See <http://Cmiskp.Echr.Coe.Int/Tkp197/Search.Asp?Skin=Hudoc-En> Case of *T v UK* (App No 24724/94) Judgment, Strasbourg, 16 December 1999. Case of *V v UK* (Application No 24888/94) Judgment, Strasbourg, 16 December 1999.

[62] *R v Secretary of State, ex p V; R v Secretary for the Home Department, ex p T* [1998] AC 409.

[63] Smith, DJ, *The Sleep of Reason: The James Bulger Case* (London, 1995); Jackson, D, *Destroying the Baby in Themselves: Why did the Two Boys Kill James Bulger?* (Nottingham, 1995).

[64] Freeman, n 58 above, 244.

[65] Collett, S, 'Beyond Reason and Understanding—The Everyday Understanding of Crime' (1993) 40 *Probation Journal* 184–187.

I want to suggest that the important question here is, who were the two boys?—Is there anything else for us to know or understand—or were they just two evil boys?

The psychiatrists who examined the two boys declared them free of mental illness or depression, although there was plenty of evidence hinting that these were very unhappy, emotionally disturbed boys who were consequently problematic in various ways. Jon's background seems chronically insecure as he got shunted back and forth between parents who suffered from periodic depression, could not cope consistently, nor decide whether to live together or apart. At the age of seven a trainee psychologist identifies him as unable to cope with the pressures on him. Robert came from a history of neglect and violence. Robert's mother was herself an abused and unloved child, had married an abusive violent man with whom she had six children. Once Robert's father left, she started drinking heavily. Bullying brothers took over disciplining Robert. Both boys stole, bullied other children, underachieved scholastically and were often truant. Neither received significant attention of helping professionals prior to the murder. Both received it in secure accommodation and radically changed their behavior. Robert moved from habitual truant to college student.[66]

The politicians' statements imply that social issues do not involve questions of right and wrong. They also imply that if the child murderers had been taught to understand the meaning of 'wrong' and condemned for their misdeeds in the past, the murder would never have happened. Furthermore, they imply that society's efforts to understand the causes of crime undermine its efforts to prevent it. Here we should note the contrasting approach of the UN Guidelines for the Prevention of Juvenile Delinquency, which chiefly discuss the systemic social and economic factors that can ensure psychological well-being and advocate a proactive, preventive approach.[67]

The premises of both the judge's and the politicians' rhetoric are totally unfounded: there is no basis for believing that the boys were born evil, as Mr Justice Morland intimated when writing of a wicked act of unparalled evil and brutality while almost totally ignoring their background. Neither is there a basis for thinking that had the boys understood the wrongness of their act and experienced condemnation for it in the past they could have avoided the murder by themselves, or that attempting to understand the etiology of the terrible crime would undermine future efforts at crime prevention. The sentence handed down and the politicians' pronouncements all worked to the same end, to absolve society and state from the moral responsibility for social problems.

---

[66] Jefferson, T, 'Book Review: The Sleep Of Reason: The James Bulger Case, by David James Smith (London, 1995). Destroying The Baby In Themselves: Why Did The Two Boys Kill James Bulger? by David Jackson (Nottingham, 1995). The Case Of Mary Bell: A Portrait Of A Child Who Murdered, by Gitta Sereny (London, 1995)' (1996) 36(2) *British Journal of Criminology* 319–324. Orr, D, 'Ten Years On: The Real Lessons of the Bulger Case' *The Independent* 11 February 2003.

[67] Cappelaere, G, 'Introduction' to *United Nations Guidelines for the Prevention of Juvenile Delinquency—Riyadh Guidelines. International Standards concerning the Rights of the Child* (Geneva, 1995) 1–8.

Children who murder are a social problem and may reflect severe social neglect. However, I suggest that we are all prone to anxiety at our vulnerability to such horrific behaviours and at the fragility of decency and humaneness in alienated social worlds where the claim that 'anything goes' is popular.[68] One is tempted to react to such anxiety by intolerance to ambiguity and uncertainty and to scapegoat of an evil 'Other'.[69] Thus, a case like this becomes an excellent bludgeon to attack those who argue the state's responsibility for social ills. The Bulger murder was a horrific and twisted cry for attention and help which was used by key players from the British establishment to promote an agenda of social alienation; can society afford to ignore the subjective meaning of the children's terrible act from their perspective or deny our responsibility for the preconditions which must be tackled if we hope to minimize such horrors in the future? There is wide recognition in the literature that the children who murdered James Bulger were failed by society.[70] This should be translated into consolidation of social rights to services for children and their families such as tutoring, psychotherapy, school counseling and day care, services which have a preventive effect and are called for by the CRC and the Riyadh Guidelines.[71]

To summarize, then: the collective memory of these murders, the causes of the offenders' behaviour, and the extent to which the state was responsive to the offenders' psychological and educational needs before the crime, is relevant not only in this case but in general, for the prevention of violence and the promotion of individual and social wellbeing.

Through either the mindful or unmindful construction of the official story and the neglect of the children's counter-stories, the judge in the Bulger case not only applied his own personal vision of human motivation, but justified a particular social philosophy through his pronouncement on reality. Under different circumstances, this philosophy would have seemed repugnant since it facilitated and excused state irresponsibility for children's twisted development. The two

---

[68] eg Winnicott, C, Sheperd, R, and Davis, M (eds), *Deprivation And Delinquency* (London, 1984) Martha Minow argues that identity politics has contributed to social alienation, see Minow, M, *Not Only for Myself—Identity, Politics and the Law* (New York, 1999) 23–28. Gerald Lopez and Peter Cicchino elucidate the sometimes subtle and sophisticated challenge of overcoming moral relativism and client–professional alienation faced by human rights advocates. Lopez, GP, 'An Aversion to Clients: Loving Humanity and Hating Human Beings' (1996) 31 *Harvard Civil Rights—Civil Liberties Law Review* 315–323. Cicchino, PM, 'To be a political lawyer' (1996) 31 *Harvard Civil Rights—Civil Liberties Law Review* 311–314. No doubt, this anxiety is exasperated by the perceived threat of postmodernism and Communitarianism in as much as they are equated with justification of an amoral social sphere. See eg Howard, RE, 'Cultural absolutism and the nostalgia for community' (1993) 15 *Human Rights Quarterly* 315–338. Cohen, S, *States of Denial: Knowing about Atrocities and Suffering* (Cambridge, 2001) 285–286.

[69] For a discussion of scapegoating and intolerance to ambiguity and uncertainty in the context of the Bulger case, see also Prins, H, 'Even a Child is Known by His Doings' (1993) 40 *Probation Journal* 88.

[70] Downing, K, 'When Children Commit Murder, Who is Really Responsible?' (1994) 158 *Justice of the Peace and Local Government Law* 51–52. Collett, n 65 above.

[71] Cappelaere, n 67 above.

children, who came from disadvantaged homes and were undoubtedly the victims not only of unique family circumstances, but of systemic and societal neglect, were not faced as human beings either by politicians or judges. Justifiably, they were held accountable for their terrible crime, but paradoxically the terrible cruelty of the crime may have motivated the rationalization of a position of state non-accountability for the causes of child and juvenile delinquency. Empathy in this case was blatantly politicized.

Accepting that it may have deeply offended public sentiment to comment about the case in ways that could have been construed as understanding the boys, I nevertheless want to suggest that trying publicly to understand the murder might have served a humanistic agenda for child and family policy that could well have prevented deaths in the future.

Conclusion

This paper opened with a personal vignette describing how the author of the vignette regained something of his human dignity denied to him by humans, through the responsiveness of a dog. The vignette's author, though disillusioned with a morality founded on intellect alone, does not despair of the law's capacity to respond to human suffering. Law is not inherently unresponsive to vulnerability and suffering and thus one should not despair of the prospect of its responsiveness to the experience of children, a social group characterized by vulnerability.

Indeed, individuals such as psychotherapists, novelists, judges, legislators and legal scholars, who are in a position to influence our personal and collective memories, can project the meanings of their choice onto our collective and personal pasts. Such projections may even become part of an ostensibly *objective* 'history', part of '*the* facts', part of '*the* true account of events'.

As legal history unfurls, stories of childhood and parenthood are written and rewritten mainly because our understanding of our own childhood and the childhood of others changes as our personal memory is perpetually reconstructed. This process does not have to be arbitrary, unconscious or unmindful.

Psychological mindedness can gradually liberate law, jurists and helping professionals from some of the legal culture's shackling of our thinking and behaviour. Irrational reductionist scepticism can give way to a more balanced approach which is ready to risk trusting children and their families despite personal and familial deviance and malfunctioning.

Having pointed out the pitfalls of *misusing* the terminology of individual rights to frame child and family policy, we saw above that the CRC provides a solid foundation upon which to construct a regime based on interdependence. What this means specifically is that the children's rights principles laid out in the CRC affirm the reciprocal attachments of the child and his or her family and community.

The arguments regarding adolescent offenders with which this paper concludes exemplify the complexity and delicacy of constructing collective memory. The most disturbing offences can be committed and often are committed by individuals who are victims not only of unique family circumstances, but also of systemic and societal neglect. These have to be faced as human beings despite the strong temptation to demonize them.

Exposing the politicization of empathy and committing ourselves to psychological mindedness may enable us to see a richer picture of the past. Our memory of the past will frame our future, and we can offer our children a more responsive and humane world in which to grow to the degree that we allow ourselves to remember the inhumanity in our past.

24

A Dual Process that Disables the Persuasive Impact of Mass Media Appeals to Obey Tax Laws

Robert Mason and Safaa Amer*

Weak persuasive mass media effects are the hallmark for efforts to foster greater tax compliance (Mason, 1987; Stalans, Smith, and Kinsey, 1991) as well as changing other behaviours that impinge on society's welfare, such as drug use (Crano & Brugoon, 2002), excessive alcohol and tobacco use (Denzon and Lipsey, 2002), and one's protection from criminal victimization (Tyler and Lavrakes, 1986).

The study of mass media effects generally stems from Lasswell's (1948) model of answering the question 'who says what, in which channel, to whom with what effect?' This model has characterized much of our research on mass communication effects for the past half century, including research on tax compliance and crime and deterrence issues generally.

Even if we accept the argument of weak effects, we must ask if we are missing something important by the adoption of Lasswell's (1948) classic mass communication model. For instance, when studying mass communication effects, Reeves, Chafee, and Tims (1982) point out that we should not only investigate what media appeals do to people, we also should examine more closely what people *do* with the messages they receive. Attention to media information allows the freedom for one to quarrel or counterargue with these messages, and counterarguing has been shown to resist or weaken persuasive appeals (Iyengar and Kinder, 1985; Roberts and Maccoby, 1973). As well, a simpler strategy for dealing with media appeals is simply to ignore them completely (McGuire, 1969).

* The American Bar Foundation supported this study. Our thanks go to Lisa Stauff and Karyl Kinsey of the Foundation who spent many hours coding and checking the open-end thought responses. The task was most difficult and required the careful, intensive work of several individuals over several weeks to capture the detail that was required. Special thanks also are due to Laurie M Robbins, Department of Communication, Santa Clara University, and Virginia M Lesser, Department of Statistics at Oregon State University, for helpful suggestions on earlier drafts of the manuscript and to Brandt Balgooyen, graduate research assistant, Department of Statistics at Oregon State University, for the graphic design of the figures. Correspondence concerning this paper should be addressed to Robert Mason, Department of Statistics, Oregon State University, Corvallis, OR 97331.

We argue in this paper that a dual process is at work to disable the persuasive impact that we and others have reported. One element is the cognitive responses to the messages; the other is a self-enhancement strategy people employ to maintain their self-worth that builds on these cognitions. The purpose of this paper is to formulate and justify our dual model and subject it to an empirical test of Oregon taxpayers.

Theoretical Background

Elements of a Persuasive Media Message

Much of the research that has examined the role of cognitive responses stems from Greenwald's (1968) argument that 'learning the cognitive response content may, indeed, be more fundamental for persuasion than the learning of communication content' (p. 149). The role of cognitive mediation is now well established in the persuasion literature (Romero, Christopher, and Insko, 1996) and the 'success' of our experimental news stories is based on the cognitive responses to them. The key to any success depends on the formulation of a credible message, since that is a feature of a news story where cognitive responses are expected to surface (Perloff and Brock, 1980) and messages to be processed (Chaiken, Wood, and Eagly, 1996). Therefore, it is important that our experimental messages are roughly equal in their ability to stimulate thinking and cognitive processing. The features considered in this study are:

- *Strong arguments.* Argument quality has been shown to foster message processing with strong arguments in relevant situations, producing more than twice as many favourable thoughts as did low-relevance situations (Petty, Priester, and Brinol, 2002; Petty and Wegner, 1983). Overall, strong arguments were more persuasive than weak ones, but the interaction between relevance and argument quality showed a significant joint effect on persuasion.

  The content of our two media news stories requires us to write them so that they not only convey convincing arguments but also comply with journalistic standards of good news writing (Cappo, 1991). We are doing this to control for the effect of argument quality when comparing the persuasive impact of each story.

- *A credible source.* News stories require a source (attribution) for quoted information. For our experiment, we sought a credible source in order to control for source credibility in the study. Highly credible sources, according to Hovland, Janis, and Kelly (1953) are those who are perceived as experts— persons who are knowledgeable and able to provide accurate information. As well, a credible source is perceived as trustworthy, ie honest and truthful. Credible sources are important for message processing in two respects: (1) they are more persuasive with persons in low involvement or low personal relevant situations (Petty, Cacioppo, and Goldman, 1981); and (2) they serve as a *peripheral* cue for message evaluation when the motivation or ability to think about a message is not strong. A peripheral cue is a persuasion strategy that allows a person to form favorable or unfavorable attitudes without engaging in effortful thinking about the message's content. This feature of message processing is in contrast to the *central* route of evaluation that involves effortful thinking (Chaiken, 1980; Petty, Cacioppo, and Schumann, 1983).

Selection of Experimental News Stories

A sanction threat and a moral appeal to pay one's tax obligation fully are the two news stories that will be employed in our experiment.

Long and Swingen (1991) note that tax authorities choose cases to present through the media that aim to create fear if one cheats on his or her taxes. As a recent example, national newspapers quoted the Internal Revenue Service (IRS) as saying that the agency had hired more than 1,000 new auditors to help stanch an estimated $250 billion annual loss of revenue from fabricated deductions and unreported income (Kristof, 2002). While additional auditors will bring in revenue that otherwise may be lost, the *Los Angeles Times* story is significant because it is a good example of a media policy that relies on sanction fear and punishment threats to deter tax cheating.

Criminologists and social psychologists, following Schwartz and Orleans' (1967) seminal field experiment, suggest that, as an alternative to sanction threats, the most powerful incentive to obey the law rests with appeals that tap internalized norms and values of right and wrong (Caldini, 1989; Roth, Scholz, and Witte, 1989; Tyler, 1990). Grasmick and Scott (1982) argue that knowingly cheating on one's taxes produces guilt from both shame and fear of legal sanctions that significantly reduces future intentions to cheat on one's taxes. The effect of shame, however, was twice as great as the fear of sanctions on estimated future compliance (Grasmick and Bursik, 1990).

Results of Cognitive Response on Self-enhancement Strategies

At one time, conventional wisdom held that the self-serving bias (or self/other contrast) was the domain of those whose self-esteem had been threatened and required restoration (Shrauger and Patterson, 1974). An alternative view more prevalent today suggests that a greater self-serving enhancement occurs because individuals are motivated to maintain a consistently positive self-image. People respond to a favourable outcome from a challenge to their self-worth by taking steps to ensure stability of their positive view of themselves, eg others will be more affected by the message than self. Consistency in maintaining one's self-worth is

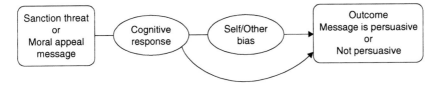

Figure 24.1. Diagram of a dual communication model for persuasive media messages

considered important because stable self-views help people achieve predictability and control over their lives (Epstein, 1973). Empirical support favours the self-consistency model (Brown, Collins, and Schmidt, 1988; Swann, Premore, and Baines, 1999).

Therefore, people are assumed to be motivated to maintain or restore a positive image of themselves through an invidious comparison between self and others. They frequently tailor their judgement of others, relative to themselves, in order to do this (Beauregard & Dunning, 1998; Brown, 1986). The role of cognitive responses is of particular interest in order to learn how media information is processed in situations that may require the formation of self-enhancement judgements. By cognitive responses, we mean those thoughts that go through an individual's head when he or she receives, comprehends and evaluates messages that serve to describe the information that is processed. If the person's cognitive responses create denial, then message rejection is the outcome if one specifies that others are influenced more than self. If the message produces favourable thoughts, then the message is persuasive if respondents specify that one's self is influenced more than others (Petty, Priester, and Brinol, 2002).

Our design is shown in Figure 24.1. Cognitive responses formed from exposure to the media messages are related to the magnitude of a self/other bias. Exposure to the media messages may be directly related to a self/other bias, but then we have difficulty explaining how this occurs without the filtering or gate-keeping effect from the internal process of cognitive activity, such as denial or agreement cognitive factors. Some cognitive factors may be sufficient to maintain one's self-worth in their own right without employing a self/other comparison.

Methods

Participants and Design

Participants were 242 Oregon taxpayers whom the state Department of Revenue (DOR) had selected for audit of their 1992 income tax returns. A control group of 144 taxpayers who were not under investigation also was selected. They had similar income sources and levels as those who had been selected for audit and were drawn from the same pool of nearly 40,000 taxpayers from which auditors had selected individuals for examination. Face-to-face interviews were completed immediately after the audit. A 70 per cent response rate was achieved for the audited sample, 62 per cent for the control group.

Measurement of the Variables

Creation of the Experimental News Stories

Two experimental news stories—one a sanction threat message and the other a moral appeal to comply with income tax laws—were written and balanced by the same headline, story length, and source or authority for the message. One news story, selected at random, was shown to each respondent during the interview.

The sanction threat message was developed from the types of sanctions employed in tax enforcement—fines, interest penalties and fraud penalties for flagrant abuse of tax laws. We adopted Rogers' (1983) model that a strong fear appeal should (1) convince the reader that there are severe undesirable consequences for not complying fully with one's tax obligation; (2) that these consequences will occur if proper actions are not followed; and (3) negative consequences can be avoided if taxpayers pay all taxes that are due.

For the moral appeal, we based our message on Bardach's (1989) analysis of the moral rationale for persuading taxpayers to comply voluntarily with tax laws. We used the only appeal that Bardach concluded stood on firm moral ground, ie 'Tax cheating is not a victimless crime. The victims are the great majority of our fellow citizens who are honest and pay what they owe with every wage and salary check' (p 61).

The president of the Oregon Certified Public Accountants (who consented to have his name and title used in this study) was the authority cited in the stories. Considered a credible source, the use of his name was employed to control for source credibility. Respondents could then focus their attention where we wanted—on the credibility of the message content. The experimental news stories are displayed in Figure 24.2.

Measurement Cognitive Response

Respondents' reaction to an open-ended question was sought immediately after they had read the experimental news story. Interviewers probed for the type of thoughts they had, how much influence the story would have on their own taxpaying and how much they would discuss the story with others (Cacioppo and Petty, 1986). The 'thought listing' of open-ended responses was transformed into statements by two coders (Brock, 1967; Perloff and Brock, 1980). First, code categories were updated by the primary coder and a researcher familiar with the survey. Ambiguous responses were checked with other researchers in order to reach a consensus in forming the cognitive response categories and their

Sanction threat

Moral appeal

State targets large tax gap

SALEM (AP) — Citing an estimated $150 million in unpaid state taxes per year, the Department of Revenue today announced plans to hire more auditors and to enforce fines and interest penalties.

The department will also recommend fraud penalties for flagrant cases of tax abuse.

The action has the support of one of Oregon's leading tax accountants. "The Department of Revenue is sending a message that you should not abuse state tax laws," said Richard Visse, president of the Oregon Society of Certified Public Accountants. He said that the risk of getting caught is now much greater and punishment is more severe.

State targets large tax gap

SALEM (AP) — Citing an estimated $150 million in unpaid state taxes per year, one of Oregon's leading tax accountants today appealed to delinquent taxpayers to restore fairness to the system.

"Tax abuse is not a victimless crime. The victims are the great majority of our citizens who are honest and who pay what they owe with every wage and salary check," said Richard Visse, president of the Oregon Society of Certified Public Accountants.

Delinquent taxpayers are exploiting their neighbors who follow the law, Visse added.

Figure 24.2. Experimental sanction threat and moral appeal news stories

operational definitions. Then, the expanded list of categories and their definitions were mailed to a third person familiar with the study who rechecked the coding scheme for completeness and reliability. Two coders, unfamiliar with the study and working independently for the third researcher, analysed verbatim responses from fifty randomly selected questionnaires. They agreed on about 95 per cent of the response frequencies for each category, so we considered the coding scheme reliable.

The content analysis produced fourteen potential cognitive responses. Fewer than five cases were observed for three of the responses and were deleted due to low sample size. Two also were deleted because the responses referred to others, not to self.

The remaining nine cognitive responses were standardized and intercorrelations subjected to a principal component factor analysis. Four factors were extracted that had eigenvalues greater than 1.0. The four factors accounted for 57.1 per cent of the common variance. In order to simplify the interpretation of the factors, a varimax rotation with Kaiser normalization was used to obtain final factor scores. The four factors describe a structure for maintaining one's self-worth after reading the experimental media message.

Regression was used in association with the factor loadings to create new variables representing the factor scores used in further analysis of cognitive responses (Johnson, 1998).

Measurement of Self/Other Judgements

After respondents had read the news story and had answered the two open-ended 'thought' questions, they were shown a five-point scale where a '1' was labelled 'no influence at all' and a '5' labelled 'a great deal of influence' and asked two closed-attitude questions:

- Well, if most Oregonians read an article like this one, how much would the information influence *their* taxpaying? How would you answer on the scale of 1 to 5, where a '1' equals no influence and '5' a great deal of influence?

- Suppose you had to rate how much a news article like this one would influence *your* taxpaying. How would you rate your answer on the scale of 1 to 5 where '1' equals no influence and '5' a great deal of influence?

The two questions were asked in random order.

The contrast in self/other judgements was obtained by subtracting each person's self-influence score from his or her other influence score. A positive score indicates a contrast favouring the message's effect on others than on self, while a negative score shows the opposite—the message impacts self more than others. The scores ranged from –4 to 4.

Appraisal of a Taxpayer Honesty Norm

An assumption underlying this experiment asserts that a norm for taxpaying honesty is widespread among taxpayers. We attempted to verify this norm by asking the following question: 'It is not so wrong to underreport certain income, since it does not really hurt anyone. Looking at the 5-point scale will you please tell me how much you agree or disagree with this statement?' Scores ranged from 'Strongly Disagree' (5) to 'Strongly Agree' (1).

This question, based on Bardach's (1989) recommended moral appeal, was asked in a battery of twelve attitude questions concerning taxpaying and the performance of government officials who administer the state's tax laws. These questions were asked before respondents had been shown the experimental news stories.

A person would have had to disagree with the statement to support an honesty norm, a step taken to reduce acquiescence when a respondent simply agrees to an attitude question (Schuman and Presser, 1982). A socially desirable effect (a bias that stems from the respondent wishing to appear to support taxpayer honesty publicly) also is a strong possibility and the reversal question wording was adopted that required the person to think about his or her answer before responding. As well, a face-to-face interview, such as ours, is particularly prone to socially desirable responses compared to telephone interviews and self-administered questionnaires (Sudman and Bradburn, 1981). The direction of both biases is expected to inflate support for an honesty norm and, therefore, care was taken to reduce the possibility of spuriously high normative responses.

The results show that 91 per cent of the sample report that they disagreed strongly or disagreed with the item. The norm appears to be widespread in our taxpaying sample, remaining above 90 per cent regardless of one's news story treatment, cognitive response factors, gender, age or educational level.

Analysis Strategy

The factor analysis in this study is considered as an exploratory examination of the structure of cognitive responses that is aimed at disabling the message's persuasive impact. A Generalized Linear Model (GLM) regression is planned for two separate statistical models.

First, scores for the full model that includes the audit group, the experimental news stories and an audit by news story interaction, as well as scores of the four cognitive factors are regressed against the response variable, an individual's self/other difference score. Next, the difference between the two experimental news stories is examined for each of the four cognitive factors. The first regression tells us which variables, if any, are related to self/other differences; the second tells us if a sanction threat or a moral appeal differs for each cognitive factor, now considered a response variable.

Results and Discussion

The Factor Analysis of Cognitive Responses

Factor loadings are shown in Table 24.1. Loadings of 0.35 or greater were considered high enough to be part of the factor.

The first factor, an Ignore Factor, had a negative loading on 'cheating is not a victimless crime', and positive loadings on 'would ignore the article' and on 'story would not change how R pays taxes'. This factor suggests that Rs enhance or maintain their self-esteem by disregarding or not paying attention to the media message. Note that the sign for the 'victimless crime' cognitive response is negative, suggesting that the moral underpinning for compliance is not supported. Assertion of self's compliance is not loaded high enough on this factor either, indicating that this response does not play a strong role in dismissing the message.

The second factor, called a Credulous Factor, had a negative loading on 'think story is a scare tactic' and positive loadings on 'feels most taxpayers are honest' and

Table 24.1. Rotated Factor Loadings for Cognitive Responses to Sanction Threat and Moral Appeal News Stories (n = 389)

Cognitive response	Factor 1 (Ignore)	Factor 2 (Credulity)	Factor 3 (Self-esteem)	Factor 4 (Contempt)
Assertion of compliance	0.183	−0.021	**0.784**	−0.045
Disapproval of noncompliance	−0.246	0.282	0.117	**0.560**
Cheating is not a victimless crime	−0.463	0.147	**0.441**	−0.155
Feels most people are honest	0.152	**0.391**	−0.357	−0.155
Feels many people cheat	0.073	−0.120	−0.050	**0.832**
Would ignore article	**0.778**	0.011	−0.045	−0.034
Story would not change how R pays taxes	0.764	0.115	**0.357**	−0.160
Agreement with article	−0.040	**0.764**	−0.113	−0.070
Think story is a scare tactic	−0.022	**−0.684**	−0.215	−0.226
Variance explained (%)	17.8	15.1	12.8	11.4

on 'agrees with the article'. Respondents who support this factor seem to maintain their self-worth by stitching together a group of internally consistent cognitive responses that support an agreement belief. For instance, by agreeing with the message, they also disagree with the suggestion that the story was a scare tactic, which is consistent with message agreement.

The third factor, a Self-Esteem Factor, had a negative loading on 'feels most people are dishonest' and positive loadings for 'R's assertion of compliance', 'cheating is not a victimless crime', and on 'story would not change how R pays taxes'. The cognitive responses to this factor clearly support a positive view of one's self. Here, we find support for the moral obligation to pay all of one's taxes as well as assertions of one's compliance. Furthermore, Rs grouped on this factor also believe that most people are not honest in their taxpaying. As well, the 'story would not change how one pays taxes' loaded strongly on both the Ignore and Self-Esteem factors, showing that that sentiment plays a positive role in both factors.

The fourth factor, called a Contempt Factor, had positive loadings on 'disapproval of noncompliance', and on 'feels many people cheat on their taxes'. This factor suggests another strategy for maintaining a positive view of one's self—the derogation of the noncompliance behavior of others.

Test of the Overall Model

The GLM SAS Type III sum of squares analysis shows that only the 'Ignore Factor' is related to the response among the four factors observed. The results are shown in Table 24.2.

Table 24.2. SAS Type III generalized linear model analysis of message and cognitive response variables on self/other differences (n = 377)

Variable	DF	Sum of squares	Mean square	F	P > F
Audit group	2	5.2792	2.6389	2.04	0.132
News story	1	1.6390	1.6390	1.27	0.261
Ignore Factor	1	7.0042	7.0042	5.41	0.021
Credulity Factor	1	0.6340	0.6340	0.49	0.485
Self-esteem Factor	1	0.5052	0.5052	0.39	0.533
Contempt Factor	1	0.7109	0.7109	0.30	0.531
Audit news story by interaction	2	6.9325	3.4663	2.68	0.070

The Ignore Factor is related significantly to self/other differences ($p < 0.021$). As we expected, neither media message was related. (The message p-value was checked as a simple term in the model without the factors, and they did not change appreciably from the non-significant p-value observed in Table 24.2.)

The audit group variable was included in the statistical model because audit group was in the experimental design. The results show that the audit group was not statistically significant ($p = 0.132$). The audit group by news story interaction was marginally significant ($p = 0.07$) and warrants further investigation.[1]

Factor scores are scalar and their relationship to self/other differences can be compared as Pearson correlations. A statistically significant correlation (adjusted for the variables in Table 24.2) was observed only for the Ignore Factor (-0.116; $p = 0.047$), suggesting that respondents high on that factor reported a low self/other bias. This appears counterintuitive and underscores the need for caution in accepting the possibility that taxpayers employ only a self/other strategy for maintaining their self-worth. For instance, those who appear to be persuaded by the Sanction Threat message, based on their low Ignore Factor score, may ignore the message anyway, since they believe that the story influences others more than self.

Effect of News Messages on Factor Scores

Statistically significant differences were observed when we regressed news story messages against Ignore Factor scores as the response variable. The GLM results are displayed in Figure 24.3.

The Sanction Threat is associated with low Ignore Factor means while the opposite is observed for the Moral Appeal. The adjusted difference, 0.230, is

---

[1] The results for the remaining variables are the same whether or not the audit variable or the interaction term is included in the model. Any effect of an audit group by news story interaction, $p = 0.07$, is supportive but inconclusive with our data.

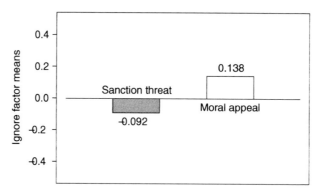

Figure 24.3. Ignore factor means for sanction threat and moral appeal news stories (n = 386)

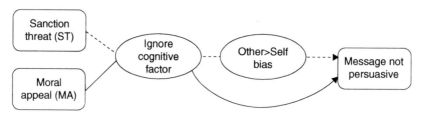

Figure 24.4. Diagram of revised dual communication model for media messages

statistically significant at the $p < 0.022$ level. The results suggest that a Moral Appeal is largely ignored, compared to a Sanction Threat, and casts doubt on a Moral Appeal having much impact in persuading people to pay their full tax obligation. Taxpayers have shown a talent for neutralizing a moral appeal in their dismissal of the media message (Thurman, St John, and Riggs, 1984) and may account for the finding we observe.

Our analysis supports the hypothesis that taxpayers use a dual strategy for dismissing a media message aimed at persuading taxpayers to pay fully their tax obligation. Figure 24.4 illustrates the results of our analysis.

For respondents exposed to a Sanction Threat, the message seems credible, for they report low Ignore Factor scores. However, they also appear to maintain their self-worth by viewing the message as influencing others, not themselves. For respondents exposed to the Moral Appeal, message rejection is straightforward by reporting high Ignore Factor scores without resorting to forming a self/other bias. The Ignore cognitive response acts like a control or a gate that shifts the process of dismissing the message to one of two routes, one featuring a self/other bias, the other not.

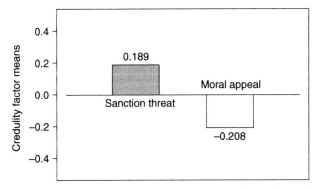

Figure 24.5. Credulity factor means for sanction threat and moral appeal news stories (n = 386)

This explanation also suggests that the Sanction Threat should be viewed as more credible than the Moral Appeal. That is what we find, as shown in Figure 24.5.

The adjusted difference, 0.397, is statistically significant at the $p < 0.001$ level. A comparison of the results in Figures 24.3 and 24.5 shows an interesting consistency that underscores our contention that each message plays a different role in disabling the persuasive force of the messages. The Sanction Threat is associated with low Ignore Factor and high Credulity Factor scores, while the Moral Appeal has high Ignore Factor and low Credulity scores.

Throughout the analysis, neither message was related to Self-Esteem or Contempt for Cheating factors. Nor did these factors play roles in accounting for self/other differences. This is viewed as evidence that the factors represent separate strategies for dealing with media messages, and one's self-worth is maintained without resorting to an invidious self/other comparison.

How Much Persuasion Is There?

We noted in our introduction that weak media effects should be expected from media messages, and our analysis shows how Denial and Credulity Cognitive factors work to diminish their persuasive impact on taxpayers. Our self/other measure provides one estimate for media persuasion since some respondents reported that they were influenced more by the story than were others. A total of thirty-four respondents, representing 9 per cent of the sample, were in this group. (They split about evenly between each message, but four Moral Appeal cases may be discounted from a direct effect of the Ignore cognitive factor because they had negative or low Ignore Factor scores.)

Such a low percentage seems trivial, but Denson and Lipsey (2000) argue otherwise. They contend that even a 2 per cent persuasive impact is not trivial when generalized to a large population. They point out that 'media interventions can be widely disseminated at modest cost so that even a small effect may involve a significant number of individuals with a high degree of cost-effectiveness' (p 250). Bardach (1989) underscores this point by noting that if only 2 per cent of delinquent taxpayers are brought into compliance through media appeals, the tax gain could run into the billions. Our estimate is higher than the Bardach (1998) value, and may be trivial but is suggestive of cost-effective media impacts, nonetheless.

Summary and Conclusions

This study compares the persuasive impact of a media Sanction Threat and a Moral Appeal in order to extend the early findings of Schwartz and Orleans (1967) to learn how taxpayers process media messages and what effect the information has on their thinking about tax compliance. Drawing upon the literature of persuasion and cognitive processing, we sought to account for the impact of a Sanction Threat and a Moral Appeal on self-enhancement strategies. Specifically, we compared the cognitive responses to the two news stories from a sample of 398 Oregon taxpayers.

Cognitive responses were obtained by a thought-listing procedure in which respondents were randomly shown either a Sanction Threat or a Moral Appeal news story and asked to tell the interviewer his or her thoughts about the story. A content analysis produced nine cognitive responses that were subjected to a principal components factor analysis. Four orthogonal factors were extracted that accounted for 57.1 per cent of the common variance. They were Ignore, Credulity, Self-Esteem, and Contempt for Cheating. A nine-point self/other difference score, ranging from –4 to 4, described the magnitude of bias or contrast in judgments concerning the influence of the Sanction Threat or Moral Appeal on self and on others. This difference represented the response variable.

Analysis showed that the persuasive impact of both news stories was disabled through different processes. A Moral Appeal appears to have been neutralized by high loadings on the Ignore Factor and low loadings on the Credulity Factor. The Sanction Threat was dismissed by a large self/other difference score in combination with low Ignore Factor and high Credulity Factor scores. Compared to a Moral Appeal, a Sanction Threat appeared more persuasive based on their location on the two cognitive factors, yet, their persuasive impact was discounted from perceptions that the story would influence others more than themselves.

Schwartz and Orleans (1967) and Grasmick and Scott (1982) argued that both types of messages produced greater compliance or greater future intentions to comply with one's taxpaying. Our results suggest that the two messages complement one another in important areas of the public's thinking about taxpaying. For instance, if one worries about the neutralizing of a Moral Appeal, then consider the advantage of a Sanction Threat because some persuasive effect is likely to come from a belief in the credibility of the message.

Our analysis underscores that much of the persuasive force of both news stories is seriously weakened. However, an estimated 9 per cent report that either story influenced respondents more than others. When generalized to the taxpaying population, we are talking about the possibility of bringing in billions to the federal treasury that otherwise would be lost (Bardach, 1989). A plan that employs both messages, rather than focusing on one versus the other, seems a reasonable policy for designing mass media appeals directed at tax compliance problems.

References

Bardach, E (1989). 'Moral Suasion and Taxpayer Compliance'. *Law and Policy* 11: 49–69.

Beauregard, K and Dunning, D (1998). 'Turning up the contrast: Self-enhancement, motives, prompt egocentric contrast effects in social judgments'. *Journal of Personality and Social Psychology* 74: 606–621.

Brock, TC (1967). 'Communication Discrepancy and Intent to Persuade as Determinants of Counterargument Production'. *Journal of Experimental Social Psychology* 3: 296–309.

Brown, JD (1986). 'Evaluations of Self and Other: Self-enhancement Biases in Social Judgment'. *Social Cognition* 4: 353–376.

——Collins, RL, and Schmidt, GW (1988). 'Self-esteem and Direct Versus Indirect Forms of Self-enhancement'. *Journal of Personality and Social Psychology* 53: 445–453.

Cacioppo, J and Petty, RE (1986). 'Social Psychological Procedures for Cognitive Response Assessment: The Thought-listing Technique'. In TV Merluzzi, CR Glass, and M Genest (eds), *Cognitive Assessment*, 309–342. New York.

Caldini, RB (1989). 'Social Motivation to Comply: Norms, Values, and Principles'. In JA Roth and JT Scholz (eds), *Taxpayer Compliance: Social Science Perspectives*, 200–227. Philadelphia.

Cappon, RJ (1991). *Associated Press Guide to News Writing*. New York.

Chaiken, S (1980). 'Heuristic Versus Systematic Information Processing and the Use of Source Versus Message Cues in Persuasion'. *Journal of Personality and Social Psychology* 39: 752–766.

——Wood, W, and Eagly, AH (1996). 'Principles of Persuasion'. In ET Higgins and AW Kruglanski (eds), *Social Psychology Handbook of Basic Principles*, 702–741. New York.

Crano, WD and Burgoon, M (2002). *Drug Prevention*. Mahwah, NJ.

Derzen, JH, and Lipsey, MW (2002). 'A Meta-analysis of the Effectiveness of Mass-communication for Changing Substance-use Knowledge, Attitudes, and Behavior'. In WD Crano and M Brugoon (eds), *Drug Prevention*, 231–257. Mahwah, NJ.

Epstein, S (1973). 'The Self-concept Revisited'. *American Psychologist* 28: 404–416.

Grasmick, H and Scott, WJ (1982). 'Tax Evasion and the Mechanisms of Social Control: A Comparison with Grand and Petty Theft'. *Journal of Economic Psychology* 2: 213–230.

——and Bursik, RJ (1990). 'Conscience, Significant Others, and Rational Choice: Extending the Deterrence Model'. *Law and Society Review* 24: 837–861.

Greenwald, AG (1968). 'Cognitive Learning, Cognitive Response to Persuasion, and Attitude Change'. In AG Greenwald, JC Brock, and TM Ostrom (eds), *Psychological Foundations of Attitudes*, 147–170. New York.

Hovland, CL, Janis, IL, and Kelley, HH (1953). *Communication and Persuasion.* New Haven.

Iyengar, S and Kinder, DR (1985). 'Psychological Accounts for Agenda-setting'. In S Kraus and RM Perloff (eds), *Mass Media and Political Thought,* 117–140. Beverly Hills.

Johnson DE (1998). *Applied Multivariate Methods for Data Analysis.* Pacific Grove.

Kristof, KM (2002, March 1). IRS to Increase Number of Audits, C1, C2. *Los Angeles Times.*

Lasswell, HD (1948). 'The Structure and Function of Communication in Society'. In L Bryson (ed), *The Communication of Ideas,* 37–52. New York.

Long, SB and Swingen, JA (1991). 'Taxpayer Compliance: Setting New Agendas for Research'. *Law and Society Review* 25: 637–683.

McGuire, WJ (1981). 'Theoretical Foundations of Campaigns'. In RE Rice and WJ Paisley (eds), *Public Communication Campaigns,* 41–70. Newbury Park.

Mason, R (1987). 'A Communication Model of Taxpayer Honesty'. *Law and Policy* 9: 246–258.

Perloff, RM and Brock, TC (1980). 'Cognitive Response to Persuasion'. In ME Roloff and GR Miller (eds), *Persuasion: New Directions in Theory and Research,* 67–99. Beverley Hills.

Petty, RE, Cacioppo, JT, and Goldman, R (1981). 'Personal Involvement as a Determinant of Argument-based Persuasion'. *Journal of Personality and Social Psychology* 41: 847–855.

—— —— and Schumann, DW (1983). 'Central and Peripheral Routes to Advertising Effectiveness: The Moderating Role of Involvement'. *Journal of Consumer Research* 10: 135–146.

—— and Wegner, DT (1998). 'Attitude Change: Multiple Roles for Persuasion Variables'. In DT Gilbert, ST Fiske, and G Lindzey (eds), *The Handbook of Social Psychology,* 323–383. New York.

—— Priester, JH, and Brinol, P (2002). 'Mass Media Attitude Change: Implications of the Elaboration Likelihood Model of Persuasion'. In J Bryant and D Zillmann (eds), *Media Effects: Advances in theory and research,* 155–198. Mahwah, NJ.

Reeves, BR, Chafee, SH, and Tims, A (1982). 'Social Cognition and Mass Communication Research'. In ME Roloff and CR Berger (eds), *Social Cognition and Communication Research,* 287–326. Beverly Hills.

Roberts, DE and Maccoby, N (1973). 'Information Processing and Persuasion: Counterarguing Behavior'. In P Clark (ed), *New Models for Mass Communication Research,* 269–307. Beverley Hills.

Rogers, RW (1983). 'Cognitive and Physiological Processes in Fear Appeals and Attitude Change: A Revised Theory of Protection Motivation'. In JT Cacioppo and RE Petty (eds), *Social Psychophysiology: A Sourcebook,* 153–176. New York.

Romero, AA, Cristopher RA, and Insko, CA (1996). 'The Cognitive Mediation Hypothesis Revisited: An Empirical Response to Methodological and Theoretical Criticism'. *Personality and Social Psychology Bulletin* 22: 651–665.

Roth, J, Scholz, J, and Witte, AD (1989). 'Expanding the Framework for Analysis'. *Taxpayer Compliance: An Agenda for Research.* Philadelphia.

Schuman, H and Presser, S (1981). *Questions and Answers in Attitude Surveys.* New York.

Schwartz, RD and Orleans, S (1967). 'On legal sanctions'. *University of Chicago Law Review* 34: 257–268.

Shrauger, JS, and Patterson, MB (1974). 'Self-evaluation and the Selection of Dimensions for Evaluating Others'. *Journal of Personality* 42: 569–585.

Stalans, LJ, Kinsey, KA, and Smith, KW (1991). 'Listening to Different Voices: Formation of Sanction Beliefs and Taxpaying Norms'. *Journal of Applied Social Psychology* 21: 119–138.

Sudman, S and Bradburn, NM (1982). *Asking Questions*. San Francisco.

Swann, WJ, Predmore, GS, and Baines, B (1999). 'The Cognitive-Affective Crossfire: When Self-Consistency Confronts Self-Enhancement'. In R Baumeister (ed), *The Self in Social Psychology* 391–401. Ann Arbor, Mich.

Thurman, Q, St John, C, and Riggs, L (1984). 'Neutralization and Tax Evasion: How Effective Would a Moral Appeal be in Improving Compliance to Tax Laws?' *Law and Policy* 6: 309–327.

Tyler, T (1990). *Why People Obey the Law*. New Haven.

—— and Lavrakas, PJ (1986). 'Cognitions Leading to Personal and Political Behaviors: The Case of Crime'. In S Kraus and RM Perloff (eds), *Mass Media and Political Thought*, 141–156. Beverley Hills.

25

Consumer Bankruptcy Reform and the Heuristic Borrower

Susan Block-Lieb and Edward J Janger

In April 2005, the US Congress enacted, and President Bush signed into law, the Bankruptcy Abuse Prevention and Consumer Protection Act of 2005 (the 'Bankruptcy Bill').[1] The Bankruptcy Bill makes radical amendments to the US Bankruptcy Code (the 'Bankruptcy Code'). These changes became effective on October 17, 2005, and have the principal effect of restricting the ability of consumers to discharge debt in bankruptcy. The Bill accomplishes this through the combined effects of a 'means test' which operates as a direct bar to access to Chapter 7 relief for certain debtors, and of a series of document production, credit counseling and attorney due diligence requirements that raise the price of obtaining access to bankruptcy court.[2]

The articulated rationale for this legislation turns on a particular view of who files for bankruptcy and why. The Bill's sponsor takes the view that bankruptcy has become a system 'where deadbeats get out of paying their debt scott-free while honest Americans who play by the rules have to foot the bill.'[3] This colloquial characterization of bankruptcy as a haven for deceitful debtors rests in turn on two empirical assumptions: (1) that rational lenders cannot distinguish high risk or dishonest borrowers from low risk honest borrowers and are therefore at their mercy; and (2) that consumer borrowers are instrumentally rational and able to translate their preferences for present and future consumption into decisions whether to borrow and whether to default.

The Bankruptcy Bill was presented by its proponents, representatives of the consumer credit industry, as protecting innocent lenders from being duped.[4] These

---

[1] PL 109–8, 109th Congress, 1st Session (2005).

[2] 11 USC §§ 707(b) (means test and attorney certification requirement) and 521 (document and credit counseling requirements).

[3] Press Release, [Senator Charles] Grassley Renews Effort To Reform Bankruptcy Code (2 February 2005), available online at <http://grassley.senate.gov/index.cfm?FuseAction=PressReleases. View& PressRelease_id=4873>.

[4] For references to lobbyists' and commentators' justifications for the Bankruptcy Bill, see S Block-Lieb and EJ Janger, 'The Myth of the Rational Borrower: Rationality, Behaviorism and the Misguided "Reform" of Bankruptcy Law' (2006) 84 *Texas Law Review* 1481.

proponents contributed vast sums to sympathetic legislators, and to legislators who they hoped would become sympathetic.[5] In this paper, we explore whether the picture of the paradigmatic debtor they paint is empirically accurate. We seek to show that the factual assertions that ostensibly motivated the Bankruptcy Bill are belied by data and the consumer credit industry's own behaviour, and we suggest an alternate story that is, we believe, both more plausible, and more problematic. Consumers do not overborrow in reliance on the availability of the bankruptcy discharge. Instead, they borrow honestly, but heuristically, often in response to aggressive solicitations, and default if (and, by and large, only if) their debt load becomes crushingly great. Indeed, consumer lenders know this, and profit by encouraging financed consumption.

In the first part of this paper, we concede that the first assumption may once have been true, at least for national credit card lenders in the late 1970s and early 1980s when these theories were first articulated.[6] However, we seek to show that legal and technological changes since 1980 have rendered it false.[7] We also seek to show that while lenders *say* that these assumptions are true, they do not *act* as if they are true. In the second part, we look at consumers and turn to behavioural decision research to suggest that far from being rational, consumers make credit decisions based on a number of heuristics that systematically bias their decision-making.[8] In the third part, we suggest a different view of reality, in which rational, profit maximizing lenders exploit the decisionmaking biases of consumers. Indeed, even under current law, the consequence of heuristic borrowing is high profits to lenders,[9] welfare losses to consumers and social deadweight loss.[10] In our view, the Bankruptcy Bill is based on inaccurate factual premises, and shifts the legal balance in precisely the wrong direction.

The Myth of the Informationally Disadvantaged Lender

The Mythic Landscape

The choice between competing positions in the US debate over bankruptcy policy turns on competing empirical claims about the paradigmatic lender and the

---

[5] S Nunez and H Rosenthal, 'Bankruptcy "Reform" in Congress: Creditors, Committees, Ideology, and Floor Voting in the Legislative Process' (2004) 20(2) *Journal of Law, Economics, and Organization* 527–557, available online at <http://jleo.oxfordjournals.org/cgi/reprint/20/2/527>.

[6] See text at n 15 below.

[7] See text at n 16 below (legal change). With regard to technological change, see MJ Furletti, 'Credit Card Pricing Developments and their Disclosure' (Federal Reserve Bank of Philadelphia, January 2003) (Payment Cards Ctr, Working Paper No 03-02, 2003), available at <http://papers.ssrn.com/sol3/papers.cfm? abstract_id=572585>; and C Yom, 'Limited-Purpose Banks: Their Specialties, Performance and Prospects' (Federal Deposit Insurance Company Working Paper FOB-2004-07.1 (June 2004) 15, available at <http://www.fdic.gov/bank/analytical/future/fob_ 07.pdf>.

[8] See text at nn 45–75 below.

[9] Board of Governors of the Federal Reserve System, 'Annual Report by the Board of Governors of the Federal Reserve System: The Profitability of Credit Card Operations of Depository Institutions' (June 2004), available at <http://www.federalreserve.gov/boarddocs/rptcongress/creditcard/2004/ccprofit.pdf>.

[10] See n 78 below.

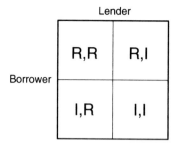

Figure 25.1. Rationality versus irrationality in consumer lending transactions

paradigmatic borrower in consumer credit transactions. Broadly speaking the debate turns on the locus of instrumental rationality. Do we live in a world of rational borrowers? Rational lenders? Both? Or neither? Whether regulation is necessary, and in what form requires on answer to this question. The possibilities are graphically depicted in Figure 25.1.

The policy tradeoffs will be discussed in more detail below, but are roughly as follows:

- If both the lender and the borrower are instrumentally rational, and have roughly equal information at their disposal, no regulation of consumer lending contracts is necessary.

- If lenders are rational, but borrowers are irrational, or subject to cognitive limitations and heuristic biases, consumer protection is in order.

- If lenders are irrational or informationally disadvantaged, and borrowers are rational, then the locus of regulation should focus on consumer incentives regarding default.

The stakes of the empirical debate are high, and the costs of disingenuousness higher.

The Myth

The proponents of bankruptcy reform in the United States have relied on economic insights from the 1970s, economic insights premised on the assumption that borrowers are rational and that lenders, while rational, suffer from an informational disadvantage—they don't know whether their borrowers are honest or dishonest.[11] Borrowers, on this view, are assumed to be rational actors who are

---

[11] MJ White, 'Why It Pays to File for Bankruptcy: A Critical Look at the Incentives Under U.S. Personal Bankruptcy Law and A Proposal for Change' (1998) 65 *University of Chicago Law Review* 685, 686, 710 (asserting that one-third of US households could benefit from filing for bankruptcy if they planned strategically, and proposing legal reforms that combine Ch 7 and 13 to improve the

able to compare the value of present consumption to the value of future consumption, and compare both to the cost of consumer debt. Most importantly, borrowers recognize that if they run into trouble, the bankruptcy discharge will give them a free walk on their debt. In this world, lenders are rational, too, but at an informational disadvantage.[12] The informational problem faced by lenders is that they cannot tell *ex ante* whether a borrower is honest (and will repay) or dishonest (and likely to file for bankruptcy).

This informational disadvantage is compounded by two further assumptions: (1) that lenders are unable to price discriminate and (2) that they are subject to adverse selection.[13] First, the claim is that credit card lenders can only charge a single rate to all of their customers (because they cannot distinguish honest borrowers from dishonest ones). Secondly, if they attempt to compensate for the riskiness of the pool by raising the interest rate they charge, the problem will be compounded because low risk borrowers will leave the pool. Low risk borrowers, it is argued, are those who need credit least, and are therefore most likely to be 'price elastic'—their demand for borrowed funds is sensitive to any increase in the interest rate. High risk borrowers are thought to be those who need credit most, and are therefore likely be 'price inelastic.' Their demand for credit is not affected by increased interest rates. Therefore, if a lender raises the price of consumer credit, the result will be that only risky borrowers will borrow.

On this theory, the bankruptcy discharge will lead to credit rationing and dead-weight loss. To the extent that this picture of the world of consumer credit is accurate, the policy prescription is simple: Eliminate the bankruptcy discharge. The result will be a greater supply of credit at a lower cost to consumers.

The Golden Age versus the Modern Age

It is important to recognize that these insights, which have been used to justify bankruptcy reform, are themselves situated in time. The relationship between opportunistic borrowers and the bankruptcy discharge was articulated by William Meckling in 1977,[14] and the relationship between imperfect lender information and credit rationing was described by Joseph Stiglitz and Andrew

equity and efficiency of the system); TJ Zywicki, 'Bankruptcy Law as Social Legislation' (2001) 5 *Texas Review of Law and Policy* 393, 406, 422 (arguing that increased bankruptcy rates are a natural result of a system that 'rewards short-term and irresponsible behavior' and places few restrictions on opportunistic use); TJ Zywicki, 'The Past, Present, and Future of Bankruptcy Law in America' (2003) 101 *Michigan Law Review* 2016, 2021–2022 (book review) (detailing how American bankruptcy law has historically been shaped by the competing interests of academics, bankruptcy professionals, and creditors); EH Jones and TJ Zywicki, 'It's Time for Means-Testing' (1999) *Brigham Young University Law Review* 177, 180 (attributing the rise in consumer bankruptcies to declining social stigma and advocating means-testing to stem opportunistic filings).

[12] See n 14 below.   [13] See n 15 below.

[14] WH Meckling, 'Financial Markets, Default, and Bankruptcy: The Role of the State' (1977) 41 *Law and Contemporary Problems* 13.

Weiss in 1981.[15] The credit card industry was still in its comparative infancy, and the broad outlines of consumer lending fit the description fairly well. Prior to 1978, the inability to price discriminate in consumer lending transactions was as much a function of legal usury limits as it was of price elasticity and adverse selection. Most states had usury laws that placed limits on the rates that banks could charge their customers. In addition, credit reporting was local rather than national and consumer credit transactions were, for the most part, local and based on local reputational information.

Starting in 1978, this picture of consumer credit markets as characterized by usury limits and limited access to credit information began to change. In 1978, the US Supreme Court decided *Marquette v Citibank*.[16] In that case, consumer lending contracts were held to be governed by the law of the jurisdiction where the lending bank was located. While this choice of law ruling might not seem like an earthshaking development, the effect was to remove usury caps from consumer lending transactions initiated by national banks. South Dakota and Delaware, among other states, quickly repealed their usury limits in reaction to *Marquette*. Not surprisingly, credit card banks, and other consumer lenders are now clustered in these jurisdictions. For example, Citibank's credit card bank is incorporated in South Dakota, and MBNA conducts its business out of Delaware.[17]

Suddenly, national consumer lending was potentially more profitable than local consumer lending, but only if the information asymmetry created by local credit reporting could be overcome. Over the last twenty-five years, technological advances and market forces have operated to make information about consumer creditworthiness available on a national scale. First, the credit reporting and data aggregation businesses have exploded. Reporting agencies, such as Trans Union, Equifax and Experian, along with data aggregators, like ChoicePoint and Axciom, have built files on virtually every American.[18] Secondly, credit scoring alleviates the need for lenders to engage in their own analyses of credit history. Lenders can now price the risk of a loan to a particular customer with a single phone call to Fair Isaacs Corporation.[19] They can even use such information to target their marketing—to decide who to solicit for a credit card. Finally, the growth of asset backed securities has allowed credit card banks to bundle credit card receivables and resell the loans to the capital markets.[20] Today, unlike 1978, consumer credit markets are characterized by unregulated interest rates, relatively solid information about credit risk, the ability to price discriminate, and the ability to manage the amount of risk carried in the lender's portfolio.

[15] JE Stiglitz and A Weiss, 'Credit Rationing and Imperfect Information' (1981) 71 *American Economic Review* 393.   [16] 439 US 299 (1978).
[17] DS Evans and R Schmalensee, *Paying With Plastic: The Digital Revolution in Buying and Borrowing* 72 (1999); see JJ White, 'The Usury Trompe L'Oeil' (2000) 51 *South Carolina Law Review* 445, 455–466.   [18] ibid, 455–466.
[19] For Fair Isaacs Corporation's description of its own products, see <http://www.myfico.com/>.
[20] Yom, n 7 above, 21 ('Since its introduction in 1987, credit card securitization has been a primary source of funding and is integral to the growth of the credit card industry.' (citations omitted)).

The Puzzle of Consumer Credit

Increased Filing Rate and Debt Loads

While credit reporting and deregulation of interest rates have removed a number of impediments from the lending side of the equation, advocates of bankruptcy reform point to a number of data points to suggest that the bankruptcy discharge increases the amount of opportunistic borrowing. First, and foremost, they point to the recent increases in the bankruptcy filing rate. Since 1978, when the Bankruptcy Code was amended and *Marquette* was decided, the number of non-business bankruptcy filings in the United States has increased from just under 200,000 to just over 1.6 million (see Figure 25.2).[21] Bankruptcy has certainly become more popular. Similarly, household debt loads have increased during the same period, nearly doubling between 1975 and 2003 (Figure 25.3).[22] The implication is that since the enactment of the US Bankruptcy Code, which (like the *Marquette* decision) occurred in 1978, consumers have become more opportunistic. The bankruptcy discharge, it is argued, has made consumers more likely to overborrow, and more likely to default and seek bankruptcy protection.

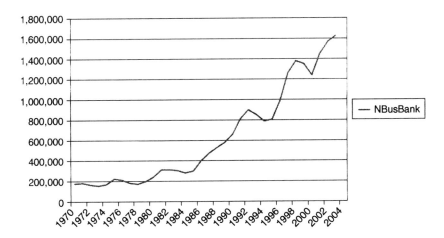

Figure 25.2. Non-business bankruptcy fillings, 1970–2003

---

[21] Administrative Office of the US Courts, available online at <http://www.uscourts.gov/bnkrpctystats/bankruptcystats.htm>. The historical data is compiled at <http://www.abiworld.org/ContentManagement/ContentDisplay.cfm?ContentID=13743>.

[22] The outstanding amounts of consumer debt are reported in Federal Reserve Board, Table G-19, available online at <http://www.federalreserve.gov/releases/g19/>. Household data is collected by the US census bureau, and is available at <http://www.census.gov/statab/hist/HS-12.pdf>. Inflation adjustments were calculated using the Consumer Price Index calculator published by the US Department of Labor and available at <http://data.bls.gov/cgi-bin/cpicalc.pl>.

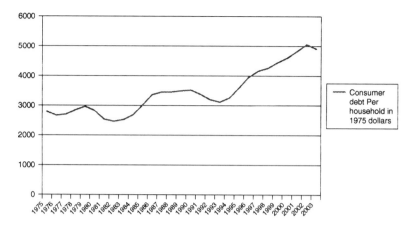

Figure 25.3. Consumer debt per household in 1975 dollars

The Paradox of Profitability

But bankruptcy filing rates and debt loads may be increasing for reasons other than debtor opportunism. According to Stiglitz and Weiss, the equilibrium in a world of rational borrowers and informationally disadvantaged lenders is one where consumer credit is constrained, where consumers are not able to borrow as much as is socially optimal. This is simply not the world that we observe two decades after Stiglitz and Weiss wrote. Instead, the absolute amount of consumer debt outstanding, and household debt loads as a function of disposable income, have increased. At the same time, the profitability of consumer lending has remained robust, with 2003 the third most profitable year (in terms of profit per dollar outstanding) ever (Table 25.1).[23]

The Mystery of the Missing Markup

With this data, the prediction of credit constraint appears shaky, but it is nonetheless possible for credit constraint, increased supply of credit, and an increasing bankruptcy filing rate to coexist, if the profitability has been driven by increased interest rates and an increased profit margin. However, even this aspect of the Stiglitz and Weiss prediction collapses when one looks at interest rates. First, interest rates have declined steadily since 1982, and are currently well below where they were in 1978 when the Bankruptcy Code was last significantly amended (Figure 25.4).[24]

[23] Board of Governors of the Federal Reserve System, 'The Profitability of Credit Card Operations of Depository Institutions' (June 2004), available at <http://www.federalreserve.gov/boarddocs/rptcongress/creditcard/2004/ccprofit.pdf>.
[24] The data in Figure 25.4 can be found in Federal Reserve Statistical Release G.19, available at <http://www.federalreserve.gov/releases/ g19/hist/cc_hist_mh.html>.

Table 25.1. Net before-tax earnings as a percentage of outstanding balances for large credit card banks (adjusted for credit card securitization), 1986–2003[1]

Year	Earnings[2]	Year	Earnings
1986	3.45	1995	2.71
1987	3.33	1996	2.14
1988	2.78	1997	2.13
1989	2.83	1998	2.87
1990	3.10	1999	3.34
1991	2.57	2000	3.14
1992	3.13	2001	3.24
1993	4.06	2002	3.28
1994	3.98	2003	3.66

1. Large credit card banks are defined as commercial banks that have assets greater than $200 million, have the bulk of their assets in loans to individuals (consumer leading), and have 90 percent of their consumer leading in credit cards and related plans. For credit card banks, outstanding balances are adjusted to include balances underlying credit card securities. Outstanding balances reflect an average of the four quarters for each year.

2. Figures may differ from those presented in prior year reports as the result of revisions to the Reports of Condition and Income.

Source: Reports of Condition and Income, 1986–2003, and data on securitizations.

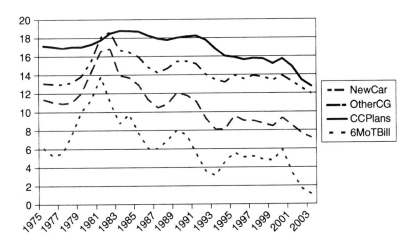

Figure 25.4. Commercial Bank Interest Rates for consumer credit, 1975–2003

In Figure 25.4, the solid line (at the top of the graph) represents the interest rate charged on credit cards. The dot-dashed line (upper middle) represents other miscellaneous types of consumer debt, and the dashed line (lower middle) represents new car loans. Finally, the dotted line (at the bottom of the graph) represents the interest rate on six-month US Treasury bills.

Of course, interest rates have fallen steadily across the board since 1990, but this is principally because of a decline in the lenders' cost of funds. A more informative number is the spread between a bank's cost of funds, or the risk free rate of return, and the rate charged to credit card borrowers. The factors which influence the size of the spread are likely to be the cost of funds (ie, the T-bill rate), the cost of underwriting loans (ie, administrative costs), and the riskiness of the portfolio of loans (ie, the default rate).

With the rate of bankruptcy filings significantly increasing, one would expect the default costs suffered by credit card issuers to rise as well. This should be reflected over time as an increase in the spread between the T-bill rate and the rate charged on consumer credit. As shown above in Figure 25.2, the filing rate went from 170,000 per year to 310,000 per year, between 1978 and 1983. Then, after 1983, the rate truly skyrocketed, to 1,600,000 per year in 2003. Paradoxically, as will be shown below, the markup on consumer credit was actually below the historic average from 1978–83, and again between 1995 and 2001.

It is possible to distinguish the decline in the general market interest rates generally from the decline in the cost of credit card debt. This difference can be seen graphically in a number of ways. First, if one plots the decline in the T-bill rate and reduces it to a trendline through the use of an ordinary least squares regression, the decline in credit card interest has a much less pronounced downward slope (Figure 25.5) than the decline in the T-bill rate (Figure 25.6).

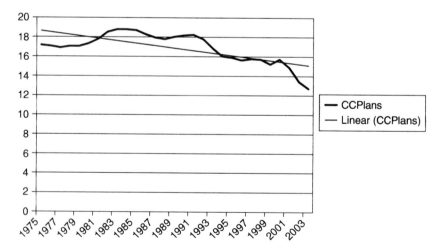

Figure 25.5. Credit card interest rates, 1975–2003

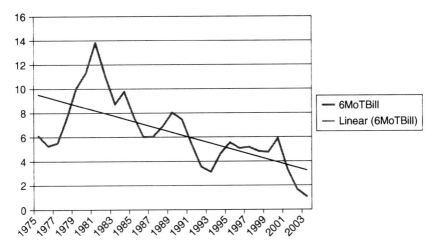

Figure 25.6. Six-month Treasury bill rate, 1975–2003

The stickiness of credit card rates can be seen in the difference between the slope in Figure 25.5[25] and the slope in Figure 25.6.[26]

Another way to show the extent to which credit card rates have not been responsive to changes in the lenders' bankruptcy costs is to look at what we call the 'credit card markup rate.' The markup (represented by the short-dashed line in Figure 25.7) is simply the difference between the T-bill rate and the credit card rate.[27] This graphic representation of consumer credit interest rates significantly undercuts the predictive value of the economic models of consumer credit.

Increasing bankruptcy filings would be expected to add to lenders' costs, and should therefore have led to the markup increasing over time. Curiously, this is not at all what happened. Instead of increasing over that same period, the interest rate spread remained almost completely flat. If one plots an ordinary least squares trendline for the period (see Figure 25.8), the predicted interest rate rises from about 11.1 per cent to 11.4 per cent over a period of twenty years. This is hardly an astronomical increase, or one that suggests a system that is broken, particularly if one recognizes that this blended rate of interest also reflects the expansion of

[25] The data in Figure 25.5 can be found in Federal Reserve Statistical Release G.19, available at <http://www.federalreserve.gov/releases/ g19/hist/cc_hist_mh.html>.

[26] The data in Figure 25.6 can be found in Federal Reserve Statistical Release H.15, available at <http://www.federalreserve.gov/releases/h15/>.

[27] The data in Figure 25.7 can be found in Federal Reserve Statistical Releases H.15 and G.19, available at <http://www.federalreserve.gov/releases/h15/> and <http://www.federalreserve.gov/releases/g19/hist/cc_hist_mh.html>.

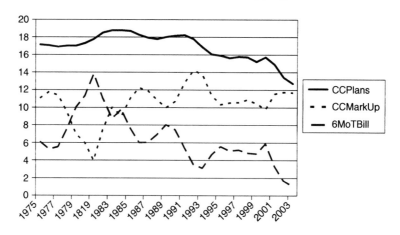

Figure 25.7. Credit card rate and credit card/T-bill spread, 1975–2003

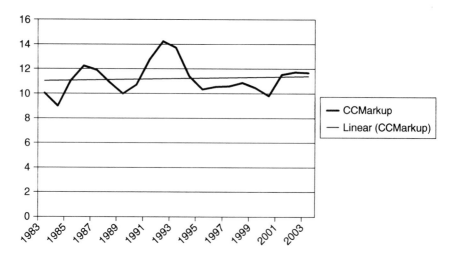

Figure 25.8. Credit card/T-bill spread, 1983–2003

consumer lending into subprime credit markets. Subprime lenders extend credit to borrowers characterized by one of the following: '(1) a FICO credit score of 660 or below; (2) two or more 30-day delinquencies during the past year; (3) bankruptcy in the last five years; (4) judgment, foreclosure, repossession, of charge-offs in the past 24-months; or (5) debt service to income ratio of 50 percent or greater.'[28]

---

[28] Yom, n 7 above, 15.

Expansion of subprime credit markets should cause the creditworthiness of the pool of borrowers, on average, to decrease and the default risk associated with the pool to increase. With increases in the default risk of the credit pool and other factors remaining equal, one would again expect an increase in the markup over time. Surprisingly, that has not happened.

What is most interesting about this data is that it does not support Meckling's prediction that the cost of consumer credit would increase if consumer bankruptcy filings increased. Paradoxically, filing rates have gone up, while interest rates and interest rate spreads have not.

Consumer Credit Today

So how can this puzzle be explained? The answer would appear to be that technology has changed the nature of consumer credit by removing, or at least significantly reducing, the informational obstacles faced by consumer lenders. They can now identify borrowers by type and price loans accordingly. This ability to price discriminate has eliminated, or, at least, substantially limited, credit constraints. Instead, lending to subprime borrowers at high interest rates has grown.[29] Moreover, since *Marquette* effectively deregulated interest rates, there is no constraint on the ability of price discriminating lenders to charge high prices to high risk borrowers.[30]

The discussion in this section rejects only one of the empirical pillars of bankruptcy reform: lenders are rational and suffer no informational impairments. This leaves two possibilities, one in which consumer borrowers are rational, and one in which consumer borrowers are subject to cognitive and heuristic biases. If consumers are rational, bankruptcy reform will act as the economists would predict; limiting access to the bankruptcy discharge would therefore make sense. If, however, consumers do not make rational borrowing decisions, the policy prescription is quite different.

The Myth of the Rational Borrower

In this section, we use behavioural decision research to cast doubt on the assumption made by economists and the proponents of bankruptcy reform that consumer borrowers are instrumentally rational. Research by cognitive psychologists suggests that consumer borrowers may be subject to a variety of cognitive limitations, heuristic biases, and inconsistencies in preferences. Each of these research results undercuts the assumption that consumers are instrumentally rational. Taken together, they wash it away.

---

[29] ibid, 17.   [30] Furletti, n 7 above, 9.

Cognitive Limitations

In a cash economy, consumer consumption is relatively straightforward, and it is plausible to assume that consumers will be able to make rational decisions based on full information. The goods are what they are, and the purchaser either has enough cash to make the purchase or not. Time elements enter in, because some goods have longer useful lives than others, but cash is simple. Either there is enough, or there is not. The availability of consumer credit significantly complicates the decisionmaking process. A consumer buyer must weigh his or her preference for present versus future consumption against the cost of borrowing, against predictions of future income. Cognitive limitations and cognitive dissonance are significant obstacles in this regard.

Financial Literacy

As a threshold matter, individuals need to be able to assess credit's cost and terms. Consumer lenders often go to great lengths to obscure the actual interest rate that they charge through the use of teaser rates, default rates, and by simply hiding the interest rate being charged on the third page of a credit card statement. As a palliative, US statutes and regulations focus on disclosure, requiring lenders to disclose the annual percentage rate and other terms to assist consumers in this process.[31]

It is not clear that disclosure of this sort is, on its own, sufficient to overcome individuals' cognitive limitations. Empirical studies of adult literacy, including financial literacy, skills in the United States raise substantial doubts on this score.[32] When thousands of adults from across the country were given tests of basic maths and basic literacy, a significant portion of the population was unable to make the comparisons necessary to assess the cost of consumer credit.[33] And while education may assist some consumers in raising the level of their financial literacy skills, financial literacy training is not widely available today, even for those still in school.[34]

In short, while consume now, pay now requires simple arithmetic, consume now, pay later requires higher math. Most people, including the authors of this paper, are not capable of computing the present value of an income stream in their heads so that it can be compared to the cost of paying cash.

Cognitive Dissonance and Confusion

Credit card purchases may also create cognitive dissonance for consumers. Sociologist Ronald Manning suggests that cash creates a tangible limit on purchasing

[31] 15 USC §§1637(c)(1)(A), 1632(c).

[32] See IS Kirsch, A Jungeblut, L Jenkins, and A Kolstad, *Adult Literacy in America: A First Look at the Findings of the National Adult Literacy Survey* (1993), available online at <http://nces.ed.gov/pubsearch/pubsinfo.asp?pubid=93275>.   [33] ibid.

[34] See RL Wiener, S Block-Lieb, K Gross, and C Baron-Donovan, 'Financial Education and Pending Bankruptcy Legislation' (2005) 23 *Behavioral Science and Law* 347 (finding that three-hour long financial literacy course significantly improved knowledge of bankruptcy debtors).

power—the empty wallet.[35] By contrast, a credit card-wielding consumer can incur credit obligations without cash outlays at the point of purchase. Bills arrive days or weeks later, and even then may demand only a minimum payment that covers very little in the way of principal.

Lawrence Ausubel, an economist, agrees that some credit card users may be confused or in denial at the point of purchase about the extent of their borrowing.[36] He finds that nearly three-quarters of active credit card accounts incur finance charges. However, he also finds that survey research indicates that 47 per cent of responding credit card users report that they 'nearly always pay in full,' 26 per cent 'sometimes pay in full,' and only 27 per cent report 'hardly ever paying in full.'[37] Because consumers underestimate the extent of their current and future credit card borrowing, they therefore 'make suboptimal decisions regarding the choice and usage of credit cards.'[38]

Behavioural research supports the confusion hypothesis.[39] Experiments show that credit card transactions lead consumers to underestimate past expenditures and, thus, inflate their perceived ability to afford the additional purchase.[40] Some of these experiments suggest that credit card customers have a more difficult time recalling past purchases than do cash customers and, as a result, find it difficult to rehearse the consequences of added credit transactions. By contrast, research finds that cash and cheque transactions instead enjoy an immediacy of payment permitting greater recall.[41]

---

[35] R Manning, *Credit Card Nation* 292 (2001) ('. . . it is clear that bank credit cards have fractured the culturally conditioned "cognitive connect" between earnings and consumption. In the process, they have profoundly changed the determinative role of work in defining one's consumption or even employment decisions.').

[36] LM Ausubel, 'The Failure of Competition in the Credit Card Market' (1991) 81 *American Economic Review* 50, 70–72, reprinted in *Advances in Behavioral Finance*, ch 21 at 560–564 (D Thaler ed, 1993).

[37] Ausubel, n 36 above, 71–72. Ausubel also supports his 'underestimation hypothesis' with claims that the consumer face high costs in searching out lower cost credit card issuers and switching credit obligations to these issuers (70–71). Others corroborate the high search and switch costs consumers face. See eg PS Calem and LJ Mester, 'Consumer Behavior and the Stickiness of Credit-Card Interest Rates' (1995) 85 *American Economic Review* 1327 (providing empirical support for the contention that cardholders face search and switch costs). Similarly, Cambridge Consumer Index has a monthly accounting of the difference between how much consumers said they would pay off debt last month and how many now report that they did pay off credit, available at <http://www.cambridgeconsumerindex.com>.

[38] LM Ausubel, 'Credit Card Defaults, Credit Card Profits, and Bankruptcy' (1997) 71 *American Bankruptcy Law Journal* 249, 261.

[39] See eg RA Feinberg, 'Credit Cards as Spending Facilitating Stimuli: A Conditioning Interpretation' (1986) 13 *Journal of Consumer Research* 348; E Hirschman, 'Differences in Consumer Purchase Behavior by Credit Card Payment System' (1979) 6 *Journal of Consumer Research* 58; D Prelec and D Simester, 'Always Leave Home Without It: A Research Note', (2001) 12 *Marketing Letters* 5.

[40] See D Soman, 'Effects of Payment Mechanism on Spending Behavior: The Role of Rehearsal and Immediacy of Payments' (2001) 27 *Journal of Consumer Research* 460, 462 (assessing the role of rehearsal and immediacy of payments); D Soman and A Cheema, 'The Effect of Credit on Spending Decisions: The Role of Credit Limit and Credibility' (2002) 21 *Marketing Science* 32.

[41] See Soman, n 40 above; J Srivastava and P Raghubir, 'Debiasing Using Decomposition: The Case of Memory-Based Credit Card Expense Estimates' (2002) 12 *Journal of Consumer Psychology* 253 (conducting experiments to test credit card users' and other purchasers' memory of recent expenditures).

If cognition is the sole difficulty, it suggests palliative solutions of a certain type. Financial literacy can be taught, and steps can be taken to limit cognitive dissonance. For example, with modern technology, finance charges can be calculated and disclosed at the point of purchase. Credit card balances could be reported on a statement that consolidated them with bank balances to show a consumer's true financial position. However, cognitive limitations do not tell the whole story.

Heuristics

Satisficing and Heuristic Borrowing

Consumers need not do the maths every time they engage in a credit purchase. Economists allow that consumer decisions may not always be fully considered. This does not necessarily mean that they are irrational or wrong. Instead, consumers may 'satisfice' or rely on a limited number of data points to make their decisions.[42] This may not be perfect, but these consumer heuristics may be sufficient to make consumer decisionmaking predictable, and 'close enough' to rational.[43] Whether decisionmaking based on heuristics, rather than full information, is 'close enough' will, of course, depend on the quality of the heuristics.

Heuristic Biases

Psychological experiments into individual judgement and decisionmaking cast doubt on these heuristics, at least insofar as they apply to consumer borrowing decisions. Some of these biases apply to consumer decisions about whether to borrow, and others to whether the borrower will repay, continue to pay interest and borrow more, or default. The starting point with heuristic borrowing lies in the work of Daniel Kahnemann and Amos Tverski on framing and endowment effects.[44]

---

[42] See eg HA Simon, 'Theories of Bounded Rationality' in CB Radner and R Radner (eds), *Decision and Organization* (1972) 161–176 ('In satisficing procedures, the existence of a satisfactory alternative is made likely by dynamic mechanisms that adjust the aspiration levels to reality on the basis of information about the environment.').

[43] HA Simon, 'Rational Decision Making in Business Organizations' (1979) 69 *American Economic Review* 493, 503 (arguing, as an alternative to the concept of utility maximization, that 'one could postulate that the decision maker had formed some *aspiration* as to how good an alternative he should find. As soon as he discovered an alternative for choice meeting his level of aspiration, he would terminate the search and choose that alternative' and calling this mode of selection 'satisficing').

[44] A Tversky, 'Rational Theory and Constructive Choice' in K Arrow *et al* (eds), *The Rational Foundations of Economic Behavior* (1996) 371, 186 ('Alternative descriptions of the same choice problems lead to systematically different preferences; strategically equivalent elicitation procedures give rise to different choices; and the preference between x and y often depends on the choice set within which they are embedded.'). Amos Tversky and Daniel Kahneman coined the concept of 'framing.' According to Tversky and Kahneman, a decision 'frame' is 'the decision maker's conception of the acts, outcomes, and contingencies associated with a particular choice.' A Tversky and D Kahneman, 'The Framing of Decisions and the Psychology of Choice' (1981) 211 *Science* 453, 456 (proposing that

Framing

Individuals do not judge their well-being in absolute terms. Instead they use a frame of reference. According to Tversky and Kahneman's 'prospect theory,' intertemporal choices depend upon departures from a reference point that is based on past consumption levels, expectations, social comparisons, and so on.[45] This prediction has been corroborated by experimental results. For example, David Bowman, Deborah Minehart and Matthew Rabin found that individuals are reluctant to alter their current consumption in reaction to shocks to income.[46] George Loewenstein agrees, finding that 'loss aversion reinforces time discounting,' and creates a 'powerful aversion' to reductions on consumption levels.[47] John Shea supports this prediction using both aggregate data and data from teachers' unions (in which wages are set a year in advance).[48] He found that consumption growth responds more strongly to future wage decreases than future wage increases. Jeffrey Fuhrer reaches similar conclusions by modelling consumer decisionmaking in terms of habit-formation.[49] He argues that habit formation explains 'hump-shaped' responses to shifts in income. While adjustments to consumption are sluggish in the short term, in the long run they respond to resource constraints.

Endowment Effects

Individuals also place a higher dollar value on the property that they own than other people's property. This is the so-called 'endowment effect'.[50] As a result,

decision frames are controlled, in part, by formulation of problem or question and, in part, by norms, habits, and characteristics of the decision maker). See also A Tversky and D Kahneman, 'Rational Choice and the Framing of Decisions' (1986) 59 *Journal of Business Science* 251.

[45] ibid.

[46] D Bowman, D Minehart, and M Rabin, 'Loss Aversion in a Consumption-Savings Model' (1999) 38 *Journal of Economic Behavior and Organization* 155.

[47] G Loewenstein, 'Frames of Mind In Intertemporal Choice' (1988) 34 *Management Science* 200. Georage Loewenstein expands on this thesis in a subsequent work co-authored with Drazen Prelec. G Loewenstein and D Prelec, 'Anomolies in Intertemporal Choice: Evidence and an Interpretation' (1992) 107 *Quarterly Journal of Economics* 573 (asserting the existence of a magnitude effect, sign effect and delay-speedup asymmetry).

[48] J Shea, 'Myopia, Liquidity Constraints, and Aggregate Consumption' (1995) 27 *Journal of Money, Credit, and Banking* 798; J Shea, 'Union Contracts and the Life-Cycle/Permanent-Income Hypothesis' (1995) 85 *American Economic Review* 186 .

[49] J Fuhrer, 'Habit Formation in Consumption and Its Implications for Monetary-Policy Models' (2000) 90 *American Economic Review* 367.

[50] See eg J Arlen, M Spitzer, and E Talley, 'Endowment Effects Within Corporate Agency Relationships' (2002) 31 *Journal of Legal Studies* 1; R Korobkin, 'The Endowment Effect and Legal Analyses' (2003) 97 *Nw U L Rev* 1227. Although loss aversion is the most widely accepted explanation for the endowment effect, R Thaler, 'Toward a Positive Theory of Consumer Choice' (1980) 1 *Journal of Economic Behavior and Organization* 39, 44, alternative theories exist. See eg Korobkin, above, 1242–1256 (reviewing literature and discussing several potential causes, including: wealth effects; loss aversion; and regret avoidance); B Inder and T O'Brien, 'The Endowment Effect and the Role of Uncertainty' (2003) 55 *Bulletin of Economic Research* 289 (theorizing that endowment effects pertain more to uncertainty than loss aversion); I Simonson and A Drolet, 'Anchoring Effects on Consumers' Willingness-To-Pay and Willingness-To-Accept' (2004) 31 *Journal of Consumer Research* 681 (testing the relationship between anchoring and endowment effects).

people tend to place a higher value on losses than equivalent gains, and exhibit a preference for avoiding the loss of property that exceeds their desire to acquire property of an equal value. Repeated experiments confirm the existence of this endowment effect in research settings.[51] Market data also confirms significant differences between actors' willingness to pay for a good and willingness to accept offers to buy, even in geographically and culturally distinct markets.[52]

The Endowment Effect in Consumer Borrowing and Consumer Bankruptcy

Survey and other empirical studies of consumer debtors in bankruptcy provide sobering reminders of the influence of sunk costs and endowment effects. Over the past twenty years, Sullivan, Warren and Westbrook have studied thousands of bankruptcy filings in more than a handful of states,[53] and found that, for a 'persistent

---

[51] See eg WL Adamowicz, V Bhardwaj, and B MacNab, 'Experiments on the Difference between Willingness to Pay and Willingness to Accept' (1993) 69 *Land Economics* 416; I Bateman, A Munro, B Rhodes, C Starmer, and R Sugden, 'A Theory of Reference Dependent Preferences' (1997) 112 *Quarterly Journal of Economics* 112; RR Boyce, TC Brown, GH McClelland, GL Peterson, and WD Schulze, 'An Experimental Examination of Intrinsic Values as a Source of the WTA-WTP Disparity' (1992) 87 *American Economic Review* 1366; DL Coursey, JJ Hovis, and WD Schulze, 'The Disparity Between Willingness to Accept and Willingness to Pay Measure of Value' (1987) 102 *Quarterly Journal of Economics* 679; DW Harless, 'More Laboratory Evidence on the Disparity Between Willingness to Pay and Compensation Demanded' (1989) 11 *Journal of Economic Behavior and Organization* 359; D Kahneman, J Knetsch, and R Thaler, 'Experimental Tests of the Endowment Effect and the Coase Theorum' (1990) 98 *Journal of Political Economy* 1325; D Kahneman, JL Knetsch, and RH Thaler, 'The Endowment Effect, Loss Aversion and Status Quo Bias' (1993) 5 *Journal of Economic Perspectives* 193; J Knetch, 'The Endowment Effect and Evidence of Nonreversible Indifference Curves' (1989) 79 *American Economic Review* 1277; J Knetch and JA Sinden, 'Willingness to Pay and Compensation Demand: Experimeal Evidence of an Unexpected Disparity in Measure of Value' (1984) 99 *Quarterly Journal of Economics* 507; JA List, 'Neoclassical Theory Versus Prospect Theory: Evidence from the Marketplace' (2004) 72 *Econometrica* 615 (limiting his confirmation of endowment effect to 'inexperienced consumers' and concluding that 'consumers with intense market experience [trading more than 12 times per month] behave largely in accordance with neoclassical predictions'); MA Strahilevitz and G Loewenstein, 'The Effect of Ownership History on the Valuation of Objects' (1998) 25 *Journal of Consumer Research* 276; E van Dijk and D van Knippenberg, 'Trading Wine: On the Endowment Effect, Loss Aversion, and the Comparability of Consumer Goods' (1998) 19 *Journal of Economic Psychology* 485; E van Dijk and D van Knippenberg, 'Buying and Selling Exchange Goods: Loss Aversion and the Endowment Effect' (1996) 17 *Journal of Economic Psychology* 517.

[52] See JF Shogren, SY Shin, DJ Hayes, and JB Kiliebenstein, 'Resolving Differences in Willingness to Pay and Willingness to Accept' (1994) 84 *American Economic Review* 225 (noting that incentive-compatible bidding systems do not eliminate endowment effect for nonmarket goods). But see JL Knetsch, F-F Tank, and R Thaler, 'The Endowment Effect and Repeated Market Trials: Is the Vickrey Auction Demand Revealing?' (2002) 4 *Experimental Economics* 257 (concluding that some Vickrey auctions cause disparity between WTP and WTA to decrease or even disappear over repeated trials); JF Shogren and DF Hayes, 'Resolving Differences in Willingness to Pay and Willingness to Accept: Reply' (1997) 87 *American Economic Review* 241. These results persist, even in geographically and culturally distant markets. SJ Kachelmeire and M Shelahata, 'Examining Risk Preferences Under High Monetary Incentives: Experimental Evidence from the People's Republic of China' (1992) 82 *American Economic Review* 1120; M Wallendorf and EJ Arnould, 'My Favorite Things: A Cross Cultural Inquiry into Object Attachment, Possessiveness and Social Linkage' (1988) 14 *Journal of Consumer Research* 531.

[53] See eg TA Sullivan, E Warren, and JL Westbrook, *As We Forgive Our Debtors* (New York, 1989); TA Sullivan, E Warren, and JL Westbrook, *The Fragile Middle Class: Americans in Debt* (New Haven,

subgroup of Americans,' 'the home itself may be the debtor's financial ruin, with its relentless demands for mortgage payments, maintenance, and taxes. For some, the refusal to abandon a home that is no longer affordable brings them to collapse.'[54]

Empirical studies suggest that the influence of the endowment effect in consumer bankruptcy cases is pervasive. Sullivan, Warren and Westbrook show that 'about half of all the debtors who file for bankruptcy own homes when they file' and are burdened with a median mortgage debt of $44,000.[55] When they compare the income, mortgage debt and non-mortgage debt for homeowners in bankruptcy with that of homeowners in the general population, Sullivan, Warren and Westbrook find that homeowners 'carry similar mortgage debts and higher non-mortgage debts than their homeowner counterparts in the general population, and they do so on substantially lower incomes.'[56]

The rationality of the decision to reaffirm secured debt turns on a comparison of the cost of the reaffirmed debt and the cost of a replacement obligation. But data shows that many consumer debtors reaffirm secured debt, whether or not the affected collateral could have been replaced for a lesser amount. For example, a rational debtor would not reaffirm a debt securing the purchase price of a car where public transportation or a cheaper used car was instead available. A rational consumer might also be unlikely to reaffirm a security agreement where the re-affirmed debt amount exceeds the collateral value because creditors generally insist that the debtor reaffirm the entire debt balance regardless of collateral value.

Yet, in their preliminary study of more than a thousand Chapter 7 cases filed in 1995 in seven judicial circuits located across the nation, Marianne B Culhane and Michaela M White found a significant number of seemingly irrational reaffirmations.[57] They report that close to 40 per cent of the reaffirmation agreements they studied involved unsecured debt.[58] Moreover, they report that, in a substantial portion of the studied reaffirmations involving secured debt, the reaffirmed debt exceeded the value of the related collateral:

> In 38% (49 of 129) of the motor vehicle reaffirmations, the amount reaffirmed exceeded the stated value of the car. Ten percent of the motor vehicle reaffirmations were for amounts 200% or more of scheduled collateral value. In 37% (17 of 46) of reaffirmations of debt secured by homes, the debtors reaffirmed an amount greater than scheduled value . . . [A]lmost 40% of the reaffirmations of homes and cars were at least partly unsecured.[59]

And these statistics relate to reaffirmations involving high value collateral.

2001). Subsequent work further refines their empirical look at consumer bankruptcy and its policy implications. E Warren and A Warren Tyagi, *The Two Income Trap* (New York, 2003).

[54] Sullivan, Warren and Westbrook, *Fragile Middle Class*, n 53 above, 200.

[55] ibid, 218.   [56] ibid, 219.

[57] MB Culhane and MM White, 'Debt After Discharge: An Empirical Study of Reaffirmation' (1999) 73 *American Bankruptcy Law Journal* 709.   [58] ibid.

[59] ibid, 730.

With agreements to reaffirm debt secured by low value household goods, Culhane and White cannot refer to valuations of the collateral in the court records. Nonetheless, they say, 'it seems likely that most of the household goods reaffirmations are less than fully secured, given the quick depreciation and low residual value of most such collateral.'[60]

Culhane and White's work also raises substantial questions about debtors' abilities to afford their reaffirmed obligations. When they computed reaffirming debtors' net disposable income available to cover reaffirmation costs, they found an average monthly deficit of $80.00.[61] Indeed, 39 per cent of the reaffirming debtors had no (zero) disposable income available for reaffirmation payments.[62]

Time Inconsistent Preferences

Behavioural psychologists have described another anomaly in individual borrowing behaviour—time inconsistent preferences. Consumer borrowing decisions involve a choice between present and future consumption. This inter-temporal choice depends on the relative weight attached to prospective well-being as compared to present consumption—the consumer's discount rate. Economists assume that the discount rate is consistent over different time periods.

Individuals may not apply a single discount rate over their lifetime. Richard Thaler asked respondents to specify the amount of money they would require in {one month/one year/ten years} to make them indifferent to receiving $15 now.[63] The responses {$20/$50/$100} imply a wildly divergent range of average annual discount rates over the three periods {345 per cent/120 per cent/9 per cent}.[64] Other studies report similar 'hyperbolic discounting' among respondents.[65] Indeed, after extensively reviewing this literature, Shane Frederick, George

---

[60] Culhane and White, n 57 above, 731.   [61] ibid, 761.

[62] ibid. Culhane and White considered the affordability of reaffirmed debts obligations according to several other indicators. They calculated ratios of reaffirmed debt to income and of reaffirmation payment to monthly income; they also considered nondischargeable debt as an additional burden on debtors' fresh start. With each of these alternative measures for assessing the affordability of the reaffirmed debt they studied, Culhane and White reached the same conclusions: they did not think that the debtors were financially able to make the payments to which the reaffirmation agreement committed them.

[63] R Thaler, 'Some Empirical Evidence on Dynamic Inconsistency' (1981) 8 *Economic Letters* 201.

[64] ibid.

[65] U Benzion, A Rapoport, and J Yagil, 'Discount Rates Inferred From Decisions: An Experimental Study' (1989) 35 *Management Science* 270; GB Chapman, 'Temporal Discounting and Utility for Health and Money' (1996) 22 *Journal of Experimental Psychology: Learning, Memory and Cognition* 771; GB Chapman and AS Elstein, 'Valuing the Future: Temporal Discounting of Health and Money' (1995) 15 *Medical Decision Making* 373; S DellaVigna and U Malmendier, *Overestimating Self-Control: Evidence from the Health Club Industry*, NBER Working Paper Series No 10819, 1–2 (September 2004), available at <http://www.nber.org/papers/w10819> (reporting comparable findings for first year of annual contract holders); JL Pender, 'Discount Rates and Credit Markets: Theory and Evidence from Rural India' (1996) 50 *Journal of Development Economics* 257; DA Redelmeir and DN Heller, 'Time Preference in Medical Decision Making and Cost-Effectiveness Analysis' (1993) 13 *Medical Decision Making* 212. Experimenters also observe preference

Loewenstein and Ted O'Donoghue contend that hyperbolic discounting 'is also evident across studies.'[66] They argue that the only remaining question is the precise shape of the inconstant discount rate, rather than the fact of its inconstancy.[67] This implies that 'people will always consume more in the present than called for by their previous plans.'[68] To enable this present consumption, consumers will borrow more than would maximize utility in the long-run.[69]

Consumers' implicit discount rates also vary depending upon the overall size of the benefit or cost at issue. Individuals do not equate the choice between $100 today and $150 in a year with the choice between $10 today and $15 in a year, implicitly assigning a higher discount rate to smaller-sized transactions. Studies varying outcome size consistently find that large outcomes are discounted at lower rates than small ones.[70] They are therefore more likely to put off consumption decisions perceived as large (ie, buying a home), but to engage in lots of incremental borrowing for present consumption in small amounts (ie, spending $50/week at the local drugstore on greeting cards, cigarettes and candy bars).

Framing shows up here, as well. Individuals' discount rates vary when the choice is framed as a decision to consume rather than save. George Loewenstein and

reversals—situations in which respondents prefer, for example, $110 in 31 days over $100 in 30 days, but also prefer $100 now over $110 tomorrow. *See* L Green, N Fristoe, and J Myerson, 'Temporal Discounting and Preference Reversals in Choice Between Delayed Outcomes' (1994) 1 *Psychonomic Bulletin and Review* 383; K Kirby and RJ Herrnstein, 'Preference Reversals Due to Myopic Discounting of Delayed Reward' (1995) 6 *Psychological Science* 83; A Millar and D Navarick, 'Self-Control and Choice in Humans: Effects of Video Game Playing as a Positive Reinforcer' (1984) 15 *Learning and Motivation* 203; J Solnick, C Kannenberg, D Eckerman, and M Waller, 'An Experimental Analysis of Impulsivity and Impulse Control in Humans' (1980) 11 *Learning and Motivation* 61.

[66] S Frederick, G Lowenstein, and T O'Donoghue, 'Time Discounting and Time Preference: A Critical Review' (2002) 40 *Journal of Economic Literature* 351, 361.

[67] ibid. See also D Read, 'Is Time-Discounting Hyperbolic or Subadditive?' (2001) 23 *Journal of Risk and Uncertainty* 5 (finding that implicit discount rates are subadditive, which means that the total amount of discounting over a temporal interval increases as the interval is more finely partitioned).

[68] See eg RH Strotz, 'Myopia and Inconsistency in Dynamic Utility Maximization' (1955) 23 *Review of Economic Studies* 165.

[69] D Laibson, A Repetto, and J Tobacman, 'A Debt Puzzle in Knowledge, Information, and Expectations in Modern Economics: In Honor of Edmund S. Phelps' (P Aghion, R Frydman, J Stiglitz, and M Woodford (eds), forthcoming), available at <http://post.economics.harvard.edu/faculty/laibson/papers/sept17.pdf>; C Harris and D Laibson, 'Hyperbolic Discounting and Consumption', *Eighth World Congress of the Econometric Society* (forthcoming), available at <http://post.economics.harvard.edu/faculty/laibson/papers/hlfeb19.pdf>.

[70] Benzion *et al*, n 65 above; Green *et al*, n 65 above; JH Holcomb and PS Nelson, 'Another Experimental Look at Individual Time Preference' (1992) 4 *Rationality and Society* 199; KN Kirby, 'Bidding in the Future: Evidence Against Normative Discounting of Delayed Rewards' (1997) 126 *Journal of Experimental Psychology: General* 54; KN Kirby and NN Marakovic, 'Modeling Myopic Decisions: Evidence for Hyperbolic Delay-Discounting with Subjects and Amounts' (1995) 64 *Organizational Behavior and Human Decision Process* 22; G Loewenstein, 'Anticipation and the Valuation of Delayed Consumption' (1987) 97 *Economic Journal* 666; A Raineri and H Rachlin, 'The Effect of Temporal Constraints on the Value of Money and Other Commodities' (1993) 6 *Journal of Behavioral Decision Making* 77; MK Shelley, 'Outcome Signs, Question Frames and Discount Rates' (1993) 39 *Management Science* 806; Thaler, n 63 above.

Richard Thaler provided a sample group with vouchers that could be redeemed at a local record store on several specified future dates, and asked participants how the value of the certificate would change if they were asked to agree to wait longer to redeem it.[71] Loewenstein and Thaler found that the participants demanded more than twice as much to delay the date than they were willing to give up to accelerate the redemption date. When conducting a different study, Loewenstein found that respondents' discount rates differ depending upon whether the change in delivery time of an outcome is framed as acceleration or delay from a temporal reference point.[72] Numerous studies corroborate this result, finding that respondents discount gains at a higher rate than losses.[73] Moreover, when researchers compare respondents' preferences as relates to a series of outcomes, they typically find that individuals strongly prefer improving sequences to declining sequences.[74]

In the consumer finance context, the problem of amount-inconsistent discount rates may explain why consumers are willing to pay large interest rates on relatively small amounts of money so long as the monthly payment remains affordable, and so long as they are not forced to focus on the length of time that it will take them to actually repay the debt. Pay day loans are a classic example, in that people are willing to pay annualized interest rates of 400 per cent or more for small loans with a stated due date of two weeks or so. While these loans appear to be short term, they are often rolled, and kept outstanding for longer periods. This may also explain resistance of the credit card industry to measures which would call attention to the length of time it will take to repay a credit card balance, when the minimum balance is paid.[75]

[71] G Loewenstein and RH Thaler, 'Anomalies: Intertemporal Choice' (1989) 3 *Journal of Economic Perspectives* 181, 187–188 and Table 1.   [72] Loewenstein, n 47 above.

[73] Benzion *et al*, n 65 above; Loewenstein, n 70 above; LD MacKeigan *et al*, 'Time Preference for Health Gains vs. Health Losses' (1993) 3 *PharmacoEconomics* 374; W. Mischel *et al*, 'Effects of Expected Delay Time on Subjective Value of Rewards and Punishments' (1969) 11 *Journal of Personality and Social Psychology* 363; Thaler, n 63 above; JF Yates and RA Watts, 'Preferences for Deferred Losses' (1975) 13 *Organizational Behavior and Human Performance* 294.

[74] See eg GB Chapman, 'Preferences for Improving and Declining Sequences of Health Outcomes' (2000) 13 *Journal of Behavioral Decision Making* 203 (posing a variety of sequences of headache pain and finding that the vast majority preferred decreasing sequence of pain); C Hsee, RP Abelson, and P Salovey, 'The Relative Weighting of Position and Velocity in Satisfaction' (1991) 2 *Psychological Science* 263 (finding that increasing wage profile was rated as highly as a decreasing sequence that conferred much more money); G Loewenstein and D Prelec, 'Preferences for Sequences of Outcomes' (1993) 100 *Psychological Review* 91 (finding that participants generally preferred to save a better thing for last); G Loewenstein and N Sicherman, 'Do Workers Prefer Increasing Wage Profiles?' (1991) 9 *Journal of Labor Economics* 67 (finding that most respondents prefer increasing wage profile to declining or flat one as relates to otherwise identical jobs); C Varey and D Kahneman, 'Experiences Extended Across Time: Evaluation of Moments and Episodes' (1992) 5 *Journal of Behavioral Decision Making* 169 (finding that subjects strongly preferred sequences involving decreasing discomfort as compared to increasing discomfort levels, even when the overall sum of discomfort was otherwise identical).

[75] J Caskey, 'Fringe Banking and the Rise of Payday Lending,' in P Bolton and H Rosenthal (eds), *Credit Markets for the Poor* (New York, 2005).

Time-inconsistent and amount-inconsistent preferences are complex phenomena. For an economist, preferences are taken as a given, and borrowing decisions made pursuant to those preferences are, by definition, rational. This logic is circular, however. In some instances the time inconsistency might be a function of a cognitive limitation, such as an inability to calculate an interest rate. In other cases, it might be a product of biased heuristics, such as an endowment effect. A consumer might feel a loss of present purchasing power very intensely. Or, it simply might be what it is, inconsistent preferences. To the extent that these cognitive limitations and heuristic biases are known to lenders and exploited, however, they may create an argument for regulation of consumer credit contracts.

Credit cards create an opportunity for present consumption in return for future payments. If one is indifferent between $15 now and $20 in a year, perhaps one would also be willing to pay $20 in a year for $15 now. If the implicit discount rate is 345 per cent for a one-year loan, that creates a significant opportunity for the marketers of pay-day loans. It suggests a perverse willingness to pay high interest for short-term loans, and an insistence on lower interest rates for long-term loans. In short, 'people will always consume more in the present than called for by their previous plans.' [76] To enable this present consumption, consumers will borrow more than would maximize their utility in the long-run. The result will be welfare loss for consumers, a windfall to consumer lenders. To the extent that consumers make inefficient intertemporal substitutions, the result will also be deadweight loss, as consumers' purchasing decisions are constrained in subsequent periods.

Rational Lenders and Quasi-rational Borrowers

In the previous two sections we have argued that, contrary to the assertions of lobbyists for the consumer credit industry, lenders are rational, while borrowers tend to be irrational. In this section we sketch the parameters of this alternative, and we think more plausible universe, suggest policy implications, and avenues for future research.

Modelling the Quasi-rational Borrower

In our view, a consumer's decision whether to borrow money to finance current consumption or to save is influenced by the answer to five questions:

- How much do I owe already?
- What is the cost of the new credit transaction?
- What is the likelihood that my income will either remain constant or increase in the next period?

[76] RH Thaler, *The Winner's Curse* (Princeton, 1992) 98.

- Which is stronger, my preference for current consumption or my preference for consumption in the future?
- What are the costs and benefits of default, including filing for bankruptcy, in the event that I cannot pay?

The cognitive limitations and heuristic biases that we described above will influence each of these decisions, and at each stage lead consumers to borrow more than the optimal level for a fully rational consumer with the same preferences.

When a consumer tries to calculate their current debt level, cognitive dissonance may cause them to underestimate the amount that they currently owe, and to underestimate the amount of unbilled activity on their card—the amount that they have already borrowed that month. Over-optimism may cause them to overestimate their ability to pay off the balance at the end of the month or to amortize the balance over a reasonable period of time.

When a consumer tries to calculate the cost of borrowing for a new purchase, the preceding problems can be compounded by the cognitive limitations discussed above. First, the terms of their existing credit arrangements may not be fully understood. Secondly, to the extent that they plan to use a new financing product to facilitate the purchase, the array of products available is confusing, and the terms are, by design, non-transparent. Thirdly, these decisions, at least where small purchases are involved, tend to be made quickly. Fourthly, calculating the cost of compound interest over time is not something that most consumers are capable of doing. As a result, it appears that many consumers simply ask themselves whether they can afford the minimum monthly payment, and assume that if they can, then they can afford the purchase.

Not only is a consumer likely to underestimate his current debt-load and the true financial cost of a financed purchase; when a consumer tries to decide whether they can afford to pay off the loan out of future income, optimism bias is likely to infect the decision. Consumers are likely to underestimate their future expenses and future borrowing, while overestimating the extent to which their income will increase over time.

When weighing the value of present consumption over future consumption, frames and hyperbolic discounting are also likely to play a significant role. First, frames come into play whenever a consumer suffers an income shock, or otherwise finds that current income is falling short of that necessary to support their current (or expected) lifestyle. A benefit of consumer credit is that it allows people to smooth consumption, if their income streams are variable. So long as this is done rationally, with a true appreciation of the costs, risks and tradeoffs, this is not problematic, but given the biases described above, and the intensity with which the framing literature tells us losses are felt, one would expect to see consumers 'overinvesting' in consumption smoothing and delaying adjustments to spending in the face of income disruptions. This is compounded by the effect of hyperbolic discounting, which causes consumers to value current consumption much more highly than future consumption. Together, these biases lead to a prediction of overinvestment in present consumption, at the expense of future consumption.

Finally, how do the cognitive limitations, heuristic biases and anomalous preferences, described above, affect a consumer's decisions when both cash and credit are short and default is in prospect? Here again, endowment effects suggest that consumers will borrow to maintain assets, even when the rational thing to do would be to sell them, either because they are not worth the price or because the consumer simply can't afford them.

The Rational Lender and the Quasi-rational Borrower

As Oren Bar-Gill has noted, in a world where borrowers engage in hyperbolic discounting, rational lenders can profit by charging high interest rates for seemingly short-term loans, and then benefiting as consumers overestimate their ability to repay, and underestimate the financial cost of the loan.[77] Awareness of these heuristics appears to define many consumer credit relations. The heavy use of revolving lines of credit, rather than term loans, disguises the long-term nature of much consumer debt. The use of teaser rates that expire after a period of time capitalizes on consumers' optimism about their ability to repay; profitability is maximized by exploiting consumers' propensity to underestimate how much they will use the line of credit in the future. In turn, consumer lenders' use of default rates and late fees maximize the penalty paid by consumers for their biased decision-making processes. The price of over-confidence bias is magnified if the default interest rate is 30 per cent, rather than the teaser rate of 5 per cent. Similar exploitation of hyperbolic discounting and optimism bias can be seen in the way health clubs price their memberships, in the time-honoured methods that book clubs (and now DVD clubs) use to entice members to join, and the way cellular telephone companies use free phones to encourage subscribers to commit for one or two years.[78]

In short, lenders are not unaware of the biases inherent in consumer borrowing and purchasing decisions. The only people who appear to be unaware of them are consumers—and ostensibly the lobbyists for consumer lenders.

Policy Implications and Future Research

The literature on judgement and decisionmaking suggests (1) that consumers will borrow more than a rational actor model predicts, (2) that they will be slow to react to signs of default, and (3) that they will be more reluctant to liquidate possessions than the rational actor model predicts. However, there have not been any studies designed to test these precise questions. While previous experiments

---

[77] O Bar-Gill, 'Seduction by Plastic' (2004) 98 *Nw U L Rev* 1373.
[78] DellaVigna and Malmendier, n 65 above, 1–2.

suggest that consumers will borrow more using a credit card than using cash, and that consumers are reluctant to liquidate assets, or limit lifestyle, no studies have compared these results to the rational actor baseline to determine whether what we are seeing is overborrowing, or an efficient compensation for risk aversion associated with cash transactions.

Assuming that these hypotheses bear out, however, the implications for bankruptcy policy and for the regulation of consumer credit are considerable. First, regulation focusing on enhanced disclosure may not, standing alone, be sufficient. While it may help eliminate some of the cognitive problems discussed above, it is not likely to alter the biased heuristics used by consumer borrowers. In any event, disclosure-based regulation should be carefully crafted to counteract consumer biases in decisionmaking. Financial literacy education, too, may help on the cognitive side and, together with notice, might limit the effect of heuristic biases.

However, in the near term, the implication of cognitive limitations, heuristic biases and inconsistent consumer preferences is that the focus for any regulation of overborrowing by consumers should not be on altering the incentives of consumers, but instead on altering the incentives of lenders. There are so many layers of cognition, bias and irrationality through which regulation focused on consumers must operate that it is very difficult to anticipate what, if any, effect the regulation will have on consumer borrowing decisions. By contrast, lenders appear to be rational, profit-maximizing actors. Altering their incentives is likely to go a lot further toward limiting the amount of harm caused by overleveraged consumer debtors.

Conclusion

Behavioural decision research suggests a behavioural model of consumer decision-making—a model in which individuals make decisions based on short cuts that lead them astray in predictable ways. A behavioural model of consumer bankruptcy law provides an alternative explanation for consumer debt levels and non-business bankruptcy filings. It suggests that consumers will purchase and borrow more than rational consumers would have, and that they will be slower to react to a default situation. It also suggests that rational lenders face market incentives to design consumer finance products and contract terms to exploit these decisional biases.

Legal and technological changes since 1978 have facilitated lender exploitation of consumer biases. The demise of usury laws and the development of national credit reporting and credit scoring systems and mass marketing techniques have permitted lenders to create a national market for consumer credit available to even the least credit-worthy members of society—at a price. Until recently, the harm caused by lender exploitation of consumer biases was tempered by the availability of the bankruptcy discharge. But, in the United States, enactment of the

Bankruptcy Abuse Prevention and Consumer Protection Act of 2005 severely limits consumer access to the bankruptcy lifeboat, and, in effect, rewards consumer lenders for taking advantage of consumers' cognitive limitations and heuristic biases.

We find the Bankruptcy Bill's focus on incentivizing rational consumer borrowers to be particularly wrongheaded. To the extent that rationality and opportunism exist in consumer credit transactions, they both appear to exist on the lender, not the borrower side of the equation. Those who would seek to reduce the bankruptcy filing rate should focus there as well.

26

Regulating Prostitution

Helen J Self

In recent years the number of prostitution-related offences has steadily increased. However, despite the obvious coercive intent reflected by this legislation, the Home Office consultation paper 'Paying the Price' is clothed in the 'victim-centred' New Labour rhetoric of 'protecting the vulnerable' and 'holistic', multi-agency partnership. To add to the confusion, the Association of Chief Police Officers has published a National Strategy which, whilst employing the same jargon, misleadingly identifies prostitution as a crime, arguing that if prostitution was given a higher policing priority, a range of more serious offences could be prevented.

These strategies play into deep-rooted public prejudice against the prostitute as 'Other'.

Background

Pathologizing Prostitution

The development of psychology as a discipline in the late nineteenth century provided a template for what was considered to be 'normal' or 'abnormal' human behaviour, much of which was grounded in notions of sexual conformity and deviance. Prostitution, therefore, provided a rich field for speculation and conjecture amongst both professionals and lay people, much of which should, in retrospect, be seen as prejudicial and harmful.

Perhaps the most notorious of the professional innovators was Cesare Lombroso who, in collaboration with William Ferrero, developed in the 1890s a theory connecting natural physiological variations in women with an inborn predisposition to criminality and prostitution. Prostitution, it was said, was the female corollary of criminality in men, resulting in a lower incidence of recorded crime amongst women. Facial features and childish behaviour were, in their opinion, sufficient evidence of a recognizable 'primitive' form of development. In one example a 9-year-old girl who lifted her skirt up in the street was categorized as a 'natural prostitute'. These assumptions fed easily into the Victorian fashion for clitoridectomy, seen at the time as a cure for 'over-sexed' masturbating females.[1]

Perhaps the most serious aspect of Lombroso's work, in terms of its eventual consequences, was the notion that criminality and immorality were diagnosable hereditary characteristics, revealing the 'born offender' for whom there was no cure. His subjects were placed into many sub-divisions, including the 'epileptic delinquent' and the 'morally insane', the latter being a hopelessly incurable recidivist who was best confined for life in a mental asylum. These questionable categories became common currency in academic circles and influenced social policy.[2] For example, in 1918 the medical expert, AF Tredgold, developed Lombroso's theories, arguing that a mixture of hereditary disorders, infectious diseases and conditions such as epilepsy, alcoholism and tuberculosis were related to feeble-mindedness, criminality and prostitution.[3] Tredgold gave evidence to the Royal Commission on the Care and Control of the Feeble Minded (1908), and the influence of his ideas can be detected in the Mental Deficiency Act 1913 which led in some instances to the incarceration of promiscuous and/or pregnant young women in mental hospitals.

Psychology had an understandable appeal for individuals engaged in categorizing and censuring the behaviour of others. For example, in 1930 the International Union of Catholic Women found that 'psycho-psychological and moral data were necessary to pierce through all the reflexes and currents of the subconscious', and concluded that prostitutes displayed 'fecklessness and marked blunting of moral faculties'. But with regard to higher faculties 'the repetition of vicious acts had strengthened in them a kind of automatism all the stronger if due to heredity tendencies'.[4] Here, the underlying moral disapproval mingled with the new-found discipline of psychoanalysis, and more worryingly still was given spurious legitimation through eugenic theories.

Sir Cyril Burt linked all together in an immense cauldron of female deviance which recognized no boundary between promiscuity and prostitution. Characteristically, he advocated the detention of 'over-sexed' adolescent girls as a protective measure against the spread of venereal disease, claiming that:

In secret, many of these loose and languid precocities become tempters of the opposite sex, purveyors of disease, and spreaders of vicious knowledge amongst their friends and casual

---

[1] C Lombroso and W Ferrero, *The Female Offender* (Peter Owen Edition, 1959).

[2] Lombroso's sub-divisions included a variety of hereditary conditions and racial characteristics as well as behavioural responses to social and environmental circumstances such as tattooing or suicide. The women of dark-skinned races were 'savage', exhibiting primordial characteristics. They were 'difficult to recognise for women, so huge are their jaws and so hard and coarse their features'. The venal women were frequently obese. The white-skinned criminal, who was characterized by asymmetric heavy features, was a reversion to the primitive state.

[3] AF Tredgold, *Mental Deficiency in Relation to Venereal Disease* (The National Council for Combating Venereal Disease, London, 1918) 7–8.

[4] League of Nations Advisory Commission for the Protection and Welfare of Children and Young People, Minutes of the Ninth Session, 9 April 1930, 91–2.

acquaintances; and with extreme cases of this kind, if only to protect society, segregation must be advocated, even perhaps at the risk of discomfort and of neurotic development in the individual . . . Moreover, since the condition is sometimes hereditary, the girl's home frequently contains other examples of the same oversexed constitution. For her, therefore, the home may be the last place in which she can be left with security.[5]

When, during the 1950s, the Home Office appointed the Wolfenden Committee to consider the law and practice relating to homosexual offences and prostitution, such misogynistic views concerning women in prostitution were common currency. Although the predominantly male committee accepted, perversely, that the client was merely responding naturally to an unsolicited offer, it assumed that some additional psychological elements had to be present in the personality of a woman who became a prostitute. Predictably, this aspect of her character was thought to require a social or medical report and the Committee recommended that the courts should be given the power to detain offenders for up to three weeks for this to be furnished.[6]

Over the early years of the twentieth century, little serious attention was given to the role of the client. But in 1962, the highly respected psychologist, Professor TNC Gibbens, from the Institute of Psychiatry, delivered a lecture on the subject of 'The Clients of Prostitutes'.[7] Some of the lifestyle circumstances he believed were responsible for propelling men into the arms of prostitutes are still familiar in today's literature, for example, the peripatetic seaman, the lorry driver, the disabled, sick, elderly or otherwise unattractive, and those men who were just not interested in, or afraid of a permanent relationship.

However, some aspects of his 1960s analysis seem dated. The sexually deviant were, in Gibbens' opinion, individuals who came from either end of a spectrum with normality at its centre, that is, those who had been either over or undercontrolled in their personal and private lives. The over-controlled, he argued, had their first sexual experience late in life, whilst the under-controlled were promiscuous, having experienced sexual relations between 14 and 15 years. Both of these groups were said to represent the casualties of society, the latter (echoing Lombroso), resembling the criminal population in many ways. Gibbens concluded that: 'Their capacity for human relationships has often withered in a cold wind rather than failed to develop for any innate reason.'

Two further groups, included soldiers who had their first sexual experience whilst abroad, and married men indulging in an 'exceptional extra-marital lapse' during a business trip. In both cases Gibbens believed that the men succumbed to temptation as a result of peer pressure but were subsequently overcome by

---

[5] C Burt, *The Young Delinquent* (London, 1952, 9th edn) 224.

[6] Report of the Committee on Homosexual Offences and Prostitution (1957), Cmd 247, s 223 (rec xxiv, 166). For elaboration of the above discussion, see also HJ Self, *Prostitution, Women and Misuse of the Law. The Fallen Daughters of Eve* (London, 2003).

[7] TCN Gibbens, *The Clients of Prostitutes* (1962, Alison Neilans Memorial Lecture for the Josephine Butler Society) copy in Women's Library, London.

feelings of guilt which they voiced when checking into the VD clinic. A degree of surprise was expressed at the discovery that quite a large group of older married men made little attempt to explain their behaviour, declaring that their wives and marriages were satisfactory. But, displaying an almost Victorian flourish, Gibbens declared that it later emerged that the 'satisfactory' wives were 'possessive' and 'neurotic', 'retiring into illness if they could not get their way or creating hysterical scenes'.

Less appealing still, in today's terms, were his comments on race. For example, the 'maladjusted Irish immigrant' whose experience of poverty had made sex seem a luxury since his main object in life was to stay alive. For the Irish labourer, hard physical work and bouts of drinking culminated in visits to prostitutes, only to be followed by anger and remorse emanating from their early Catholic education and what was considered in retrospect to have been a waste of money. The West Indian immigrant was said to have the same outlook.

Gibbens finally pigeonholed himself when he speculated that an element of the client's relationship with the prostitute was one of passivity: 'it is essentially a relationship in which someone else gives something, and one obtains it with minimum effort'. It is somewhat depressing to read his conclusion that: 'In the family background of clients...one finds fairly often a dominant and rather possessive mother', the father being either dead or a much less important figure for whom the mother has not encouraged any respect.

The thread which unites this range of views is a depressingly common form of prejudice which connects prostitution with numerous disorders. These include moral, spiritual, mental and physical disorders, juvenile delinquency, criminality, public disorder, contagion and death. All of which apparently flow from the behaviour of young women.

It was not until the 1980s, when the emergence of kerb crawling was recognized as a social menace, that the client took on a more prominent politically controversial role, requiring legislation. These changing priorities will unfold as we examine the current situation and the additional legislation of the past twenty-five years.

The Law

The current statutory definition of prostitution as laid out in the Sexual Offences Act 2003 is: 'The exchange of sexual services for some form of payment—usually money or drugs. This can take place on the street or in massage parlours or saunas, through escort agencies or at private addresses'.[8] In section 51(2) of the Sexual Offences Act 2003 the word 'prostitute' is defined as 'a person (A) who on at least one occasion and whether or not compelled to do so, offers or provides sexual

---

[8] (Home Office, 2004b).

services to another person in return for payment or a promise of payment to A or a third person'.[9] However, what constitutes a *sexual service* is not clearly defined.

One of the central peculiarities of the law as it applies to prostitution is its contradictory nature. On the one hand we have a long history of Public Order Acts which identify prostitutes as vagrants and street-walkers who loiter or solicit in public places, they are generally seen as a nuisance and a threat to free commerce and social order.[10] This aspect is currently addressed by the Street Offences Act 1959, with its cautioning system and inbuilt presupposition of guilt. An extension of this approach is to be found in the Sexual Offences Act 1985 which criminalizes kerb crawlers. On the other side we have the protective legislation which developed as a result of the nineteenth-century campaign for the repeal of the Contagious Diseases Acts.[11] These Acts, which applied to a number of military ports and towns in England and Ireland, legitimated the medical examination and registration of women believed to be prostitutes and were intended to protect the forces from venereal disease. This campaign was of great importance, because it set in motion a stream of Criminal Law Amendment Acts (consolidated in the Sexual Offences Act 1956 and reformed in the Sexual Offences Act 2003).[12] One of the principal aims of this legislation has been the protection of vulnerable people (primarily women and children) from abuse through prostitution and trafficking.[13] I wish to emphasize that the abuse of children, rather than adult women, set in motion both the original Criminal Law Amendment Acts and our more recent reforms. So we need to tease apart society's attitudes to adult women in prostitution, for whom there is often little sympathy, and our understandable concern to protect those who we perceive as vulnerable.

[9] See also K Stevenson, A Davis, and M Gunn, *Blackstone's Guide to The Sexual Offences Act 2003* (Oxford, 2004) 122.

[10] Vagrants Act 1824; Metropolitan Police Act 1839; Vagrancy Act 1898; Town and Police Clauses Act 1947.

[11] (1864, 1866, and 1869).

[12] Criminal Law Amendment Act 1885; Vagrancy Act 1898; Incest Act 1908; Criminal Law Amendment Act 1912; and Criminal Law Amendment Act 1922. These Acts were consolidated in the Sexual Offences Act 1956.

[13] Following the Criminal Law Amendment Act 1885, an international social purity movement ran in parallel with the Victorian–Edwardian campaign, leading to a series of international instruments aimed at the protection of women and children from abuse through prostitution and trafficking. These statutory instruments included: the International Agreement for the Suppression of the White Slave Traffic, signed at Paris, 18 May 1904, ratified at Paris, 18 January 1905 by Great Britain, Germany, Denmark, Spain, France, Italy, Russia, Sweden, Norway, Switzerland, Belgium, the Netherlands, and Portugal. Treaty Series No 24. HMSO 2689; the International Convention for the Suppression of the White Slave Traffic, signed at Paris, May 1910 by Austria and Hungary, Great Britain, France, Belgium, Brazil, Denmark, Spain, Italy, the Netherlands, Portugal, Russia, Sweden. Treaty Series 1912 No 20; the League of Nations Convention on the Traffic in Women and Children, Geneva, 18 October 1921; the League of Nations Convention on the Traffic in Women and Children, Geneva, 18 October 1921; the League of Nations Convention for the Suppression of the Traffic of Women of Full Age, 1933; and the United Nations Convention for the Suppression of the Traffic in Persons and the Exploitation of the Prostitution of Others, 1949.

Recent Changes

Two important milestones, which focus upon the needs and vulnerability of children, mark the end of the 1980s. First, the United Nations Convention on the Rights of the Child and, secondly, the Children Act 1989 (both define children involved in prostitution as under the age of 18). Taking advantage of these initiatives, the Children's Society launched a campaign against the prosecution of children for loitering or soliciting, arguing that it was wrong to give *children* criminal records when we ought to be prosecuting the men who abused them.[14]

Barnardo's capped this with its Streets and Lanes project, which investigated the grooming and illegal detention of children for the purpose of prostitution by a pimp/boyfriend.[15] The police picked up on these campaigns, and under the guidance of Dr Tim Brain (now Chief Constable of Gloucestershire and police spokesperson on prostitution), the Association of Chief Police Officers (ACPO) published new guidelines for dealing with children involved in prostitution. This was to entail a multi-agency strategy, through which the Police would be actively supported by the Probation Service, the Crown Prosecution Service, Health, Social and Education Services and voluntary agencies. Prosecution was to remain available as a last resort.

These developments represented the beginning of an important ideological shift within the oppressive arm of the law, which meant withdrawing from the idea of street-workers as a public nuisance and moving towards a wider definition of *all* women in prostitution as '*victims*' or '*vulnerable groups*' preyed upon by men, featuring the client as well as the pimp as abusers. Antagonism towards men was reinforced by the emergence of anti-pimping societies such as the Coalition for the Removal of Pimping (CROP), the establishment of a 'John school' in Yorkshire, renewed concern over trafficking, and feminist support for the Swedish approach to legislation which sees prostitution as a form of violence against women.[16]

When New Labour was elected in 1997, the Home Secretary, Jack Straw, voiced his concern for the 'victims' of crime and the Home Office responded to the growing public anxiety over domestic violence, paedophilia, sexual offences and child prostitution by announcing a 'review of sex offences'. The announcement was prefaced by a statement insisting that the review would *not* be looking at 'decriminalizing prostitution' (which was not an offence anyway), although it would cover homosexual offences, flashing and sexual abuse. Consequently, the Home Office Steering Committee's external reference group did not include

---

[14] M Lee and R O'Brien, *The Game's Up: Redefining Child Prostitution* (1995).

[15] Barnardo's, *Whose Daughter Next? Children Abused Through Prostitution* (1980).

[16] The first UK John school project was organized by the radical feminist Julie Bindel. The experiment was conducted by Leeds Metropolitan University in cooperation with the West Yorkshire Police, the rationale being that a client arrested for kerb crawling is given the option of prosecution or a day's course during which he is confronted with the consequences of his anti-social behaviour. It was abandoned by the police after a trial period.

representatives from organizations working in the field of sexual health, outreach work, or sex-work projects, whilst it did include representatives from a number of NGOs with only a passing interest in the subject, such as the Soroptimists. There then followed a protracted and frustrating correspondence between the Home Office and concerned organizations, including the UK Network of Sex Work Projects and the Josephine Butler Society (JBS), pointing out that it was just not feasible for the Home Office to review and reform the 1956 Sexual Offences Act, *without* reference to prostitution.[17] Moreover, any recommendations leading to a change in the law relating to prostitution should only emerge as a result of a comprehensive review of all the legislation pertaining to prostitution. Such a review was well overdue and should include an examination of the extent to which *the law and its application* contribute towards the vulnerability of sex workers.

In July 2000, the Home Office published its report, *Setting the Boundaries— Reforming the law on sex offences*, and the Bill which implemented many of its recommendations was taken through the House of Lords, mostly on Thursday afternoons, and was largely ignored by the press and the public.[18]

Meanwhile, the piecemeal development of the law applying to prostitution continued. Most significantly, the Crime and Disorder Act 1998 provided a new tool for the police in the guise of the Anti-Social Behaviour Order, the infamous ASBO, which reintroduced imprisonment for loitering or soliciting, despite the fact that this penalty had been repealed in the Criminal Justice Act 1982.[19] A further section brought the banning of prostitutes' cards in telephone boxes, whilst the power to arrest kerb-crawlers was introduced in the Criminal Justice and Police Act 2001.[20] Finally, a new group of anti-trafficking offences were placed as a temporary measure in the Nationality, Immigration and Asylum Act 2002, later to be transferred to the Sexual Offences Act 2003.[21]

Regardless of the lack of debate, and the repeated assurances that prostitution was not part of the sex offences review, the Sexual Offences Act 2003 introduced a number of important prostitution-related reforms. These included the creation of gender neutral offences, statutory definitions of prostitute, prostitution and brothel, the new trafficking offences, the redrafting of offences of 'exploitation for the purpose of prostitution', a new offence of running a brothel, an offence of accepting a sexual service from a person under 18 and many increased penalties.[22] It also provided the option of withdrawing driving licences from kerb-crawlers.

---

[17] The history of the JBS stretches back to Josephine Butler's 19th-century campaign for the repeal of the Contagious Diseases Acts. In 1915, the Ladies National Association, founded by Josephine Butler in 1869, merged with the British Branch of the Abolitionist Association and became the Association of Moral and Social Hygiene (AMSH), which changed its name to the Josephine Butler Society in 1962.

[18] *Setting the Boundaries: Reforming the law on sex offences* (Home Office, London, 2000) vols I and II.

[19] Crime and Disorder Act 1998, s1; Criminal Justice Act 1982.

[20] Criminal Justice and Police Act 2001, ss 46 and 71.

[21] Nationality, Immigration and Asylum Act 2002, ss 143–146.

[22] See *Blackstone's Guide to The Sexual Offences Act 2003*, n 10 above.

Whilst the Bill wound its way through the House of Lords, activists proceeded to lobby its members and persuaded a cross-party group of Lords and Baronesses to demand that the government should implement recommendation 53 of *Setting the Boundaries*: 'that there should be a further review of the law on prostitution'.

Although the Home Office capitulated on this demand, any feeling of triumph was short lived. It was not long before it became apparent that this exercise would be equally frustrating, since the remit was once again constrained within a victimization paradigm, leaving no room for individual autonomy. Consequently, any meaningful scrutiny of the legislation, or the counter-productive nature of the legal framework, was compromised.

When the consultation paper *Paying the Price* was published in 2004, the subject of prostitution was presented in terms of addressing the needs of the vulnerable.[23] It therefore strengthened and built upon the assumptions adopted in *Setting the Boundaries*, that sex workers were invariably victims and prostitution intrinsically harmful. This was made explicit by the framework adopted, which focused on the abuse of women and children, harassed local communities, drugs, links with serious crime and exiting programmes.

The key issues within the report are defined by the question: What is prostitution, how prevalent is it and how can we prevent it? Connected problems being the pimp, the user and the problems created by the existence of a sex trade, followed by government and voluntary action to address the consequences. The paper concludes with 'considering the options': a survey of selected legal approaches from around the world, but without including any positive feedback from more liberal countries, for example, the Netherlands, Germany, Brazil, Canada or New Zealand.

Each chapter of the report is headed by a small vignette, illustrating the abuse and victimization of those involved. Belinda Brooks-Gordon has commented on the extent to which children have informed this debate, pointing out that even the cover picture of a sorrowful child contributes to this melancholy impression. Lost and forlorn, she stands there, head to one side, dressed in blue, with a soft mauve background. The embodiment of sorrow.[24] Yet child abuse was extensively discussed in the previous review and during the parliamentary debates which accompanied the passage of the Bill, so why do it again?

The text is then peppered with highlighted examples of how various NGOs are addressing the issues. These are frequently aimed at children and include the NSPCC, YWCA, Sure Start, Child Line and Jig Saw. They feature programmes which offer 'holistic' approaches, counselling for victims, prevention and exit programmes. Consequently the conflicting needs of women and children are conflated, encouraging us to infantilize adult women and see them as people who require firm guidance and strict discipline. Indeed, if the offender is unwilling to

---

[23] *Paying the Price: a consultation paper on prostitution* (Home Office, London, 2004).
[24] B Brooks-Gordon, *Response to Paying the Price: A Consultation Paper on Prostitution* (2004). Dr Brooks-Gordon has conducted extensive research into the role of the client.

adopt the role of victim, submit to drug testing and accept 'treatment', then guidance and discipline will inevitably follow.

However, chapter 8 of the report changes our perceptions, by providing the links with serious crime which are seen to require and legitimate legal interventions against individual sex workers, leading us into a far more sinister and threatening world of adult criminal activity. To quote:

> Prostitution undermines public order and creates a climate in which more serious crime flourishes. Street prostitution is often associated with local drug markets, bringing class A drugs and gun culture to local communities. It is believed that those who control prostitution also tend to be connected to other forms of serious crime. Dealing effectively with prostitution could have a dramatic effect on dealing with more serious crime and help to stifle drug supply.[25]

The Police Strategy

The Home Office report was a gift to the police who responded with their own: 'National Strategy for Policing Prostitution: Guidelines for dealing with exploitation and abuse through prostitution.'[26] The authors state in their report that the law on prostitution is clear, which indeed it is. And to reinforce this statement Lord Denning is quoted on the duties of the Chief Constable, saying that: '*In all things he is not a servant of anyone save the law itself*'. Yet, the authors wilfully misinterpreted the law. Prostitution, which has never been a crime, is redefined three-dimensionally. It becomes a 'victim centred crime', a 'signal crime' and a 'market crime'. Admittedly, these terms are euphemisms or pointers, nevertheless the dark spectre of criminality is played upon relentlessly in an effort to enhance the profile of prostitution as a policing priority. The argument being, that if increased resources were ploughed into this Cinderella area, many more serious offences could be tackled.

'Policing Prostitution' echoes the 'vulnerable, abused victim' mantra of the Home Office papers and is filled with references to 'holistic' and 'multi-agency' approaches. In it, sex workers are portrayed as victims and/or 'drug addicts' who require help in order to 'detox' and to 'exit'. The prostitute remains, contradictorily, both a threat to law and order and the object of compassion. However, this is compassion with strings attached to it. It requires the passive acceptance by offenders of the 'the sick role'—the individual must perceive themself as a person who is mentally and physically ill and in need of treatment. Without any willingness to reform on the part of the offender, the full coercive weight of the law will descend upon them.

In this country we are increasingly applying a 'carrot and stick' approach to areas of low-level criminality. For example, there is now compulsory drug testing

---

[25] *Paying the Price*, para 8.1.
[26] This paper, which is not generally available, was written by Dr Tim Brain, Tony Davis, and Ann Phillips.

and treatment for women arrested for loitering or soliciting, with the alternative being an ASBO and the threat of up to five years' imprisonment for non-compliance. As one homeless person put it, the system 'coaxes and wheedles at one end and swipes you raw at the other'.

Unfortunately, and despite a growing campaign for the recognition of sex work, the police and the Home Office are unwilling to contemplate the idea that there is any element of free choice involved, arguing that even those who have 'chosen' only do so under the constraints of poverty and inequality, having been coerced by circumstances out of their control. Prostitutes and 'trafficked' women are portrayed as passive, ignorant individuals forced into 'modern-day slavery'.

It would not matter so much if the multi-agency, holistic approach was entirely benign. But in reality local authorities see it as a godsend. Take, for example, the case of Birmingham City Council. A Legal Services Briefing from Birmingham 2002/2004 reveals the potency of the multi-agency networking measures which can be used to force prostitutes off the streets and out of business, resulting in a dramatic decrease in the number of women causing 'harassment, alarm and distress' to residents.[27] In 2001, Birmingham City Council set up a Partnership Action Group which reported to the Member Level Street Prostitution Panel. The Partnership Group met monthly and implemented a wide range of measures designed to address the adverse effects of street prostitution upon local communities.

In collaboration with the Police, Probation Service and Birmingham Magistrates' Court they produced a Legal Proceedings Chart detailing legal action against kerb-crawlers, pimps and street prostitutes which was sent to the Home Secretary, with recommendations for enhancing penalties for kerb-crawlers. Legal action was taken against twenty prostitutes, in the form of ASBOs. Warning letters were issued and efforts made to involve the Health Service and voluntary organizations. Only five of the women disobeyed the court order and were sentenced to prison, but this was suspended in order to give them a 'last chance'— meaning they were obliged to obey the original order or be committed to prison. The Health Service made renewed efforts to take the women off the streets. Only two workers re-breached the order and were given 28-day prison sentences.

As a result of this strategy, the number of street workers were reduced from fifty to five per day. Which was, of course, seen as a great success, but it would be interesting to know how the women taken off the streets had fared. It would be rather surprising if their legal, social, employment, family and health problems had been solved. Perhaps they had merely moved to other geographical areas or to indoor work. However, the Legal Service Briefing finishes: 'The City Council and indeed local authorities, in partnership, face a significant challenge to reduce anti-social behaviour in our communities. There is a major new role for legal services to support and drive this process forward.'

[27] Birmingham City Council Legal Services Briefing, *Crime and Disorder Anti-Social Behaviour 2002/2004*. This document is available on the internet.

Demonizing the Client

Following the successful implementation of the Street Offences Act 1959 and a steep increase in car ownership, attention began to focus upon the activities of clients who cruised around residential areas in search of prostitutes, creating congestion and harassing local women. In 1984 the Criminal Law Revision Committee recommended new legislation to deal with the issue and the Sexual Offences (Kerb Crawling) Act 1985 was passed. Hostility towards the client was amplified once the Barnardo's campaign (mentioned above) got under way and the pimp/boyfriend emerged as the perpetrator of crimes which, quite apart from living on the earnings of prostitution, involved the abduction of minors, illegal detention, rape, violence and theft. Anxiety increased still further as a result of the growing international concern over sex-tourism and trafficking. The combined impact of these concerns led many anti-prostitution campaigners (mostly religious and radical feminist groups), to believe that the only way to tackle the problem of 'sexual slavery' was to 'target the demand' and they have campaigned tirelessly towards this end.

The resulting re-configuration of the 'client' alongside the pimp, as an abuser of vulnerable, underage girls and damaged women has encouraged a coalition of academics and sex workers rights organizations to examine more closely the role and motivations of the client, especially in relation to differing interpretations of female autonomy and human rights. It is easy, therefore, for analysts to 'cherry pick' those views which support their case from an array of diametrically opposed views which are presented as the 'truth' about prostitution. (This, I would suggest, is something that the Home Office has been guilty of in *Paying the Price*.) For example, prostitution as a form of abuse is supported by the work of Julie O'Connell Davidson who, in *Prostitution, Power and Freedom*, states that she is firmly of the opinion that 'prostitute use' is an oppressive act.[28] This stance inevitably limits her analytical scope, since she is then obliged to fit the evidence gained from her interviewees into an abusive mould.

In analysing the power dynamics between prostitute and client, O'Connell Davidson expands upon the theories of Robert Stoller who argues that the client is playing out a fantasy which, in Freudian terms, is characterized by the wish to debase the object of sexual desire. Consequently, triumph, mastery and dehumanization are at the core of any prostitute/client contract, regardless of the form the encounter takes. For instance, it is said to be the extreme powerlessness of the child prostitute which is eroticized by the sex tourist. The child is anxious to please and does not negotiate terms. Similarly, it is argued, the client who professes loneliness as his motive, or who patronizes the dominatrix is still purchasing the right to dominate, whereas the married man eroticizes the danger

---

[28] J O'Connell Davidson, *Prostitution, Power and Freedom* (Cambridge, 1998).

of being caught and the secrecy involved in cheating his wife by having sex with a 'dirty whore'.

However, the more pragmatic analyst will attribute mundane motives. Hilary Kinnell of the Network of Sex Work Projects argues that many of the men who visit sex workers simply enjoy their company, they may crave variety in women and sexual experience, or merely find it is simpler to purchase something that might otherwise be denied after an evening of socializing.[29] The relative certainty of the outcome and the lack of emotional commitment are powerful attractions.

By limiting its remit to the protection of the vulnerable, the Home Office has also narrowed its scope (this I believe to be intentional), but as Brooks-Gordon has observed, it is nonsensical to exclude all reference to the client, or to omit mentioning the increasing number of men who sell sex to other men, men who sell sex to women and women who sell sex to couples.[30] As a result of narrowing the discussion, the Home Office has been able to ignore large areas of concern, including sex workers' health and safety, academic work which does not fit the required mould and even the effectiveness, or inadequacy, of current legislation, whilst at the same time it has promoted a police-led agenda which repeals and reforms nothing but promotes public acceptance of the criminalization of men. Sadly, one can only conclude that the consultation paper represented a lost opportunity.

Conclusion

To sum up my concerns:

(1) In *Paying the Price* the Home Office fails spectacularly to review the law relating to prostitution as suggested in section 53 of *Setting the Boundaries* (it does not even criticize the use of the term 'common prostitute').

(2) The paper is directed towards the street trade and largely ignores the off-street venues where most prostitution transactions take place.

(3) It is an emotive document which focuses upon abuse and victimization, especially of children, leading to the conflation of women and children and the infantilization of adults.

(4) It is manipulative: using the language of compassion and wholeness, asking questions which are difficult to respond to without addressing and endorsing the negative framework adopted.

(5) It emphasizes vulnerability, whilst obscuring a coercive agenda which includes mandatory drug tests and treatment.

---

[29] B Brooks-Gordon (ed), *The Price of Sex: Prostitution, Policy, and Society.* (Collumpton Devon, 2006) 198.

[30] B Brooks-Gordon, 'Clients and Commercial Sex: Reflexions on Paying the Price: A Consultation Paper on Prostitution' (2005) *Criminal Law Review* 425–443.

(6) It replaces choices apparently made under the constraints of poverty and deprivation, with an equally dubious choice between adopting the role of victim or offender, which will do little to relieve the stigmatization of sex workers. This course of action could only be acceptable if it was backed by the necessary financial and practical resources needed to give offenders real opportunities.

(7) It demonizes men, in a way which will encourage the creeping criminalization of the client, asking slanted questions such as, 'What can we do to ensure that those who go to prostitutes are fully aware of the implications of their activities?'

(8) It plays upon the fear of serious crime, which has predictably encouraged the police to appeal for increased resources. This will increase the pressure upon women in the sex trade.

(9) It cherry-picks research, using, and I believe commissioning, only what supports the official view, whilst ignoring or suppressing what does not.

For example, Belinda Brooks-Gordon's work on clients was misrepresented, as was my history of the law and almost anything which would have helped to provide a broad and balanced discussion. The Home Office, like Wolfenden and many others before, adopted the view that no individual in their right mind could willingly resort to prostitution as an occupation.

So, despite official recognition of gender neutrality, the prostitute or sex worker remains the 'other', a socially unacceptable sick 'female', outside the margins of respectable society.

In January 2006, the Home Office published 'A Coordinated Prostitution Strategy and a summary of responses to *Paying the Price*'. The proposed 'national strategy' it contains has already been adopted, but some legislation is anticipated which will make it legal for two women and a maid to work together and which will reform the Street Offences Act 1959, adapting it to fit the proposed multi-agency strategies.[31]

---

[31] For further analysis, see n 30 above.

27

Psychoanalysis and the Nazis[1]

Stephen Frosh

The history of psychoanalysis in Germany during the Nazi period has been a source of some controversy and heart-searching within the analytic community over the past twenty years. Prior to that, with the exception of early revelations concerning CG Jung's collaboration with the Nazis (Léon, 1946) and a rather negative report to Ernest Jones from John Rickman in 1946 (reprinted in Brecht *et al*, 1985), there had been a ferocious silence over events between 1933 and 1945. 'Ferocious' here, because the silence not only covered up a troubled history, but also repressed a set of contradictions and tensions which have relevance both to the social history of psychoanalysis as a profession, and also to its theoretical positions. Both this history and these theories are heavily invested in by psychoanalysts and others committed to the discipline, the benign nature of which is to some extent called into question if one argues—as it is possible to do—that psychoanalysis fell rather easily into Nazi hands. Thus, 'not speaking' about the Nazi period was one of those functional defences arising out of a partially unconscious awareness of the problems which could have been caused by speaking too clearly. The silence not only served to create a space to get on with post-war reconstruction; it was also a way of holding together a movement which might easily, faced with its own destructive impulses, fragment.

Since about the mid-1970s, there has been an opening out of work on the Nazi period, with a major spur to action being the meeting of the International Psychoanalytic Association in Hamburg in 1985, although this produced disappointment in some Jewish analysts that the issues of the Nazi Holocaust were not fully attended to (Moses and Hrushovski-Moses, 1986). This work has had practical ramifications in the structures and splits in contemporary German psychoanalysis, but it also says a considerable amount about the fundamental assumptions of psychoanalysis, the conditions under which it can survive, those under which it can thrive, and the moral standing of its practitioners. None of

---

[1] This paper is based on S Frosh (2003) 'Psychoanalysis, Nazism and "Jewish Science".' *International Journal of Psychoanalysis* 84: 1315–1332. An extended account of this material is in S Frosh (2005) *Hate and the 'Jewish Science': Anti-Semitism, Nazism and Psychoanalysis.* London: Palgrave. Reprinted material is used with permission.

these issues has gone unnoticed, although often they become somewhat swamped by the political and transferential realities of the psychoanalytic scene. In addition, there is the relatively silenced question of psychoanalysis as a 'Jewish science'. This was, of course, the way it was catalogued by the Nazis and the notion of it as 'Jewish' therefore has strong antisemitic connotations; but there are also many serious Jewish scholars interested in the links between psychoanalysis and Jewish thought (eg Bakan, 1958; Diller, 1991; Gillman, 1993; Klein, 1985; Roith, 1987; Yerushalmi, 1991), making any simple repudiation of the 'Jewish science' idea difficult to sustain.

The idea that psychoanalysis might at least have a strong Jewish connection, even if one might baulk at the idea of it being a Jewish 'science', is in fact not particularly contentious. Sociologically and philosophically, in its membership, its practices and its mind-set, psychoanalysis was constructed out of the energy released from the antisemitic as well as the theocratic restrictions of the past. With the resurgence of the antisemitic part of this in its newly virulent twentieth-century European form, these issues became key once more: psychoanalysis was to be damned because of its Jewish origins and structure, and if it was going to be rescued, then—so at least some of the thinking went—its Jewishness (including its Jewish membership) would have to be discarded. It is with how this process was played out in Nazi Germany that this paper is concerned.

Appeasing the Nazis

By the early 1930s, German psychoanalysis and specifically the Berlin Psychoanalytic Institute (BPI), was a model for how psychoanalysis might be practised and developed in an advanced society. The BPI had been founded by Ernst Simmel and Max Eitingon in 1920 and was bankrolled by Eitingon, who in the early 1930s was also President of the German Psychoanalytic Society (DPG). It was explicitly social reformist in attitude and approach, and had amongst its members some of the stars of the movement to combine socialism or Marxism and psychoanalysis—Wilhelm Reich, Otto Fenichel, Erich Fromm, Edith Jacobson, Ernst Simmel, Siegfried Bernfeld and others, most of them Jews. It also adopted a programme of developing psychoanalysis so that it could be of benefit to working people, with a substantial commitment to low cost psychotherapy. Otto Fenichel ran the famous 'Children's Seminar' at the BPI, the 'children' of the title referring to their position in the hierarchy of analysts rather than their focus, for the purpose of this seminar was to study relations between psychoanalysis and politics, particularly socialism (Jacoby, 1983). The BPI thus enacted both a commitment to psychoanalytic practice and education, and an attempt to make psychoanalysis of cultural and political relevance—a serious yet immensely exciting affair. Goggin and Goggin (2001, 19) comment, 'it is not too much to say that by 1930 the BPI had established itself as a role model for the profession'. Yet, within a remarkably short time after the accession of the Nazis to power in 1933, all this had gone.

The story of how this happened is quite complex, and its underlying dynamics are even more so. There are also continuing uncertainties over the role of certain important protagonists, including Freud and Anna Freud themselves. Mixed up in the narrative is the provocative figure of Jung, and a subsidiary plot is provided by the machinations around Wilhelm Reich. Ernest Jones is at times both villain and hero. Three names recur: Matthias Göring, Felix Boehm and Carl Müller-Braunschweig, the first of these a cousin of the top Nazi politician, who took over the psychotherapy movement as a consequence; the other two being non-Jewish ('Aryan') psychoanalysts who were instrumental in the collaboration with Nazism in the 1930s and who survived the war, in Müller-Braunschweig's case going on to head the new psychoanalytic organization in West Germany. The story is one of failed appeasement and muddled thinking, not especially scarce commodities in the 1930s, with a contributory undertone of self-deception.

The history has been reasonably well documented in recent years, particularly in Brecht *et al* (1985), and can only be summarized briefly here. Hitler was elected Chancellor of Germany at the end of January 1933 and rapidly consolidated his power. Within months the opposition had been largely defeated, the mechanisms of terror had been put in place, and the writing was on the wall for Jews, Communists and other anti-Nazi elements. The psychoanalysts panicked. Max Eitingon, then President of the DPG, went to consult with Freud, leaving Boehm and Müller-Braunschweig in temporary charge. These two immediately began a process of negotiation with the Nazis, hatching a plan for Eitingon to be replaced as leader of the DPG and for the Jewish members to resign. Freud himself, when consulted by Boehm, agreed that he could take over the DPG if he could get a majority to vote for him, apparently hoping that hiding the Jewish culture of psychoanalysis behind the 'Aryan' figure of Boehm might be enough to appease the Nazis. This was also the view of Ernest Jones, President of the International Psychoanalytic Association, who in the early period of the Third Reich was strongly committed to an approach which would protect the interests of German psychoanalysis even at the expense of its individual members—that is, its Jewish members. Even though the DPG opposed Boehm's move, Eitingon resigned at the meeting of 6 May 1933 and shortly afterwards left Germany to live in Palestine. By the end of 1933 a further twenty or so Jewish analysts had left the country and, in a symbolic act of great significance in bringing home to them the new State's attitudes, Freud's books had been publicly burnt. Simmel, a past chairman of the Association of Socialist Doctors, had also been arrested in the summer of 1933, increasing the anxiety of the DPG (Brecht *et al*, 1985, 112). Boehm and Müller-Braunschweig were hard at work, following an appeasing plan: 'the DPG went its way eliminating step by step whatever endangered it as an institution, in the hope of saving itself and psychoanalysis at the same time' (ibid). They had met with the Nazi Ministry of Culture in September 1933 to discuss the conditions under which the DPG could be preserved, and by November 1933 all the offices of the DPG had been taken over by non-Jewish members, while only non-Jewish candidates for membership were approved.

To the Nazis, psychoanalysis was a prime example of the corrosive nature of Jewish thought, its degenerate capacity to poison the sources of idealism and feeling for race and nation and, especially, 'to strike the Nordic races at their most vulnerable point, their sexual life' (Deutsche Volksegesundheit aus Blut und Boden, 1933, quoted in Brecht *et al*, 1985, 101). Psychoanalysis 'belonged to the overrationalized corruptions of late capitalism, its alleged obsession with sexual drives plaguing primitive peoples like the Jews making it a proper therapeutic method only in rare cases' (Cocks, 1997, 60); the practice of psycho-analysis could thus be seen as actively anti-social. Defending psychoanalysis against this onslaught, Boehm and Müller-Braunschweig therefore saw themselves as faced with the task of persuading the Nazis that psychoanalysis was not necessarily 'Jewish', but could be utilized in the service of the state. From Boehm's own account (Brecht *et al*, 1985, 132–137), a great deal of his energy went into persuading Nazi functionaries that psychoanalysis was not dependent on the fact that Freud, a Jew, had founded it, but rather stood independently of this on its merits. Moreover, whereas the Nazis were inclined to see it as a 'subversive' discipline, Boehm himself attempted to persuade them that 'I had never known psychoanalysis to have a destructive effect on love of country' (ibid, 132). Müller-Braunschweig wrote a famous 'Memorandum' on psychoanalysis for the Nazis, published in a slightly adapted form in October 1933, under the title 'Psychoanalysis and *Weltanschauung*' in *Reichswart*, a 'rabid anti-Semitic publication' (Nitzschke, 1999, 357). In this article, the basis of psychoanalysis is asserted to be not just the understanding of sexuality, but of ego-instinct conflicts in general; this particular slant allows Müller-Braunschweig to use the language of 'mastery' so resonant with the Nazis—the unconscious can be 'mastered', the patient can achieve 'mastery of himself'. Then comes an infamous passage, taken generally as an example of the slippage in Müller-Braunschweig's thinking between an analytic stance and one in which service to the Third Reich could come to predominate.

Psychoanalysis works to remodel incapable weaklings into people who can cope with life, the inhibited into confident types, those divorced from reality into human beings who can look reality in the face, those enslaved by their instincts into their masters, loveless, selfish people into people capable of love and sacrifice, those indifferent to the totality of life into those willing to serve the whole. Thus it does outstanding work in education, and is able to give valuable service to the principles, only now mapped out anew, of a heroic, constructive conception of life, attuned to reality. (ibid)

This last sentence in particular shows the direction of the argument, calling as it does on the ('only now mapped out anew', ie Nazi) 'heroic' conception of life and advancing the idea that psychoanalysis, despite its past faults, can contribute to this. Interestingly, the key advocate of 'neo-analysis' in the DPG before and after the war, Harald Schultze-Hencke, published a very similar article at about the same time as that by Müller-Braunschweig. In this, he too argued that the goal of psychotherapy should be to 'free the powers of fitness and proficiency within the individual' and contended 'that the achievement of this kind of psychological health was a duty each individual owed to his community and that its mainten-ance was the corresponding duty of the psychotherapist' (Cocks, 1997, 87). Psychological health was defined 'in terms of blood, strong will, proficiency, discipline, community, heroic bearing, and physical fitness' (ibid); from here to the idea of an accommodation with the Nazis' projected 'German psychotherapy' was an easily managed step.

With the support of Jones, Boehm and Müller-Braunschweig thus followed a tactic of attempting to persuade the Nazis that psychoanalysis could be divorced from its Jewish origins and its socialist associations, so as to try to ensure its survival in Germany. Boehm and Müller-Braunschweig were left in no doubt by the Nazis that the proportion of Jewish analysts in the DPG made it very likely that their organization would be banned, and that for the sake of the survival of the DPG, the Jewish analysts had to go. Again with the active connivance of Jones, the DPG was 'Aryanized' by the end of 1935, nearly three years before other Jewish professionals, such as lawyers and doctors, were excluded from their equivalent organizations. By 1936, Fenichel could comment that the 'Aryan' members of the DPG 'are avoiding any contact—both the slightest professional contact as well as personal contact—with their non-Aryan colleagues: an almost incredible example of the devil, who will grab your whole hand when you stretch out your little finger' (Eickhoff, 1995, 950). The exclusion of the Jews was thus embraced with some enthusiasm by their non-Jewish erstwhile colleagues, whether through fear of being associated with the specifically derogated marginality of the Jews, or through active antisemitism. Although, ironically, there was a beneficial outcome of this in that most of the Jewish analysts, deprived of their livelihood, left Germany before the Holocaust, and so were saved (although fifteen did die in the concentration camps, as Jones confirmed at the first post-war International Congress—A Freud, 1949)—and although Jones played a heroic part in getting them out and in finding them places to go—this was not the motivation at the time; rather, the vain hope of appeasing the Nazis was the conscious purpose of this collusive strategy. One might wonder, in addition, whether behind this there was a darker strand, a point which will be returned to below.

The pressure to resign 'voluntarily' under which the Jewish analysts were put can be seen as an only slightly more benign version of the famously brusque treat-ment meted out by the psychoanalytic movement to its errant scion, Wilhelm Reich. Reich had joined the Communist Party in Berlin in 1930 and caused dissent within it both because of his particular views on the gravity of the working class defeat with the advent of Hitler, and because of his promotion of sexual liberation (Sharaf, 1983). His political radicalism was also of concern within the psychoanalytic movement, with Freud himself being noticeably critical— although some of the problems here concerned Reich's opposition to Freud's theory of the death drive. With the arrival of the Nazis in power, however, the threat posed by 'political' activity to the safety of psychoanalysis within Germany was seen by Freud as well as by Jones as potentially extremely damaging, with Reich (who in fact left Germany for Vienna in March 1933 and a month later embarked on some hectic to-ing and fro-ing around Scandinavia) as the most obvious representative of this tendency. Anna Freud's letter to Jones of 27 April, 1933, shows the reasoning:

Here we are all prepared to take risks for psychoanalysis but not for Reich's ideas, with which nobody is in agreement. My father's opinion on this matter is: If psychoanalysis is to be prohibited, it should be prohibited for what it is, and not for the mixture of politics and psychoanalysis[2] which Reich represents. My father can't wait to get rid of him inasmuch as he attaches himself to psychoanalysis; what my father finds offensive in Reich is the fact that he has forced psychoanalysis to become political; psychoanalysis has no part in politics. (Steiner, 2000, 128)

Promotion of the idea that 'psychoanalysis has no part in politics' was a key element in the defence of psychoanalysis against the Nazi critique of its inherently destabilizing nature, and was precisely the line taken by Boehm and Müller-Braunschweig in their negotiations with the Nazis. Boehm, for example, noted in 1934 that 'Reich had often come out publicly as a Communist and as a psychoanalyst, presenting his opinions as the results of psychoanalysis...I had to fight against this prejudice' (Brecht *et al*, 1985, 120). As it turned out and as Reich and a few others were prescient enough to see, this 'non-political' attitude effectively paved the way for a partial Nazification of psychoanalysis, while depriving psychoanalysis of its crucial critical role. It also resulted in the 'secret' expulsion of Reich from the DPG and the IPA, which Reich seems to have known nothing about it until he arrived at the Lucerne Congress of August 1934, when Müller-Braunschweig informed him that he had been expelled from the DPG a year earlier; over the course of that Congress it became apparent to Reich that the leadership of the IPA endorsed this decision. Jones later claimed that Reich had resigned from the IPA at that Congress, but this, it seems, was never Reich's view (Sharaf, 1983, 188).

Jacoby (1983) has discussed some of the complex politics surrounding Reich at this time, pointing out that he did not have the unequivocal support even of the 'political' Freudians, notably Fenichel. However, the key point here is not so much how difficult Reich was even for those who might be seen as potentially aligned with him, but rather that from Freud down, the early period of Nazi rule in Germany was seen as requiring extreme caution about political involvement of any possibly subversive kind—and that the consequences of this were that the

---

[2] Nitzschke's (1999, 355) translation is 'a hodgepodge of politics and analysis'.

politics of the psychoanalytic movement itself came to be played out under the shadow of Nazi demands.

It is worth noting a few more of the ambiguities in Ernest Jones' actions at this point. That he followed a policy of appeasement of the Nazis in the early period of the Third Reich is not in doubt, though in the context of the time this was less indefensible than it now seems, and it is also true that Jones' skilfulness and energy in finding routes out for endangered Jewish analysts was exemplary. On the other hand, he clearly played a double game. Supporting Boehm, he wrote to him in July 1934 to warn him of what might happen at the forthcoming Psychoanalytic Congress in Lucerne, in which his activities in negotiating with the Nazis were bound to come under attack. Revealing both personal prejudices and the acceptable language of the time (which may also have indicated some of his own ambivalence towards the Jewish dominance of psychoanalysis), Jones included in his letter the following piece of gentile solidarity.

You will know that I myself regard those emotions and ultra-Jewish attitude very unsympathetically, and it is plain to me that you and your colleagues are being made a dumping-ground for much emotion and resentment which belongs elsewhere and has displaced in your direction. My only concern is for the good of psychoanalysis itself, and I shall defend the view, which I confidently hold, that your actions have been actuated only by the same motive. (Brecht *et al*, 1985, 78)

Jones had previously expressed some similar sentiments (without the aside on ultra-Jewish attitudes) to Anna Freud. In a letter of 2 October 1933, he commented that, 'After the interview [with the DPG leaders] my impression of the Germany situation has slightly altered and I don't feel that the people concerned are quite so villainous as it has been suggested to me here.' Boehm in particular, whose 'initial action was very debatable' was seen as 'having saved Psycho-analysis in Germany from a horrific explosion that threatened early in August...which would have probably ended in the dissolution of the Society and Institute and the internment of most of its members in concentration camps' (Steiner, 2000, 53–54). On the other hand, he also noted two somewhat different appeals of Nazism to the two leading figures in the DPG.

Müller-Braunschweig was pretty objective. He showed no signs of any anti-Semitism, but evidently felt rather German. I suppose his leanings towards idealism draw him a little to that somewhat neglected aspect of Hitlerism. Boehm, on the other hand, was more sceptical about the Government but did show some indications of anti-Semitism, possibly associated with the unfortunate discovery of his unhappy grandmother. (ibid)

This differentiation, between Müller-Braunschweig's tendency towards a generally nationalist feeling infused with the heritage of German Romanticism and Boehm's more active anti-semitism, was played out in many other spaces in German society, including the wider psychotherapeutic and psychiatric professions (Cocks, 1997), with the effect of encouraging collaboration with the Third Reich. Interestingly, by 1935 Jones had reversed his assessment of which of the two German analysts showed the more obvious anti-semitic tendencies. Writing again to Anna Freud, he portrayed Boehm as a weak and inadequate leader: 'He has neither the personality required to manage a group nor a sufficiently quick grasp of the essentials of the strategic situation' (Brecht *et al*, 1985, 131). Müller-Braunschweig, on the other hand, was infected rather more with the times: 'Müller-Braunschweig is busy coquetting with the idea of combining a philosophy of Psycho-Analysis with a quasi-theological conception of National-Socialistic ideology ... No doubt he will proceed further along these lines, and he is definitely antisemitic, which Boehm is certainly not' (ibid). Who was, and who was not, and for what reasons, is a complex question, but Jones' acuity in most areas is not to be doubted, and clearly at different moments in the 1930s he was persuaded of the anti-semitism of each of the two main DPG leaders. In his 1946 report, Rickman confirms the Nazi taint in Müller-Braunschweig: 'I believe his personality has deteriorated during the Nazi regime ... and I think he is "dark grey" '—Boehm was seen as possibly 'black', meaning completely corrupted (Brecht *et al*, 1985, 237–238). Within four years of Rickman's report, however, Müller-Braunschweig was back in favour and Jones acted in his support.

Anti-semitism Bites

The role of CG Jung in supporting Nazism in the 1930s, when he was Chairman of the 'International' General Medical Society for Psychotherapy, is well known. However, the focus here is on what happened to the psychoanalysts, whose fate became tied up with the leader of the *German* Medical Society for Psychotherapy (the umbrella organization for German psychotherapists of all kinds)—Matthias Heinrich Göring. MH Göring was a psychiatrist and had undergone Adlerian analysis; he was also a member of the Nazi Party from 1 May 1933 onwards, and he was seen by the psychotherapists in Germany as a potentially protective figure because of his relationship with Reichsmarshall Hermann Göring. Writing in response to the invitation to take on the leadership of the German psychotherapists, he phrased his own views as follows (Cocks, 1997, 103).

In the interests of our society I wish to accept your offer, because I am a National Socialist not in name only but wholeheartedly in the spirit of Adolf Hitler, because moreover I bear the name of the Prussian Minister-President and am related to him. Also in the interests of National Socialism I must not refuse, for I believe that we psychotherapists have a great mission in the new state ... we are called to educate children and adults in the right spirit.

From the very start, therefore, the psychotherapists in the Third Reich pinned their colours to a masthead already painted in the Nazi red and black.

It was rapidly apparent that the future survival of psychoanalysis in the Third Reich would be bound up with the psychotherapists and hence with the person and organization of Göring rather than with the continuation of the DPG, and indeed the psychoanalysts took it upon themselves actively to seek the protection that Göring's name offered. As early as 1934, Boehm and Müller-Braunschweig and some of their non-Jewish colleagues met with the Jungians and with other psychotherapists to discuss joining together under a planned new institute headed by Göring. In February 1936, Boehm was told by the Ministry of Culture that psychoanalysis would be allowed to continue if the Berlin Psychoanalytic Institute would join with other branches of psychotherapy in an organization under Göring's leadership, with a commitment to developing a 'New German Psychotherapy' (Goggin and Goggin, 2001, 104). Boehm met with Anna Freud to discuss this, apparently gaining support from her, and the German Institute for Psychological Research and Psychotherapy—known, colloquially and lastingly, as the Göring Institute—was set up on 26 May 1936. In July 1936, Göring, Boehm and Müller-Braunschweig met with Jones and Brill to gain the approval of the IPA, promising that the independence of psychoanalysis would be maintained within the Institute. This promise, however, was not kept: psychoanalytic training came to be combined in most important respects with that of other psychotherapies. The DPG handed its building over to be the base for the Göring Institute; the experience of the remaining analysts was thus that their 'home' had become occupied, and they were allowed only shared and partial use of it. In October 1936, Göring gave his inaugural remarks on the new German psychotherapy, which was to be founded on a non-Freudian, pro-Nazi and anti-semitic basis; reading of *Mein Kampf* was made an obligatory part of the training and the remaining Jews were excluded (although neither of these last two moves was fully enforced, and some Jews and half-Jews survived in the Göring Institute until the end of the war—Cocks, 1997, 104, 273). Otto Fenichel, in his typically scathing way, described Boehm's subsequent attempt to patch things up with Freud. After an occasion at the Göring Institute when 'people had to "fall in"', whilst Göring gave a lecture on the Jewish libido conception of Freud and the Aryan one of Jung', Fenichel states:

Böhm had such a bad conscience that he went to Vienna to assure Freud of his loyalty and to obtain absolution. He was not given it; Freud said to him: 'Different peoples, with different destinies, have developed a capacity, varying in strength, of holding on to their convictions, even if they have to be abandoned on the outside. Our Jewish people have had the misfortune, or fortune, of accumulating a host of experiences of this kind ... Other peoples are less capable of resisting, and when they give in on the outside, they eventually give in on the inside too. It will all depend on what you hold onto inside.' After Böhm had left he said he did not believe that analysis would last in Germany: 'They are a submissive people.' (Fenichel, *Rundbrief* of 30 November 1936, in Eickhoff, 1995, 951)

Freud's assertion of a mode of Jewish superiority is notable here, in the light of the continuing attempt to appease the Nazis and to accommodate to their own ideology of racial superiority.

A Non-Jewish Psychoanalysis

The Göring Institute had a surprisingly important place in the hierarchy of the Third Reich, apparently invested with the expectation that it could serve the needs of the German people in developing a Nazified psychotherapeutic process serving national ideals. Throughout the war, it was involved in psychotherapy and leadership training (particularly with the Luftwaffe), and attracted a substantial budget (Cocks, 1997, 335–338). While its practical activities were probably valued as a contribution to the war effort, it was its efforts towards the development of a Nazified psychotherapy which distinguished it most—as its proponents were the first to acknowledge. In a newspaper interview from May 1939 (Brecht *et al*, 1985, 151), Göring answers the question of, 'how *psychoanalysis*, a very modern branch of medicine, could once have had *so destructive an effect?*' His answer is that, 'since Freud, it has been almost exclusively the domain of *Jewish doctors.*'[3] Freud, as a Jew, could not understand that the unconscious is not a domain of repressed sexual activity, but the 'foundation of life', the source of creativity.

It is clear that it is precisely in a field of work like that of the mind that Judaism could bring its destructive influence to bear most fruitfully. For the Jews, psychotherapy became a business, and the poisoning of mental life a necessity, so that they could then undertake to cure the poison. *Today a thoroughly German form of psychotherapy has been developed.*[4]

The 'new German psychotherapy' aimed to 'strengthen belief in the meaning of life and reinforce the link with the higher world of values; it was to convey to the patient the consciousness of being bound and incorporated into the common destiny of the German people' (Brecht *et al*, 1985, 152). It is clear from this that what was being proposed was a psychology without the critical doubt so central to Freud—without, that is, something of what might be thought of as its 'Jewish' heritage. Instead, the objective of psychotherapy was to facilitate in the patient the discovery of an unconscious energy and purpose which could be activated in the service of the German state. That the orientation of the work was towards the collective and not the individual is evidenced both in the expressed aims of the 'new German psychotherapy' and in some of its practices, for example, its involvement with 'euthanasia', something leading members of the Institute, including Boehm, came to accept as a solution for the 'untreatable' patient (Goggin and Goggin, 2001, 123). The relevant point here, however, is that despite this apparent displacement of key psychoanalytic assumptions and ethical values in favour of a Nazified psychotherapy, and even after the formal dissolution of the DPG in 1938 (which was connected with an intercepted letter of homage from Müller-Braunschweig to Anna Freud in Vienna), psychoanalytic

---

[3] Emphasis in original.   [4] Emphasis in original.

activity continued within the Göring Institute in an explicit manner. Brecht *et al* (1985, 154) note:

In fact the training of psychotherapists was to a great extent the responsibility of the 'Berlin psychoanalysts'. After the events of 1938 they did indeed lose some official responsibilities and were partially restricted in their teaching activities. But they were able to keep their influential position and expand it through clever staffing policies.

They managed to keep the Polyclinic, the heart of the Institute, as their responsibility. Thus, the psychoanalysts continued to have an impact in the Göring Institute. Boehm led the programme for homosexual soldiers; Werner Kemper helped work out treatment programmes for soldiers suffering from war neuroses; Müller-Braunschweig remained responsible for lecture organization and the teaching programme of the Institute. Even the Goggins acknowledge that the training programme involved training analysis, supervision and 'conventional-sounding' courses (2001, 109) and that 'between 1938 and 1945 Working Group A [the Freudians] had trained thirty-four people' (112). Chrzanowski (1975), in a relatively early interview-based study, notes that, 'Neither the people inside the Institute nor organised German psychiatry outside of the Institute believed that psychoanalysis had been extinguished' (496).

Our research demonstrates that those analysts who remained in Germany, under the Nazis, were doing 'regular analytic work' during the critical years. Not one person interviewed by us expressed the slightest doubt that he had continued to function as a psychoanalyst throughout the Hitler years. We have no doubt as to their sincerity. (494–495)

Chrzanowski does point to the mutual fears of betrayal by analysts and patients as powerful factors interfering with the therapy; however, while this is of considerable importance, it does not in itself imply that the activity being engaged in was not psychoanalysis.

As Cocks (2001) notes, none of this means that all the analysts were Nazis or Nazi sympathizers, but it does reveal a degree of social blindness, moral cowardice and self-seeking which, it seems, even thorough-going orthodox personal analysis had not been able to remedy. What seems clear is that during the period of the Göring Institute, non-Jewish analysts carried on with their work as best they could, with varying degrees of collaboration with the aims of the new German psychotherapy, including implication in the euthanasia programme. No-one, with the pre-war exception of Edith Jacobson (who was imprisoned for subversive activities and whom Boehm successfully prevented Jones from supporting) and the wartime martyr John Rittmeister, rebelled, although few actually joined the Nazi Party. Psychoanalytic training activities continued, even though Göring himself exercised personal censorship of Freudian terms and concepts and the members of 'Workgroup A' (the psychoanalysts) accordingly had to resort to euphemisms (eg 'depth psychotherapy' instead of 'psychoanalysis'). Some cases were handled by depth analysis including free association and the use of the analytic couch. Whether one likes what it became or not, psychoanalysis was going on, albeit 'in a most peculiar way' (Rittmeister, 1939).

Conclusion

There are numerous ways of understanding the somewhat sorry tale of psychoanalysis in Germany in the Nazi period. At the simplest level (which is not to say that it does not have its own complexities), it is a story of individuals faced with circumstances hostile to the continuation of their professional work, who were also caught up more or less strongly in a phenomenon of stupendous power, with its threat and its excitement. At the very least, these individuals went along with the dictates of the Nazi machine, retaining what dignity they could (less as time went on), plying their trade and preserving their profession as much as possible. This may have been ignoble, but perhaps not more so than those who did exactly the same in other walks of life. Psychoanalysts were certainly no more malevolent than many others who should and might have done better, being representatives of a class or professional group which was built upon self-reflection or accurate analysis of personal and political situations, or which had around it a clear ethical framework: lawyers, doctors, academics. Whilst there were heroes of resistance in all these fields, as a group they did not cover themselves with glory; psychoanalysis may not have had many heroes, but it also had relatively few perpetrators of Nazi abuses, and at least most of its Jewish representatives escaped.

However, there is something else to be explored here, which has been the rationale for this paper: psychoanalysis had some kind of special status not (or not *just*) because it is premised on an idea of awareness of personal motives, but more (or also) because of its position as a paradigmatic 'Jewish science'. As noted earlier, this was a term of Nazi abuse and carried with it all the racist connotations that are instantly recognizable: something corrupting, parasitic, demeaning and impure, which should be wiped out. However, psychoanalysis was also seen by many of its *practitioners*, including Freud himself, as having a special connection with Jewish culture, history and identity, a connection which had made psychoanalysis 'Jewish' well before the Nazis made this an index of abuse. Not only were the vast majority of European psychoanalysts secular Jews, but analysts and others alike could see that Jewish assumptions and ways of thinking were key elements of the psychoanalytic approach, however much it hungered for the apparent objective universalism of 'science'. Under such circumstances, it might have been possible to hope that German psychoanalysis, with its outstanding history of political engagement, would provide a source of political and cultural resistance to Nazism; in the name of its own values and origins it might have resisted appeasement even if that meant exile (as happened in France, the Netherlands, Norway and even Austria). In fact, as soon as it was tested, the opposite was the case.

There is little doubt about the antisemitism of some of the players in this game: Jung, Göring, Müller-Braunschweig, probably Boehm; this has been attested to elsewhere in this paper. More profoundly, however, there was an antisemitic *movement* at work, which fed off and into Nazism and represented a serious attempt to rewrite the future of psychoanalysis. Jung thought he could bid for it and become the dominant force in an 'Aryanized' depth psychology; the Göring Institute was the institutional centre for the more formal attempt to put it into practice as a 'new German psychotherapy'. But what may be dimly perceived in all the scheming, the appeasement and collaboration, the forced resignations and (at least in the case of Wilhelm Reich) secret expulsions, is the enactment (albeit probably guilt-ridden, as Müller-Braunschweig revealed in Vienna) of a wish to eradicate the Jewishness from psychoanalysis. This *consciously* involved opposition to Freud and the centrality of sexuality, it also meant *consciously* replacing the Freudian critical stance and the theory of the opposition between individual desire and social order with an approach that gave primacy to the interests of the latter—recast as the 'Aryan nation'—and asserted that individuals could be psychologically enriched by falling in with these interests. It also meant constructing a theory of leadership congruent with the Nazi 'Führer-fixation', and converting a theory of necessary psychic conflict into one in which wholeness and integrity, in the service of the state, is possible. All this was *conscious* and can be read out from the writings of the representatives of psychoanalysis in the Third Reich.

The *unconscious*, however, was also at work, as it always is. What could have been the meaning, for gentile psychoanalysts, of finding themselves caught in the web of a 'Jewish science', subservient to its demands and, through their own transferences and the trust they had put in mainly Jewish training analysts (not to mention their institutional idolizing of Freud), personally implicated in this Jewish cultural product, at a time and in a place in which things Jewish had become the defining mark of corruption, antisocial activity, parasitism and defilement? If Jewish analysts felt at home with psychoanalysis because of its compatibility with their culture, however much they had repudiated the beliefs of Judaism as a *religion*, then non-Jewish analysts were always likely to have a sense of marginality within their chosen profession, have the tables turned, as it were, be the uncomfortable outsiders who have to learn the rules to 'pass'—the reverse of the usual social situation. Once the Nazi hegemony was established, as it was in Germany extraordinarily quickly, these same non-Jewish analysts found themselves in a bind: hold out heroically as representatives of a Jewish culture to which they would always be outsiders, but to which they had given themselves through their training and professional affiliation, or join the new path and become central, insiders again. Coupled with the general uncertainty about whether appeasement was an appropriate political policy, and added to the genuine dangers of speaking out, of resistance; and mixed in with some no-doubt unconscious fratricidal urges towards their Jewish analytic peers; and perhaps enraged by the loss of so many senior Jewish analysts, whose disappearance might have been experienced unconsciously as abandonment at a time of need; it perhaps did not require more than an average dose of moral turpitude and self-serving ambition to side with the apparent historical victors. Psychoanalysts of the Third Reich kept going throughout the Nazi period, quietly most of the time, doing good sometimes, but collaborating, losing their way, corrupting the psychoanalytic movement. They did so not only for all the compelling reasons that make it so hard to resist totalitarianism, but also because it was a form of revenge against the Jews.

References

Bakan, D (1990, orig pub 1958). *Sigmund Freud and the Jewish Mystical Tradition*. London.
Brecht, K, Friedrioch, V, Hermanns, L, Kaminer, I, and Juelcih, D (eds) (1985) *'Here Life Goes On in a Most Peculiar Way': Psychoanalysis before and after 1933*. Hamburg.
Cocks, G (1997). *Psychotherapy in the Third Reich*, 2nd edn. Oxford.
——(2001) 'The Devil and the Details'. *Psychoanalytic Review* 88: 225–244.
Chrzanowski, G (1975) 'Psychoanalysis: Ideology and Practitioners'. *Contemporary Psychoanalysis* 11: 492–499.
Diller, J (1991) *Freud's Jewish Identity: A Case Study in the Impact of Ethnicity*. London.
Eickhoff, F (1995) The Formation of the German Psychoanalytical Association (DPV): Regaining the Psychoanalytical Orientation Lost in the Third Reich'. *International Journal of Psycho-Analysis* 76: 945–956.
Freud, A (1949) 'Report on the Sixteenth International Psycho-Analytical Congress'. *Bulletin of the International Psychoanalytic Association* 30: 178–208.
Gilman, S (1993) *Freud, Race and Gender*. Princeton.
Goggin, J and Goggin, E (2001) *Death of a 'Jewish Science': Psychoanalysis in the Third Reich*. West Lafayette.
Jacoby, R (1983) *The Repression of Psychoanalysis*. New York.
Klein, D (1985) *Jewish Origins of the Psychoanalytic Movement*. Chicago.
Léon, M (1946) The Case of Dr Carl Gustav Jung: Pseudo-scientist Nazi Auxiliary. *Report to U.S. Department of State and Nuremberg Tribunal*.
Moses, R and Hrushovski-Moses, R (1986) 'A Form of Group Denial at the Hamburg Congress'. *International Review of Psycho-Analysis* 13: 175–180.
Nitzschke, B (1999) 'Psychoanalysis during National Socialism: Present-Day Consequences of a Historical Controversy in the 'Case' of Wilhelm Reich'. *Psychoanalytic Review* 86: 349–366.
Rittmeister, J (1939) Letter to Alfred and Edith Storch, Münsingen, 15 October 1939.
Roith, E (1987) *The Riddle of Freud*. London.
Sharaf, M (1983) *Fury on Earth: A Biography of Wilhelm Reich*. London.
Steiner, R (2000) *It is a New Kind of Diaspora: Explorations in the Sociopolitical and Cultural Context of Psychoanalysis*. London.
Yerushalmi, Y (1991) *Freud's Moses*. New Haven.

Index